EUROPEAN WRITERS
The Age of Reason and the Enlightenment

EUROPEAN WRITERS

The Age of Reason and the Enlightenment

GEORGE STADE
EDITOR IN CHIEF

Volume 3

RENÉ DESCARTES

TO

MONTESQUIEU

CHARLES SCRIBNER'S SONS / NEW YORK

Copyright © 1984 Charles Scribner's Sons

Library of Congress Cataloging in Publication Data
(Revised for volumes 3 and 4)
Main entry under title:

European writers.

    Subtitle varies: v. 3–   . The Age of Reason and the
Enlightenment.
    Includes bibliographies.
    Contents: v. 1. Prudentius to Medieval Drama—
[etc.]—v. 3. René Descartes to Montesquieu—v. 4.
Voltaire to André Chénier.
    1. European literature—History and criticism—
Addresses, essays, lectures.   I. Jackson, W. T. H.
(William Thomas Hobdell), 1915–   . II. Stade, George.
PN501.E9   1983   809′.894   83–16333
ISBN 0–684–16594–5 (v. 1–2)
ISBN 0–684–17914–8 (v. 3–4)

PRINTED IN THE UNITED STATES OF AMERICA

The paper in this book meets the guidelines for permanence and durability of
the Committee on Production Guidelines for Book Longevity of the Council
on Library Resources.

EDITORIAL STAFF

G. MICHAEL McGINLEY, *MANAGING EDITOR*

H. ABIGAIL BOK, *Associate Editor*

WILLIAM L. C. BROADDUS, *Editorial Assistant*

JOHN CANTRELL, *Editorial Assistant*

CHRISTIANE L. DESCHAMPS, *Associate Editor*

ELIZABETH ELSTON, *Assistant Editor*

W. KIRK REYNOLDS, *Editorial Assistant*

STEVEN A. SAYRE, *Assistant Editor*

JOEL HONIG, *Associate Editor*

ELIZABETH I. WILSON, *Associate Editor*

JENNIFER E. ATKINSON, *Copyeditor*

WILLIAM H. FARICY, *Copyeditor*

EMILY GARLIN, *Proofreader*

WILLIAM M. HOFFMAN, *Copyeditor*

ELIZABETH C. HULICK, *Copyeditor*

MARCIA MERRYMAN-MEANS, *Proofreader*

VALERIE MURPHY, *Proofreader*

DIANA NORDERHUS, *Proofreader*

DENNIS J. POWERS, *Copyeditor*

EVA GALAN SALMIERI, *Proofreader*

JANET HORNBERGER, *Production Manager*

MARSHALL DE BRUHL, *DIRECTOR, REFERENCE BOOKS DIVISION*

v

LIST OF SUBJECTS

Volume 3

Volume 4

INTRODUCTION

*E*UROPEAN WRITERS WAS conceived as a companion to the eight-volume *American Writers* (1974–1981), the eight-volume *British Writers* (1979–1984), and the two-volume *Ancient Writers: Greece and Rome* (1982). These four sets, so far, comprise the Scribner World Literature series. The two volumes of *The Age of Reason and the Enlightenment* are the third and fourth installments of this chronological reference set that will be completed in twelve volumes. The first two volumes, *The Middle Ages and the Renaissance*, were published in 1983.

The articles in *The Age of Reason and the Enlightenment* are each approximately fifteen thousand words long. With one exception, the articles are each devoted to a single writer, from René Descartes, who was born at the end of the sixteenth century, to André Chénier, who died at the end of the eighteenth century. In style and scope the articles were written expressly for the general reader; that is, for high school, undergraduate, and graduate students, as well as for their teachers; for librarians and editors; for reviewers, scholars, and critics; for literary browsers; for anyone who wants to repair either an erosion or a gap in his reservoir of knowledge. The article that can at once inform the beginner and interest the specialist has achieved its goal.

In pursuit of this goal, the authors of the articles give an account of their writer's works; his life; his situation, social and literary; the relations among these. But from article to article the emphasis varies, as from writer to writer the relative interest or importance of his life, works, and situation vary. Voltaire, for example, had an immediate and powerful impact on his contemporaries; their reactions to his work (and his reaction to their reactions) are part of his story. Giovanni Battista Vico, by contrast, was relatively unread during his life time; what in his work his contemporaries were unable or unwilling to assimilate is part of his story. Some writers, such as Jean Jacques Rousseau, were vivid and fascinating personalities, their lives inextricably connected to their works; it is hard to think of the works without thinking of the man. Other writers, such as Christoph Martin Wieland, only became vivid through their works; it is hard to think of the man at all. These differences, among others, are reflected in the articles that follow. The articles vary in the amount of space devoted to biography, analysis of individual works, political

INTRODUCTION

events, and literary precoursers or successors. But whatever the emphasis, the works come first: other matters are discussed to the extent that they inform the works.

Because the authors of the articles vary in their methods and points of view, the experience of reading through a volume of *European Writers* is not the same as reading through an encyclopedia or a volume of literary history or a collection of essays by a single hand. An encyclopedia properly strives for a uniform neutrality of style and attitude; it contains essays on small matters as well as large ones. In a literary history, works and writers are pressed into their relative positions by the force of an overriding thesis. In a collection of essays there is at least the continuity of the author's personality and values. The articles in *The Age of Reason and the Enlightenment*, however, are not uniform in style and attitude, not shaped by a single thesis or set of values. But if you believe—as I do—that reality, in this case the literary reality of an age, does not lend itself to containment within a single mind or conceptual order, you will find a certain appropriateness to the variety of perspectives comprised in *The Age of Reason and the Enlightenment*.

The writers, works, conventions, and recurrent themes of any literary era move through time at different paces and at all angles to each other. The separate works, as we spread them out in imaginative space, intersect, intertwine, overlap, aggregate in larger structures, then fall apart or regroup, as we redirect our attentions, as our roving glances reverse the positions of foreground and background. In social space, works (like writers) court, challenge, and snub each other. When read sequentially, the articles in *The Age of Reason and the Enlightenment* together reflect the polymorphous relations among the literary realities of that era. Just the same, as we read the articles one by one, we get a deepening sense of the undeclared subject beyond the subject of the individual pieces. We get a sense of the temper of the times, the nexus of fears, hopes, and obsessions that makes an era what it is and that finds its most vivid expression in the words of its great writers. In sum, the essays presented here may vary in a number of ways: each is a separate performance; each sticks to its own subject; each can be read aside from the rest. But together they provide a complex and particularized sense of an age, even if that sense cannot be formulated in a neat set of interlocking propositions. In his preface to a study entitled *The Enlightenment*, Norman Hampson notes that "within limits, the Enlightenment was what one thinks it is." But only within limits: after his preface Mr. Hampson goes on to show just how strong were the family resemblances among the thoughts and attitudes of Enlightenment writers.

From our perspective at least, especially if we look only toward the writers who still seem to talk to us, the period from England's Glorious Revolution of 1688 to the French Revolution of 1787 feels like a unit, like a time during which something gradually jelled, hardened, and then crumbled under the impact of violent blows, intellectual and political. And the immediatley preceding half-century (again from our foreshortened perspective), the period during which Corneille, Molière, Pascal, Racine, and, above all, Descartes, Newton, and Locke began to write, seems to have stirred in the active ingredients that produced the Enlightenment.

INTRODUCTION

In 1637, a year after his fortieth birthday, Descartes published his first work, the *Discourse on Method.* He begins by observing that "the power of forming a good judgment and of distinguishing the true from the false, which is properly speaking what is called Good sense or Reason, is by nature equal in all men." Not only, he continues, is reason "to be found complete in each individual"; it is also "the only thing that constitutes us men and distinguishes us from the brutes." Although to be human is to reason, Descartes continues; although he was an eager reader from his childhood on; although he attended a celebrated school and learned there all that the other students learned, and more; although he read contemporary authorities in rhetoric, mathematics, theology, science, and philosophy—his efforts had "no effect other than the increasing discovery of my own ignorance." As for philosophic reasoning, he could say no sure thing but "that it has been cultivated for many centuries by the best minds that have ever lived, and that nevertheless no single thing is to be found in it which is not subject to dispute, and in consequence which is not dubious."

Philosophers, Descartes concluded, were like other people in that they were more likely to be persuaded by custom and example, by taste and authority, than by any certain knowledge. The first step to be taken by the seeker after truth, then, is "a resolve to strip oneself of all opinions and beliefs formerly received." The second step, for Descartes, was a resolve "to seek no other science than that which could be found in myself, or at least in the great book of the world." Out of these resolutions came Descartes's famous Method, the first precept of which was "to accept nothing as true which I did not clearly recognize to be so."

It is hard for us now to feel how exhilarating these first few pages of the *Method* were, how many new avenues of thought and action they unclogged. But the first generation of Enlightenment figures could feel it, and they knew how to put their feelings to work. Descartes's *Method* contains in embryo much of the whole Enlightenment program: its secular faith in unaided human reason; its belief that men and women everywhere and at all times share a common human nature; its cosmopolitanism; its brief for religious and political tolerance; its daring and self-confidence; its trust in nature, "the book of the world," as being such that human understanding could read it; its skepticism of authority and received opinion; its empiricism and eclecticism; its bent toward criticism and analysis; its predilection toward amateurism; even its weak sense of history; its preference for the typical over the individual; above all, its assurance that humankind was ready and able to begin again, to construct a new mental and social world, one in which humanity could live unsponsored, free, and responsible—but only to itself.

By the time that the Enlightenment was in full swing, the more influential writers had rejected much of Descartes, especially his pious conclusions, his doctrine of innate ideas, and his absolute separation of the mind from the body. The *philosophes* were more likely to turn to Locke, Newton, and Hume for argument and evidence in their attempts to construct a system of natural law, of natural religion, of natural morality that would be consistent with both reason and experience. But we can get some sense of the continuities throughout the period we are considering by a look at an essay written near

INTRODUCTION

the end of it. Immanuel Kant is above all others the philosopher who sorted out and systematized that loose bundle of attitudes we call the Enlightenment; in 1784 he published an essay entitled "Was Ist Aufklärung?"—which we translate "What is Enlightenment?" although English speakers did not naturalize the name "Enlightenment" until the nineteenth century. Kant answers this question in his first paragraph:

> Enlightenment is man's release from his self-incurred tutelage. Tutelage is man's inability to make use of his understanding without direction from another. Self-incurred is this tutelage when its cause lies not in lack of reason but in lack of resolution and courage to use it without direction from another. *Sapare aude!* "Have the courage to use your own reason!—that is the motto of the Enlightenment."

Kant also observed that although he lived in an age of Enlightenment, his was not an enlightened age. Not everyone was reasonable or had much faith in reason. The great subject of the dramatists and novelists was the conflict between will and honor, on one side, and passion, especially sexual passion, on the other. Passion increasingly won. By the end of the period even the *philosophes* regularly turned their skepticism upon themselves. Diderot liked to quote Pierre Bayle's remark that "the grounds for doubting are themselves doubtful; we must therefore doubt whether we ought to doubt." Some of the period's great writers, like Fénelon, tried to recapture what the *philosophes* were out to destroy; others, like René Lesage, tried to squeeze out a space for themselves between the contending conservative and Enlightenment forces; still others, like the marquis de Sade, held up to the Enlightenment its negative image, reason pushed to its conclusion in madness, nature become monstrosity, perversity the norm. And others, like Johann Gottfried von Herder, began to approach the momentous nineteenth-century presumption, still with us, that human beings are not everywhere and at all times essentially the same, but products of this time and that place, products of history, created and re-created by changing circumstances. And when Rousseau opens his *Confessions* by announcing that he has set out on an enterprise that has no precedent and will have no imitators, when he tells us that his subject is "simply himself" and that he is like no one else in the whole world, we are moving from an age that valued the universal and the general to one that values the unique and the particular; we are moving from an age that was justified in considering itself classical to one that was triumphantly romantic.

Enlightenment values were not shunted aside forever. Suitably chastened, they moved back to the center during the nineteenth century in what we call "liberalism." Certainly Hayden V. White is correct in saying that "the crisis into which Liberal society entered during the twentieth century was, ultimately, a crisis of the Enlightenment tradition." The vicissitudes of the Enlightenment tradition are of particular concern to Americans, whose nation was constituted on a base of Enlightenment values. Our Founding Fathers, Jefferson, Franklin, Madison, Hamilton, and Washington, were all influenced by British and European writers of the era that is the cumulative subject of

INTRODUCTION

The Age of Reason and the Enlightenment. Our declaration of national identity is one of the most eloquent of Enlightenment documents:

> We hold these truths to be self-evident, that all men are created equal, that they are endowed by their Creator with certain inalienable Rights, that among these are Life, Liberty, and the pursuit of happiness.—That to secure these rights, Governments are instituted among Men, deriving their just powers from the consent of the governed. . . .

GEORGE STADE

CHRONOLOGY OF THE AGE OF REASON AND THE ENLIGHTENMENT

1534–1536	John Calvin's *Institutes of the Christian Religion*
1543	Publication of Copernicus' *On the Revolution of Heavenly Bodies*, which gives his theory that the earth revolves around the sun
1545–1563	Council of Trent meets periodically to define Catholic doctrine and reiterate papal authority
1547–1584	Ivan IV (the Terrible), czar of Russia
1564	Deaths of Michelangelo and John Calvin
1568	The Netherlands revolts against Spain, which acknowledges Dutch independence in 1648
1572	Saint Bartholomew's Day massacre, in which thousands of Huguenots are murdered
1580	First two books of Montaigne's *Essays* mark beginning of a new literary genre
1583–1584	William of Orange, king of the Netherlands; assassinated on orders of Philip II of Spain
1588–1590	Defeat of the Spanish Armada by the English
1588–1610	Henry IV, first Bourbon king of France; converts to Catholicism in 1593 in effort to end religious wars
1596–1650	René Descartes
1598	Edict of Nantes grants religious freedom in France; ends civil war between Huguenots and Catholics
1598–1605	Boris Godunov, czar of Russia
ca. 1600–*ca.* 1750	Baroque period in art
1606–1684	Pierre Corneille
1609–1619	Kepler's laws accurately describe the revolutions of the planets around the sun
1610	Galileo's *Sidereus nuncius*
1613–1680	François VI, duc de La Rochefoucauld
1618–1648	Thirty Years' War, in which Protestants revolt against Catholic oppression throughout Europe (mainly in Germany); ended with the Treaty of Westphalia
1621–1695	Jean de La Fontaine
1622–1673	Molière (Jean Baptiste Poquelin)
1623–1662	Blaise Pascal

CHRONOLOGY OF THE AGE OF REASON AND THE ENLIGHTENMENT

1627–1704	Jacques Bénigne Bossuet
1633	Galileo forced by the Inquisition to retract writings in support of Copernican planetary system
1636–1711	Nicolas Boileau-Despréaux
1639–1699	Jean Racine
1645–1696	Jean de La Bruyère
1651–1715	François de Salignac de la Mothe-Fénelon
1661–1715	Louis XIV, crowned at the age of five in 1643, rules France; construction of Versailles begins
1665	Great Plague in England
1668	Triple Alliance between England, the Netherlands, and Sweden against France
1668–1744	Giovanni Battista Vico
1668–1747	René Lesage
1678	Madame de La Fayette's novel *La princesse de Clèves* marks beginning of a new literary genre
1682–1725	Peter I (the Great), czar of Russia
1683–1699	War of European powers against the Turks
1685	James II succeeds Charles II
	Edict of Nantes revoked by Louis XIV; Huguenots flee France
1686	First book of Newton's *Principia—De motu corporum* proposes theory of gravitation
1688	William of Orange is invited to England after Protestants call for the Glorious Revolution; James II is allowed to escape to France
1689–1702	William III and Mary II rule England
1689–1755	Montesquieu
1694–1778	Voltaire (François Marie Arouet)
1695	Fénelon's controversy with Bossuet
1697–1763	Antoine-François Prévost
1699	Pope Innocent XII condemns Fénelon's *Maximes des Saints*
	Alliance between Peter the Great, Frederick IV (Denmark), and Augustus II (Poland and Saxony) formed against Charles XII (Sweden) to end Swedish dominance in the Baltic area
1700–1721	Northern War
1700	German Protestants adopt Gregorian calendar
1701–1714	War of the Spanish Succession; concluded by the Peace of Utrecht, which marks the end of French expansion and the rise of the British Empire
1705	Peter the Great founds Moscow University
1707	United Kingdom of Great Britain formed after England, Wales, and Scotland are joined by the Act of Union
1707–1793	Carlo Goldoni
1709	Charles XII defeated at Poltava
1711	Berlin Academy established; Gottfried Wilhelm Leibniz appointed president
1712–1778	Jean Jacques Rousseau
1713–1784	Denis Diderot
1715–1774	Louis XV, king of France
1718	Quadruple Alliance (Britain, France, the Netherlands, and the German Empire) in war against Spain
1724–1803	Friedrich Gottlieb Klopstock
1725	Vico's *New Science*
	Peter the Great founds the Academy of Sciences at St. Petersburg

CHRONOLOGY OF THE AGE OF REASON AND THE ENLIGHTENMENT

1729–1781	Gotthold Ephraim Lessing
1732–1799	Pierre-Augustin Caron de Beaumarchais
1733–1813	Christoph Martin Wieland
1738	Daniel Bernoulli's *Hydrodynamica*
1740–1748	War of the Austrian Succession
1740–1786	Frederick II (the Great), king of Prussia
1740–1841	The marquis de Sade
1741–1803	Choderlos de Laclos
1744–1803	Johann Gottfried Herder (von Herder)
1749	The comte de Buffon's *Histoire naturelle* (44 vols.) proposes important theories and questions on evolutionary biology
1749–1803	Vittorio Alfieri
ca. 1750–ca. 1850	Industrial Revolution
1751–1772	Publication of the *Encyclopédie* (28 vols.), edited by Diderot and Jean d'Alembert; six-volume supplement published 1776–1777
1752	British adopt Gregorian calendar
1755	Great earthquake in Lisbon
	Samuel Johnson's *Dictionary of the English Language*
1756–1763	Seven Years' War; Britain and Prussia defeat France, Spain, Austria, and Russia
1756–1791	Wolfgang Amadeus Mozart
1762–1794	André Chénier
1762–1796	Catherine II (the Great), czarina of Russia
1762	Rousseau's *The Social Contract*, which encouraged the rise of antimonarchical republicanism
1767–1830	Benjamin Constant
1772–1795	Partition of Poland between Austria, Prussia, and Russia ends Polish independence
1781	Immanuel Kant's *Critique of Pure Reason*
1789–1799	French Revolution

CONTRIBUTORS TO VOLUMES 3 AND 4

HUBERT F. BABINSKI
ANDRÉ CHÉNIER

GENE BLUESTEIN
*California State University,
Fresno*
JOHANN GOTTFRIED VON
HERDER

JULES BRODY
Harvard University
NICOLAS BOILEAU-DESPRÉAUX

RICHARD DANNER
Ohio University
JEAN DE LA FONTAINE

HUGH M. DAVIDSON
University of Virginia
BLAISE PASCAL

DANIEL B. DODSON
Columbia University
GOTTHOLD EPHRAIM LESSING

OTIS FELLOWS
Columbia University
ALAIN-RENÉ LESAGE

ROBERT J. FRAIL
Columbia University
JACQUES BÉNIGNE BOSSUET

PAUL H. FRY
Yale University
JEAN JACQUES ROUSSEAU

NATHAN GROSS
PIERRE CORNEILLE

JOSUÉ HARARI
*The Johns Hopkins
University*
MONTESQUIEU

MICHAEL HAYS
Columbia University
CARLO GOLDONI

MICHAEL HOOKER
Bennington College
RENÉ DESCARTES

DONALD R. KELLEY
University of Rochester
GIOVANNI BATTISTA VICO

PAULINE KRA
Yeshiva University
JEAN DE LA BRUYÈRE

JOHN A. McCARTHY
University of Pennsylvania
CHRISTOPH MARTIN WIELAND

JANE McLELLAND
University of Iowa
MONTESQUIEU

GITA MAY
Columbia University
DENIS DIDEROT

JULIUS A. MOLINARO
University of Toronto
VITTORIO ALFIERI

HAROLD E. PAGLIARO
Swarthmore College
FRANÇOIS VI, DUC DE
LA ROCHEFOUCAULD

BRIGITTE PEUCKER
Yale University
FRIEDRICH GOTTLIEB
KLOPSTOCK

JEANINE P. PLOTTEL
Hunter College
THREE FRENCH NOVELISTS:
ANTOINE-FRANÇOIS PRÉVOST,
CHODERLOS DE LACLOS,
BENJAMIN CONSTANT

JOHN RICHETTI
Rutgers University
SADE AND THE FRENCH
LIBERTINE TRADITION;
PIERRE-AUGUSTIN CARON DE
BEAUMARCHAIS

JEAN SAREIL
Columbia University
VOLTAIRE

BERTRAM EUGENE
SCHWARZBACH
FRANÇOIS DE SALIGNAC DE LA
MOTHE-FÉNELON

MICHAEL SEIDEL
Columbia University
MOLIÈRE

MICHAEL WOOD
University of Exeter
JEAN RACINE

EUROPEAN WRITERS

The Age of Reason and the Enlightenment

RENÉ DESCARTES

(1596–1650)

RENÉ DESCARTES, "the father of modern philosophy," was one of the pivotal characters in the intellectual transition from the Middle Ages to the Renaissance. His revolutionary picture of the sciences as constituting a unified whole liberated the scientist from medieval dogma and was the single most significant contribution to the sciences until the publication of Sir Isaac Newton's *Principia* more than half a century later. Equally important as the scientific doctrines are their underpinnings in the metaphysical view of the universe that Descartes propounded. With the publication of the *Meditations* in 1641, Descartes changed man's conception of the world.

This essay will attempt to provide a three-dimensional picture of Descartes. Interspersed throughout a sketch of his life are discussions of the major historical and philosophical trends that Descartes challenged. Most important, the reader will be introduced to Descartes's monumental work, the *Meditations,* and will have the opportunity to explore this treatise with a certain degree of philosophical rigor. The motivations for Descartes's views will also be discussed in order to help the reader appreciate him not only as a great philosopher and scientist but also as a man—one of those rare men whose thoughts and speculations have come to shape our vision of the world.

René du Perron Descartes was born at La Haye, Touraine, on 30 March 1596, the third son of Joachim Descartes. His father had chosen the profession of law, and had obtained the independent judicial appointment of counsellor to the Parlement of Britanny. His mother died of a lung infection a few days after his birth. He tells us, "I inherited from her a dry cough and a pale complexion, which I retained to the age of more than twenty, and which caused all the doctors who saw me before that time to condemn me to die young" (*Oeuvres de Descartes* 1:300–301).

At the age of eight, Descartes was sent to the Jesuit school of La Flèche in Anjou. La Flèche had recently been founded by Henry IV to offer a superior education to the sons of the nobility. The king was so committed to the school that he directed in his will that his heart be buried there—a directive that was carried out six years after the young Descartes arrived, in a ceremony that found him one of twenty-four young gentlemen who walked in the funeral procession.

Descartes was apparently quite happy at La Flèche; he speaks highly of his life there. Indeed there was one event that seems to have made a lasting mark on him. On the anniversary of the death of Henry IV, the *Henriade* sonnets (as they were called) were read by the students celebrating various advances in the sciences. One sonnet, "On the Death of King Henry the Great and on the Discovery of Some New Planets or Stars Moving Around Jupiter, Made This Year by Galileo, Celebrated Mathematician of the Grand Duke of Florence," seems to have caught the attention of the young Descartes. For not only was the discovery of the moons of Jupiter important, but the use of the telescope was enlarging man's view of the universe. Descartes was wholly in favor of this expansion of man's horizons, and it is not unusual that a young man's curiosity might be piqued by such discoveries. Descartes remained interested in the heavens throughout his life, his interest culminating in such works as *Le monde,* the *Meteors,* and the *Dioptrics.* From this celebration at the *Henriade* Descartes grew to respect Galileo as he did few other men, and as we shall see, Galileo's condemnation would have a profound effect on Descartes's published works.

While at La Flèche, Descartes was considered an extraordinary student; teachers and fellow classmates acknowledged his remarkable talents. Yet after eight and a half years, he left the school resolved to forsake the study of books forever because he thought they were a waste of time. In his own words:

I have been nourished on letters since my childhood, and since I was given to believe that by their means a clear and certain knowledge could be obtained of all that is useful in life, I had an extreme desire to acquire instruction. But so soon as I had achieved the entire course of study at the close of which one is usually received into the ranks of the learned, I entirely changed my opinion. For I found myself embarrassed with so many doubts and errors that it seemed to me that the effort to instruct myself had no effect other than the increasing discovery of my own ignorance. And yet I was studying at one of the most celebrated Schools in Europe, where I thought that there must be men of learning if they were to be found anywhere in the world. I learned there all that others learned; and not being satisfied with the sciences that we were taught, I even read through all the books which fell into my hands, treating of what is considered most curious and rare. Along with this I knew the judgments that others had formed of me, and I did not feel that I was esteemed inferior to my fellow-students, although there were amongst them some destined to fill the places of our masters. And finally our century seemed to me as flourishing, and as fertile in great minds, as any which had preceded. And this made me take the liberty of judging all others by myself and of coming to the conclusion that there was no learning in the world such as I was formerly led to believe it to be.

(*The Philosophical Works of Descartes* 1:83–84)

It was for these reasons that Descartes "abandoned the study of letters, and resolved to seek no other science than I could find within myself or in the great book of the world."

At the age of sixteen and a half Descartes returned to his family in Rennes. He was now obliged to decide on a career. He pondered the possibilities, apparently at great length, but was unable to convince himself of the suitability of any of the traditional occupations for a person of his standing. He spent two years at home and finally settled on joining the army. His father sent him to Paris, a necessary preliminary to his service.

In Paris he became reacquainted with an older schoolmate, Père Mersenne, who was at the time a Franciscan monk in a Minorite convent. His conversations with Mersenne caused Descartes to return to those matters that had preoccupied him at La Flèche. He began to wrestle with the two conflicting parts of his mind—the one part with its aversion to book learning and the other with its craving for "intellectual occupation." Descartes's need to effect a fusion of these two divided parts prompted a search that eventually led to the formation of his famous method. It was only a year after Descartes's renewed friendship with Mersenne that the latter left Paris to take up a professorship in philosophy at Nevers. Descartes disappeared from Paris after Mersenne left and turned up in the army several months later.

It is fair to say that Descartes's military career was not a particularly distinguished one. He first took service under the banners of

Maurice of Nassau (May 1617); two years later he passed into temporary service with the Catholic emperor Ferdinand. If Descartes ever fought in battle, was wounded, or indeed drew a sword, it is not recorded. There is but one surviving anecdote concerning his military career. One day, as Descartes was walking down a street in Breda, a placard on a wall caught his eye. The placard contained a mathematical problem with an invitation to solve it. Descartes was familiar with the diagram, but the terms were in Flemish. He asked a bystander for translation. The bystander happened to be the famous mathematician Isaac Beeckman, who answered that he would provide one only if Descartes would provide a solution. The next day Descartes called on Beeckman with the problem solved.

Beeckman was eight years older than Descartes, and he assumed the role of teacher in their relationship. He was fond of comparing Descartes to a top that remains upright while spinning. "René," he wrote, "makes me think that a man could hold himself upright in space." The first result of Beeckman's influence was Descartes's treatise on music, the *Compendium musicae* (completed 1618). Descartes dedicated the work to his friend with the stipulation that it would be kept secret, as he felt it was unsuitable for publication. The work was not published until 1650, after Descartes's death. Because of Beeckman, Descartes was once more drawn toward the intellectual life. He wrote:

> To speak truthfully, you alone have drawn me from my idleness and made me remember what I had learned and almost forgotten; when my mind was wandering from serious occupations, you brought it back to the right path. If I produce anything of merit, you will be entitled to claim it entirely for yourself.
>
> (*Oeuvres* 1.14)

But by 1630 Descartes would regret having made such a statement of indebtedness. Beeckman bragged to Mersenne and others that it was he who was the source of Descartes's ideas. In an uncommon fit of temper, Descartes requested that Beeckman return the manuscripts in his possession and wrote to him:

> When you boast of such things in front of people who know me, it injures your reputation. . . . And you have shown my letters as testimony for naught because one knows that I am accustomed to instructing myself even with ants and worms, and one will think that this is how I used you.
>
> (1.144–145)

The quarrel soon passed, and they were friends again a year later.

Beeckman left Breda for Middleberg on 2 January 1619, leaving behind a Descartes who was full of creative energy. For several months Descartes stayed in or around Breda, consumed in his work. Finally, at the end of April he set off for Germany, where he spent almost six months touring the country. By winter he had settled at Neuberg on the Danube. There he rented a heated room, his *poêle,* and spent long hours locked inside in contemplation. He became more and more convinced that there was something important to come of his studies, a conviction that caused him to push himself even harder.

On 10 November 1619, Descartes found what he had been looking for. Having worked himself into an almost delirious state, he was struck with a "blinding flash" of insight and he realized his discovery—that all of the sciences should be studied as a unified whole. He described the significance of this idea twenty years later in *Discours de la méthode* (*Discourse on Method*, 1637):

> Those long chains of reasoning, simple and easy as they are, of which geometricians make use in order to arrive at the most difficult demonstrations, had caused me to imagine that all those things which fall under the cognizance of man might very likely be mutually related in the same fashion; and that, provided only that we

abstain from receiving anything as true which is not so, and always retain the order which is necessary in order to deduce the one conclusion from the other, there can be nothing so remote that we cannot reach to it, nor so recondite that we cannot discover it.

(Philosophical Works 1.92)

The significance of Descartes's discovery should not be underestimated. The discovery of the unity of human knowledge was a major (if not *the* major) breakthrough of the modern era.

The evening of 10 November was one of the most important in Descartes's life. The *Discourse on Method* refers to the three dreams in which his "vocation" was revealed. Descartes wrote out in minute detail a description of these dreams, which is now unfortunately lost to us. We have, however, an account (paraphrased below) of them by Descartes's earliest biographer, Adrien Baillet.

In the first dream Descartes struggles against a strong wind that constantly whirls him about as he tries to reach the church of the college (presumably La Flèche) in order to say his prayers. At one point, as he is turning to bow to someone he has neglected to greet, the wind blows him violently against the church. Someone yells to him from the middle of the courtyard, telling him that an acquaintance of his has a gift for him—a melon. At this point Descartes awakened and rolled over on his right side. He prayed to God for protection from the effects of the dream.

He then had a second dream—of a burst of noise like a crack of thunder—and awakened from it to see thousands of sparks in his room.

His third dream, unlike the first two, contains nothing frightening, but is much more complicated. In this dream, Descartes notices a book on a table. He goes over to it, opens it, and is delighted to find that it is a dictionary. He then finds a second book, a collection of poems entitled *Corpus poetarum.* Out of curiosity he opens the book and the line "Quod vitae sectabor iter?" (What path shall I follow

in life?) catches his eye. As Descartes is reading, an unknown man hands him some verses beginning with the words "Est et non." Descartes tells the man that he knows the poem well, that it comes from the *Idylls* of Ausonius, one of the authors in the bulky dictionary on the table. As Descartes goes to the table to fetch the book, the man asks him where he got it. Descartes is unable to answer and notices that the book has disappeared. No sooner does he say so than it reappears on the other end of the table. But this book is slightly different from the dictionary he saw before. He searches for the passage from Ausonius beginning "Est et non," but he cannot find it. At this point both the book and the man disappear, yet Descartes does not awaken. While still asleep, he proceeds to interpret the significance of the dream. He judges that the dictionary signifies all the sciences, and that the *Corpus poetarum* signifies the unity of philosophy with wisdom. The words "Est et non," which are the "Yes and No of Pythagoras," represent truth and falsity in human achievement in the secular sciences; the section beginning "Quod vitae sectabor iter?" marks the good advice of a wise person, or even moral theology.

Descartes believed that the first two dreams were admonitions touching his past life. The melon offered in the first dream symbolized solitude. The wind that whirled him around toward the church was an evil genius who, according to Baillet, "was to throw him by force into a place where it was his design to go voluntarily." Finally, the lightning of the second dream was nothing less than the spirit of truth descending on him (*Oeuvres* 6.9).

It is interesting that many of those whom Descartes told of his dreams counseled him to keep them a secret, lest he be thought a madman. Yet these very dreams told Descartes what path to follow. He had found the synthesis that he had sought for so long. With the sciences now unified in his thinking, he was able to fuse his own divided thoughts. Not only had he found what he saw as the correct way of interpreting the sciences, but his method—always proceeding from the most simple to the most complex, and never assuming the truth of anything that has not been proven to be true—assured his concept a validity that was not present before this point in the history of ideas. His method supplied a degree of certainty to our metaphysical picture of the world, and it was this certainty that Descartes saw as all important.

During the following years Descartes spent much of his time traveling. By 1628 he had settled in Paris and prepared to reveal his discovery. Monsieur de Baigne, the papal nuncio, had invited a group of scholars to listen to a lecture by Chandoux—"an extremely capable professor of chemistry"—who was to speak against the Aristotelian system of scientific inquiry. His lecture was eloquently delivered and urged opposition to what he called the "yoke of scholasticism." He went on to propose another system to replace the one currently taught in the schools. The lecture was received enthusiastically by everyone in the hall except Descartes. His coolness was noticed by Cardinal de Bérulle, who requested that Descartes explain his dissatisfaction with the lecture. Descartes responded that the cardinal was surely a more capable judge than he concerning matters such as these, and asked to be excused. The cardinal, seconded by the nuncio, urged him to voice his opinion, making it clear that Descartes could not refuse.

Descartes began by praising Chandoux for his attempt to pull philosophy away from scholasticism. He then pointed out that unless any system, including the one propounded by Chandoux, had some foundation in certainty, it could be only a plausible system, not one that could be considered metaphysically true. At this point the audience began to voice its dissent. Descartes urged the audience to bear with him. He proceeded to take a statement that was widely considered to be true, and by "twelve evident reasons" showed that it was false. He did likewise with a proposition that everyone considered false. Just what these

"twelve evident reasons" were is lost to us now, but they apparently had quite an impact on the audience. Descartes went on to argue that any system not grounded in certainty would be caught in paradoxes, and hence could be called only a plausible system. Entreated to tell the audience what his method was, Descartes gave only several hints and apologized because his theory was incomplete. His performance at this public lecture had a profound effect on everyone in the room. Chandoux, who felt he had been humiliated by Descartes, gave up the study of philosophy altogether. He was hanged a few years later for passing counterfeit money. Cardinal de Bérulle took Descartes aside after the lecture and convinced him that he must go forth and complete his method, telling him that it was God's will for him to do so.

At the end of 1628 Descartes left Paris for Holland to begin what he called a self-imposed exile, which lasted almost twenty years. The immediate cause of his move was the difficulty of maintaining in Paris the anonymity he thought was essential to his work. Descartes found Holland an almost ideal place to study. He wrote to his friend Balzac:

> Here I sleep ten hours every night without being disturbed by any care. After my mind has wandered in sleep through woods, gardens, and enchanted palaces where I experience every pleasure imaginable, I awake to mingle the reveries of the night with those of the day.
>
> (*Oeuvres* 1.86)

In another letter to Balzac, Descartes praised city life because it ensured his all-important anonymity. And in 1639 he wrote Mersenne:

> I work very slowly, because I take much more pleasure in instructing myself than in putting into writing the little that I know. . . . I pass my time so pleasantly in instructing myself that I never set myself to writing my Treatise except by constraint, and in order to acquit myself of the resolution I have taken, which is, if I live, to put

myself in a condition to send it to you in the beginning of the year 1633.

(1.190)

While Descartes was in Holland he went to great lengths to protect his privacy. Only Mersenne knew of his whereabouts for long periods of time. His life was a shuttle back and forth between the anonymity of the city and the quiet of the country. But whenever he felt that someone was looking for him, or that he was in danger of being found, Descartes would move. He didn't want to waste time explaining or justifying his thoughts to others and, above all, he needed the time to refine them.

In July 1633 Descartes wrote Mersenne that his treatise was almost finished and that he would send a completed copy to him by the end of the year. Just as all was ready, Descartes learned of the fate of Galileo. The church had just condemned Galileo's *Dialogue Concerning the Two Chief World Systems.* It forced the author to sign a formal abjuration of his belief in the Copernican system and imprisoned him for an indefinite term. It also ordered copies of the work to be publicly burned. So distressed was Descartes, a devout Catholic, that he wrote Mersenne:

I was so astounded that I have half a mind to burn all my papers or at least not to show them to anyone. I cannot imagine that an Italian, and especially one well thought of by the Pope from what I have heard, could have been labeled a criminal for nothing other than wanting to establish the movement of the earth. I know that this had been censured formally by a few Cardinals, but I thought that since that time one was allowed to teach it publicly even in Rome. I confess that if this is false then all the principles of my philosophy are false also. . . . And because I would not want for anything in the world to be the author of a book where there was the slightest word of which the Church might disapprove, I would rather suppress it altogether than to have it appear incomplete—"crippled" as it were.

(1.241–242)

Mersenne was never to see a copy of the work referred to in the letter. *Le monde* would not be published until after Descartes's death. One might imagine that the shock over Galileo would have caused Descartes to cease his work altogether, but fortunately he did not. Descartes embarked on another project. In March 1636 he wrote Mersenne to ask him to arrange for the printing of a volume that would contain four treatises, entitled *Project of a Universal Science, Which Can Raise Our Nature to Its Highest Degree of Perfection; also Dioptrics, Meteors, and Geometry, Wherein the Most Curious Matters Which the Author Could Select, In Order To Give Proofs of the Universal Science He Sets Forth, Are Explained in Such a Manner That Even Those Who Have Not Studied May Understand Them.* The book was published in 1637, although not in Paris; and it bore the more modest title *Discourse on the Method of Rightly Conducting the Reason and Seeking Truth in the Sciences. Next to the Dioptric, the Meteors, and the Geometry, Essays in This Method.*

This first published work by Descartes astounded many of those who read it. A work of far-reaching genius, it was accessible to many nonscholars because it was written in French, almost unheard of at a time when all "serious" books were written in Latin. Concerning this, Descartes wrote:

If I write in French, which is the language of my country, rather than in Latin, which is that of my preceptors, it is because I hope that those who use only their natural reason will be better judges of my ideas than those who only believe in ancient texts; and as for those who join good sense with study, those alone whom I desire as judges, they will not be so partial toward Latin that they will refuse to understand my reasoning just because I explain things in the vulgar tongue.

(6.77–78)

The cornerstone of the *Discourse* is Descartes's formulation of the four rules of method. An examination of these rules should lead the reader more closely to modern scientific method than any other single work, for it is these rules that in fact define scientific method. Descartes writes:

The first of these was to accept nothing as true which I did not clearly recognize to be so: that is to say, carefully to avoid precipitation and prejudice in judgments, and to accept in them nothing more than what was presented to my mind so clearly and distinctly that I could have no occasion to doubt it.

The second was to divide up each of the difficulties which I examined into as many parts as possible, and as seemed requisite in order that it might be resolved in the best manner possible.

The third was to carry on my reflections in due order, commencing with objects that were the most simple and easy to understand, in order to rise little by little, or by degrees, to knowledge of the most complex, assuming an order, even if a fictitious one, among those which do not follow a natural sequence relatively to one another.

The last was in all cases to make enumerations so complete and reviews so general that I should be certain of having omitted nothing.

(*Philosophical Works* 1.92)

Descartes goes on from this point to describe how following these simple rules leads to the establishment of a system whose foundation is certainty.

The *Discourse* is a most interesting work. It is organized into six chapters, each of which treats a completely different subject. These chapters are followed by three separate works—*La dioptrique* (the *Dioptrics*), *Météores* (the *Meteors*), and *La géométrie* (the *Geometry*)—each of which is an attempt by the author to extend the method to matters of current scientific interest. The first six chapters of the *Discourse* comprise a work that is part biography, part philosophy, part science. Chapter 1 is concerned almost exclusively with Descartes's life at La Flèche and explains his rejection of the "schools" and academic life. Chapter 2 concerns the three dreams of

10 November 1619 and contains the four rules given above. Chapter 3 concerns the best way to conduct one's life. Chapter 4 is given over to more purely metaphysical speculation and contains the "I think, therefore I am," which may be the most famous adage in the history of philosophy. In chapter 5 we find a discussion of physics and biology, and chapter 6 serves as a conclusion.

Concerning the *Discourse*, Descartes wrote to a friend: "My only purpose in printing at this time is to prepare the way for another work which I hope to bring out in case the public should desire it, and I think that they will. I am testing the waters" (*Oeuvres* 1.300–301). The publication was most certainly successful in "testing the waters." It plunged Descartes into a controversy with all manner of learned men. It seemed that the public would want another work.

In November 1639 Descartes wrote Mersenne:

I am now working on a discourse in which I try to clarify what I have hitherto written on this topic. It will be only five or six printed sheets but I hope it will contain a great part of Metaphysics. To make it as good as possible, I plan to have only twenty or thirty copies printed, and send them to the twenty or thirty most learned theologians I can find, so as to have their criticisms and learn what should be changed, corrected or added before publication.

(*Descartes: Philosophical Letters* 68)

This letter marked the first announcement of what was to become one of the most influential works in the history of philosophy. Descartes did in fact distribute copies to some of the learned men of the time. Among them were Mersenne, Pierre Gassendi, Thomas Hobbes, Antoine Arnauld, Pierre Bourdin, and the Jesuit fathers of the Sorbonne. Descartes explained to them that their objections to the work, *Meditations on First Philosophy*, would be published together with his replies. In August 1641 the text of the *Meditations* and the

"Objections and Replies" (which constitutes the largest portion of the book) was published in Paris. The *Meditations* is Descartes's most representative work. It provides a nearly complete expression of his epistemological and metaphysical doctrines.

In order to understand the motivations behind the *Meditations,* and before examining it in detail, it is useful to look at the social and intellectual context in which it was produced. The sixteenth century was a period of considerable intellectual upheaval for a number of reasons. Chief among these were the effects of the recent explorations by European seamen who returned with stories of strange cultures and foreign lands where beliefs, values, and ways of living were at wide variance with established customs at home. The overturn of Ptolemaic astronomy following the publication in 1543 of Copernicus' heliocentric theory of planetary motion and the Protestant Reformation brought about by Martin Luther's challenge to the authority of the Catholic church also had an unsettling effect on the confidence with which people held the philosophical and religious beliefs they had grown up with.

The overthrow of the geocentric theory in astronomy tended to undermine the confidence of intellectuals in the security of scientific theory. If a belief that had existed for a thousand years and seemed obviously true could be subverted in such a short period of time, it was not clear whether any of the other accepted opinions regarding the nature of the physical world could still be held with confidence. Even more disturbing was the confusion engendered by the Protestant Reformation regarding the question of religious truth. Prior to Luther's time there was no question about the methodology for settling disputes in matters of religion. In the Catholic church the pope was the final authority on religious questions, and when he spoke ex cathedra on the interpretation of Scripture, he spoke as God's representative on earth. However, Luther's challenge cut at the very heart of religious dogma. Whereas the Catholic church held the pronouncements of papal authority to be the sole criteria of religious truth, Luther claimed that what was true in religion was what one's conscience compelled one to believe after thorough and careful reading of Scripture. That Luther's judgment of religious truth was accepted by many would have been sufficient in itself to cause a general intellectual upheaval. The real damage done by Luther was much more severe: he had raised the question of the adequacy of any putative criterion of truth.

The problem posed by Luther's challenge was this: How can we adjudicate disputes between competing criteria of truth? In attempting to answer the question, one quickly sees that what is needed is some criterion to enable us to select among competing criteria. The possibility of selection raises the further question, however, of how one would defend challenges to the criterion in question. If Luther were asked "How do you know that your conscience is what is right to believe in religious matters?" he would respond that he was convinced of this because his conscience compelled him to believe it. Similarly, a spokesman for the Catholic church would argue that the pope is the final authority on matters of religion because that is what the pope says, and he speaks for God. Appeal to advocates will not help solve the problem, but neither does it appear that the answer lies in the search for some independent standard of adjudication. Any criterion that we select for objective determination of the matter will itself be open to challenge, and additional criteria will be needed to defend it. The task is obviously a hopeless one. Recognition of this fact led naturally to the skeptical conclusion that one person's opinion is as good as another's and that no rational means can be found for proving any one opinion correct over another.

In accounting for the general intellectual upheaval of the time, something else is as important as the revolutions in astronomy and religion: the discovery in the middle of the sixteenth century of the manuscript of Sextus Empiricus, a third-century skeptic. Sextus distinguished two varieties of skepticism: academic skepticism and Pyrrhonian skepticism. Academic skepticism maintains that no one knows anything, but that some opinions are probably more true than others, and it is prudent to act on those opinions that have probability in their favor. Pyrrhonian skepticism denies that some opinions are more probable than others. It does this in virtue of a problem like Luther's: the impossibility of defending criteria of the adequacy of criteria themselves. The problem, according to Pyrrhonian skeptics, is that one who maintains that some opinions are more probable than others must have some means of assessing relative probability. The difficulty is that there is no way to be sure that any criterion of probability is correct. Again we need a criterion to validate a criterion of probability, and no such criterion is available. Were a candidate offered, we would have the additional problem of validating it, and so on. The problem, as before, seems unsolvable. The effect of recognizing as much is often intellectual despair.

Sextus' catalog of skeptical arguments was made known to sixteenth-century Parisians through the works of Michel de Montaigne, particularly his *Apology for Raymond Sebond* (1576). Montaigne's arguments for skepticism gained popularity, and it became quite widely held that any intellectual doctrine could be defended or defeated by one possessed of sufficient intellectual tools. Reason came to be seen as inducive to an attitude of skepticism.

It was probably in response to the popularity of skepticism and the apparent hopelessness of any attempt to acquire concrete human knowledge that Descartes believed any attempt to construct a philosophical system was doomed to failure without indubitable and certain foundations. At any rate there is no

doubt that in the First Meditation he is at pains to discover a proposition that he can know with certainty and that can form the basis of his philosophical system.

The subtitle that Descartes gives his First Meditation is "What Can Be Called into Question," and is, as one might guess, a direct result of his first rule of method from the *Discourse*. He begins by telling the reader that it will be necessary to take a fresh look at all accepted opinions:

> But inasmuch as reason already persuades me that I ought no less carefully to withhold my assent from matters that are not entirely certain and indubitable than from those which appear to me manifestly to be false, if I am able to find in each one some reason to doubt, this will suffice to justify my rejecting the whole. And for that end it will not be requisite that I should examine each in particular, which would be an endless undertaking; for owing to the fact that the destruction of the foundations of necessity brings with it the downfall of the rest of the edifice. I shall only in the first place attack those principles upon which all my former opinions rested.
> (*Philosophical Works* 1.145)

That "reason already persuades me" demonstrates Descartes's acceptance of and reliance on the conclusions reached in the *Discourse*. He now begins a survey of his opinions: "All that up to the present time I have accepted as most true and certain I have learned either from the senses or through the senses . . ." (1.145). But, he then reminds himself, we have at times caught our senses deceiving us (such things as optical illusions "deceive" the senses), and a wise man never trusts what has once deceived him. But it is not only such things as distant objects (if you look at a coil of rope from a distance, you might mistake it for a snake) and optical illusions that give us reason to doubt the senses; there is something even more misleading. It is possible to be asleep and dream that one is having sensory impressions when in fact one is not: "How often has it happened to me that in the night I dreamt that I found myself in this particular place, that I was dressed and seated near the fire, whilst in reality I was lying undressed in bed!" (1.145–146).

The importance of this realization should not be underestimated; it is the first step in the "radical" Cartesian program of hyperbolic doubt (doubting everything that can be doubted), which is mandated by the first rule of method. The extension of this argument, or realization, proves to be equally interesting. The question that Descartes raises is this: How can we be sure of what is real and what is not real if we cannot distinguish dream life from nondream life? What mark is there that distinguishes the dream world from the real world? What criterion can we use to adjudicate the distinction? A brief survey of the possible criteria will serve to demonstrate the problem. One might respond that one knows one has been dreaming because at the end of a dream one awakens. But surely it is possible to dream that one is waking up. Another answer is the familiar pinching test. If you pinch yourself, you can be sure you're awake. But surely this won't work either. It is entirely possible to dream that you are pinching yourself. Many philosophers have considered the question about dreaming. It seems that there is no test, no criterion, that one can rely on to distinguish dream life from the real world.

The dream argument against the certainty of knowledge should appear very potent at this point, but Descartes noticed there were some truths, not dependent on the senses, that seemed to be outside its scope:

> That is possibly why our reasoning is not unjust when we conclude from this that Physics, Astronomy, Medicine and all other sciences which have as their end the consideration of composite things, are very dubious and uncertain; but that Arithmetic, Geometry and other sciences of that kind which only treat of things that are very simple and very general, without taking great trouble to ascertain whether they are actually exis-

tent or not, contain some measure of certainty and an element of the indubitable. For whether I am awake or asleep, two and three together always form five, and the square can never have more than four sides, and it does not seem possible that truths so clear and apparent can be suspected of any falsity [or uncertainty].

> (1.147)

Had Descartes found his core of certain truths? He would have, had he been armed with only the dream argument, but he advanced an even more powerful argument at this point: the second "radical" step in the program of hyperbolic doubt, which we will call the move to the evil demon.

Descartes argues in the second "radical" step that there is "implanted in my mind" an idea that there is an all-powerful God, one who can bring about any state of affairs. What would prevent such a God from bringing it about that one is always deceived?

> But how do I know that He has not brought it to pass that there is no earth, no heaven, no extended body, no magnitude, no place, and that nevertheless [I possess the perceptions of all these things and that] they seem to me to exist just exactly as I now see them? And, besides, as I sometimes imagine that others deceive themselves in the things which they think they know best, how do I know that I am not deceived every time that I add two and three, or count the sides of a square, or judge of things yet simpler, if anything simpler can be imagined?

> (1.147)

Descartes admits that God probably wouldn't do such things, but then asserts that the postulation of such an evil demon provides grounds for the doubt of all opinions, and that these opinions cannot be trusted if one's quest is certainty. His conclusion of the First Meditation includes the following:

> I shall then suppose, not that God, who is supremely good and the fountain of truth, but some

evil genius not less powerful than deceitful, has employed his whole energies in deceiving me; . . . I shall remain obstinately attached to this idea, and if by this means it is not in my power to arrive at the knowledge of any truth, I may at least do what is in my power [i.e., suspend judgment], and with firm purpose avoid giving credence to any false thing, or being imposed upon by this arch deceiver, however powerful and deceptive he may be.

(1.148)

As if to reinforce the conclusion of his First Meditation, Descartes begins the second, "The Nature of the Human Mind: It Is Better Known Than the Body," with the following:

The Meditation of yesterday filled my mind with so many doubts that it is no longer in my power to forget them. And yet I do not see in what manner I can resolve them; and, just as if I had all of a sudden fallen into very deep water, I am so disconcerted that I can neither make certain of setting my feet on the bottom, nor can I swim and so support myself on the surface. I shall nevertheless make an effort and follow anew the same path as that on which I yesterday entered, i.e. I shall proceed by setting aside all that in which the least doubt could be supposed to exist, just as if I had discovered that it was absolutely false; and I shall ever follow in this road until I have met with something which is certain, or at least, if I can do nothing else, until I have learned for certain that there is nothing in the world that is certain. Archimedes, in order that he might draw the terrestrial globe out of its place, and transport it elsewhere, demanded only that one point should be fixed and immoveable; in the same way I shall have the right to conceive high hopes if I am happy enough to discover one thing only which is certain and indubitable.

(1.148)

Descartes then begins a survey of the possible truths. He again rejects all sensory data and all mathematical truths, but fixes upon the one thing that constantly reappears in his doubts about the world, the "I" that refers to himself:

But how can I know there is not something different from those things that I have just considered, of which one cannot have the slightest doubt? Is there not some God, or some other being by whatever name we call it, who puts these reflections into my mind? That is not necessary, for is it not possible that I am capable of producing them myself? I myself, am I not at least something? But I have already denied that I had senses and body. Yet I hesitate, for what follows from that? Am I so dependent on body and senses that I cannot exist without these? But I was persuaded that there was nothing in all the world, that there was no heaven, no earth, that there were no minds, nor any bodies: was I not then likewise persuaded that I did not exist? Not at all; of a surety I myself did exist since I persuaded myself of something [or merely because I thought of something]. But there is some deceiver or other, very powerful and very cunning, who ever employs his ingenuity in deceiving me. Then without doubt I exist also if he deceives me, and let him deceive me as much as he will, he can never cause me to be nothing so long as I think that I am something. So that after having reflected well and carefully examined all things, we must come to the definite conclusion that this proposition: I am, I exist, is necessarily true each time that I pronounce it, or that I mentally conceive it.

(1.149–150)

What is certain for Descartes is that as long as the I thinks, the I exists. This is the famous *cogito ergo sum* (I think, therefore I am). The argument he presents can be looked at in the following way: in the First Meditation Descartes examines several doubt-makers within his method of hyperbolic doubt, each of which is designed to strip away those opinions that are not certain. They are: (1) my senses are deceiving me, (2) I am dreaming, (3) God is deceiving me, and (4) an evil demon is deceiving me.

What Descartes notices about the doubt-makers is that each assumes the proposition "I exist." None of the reasons that Descartes can adduce for doubting what he previously believed provides any reason for doubting the truth of his own existence. In fact, "I doubt that I exist" embodies "I exist," because doubting requires some agent. Doubting cannot be carried out without something to do the doubting. Therefore, Descartes concludes, no unclouded mind could rationally hold that the proposition "I doubt that I exist" is true.

The question that Descartes has to settle is just what sort of being this I is. He begins with an assessment of the corporeal side of his existence and quickly rejects it as part of his *essence*. This term is introduced in a technical sense in Cartesian philosophy: the essence of an object is that property or set of properties without which the object would cease to continue as that object. For example, we might say that the essence of a nail is that it exists in the universe, and that it is made of matter; clearly, if the nail didn't exist in the universe, we would be hard pressed to identify it as a nail.

There are two reasons for Descartes's rejection of body as a part of his essence. The first is the familiar evil demon argument: the "malign spirit" could be deceiving him into believing that he has a body when in fact he doesn't. The second reason is that Descartes can imagine himself without a body; therefore the body cannot be a part of his essence. If you couple the first reason with Descartes's insistence that we accept only the certain, his rejection of body as the essence of the I is an obvious move. He then continues the search for the elusive essence of the I:

I find here that thought is an attribute that belongs to me; it alone cannot be separated from me. I am, I exist, that is certain. But how often? Just when I think; for it might possibly be the case if I ceased entirely to think, that I should likewise cease altogether to exist. I do not now admit anything which is not necessarily true: to speak accurately I am not more than a thing which thinks, that is to say a mind or a soul, or an understanding, or a reason, which are terms whose significance was formerly unknown to me. I am, however, a real thing and really exist;

but what thing? I have answered: a thing which thinks.

(1.151–152)

Descartes thereby identifies himself as thinking substance, distinct from nonthinking or corporeal substance. The answer to the question What sort of thing is the I? is *sum res cogitans* (I am a thing that thinks).

At this point Descartes goes on to consider the nature of corporeal objects, taking as his example a piece of wax. He notes that the wax possesses many properties, including smell, color, texture, shape, and temperature, but he also notices that it is possible for the wax to lose its color, change its shape, lose its smell, and so on, and still lay claim to being the same piece of wax. But what then is the wax—what is its essence? "Let us attentively consider this, and, abstracting from all that does not belong to the wax, let us see what remains. Certainly nothing remains excepting a certain extended thing which is flexible and movable" (1.154). But what are these properties? Descartes tells us that they are accessible only through the intellect, for there are too many possibilities encompassed by extension, flexibility, and changeability. And he concludes:

It is now manifest to me that even bodies are not properly speaking known by the senses or by the faculty of imagination, but by the understanding only, and since they are not known from the fact that they are seen or touched, but only because they are understood. . . .

(1.157)

Descartes therefore feels comfortable asserting that as a *res cogitans* his mind is more "easily or manifestly perceptible" than are bodies. Another conclusion that the reader is to absorb sub rosa is that there are two distinct sorts of substance in the world: minds, whose essence is thinking; and bodies, whose essence is extension. This last point is treated much more fully in the Sixth Meditation.

Descartes begins his Third Meditation, "Concerning God: That He Exists," by establishing a general rule: "that all things which I perceive very clearly and very distinctly are true" (1.158). Perhaps the best account of what Descartes means here by "clear" and "distinct" can be found in a later work of his, the *Principia philosophiae* (*The Principles of Philosophy*, 1644), where he writes:

> For the knowledge upon which a certain and incontrovertible judgment can be formed, should not alone be clear but also distinct. I term that clear which is present and apparent to an attentive mind, in the same way as we assert that we see objects clearly when, being present to the regarding eye, they operate upon it with sufficient strength. But the distinct is that which is so precise and different from all other objects that it contains within itself nothing but what is clear.
>
> (*Philosophical Works* 1.237)

In other places Descartes tells us that the "clear and distinct" are perceived by the "natural light of reason." At any rate it is important to understand the Cartesian move to clear and distinct knowledge. Descartes wanted to claim any knowledge that he perceived clearly and distinctly as true knowledge—an application of the general rule that was presented earlier. His reliance on clear and distinct knowledge caused a serious problem for him—a problem known as the Cartesian Circle—which we will examine later.

At this point in the Third Meditation, Descartes begins examining the ideas that he had on his mind. He observes that he had an idea of God. But from whence comes this idea? He notes that ideas are only representations:

> For just as this mode of objective existence pertains to ideas by their proper nature, so does the mode of formal existence pertain to the causes of those ideas (this is at least true of the first and principal) by the nature peculiar to them. And although it may be the case that one idea gives birth to another idea, that cannot continue to be

so indefinitely; for in the end we must reach an idea whose cause shall be so to speak an archetype, in which the whole reality [or perfection] which is so to speak objectively [or by representation] in these ideas is contained formally [and really]. Thus the light of nature causes me to know clearly that the ideas in me are like [pictures or] images which can, in truth, easily fall short of the perfection of the objects from which they have been derived, but which can never contain anything greater or more perfect.

> (1.163)

Descartes's proof of God's existence follows directly from these conclusions. The steps are:

1. I have an idea of God, an infinitely perfect being.
2. This idea of God has formal existence.
3. Whatever has formal existence must have a formally existing cause.
4. There must be as much total perfection in the cause of an idea as there is in the idea itself.
5. My idea of God has infinite total perfection.

Therefore:

6. God has formal existence.

An intuitive way to understand this proof is as follows: Descartes had an idea of God. This idea had to have come from somewhere. The cause of an idea must be at least as perfect as the idea itself; as the idea is of a supremely perfect being (God), the cause of the idea must be at least as supremely perfect. Therefore, for Descartes to have had an idea of God (a supremely perfect being), God must exist.

Descartes saw himself as proving the existence of God. It is important to note here that Descartes remained faithful to his method up to this point in the *Meditations*. Following his dictum to accept nothing as true that one could find the least reason to doubt, he searched his opinions and established the certainty of "I exist." He then established that this I must be a thinking thing essentially, and that it has in it *ideas.* Now, these ideas must come from somewhere, especially the idea of God. Where do they come from? Well, at least in the case of God, the only way to explain the existence of the idea is to allow for the existence of the source of the idea, since ideas can be nothing more than imperfect representations of their subjects. Descartes built his universe up from the most simple (the *sum* of the Second Meditation) to the point at which he established the existence of God.

Descartes concludes the Third Meditation:

> —a God, I say, whose idea is in me, i.e. who possesses all those supreme perfections of which our mind may indeed have some idea but without understanding them all, who is liable to no errors or defect [and who has none of all those marks which denote imperfection]. From this it is manifest that He cannot be a deceiver, since the light of nature teaches us that fraud and deception necessarily proceed from some defect.
>
> (1.171)

Descartes enters into the Fourth Meditation, "Truth and Falsehood," with the assertion that God can be no deceiver. The burden of the meditation is to prove the assertion. Up to now in the *Meditations*, Descartes has proven the existence of God, but he has yet to dismiss the evil demon argument, or the deceiving God argument. It is at least possible at this point in the evolution of the Cartesian system that there be both a good God and an evil one, or that there exists a God who is a deceiver. Descartes needed to establish that there is but one God, and that he is supremely perfect, which would in one stroke rule out the possibility of the existence of both the evil demon and the deceiving God.

The problem, quite simply put, is that Descartes noticed there was evil and error in the world, and this was manifestly incompatible with an all-powerful veracious God. Why is the existence of error and evil in the world incompatible with a veracious God? Descartes begins by noting that any faculty he possesses must have come from God:

> In the next place I experienced in myself a certain capacity for judging which I have doubtless received from God, like all the other things that I possess; and as He could not desire to deceive me, it is clear that He has not given me a faculty that will lead me to err if I use it aright.
>
> (1.172)

As Descartes rightly notes, it seems to follow that it is impossible to go wrong. But this is obviously a ludicrous conclusion. People do go wrong; they are susceptible to error. The question is: Why would an all-powerful veracious God have given us an imperfect faculty (imperfect in that we can be deceived through its use); and isn't the fact that we are deceived reason enough to conclude that God in fact condones such deception and is therefore a deceiver? The argument for God as a deceiver seems quite powerful.

Descartes begins the refutation of this argument by noting that so long as he thinks only of God, he can discern no cause of error or falsehood. The problem begins when he contemplates himself and matters concerning himself. God, Descartes reminds us, is the supremely perfect being; and just as we have an idea of God, we also have an idea of nothingness or nonbeing. The first attempt to resolve the problem of error goes like this:

> I am in a sense something intermediate between God and nought, i.e. placed in such a manner between the supreme Being and non-being, that there is in truth nothing in me that can lead to error in so far as a sovereign Being has formed me; but that, as I in some degree participate likewise in nought or in non-being, i.e. in so far as I am not myself the supreme Being, and as I find myself subject to an infinitude of imperfections, I ought not to be astonished if I should fall into error. Thus do I recognize that error, in so far as it is such, is not a real thing depending on God, but simply a defect; and therefore, in order to fall into it, that I have no need to possess a special faculty given me by God for this very purpose, but that I fall into error from the fact that the

power given me by God for the purpose of distinguishing truth from error is not infinite.

(1.172)

The answer to the question "How is error possible?" seems to come down to the answer "Because I am not God." That is, man is susceptible to error because he is not infinitely capable of applying the faculty of right judgment to all decisions that he must make. Only God is capable of doing so.

The next phase of the meditation is to examine the nature of error in man more closely. Descartes tells us that it depends on two concurrent causes: the faculty of cognition and the faculty of choice, or free will. God has given humankind an infinite faculty of choice, but we do not have infinite understanding, as this is reserved for God alone. We are therefore prone to error, not because God has restricted our choice or determined that we should err—indeed we are always free to choose rightly—but rather because we choose on the basis of insufficient information. Choices that we make are prone to error because our will extends much further than our understanding. When we do perceive something clearly and distinctly, there is no doubt that we understand it; God guarantees this. But what happens is that we are constantly making decisions, exercising our faculty of choice, on the grounds of nonunderstanding:

Whence then come my errors? They come from the sole fact that since the will is much wider in its range and compass than the understanding, I do not restrain it within the same bounds, but extend it also to things which I do not understand: and as the will is of itself indifferent to these, it easily falls into error and sin, and chooses the evil for the good, or the false for the true.

(1.175)

Descartes's conclusion then is that God is no deceiver. He provides an analysis of error that at once allows error to exist in men and preserves the veracity of God. What of those who complain that by giving us such a widely ranging faculty of choice, God in fact placed error in the world and hence could be seen as a deceiver? Descartes replies:

I have further no reason to complain that He has given me a will more ample than my understanding, for since the will consists only of one single element, and is so to speak indivisible, it appears that its nature is such that nothing can be abstracted from it [without destroying it]; and certainly the more comprehensive it is found to be, the more reason I have to render gratitude to the giver.

(1.177)

Descartes concludes the Fourth Meditation:

. . . it seems to me that I have not gained little by this day's Meditation, since I have discovered the source of falsity and error. And certainly there can be no other source than that which I have explained; for as often as I so restrain my will within the limits of my knowledge that it forms no judgment except on matters which are clearly and distinctly represented to it by the understanding, I can never be deceived; for every clear and distinct conception is without doubt something, and hence cannot derive its origin from what is nought, but must of necessity have God as its author—God, I say, who being supremely perfect, cannot be the cause of any error; and consequently we must conclude that such a conception [or such a judgment] is true. Nor have I only learned to-day what I should avoid in order that I may not err, but also how I should act in order to arrive at a knowledge of the truth; for without doubt I shall arrive at this end if I devote my attention sufficiently to those things which I perfectly understand; and if I separate from these that which I only understand confusedly and with obscurity. To these I shall henceforth diligently give heed.

(1.178–179)

In the Fifth Meditation, "The Nature of Material Things: God's Existence Again Consid-

15

ered,'' Descartes revives a theme from the First Meditation in considering the question of the certain existence of material objects. But, he tells us, before we can entertain the question, we must consider the ideas possessed in the mind about these objects. In our examination of these ideas we must determine which are distinct and which are confused.

Descartes notes that there are some ideas of objects which are such that even if they have no existence, they cannot be called non-entities. As an example he cites the triangle:

> . . . when I imagine a triangle, although there may nowhere in the world be such a figure outside my thought, or ever have been, there is nevertheless in this figure a certain determinate nature, form, or essence, which is immutable and eternal, which I have not invented, and which in no wise depends on my mind, as appears from the fact that diverse properties of that triangle can be demonstrated, viz. that its three angles are equal to two right angles, that the greatest side is subtended by the greatest angle, and the like, which now, whether I wish it or do not wish it, I recognize very clearly as pertaining to it, although I never thought of the matter at all when I imagined a triangle for the first time, and which therefore cannot be said to have been invented by me.
>
> (1.180)

What he concludes is: That which we clearly and distinctly understand to belong to the true and immutable nature of anything, essence or form, can be truly affirmed of that thing.

This principle is a very close relative of the general rule discussed earlier. Although we will not consider the ramifications of the principle (it has a long and rich philosophical tradition), we should note that it is the foundation of Descartes's ontological proof of God's existence, and will enable him to prove the existence of material objects. Descartes states:

> But now, if just because I can draw the idea of something from my thought, it follows that all which I know clearly and distinctly as pertaining

to this object does really belong to it, may I not derive from this an argument demonstrating the existence of God?
>
> (1.180)

Descartes continues with his famous ontological proof of God's existence:

1. God is a total of all perfections.
2. Existence is a perfection.

Therefore:

3. God exists.

He then writes:

> I clearly see that existence can no more be separated from the essence of God than can its having its three angles equal to two right angles be separated from the essence of a [rectilinear] triangle, or the idea of a mountain from the idea of a valley; and so there is not any less repugnance to our conceiving a God (that is, a Being supremely perfect) to whom existence is lacking (that is to say, to whom a certain perfection is lacking), than to conceive of a mountain which has no valley.
>
> (1.181)

By ''a mountain which has no valley,'' Descartes means an uphill slope without a downhill slope.

Descartes thus holds that God exists precisely because it is inconceivable that he does not exist, if we ponder his essence. Yet how did we discover his essence? We perceived it clearly and distinctly:

> But after I have recognised that there is a God—because at the same time I have also recognised that all things depend upon Him, and that He is not a deceiver, and from that have inferred that what I perceive clearly and distinctly cannot fail to be true.
>
> (1.184)

Descartes holds that God exists because he clearly and distinctly perceives that God's existence is necessary, as it is a part of his essence. But recall that Descartes's reason that clear and distinct ideas are necessarily true is God's veracity. It is hard to see how Descartes can have it both ways. Either he should use clear and distinct ideas to validate God's existence, or he should use God's existence to validate clear and distinct ideas.

As it stands the reasoning is circular. One cannot say that the reason for A's being true is B, while at the same time holding that the reason for B's being true is A. This is the famous Cartesian Circle, which is complex and has no easy solution.

Descartes concludes his Fifth Meditation:

> And so I very clearly recognise that the certainty and truth of all knowledge depends alone on the knowledge of the true God, in so much that, before I knew Him, I could not have a perfect knowledge of any other thing. And now that I know Him I have the means of acquiring a perfect knowledge of an infinitude of things, not only of those which relate to God Himself and other intellectual matters, but also of those which pertain to corporeal nature in so far as it is the object of pure mathematics [which have no concern with whether it exists or not].
>
> (1.185)

In the Sixth Meditation, "The Existence of Material Things: The Real Distinction of Mind and Body," Descartes proves the existence of the material world, thus fulfilling his promise to explain the most complex problems only in terms of the most simple truths. He moves from the simple truth of *cogito ergo sum* to a reconstruction of the rational world. Thus the Cartesian universe will satisfy the quest for certainty that Descartes mandates in his *Discourse*.

Briefly, Descartes's proof of the external world is: There is an inclination to believe in an external world because there must be objects of sensations; and since a veracious God would not allow him to be deceived in a matter such as this, the external world must necessarily exist. At the end of the Fifth Meditation, Descartes argues that the existence of the external world is at least possible, and by the Sixth he argues that this possibility is an actuality, the appeal to God's veracity being the step of the argument that validates its legitimacy. If God is truly veracious, then the material world must exist, as Descartes clearly and distinctly perceives it must.

Descartes also argues for the "radical" distinction between the mind and the body—between the two sorts of substance in the Cartesian universe. He argues that they are distinct precisely because he can imagine the two as separate:

> Because I know that all things which I apprehend clearly and distinctly can be created by God as I apprehend them, it suffices that I am able to apprehend one thing apart from another clearly and distinctly in order to be certain that the one is different from the other, since they may be made to exist in separation at least by the omnipotence of God.
>
> (1.190)

Descartes goes on to argue that because his essence is thinking, it cannot also be extension, and therefore the two must be distinct:

> . . . and, therefore, just because I know certainly that I exist, and that meanwhile I do not remark that any other thing necessarily pertains to my nature or essence, excepting that I am a thinking thing, I rightly conclude that my essence consists solely in the fact that I am a thinking thing [or a substance whose whole essence or nature is to think]. And although possibly (or rather certainly, as I shall say in a moment) I possess a body with which I am very intimately conjoined, yet because, on the one side, I have a clear and distinct idea of myself inasmuch as I am only a thinking and unextended thing, and as, on the other, I possess a distinct idea of body, inasmuch as it is only an extended and unthinking thing, it is certain that this I [that is to say, my soul by which I am what I am], is entirely and absolutely distinct from my body, and can exist without it.
>
> (1.190)

The mind and the body are distinct but closely bound. He explains:

> I am not only lodged in my body as a pilot in a vessel, but . . . I am very closely united to it, and so to speak so intermingled with it that I seem to compose with it one whole. For if that were not the case, when my body is hurt, I, who am merely a thinking thing, should not feel pain, for I should perceive this wound by the understanding only, just as the sailor perceives by sight when something is damaged in his vessel.
>
> (1.192)

The entire analysis of the mind/body distinction is perhaps best summarized in this way:

> In order to begin this examination, then, I here say, in the first place, that there is a great difference between mind and body, inasmuch as body is by nature always divisible, and the mind is entirely indivisible. For, as a matter of fact, when I consider the mind, that is to say, myself inasmuch as I am only a thinking thing, I cannot distinguish in myself any parts, but apprehend myself to be clearly one and entire; and although the whole mind seems to be united to the whole body, yet if a foot, or an arm, or some other part, is separated from my body, I am aware that nothing has been taken away from my mind. And the faculties of willing, feeling, conceiving, etc. cannot be properly speaking said to be its parts, for it is one and the same mind which employs itself in willing and in feeling and understanding. But it is quite otherwise with corporeal or extended objects, for there is not one of these imaginable by me which my mind cannot easily divide into parts, and which consequently I do not recognise as being divisible; this would be sufficient to teach me that the mind or soul of man is entirely different from the body, if I had not already learned it from other sources.
>
> (1.196)

The *Meditations* are the rules of method worked out. They are an attempt to provide a bedrock of certainty for opinions about the world. Descartes was challenging scholastic doctrines by establishing the validity of the rational universe, both physical and spiritual. His method of hyperbolic doubt was largely successful in clearing away most of the usual stumbling blocks. But even the great Descartes was himself guilty of dogmatic positions. His rejection of the certainty of sensory data forced him to reject the empirical scientific method and brought him in direct conflict with a group of philosophers organized around Pierre Gassendi.

The publication of Sextus Empiricus' texts in 1621 had a profound impact on the intellectual world of the time. One of the philosophers most deeply affected was Gassendi, a young faculty member at the University of Aix. It was Gassendi's aim to use the wisdom of the ancients as a weapon against the scholastics. In 1624 he published his *Arguments Against the Aristotelians*, a work that challenged the foundations of scholastic teachings and cemented his reputation in the French intellectual community. In the 1630's he began a project reviving the philosophy of Epicurus, most notably his atomism.

Gassendi and Descartes were quite famous combatants. Gassendi's "Objections" to the *Meditations* were well received in the intellectual circles that also served as the forums of philosophic debate. He was the first to point out the Cartesian Circle, as well as one other famous Cartesian problem. Gassendi noticed that Descartes's proof of the existence of the self, the *cogito ergo sum*, could apply not only to thinking but to any other active verb as well. Using Descartes's argument, one could prove the *sum*, the "I am," not only by thought (as in the *cogito*) but also by activities such as walking, talking, or any other that requires an implied subject. Consequently, "I walk, therefore I am" is every bit as valid a proof of the "I am" as is "I think, therefore I am." Descartes never found a way out of this problem; his answers in the "Replies to the Objections" are disappointing.

Gassendi was a philosopher committed to the rise of empirical science. He was one of the first modern philosopher-scientists to insist that the confirmation of scientific theories was dependent on their conformity with observed phenomena. Gassendi held that the philosopher-scientist had an obligation to examine various hypotheses by subjecting them to experiments and tests. It was Descartes's belief, however, that the answers to questions of science could be arrived at without such experiments—that the "true" answers would be obtained not by checking their conformity with the "real" world, but by checking their conformity with certain metaphysical principles that the theorist held. As one might guess, this sort of rationalistic science at times formed hypotheses about the world that observation did not bear out.

There is one surviving anecdote concerning Descartes and Gassendi that demonstrates the inevitable clash between two such radically different approaches to science. In attempting to work out a complete theory of the physical world, Descartes formulated several theories of motion, to which he was committed because of his background in metaphysics. His fourth "law" of motion held that in any collision, the larger of the two bodies colliding would always win out. Gassendi noted that if the larger of the two bodies was at rest, Descartes was committed to holding that this body would continue at rest, no matter how fast the smaller body was moving. Gassendi set up the following test of Descartes's fourth law of motion: he placed a cannonball at rest in the middle of a floor and aimed a musket at it. When the musket ball, which was much smaller than the cannonball, struck the cannonball, the cannonball began to move. This result was clearly opposed to the hypothesis of the Cartesian theory, and Gassendi concluded that Descartes's fourth law was inaccurate. Descartes, of course, responded that Gassendi's test proved nothing, for all it showed was that the cannonball "appeared" to move, not

that it really moved at all—Gassendi merely saw it incorrectly. At this point Descartes reiterated his proof of the fourth law and denied the validity of Gassendi's conclusion.

As one can see from the above, the differences between the two conceptions of the role of science are irreconcilable. Gassendi saw the purpose of science as explaining the observed phenomena of the world around us, while Descartes saw it as a reflection of his theories about the material world—"the way that it should be." That these two conceptions would clash—and clash in a grand way—should not be surprising; indeed, these differences actually helped to further the cause of science in the seventeenth century.

With the publication of the *Meditations*, Descartes had gone a long way toward establishing a substantial reputation for himself. The Cartesian school of thought soon became the rage in intellectual circles across the Continent. As Descartes's popularity grew, so did his circle of acquaintances. Among his friends was Heinrich Reneri, a professor of philosophy at the University of Utrecht. Reneri considered himself a close friend and disciple of Descartes's, and he said as much to both colleagues and students. Reneri died suddenly at an early age, and at his funeral, Amelius, a professor of history and rhetoric, delivered the eulogy. He took the occasion to praise Descartes above all else, thinking that this would have pleased Reneri, and called Descartes "the only Atlas and Archimedes of our age." This was praise that offended several in the audience, particularly Gysbertus Voetius, pastor of the Reformed Church of Utrecht.

Voetius possessed neither remarkable intellectual gifts nor personal charm. But he did possess a fanatical resentment of the Cartesian school and a personal hatred for Descartes himself. His first salvo against Descartes was to publish a pamphlet under the title *Theses on Atheism* in which he attacked the "new philosophy," the Cartesian philosophy, as being committed to atheism. He reasoned that Cartesian doubt led to skepticism; people who propounded skepticism were of course skeptics, and skeptics were but atheists in disguise. In order to gain more support for his crusade, Voetius attempted to enlist the aid of some prominent theologian. He settled on Mersenne, not knowing that he was Descartes's most trusted friend, and wrote a letter requesting the good father's assistance. Mersenne promptly delivered the letter to Descartes, who read it and sent it back to its author.

In 1641 Voetius was appointed (by rotation) to the rectorship of the University of Utrecht. By 1642 he managed to get the University Senate to reject the new philosophy, and reaffirm its commitment to scholasticism. It was at this point that Descartes entered into the controversy directly. In a letter to the Reverend Father Dinet, provincial of the Jesuits, he wrote:

> A man who passes in the world as a theologian, having, by vigorous abuse of all who differ from him, in a style of broad humor, which takes the ear of the vulgar, gained credit for an ardent zeal for religion; and who likewise, by continually putting out little pamphlets—though not worth reading—and citing many authors—though these so often are against his position that it is likely that he knows them only from the table of contents; and by speaking with great confidence, though very much at random, concerning every branch of knowledge, passes for learned among the ignorant.
>
> (Oeuvres 7.584)

Voetius responded by citing Descartes and calling him up before the courts of Utrecht. Descartes, claiming to be a French citizen and viewing the whole matter as ridiculous, responded that the courts had no jurisdiction in this case, and did not attend the trial. The decision of course went against him. Descartes was found guilty of libel (because of the letter to Father Dinet) and was sentenced to be burned at the stake. Voetius went so far as to request that the pyre be large enough to be seen several miles away.

At this point Descartes fled to the Hague and placed himself under the protection of the French ambassador. The dispute was resolved on 11 June 1645 in a decree imposing silence on both Descartes and Voetius, which of course neither party heeded. The battle raged on for several more years, although not much more came of it.

While Descartes was having his problems with Voetius, he met Princess Elizabeth of the Hague. Elizabeth was a young woman of twenty-two who reportedly spoke six languages and was quite adept in mathematics. She wanted to meet Descartes after having read and been favorably impressed by his *Meditations*. Descartes and Elizabeth soon formed a warm friendship that generated a good deal of correspondence. He demonstrated his respect and admiration by the effusive dedicatory letter to her, which praises her intelligence and charm, in his *Principles of Philosophy*, his third published work.

Descartes's *Principles* is a masterly work; therein he explicates more fully the philosophical system that he set forth in the *Meditations*. The work is organized into four parts: part 1 concerns the principles of human knowledge; part 2, the principles of material things; part 3, the visible world; and part 4, the earth. In a letter to the abbé Claude Picot, the French translator of the *Principles* (which were written in Latin), Descartes wrote:

> I would like to explain here what seems to me to be the order which should be followed in our self-instruction. To begin with, a man who as yet has merely the common and imperfect knowledge which may be acquired by the four methods before mentioned, should above all try to form for himself a code of morals sufficient to regulate the actions of his life, because this does not brook any delay, and we ought above all other things to endeavor to live well. After that he

should likewise study logic—not that of the Schools, because it properly speaking is only a dialectic which teaches how to make the things that we know understood by others, or even to repeat, without forming any judgment on them, many words respecting those that we do not know, thus corrupting rather than increasing good sense—but the logic that teaches us how best to direct our reason in order to discover those truths of which we are ignorant. And since this is very dependent on custom, it is good for him to practise the rules for a long time on easy and simple questions such as those of mathematics. Then when he has acquired a certain skill in discovering the truth in these questions he should begin seriously to apply himself to the true philosophy, the first part of which is metaphysics, which contains the principles of knowledge, amongst which is the explanation of the principal attributes of God, of the immateriality of our souls, and of all the clear and simple notions which are in us. The second is physics in which, after having found the true principles of material things, we examine generally how the whole universe is composed, and then in particular what is the nature of this earth and of all the bodies which are most commonly found in connection with it, like air, water and fire, the loadstone, and other minerals. It is thereafter necessary to inquire individually into the nature of plants, animals, and above all of man, so that we may afterward be able to discover the other sciences which are useful to man.

(*Philosophical Works* 1.210–211)

Perhaps the best statement of the organization of Cartesian philosophy is given in the same letter to Picot, where Descartes writes: "Thus philosophy as a whole is like a tree whose roots are metaphysics, whose trunk is physics, and whose branches, which issue from this trunk, are all the other sciences" (1.211). Descartes saw his *Meditations* as establishing the "roots" of this tree, and the *Principles* were the "trunk." In the same letter to Picot, Descartes advises that no one read his *Principles* without first having read his previous works.

The explication of the physics in the *Principles* drew fire from many quarters. The most severe criticisms focused on part 2 of the work, and were aimed by none other than Gassendi. In part 2 Descartes sets forth his controversial laws of motion, one of which (the fourth) we have already discussed. But Descartes seems to have had another goal besides stabilizing the "trunk" of his philosophical tree. He seems to be counterattacking the school that was establishing itself around Gassendi. As previously noted, Gassendi revived the notion of Epicurean atomism in the seventeenth century. In part 2 Descartes challenges the notion of atoms, and provides a proof of their nonexistence. He insists that whatever is material is necessarily divisible, and hence the idea of an indivisible material atom is nonsensical. The controversy raged on for years, with neither Descartes nor Gassendi willing to admit defeat.

Descartes and Elizabeth's correspondence grew more and more technically philosophical following the publication of the *Principles*, eventually resulting in the last work that Descartes was to publish in his lifetime, the *Passions de l'âme* (*The Passions of the Soul*, 1649). There he seeks to explain how all psychological manifestations can be reduced to mechanical causes. One should read Descartes's *Passions* as his attempt to complete the picture of philosophy set forth in the *Principles*. In 1647 circumstances required that Elizabeth leave the Hague. She became the abbess of the Lutheran abbey of Hervorden, in Westphalia. Her correspondence with Descartes continued until his death.

In the summer of 1647 Descartes left the Netherlands for Paris, where he met Blaise Pascal. The two apparently became close friends, although little is known about their relationship. While in Paris, Descartes also made a number of close friends at the royal court and secured the promise of a pension from the crown.

After returning to Holland in May 1648,

Descartes was persuaded to go back to Paris by the crown's promise of a handsome pension. Once there he realized that there would be no pension, since the rebellion of the Fronde had broken out. Dejected and unsure of what to do, he again returned to Holland.

In Sweden, Queen Christina took an interest in the new philosophy. She had never met Descartes, but one of her advisers, Pierre Chanut, was a friend and correspondent of his. Christina began by reading the *Meditations*, asking Chanut to help her through them. By 1647 Descartes and Christina were corresponding and were cultivating a friendship. In 1649 Christina invited Descartes to visit her in Sweden, and at the beginning of October he arrived in Stockholm.

Descartes tutored Christina in philosophy and found her an eager student—so eager, in fact, that she resolved to keep him in Stockholm by offering him a pension, a title, or whatever else he desired. But before any arrangements were made, the Swedish winter began and Chanut was taken ill with an inflammatory disease of the lungs. Descartes nursed him to the point of recovery until on 2 February 1650 he himself was struck by the same illness. Descartes, who had a history of weak lungs, died holding the hands of his two friends, Chanut and Christina, on 11 February 1650.

Descartes not only unlocked the door of scientific progress by releasing the seventeenth-century scientist from medieval dogma, he completely revised the metaphysical view of the universe. He originated a method of inquiry, a systematic program that, if correctly followed, would validate progress in any number of fields—science, epistemology, or metaphysics. The *Meditations* stand as one of the great masterworks in the history of philosophy; and Descartes stands as one of the greatest intellectuals in the history of thought.

Selected Bibliography

EDITION

Oeuvres de Descartes. 12 vols. Edited by Charles Adam and Paul Tannery. Paris, 1897–1913. Reprinted 1964.

TRANSLATIONS

Descartes: Discourse on Method, Optics, Geometry, and Meteorology. Translated by Paul J. Olscamp. Indianapolis, 1965.

Descartes: Philosophical Letters. Translated and edited by Anthony Kenny. Oxford, 1970.

Descartes: Philosophical Writings. Translated by G. E. M. Anscombe and Peter Geach. Edinburgh, 1954.

The Essential Descartes. Edited by Margaret Wilson. New York, 1969.

The Philosophical Works of Descartes. 2 vols. Translated by Elizabeth Haldane and G. R. T. Ross. Cambridge, 1911–1912. Reprinted New York, 1955.

BIOGRAPHICAL AND CRITICAL STUDIES

Beck, L. J. *The Metaphysics of Descartes: A Study of the "Meditations."* Oxford, 1965.

Curley, E. M. *Descartes Against the Sceptics.* Cambridge, Mass., 1978.

Doney, Willis, ed. *Descartes: A Collection of Critical Essays.* New York, 1967.

Frankfurt, Harry. *Demons, Dreamers, and Madmen: The Defense of Reason in Descartes' "Meditations."* Indianapolis, 1970.

Hooker, Michael, ed. *Descartes: Critical and Interpretive Essays.* Baltimore, 1978.

Kenny, Anthony. *Descartes: A Study of His Philosophy.* New York, 1968.

Lowndes, Richard. *Descartes: Life and "Meditations."* London, 1878.

Vrooman, Jack. *René Descartes: A Biography.* New York, 1970.

Williams, Bernard. *Descartes: The Project of Pure Enquiry.* London, 1978.

Wilson, Margaret. *Descartes.* Boston, 1978.

MICHAEL HOOKER

PIERRE CORNEILLE
(1606–1684)

IN THE THIRTY-TWO plays he wrote between 1629 and 1674 Pierre Corneille transformed French tragedy and laid a foundation for modern comedy in France. He put on the stage startlingly new types of heroism and utilized unprecedented modes of engendering emotions. His plays remained unrivaled in popularity until the tragedies of Jean Racine, which, in the late 1660's, emphasized the power of unrestrained passions and imitated ancient Greek tragedy. Corneille's heroes and heroines elicited, by their dazzling nobility and feats of courage and sacrifice in the face of frightful consequences, the admiration of a public that included the aristocrats, who set standards of taste, and the professional men of letters, who determined canons of form. Despite changes in taste and regime, Corneille's four early tragedies—*Le Cid* (1637), *Horace* (1640), *Cinna* (1641), and *Polyeucte* (1643)—were frequently performed in the late seventeenth century and the eighteenth century. With *La mort de Pompée* (*Pompey's Death*, 1644) and the comedy *Le menteur* (*The Liar*, 1643), they still hold a central position in the French classical repertoire. In occasional revivals, such early comedies as *La place royale* (*The Royal Square*, 1634) and *L'Illusion comique* (*The Comic Illusion*, 1635) and the tragedies *Rodogune* (1645), *Nicomède* (1651), and *Othon* (1664) reveal ingenuity of plot, striking characters, and thrilling speeches that continue to surprise a French audience brought up on Corneille's acknowledged masterpieces but not aware of similar qualities in the neglected plays.

The four great tragedies differ from most of Corneille's other tragedies. They deal primarily not with the qualities requisite in a monarch or with struggles to gain political power for its own sake—the obsessive themes of many of the plays composed after *La mort de Pompée*—but with transformations experienced by men and women who, suddenly disillusioned with the values habitually or conventionally regulating their thought and behavior, discover other means of governing themselves and of setting new examples of dealing with other people and of shaping events. Challenged by conflicting codes of honor and passion, they undergo formidable psychological struggles before they repudiate values predicated on previously unquestioned convention or on deceit, and they display an active commitment to attitudes and priorities conducive to genuine happiness, honor, and self-respect. Corneille's tragedies all contain repeated appeals to ideals of duty and honor—duty to various traditional codes of behavior that are taken for granted until the protagonists discover the painful consequences of constant fidelity to duty. The genuinely heroic character redefines himself with respect to duty and personal honor, and by choosing values that he more fully understands because of his experience, he infuses the values with new significance and energy, thereby providing an unparalleled model of a man inseparable in thought and action from his most cherished beliefs. These plays exert a strong appeal because audiences admire the heroism in such behavior, experiencing wonderment that such behavior may be possible, and because the protagonists provide models that can be emulated as ideals, in imagination if not in fact.

Corneille is the first French dramatist to develop his ethical and political thought through a long series of plays. He converted a popular entertainment into a source of serious moral exploration that reflected the theoretical and practical concerns of the surviving feudal nobility of his times. In figures like Rodrigue and Chimène (protagonists of *Le Cid*), Horace, Emperor Auguste (in *Cinna*), and Pauline (in *Polyeucte*), he created paradigms of action who struggle to choose ethical bases for behavior. Corneille's dynamic theater deals with active processes—transformation, doubt, and search for values and identity. This theater grapples with the disturbing preoccupations of the baroque or Counter-Reformation period that surface in works as various as Montaigne's *Essays*, Cervantes' *Don Quixote*, and Descartes's *Meditations:* Who am I? By what means can I define myself? How do I relate to the world around me, to the physical universe, to the moral order, to God? Corneille's answers, as problematic as the questions themselves, always invite further critical, skeptical thought.

These concerns are not apparent in the life of the dramatist. He seems to have kept quite separate his personal life and the philosophical tendencies of his theatrical productions. His early years in no way indicate any ambition for a life in the limelight. Born on 6 June 1606, he attended a Jesuit school in his native Rouen, trained for the law, was granted his degree in 1624, and obtained two official positions in the Rouen judicial establishment (which he held until 1650, long after his recognition as the leading playwright of France).

According to legends (that he himself may have spread), he was a dashing young man about town. Despite his success in Paris, he maintained his residence in Rouen until 1662, when both he and his younger brother, Thomas, also a dramatist, moved to the capital. (Residence in Paris was made a condition of his election to the French Academy by that body of savants in 1647.) His private life was led mostly in Rouen, where he married in 1641, raised a family, and was constant in his Catholic devotion and service in his parish. His public activities in Paris brought him recognition and wealth. There he earned the enmity of jealous rivals and the admiration of friendly critics, such as Guez de Balzac and Jean Chapelain, and of the aristocratic circle gathered in the salon of the marquise de Rambouillet, which was the center of Parisian aristocratic refinement in the 1630's and 1640's. Corneille could hold his own among critics and noble amateurs of literature and the arts; he could compose playful verse to celebrate a beautiful woman, in the vein of Petrarchist preciosity. Apparently he could also engage in flirtation as a harmless amusement that the conventions of the Hôtel de Rambouillet and other salons kept within virtuous bounds: his eye for beautiful women is suggested by a series of poems, published in 1660, written to woo the actress Thérèse Gorla (better known by her stage name, Marquise Du Parc). This evidence of gallantry does not, however, convey any sense of triumph.

Although Corneille enjoyed the attention of admirers in Paris, he returned to Rouen for the tranquillity in which he could compose plays, answer critics—most notably in three *Discourses on Dramatic Poetry* (1660)—and engage in nonsecular literary pursuits. One such effort was his monumental translation from Latin of Thomas à Kempis' *Imitation of Jesus Christ*, more than thirteen thousand lines of poetry on which he worked during the 1650's when he had retired from the theater after the failure of *Pertharite, roi des Lombards* (1652). The choice of this project indicates something about his personal values and the Christian life he preferred in a way that none of the plays does. In fact it is virtually impossible to use what is known of his life to comment on the plays, and vice versa. That applies to his entire dramatic output, from the early comedies to the final tragedies.

Nothing in the early biography even suggests that Corneille had intended to become a playwright; and although rumors circulated that the plot of *Mélite,* his first comedy, performed in 1629, was based on a real episode in his life, no proof substantiates the claim. On the contrary, Corneille seems to have been suddenly inspired to compose a play by the visit to Rouen of a theatrical troupe from Paris led by Guillaume Montdory. Without warning, the comedy and the ambition it suggests burst forth like one of his own later hero's stunning revelations. For *Mélite* was a revelation emblematic of his career as a series of experimental presentations of unexpected, innovative forms and subjects.

In 1629 comedy as a dramatic genre barely existed in France. Crude farces—remnants of traditional plots and stock characters dating back to the Middle Ages—were produced by itinerant performers at seasonal fairs and, more permanently, in booths set up in Paris along the Pont-Neuf and outside the old walls near the abbey of Saint Germain on the Left Bank. Farces of virtually no literary value were also to be seen at the Hôtel de Bourgogne, the single regular theater in the city. Comic, farcical, and relatively vulgar passages were also interspersed among serious scenes in tragicomedy and dramatic pastoral, the two most popular theatrical genres of the late 1620's and early 1630's. But as far as comedy of manners is concerned, it was as though the Renaissance had not happened in France: there simply were no such plays, lacking serious political overtones but with plots borrowed from Renaissance novellas and deriving ultimately from Roman comedy, dealing with love affairs and marriages among young people opposed by their elders, with additional obstacles such

as intercepted letters, feigned and real madness, confused identities, and general misunderstandings. (A model for such a play did exist—in pastoral form, however—in Honorat de Racan's *Bergeries,* published in 1625 but unplayable because of its length, nearly three thousand lines, and complications of plot.) Corneille virtually invented the comedy of manners for seventeenth-century France, preparing the way for Molière and, in tragedy, for Racine. *Mélite* succeeded in Paris because of its innovativeness, its witty and unbombastic language, and the surprising skill with which the amateur from Normandy composed poetry. Corneille's triumph led him to visit Paris for the first time. His delight in applause, as well as remuneration, was stimulated. He came into contact with theoreticians of dramatic poetry and became aware of neo-Aristotelian theory and rules: he was no longer an amateur or an innocent.

Corneille began a long association with Montdory's actors, called the Troupe du Marais after the newly fashionable neighborhood on the right bank, built over marshy ground (*marais*) where the theater was located. After another experiment testing his skills in a different dramatic genre in the tragicomedy *Clitandre* (1631), Corneille composed variations on *Mélite* in four more comedies, of which the last, *La place royale* (1634), marks a serious turning point. The protagonist, Alidor, is no typical lover: disregarding his lady's desires, he gives her up to a rival in order to preserve his independence. Instead of achieving contentment as it is usually defined in comedy, Alidor chooses another source of happiness. Corneille suddenly introduces into comedy extraordinarily serious, problematic questions of ethics. Alidor subjects passion to analysis, asks himself what he really wants, challenges his will to exercise control and to prefer what reason dictates. Asserting independence from sentiment and convention, he defines himself by his thought and consequent behavior as a free man. He knows and repudiates his weakness, while he amazes the other characters and the spectators. The Cornelian tragic hero and strategy of producing admiration before acts of will and independence first appear in Alidor, protagonist of a comedy.

By this time Corneille was part of the literary circle sponsored and dominated by Cardinal de Richelieu, Louis XIII's chief minister. Richelieu had ambitions of producing tragedy according to the neo-Aristotelian rules governing unity of time, place, and action. Such works, he believed, would grace French culture and provide instruments of political indoctrination as well, since the stage afforded opportunities for public exhibition of virtues to be celebrated and misdeeds to be condemned in a well-ordered state. Richelieu desired to codify language and the arts as part of a general centralizing of control over all aspects of public activity. As power was increasingly wrested from the feudal nobility by the crown, so patronage of cultural endeavors, with a concomitant restriction on subject matter and the mode of execution, was to be the affair of a ministry serving the king. In effect the cultural program inaugurated by Richelieu, who died in 1642, a few months before the death of Louis XIII, was a forerunner of that initiated by the young Louis XIV, who, with his minister, Colbert, became in the 1660's and 1670's the grandest of all patrons of the arts. Under Louis XIV, cultural achievements were to reflect the glory of the Sun King's political and military accomplishments. Richelieu founded the Académie Française in 1635 as an authoritative body of savants charged with responsibility for regulating standards of usage—grammar and vocabulary—for the French language. The academy was ultimately intended to ensure linguistic unity within the various provinces of the kingdom, in another aspect of Richelieu's efforts to centralize all aspects of the nation under the crown. (In fact such unity was not imposed until Napoleonic reforms in the early nineteenth century, and even then not entirely.)

The five poets whom Richelieu gathered around him in his magnificent Palais Cardinal (now the Palais-Royal)—in which he had a theater constructed—were to accomplish for dramatic art what the academy was to do for language in general. They tried to put into practice the results of debates by literary theoreticians over the neo-Aristotelian unities as well as conventions dictating the proprieties of behavior on the stage. Tragedy and tragicomedy in the 1620's and early 1630's were unruly forms. Plays were not expected to conform to codified regulations. Typical are the plots of the prolific Alexandre Hardy, who wrote for the Hôtel de Bourgogne until around 1630. They could involve long periods of time and several locations; they might contain several unrelated subplots, as well as violent actions acceptable to the sensibilities of the 1620's but offensive both to the official sensibilities Richelieu chose to promote and to the refined ones cultivated in aristocratic salons like Madame de Rambouillet's.

Under the minister's sponsorship, several tragedies and pastorals were composed according to the rules, most notably by one of his five poets, Jean Mairet, whose *Sophonisbe* and *Sylvanire* are the first examples of "regular" tragedy and dramatic pastoral in France. Jean de Rotrou, not part of the group of five but close to their activities, produced *Hercule mourant* (*Dying Hercules*) in 1634. Based on a tragedy by Seneca, it concentrates the death of Hercules in a few hours and in one place; but, true to the Senecan tradition, the play contains violence and lengthy moralizing. When Corneille chose a subject for his first effort in tragedy, he looked not to Roman history, like Mairet, but to Greek myth as treated by Seneca. Ironically, Corneille's later plays dealt with mostly Roman subjects, whereas his subsequent mythological tragedies number only a handful. Richelieu might have been pleased with Corneille's *Médée* (*Medea*, 1635) on formal grounds, since it respects the unities to the same extent as its model, Seneca's *Medea*. But the minister could hardly have approved of the behavior of the characters, who

26

violate every rule of morality. Corneille puts on the stage a duplicitous tyrant in Créon; an unfaithful husband who deserts his wife for political expediency in Jason; a sexually obsessed princess in Créuse; a lovesick, powerless king in Égée. Médée herself is resolutely confident of her sorceress' powers to cut through the ruses and deceits of tyrant, husband, and rival, to denounce their unworthy, ignoble behavior and to punish them for it. Médée is a monster who sees clearly into her enemies' devices and her own strength of will to challenge king, kingdom, and universe. She opposes herself—"Myself, I say, and that is enough"—to Fortune, engendering in the audience both admiring wonder and astounded horror. Corneille respects the formal rules governing the construction of tragedy, but he uses the concentration that the rules produce to intensify dramatic effects and to raise questions that Richelieu could not have envisaged when he encouraged his poets to produce works for the public stage.

That problem may underlie the quarrel concerning the merits of *Le Cid* and Corneille's assertion of independence from both Richelieu's patronage and the pundits of the Académie Française. Corneille himself may have wondered about limits and asked himself which subjects and devices were appropriate for tragedy. *L'Illusion comique*, produced in 1635 and perhaps written at the same time as *Le Cid*, violates every rule: it mixes tragedy, comedy, real life, magic, theatrical performance, genuine heroism, and hyperbolic boasting that mask cowardice, noble values, and base motives. Within a parody of Senecan tragedy and of Corneille's own comedies, it presents a figure of authority who, contrary to the conventions of the dramatic genres parodied, regrets his error in opposing his son's desires. Traditional reason here acknowledges the power of youthful passion and respects the impulses of willfulness. The confusion of modes and values that characterizes this "strange monster," as Corneille calls it, recurs in *Le Cid*, which provoked a scandalous

argument among partisans and opponents, including members of the Académie. Richelieu could use that body for purposes of political manipulation. The dispute over *Le Cid*, which Richelieu finally had to stop by personal intervention, may have begun as his attempt, under cover of a literary quarrel, to distract from the dangerous, possibly subversive nature of the play and to put Corneille on warning.

Le Cid was acclaimed as a masterpiece when it was first performed. Audiences found it beautiful: "Beautiful, like the *Cid*" entered French as a proverbial expression. The crush at the Marais Theater to see Montdory as Rodrigue was so great that aristocrats who would not be turned away were seated in the wings and on the stage (a practice retained in Paris theaters, despite protests by actors and playwrights, until 1759). The play contained thrilling poetry, noble and heroic characters, exciting and surprising situations—and dubious politics. Delighted audiences might applaud, critics might condemn (on grounds of improbability and offense to decency), and Richelieu might find subversive, the same sequence of episodes: the count de Gormas challenges royal Spanish authority by slapping an elderly nobleman, Don Diègue, whose son, Rodrigue, kills the count in a duel to avenge his father's honor, despite the king's displeasure. (Richelieu was also irritated, for Rodrigue's duel set a poor example in France, where the minister had outlawed dueling.) Her father's death notwithstanding, the count's daughter, Chimène, continues to love Rodrigue but vows to pursue vengeance. Rodrigue's amazing defeat of an invading Moorish army prompts the king to exempt him from ordinary justice, and after Rodrigue defeats Chimène's champion on the field of honor in single combat, the king predicts that the lovers' marriage will occur. Richelieu might even have found fault with the king's behavior: instead of exercising authority, he fails in act 2 to judge between two subjects demanding justice, Chimène and Don Diègue; in act 4 he tricks Chimène into admitting her love, and he accepts her proposal for a duel; he even visits a subject, Chimène, in act 5. The conclusion is also ambiguous, with Chimène's protests undercutting the king's promise to Rodrigue of marriage to Chimène after a decent interval. In effect the play is constructed to produce a series of shocks and surprises, at nearly each of which the authority of the crown is rendered dubious. *Le Cid* begins in the manner of comedy with a conversation about the marriage with parental approval of two young people in love; it becomes a serious conflict with increasingly grave political dimensions that Richelieu must have observed and deplored.

The change in the nature of the action is reflected in the transformations of the hero, who grows from an untested young man, to the upholder of family honor against Spain's greatest swordsman (who is also his beloved Chimène's father), to the Cid, or supreme chieftain, as the defeated Moors hail him on the battlefield. Each development is accompanied by difficult struggles—both moral and physical—and each stage produces ethical dilemmas. Corneille concentrates Rodrigue's transformations in three specific moments: the reflective stanzas, known as the *stances*, concluding act 1 (1.6.291–350); act 3, scene 3, while he overhears Chimène declare that her father's death at Rodrigue's hands has not destroyed her love; the interval between acts 3 and 4 during the battle with the Moors, which he recounts to the king (4.3.1257–1329).

Rodrigue's poetic monologue—the stances —occurs soon after a soliloquy by his father, "Oh rage, oh despair, oh hateful age!" (1.4.237–260). Don Diègue's earlier speech contains the theme of transformation, but in negative terms: he grieves that age has so physically deteriorated him that a man in his prime can outrageously sully his honor. Desire for revenge is his immediate response; no reflection intervenes. If his own arm cannot wield the avenging sword, his son's will strike instead. The old man's blood-and-thunder

monologue introduces the terms that Rodrigue's soliloquy treats meditatively: only physical force may purge moral degradation; the "bras" (arm) may restore lost honor; spiritual or moral means associated with "âme" (the soul) may not. Diègue's words to his son permit no hesitation; he gives voice to the code of honor: "Die or kill." The stances, like Don Diègue's monologue, move from passivity and paralysis to determination. The energy in the final stanza duplicates Diègue's outburst when his son enters: "Rodrigue," he demands, "have you courage?" Rodrigue's answer indicates a bravado characteristic of a heedless comic figure like the matamore in *L'Illusion comique*. The lines are often cited as typical of the Cornelian character's boundless energy and unquestioned sense of self-worth: " 'Rodrigue, have you courage?' 'Anyone but my father would experience it on the spot' " (1.5.261–262).

This instinctive boast produces a quasi-comic effect in a process of ego inflation and sudden letdown. Don Diègue excites his son's curiosity by narrating the affront to his honor—a slap across his face—while he delays identifying the culprit, so that Rodrigue must interrupt to demand the name. His father cites the law of honor to a speechless Rodrigue: Chimène's father must be destroyed. Rodrigue's energy gives way to paralysis.

At the beginning of the stances, he is in shock:

> Pierced to the depths of my heart by a blow that is as unexpected as it is deadly, wretched avenger of a just cause and unfortunate victim of an unjust unyielding necessity, I remain immobile, and my stunned soul yields to the blow that kills me. So near to seeing my passion rewarded, oh, God, the strange anguish! In this insult my father is offended, and the offender is Chimène's father.
>
> (291–300)

No longer looking forward to his first duel, he detests his predicament and indulges in self-pity, describing himself as wretched, unfortunate. He remains motionless physically and psychologically. In the second and parallel stanza he sees himself as "reduced," constrained and diminished by the choice between love and honor, both infinite and absolute values: "Des deux côtés mon mal est infini" (On both sides my pain is infinite: 307). These are terms of a typically Cornelian dilemma: honor and duty are transcendent, eternal values opposed to passion. These are not abstract terms; they are laden with significance and emotion for the characters and audience of the 1630's and 1640's. (In the plays composed during the 1660's and 1670's, however, such terms occur as clichés or formulas, as though Corneille were ringing conventional changes on what had originally been deeply dramatic, passionate conflicts, and as though he were making a devastating comment about characters who could resolve the opposition of duty and passion coldly.) The image in Rodrigue's second stanza reveals an inexperienced young man suddenly aware of his infinitely small moral force as he is trapped between two infinitely vast moral values, commitment to a beloved woman and obligation to family honor. The tragic vision of helplessness arouses compassion for Rodrigue, who reacts to his dilemma, so far, with his soul, the source of feelings, not his mind. Although the opposition of values—father, mistress; honor, love—appears reasonably ordered, and although Rodrigue seems to weigh the merits of each side, no rational argument occurs. Instead Rodrigue's extraordinary anguish precludes rational decision: "Oh God, the strange pain!" (308), he repeats. He addresses as a cause of woe the very sword he had enthusiastically seized from his father to kill the still unnamed enemy. His first decision is also not rational: suicide satisfies no one; and the argument that failing to claim vengeance will make him unworthy of Chimène, who will despise him as a coward, leads to no rational solution. At the conclusion of the suicide stanza he evokes his soul: "So

then, my soul, since I must die, let us die at least without offending Chimène" (329–330).

Then his energy suddenly resurfaces. Attention shifts from soul to arm, from self-pity and passivity to belligerence and active defense of traditional values. The context of the psychological struggle also changes. He no longer sees himself caught between two infinite values; now that he is aware of Spain and of future generations, his context is defined by a place and time where honor is the highest value. The energy with which he had entered recurs more intensely, now directed to an appropriate object: his glory as the instrument of restoring his family's honor before the admiring witness of Spain for all time to come. Rodrigue is decisively transformed in the final two stanzas. In effect, however, a restoration to traditional values is accomplished, not a discovery of something new: "I will give my blood as pure as I received it" (344). Under shock, his soul, forgetting the aristocratic code, had failed to respect the basis of all reasoning for a nobleman, the honor on which are predicated all other values and the civil order. Rodrigue's first transformation reinforces the power of ancient codes of behavior. Rediscovering the meaning of honor, he strides off to exact vengeance and to display unprecedented devotion to the system of obligation underlying the social caste. This commitment is expressed in terms of physical force, of violence in the unquestioning service of an ethical law. After Rodrigue's momentary stage of doubt on the threshold of heroism, Corneille may be expected subsequently to present him as consistent with his transformed manner, his fidelity to the past, and his devotion to an image of himself before the admiring judgment of future generations.

But Corneille is a strategist of surprise. Rodrigue in act 2 strikes in the heat of enthusiasm, energetically provoking the count with challenges phrased in the popular language of comedy. His declarations of courage make Chimène's father acknowledge Rodrigue's transformation into an admirable hero acting upon authentic values. Ironically, the count is punished for his violation of those values in Rodrigue's first exercise in their defense. But when Rodrigue next appears, in act 3, he seems physically and morally exhausted, and he desires condemnation and punishment by Chimène. This retrogression to passivity proves temporary; once Rodrigue, hiding behind a tapestry—a situation smacking of comedy—hears Chimène confess her love, he seizes the initiative, leaping forth to attack her verbally and forcing her to admit her love and, therefore, to abandon fidelity to the code of honor that dictates a vengeance she abhors. Knowledge of her passion transforms him again; he pursues the advantage of his knowledge like a duelist seeking the weak spot in his adversary's defense. This encounter is marked by cruel aggression. The shock of seeing Rodrigue in her home weakens Chimène, and with every ironic line he callously strikes where she is most vulnerable. He virtually mocks her inability to kill him, as he had taunted her father. The bloodstained sword, offered in a sarcastic gesture, reminds Chimène of her helplessness. Rodrigue invokes honor and duty to justify his action and even recapitulates the stages of the stances, with some major misrecollections, to show that, after hesitation, he acted to join faith with ancient values. He in fact declares his own heroism and sacrifice of sentimental values to the feudal caste order, as he tries to reduce Chimène to admitting she cannot follow her own commitment to that code.

Rodrigue's account of his decision to avenge his honor also follows that strategy. His revisionist version emphasizes Chimène's part in the argument of worthiness: but he does not state that he considered suicide to avoid her displeasure, nor that he challenged the count to gain honor before Spain and posterity. He makes the decisive argument seem his unworthiness of Chimène should he refuse to defend his honor. Rodrigue misrepresents the stances to make Chimène acknowledge his commitment to the code of honor and her inability to duplicate that commitment in action.

Although Chimène responds in the same appropriate language, her failure to exercise her duty is clear. Words like "gloire," "honneur," "devoir," "digne," "générosité" lack the energy Rodrigue had shown at the end of the stances. She is going through motions to accomplish an obligation she in fact hates: "This frightful duty, whose order kills me" (925). She repeats the argument of worthiness: "By offending me, you showed yourself worthy of me; I must, by your death, show my worthiness of you" (931–932). Rodrigue cruelly seizes on this, repeatedly offering Chimène the chance to kill him, until he finally obtains a direct avowal of love. The lyrical ending of the confrontation exalts Rodrigue's sense of triumph, as Chimène deplores her paralysis and expresses despair should she somehow succeed against her hopes in obtaining Rodrigue's death. For Rodrigue, a "miracle of love" has been revealed; Chimène discovers, in contrast, a "height of misery"—ultimate wretchedness.

Rodrigue's maneuvers in this scene shock the audience as well as Chimène and her confidante, Elvire. His appearance in the house of the murdered man is disturbing. Corneille keeps producing the sense of bewilderment and outraged sensibilities, uniting the audience in sympathy with Chimène. Although Rodrigue's fidelity to the code of honor deserves admiration, his disregard for Chimène's feelings and his attempt to make her abandon the code are dismaying. Rodrigue is a problematic hero—not the unequivocally admirable son, the unidimensionally respectful suitor, or the single-minded servant of the crown. The play caused controversy in 1637: questions of behavior and politics—not of language—provoked strong reactions. Rodrigue becomes conscious of his power, which is real enough; it is power in action. But he resembles Alidor, the hero of *La place royale*, who, within reach of happiness through a marriage, prefers to exercise his will and to bewilder everyone by his uniqueness (without concern for the sentiments of his fiancée). Alidor, a supreme egotist, celebrates self-sufficiency from a comic perspective as Médée does from the direction of serious tragedy. Egotism and the power of the will—wondrous qualities—may also be the characteristic failings of a character caught in both comic and tragic situations.

The transformation of Rodrigue along these lines continues in the remainder of the play. In act 3, scene 6, Don Diègue proposes a political metamorphosis intended to silence Chimène: Rodrigue must drive off the Moors and save Spain. When he next appears at court, the king pardons him, anxious to hear of his exploits and to make Chimène renounce claims upon the life of the kingdom's new hero. The king becomes a party to Chimène's humiliation. Corneille introduces a quasi-comic trick as the court deceitfully pretends sadness on Chimène's arrival, as though Rodrigue had been killed. (The ruse is especially low in the immediate context of Rodrigue's long, thrilling account of the battle. Long before Victor Hugo, Corneille joined grotesque to sublime.) Chimène swoons, but on learning the truth she demands a champion to defend her honor in a duel with Rodrigue and to give the lie to the appearance of love for Rodrigue caused by her swoon. This reaction to the king's ruse foreshadows the end. Chimène also undergoes transformation. She grows into a woman whose fidelity to traditional values makes her perform a brave act as impressive and stunning as Rodrigue's defeat of the Moors: she renounces him and stands in isolation against king, Cid, infanta, court. Her resolve and nobility inspire admiration even more than that for the play's titular hero.

The power of Chimène's determination can be appreciated only in the context of the final scene: despite pressure to marry Rodrigue from the king's daughter, Rodrigue, and the king himself, and despite her own admission of love, Chimène seems opposed to wedding the man who is both the state's hero and her father's assassin. Is the play a tragicomedy, as it was called in 1637 and in all printed editions until 1660, with a happy ending, or is it a tragedy with the characters forever unsatisfied in their desires, ambitions, or visions of the ideal life? Although in Spanish tradition the Cid did wed his Ximena, few of Corneille's contemporaries knew the legends and poems associated with the medieval Spanish national hero, including Corneille's source, *Las mocedades del Cid* by Guillén de Castro. Their response would be governed by the strategy of the play's conclusion. Corneille creates during the final moments a recapitulation of Chimène's resistance to Rodrigue. He brings back to the stage the infanta, who, in order to repudiate her own love for Rodrigue, a man not of royal blood, once before had encouraged the young nobleman to court Chimène. She had helped him overcome Chimène's initial disdain: "She loves Rodrigue, and she accepted him from my hand, and through my efforts Rodrigue overcame her disdain" (1.2.67–68). At the conclusion the infanta again leads Rodrigue to Chimène, even though she herself might now marry the Cid—no longer a simple nobleman but a conqueror of kings—as she had argued in her stances (5.2.1565–1596). She acts, however, according to a code of honor that respects the consequences of her acts: she sponsored their love; therefore she will exercise the will appropriate to a princess of Spain and renounce any claim to Rodrigue: "Dry your tears, Chimène, and receive without sadness/This noble conqueror from the hands of your princess." But now Chimène has genuine reasons to disdain the man who killed her father and forced her to confess her passion for him nonetheless, a confession he again seeks to elicit during his last speech to her.

Rodrigue begins with a two-verse preface to the king, asking pardon for speaking and kneeling to Chimène. Then he addresses Chimène at length. The form of his speech—the preface to the king, the long remarks to Chimène—makes the audience notice the surprising form of Chimène's speech, for it is just the opposite of Rodrigue's. She virtually dismisses him in half a verse—"Get up, Rodrigue" (1801)—which may express contempt; then she ignores him to address the king at length.

The content of the speeches is also revealing. Rodrigue again evokes his power to perform miraculous feats of valor—a reminder that he vanquished the invading Moors and that in his first duel he defeated Chimène's father; he repeats the offer of his unconquerable person to the justice of Chimène: only she may kill him. This repeats his argument in act 3, scene 4, when, knowing of her persistent love, he cruelly forced her to acknowledge her inability to take justice into her own hands and kill him. In act 5 he had also prompted her to order him not to allow her champion, don Sanche, to defeat him. Now, confident that she will again refuse the offer and admit her love, he publicly dares her to take his life. She rises to the challenge—by heroic resistance. In this public embarrassment she refuses to submit, as she had twice before, in private, in acts 3 and 5. She gains in stature during her speech, which contains stunning surprises. She follows the abrupt dismissal of Rodrigue with an admission that she cannot disclaim a love that she just inadvertently confessed; this statement suggests that Rodrigue has indeed forced Chimène to acquiesce. Suddenly Chimène objects to marriage, with newly discovered strength to resist. She refuses to serve as a pawn of the state and to be a reward given Rodrigue for his battlefield exploits. She also evokes a picture of her murdered father, denying that she can bear being touched by a man stained with that blood. Both arguments must have offended sensibilities in 1637: the first challenges the state—Spain in the fiction on stage or France under Louis XIII and Richelieu—whose interests must be satisfied to preserve order; the second openly refers with distaste to sexual relations.

The conventions in 1637 were not as rigorous as they became in the 1660's, when Corneille in fact toned down Chimène's speech. Sexual submission plays an important part in other plays: in Mairet's *Sophonisbe*, Massinisse's consummation of marriage with the heroine seals his revolt from Rome; and in Tristan L'Hermite's *Mariamne*, the heroine refuses to submit to her husband, Hérode, thus sealing her fate. But Sophonisbe and Mariamne are married women, with previous sexual experience; Chimène's allusions are shocking because she is unmarried. Her boldness is as shocking and impressive as Rodrigue's valor in battle, for she challenges the entire court, the state—and the audience as well, winning its respect by an act of temerity that breaks with conventional sensibilities. She duplicates Rodrigue's earlier violation of the conventions, the code of decency governing what might be spoken and done on the stage. But unlike him, she gains the audience's sympathy and admiration.

Chimène grows isolated as the only character remaining faithful to traditional values of honor and duty. Although she may claim to maintain these values as a pretext to avoid submission to Rodrigue, she stands apart from the king, who invites her to abjure revenge—honor as traditionally understood—because for political reasons he must satisfy Rodrigue. Out of necessity or expediency, others may compromise values; Chimène will not. Rodrigue promises military conquests in response to the king's proposal: he will boundlessly serve the state in order to regain Chimène's favor. He does not understand that his heroic exploits, for which the king compromises values, will not make her renounce her inflexible attitude: she is wedded to eternal values of honor and to the moment when her father was killed.

The king's last speech emphasizes hope in the effects of time, in Rodrigue's heroic exploits, and in the efficacy of the king himself. The king, however, is no persuasive figure of authority and wisdom. He has been consistently ineffective. The origin of the quarrel between Don Diègue and the count is a challenge of the king's appointment of the old man as his son's tutor—the wrong choice, if Diègue's subsequent behavior is any criterion. The figure of the king has a foot in comedy; he has something of the well-meaning, ineffectual type whom Molière would develop into a Chrysale, the browbeaten father in *Les femmes savantes* (1672). Thus it even seems appropriate that the king never observes his own daughter's infatuation with Rodrigue.

Chimène's opposition to king, court, and Spain itself evokes unqualified admiration. The king and Rodrigue anticipate future events in conformity with transformed values; Chimène looks back to a past with which she cannot break. She embraces the burdens of its values, traditions, codes of honor, and obligation, as she assumes the consequences of a violent act she did not initiate. She may even hate her obligations, as she admits to Rodrigue in act 3; she maintains fidelity to them, though they deny her conventional happiness. Unlike other, later Cornelian heroes, who overcome the past while aspiring to newly forged values, Chimène exercises her will to denounce changed values. In that sense she is as tragic as any Racinian heroine doomed by her past—without experiencing the self-deception that allows Racine's characters to pretend that the consequences of past acts do not destroy them in the present. She is lucid and honest throughout, and worthy of comparison with the archetypal tragic heroine, Sophocles' Antigone, for in her behavior she remains true to an unchanging moral order that she will not compromise for the convenience of a king or the civil order.

It is legitimate to wonder whether Chimène's attitude concerning the king's compromise and political necessity should not produce an ethical insight like that engendered by Sophocles' tragedy: that the civil order deteriorates once respect for the absolute moral order is compromised; that the stability of the civil order is predicated upon the unchanging moral order. Although Corneille's ethics may be evolutionary, belonging to a vision of the political order in which the compromise to necessity and the transformation of values contribute to happiness, nevertheless his ethics also contain an element of absolute, rigorously unyielding, tragic vision. In this sense *Le Cid* is a tragicomedy, not in the sense of plot or ending, but in the dual tragic and comic, absolute and relative, modes of perception and ethics that are applied. Chimène belongs to the tradition of Antigone, of Corneille's own Alidor, who refuses to compromise his liberty, and of his Médée, who opposes Créon, the tyrant of Thebes, a Senecan variant of Sophocles' tyrant. Corneille's kings—beginning with the weak, dependent ruler of Spain and extending to the last king, Orode, in *Suréna* (1674)—perhaps originate in this Créon. They all compromise strict ethical standards to maintain a civil order that, no longer founded upon rigorous moral bases, may no longer be worth preserving.

The king of Spain behaves according to *raison d'état*. At the end, although he does not overtly banish Rodrigue from the court, sending him to pursue the Moors amounts to an exile under the pretexts of service to the state and of absence to allow for Chimène's consolation. Rodrigue constitutes a danger to a weak king. (This theme also reappears with frequency in the later plays, most notably in *Nicomède* and *Suréna*.) During twenty-four hours, the transformation from an untested young man into the destroyer of Spain's military chief and the savior of the kingdom has also made him a feudal power commanding a large independent army. The king, for all his apparent favoritism, may recognize that Rodrigue's growth into a hero includes consequences that might be directed against the crown.

Rodrigue's exploits stir wonder—admiration—and also raise questions concerning their ethical dimensions or implications. The events in Corneille's next produced play, *Horace* (1640), may provoke admiration of another sort and engender stronger sentiments of horror and repulsion. We might wish in imagination to emulate Rodrigue's acts in the service of his country, although not his private life. In the case of Horace, neither public nor private behavior produces a wish for resemblance. The judgment of the late-seventeenth-century moralist Jean de La Bruyère that Corneille depicts men as they should be, Racine as they are, is hard to reconcile with a play in which heroic deeds committed in the name of ideals border on barbarism and culminate in fratricide.

After the quarrel with the Académie over *Le Cid*, Corneille left Paris for Rouen, where he produced the best answer to his critics: not one but two tragedies, *Horace* and *Cinna, ou la clémence d'Auguste* (*Cinna, or The Clemency of Augustus*), composed according to the formal rules allegedly violated in *Le Cid.* These plays created stunning aesthetic effects and made complementary political statements about the ethical bases of the civil order. Both deal with heroes in fateful situations, who discover inner moral resources and provide paradigms of commitment in action to values. One paradigm, Horace, is to be feared; the other, Auguste, emulated. Both plays might be compared with Vergil's *Aeneid*, whose hero, father of the Roman state, serves as a model to Vergil's patron, the historical Emperor Augustus. Horace comes to resemble Aeneas during his affair with Dido in Carthage, out of control and forgetful of his sacred mission to bring the gods of Troy to Italy, and again during the last cantos of the poem, when his task of founding Rome grows confused with his desire to avenge the death of the young man Pallas. In the last action of the epic, Aeneas repudiates the compassion that has characterized him throughout the poem—the compassion and respect for law that made him worthy of the gods' choice as the survivor of Troy and founder of Rome. Aeneas' final acts contradict his father's command made in Hades, where he reveals this truth: the Roman genius is in law and in both sparing and converting defeated peoples.

The serious political dimension in Corneille's plays produced in the 1640's marks a distinct turn from tragicomedy to genuine tragedy. These works all pose the classic dilemma of the violated or threatened relationship between civil order and moral order. The civil order is predicated upon respect for a moral order that posits the values represented in a dominant ideology or mythology. When those values are debased or taken for granted, or used as pretexts to cover selfish and morally suspect motives, the civil order is threatened with disintegration. In his Roman plays, Corneille introduced into French tragedy the moral plot not only of the *Aeneid* but of much more ancient Greek tragedy, particularly the Sophoclean type represented in *Ajax, Antigone,* and *Oedipus at Colonus,* and reflected as well in the ethical vision of Thucydides. Corneille's ethical and political philosophy places him solidly in the classical tradition, even though most of his subjects are not drawn from Greek sources.

Horace concerns the struggle for political domination between the sister-cities of Rome and Alba. Three warrior-champions from each side are to decide in combat their cities' destinies. They turn out to be two sets of brothers, the Horatii and the Curiatii, whose families are closely related by friendship and marriage. The Roman Horatii defeat the Alban brothers, with only one man, Horace, surviving. His victory is marred, however, as he murders his sister, Camille, in violent reaction when she curses Rome, whose champion, Horace, has killed her lover, Curiace. In the final act Horace is absolved of his crime by the Roman king. It is apparent that Horace has become a kind of sacred monster whose extraordinary courage, cunning, and devotion to Rome produce acts of physical grandeur and moral debasement. In comparison with Horace's irrevocable murder of Camille, Rodrigue's cruel aggression toward Chimène seems inconsequential. The Roman hero's action is bewildering: no one, on the stage or in the audience, knows how to respond to or judge a deed without precedent—except for the fratricide of Remus by Romulus. That murder, which occurred in the mythological past, underlies the very foundation of Rome, and Corneille may by implication be raising questions about the ethical validity of Roman attitudes, including Stoicism in the face of irrevocable deeds and destiny, as well as about the Roman state itself. And Rome may be a metaphor for the modern kingdom of France under Richelieu.

Horace also risks forgetting his goal, the defeat of Alba so Rome may rule by law, when he takes law into his hands and kills Camille. Defending Rome against curses may be correct, but Horace's unrestrained violence in executing a defense is also an inappropriate and ill-omened foundation to Roman power—like Aeneas' murder of Turnus and Romulus' fratricide. *Horace* and *Cinna* are political plays whose reflections of the heroic and the flawed aspects of the Roman ideal stir emotions in order to instruct audiences about the function of moral values in the individual men who compose civil and well-ordered states.

Like Aeneas, Horace vows to measure up as the man of destiny summoned mysteriously by the gods and challenged to develop the necessary character—discipline and submission to the necessities of his mission—that permits extraordinary accomplishments. Chosen to fight for his state in a duel that must break the ties uniting two families and for which he must stifle all natural human emotions of love, he declares without hesitation: "Rome has chosen my arm, I question nothing." He accepts the selection and the consequent personal misfortune as his fate, and he insists upon the glory implicit in honoring his obligation to Rome. Horace heroically converts the rigors of fortune into a source of intense moral satisfaction—pride—by identifying his will with that of the state, its gods, and its fate. He surpasses a passive Stoicism and pits himself in a superhuman manner against whatever trials fate may have in store for him. Horace is typical of the Cornelian hero, who welcomes the tragic dilemma as a test of his moral and physical powers, and who exhibits disdain for its frightening aspects. This hero considers the fateful situation a necessary consequence of decisions and events, but also as the opportunity awaiting him—his unique opportunity—to become the hero he is capable of being.

Horace's behavior exemplifies the extraordinary, even excessive extent to which the Cornelian hero is committed to honoring his *devoir*—duty or obligation—as he understands it. According to this central concept of Cornelian tragedy, the individual submits to moral demands imposed by a national or caste conscience, the ethical values common to a state, community, or clan, reaching back in time to the group's quasi-mythological origins. The *généreux*—the nobleman—remains faithful to the values of his race or clan, such as the Roman family, and guarantees the survival of the community and the preeminence within it of those who serve the laws. In effect the nobility constantly defines its aristocratic nature by practicing such a code, while restraining individual desires and passions whenever necessary. *Devoir* as an absolute moral consciousness asserts itself intuitively in the nobleman whom training or discipline has prepared for the morally correct choice in a crisis, when rational judgment falters under the pressure of painfully conflicting passions and duties.

Corneille's heroes, like Horace, in their devotion to moral obligation, surpass the neo-Stoicism popular in the Renaissance, such as marks the tragedies of Robert Garnier (active 1567–1583). Corneille was familiar with all the major sources of this philosophy—Senecan tragedy and moral literature, Roman historians including Plutarch in Jacques Amyot's popular translation—as well as with the neo-Stoicism of Montaigne's *Essays*. But he also knew the most successful dramatic works of the 1620's and 1630's, in which neo-Stoicism and its commitment to duty and to acceptance of the inevitable are virtually absent: the violence-laden plays of the prolific Alexandre

Hardy (active *ca.* 1605–1628) and Théophile de Viau's *Amours tragiques de Pyrame et Thisbé* (*ca.* 1620). Even in Mairet's *Sophonisbe,* the first tragedy composed in Richelieu's circle to conform to the rules of the unities, the protagonists abandon themselves to passion and knowingly flout their duty. Unlike Corneille's heroes, Mairet's engage in scheming and self-deception to satisfy passions opposed by Rome. In effect, *Sophonisbe* anticipates Racine's tragedies of the 1660's and 1670's, where, in a reversal of typical Cornelian heroic behavior, the denial of their duty by impassioned, violent characters produces tragic consequences. Were it not for the popularity of Corneille's treatment of neo-Stoic duty, even to the point of excess, French tragedy might have taken the path suggested by Mairet's play long before the advent of Racine.

Of course, not all of Corneille's characters behave like Horace. That exceptional man's moral stance is enhanced by the presence of an entire gamut of attitudes toward their fate shown by the other characters. These attitudes range from total opposition—by Camille, Horace's sister—through resolute but sorrowful Stoic acceptance of obligations to both country and family—by Curiace and his sister, Sabine, Horace's wife—to the case of Horace's elderly father, the paterfamilias, who, despite a moment of sentimentality toward Curiace's family, comes closest to Horace's own celebration of duty as an opportunity to display uncommon values and to acquire extraordinary honor. This scale provides a context in which the extreme positions of Camille and Horace provoke in the audience a sense of wonder and admiration; but these characters also seem abnormal, even barbaric and monstrous. Horace's enthusiasm for the battle contrasts with Curiace's humane regret that he must kill, or be killed by, the men he most loves in Rome; and even the armies and rulers of Rome and Alba regard the conflict between two sets of brothers as loathsome and as exceeding the limits of moral obligation.

Equally monstrous is Camille's outburst of curses against her homeland at the end of act 4, after Horace has perversely commanded her to acknowledge his achievement as the savior of Rome and to ignore the fact that he has killed her lover. The confrontation between brother and sister at the extreme, opposed ends of the scale of attitudes toward duty provides the most provocative, ethically problematic event of the drama. The other principal action, the offstage fight between the Horatii and Curiatii, is narrated in two long messenger speeches; but Horace and Camille commit acts of violence in full view of the audience. Corneille provides the spectators with no mitigating effects, as in those eyewitness accounts that include the reporter's own reactions as a means to manipulate the audience's response. Camille uses unusually violent language (4.5.1301–1318), and Horace, his sword upraised, menacingly pursues her off the stage into the wings to kill her. The audience hears her dying shout: "Ah, traitor!"

These extraordinary outbursts of passion are inevitable concomitants of the characters' extreme identification with duty to the state and to a lover. Corneille knew that he risked offending the audience's sensibilities and that some diehard critics, those who had attacked *Le Cid,* would also find in the murder a violation of the rule governing unity of action: at the end of act 4, when the apparent main event has been completed, Horace suddenly faces a new peril because of his rage. In fact when the hero loses his temper, Corneille is using a convention that is a throwback to the earlier, "unruly" tragedy, that of Alexandre Hardy in the 1620's, for instance. This device survived in the plays of Corneille's contemporary Tristan L'Hermite, whose Herod (in *Mariamne*) and Nero (in *La mort de Sénèque—The Death of Seneca*) cannot restrain their inherent violence. Corneille uses the older convention, however, not to flout the critics but to bring to a head the incipient flaw in Horace that is always present in a man of "vertu farouche" (savage virtue, or savage manliness, as the oxymoron might more properly be rendered). Corneille used this phrase to describe Horace in the *examen*, or study, he prepared as a preface published in the 1660 edition of his works. "Farouche" derives from the Latin *ferox*, basis of the English "ferocious." Horace, as a tragic hero, succumbs to his nature, which suddenly emerges in full fury and casts doubt upon the value of his previous acts. He may have made possible Rome's political supremacy, but if he succumbs to an irrational impulse to destruction—even to self-destruction, should one consider Camille the mirror image of her brother—then he threatens the rule of law and self-control that, according to Anchises' vision in the *Aeneid*, lies at the heart of Roman virtue and legitimizes Rome's claim to world power.

Corneille is concerned less with the fall of a tragic hero than with the revelation of dangers implicit in the nature of an extraordinary man whose stupendous acts evoke both horror and admiration. Horace's glorious exploits lack the ethical dimension of civilized beings serving a civil order predicated upon an acknowledged and respected, even sacred, moral order. In Corneille's theater the outstanding example of a man who founds such a civil order upon a newly discovered moral order is the emperor Auguste in *Cinna, ou la clémence d'Auguste*, the other tragedy composed in Rouen during the aftermath of the quarrel concerning *Le Cid*. The dual title suggests that this play, which may be Corneille's greatest dramatic achievement, concerns two men whose fortunes are inextricably connected. Since these men are emperor and subject—or ruler and citizen—the link between them stands as a metaphor for the relationship of the secular power and the citizenry. In effect Auguste discovers that his own behavior and values—products of his ethical defects and virtues—provide paradigms of action for all of his subjects to follow. He learns that he is responsible for both the corruption and the glory of Rome.

The plot alternates between a conspiracy to assassinate Auguste and the emperor's soul-searching, first over his desire to abdicate, then over his sense of responsibility for the moral chaos in Rome. That moral chaos is evident in Cinna himself, for he leads the conspiracy not to serve the political ideal of destroying a dictator to restore the Roman Republic, but because Émilie, his mistress, has set as the condition for marriage to Cinna Auguste's death in revenge for his assassination of her father. Ironically, Auguste asks Cinna and another conspirator, Maxime, to advise him concerning abdication; and to reward what he mistakenly assumes is Cinna's sincerity, the emperor showers him with more political favors, including the right to marry Émilie! Cinna's confusion becomes apparent as he recognizes Auguste's generosity and his own total dependence on the emperor's favor for his status in Rome, but he nevertheless promises Émilie to carry out her command for vengeance. When Auguste learns of the conspiracy from Maxime's servant, he meditates on the failure of his reign to inspire genuine gratitude, concluding that the fault lies in his own behavior: he set the tone for conspiracy, murder, and parricide by his own political executions and banishments. But he refuses to follow his wife Livie's advice to set a new tone in politics with clemency. After confronting Cinna with the facts of Cinna's enormous debt to him and of the conspiracy, Auguste learns of Émilie's involvement and, finally, of Maxime's. In an astounding act, he conquers his desire for vengeance, and he extends pardon and renewed friendship to the conspirators. Auguste's brilliant act inspires them to convert to the new model of thought and behavior that, Livie prophesizes, will endure as the foundation of Roman dominion. The conclusion of *Cinna* provides an antithesis—and antidote—to the problematic ending of *Horace*. It celebrates the divine aspect of Vergil's hero Aeneas, model for Augustus, as the conclusion of *Horace* exposes the monstrous side of Aeneas.

Cinna is also the first of Corneille's plays to deal overtly with the Machiavellian themes of power obtained at any cost and of the workings of Fortune. Both themes are of course prominent in the Roman historians whom Machiavelli studied and in Renaissance thought in general. Auguste's case as tyrant, then as benevolent despot, differs significantly from Corneille's later creations, for he discovers that he has in fact followed Machiavelli's advice to seize and maintain power by suspending normal Aristotelian (or Christian) moral standards and committing acts of force. His strong conscience grows increasingly active, and he becomes critical of power that can be held only by violent means. Corneille's later Machiavellian characters lack that self-awareness and self-condemnation. They are better typified by Cléopâtre in *Rodogune,* who is not to be confused with the more familiar queen of Egypt in *La mort de Pompée.* Cléopâtre stops at nothing, including poisoning a son, to keep the Syrian throne. The seekers of power in the late plays produced in the 1660's and 1670's are likewise not impeded by conscience. But Auguste seeks to end the reign of violence, and his miraculous discovery of a new ethical basis for the Roman civil order is Machiavellian—for it guarantees his safe exercise of power—even as it is truly benevolent toward Rome itself.

Auguste also escapes from the instability of Fortune, which he finds to be a function of his values and conduct and therefore within his control. He creates an ideology based upon his responsibility for governing himself and relationships among men and states. He surpasses Machiavelli's solution to the problem of Fortune through prowess, calculated risks, and impressive actions that produce wonder. Auguste also creates a community of values and benevolent conduct; he fashions a moral order with himself at the center, to rival the Aristotelian and Christian orders that Machiavelli suspends for his prince.

Auguste had feared that Fortune might topple him from the heights of power, from which, in a verbal paradox, "he aspires to descend" (2.1.370). Corneille drew inspiration for *Cinna* from Montaigne's essay "Various Outcomes of the Same Plan" (1.24), about the effects of accident or Fortune on all events, despite intentions, advice, or precautions. The idea of Fortune contradicts the assumption of a predictable moral order: it is a Renaissance equivalent of the absurd. Auguste suffers from his understanding of Fortune; although he would like to escape—or revolt—from it, abdication is too great a price. Corneille has created a significant variation on the traditional wisdom that the gods strike down the mighty and prosperous. He casts this tragic theme in political, secular terms, since Auguste equates Fortune with the Romans' lack of rational predictability: neither the love nor the fidelity of capricious men can be guaranteed. In his baroque vision of the court in act 2, everything is illusory and deceitful, even power, whose brilliance ("éclat") dims in Auguste's eyes because it cannot permanently control hearts and minds. The political fortunes of his predecessors also obsess Auguste: the dictators Sulla and Julius Caesar met ends inappropriate to their characters and lives.

Auguste does not understand in act 2 that Fortune ceases activity if the ruler provides values that produce happiness, which includes the satisfaction of desires—physical, psychological, moral. The ruler defines and clarifies these values in the manner of Plato's philosopher-king, who governs by wisdom and example. Auguste later discovers, or invents, a system of values in which he invites his erstwhile enemies, Cinna and Émilie, to participate as they pardon the traitor Maxime. He opposes clemency to conventionally practiced punishment, which breeds further disloyalties. With a radical, innovative moral value, Auguste distinguished himself from the entire universe of men whose behavior reflects primitive vengeful impulses. A moment before, Auguste had believed himself cut off from all men, as he learned of betrayal by those Romans in whom he had most confided. In fact, however, in his values he was not an isolated case, for he and the traitors followed the same failed system of moral values. The extent of the emptiness of these values is indicated by Cinna's quarrel with Émilie over credit for the plot to kill Auguste in act 5, scene 2. They invoke Roman values—honor, duty, nobility, liberty; but Cinna has conspired against his political patron to win Émilie in marriage, and Émilie schemes not to restore Roman freedom, but for reasons of vengeance. (Not incidentally in a play dealing with parricide, Émilie's father had been Auguste's own tutor, his instructor in moral behavior and values.) To restore significance to ancient values a truly noble act is necessary, one that repudiates personal vengeance and establishes an ethical model for emulation. Otherwise, Auguste is doomed—and Rome is doomed with him. For Auguste in act 5 is on the brink of perpetuating the error of exacting a harsh vengeance to serve failed and misunderstood values.

In this light *Cinna* is a tragedy of error and recognition, without the calamitous consequences that follow erroneous thought and action in Sophocles and Racine. (Whether *Cinna* arouses pity and terror is, however, another matter.) Of the major characters, Auguste and Cinna commit and recognize grievous errors of judgment. The initial recognition of error produces in neither a change of moral standards or conduct. Auguste's error concerns his conception of Fortune and his role in determining it. He remains passive and introspective until the very end, which is peculiar, given the depictions of him in act 1. The first subject introduced is Émilie's desire to avenge her father's death upon Auguste, whom she envisions on a throne in glory, while her father bleeds to death: "When I consider Auguste amidst his glory, and you reproachfully recall to my saddened memory that, killed by Auguste's own hand, my father lies upon the bottom step of Auguste's throne" (1.1.9–12).

Cinna's long tirade also portrays him as monstrous (1.3.163–240). The whole first act projects an impression of Auguste as a tyrant constantly engaged in furious, irrational bloodshed. But when act 2 begins, Auguste, seated upon his throne, appears quite different. He speaks in calm, solidly constructed verses, unlike the excited, uncontrolled thoughts of Émilie and Cinna in act 1; and moral insight pervades his great speech as though he had looked coolly at his situation and judged himself.

Corneille characterizes Auguste in that speech (2.1.355–404) as an analyst of the political and ethical consequences of action who cannot act because of the insecurity discovered in examples of Fortune provided by recent history. He finds no reasonable or predictable cause-and-effect relationship between intentions and acts, on the one hand, and consequences, on the other. Auguste depends for guidance on others, dead and alive: on Sulla and Julius Caesar, and on Cinna and Maxime. Ironically, Auguste seeks a decision from the worst possible source. The irony is increased by the fact that he has just dismissed all the courtiers but these two and has derogated the courtiers' value. Corneille uses stage movement to indicate the grandeur of Auguste's court and power. When act 2 begins, the courtiers are onstage but are dismissed by Auguste. He does not know that he has retained as advisers two of the most dangerous, importunate men at court. That serious error lends irony to the following scene, as Auguste acts out unwittingly his tragic failing of depending upon other men for example and advice instead of looking for criteria within himself.

The virtuosity with which Corneille constructs Auguste's great speech makes the point even more ironically. All the sentences end with moral insight: power disappoints; the human spirit always aspires to new goals; history provides examples of Fortune but is an untrustworthy mirror of destiny. Wisdom of this sort, however, does not provide the decisiveness needed for action. Auguste passively submits to conspirators, who base their arguments on past example and moral principles. The discussion of monarchy and republican government by Cinna and Maxime occupies most of act 2; Auguste passively listens. The final ironic twist occurs after Auguste accepts Cinna's brief for monarchy as the solution to a chaotic state, rewards him handsomely, and leaves. Cinna then reiterates to Maxime his intention to kill the emperor. All the political argument was pretextual rhetoric without moral commitment. Such is Auguste's most trusted adviser, and that is the measure of his error.

When in act 4, in his next appearance, Auguste confides only in himself, he makes more mistakes. The monologue in act 4, scene 2 begins and ends passively, with pleas to heaven and Rome. This rhetoric indicates his incapacity for decision and action: his own mind is stunned by the monstrosity of the ungrateful, deceitful Cinna, and Auguste is consequently blind to the significance of the moral truths that occur during the monologue and in Livie's subsequent proposal of clemency as a calculatedly brilliant alternative to the usual cruelty.

Auguste's monologue is one of two equivalents of Rodrigue's stances (the other is Cinna's soliloquy in act 3, scene 3); the form, however, is not lyric but epic, drawing upon Roman history. Auguste reflects upon his habitual violent manner of coping with problems of life and death (4.2.1130): "Look into yourself, Octave, and stop complaining." He addresses the call for introspection not to himself as the emperor Auguste but to Octave, Julius Caesar's adopted son, whose ruthlessness as a triumvir has provided a paradigm for conduct in Rome. The images of blood shed to gain and consolidate power lead to a repetition of the initial vision of Auguste in the play: he sees, as Émilie did, his tutor killed by his hand, and the tableau of action is even more explicit:

> Summon within your mind, after so much bloodshed, the bloody images of your banishments, recall how you yourself became the slaughterer of those near and dear to you, driving the dagger yourself into your tutor's breast, and then dare to accuse Fate of injustice when you see those nearest and dearest to you take arms to punish you.
> (1137–1142)

Corneille makes Auguste move radically from one extreme position to another, allowing Auguste some justification for each. The overall result bespeaks a moral confusion like Émilie's (and like Cinna's in act 3). He experiences profound insights and recognizes a tragic paradox: although weary of cruelty, he understands that he furnishes the paradigm that Rome follows in seeking his death. He does not know how to stop; violence is ingrained in his character—or in his nature. He does not realize yet that he must impose discipline upon his nature to forge a newly ethical character lest he resemble Horace and the wrong Aeneas. Instead, Auguste chooses a pseudosolution to the dilemma of recognizing error without knowing how to correct it: death for himself and for Cinna. This quasi-Stoic submission to the insolubility of the paradox reflects a despairing sense that life without nobility must be worthless, as well as reflecting his characteristic impulse for violent revenge. The quasi-Stoic posture, emphasized in the repetition of "Meurs" (Die), indicates a refusal to cope with the problem in his own soul, a problem of his character and not of Fortune, while the "brilliant" ending he proposes resembles all the actions associated with power to which he had attributed little merit in act 2. Finally, however, even his fantasy is denied, and Auguste remains passive before all the antithetical courses of action that he proposes. His insights concerning his responsibility as provider of a paradigm of destructive conduct and his incapacity to refrain from the behavior he condemns lead nowhere decisive; the struggle resulting from his consideration of his own life—not the examples of Sulla and Caesar—bewilders him. His sudden intuitions blind him morally. That is when Corneille furnishes a genuine solution in the advice of Auguste's wife.

PIERRE CORNEILLE

Livie proposes pardoning Cinna to embarrass him into admitting Auguste's moral superiority: Auguste's control over his passions marks his fitness to govern others, and his boundless magnanimity, his greatness of soul, will move Rome to love Auguste. This is, in effect, the solution Auguste discovers at the conclusion, but Corneille makes him refuse the advice coming from someone else, even from the person closest to him. This is peculiar, for Auguste has just, albeit rhetorically, asked for a sign to direct his action. Auguste refuses advice and will no longer consult with anyone, after Cinna's betrayal.

Auguste here commits a genuine tragic error: armed with knowledge and self-knowledge, which bring him blindness instead of enlightenment, he acts irrationally when the solution is offered. A Sophocles or a Racine would generate pity and fear by presenting some ironic prediction of a calamitous consequence of the refusal to see truth and act honestly upon it. Corneille permits no such tragic emotions. Auguste's rebuffs to Livie serve to spotlight Auguste's tyrannical nature; he is generous to a fault, full of moral insight, and a tyrant nonetheless. Auguste is a variation of the stage tyrant of Renaissance and seventeenth-century tragedy: inflexible, irrational, subject to the whims and passions that amount to his Fortune. Corneille uses Auguste's advantages of generosity and moral insight ironically to emphasize his failure to deal with the problem he perceives, to overcome the tyrant's limitations he finds and hates in himself. The outburst of his tyrannical nature in the scene with Livie precludes the production of pity and fear or, in the Cornelian manner, admiration inspired by a grand gesture. He is closer to Tristan L'Hermite's Hérode in *Mariamne* and Néron in *La mort de Sénèque* than to the Machiavellian prince.

Like Auguste, Cinna understands a truth about himself and his imperial patron, but does not act in accordance with that moral insight. Corneille places antithetical terms in Cinna's monologue at the physical center of the play (3.3.865–905): commitment to serve Émilie's vengeance in order to possess her; awareness of Auguste's virtuous generosity. Cinna expresses the dilemma in terms of *générosité*, nobility that obliges one to honorable behavior; but he falls short of a *généreux*: he is servile, to Émilie and to Auguste by turns. He cannot decide which commitment to honor. This situation could be tragic, producing pity and fear—or even admiration, at the awakening of Cinna's noble instincts; but Corneille arranges the speech to make Cinna's noble sentiments appear inauthentic. Cinna's awareness of Auguste's worthiness to reign follows from generous gifts—*bontés*—just bestowed on himself, not from a perception of virtue in Auguste. His own ingratitude offends Cinna because he realizes that his status in Rome depends upon Auguste's patronage. (Auguste himself confronts Cinna with an even stronger version of this truth in act 5.) Cinna is not generously, nobly, independently disinterested as he weighs the merits of "les douceurs de l'amour, celles de la vengeance" (the pleasures of love, those of vengeance: 877) or even "la gloire d'affranchir le lieu de ma naissance" (the glory of setting free the place of my birth: 878) against treachery committed upon "a magnanimous prince who holds so dear the little that I am worth, who loads me with honors, who overwhelms me with wealth, who, seeking advice for his rule, takes only mine" (881–884). Nor is he disinterested as he plots to kill Auguste: no ethical purpose motivates him, such as love of freedom and restoration of the Republic; lust for Émilie does. That ethical motives serve as pretexts to cover selfish ones becomes clearer as Cinna declares: "May Rome's enslavement endure forever!" (886) if freedom costs the life of the man who raised Cinna from nullity to power and honor. Such a statement reaffirms Cinna's mercenary, dependent, servile nature.

He also bases service to Émilie on the expectation of reward: the repeated vows in act 3, scene 4, suggest that he has contracted to serve Émilie, and his sense of honor in executing the vows inspires little respect since he no longer can feign hatred for Auguste. Cinna is a false *généreux* with a rich vocabulary and bankrupt values. Thus when he tries to persuade Émilie to abandon revenge, his language rings hollow: "A noble soul, whom virtue directs, flees the names of ingrate and traitor" (969–970).

Émilie's accusation of servility strikes the target: "[A truly Roman heart] dares everything to seize the hateful life of whoever would enslave it. It flees the shame of slavery even more than death itself" (979–981). Of course Émilie considers secondary the question of freedom and submission; she conspires and seduces Cinna to avenge a father's death. Émilie recalls Cinna's ancestry to shame him, to remind him that his dignity needs no imperial patronage: Cinna descends from Pompey the Great, enemy of Julius Caesar. However, the values of noble ancestors are meaningless in the abstract: they must be exercised and renewed if the noble ethos is to have any significance.

A confused opposition of values and goals typifies Émilie, too. Corneille begins the drama with an unusual introductory prologue, a self-portrait by Émilie resembling a Roman Fury who weighs motives and goals against dangers to herself and her lover. Émilie manipulates Cinna's love to obtain an instrument of vengeance; she commands her desire for him to support the lust for revenge. She is the rare Cornelian character who wants to satisfy both honor and passion. Her force precludes pity; her resolution can generate no fear; but her opposition to Auguste's power may command admiring wonder. After the monologue Corneille undermines that response by having Émilie repeat the stages of the monologue in a conversation with a confidante, adding the idea that assassination will free Rome and restore the Republic. The patriotic motive surprises and may even irritate an audience, because it did not occur in the monologue and because Émilie emphasizes

her own glory as a self-sacrificing benefactress rather than the benefits to Rome of liberty: "Let us unite with the sweetness of avenging our kin the glory of punishing tyrants, and let us make all Italy acknowledge: 'Rome's freedom is Émilie's handiwork; her soul was touched, her heart was captivated, but she gave her love only at the price of freeing Italy.'" She introduces patriotism as a pretext because it is more universally accepted (1.2. 107–112) and glorious a motive than revenge. Corneille points out the gap between a personal obligation and a patriotic duty. Émilie does not pursue the man who proscribed Romans opposed to his rule—not the man whose bloody deeds Auguste himself recalls in his act 4 monologue nor the dictator whose crimes Cinna recounts in a moment: she hates the assassin of her father. She has initiated a grand scheme to kill for personal vengeance under patriotic cover; she has taken into her hands Fortune—for herself, Cinna, Auguste, Rome; and she proves as arbitrary, capricious, and unjust as the Fortune that Auguste recognizes and wishes to escape.

Corneille emphasizes Émilie's dishonesty by giving her noble language a dubious, cant-like quality: "vertu," "gloire," "digne" (virtue, glory, worthy); "Whoever holds life for little is master of his own." Cinna's speech repeating his tirade exhorting the conspirators produces the same effect: the bloody tableaux of Auguste's crimes and Cinna's listing of his ancestors' noble achievements that his single act of liberation will equal—all serve to conceal his real interest, passion for Émilie. Corneille has composed a remarkable speech, vivid, horrifying, effectively exciting desires to punish a monster like Auguste; but Corneille undermines the intention. Cinna observes that all the conspirators seem to serve a woman, even to avenge a father (1.3.145–152); and he expresses his one genuine concern about the outcome: surviving or not, he will be content so long as he serves his mistress. In less poetic terms: the destiny of Rome be damned; only Émilie matters. Corneille reveals the egotism of an apparently heroic enterprise. The moral chaos of Émilie and Cinna threatens Roman civilization as much as the crimes attributed to Auguste, including the parricide that Émilie imitates as she seeks to avenge it.

Corneille indicates something rotten in the state of Rome. The moral order is represented as in virtual collapse while the civil order approaches chaos. Auguste is so bewildered by his failure to co-opt Rome by good works that he seeks advice from conspirators. Cinna, boasting of descent from Pompey the Great, lacks Pompey's values. Auguste's monologue exposes moral bankruptcy, endless bloodbaths, instability long after the civil wars. Somewhere in that fratricidal struggle, the sense of Roman patriotism was lost, and Auguste discovers that his people deem him not the father of his country but its destroyer. Corneille protrays Rome here as a degenerate state where public motives conceal violent personal desire, where noble sentiment is subordinated to vengeance and sexuality. Even when they recognize and condemn their un-Roman passions, these Romans cannot convert moral disgust to positive, redemptive action. It takes a tremendous effort of will to repudiate instinctive desires and to reinstate—or create—genuine values of order and civilization. Only Auguste makes the attempt, and he comes to it by a stroke of intuition: that is perhaps the sign of his difference, his intellectual and moral superiority, or, in a Vergilian manner, his genius and example, which preside over Roman empire and civilization.

At the conclusion Auguste establishes an unprecedented model for conduct by breaking with the past and by opposing himself to Heaven, Hell, Fate, Destiny, Fortune. He discovers ethical resources that distinguish him from all previous Romans, including Caesar and Sulla, and confirm him as the model to which all future Romans will aspire. Through discipline and will, he surpasses himself, becoming master of self and arbiter of values, as well as master of empire. His action stuns the audience and the characters, for whom terms like "generosity," "honor," and "duty" have acquired genuine meaning in Auguste's acts; they provide an ethical basis for conduct in Roman civilization. These enduring values touch the characters with a secular grace, allowing moral rebirth. "O virtue unprecedented," exclaims Cinna (5.3.1731). The radical new precedent, replacing the model of bloodshed, allows Auguste to escape the caprices of Fortune represented in the play by Émilie and the conspiracy that Cinna had characterized as being "without precedent." Corneille stresses the exemplary virtue of Auguste's clemency, which illuminates the Roman soul and banishes misconceptions about the nature of Rome as intended by Fate: monarchical empire, not republic.

Auguste's unparalleled example immortalizes him—like founding father Aeneas—as an inspiration to Romans and to rulers for all time to come, including the princes of seventeenth-century Europe. The temporal perspective expands in Livie's prophecy (5.3.1753–1774). This is not propagandizing mystification but a clear statement of Auguste's resolution of his dilemma, which is emblematic of Rome's. He has escaped Fortune and discovered an identity between his will and Fate. (Such knowing complicity between humans and Fate is uncommon in tragedy, although it occurs in Sophocles' last tragedies, *Philoktetes* and *Oedipus at Colonus*.) According to Livie, Auguste has found the divine will for Rome; his example makes possible Rome's acceptance of its Fate as a monarchical empire. Auguste's intuitive discovery of clemency is not a manipulative, expedient—or baldly Machiavellian—political act, as Livie had proposed it be used in act 4. It is political in the higher sense that it transforms the state by converting the citizens and by providing an ideology-mythology to furnish the moral justification without which no civil order may endure. Auguste becomes a type of Platonic philosopher-king—not a Machiavellian prince—by a revelation whose moral brilliance stuns Rome into an equally intuitive conversion to values of self-discipline and pardon of the human flaws associated with anticultural instinctive urges. Clemency henceforth defines Auguste's nature. Civilization replaces chaos: the plague is lifted from Thebes/Rome as Auguste/Oedipus discovers the truth about the gods' intentions for him and the culture he shapes by example.

Such an ending may seem improbable. Corneille runs the risk of violating the verisimilitude demanded by his period's theorists and derived from Aristotle's notions of probability. The audience, however, is so astonished by Auguste's rhetoric and revelation of his self-sufficient power that normal criteria of disbelief are suspended. Émilie and Cinna seize intuitively the truth of Auguste's values, which replace exhausted pseudovalues and enable them to become true *généreux*—true Romans. Auguste's action annihilates civil rivalries and hatred—whose greatest victim must always be Rome itself—and permits the descendants of ancient enemies to live in harmony as his own children. Auguste is transformed into a patriarchal god who legislates the moral code, all within a few moments in a burst of ethical illumination. The glory surrounding Auguste, with which Émilie had first pictured him, has been turned into a quasi-divine aura that extends to Émilie, Cinna, Maxime, and all Rome.

The nobleman is thus redefined in this play. He allows himself to be transformed by embracing other values and ethical codes of behavior; he breaks with a past whose paradigms preclude authentic service to causes conducive to civilization. Corneille must have made his point to Richelieu. The brilliant éclat of Auguste's astonishing act does not blind: it enlightens the mind and illuminates the soul; it produces neither pity nor terror, but an admiring wonder before the human capacity to choose the outcome—the *événement* of Montaigne's essay—that will be his Fate.

The series of conversions in *Cinna* can occur because of control over primitive impulses. A Freudian reader of Corneille might discover that his characters often express or project desires that are normally repressed or denied in civilization. In subsequent plays Corneille deals with conversion to values promoting happiness, but not always with a sense of finality and success. Although the vocabulary of duty, honor, glory, and passion remains constant, the plots and characters follow no formula. After *Cinna* there is always room for skepticism: not every character converts sincerely, just as some in the audience cynically scoff at heroic values. Some characters and people belong not to the world of truth that is tragedy but to the deceit-ridden world of comedy.

Corneille's next tragedy after *Cinna*, *Polyeucte*, is structured according to the opposition of those two modes: as the world of eternal truth opens to Polyeucte with baptism, he flees the deceitful snares of the senses. The play concerns the conversion to Christianity of Polyeucte, an Armenian nobleman who has recently married Pauline, daughter of the Roman governor, Félix. Although Pauline loves her husband, she still feels a strong attraction to Sévère, whom she once passionately loved, but whom she renounced at her father's command. Sévère has become the emperor's favorite courtier and friend, and he visits Armenia ostensibly on an imperial mission but really to seek out Pauline, whose marriage he has not yet learned of. Both Pauline and Sévère remain constant in their submission to honor and duty: Pauline to marital obligations, Sévère to his respect for Pauline. Polyeucte, however, imprisoned and sentenced to die for openly embracing Christianity and committing sacrilege against the state's pagan religion, matches Sévère's nobility and Pauline's self-sacrifice by commanding the former lovers to marry. Pauline's refusal again proves her love for her husband and her commitment to honor obligations. The example of Polyeucte's martyrdom—another, even higher form of commitment to values—induces her to convert; Félix, too, announces his conversion (which may not be sincere, for all of his behavior is motivated by political expediency). The play ends with Sévère's indication that he will try to influence the emperor to relax his persecution of Christians.

Corneille develops systematically the dichotomy between Polyeucte's new vision of eternal truth and his strong sensual attachment to his wife, but without suggesting that Polyeucte has not completely repudiated the latter. After the first scenes he experiences no real struggle, not even during his stances delivered at the beginning of the fourth act, while he is in prison meditating on what in his martyrdom he must give up on earth and what he will receive in heaven. His election of Christian values occurs while he is offstage after act 1, and he in no manner duplicates the process of soul-searching that Auguste experienced. He does realize the relative (as opposed to absolute) worth of what he has renounced, for Pauline's physical beauty is matched by her moral virtues. She honors and submits to traditional values of obligation and obedience on which the male-dominated society is based—to father and to husband—although she expresses opposition to Félix and Polyeucte. She is a victim of duty who has always sacrificed her choice to her father's political interests. But, ironically, in a theater where duty and raison d'état are supposed to reign supreme, those values prove antithetical to the production of happiness for all concerned in this play. Pauline's obedience turns out to be misguided, for Félix had seriously erred in ordering her to break off her romance with Sévère because he was poor and could not further Félix's political ambitions. Sévère has become the second most powerful man in the empire by exercising the moral virtues Pauline had recognized in him. Pauline's duty is linked first to her father's false political values. Then, when Polyeucte gives her to Sévère, she rebels against a husband who also abuses

her duty to him: he misjudges her, associating her exclusively with the deceitful, sensual mode of existence, as though she were not capable of resisting her attraction to Sévère and of maintaining marital fidelity to her martyred husband.

The play may be called Polyeucte, but it concentrates to a very large degree on Pauline's struggles to recognize correct values, not because they are husband's, father's, or lover's, but because they are true. The example of Polyeucte's martyrdom opens her eyes to vision: she is baptized in her husband's blood—offstage, of course, to avoid offending sensibilities—and she is touched by divine grace. Pauline converts to the faith that leads to truth and bliss, according to the dominant religious ideology of Corneille's period; all other values, including duty to father and state, are relatively worthless. Pauline's illumination and insistence on her decision place her in the tradition of Cornelian heroines. In effect, the character of Pauline marks a return to the prominence of female characters in Corneille's first tragedies, Médée and Le Cid. In Horace and Cinna, although Sabine, Camille, and Émilie are important and act with heroic moral energy, by comparison with Médée, Chimène, and the infanta they undergo less of a psychological struggle between two sets of antithetical values. With Pauline, Corneille begins another line of heroines who tend to dominate the plays they are in, even when not the titular protagonist: the Syrian queen, Cléopâtre, and the Parthian princess, Rodogune, in Rodogune; Theodora, princess of Antioch, in Théodore, vierge et martyre (1645–1646); the exiled Armenian queen, Laodice, in Nicomède; Rodélinde, wife of the deposed Lombard king, in Pertharite (1651–1652); Oedipus' sister, Dircé, in Oedipe (1659); the Jewish queen, Bérénice, in Tite et Bérénice (1670); and Suréna's sister, Palmis, and the Armenian princess, Eurydice, in Suréna, to name some of the most striking examples.

After Cinna Corneille occasionally returned

to comedy, composing plays that are strictly comedies, with plots mainly concerning marriage, without the psychological struggles whose resolution produces admiration and conversion to new values. Such plays are *Le menteur (The Liar)* and its sequel, *La suite du menteur* (known as *Liar II,* 1644), in which the protagonist invents a heroic past worthy of a Rodrigue and grows increasingly entangled in his schemes. But the tragedies written after *Cinna* also include characters who belong to the less noble mode of comedy. They are deceitful, usually incapable of genuine conversion, and interested only in political advancement. They could be called Machiavellian, but their schemes fail, and they lack the essential heroism and unshakable will for good or evil of the true Machiavellian. Félix is a typical representative of this class of character; although a Roman, he lacks the solid moral core of the other characters—Pauline, Sévère, Polyeucte—and he cannot appreciate the honesty and virtue of Sévère. Like the protagonist of *Le menteur,* Félix gets tripped up by his own schemes.

The distinction between characters who belong to Cornelian tragedy and those tainted by comedy—by deceit, emphasis on sensuality and marriage, failure to recognize and respect virtue, desire for political power irrespective of genuine qualifications—is apparent in Corneille's fourth Roman tragedy, *La mort de Pompée (Pompey's Death)*. Its characters fall into two groups: Romans and Egyptians. Jules César and Pompée's widow, Cornélie, embody the Roman virtues of self-discipline and respect for the enemy. Their desire for satisfaction—in his case, sexual; in hers, vengeful—is tempered by a sense of priorities and by honor. The Egyptians cannot appreciate or emulate Roman values: Ptolomée schemes and fails to grasp César's policy of generosity; Cléopâtre relies on sex appeal to seize power with César's support. But she never has a chance: Corneille's César will not succumb to this Cléopâtre's wiles, for his mind is on the injustice done his enemy, Pompée, by Ptolomée, who has had him assassinated, thinking to curry César's favor by the murder. César is more concerned with treating Cornélie with the dignity due a true Roman matron than with enjoying sexual delights.

César is perhaps the least ambiguous Cornelian hero. He establishes his majesty when he enters, treats the Egyptians as they deserve, and reveals that sexuality will not compromise his rendering of justice. He knows his values; the struggle to recognize and initiate them belongs to the past. In César and Cornélie, the values are demonstrated in action. *La mort de Pompée* is thus a fitting sequel to the preceding tragedies in which ethical values are discovered through intuition following moral anguish; the plot presents an exhibition of the permanence of the Roman moral program and the Egyptians' inability to respond. It is at once an apotheosis of Cornelian moral values—with no ambiguity—and a sad observation that in a world of Egyptians, those values remain incomprehensible except to a privileged few.

La mort de Pompée opens the way to the mixture of tragic and comic, noble and morally despicable characters found in Corneille's subsequent theater. An idea of such a mixture can be grasped just from a description of the characters in *Nicomède,* a tragedy popular during the civil wars—the Fronde, or "Slingshot," wars—of the early 1650's, when Richelieu's successor, Cardinal Mazarin, along with the regent, Queen Mother Anne of Austria, and the young Louis XIV were threatened by an unlikely coalition of princes of the blood, aristocrats, and members of the Paris Parlement. Both parties had mixed motives, and a similar confusion affects Corneille's drama. The hero is an idealized nobleman, a prince of Bithynia, a Roman satellite on the Black Sea. His military victories have won kingdoms for his father, but his open hostility to Rome has made him a dangerous asset to King Prusias of Bithynia. By all rights—primogeniture, proven moral virtue, and military capability—Nicomède should be guaranteed succession to the throne. But Prusias is under the thumb of Rome. The Roman representative, Flaminius, acts not to defend Roman political interests but out of personal hatred of Nicomède, because Nicomède's hero and paradigm is Hannibal, who defeated and killed Flaminius' father. Prusias is also dominated by his second wife, Arsinoé, archetypal stepmother to Nicomède but doting mother to her own son, Attale, and conniving, hypocritical wife to Prusias. (Molière could not have chosen a better model for Beline, the stepmother in *Le malade imaginaire*.) She inveigles Nicomède to leave his military outpost—virtually to desert his duty—and enter the capital. The quarrel she thereby provokes between father and son will leave Nicomède disinherited and assure to her own son both the royal succession and a marriage to Laodice, the Armenian queen, to whom Nicomède is engaged. Nicomède's virtue, however, inspires Attale to emulate him. When Nicomède is imprisoned and about to be sent as a hostage to Rome, Attale in disguise frees him. At the conclusion Prusias and Arsinoé seem to convert to virtue, although they have no choice since Attale has deferred to Nicomède, and they are in Nicomède's power. Laodice and Nicomède will marry. Even Flaminius renounces his hatred of Hannibal's disciple. In fact, Hannibal is nowhere mentioned in the last scene, as though Nicomède had outgrown the need to imitate a master; he now has proved worthy of having another prince, Attale, emulate him.

The characters span a gamut from noble and honest to base and conniving, and the dialogue also ranges from highflown protestations of virtue and honor by Nicomède and Laodice to hypocritical posturing by Arsinoé. *Nicomède* also contains superb examples of Corneille's comic dialogue as Nicomède engages in ironic repartee with his stepmother and as he takes advantage of his half brother's failure to recognize him on his return to the capital. (Attale had never seen him, since the younger prince had been kept a hostage in Rome.) For all his virtue, even Nicomède mixes comic with noble language, as though Corneille were subjecting his hero to the temptations of scoring easy points against unworthy opponents.

Corneille's later heroes are indeed undermatched. No one in *Tite et Bérénice*, for example, can come up to the nobility of the Jewish queen, certainly not her rival for Tite's love, Domitie, or the emperor's brother, Domitian. They are interested only in gaining power for power's sake, whereas Bérénice returns to Rome from exile after Tite's accession, only to assure herself of his continuing love for her; she determines to leave as a sign of her own will and of her control over her honor, in opposition to the will of Rome and even of Tite. Power over the self is more important to her than power over the state is to Domitie and Domitian. In effect, they are unworthy of ruling because they lack self-discipline: Bérénice, like Nicomède, appreciates the lesson of Auguste; Domitie and Domitian do not.

Much of Corneille's later theater is dominated by the theme of power sought for its own sake by those who lack the requisite virtue and self-control to exercise power properly. The hero is the exception to such characters (although in at least one play, *Othon*, 1664, no such hero exists). Corneille kept transforming this theme and experimenting with dramatic forms, including "machine plays" such as *Andromède* (1650) and *La toison d'or* (*The Golden Fleece*, 1660), whose success could be attributed to spectacular stage effects produced by flying machines and rapid changes of decor and to demonstrations of miraculous physical prowess, rather than exhibitions of ethical superiority, insight, or resolution. But even in *Andromède*, Perseus proves morally superior and worthier of power than the king and queen whose daughter he rescues: he is the slayer of a monster who exposes monstrous vices in the rulers who do not exercise power justly. In these later plays Corneille's implicit comment on the nature of authority and on those who seek and exercise it becomes harsher, and that may explain why the plays were less popular, some of them actually failures. He surely suffered no loss in creative powers. Although the plots of some late plays are Byzantine in complication, some underlying, rationally conceived substructure always provides vigorous drama and insight into values and into the failure of those desiring power to exercise truly aristocratic values that command admiration and wonder. The poetry of *Suréna* (1674) was as beautiful and modern for its time as the verse of *Le Cid* was in 1637. But *Suréna* failed, and Corneille wrote no more for the theater. He remained in Paris, where his popular plays continued to be performed; they were also presented at Versailles before the court of Louis XIV. He died in 1684.

Corneille's last plays did not please a large audience; and Racine eclipsed him as the leading tragic poet of France. Racine did not have to forge a poetic diction for the tragic stage nor train a public to consider theater a serious, enlightening, philosophical, and perhaps even politically necessary activity meant to please and instruct. Corneille had developed the language and shaped the audience. Racine readjusted balances between emotion and rational control, emphasizing passion at the expense of virtue in his characters; he explored and exposed the reason known only to the heart, both celebrating and deploring love; and he presented a different tragic vision of man and the moral universe, one that produced tears of pity and terror, not thrills of admiration (and caution), before extraordinary ethical values, thought, and conduct. For that experience, as firmly rooted in the Greco-Roman philosophical and poetic traditions as was Racine's tragedy, one turns—as in the seventeenth century—to Corneille's unprecedented and enduring achievement.

Selected Bibliography

EDITIONS

INDIVIDUAL PLAYS
Modern editions of individual plays are available in the Classiques Larousse and Nouveaux Classiques Larousse series: *Le Cid, Horace, Cinna, Polyeucte, La mort de Pompée, Nicomède, Rodogune, Attila, Sertorius, L'Illusion comique, Le menteur.*

Le Cid, tragicomédie. Paris, 1637.

Horace, tragédie. Paris, 1641.

Cinna, ou la clémence d'Auguste, tragédie. Paris, 1643.

Polyeucte, martyre, tragédie. Rouen and Paris, 1643.

Nicomède, tragédie. Paris, 1651.

Suréna, général des Parthes, tragédie. Paris, 1675.

COLLECTED WORKS
Le théâtre de P. Corneille. 3 vols. Paris, 1660. Includes twenty-three plays, three treatises; critical discussion of each play.

————. 4 vols. Paris, 1666. Includes all the plays. Last edition published in Corneille's lifetime.

Théâtre de Pierre Corneille. 12 vols. Edited by Voltaire. Geneva, 1764.

Oeuvres de P. Corneille. 12 vols. Edited by Ch. Marty-Laveaux. Paris, 1862–1907. The basic modern edition. Contains all variants.

Théâtre complet de Corneille. 3 vols. Edited by Maurice Rat. Paris, 1941. Handy format.

————. 2 vols. Edited by Pierre Lièvre and Roger Caillois. Paris, 1950. Elegant and handy edition.

Oeuvres complètes de Pierre Corneille. Edited by André Stegmann. Paris, 1963. A serious one-volume edition for students.

TRANSLATIONS

The Chief Plays by Pierre Corneille. Translated by Lucy Lockert. Princeton, 1957.

Le Cid. Translated by James Schevill, with Robert Goldsby and Angela Goldsby. In *The Classic Theatre,* edited by Eric Bentley. Garden City, N.Y., 1961.

The Cid, Cinna, The Dramatic Illusion. Translated by John Cairncross. Harmondsworth, 1975. The best translations of the latter two works.

Moot Plays by Pierre Corneille. Translated by Lucy Lockert. Nashville, 1959. Contains *La mort de Pompée, Héraclius, Don Sanche d'Aragon, Sertorius, Othon, Attila, Pulchérie, Suréna.*

BACKGROUND STUDIES

Adam, Antoine. *Histoire de la littérature française au 18e siècle.* 5 vols. Paris, 1948–1956.

Bénichou, Paul. *Morales du grand siècle.* Paris, 1948. Translated as *Man and Ethics.* Garden City, N.Y., 1971.

Borgerhoff, E. B. O. *The Freedom of French Classicism.* Princeton, 1950.

Couton, Georges. *Corneille.* Paris, 1958. Revised 1969.

Dort, Bernard. *Pierre Corneille, dramaturge.* Paris, 1957.

Doubrovsky, Serge. *Corneille et la dialectique du héros.* Paris, 1963.

Herland, Louis. *Corneille par lui-même.* Paris, 1958.

————. *Horace, ou la naissance de l'homme.* Paris, 1952.

Maurens, Jacques. *La tragédie sans tragique: Le néo-stoïcisme dans l'oeuvre de Pierre Corneille.* Paris, 1966.

Moore, W. G. *The Classical Drama of France.* Oxford, 1971.

Nelson, Robert J. *Corneille and Racine: Parallels and Contrasts.* Englewood Cliffs, N.J., 1966.

————. *Corneille's Heroes and Their Worlds.* Philadelphia, 1963.

Pocock, Gordon. *Corneille and Racine: Problems of Tragic Form.* Cambridge, 1973.

Rousset, Jean. *La littérature de l'âge baroque en France: Circé et le Paon.* Paris, 1953.

Starobinski, Jean. *L'Oeil vivant.* Paris, 1961.

Stegmann, André. *L'Héroïsme cornélien: Genèse et signification.* 2 vols. Paris, 1968.

Yarrow, P. J. *Corneille.* London, 1963.

NATHAN GROSS

FRANÇOIS VI

DUC DE LA ROCHEFOUCAULD

(1613–1680)

FRANÇOIS VI de La Rochefoucauld, remembered chiefly for his book of maxims, *Réflexions ou sentences et maximes morales* (first published after his fiftieth birthday), was born in Paris on 15 September 1613. He was the oldest child of the fifth comte (later duc) François V de La Rochefoucauld and Gabrielle du Plessis-Liancourt. Both parents were members of well-established aristocratic families. Shortly after his birth La Rochefoucauld (formally the prince de Marcillac, until he succeeded to the dukedom upon his father's death in 1650) was taken by his mother to the family estates in the west of France. These included Verteuil, the chief residence, close to Ruffec, and the castle of Marcillac, near Angoulême. His father remained in Paris to be near the court of King Louis XIII. There the aristocrats of France competed for the royal largesse; and the crown gave and withheld its gifts, in an effort to control the restless and ambitious nobility.

La Rochefoucauld was never a serious formal student, though he seems to have read and discussed the literature of the day, which included his favorite, *L'Astrée*, a prose romance by Honoré d'Urfé. Made up of many elements that together imply an ideal of upright behavior in love and adversity, the work represents chivalry in a pastoral setting as it tells of Celadon's undying love for Astrée. Mistakenly believing him to have been unfaithful, Astrée dismisses Celadon, who then tries to drown himself. Saved by three nymphs of the court—ruled over by Queen Amasis—Celadon resists their seductive maneuvers. Then he faces many dangers (extended over several volumes of the work) and is wounded in battle, before his fidelity as a lover has been appropriately demonstrated to Astrée. Though the work was satirized by the novelist Charles Sorel as *Le berger extravagant* (1627), it proved immensely popular and was widely regarded as a book that would improve the moral tone of society. Like Sorel, many twentieth-century readers might find it insipid, but for La Rochefoucauld *L'Astrée* seemed to represent a world of romance, the attractiveness of which survived his most dispassionate and impersonally expressed observations of human nature.

Apart from such reading as he chose to do and his modest formal education, which would typically have included dancing, fencing, and a little Latin, mathematics, and music, the introspective author of the *Maximes* seems to have been most influenced by the idea of family, which the aristocrats of seventeenth-century France believed more important than the idea of country. He was

51

also influenced by the life of the court, into which he was drawn soon after his marriage at age fourteen, and by his sometimes complicated relationships with several important women of the age, including Anne of Austria (wife of Louis XIII), the duchesse de Chevreuse, the duchesse de Longueville, the marquise de Sablé, the marquise de Sévigné, and the comtesse de La Fayette, each of whom represented for him a different interest or mixture of interests—political, intellectual, and personal.

Obviously, La Rochefoucauld brought something of himself to these various relationships. The view that sees him as a reflective and idealistic young man, who thought of love and war as opportunities for unselfish service and deferred fulfillment, is probably sound. It is certainly attractive as a basis for explaining many of the actions of his early life, especially his first missions on the queen's behalf—against the authority of the king and his chief minister—during which La Rochefoucauld exposed himself to the king's displeasure more to serve an idealized lady, it seems, than to make his own way in the world. Even the late *Maximes* may to some extent be accounted for by this view of him as a former idealist, both by those who regard them as fundamentally cynical statements—the statements of a thwarted idealist, one might argue—and by those who regard them as showing that even the best of men fail in the attempt to measure up to a very high standard of behavior, because self-knowledge is almost always insufficient to overcome blind self-concern: "We are far from knowing all that our passions lead us to do" (*Maximes* 460).

To this last suggestion it should be added that, until recently, the majority of the many commentators on the *Maximes* have regarded them as too cynical in their reading of human nature, though admirable nevertheless, both in psychological penetration and in style. So, for example, La Rochefoucauld's enemy Jean François Paul de Gondi, Cardinal de Retz, in a brief prose portrait of the author, says the *Maximes* show too little faith in virtue. And the woman who was to become La Rochefoucauld's closest friend during the last fifteen years or so of his life, Marie-Madeleine Pioche de La Vergne, comtesse de La Fayette, wrote in a letter, composed soon after reading the *Maximes*, that one must have corruption in mind and heart for all they contain to be imaginable. These judgments are fairly typical of responses to La Rochefoucauld's chief work down through the years, though from the very beginning some readers believed the *Maximes* represented human motives and actions with great accuracy.

Despite widespread objections to La Rochefoucauld's rendering of human nature, the *Maximes* have been much read, discussed, imitated, and translated since their first appearance in a pirated version issued by a Dutch publisher in late 1663 or early 1664. (La Rochefoucauld published the first authorized edition in 1665.) By 1670, John Davies had translated some of the maxims into English. In her *Miscellany, Being a Collection of Poems by Several Hands, Together with Reflections on Morality, or Seneca Unmasqued* (1685), Aphra Behn offered an English translation of 395 of the 504 maxims of the fifth, and last, authorized edition (1678) before La Rochefoucauld's death.

Meanwhile, in France various works having much in common with the *Maximes* were being published. These either owed a special debt to La Rochefoucauld's work or shared with the *Maximes* a concern with the motives controlling human behavior. Among them are *Maximes et pensées diverses* (1678), written for the most part by Madeleine de Souvré, marquise de Sablé; *Caractères de Théophraste* (1688)—especially those observations grouped under the heading "De la cour"—by Jean de La Bruyère; . . . *Réflexions et maximes* (1746) by Luc de Clapiers, marquis de Vauvenargues; and *Pensées, maximes et anecdotes* by Sébastien Roch Nicolas, known as de Chamfort, published in 1795.

During the first decade of the eighteenth century, Jonathan Swift produced "Thoughts on Various Subjects" (1711), which are in the style of La Rochefoucauld's *Maximes,* as are Swift's "Further Thoughts" (1727). Other seventeenth- and eighteenth-century English writers who tried their hands at the kind of aphoristic paradox typical of the *Maximes* are George Saville, marquess of Halifax; Philip Dormer Stanhope, earl of Chesterfield; and William Shenstone. Indeed, the *Maximes* have continued to attract imitators of great reputation—Oscar Wilde, Ambrose Bierce, and George Bernard Shaw, for example—and gifted translators—Louis Kronenberger and Constantine FitzGibbon.

Historians and critics (and, more recently, scholars in linguistics) have tried to discover what it is that makes La Rochefoucauld's *Maximes* as engaging as they have proved to be. No generally accepted view has been provided, but most agree with Voltaire, who says in *Le siècle de Louis XIV* (1751) that they are effective for their accurate representation of human nature and their precision of language. Though many have argued with the rather more explicit view expressed by Swift, in his *Verses on the Death of Dr. Swift* (1739), that the *Maximes* are persuasive because they correctly represent human nature and its failure, few would accept Jean Jacques Rousseau's judgment that they have never been liked by really decent people. And yet many of La Rochefoucauld's readers have experienced the discomfort and annoyance, along with the pleasure, of facing new truths about human nature, or truths they have only fleetingly or dimly acknowledged. Such discomfort may have contributed to Rousseau's conclusion. La Rochefoucauld himself notes the disturbance that his work caused: "What arouses so much in the way of objection to maxims that reveal the human heart is our fear of being exposed ourselves" (*Maximes* 524).

Probably no reader of the *Maximes* entirely escapes the sharp intrusions of some order of new truth into consciousness. Time and again they force us to acknowledge that we are ignorant of ourselves: "We would hardly long for things so much if we knew exactly what we longed for" (*Maximes* 439). Or they make us see that we are much less high-minded than we might like to imagine: "In most men gratitude is only a secret wish for greater benefits" (*Maximes* 298). Very occasionally La Rochefoucauld calls attention to mankind's good side: "Our merit wins us the esteem of the worthy, our success the esteem of the world" (*Maximes* 165). But even here he chides the world for preferring success to merit, and in a sense he chides us and himself as well. Nevertheless the acerb quality has not kept Swift and other readers from seeing in the *Maximes* an accurate representation of humankind— a representation that is finally constructive, in that La Rochefoucauld's implicit ideal throughout the work is self-knowledge, and its corollary, self-direction, though he holds out little hope for either. What he refers to as "self-love" (amour-propre) gets in the way.

When La Rochefoucauld married Andrée de Vivonne, the daughter of the former grand falconer of France, in 1628, he and his wife were acting, or being made to act, in their families' interests, which probably they would not have understood to be separate from their own. The marriage had been arranged by his father and Andrée's widowed mother. From the point of view of the La Rochefoucaulds, it was a good match, in that the wife, who was probably about the same age as her fourteen-year-old husband, brought with her a sizable dowry and the appropriate social credentials. Andrée and François could be expected to have children and to see to the continuation of the La Rochefoucaulds as a French family of consequence in other ways.

Although both had been reared in the feudal tradition that required allegiance to one's lord—in their case the head of the royal family and those closely connected with it—aristocrats like the La Rochefoucaulds sometimes suspended such allegiance, temporarily, to promote their family interests. The king's authority was unsettled, and the French nobility took full advantage of the fact to serve their own purposes. On the other hand, strong representatives of the crown, like Armand du Plessis, Cardinal de Richelieu, chief minister and effective ruler of France from 1624 until his death in 1642, and King Louis XIV, who assumed complete control of the government upon the death of his chief minister, Jules Mazarin, in 1661, were able to give reality to their view that the king of France was in important ways an absolute ruler. It was this issue of royal authority—intensified by two long regencies and a weak kingship spanning roughly fifty years of the century from 1610—that gave rise to the court intrigues and ill-defined civil wars in which the nobility participated, La Rochefoucauld among them.

In 1628, shortly after their marriage, the young couple moved from the family estates in the Angoumois of western France to Paris, in order to be near the court, where, like other nobles, they worked for their own advancement. Though there is some indication that Andrée participated in court life—chiefly the fact that La Rochefoucauld sought for her the right to a seat in the queen's audience room, a privilege that in aristocratic eyes would enhance his prestige no less than hers—she seems to have avoided involvement in the intrigues that harried the royal authority. La Rochefoucauld begins one of his maxims "Men realize they should not speak much of their wives" (*Maximes* 364). In abiding by this convention of silence, he denies us information about Andrée that no other source has provided. She neither wrote much about herself nor moved others to write much about her. Before she died in 1670, she had borne seven children. Such evidence as we have suggests that she was a generous and equable mother and wife, who protected the family resolutely and accepted her husband's many sexual infidelities. La Rochefoucauld makes no exception to the view that "There are successful marriages, but no really happy ones" (*Maximes* 113).

When La Rochefoucauld first joined the many aristocrats who attended Louis XIII at the ancient palace of the kings of France, the Louvre, he was far from being a practiced courtier and lover. For all the early maturity required by the times, in some ways he was as young as his years (by twentieth-century standards), acting in accordance with youthful fantasies despite his responsibilities. It was not only that he imprudently committed himself to Queen Anne's service. He also involved himself, through the queen, with Marie de Rohan-Montbazon, duchesse de Chevreuse, thirteen years his senior; she persuaded him to assist her in intrigues against Richelieu, whom she and many others (Anne among them) regarded as a self-serving tyrant. At the time, La Rochefoucauld was well aware that the duchesse had once been banished from the court for her part in a plot against the cardinal and the king, and that she was enjoying the steady companionship of one of her many lovers (among whom La Rochefoucauld almost certainly came to be included).

During this time he also came to know and admire the young Marie de Hautefort, about three years his junior, who was maid of honor to Queen Anne and a favorite of the king in an innocent way. Marie seems to have had the rare ability to be familiar without being intimate, and she was liked by many. In 1635 La Rochefoucauld wrote a letter declaring his undying love for her. It was to be given to her by her brother, but only if the ardent La Rochefoucauld were killed in a pending battle. He survived, and the letter was never delivered. Perhaps it was with the impression of his former self at court in mind that La Rochefoucauld wrote many years later, "When young people first enter the world, they should seem either timid or careless; an assured, self-contained manner usually turns into impertinence" (*Maximes* 495).

The court of Louis XIII was in many ways demanding and complicated. When his father, the capable and popular Henri IV, was assassinated in May 1610, Louis was not yet ten years old. His mother, Marie de' Medici, a strong and domineering woman, effectively extended her regency beyond 1614, the year in which Louis was formally declared of age. In 1617, angered by his continued exclusion from state affairs, the young king instigated the assassination of his mother's politically influential favorite, Concino Concini, marquis d'Ancre, after which Louis exiled his mother to Blois. The queen tried twice, without success, to wrest power from her son; but by 1620 the two were nominally reconciled through the efforts of her chief adviser, Richelieu. In 1624 Louis appointed Richelieu his own chief minister.

Before his service to Queen Marie, Richelieu, a dutiful third son, had occupied the poor bishopric of Luçon, near La Rochelle—it was a family holding—until gradually he called attention to himself as a masterful administrator. Though Louis distrusted the cardinal for his long association with Marie de' Medici, he gave his minister an almost entirely free hand, so that Richelieu won the king's swift approval for his plans, with rare exceptions.

Richelieu has been accused of flattering Queen Marie in order to win favor, of always acting out of intense personal ambition, and even of having attempted the seduction of Louis's wife, Anne, whom the king had married in 1615, when he was fourteen. The cardinal was certainly ambitious, and he very likely flattered Louis's mother. But the fact remains that he held France together during his tenure as minister, working tirelessly and adroitly to overcome enormous problems of state: a court headed by a less-than-competent king; a group of ambitious nobles who put their family interests above those of France; religious wars that kept France, and Europe generally, in a fever for the thirty years preceding 1648; and the will of the Spanish and Austrian Hapsburgs to rule all of Europe.

Most historians are agreed that in protecting royal authority against the ambitious aristocracy as consistently, and often as ruthlessly, as he did, Richelieu was acting on

principles intended to support the stability and the safety of France. But many of the nobles of his day, who like the La Rochefoucaulds might trace their aristocratic descent in a direct line through twenty or more generations, thought him a self-serving upstart—his family had been aristocrats for only three generations—and they allowed the gnawing fact of his ascendancy at court to serve as an excuse for working against his administration and, though they denied the charge, against the king himself.

Queen Anne, the daughter of Phillip III of Spain and Margaret of Austria, was a Hapsburg. She and Richelieu had inevitably become enemies, in part because he thought, with some justice, that she was more sympathetic to her father and brother than to France, and in part because Anne knew that Richelieu sought to intensify the coolness that Louis had displayed toward her from the first. The cardinal's aim was to keep her from becoming what she most wanted to be—her husband's close adviser. Indeed, it seems possible that Louis might have won her complete loyalty, though there are unanswered questions about their relationship. But matters took a different turn.

In 1626, with her close ally the duchesse de Chevreuse, Queen Anne was to some extent involved in a plot that anticipated her marriage to Louis's brother, Gaston, duc d'Orléans, at such time as her husband, who was chronically ill, might die. Closer to the queen's real interest was the plan to do away with Richelieu. These arrangements, made with the knowledge and approval of Spain, England, Holland, and Savoy, were nipped in the bud because the comte de Chalais, brought into the conspiracy by the duchesse de Chevreuse (whose lover he then was), spoke too freely. And when, as a result of what Chalais was overheard to say, the duc d'Orléans was questioned, he exposed the entire plot, making Chalais out to be the chief conspirator.

With the king's approval the cardinal forced the duc d'Orléans to sign a statement of submission to Louis; and he rudely interrogated the queen, banished the duchesse de Chevreuse, and had Chalais beheaded. Though neither Louis nor Richelieu would do more than make the queen and the king's brother uncomfortable, despite their deep involvement in a plot that might have destroyed the cardinal and brought foreign troops to France, the comte de Chalais, and later Henri, duc de Montmorency, who joined another conspiracy against Richelieu, were executed.

In 1630 Anne joined her mother-in-law, Marie de' Medici—by then jealous of Richelieu's power and angered by his disregard of her—in another attempt to overthrow the cardinal. The queen mother persuaded her son that Richelieu must be dismissed. Louis, having agreed to sign the necessary warrant the next day, went off to his hunting lodge at Versailles. The news that Richelieu was to be ousted spread quickly through the court, and many were frank in their censure of the cardinal and in their praise of Marie, expressions of opinion that were duly reported to Richelieu.

After a night's sleep away from his strongwilled mother, Louis decided it was in his own best interest to keep the cardinal in place. Only he could stop the nobles from overpowering the monarchy, and Louis with it. It was quickly made known that Richelieu was to remain as chief minister. Some who had spoken too freely against him fled. Others were jailed, exiled, or executed. With her son's approval Marie was banished to Compiègne; but fearing a worse punishment, she first fled to Brussels and then spent the remaining eleven years of her life in extreme poverty, traveling from court to court.

La Rochefoucauld escaped any direct involvement in either of these plots, which came to be known as the Chalais Conspiracy and as the Day of the Dupes, respectively. The first was concocted shortly before he came to court, and the second while he was away from court on his first tour of military service, during which period he fought at Carignan (August 1630). But he was shortly to plunge into very similar activity. La Rochefoucauld's father, who was at court in 1630, had aligned himself with the queen's party, with the result that after Louis decided to keep Richelieu as his chief minister, François V was exiled to a house he owned at Blois—a mild punishment, all things considered. It might be supposed that the father had set the son a bad example, as in one sense he had. But La Rochefoucauld's long immersion in the politics of intrigue, more than ten years of it on Queen Anne's behalf, cannot be explained entirely by this means. In fact, La Rochefoucauld's father often advised him against his continuing participation in the badly conceived and maladroitly executed plots that marked the life of France until well into the reign of Louis XIV. The father could understand an aristocrat's interest in short-term alliances that might improve the wealth and status of his family, but he could not see that his son's steady involvement against the royal ministers—first Richelieu, then Mazarin—could bring anything but trouble.

In addition to a strong (if romantic) sense of loyalty, a sensitive intelligence, wealth, and position, young La Rochefoucauld seems to have been fortunate in his looks and bearing. Years later, after he had left the court, he published a self-portrait (1659). He begins his contribution to this popular genre with a description of himself, which there is no reason to doubt and some reason to believe:

I am of medium height, easy-moving and well-proportioned. I have a dark, smooth complexion. My forehead is high and fairly wide; my eyes are black, small and deep-set, and my eyebrows, black and heavy, but well shaped. I would find it hard to say what kind of nose I have. It is neither pug nor Roman, neither big nor pointed, as far as I can tell. All I know is that it is more nearly big than small, and that it is just a little too long. I have a large mouth, and my lips, usually red, are neither well nor badly shaped. I have white teeth, fairly well set. I have been told my chin is too big: I have just been feeling it, looking at myself in the mirror to see what it's really like, and I still don't know what to say. As for the shape of my face, it is either square or oval; it would be very hard for me to say which of the two it is. My hair is black and naturally curly, and it is full and long enough for me to say I have what is called a good head. There is something melancholy and proud in my bearing; as a result, most people think I am scornful, but I am not at all like that. I move energetically, in fact a little too energetically, so that I make many gestures in speaking.

La Rochefoucauld goes on to say that he has been frank in appraising his looks and that he imagines others will agree with him. Engravings and paintings of him bear out much of what he says.

Having been to the wars, the well-endowed La Rochefoucauld reentered the court at eighteen, ready to serve the queen, as various of his contemporaries testify. And La Rochefoucauld himself tells us in his *Apologie* (written in 1649–1650 but not published during his lifetime) and in his *Mémoires* (1662) that he early committed himself to the queen, who graciously accepted his unqualified willingness to serve her. For a time, at least, his motives, judged by any usual standard, appear to have been largely altruistic—he worked and risked his political future, and perhaps his physical well-being, for the sake of someone else. Still, he hoped to be rewarded for his services. But no reward was given him, and he came to feel ill-used by Queen Anne.

During the decade 1633–1643 La Rochefoucauld served Anne chiefly by delivering sometimes seditious letters and messages to her friend and agent with connections abroad, the duchesse de Chevreuse, whose place of exile from the court was conveniently located between Paris and La Rochefoucauld's estate in Poitou. It was a dangerous business. Anne persisted in her aim of overthrowing Richelieu and helping her brother, Philip IV of Spain, in his efforts to overpower France. During this period La Rochefoucauld also served in the French army against Spain—in Flanders in

1635, in France itself when the Spanish attacked in 1637, and again in Flanders in 1639. He seems not to have felt it was a contradiction to work for the queen against Richelieu and to soldier for France against Spain. Both were honorable causes.

Though Richelieu knew La Rochefoucauld was somehow involved on the queen's behalf, the cardinal was relatively lenient, perhaps because he thought the young man too far from the center of intrigue to be really dangerous. He may also have thought it important that after his exile to Blois, La Rochefoucauld's father had become tractable, even helpful to Richelieu; so he might have relied on the father to require his son to behave sensibly. Nevertheless, there was some considerable trouble at one point, when the queen's gentleman cloakbearer, Pierre de Laporte, was found to be carrying a letter to the exiled duchesse de Chevreuse. The letter itself was not incriminating; but the interrogations that followed revealed something—not all—of the scope of Anne's intrigues. The queen's party managed things well enough that Richelieu could not prove the worst that she had done, and as a result neither she nor the duchesse de Chevreuse was for the time, at least, in real trouble. But owing to a mixup in signals, the duchesse took alarm and fled to Spain, then to England, disguised as a man. This desperate action implied that there was more to the plot than had been disclosed; and La Rochefoucauld, who was known to have befriended the escaping enemy of the crown, was sent to the Bastille. He was released a week or so later, but his brief imprisonment began to intensify and refine his view of things.

By this time (1637) La Rochefoucauld and his wife had two sons and a daughter, and they were to have a second daughter in the following year. The short time he spent in the Bastille, where he saw many friends and acquaintances charged with serious crimes against the crown, moved him to conceive the "... frightening image of the Cardinal's domination," he writes in his *Mémoires*. After his discharge, La Rochefoucauld was exiled to his home. He was relieved to be there, experiencing simple pleasures with his wife and children, and with his fellow exiles in the country as well. He says of this period—again in the *Mémoires*—"I felt blessed in my family."

Referring to a slightly later time (1639), La Rochefoucauld tells of another experience that raised questions in his mind. When he was praised in military reports to the cardinal, following an action in Flanders, Richelieu offered him the rank of *maréchal de camp* (brigadier-general), as a promise of things to come. But the queen put a stop to his acceptance. Perhaps she understood better than her willing servant—his fellow courtiers had named him the "Queen's Martyr" after his detention in the Bastille—that the cardinal was trying to win him over, though obviously La Rochefoucauld might have felt he was being appropriately repaid for services to the crown, with no question of his continuing independence. As a result of the incident and others like it, La Rochefoucauld seems to have concluded that his relationship to the queen was not as uncomplicated as he had supposed. Nevertheless he continued to serve her.

In December 1642 Richelieu died, and Louis XIII died in May 1643. In the interim La Rochefoucauld left home for the court, intending to be near the queen, from whom he anticipated preferment as authority and power were realigned in the new government. His hopes ran high. The queen was at last in a position to help him, and he and France were free of Richelieu. But for all the relief La Rochefoucauld may have felt at the minister's death—in a typically impersonal passage he refers in the *Mémoires* to the possible " . . . pleasure [the cardinal's] enemies felt on their liberation from so many persecutions"—he credits Richelieu with being the first to understand thoroughly the power of royal authority and the first to know how to make it available to the sovereign. Given the late date of the *Mémoires* (1662), it is possible La Rochefoucauld came to this opinion only slowly. It

seems worth pointing out here that he also offers the view that "Our willingness to think the worst of people without examining issues is the result of pride and laziness. We want to find people guilty; we don't want the trouble of evaluating their offenses" (*Maximes* 267).

At court La Rochefoucauld was to be disappointed, and ultimately frustrated and defeated. The queen was somewhat distant, putting him off, he felt. He had expected better, after more than ten years of service. On the other hand, she had urgent problems of her own. Her husband's will encumbered her regency with a council whose approval she would require before she took official actions. Fortunately for her, the parlement, the chief judicial body—with the responsibility for considering such issues—declared Louis's will unconstitutional. But she could not single-handedly govern France and protect the interests of her four-year-old son, Louis XIV, until he should come of age. For a number of reasons, she turned to Giulio Mazarini, or Jules Mazarin, as he chose to be known in France. Before this time Mazarin had served the pope, and later Richelieu, who, shortly before he died, nominated the Italian to be his successor. Mazarin was handsome, soft-spoken, and persuasive. Richelieu had found him very efficient in handling affairs of state and extremely loyal. Anne too was to find Mazarin efficient and loyal. Indeed, their relationship became very close, and it is possible—though not likely—that they were secretly married. Mazarin had been made a cardinal in 1641 but was never ordained.

La Rochefoucauld's first responses to Mazarin's prominence at court suggest that he underestimated both the cardinal's ability and Anne's growing dependence on him. Ultimately, La Rochefoucauld came to dislike him intensely, as the *Apologie* makes clear. At the heart of the matter, probably, was Mazarin's success in filling a position very like the one La Rochefoucauld had hoped to occupy. Whereas Mazarin chose a course of action and followed it with skill and daring, La Rochefoucauld was likely to wait out occasions, responding to them, for the most part—though he did so with intelligence and with great physical courage—when it was called for. But he neither invented nor implemented large political designs. His adversary Cardinal de Retz states clearly in his portrait of La Rochefoucauld what other contemporaries imply: "he has never been capable of handling any business of significance, and I don't know why, because he has qualities that in others would have compensated for the ones he lacks. . . . He has always been affected by irresolution, but I don't know to what I should attribute it. . . ."

A few years after finally giving up the idea that Queen Anne was his committed patroness, La Rochefoucauld began (probably in 1646) a serious relationship with the beautiful Anne-Geneviève de Bourbon-Condé, duchesse de Longueville. She was the sister of Louis II de Bourbon, prince de Condé (the Grand Condé), the head of a collateral branch of the royal house of Bourbon and one of the most famous generals of France. From one point of view, La Rochefoucauld reached above himself socially in his relationship with the Condés. Though he says in his *Mémoires* that he set out deliberately to seduce Anne-Geneviève, it seems fair to both of them to suppose that despite her religious upbringing and her reputation for virtue, she was ready for the relationship that he offered. It is quite possible that he loved more than she, and tried to hide it by posing as a calculating lover in the *Mémoires*. By 1646 she had borne her husband—who was then almost twice her age, in his fifties—six children. According to one prevalent view, she had done her duty as a wife and might now take a lover of appropriate rank to please herself. Her husband had certainly pleased himself in such matters.

She and La Rochefoucauld found each other's company congenial, in part because of common political interests. They wanted to overthrow Mazarin and were attracted by the idea of involving themselves in the dynamics of government affairs, both for the immediate pleasure of such involvement and for the advantages that might accrue to themselves and their families. They also were lovers. In 1649 she bore their son, named Charles-Paris; but La Rochefoucauld's paternity was never acknowledged publicly, and the child was known by the Longueville surname.

For whatever reason—greater social position, perhaps, or greater ambition and capacity for intrigue—Anne-Geneviève dominated the relationship, at least its political side, and probably the emotional side as well. It was she who set the example for him by committing herself to work against the crown in the civil strife of January through March 1649, known as the First War of the Fronde, which was the first in a series of uprisings extending to 1653, attempts by various entrenched middle-class and aristocratic elements to thwart the central government's imposition of new taxes on them, or its collection of established taxes in what was a period of economic depression. (The war took its name from a child's catapult or slingshot [*fronde*], which had earlier been used in defiance of civil authority.) The First Fronde was led by the bourgeois parlement and a few ambitious nobles. Private interests apart, the Frondeurs may be thought of as trying to overthrow the regency government of Anne and Mazarin—they insisted they were loyal to the young king—in order to win back certain powers and privileges taken from them by Richelieu. Their ultimate defeat in 1653 helped prepare the way for the absolutism of Louis XIV.

By 1648 La Rochefoucauld's disappointed ambition had led him to argue with Mazarin about rewards promised and withheld. In 1646 he had once more served the crown in Flanders, to some extent because he had been led to believe the appointment as brigadier-general would be offered to him a second time. Ironically, it was the seriousness of a wound he received that seems to have accounted for his not being given the reward. In 1648 he had put down a minor rebellion in Poitou, in anticipation of the ducal privilege of his wife's right to sit in the presence of the seated monarch. He was again disappointed, and it was then (December 1648) that he argued with Mazarin. By this time the duchesse de Longueville had joined the Frondeurs. La Rochefoucauld joined too, and toward the end of the First Fronde, in February 1649, he was again wounded, during the seige of Paris—a musket ball hit him in the throat. Cardinal de Retz, a leading Frondeur at the time (he later changed sides), records in his *Mémoires* that the wounded La Rochefoucauld said he would have stopped the duchesse de Longueville from getting into the nasty business of the Fronde if he had come back from Poitou two months earlier.

After their defeat La Rochefoucauld's relationship with Anne-Geneviève continued. With his help she, her brother, and others tried in various ways to take advantage of the relatively weak position of the regency following the Peace of Rueil, which ended the First Fronde on 30 March 1649. As a result of this connection with the powerful Condés, which seems to have satisfied part of his need to be close to the center of power, in alliance with an attractive woman of consequence, La Rochefoucauld was deeply involved in the later wars against Queen Anne and Mazarin. They did not come to their effective end until late 1652, and some opposition to the crown continued until the autumn of 1653. By this time the rebel armies had been defeated—the Grand Condé fled to Brussels—and La Rochefoucauld had sustained a terrible musket wound, the shot barely missing his eyes as it pierced his cheeks and nose. He was months recovering, and then his sight was poor.

La Rochefoucauld's ambition took various forms. He wanted to be loved and respected by a beautiful woman, preferably one close to the throne, to be appointed to high military rank, to be given a defined place of dignity in the court, to be well regarded for his political and psychological understanding. He had penetration enough to realize that even "the rulers of the world are in no position to give us physical well-being or peace of mind . . ." (*Maximes* 542), yet he sought improbable satisfactions from them. In certain ways his experience left him remarkably unchanged. In others he was the chief beneficiary of acute introspection—his own best pupil.

La Rochefoucauld never gave up ambition for family, and in this regard he was like his fellow aristocrats. For example, he saw to the reconstruction of the family residence of Verteuil, which Mazarin's troops had destroyed during the wars. In the process of effecting economies to make the renovation possible, and to ensure that his son François VII would inherit a solvent dukedom, he seems to have decided that his three daughters would have no dowries, which almost certainly meant they would not marry, at least not within their own social class.

But unlike most of his fellow aristocrats, La Rochefoucauld seems to have been capable of risking everything, including family, for the sake of a principle. For instance, he refused to separate himself from the nearly defeated Grand Condé, though he knew his powerful colleague did not have La Rochefoucauld's interests much in mind toward the end of the Frondes. And after he had been temporarily blinded by the musket shot he refused to ask the king's pardon, the formula that would have resulted in immediate amnesty. He was thereafter declared guilty of treason against the king (*lèse majesté*), and his titles were revoked and his property confiscated. All was later restored.

In these instances La Rochefoucauld repudiated the self-serving quality of ambition by refusing to evade its unfortunate consequences. He would not deny Condé—his effective patron—or ask favors of the crown, whose authority he had opposed. To think of him as naive in his resistance to following a safe course—as if he intended to live up to the ideal standard of a Celadon, or of a just and upright man (*honnête homme*), which was at the center of a tradition of aristocratic behavior with which he was familiar—is probably seeing the matter too simply, though there was undoubtedly something of this motivation for his behavior. At this point he was not a chivalrous gentleman primarily, but a man whose increasing knowledge had helped him to understand that self-interest works subliminally to dominate most human actions. As the Wars of the Fronde ended, he might have decided on an immediately self-serving course; but it would have offended his sense of himself, one may suppose, to find that in the extremity he acted to support the conclusion that "Philosophy triumphs easily over past and future misfortunes, but the misfortunes of the day triumph over philosophy" (*Maximes* 22).

La Rochefoucauld was to have a very satisfying friendship with the comtesse de La Fayette, but he seems never to have enjoyed quite the fulfillment he hoped for in any of his relationships with women or to have eased his need by understanding himself in this regard, though he probably went some considerable distance toward such understanding. Apparently his wife did not engage his amorous imagination very much. The idealized Queen Anne proved to be a remote and inaccessible presence when La Rochefoucauld moved from fantasies to real cases. The duchesse de Chevreuse used up lovers as her various political and private needs might require, so that whatever intimacy La Rochefoucauld may have experienced with her could not long have satisfied him. And his relationship with Marie de Hautefort presumably did not get past the epistolary stage, with the one important letter undelivered. There were other women, but none measured up to his high expectations, or so it seems.

The woman to whom he had been attached for some years, the duchesse de Longueville, estranged herself from him in 1651 by taking another lover, the duc de Nemours. Deeply hurt—his pride wounded and his gentler sensibilities bruised—La Rochefoucauld apparently made no effort to continue or renew the

relationship, though it seems clear his feeling for her ran deep. In fact, he was vengeful enough to support the renewal of a liaison between Nemours and Condé's established mistress, the duchesse de Châtillon, without interruption of her more recently begun relationship with Condé. In these circumstances the two women were rivals not only for Nemours's love, but also for the exercise of political influence. At one point in the affair, La Rochefoucauld got the duchesse de Châtillon to persuade Condé to offer Mazarin terms for peace highly advantageous to La Rochefoucauld's interests. The peace was never effected, though Mazarin, apparently stalling for time, at least pretended to find the terms agreeable. Despite the disappointment, La Rochefoucauld claims to have been gratified by his maneuvers. As the designer and director of this complex arrangement, ". . . the Duc de La Rochefoucauld [had] nearly complete control over all those involved . . . ," he says a little haughtily in the *Mémoires.*

But surely he was deluding himself. As he knew when he wrote the *Mémoires*, he had been in no position to control anyone for very long. He was shortly to receive the wound that almost cost him his sight, and Anne-Geneviève was to lose Nemours irrevocably. He was killed in a duel just weeks after he, like La Rochefoucauld, had been wounded in the battle of the Faubourg Saint-Antoine in 1652. Altogether, La Rochefoucauld seems much closer to the truth in this instance when he says, "We think we are in charge of things when we are in fact being led, and while we head in one direction with our minds, we are unconsciously [*insensiblement*] pulled in another by our feelings" (*Maximes* 43).

Though Anne-Geneviève held out against the queen and Mazarin for some time after most other Frondeurs had given up, she held out futilely. Then she reverted more and more to the self-constraining religious attitudes she had adopted early in life; and finally she sought consolation in Jansenism, at the convent of Port-Royal in Paris, to which Madeleine de Souvré, marquise de Sablé, and other prominent persons had also attached themselves. Though La Rochefoucauld leaves no indication that he ever was much interested in any religion, he shared with the Jansenists (followers of Cornelius Jansen) certain elements of a world view held by a good many of his contemporaries. The view, essentially Calvinistic, is dominated by the conviction that will and reason are generally insufficient to cope with the evil in human nature—the self-serving actions of mankind, along with its capacity to deceive itself about its own motives, for example. But it seems unlikely that La Rochefoucauld would have agreed with Anne-Geneviève or any other Jansenist that given the insufficiency of mankind's will and reason, divine grace might effect salvation. It would have been more like him to regard human beings as largely helpless in the face of their passions, and to think all must cope with the predicament as well as might be. For La Rochefoucauld, fortune may occasionally intervene in human affairs; but God's presence is nowhere apparent, unless one discovers it in the rare instances of human greatness or in the even rarer cases of human goodness.

Not quite forty years old when the Wars of the Fronde ended, La Rochefoucauld found his career in the politics of the court at an end. When, a year or so later, his titles and estates were restored, he went home to his disordered holdings in poor health, with little of the money he needed to repair his properties. For the most part he was to divide the remaining years of his life between his estates in the west of France and Paris. Helped by Jean de Gourville, who began his career as valet in the service of the La Rochefoucaulds before becoming a nationally prominent financier, the family's financial position was improved, though it was never to become entirely satisfactory during La Rochefoucauld's lifetime, despite his eldest son's marriage to a wealthy cousin. But Verteuil was restored, and the family survived as a strong aristocratic entity.

In Paris, La Rochefoucauld came only to the outer edges of the powerful court of Louis XIV and Mazarin, though he was ultimately reconciled to the royal favor, a fact marked by the award to him of the knightly Order of the Saint-Esprit, in 1661. Much of his time was spent in the company of socially and intellectually influential women. Among them were Catherine de Vivonne, marquise de Rambouillet, in whose salon La Rochefoucauld no doubt tried and refined certain of his psychological views of human nature; the marquise de Sablé, who collaborated with La Rochefoucauld by helping him to test some of his maxims before publication; Marie de Rabutin-Chantal, marquise de Sévigné, famous for her letters, one of which records with warm approval her friend La Rochefoucauld's coment on his mother's death in 1672—"She is the only woman who never stopped loving me"; the comtesse de La Fayette, to whose novel concerning the nature of marriage for a woman of her own class—*La Princesse de Clèves*—La Rochefoucauld made a contribution, either as a collaborating author or as an editor. He also enjoyed the company, in some cases the friendship, of several of the leading men in literary life, including Pierre Corneille, Charles de Marguetel de Saint-Denis de Saint-Évremond, Jean-Baptiste Poquelin, known as Molière, and Nicolas Boileau-Despréaux.

It was during these years after the Fronde that La Rochefoucauld produced all of his works, except for the *Apologie de M. le Prince de Marcillac*, not published until 1855. He decided against publication even though the most obvious purpose of any apologia—the very reason for writing it—is to explain oneself to others. It seems likely that a secondary purpose—to set down clearly the truth about oneself beneath the surface—so dominated his effort that the *Apologie* proved to be too revealing. It undercut the effect it was intended to produce: the representation of a straightforward and truthful La Rochefoucauld, who behaved reasonably during the First Fronde.

The *Portrait de La Rochefoucauld par lui-*

même, published in 1659, is an example of a genre that became fashionable during the 1650's, probably in imitation of portraits in the novels of Madeleine de Scudéry, particularly *Le grand Cyrus* (1649–1653) and *Clélie* (1654–1660), which portray persons contemporary with the novelist, thinly disguised as Romans, Greeks, or Persians. The genre, which was very popular in the salons, took the form of either a self-portrait or a portrait of someone else, like La Rochefoucauld's *Portrait du Cardinal de Retz* (1675).

As has been suggested, La Rochefoucauld's self-portrait seems to be essentially accurate in its physical description. The remainder of the piece may be no less accurate, but it is highly selective. In describing a face, one does not reasonably omit references to mouth, nose, eyes, hair, and coloring. But no such precisely identified categories cover the psychological side of things. Among the subjects La Rochefoucauld chooses to consider as he characterizes himself are his dominant mood—it is melancholic, he tells us—his love of good conversation and reading, his lack of worldly ambition, his openness to reasonable criticism, his commitment to gentlemanly, upright behavior, his abandonment of gallantry, and his deep understanding and keen approval of real love in its strongest, most delicate forms. It has been suggested that the self-portrait was in part intended to inform Mazarin that La Rochefoucauld was beyond all doubt politically benign, without ambition. It has also been suggested that he was not quite consciously advertising his deep need to be loved and his capacity for loving. Both suggestions seem accurate.

In *Le siècle de Louis XIV* (1751), Voltaire says that La Rochefoucauld's *Mémoires* are read, but that his *Maximes* are known by heart. His observation, accurate for his own and the preceding age, is still representative. The highly respected editor of the Pléiade edition of La Rochefoucauld's works points out that the *Mémoires* were written for a tight circle of his friends. And indeed, though they are full of detail about the Fronde, they assume that the reader already knows a good deal about persons and events that make up its extended actions. Without such information one may become lost in the intricacies of motivation, shifting human relationships, plot, and counterplot.

Though no one knows precisely when the *Mémoires* were written, it is clear that La Rochefoucauld produced all six parts of the work after the time of the Fronde. Parts 3 through 6, covering the period March 1649–October 1652, were written first. In these sections La Rochefoucauld writes in the third person, referring to himself as the prince de Marcillac before his father's death and as the duc de La Rochefoucauld afterward. Later he wrote parts 1 and 2, covering the period 1624–1649, but he wrote them in the first person. Despite this important rhetorical difference, all six parts are dominated by an impersonal voice, with the private La Rochefoucauld not much in evidence. Nevertheless, the informed reader can often identify the people he cared most about, as well as those who most disappointed or angered him.

While composing the *Mémoires*, La Rochefoucauld allowed certain of his friends to read and comment on his work. (One embarrassing result was the unauthorized publication of the biographically sensitive *Mémoires* in 1662 and afterward.) There were various accepted standards to which he probably wrote, and to some extent his friends no doubt judged his efforts by them. His fastidiousness seems to have found the *précieux* salon of the marquise de Rambouillet congenial, from his earliest experience of it in the 1630's. The *Mémoires* are explicitly dedicated to *préciosité*, which began with the decision, moral in its origins, to elevate life above merely natural impulses and to achieve delicacy of taste, feeling, manners, and language, with a cultivated understanding as the real basis of this achievement.

Among the many wide-ranging derivatives of this commitment were the view that women, typically subjugated by marriage, should be given the chance for the greater independence represented by trial marriage, divorce, and birth control; and, more relevant to the style of the *Mémoires*, the principle that language should be precise and clear, the inevitable product of the *précieux* moral sensibility, controlled by understanding and taste. Obviously such a moral-critical school might be guilty of excesses, and Molière made the most of the probability in his derisive one-act play *Les précieuses ridicules* (1659). But there might also be *véritables précieuses*, as Molière was careful to point out in his preface, though he did so almost certainly for political reasons.

It has been said in praise of La Rochefoucauld's prose that it is muscular, sensitive to nuance, and classically lucid. These qualities undoubtedly owe most to his natural endowments as a literary artist. But they also owe something to the standards of *préciosité* and to the psychologically related ideals of cultivated behavior associated with such works as *L'Astrée* and to the aristocratic theory of the *honnêtes gens,* who in their social relations are expected to behave with prudence and the self-control that indulges the needs of others—capacities for disciplined sensitivity that derive principally from self-knowledge. But for all its good style, the *Mémoires* are not a work for the general reader, a conclusion reinforced by the fact that the *Maximes* have been translated into English many times since their earliest appearance, whereas there is no recognized translation of the *Mémoires.* Though elements of both works may be traced to the same sources, it is in the *Maximes* that La Rochefoucauld speaks out of his knowledge of himself.

It was chiefly in the salon of the marquise de Sablé that La Rochefoucauld offered early versions of many of the 641 maxims now attributed to him. By the time he began to write them, he had learned firsthand something about love, war, politics, and —from his own aristocratic point of view—family responsibility. It seems correct to suppose his contemporaries had good reason to decide that he was keenly introspective and a penetrating observer of those around him, opinions borne out by the relatively early *Apologie* and the later *Portrait . . . par lui-même.* He was a leader in the sophisticated salon game of analyzing human motives, his natural skill having been improved by his quite varied experience, including his participation in the give and take of conversation in the salons. These facts do not explain the *Maximes,* of course; but they provide some basis for reading them at more than one level, and they help to make plausible certain alternatives to the simple view that they are psychologically reductive statements because they explain too much of human motivation by means of self-love.

Certain of the maxims may now seem merely routine observations on the human condition or on human behavior. For example: "It takes great ability to know how to hide one's ability" (*Maximes* 245); "We often annoy others, even when we think it would be impossible to do so" (*Maximes* 242); "Our changes of feeling are even stranger than the caprices of fate" (*Maximes* 45). But even such of the maxims as may seem to us less than extraordinary are likely to have stimulated a new perception in La Rochefoucauld's seventeenth-century reader, because he was able to penetrate a territory of the mind that was then largely uncharted and to convey what he had found in a paradoxical form that stimulates cognition.

Short, pithy statements written by a single learned hand have been produced since classical times. (Proverbs, a distinctly different art form, are folk sayings, modified by generations of use.) These statements produced by a single hand have been variously called aphorisms, apothegms, epigrams, maxims, sentences, and precepts. Most are extremely brief—a short sentence or two. But writers as far apart in time and place as Hippocrates and Francis Bacon have produced maxims that are at least fleetingly discursive; they may use a hundred words or more to make their point.

Scarcely ten of La Rochefoucauld's 641 maxims are in any sense discursive. Far and away the great majority of them are extremely brief, and they make use of paradox to convey their point tellingly: "Old men like to offer good advice to console themselves for being in no condition to set bad examples" (*Maximes* 93); "People all speak well of their hearts, but none presume to speak well of their minds" (*Maximes* 98); "Most virtuous women are like hidden treasures, safe only because they are not sought" (*Maximes* 368).

One cannot say with certainty how paradox works, but part of its success seems to depend on its requiring us to consider two contradictory views, both of which we believe at different levels of mind or in different moods, probably without consciousness of the contradiction, and perhaps without consciousness that we hold both views. In the last maxim quoted, the term "virtuous women" makes chastity a moral absolute; "safe only because . . . not sought" makes virtue relative. Though we may prefer one, most of us probably hold both views, in the sense just indicated. The maxim disturbs this double view, ostensibly by rejecting the absolute standard of virtue and preferring the relative. But obviously a woman sought may not love in return. What the paradoxical maxim does, finally, is to repudiate the clear distinction between "self-control" (virtue) and "self-indulgence" (taking opportunities), so that neither static principle may be taken to represent the mind ("feelings") in action. Paradoxical maxims generally destroy fixed and received prescriptions by this means, leaving the reader either free to reconsider an issue of human nature only nominally settled, or psychologically burdened with the responsibility for doing so.

Though the *Maximes* describe rather than provide a norm for human behavior, they certainly imply the hope that men and women may improve their generally inaccurate ways of seeing and thinking about things. But "As a result of inertia and habit, the mind holds on to whatever is easy and comfortable: this ten-dency invariably places a limit on our perceptions, and we never take the trouble to stretch our minds as much as we might" (*Maximes* 482). The *Maximes* tell us again and again that it is "self-love" or "self-interest" or the desire to "preserve" ourselves that underlies such psychological conservatism. But to conclude, therefore, that they are primarily cynical and reductive is to miss their most important truth. They show us many of the various ways in which we delude ourselves by accepting our own avowed or nominal motives as the operative ones, when in fact they are not. The *Maximes* demonstrate less that mankind is self-loving above all than that men and women do not understand themselves very well—even those who, like La Rochefoucauld himself, have begun to search below the surface of such terms as "love," "goodness," "virtue," "bravery," "self-respect," "hate," "cowardice," "gratitude," "fidelity," and so on. Unconscious processes, apparently effected by some fundamental animal need in each of us to keep us going as we are, dominate our behavior.

Maxim 563, which was given first place (it was number 1) in the initial authorized edition of 1665 but removed from later editions by La Rouchefoucauld, characterizes "self-love" not primarily as a self-serving agent of the mind, but as a subconscious being difficult to know because it is almost impossible to

. . . penetrate the deeps or pierce the darkness of its abysses. . . . But the obscurity that conceals it from itself never keeps it from seeing clearly . . . [dangers to itself] beyond its own limits; in this regard it is like our eyes, which can see everything but themselves. . . . It is capricious, though incapable of changes resulting from forces outside itself. . . . It thrives everywhere, in all circumstances, living off everything, off nothing; it accommodates itself to all things and to their absence. It even goes over to the enemy, joins in their plans, and what is really surprising, like the enemy, it hates itself. . . . In short, it wants only to exist, and so long as it does, it is [even] willing to be its own enemy. . . .

La Rochefoucauld's "self-love" represents a dark side of the mind beyond our appreciable knowledge or control, a principle of blind survival that distorts both what it observes and the way in which it understands, in order to preserve itself—that preservation being its only purpose. It is utterly without dignity or concern for principle. It is not ordinarily receptive to "truth," in that any confrontation with hard evidence indicating the reasonableness of some change in self-love results in rejection of the evidence or in its false (rationalizing) interpretation. When self-love is not threatened, ideal standards of human behavior seem possible, La Rochefoucauld believes. But to the extent that such standards imply a redefinition of that hidden side of the mind, we do not, except rarely, act in accordance with the ideal, though we may delude ourselves that we do.

It is always unfortunate, and in some ways surprising, to La Rochefoucauld that "Virtues are lost to self-interest as rivers are lost to the sea" (*Maximes* 171). But he continues to hope that experience—provided by fortune or chance—will thrust us into circumstances that may help us to think new thoughts. Though such opportunities need not result in a better understanding of ourselves, sometimes they do: "Most men, like plants, have hidden qualities that chance makes known" (*Maximes* 344); "Circumstances allow others to learn about us, and us even more to learn about ourselves" (*Maximes* 345); "To be great, one must know how to take advantage of whatever chance may bring" (*Maximes* 343).

Obviously, one cannot say how and to what degree La Rochefoucauld's natural talents as psychologist and literary artist were reinforced by the persons and events in his life—that is, by the circumstances that chance had arranged. But the autonomous, self-serving predisposition of many of those he had come to know at court and in the Wars of the Fronde—including the many sides of himself he encountered in altering circumstances—

must have contributed much to his far-reaching conclusion that the mind is profoundly governed by a nearly intractable dark side. Generally his contemporaries had neither his penetration nor his gift for reporting observations on human nature in the paradoxical turns that often shock the reader into new perceptions. But the record suggests that many of them saw in the *Maximes* a psychology that they themselves had observed during the years immediately preceding its publication. One early comment is particularly close to the mark. It was made by Marie de Hautefort, who had become the duchesse de Schomberg—the woman to whom La Rochefoucauld had written a love letter before going into battle in 1635, giving it to her brother to be delivered only if he should die. She observes in a comment to the marquise de Sablé that she is convinced La Rochefoucauld was right to represent human behavior as determined, beyond our immediate control.

Theoretically, at least, the *Maximes* identify two distinct, though ultimately related, forces that may oppose self-love. One is "virtuous behavior," which derives both from the formally expressed and the unspoken ideals of La Rochefoucauld's own social class—including the code of *honnêteté* and the theories generated in the *précieux* salon of the marquise de Rambouillet—and from his essentially individual view of things. Because the virtues "lose themselves in self-love," it is not clear in the world of the *Maximes* whether they represent potentially "real" behavior, presently checked by self-love, or whether they are delusory values, ultimately rationalizations that in fact protect self-love. Certainly they are at least temporarily delusory. So, for example, La Rochefoucauld says, "The aversion to lying is often an unconscious wish to increase the value of our testimony and to give religious weight to our statements" (*Maximes* 63). Indeed, his maxims generally show that nominal virtue is self-interest in disguise, with the disguise a means by which we deceive both others and ourselves. The second force that may oppose self-love is self-knowledge, which includes the possibility that we will gain some control over the domination by self-love of our behavior, and act virtuously. But La Rochefoucauld does not go very far in this direction. In the *Maximes* he writes as if his primary function were to document the ways in which self-love exercises its amoral authority over us. He says relatively little about the means of acquiring the will to act independently or about the likely quality of such independent action.

When the comtesse de La Fayette said that their author must have had corruption in his mind and heart for the *Maximes* to have been imaginable, she underestimated him, overlooking the possibility that he was an accurate observer of humanity. In fact, it is reasonable to suppose that in writing the *Maximes*, La Rochefoucauld did his best to assume the role of a dispassionate analyst. He was indeed a moralist whose high aim was the deliverance of human motivation into the conscious mind, where it might be controlled. But, generally speaking, he abandoned any fixed moral point of view as he examined and characterized human behavior. The concerned idealist in him was always awake; but in the *Maximes*, at least, La Rochefoucauld writes much as if the idealist's work cannot begin until the analyst's work has been completed.

Along with the *Apologie*, the *Portrait . . . par lui-même*, the *Mémoires*, and the *Maximes*, the nineteen *Réflexions diverses* complete the list of La Rochefoucauld's works, except for a brief portrait of Cardinal de Retz, some letters, and a few fragments. The *Réflexions* are very short prose essays written in an easy, relaxed style. To judge from various kinds of internal evidence, including La Rochefoucauld's use of late versions of some of his own maxims, these essays occupied him almost until his death. Seven of them were first published in 1731; the rest did not appear until 1863. Though no one knows how early in his life he began to produce them, the *Réflexions* are generally regarded as the work of La Rochefoucauld's maturity. They cover subjects like "truth," "society," "conversation," "trust," "love and the sea," "jealousy," "love and life," "taste," "falseness," "nature and fortune," and "retirement"—all of which La Rochefoucauld handles with the unpretentious assurance of one who has experienced a great deal in the consideration of himself and in the world of human affairs. In various contexts he weighs what one owes to oneself and what one owes to society. Though in the *Réflexions* he continues to see human behavior as he saw it in the *Maximes*, his general aim in these essays—reminiscent of the *honnête homme* who has immediate obligations to society—is to identify and praise balanced and controlled behavior, making part of his judgment about such behavior rest on its likely consequences for the world.

The *Réflexions* seldom surprise the reader with new penetrations. Yet La Rochefoucauld's cumulative effect in these essays is impressive. He explores the general unwillingness to give up moribund human relationships (*Réflexions* 9); he explains the need of society for those who have good taste and good judgment to speak their conclusions impartially, without undue concern for what others may think (*Réflexions* 13); and he commends that rare ability to be strong enough to keep a secret, even from a friend, if one has promised confidentiality, though he also remarks that few secrets are for all time (*Réflexions* 5). More generally, he talks about the importance of self-confidence in human affairs, and of one's demeanor and capacity to listen in conversation. Nothing he says seems trivial, probably because the context in which even his most obvious conclusions occur has a mature quality. Only a mind well endowed by natural gifts and experience could have written the *Réflexions*. Excellent critics have found them a pleasure to read at a leisurely pace.

La Rochefoucauld's late years were full, giving him both pleasure and pain. He continued to write, spending time on revisions of the *Maximes*, authorized editions of which appeared in 1665, 1666, 1671, 1675, and 1678.

And, as has been suggested, he probably worked on the *Réflexions diverses* as well during this period. But he thought of himself as slothful at times, and there were periods of profound boredom.

In Paris his social life was made pleasant by the comtesse de La Fayette. She and La Rochefoucauld had become friends shortly after the first appearance of the *Maximes.* They were regularly in each other's company; though the relationship was very close, the nature of its intimacy was not made clear to others. In addition to the obvious pleasures of human companionship, they enjoyed a literary association, chiefly the collaboration on her novels.

There were also salon meetings, dinners, readings, and visits to parks, the theater, and other places, where he might meet new acquaintances but much more likely see old friends, like the prince de Condé, and old enemies, like Cardinal de Retz. La Rochefoucauld turned down the suggestion that he apply for membership in the already famous Académie Française, which had grown out of informal meetings attended by men of letters, including his father's secretary, Jacques de Sérizay. The shift from informal to formal status for these meetings and the group who attended them was effected by Richelieu. The Academie was officially registered by the Paris parlement in 1637, with Sérizay as its first director. La Rochefoucauld was not an academician and was probably ill-suited to membership in any formally convening organization, including the court. His forte was in observing things as an intimately informed outsider.

Mixed with the pleasures of activity during these years were anxieties, losses, and physical discomforts. His wife died in 1670; La Rochefoucauld left no record of what he may have felt about her passing. In 1672 three of his sons were wounded in battle; the oldest lived to succeed his father, but neither his fourth son (Jean-Baptiste) nor Charles-Paris de Longueville recovered. La Rochefoucauld's mother had died the previous month, and he felt the loss deeply, as the marquise de Sévigné's brief report indicates. Even with the help of the comtesse de La Fayette and the influential financier Gourville, La Rochefoucauld had frequent trouble with his creditors until he died. Though he once more joined the army, in the summer of 1667, he was made to realize he was not fit for service. His eyes had given him trouble ever since he received the wound across his face, in 1652, and he often suffered excruciating pain from gout, which was ultimately the cause of his death.

La Rochefoucauld says, "We cannot look steadily at the sun nor at death" (*Maximes* 26), and he believes that "Few people have any understanding of death; they do not usually face it resolutely, but stupidly and conventionally, and most die simply because they cannot hinder death" (*Maximes* 23). But his essay on retirement (*Réflexions* 19) and a letter by the marquise de Sévigné to her daughter suggest his own gradual disengagement from life, accomplished gracefully (perhaps somberly at times) because he had read the signs—the world was moving on without him—and he had the understanding necessary to accept the painful fact and what it implied for him. In this late period of life, he says, the old do best, finally, " . . . to forget the world, which is in fact inclined to forget them . . ." (*Réflexions* 19). He seems to have sought peace within himself, believing that if he could not find it there, it was " . . . futile to look for it elsewhere" (*Maximes* 571).

La Rochefoucauld died on 17 March 1680. The marquise de Sévigné wrote to her daughter more than once to say that Marie-Madeleine de La Fayette was unable to get over the loss. Others who loved him no doubt mourned him too. The world went on without him, as it had shown him very clearly it could do. But La Rochefoucauld the man had been as engaging to some as the *Maximes* have been to generations of readers. His greatest strength was to see beneath the surface of things, observing what the subliminal mind intended rather than what the literal mind said. In one sense this strength was also his weakness. His point of view, as an author and as a man, sometimes upset the psychological equilibrium of those he addressed, just as it might leave La Rochefoucauld himself somber and uncertain, too close for comfort to the abysses of the mind from which he wrested his most effective paradoxes. But his acute and sensitive perception included the capacity to understand the feelings of others, and to write with impersonal and abstract precision about human actions and the motives that engender them.

Selected Bibliography

EDITIONS

MAXIMES AND RÉFLEXIONS DIVERSES

Sentences et maximes morales. The Hague, 1664. Actually printed by the Elzeviers on their presses in Leiden, this pirated edition stimulated La Rochefoucauld to publish an authorized edition.

Réflexions ou sentences et maximes morales. Paris, 1665. This is the first authorized edition; it includes 317 maxims, the essay on death, and an index.

————. New ed. Paris, 1666. Numerous changes distinguish this second authorized edition from the first, including a reduction in the number of maxims to 302.

————. 3rd ed. Paris, 1671. Changes in this third authorized edition include an increase in the number of maxims to 341.

————. 4th ed. Paris, 1675. This fourth authorized edition contains 413 maxims, the additions being the chief difference between this and the third edition.

————. 5th ed. Paris, 1678. This edition, the last to be published in La Rochefoucauld's lifetime, contains 504 maxims.

Réflexions ou sentences morales. 6th ed., enlarged. Paris, 1693. Apparently arranged by the comtesse de La Fayette's secretary, Jean de Segrais, this posthumous edition contains fifty new maxims, of which twenty-one are variants on maxims already published. How much work, if any, La Rochefoucauld may have done on this edition is not known.

La Rochefoucauld: Maximes & réflexions diverses. Edited by Henry A. Grubbs, Jr. Princeton, 1929. The introduction to this edition, which includes very brief biographical and critical sections, is in English. The editor's notes are also in English.

La Rochefoucauld: Maximes. Edited by Frederick C. Green. Cambridge, 1945. The introduction to this edition, which includes biographical and critical information and judgments, is in English. Except for textual variants, the editor's notes are in English.

La Rochefoucauld: Maximes et réflexions. Edited by Roland Barthes. Paris, 1961.

Maximes. Edited by Jacques Truchet. Paris, 1967; 2nd ed., 1972.

La Rochefoucauld: Réflexions, ou sentences et maximes morales; Réflexions diverses. Edited by Dominique Secretan. Geneva, 1967.

MÉMOIRES

Mémoires de M.D.L.R. sur les brigues à la mort de Louys XIII, les guerres de Paris et de Guyenne, et la prison des princes. . . . Brussels, 1662. Actually published in Amsterdam, this unauthorized edition embarrassed La Rochefoucauld, as had an even earlier unauthorized edition of parts 3–4, of which there is no known copy. La Rochefoucauld would not publish an authorized version, so the pirated editions continued to appear, in 1663, 1664, 1665, 1669, 1688, and 1700.

Mémoires du duc de la Rochefoucauld. Paris, 1817. This is the first edition based on a complete manuscript by La Rochefoucauld.

COLLECTED EDITIONS

Oeuvres de La Rochefoucauld. 4 vols. Collection des Grands Écrivains de la France. Edited by D. L. Gilbert et al. Paris, 1868–1883. This still useful edition includes (apart from the four volumes) an album (1883) that contains La Rochefoucauld's coat of arms in a color illustration, a portrait of La Rochefoucauld, and other items of interest.

La Rochefoucauld: Oeuvres complètes. Bibliothèque de la Pléiade. Edited by L. Martin-Chauffier. Paris, 1950. Revised and enlarged by Jean Marchand, 1964.

LA ROCHEFOUCAULD

TRANSLATIONS

With few exceptions, like the editions by Davies and Behn listed below, the earliest English translations of La Rochefoucauld's *Maximes* were published anonymously until the nineteenth century. Translations of the other works are hard to come by. Bolton (see below) translates the *Réflexions diverses* as well as the *Maximes,* and the biography by Bishop (see below) includes a translation of the *Portrait . . . par lui-même* and the opening section of the *Apologie.* I have not found a translation of the *Mémoires.* (An anonymous book in English that draws on pirated material and claims, inaccurately, to be a translation of La Rochefoucauld—*An Historical Account of the Late Troubles During the Wars of Paris*—was published in London in 1686.) What follows is a list of only some of the best-known English translations of the *Maximes.*

Behn, Aphra. *Miscellany, Being a Collection of Poems by Several Hands, Together with Reflections on Morality, or Seneca Unmasqued.* London, 1685. This collection includes 395 of La Rochefoucauld's maxims; it is based on the fifth edition (1678).

Bolton, A. S., trans. *The Maxims and Essays of La Rochefoucauld.* London, 1884.

Davies, John. *Epictetus Junior, or Maximes of Modern Morality in Two Centuries.* London, 1670. This translation is based on the Hague edition of 1664, which contains 188 maxims. Davies translated them all, dividing two maxims so that they become four in the translation, for a total of 190. To these he added eleven of his own composition.

FitzGibbon, Constantine, trans. *The Maxims of the Duc de la Rochefoucauld.* London, 1957.

Kronenberger, Louis, trans. *The Maxims of La Rochefoucauld.* New York, 1936; 1959.

Pratt, Kenneth, trans. *Maxims of La Rochefoucauld.* Halifax, 1931. In this edition the French and Pratt's English translations are on facing pages.

Scott, Walter, trans. *The Maxims of La Rochefoucauld.* London, 1901.

Stevens, Frederick G., trans. *The Maxims of François duc de La Rochefoucauld.* London, 1939. In this edition the French and Stevens' English translations are on facing pages.

Tancock, L. W., trans. *Maxims.* Harmondsworth, 1959.

BIOGRAPHICAL, CRITICAL, AND HISTORICAL STUDIES

Ansmann, Liane. *Die "Maximen" von La Rochefoucauld.* Munich, 1972.

Bishop, Morris. *The Life and Adventures of La Rochefoucauld.* Ithaca, N.Y., 1951.

Bonney, Richard. *Political Change in France Under Richelieu and Mazarin.* New York, 1978.

Bourdeau, Jean. *La Rochefoucauld.* Paris, 1895.

Brix, Ernst. *Die Entwicklungsphasen der "Maximen" La Rochefoucaulds vom Manuskript bis zur fünften und letzten authentischen Ausgabe (1678).* Erlangen, 1913.

Bruzzi, Amelia. *La formazione delle "Maximes" di La Rochefoucauld attraverso le edizioni originali.* Bologna, 1968.

Church, William F. *Richelieu and Reason of State.* Princeton, 1972.

Culler, Jonathan. "Paradox and the Language of Morals in La Rochefoucauld." *Modern Language Review* 68 (January 1973), 28–39.

Deyon, Pierre. "Relations Between the French Nobility and the Absolute Monarchy During the First Half of the Seventeenth Century." In *State and Society in Seventeenth-Century France.* Edited by Raymond F. Kierstead. New York, 1975.

Doolin, Paul Rice. *The Fronde.* Cambridge, Mass., 1935.

Fink, Arthur H. *Maxime und Fragment Grenzmöglichkeiten einer Kunstform.* Munich, 1934.

Ford, Franklin L. *Robe and Sword: The Regrouping of the French Aristocracy After Louis XIV.* Cambridge, Mass., 1953; New York, 1965.

Grubbs, H. A. "The Originality of La Rochefoucauld's *Maxims.*" *Revue d'histoire littéraire de la France* 38: 18–59 (January–March 1929).

Hess, Gerhard. *Zur Entstehung der "Maximen" La Rochefoucaulds.* Cologne, 1957.

Hippeau, Louis. *Essai sur la morale de La Rochefoucauld.* Paris, 1967.

Krailsheimer, A. J. *Studies in Self-Interest: From Descartes to La Bruyère.* Oxford, 1962.

Kruse, Margot. *Die "Maxime" in der französischen Literatur. Studien zum Werk La Rochefoucaulds und seiner Nachfolger.* Hamburg, 1960.

Lafond, Jean. *La Rochefoucauld: Augustinisme et littérature.* Paris, 1977.

Lewis, Philip E. *La Rochefoucauld: The Art of Abstraction.* Ithaca, N.Y., 1977.

Lough, John. *An Introduction to Seventeenth-Century France.* London, 1954.

Magne, Émile. *Le vrai visage de La Rochefoucauld.* Paris, 1923.

Marchand, Jean. *Les manuscrits des "Maximes" de La Rochefoucauld, histoire, classement et description.* Paris, 1935.

Moore, W. G. "The World of La Rochefoucauld's *Maximes.*" *French Studies* 7:335–345 (October 1953).

———. *La Rochefoucauld: His Mind and Art.* Oxford, 1969.

Mora, Edith. *La Rochefoucauld: Un tableau synoptique de la vie* et des oeuvres. . . . Paris, 1965.

Pagliaro, Harold E. "Paradox in the Aphorisms of La Rochefoucauld and Some Representative English Followers." *PMLA* 79:42–50 (March 1964).

Ranum, Orest. "Richelieu and the Great Nobility: Some Aspects of Early Modern Political Motives." *French Historical Studies* 3:184–204 (Fall 1963).

Rosso, Corrado. *Virtù e critica della virtù nei moralisti francesi. La Rochefoucauld, La Bruyère, Vauvenargues.* Turin, 1964.

Schalk, Fritz. "Das Wesen des französischen Aphorismus." *Die neueren Sprachen* 41:130–140 (April 1933); 41:421–436 (November–December 1933).

Starobinski, Jean. "La Rochefoucauld et les morales substitutives." *Nouvelle revue française* 163–164; 16–34, 211–229 (July–August 1966).

Sutcliffe, F. E. "The System of La Rochefoucauld." *Bulletin of the John Rylands Library* 49:233–245 (Autumn 1966).

Tapié, Victor-L. *France in the Age of Louis XIII and Richelieu.* Translated and edited by D. McN. Lockie. London, 1974.

Thweatt, Vivien. *La Rochefoucauld and the Seventeenth Century of the Self.* Geneva, 1981.

Zeller, Sister Mary Francine. *New Aspects of Style in the "Maximes" of La Rochefoucauld.* Washington, D.C., 1954.

BIBLIOGRAPHIES

Cioarnescu, Alexandre, ed. *Bibliographie de la littérature française du dix-septième siècle.* Vol. 2. Paris, 1966.

Cabeen, David C., ed. *A Critical Bibliography of French Literature.* Vol. 3, *The Seventeenth Century,* edited by Nathan Edelman. Syracuse, N.Y., 1961.

Marchand, Jean. *Bibliographie générale raisonnée de La Rochefoucauld.* Paris, 1948.

Vedvick, J. D., ed. *French 17. An Annual Descriptive Bibliography of French Seventeenth-Century Studies.* Seventeenth-Century French Division, Modern Language Association of America. Fort Collins, Colo. 1953–   .

HAROLD E. PAGLIARO

JEAN DE LA FONTAINE
(1621–1695)

INTRODUCTION

JEAN DE LA FONTAINE, the most versatile and most widely celebrated nondramatic poet in seventeenth-century France, has often experienced the misfortune of having the artistry of his works obscured by a host of myths, half-truths, prejudices, and nonaesthetic issues. It would appear that until recent decades the typical reader of La Fontaine tended to underestimate his literary skill, perhaps praising the *Fables* for their surface qualities but finding the author's private life and relationships more interesting than the masterful poetry and prose. Images of the man perpetuated across the ages have depicted La Fontaine as a lazy dreamer, an indifferent or absent-minded husband, a neglectful or incompetent father, a member (with such famous contemporaries as Jean Racine, Molière, and Nicolas Boileau) of a classical school of literature that never existed in the manner some have imagined.

In fact, we know relatively little about La Fontaine the person. He left no memoirs, few letters; his large literary corpus is for the most part an uncertain source of autobiographical allusions. But what we will never learn about the artist can be richly compensated for by knowledge of his art, an awareness readily available to anyone sensitive to literary language who is willing to read the works carefully and without preconceptions. Though the first point should go without saying, the second is perhaps an essential cautionary remark, for, as David Lee Rubin has recently pointed out, "La Fontaine's work runs a grave risk of being taken for granted, underread, misread and finally misjudged." The traditional misunderstanding of La Fontaine's literary talents can doubtless be partly explained by the attitude of readers who imagine his verses to be essentially for children. Generations of youngsters in France have memorized some of La Fontaine's best-known poems in school, but their preadolescent experience has only rarely been replaced by adult appreciation.

Fortunately, La Fontaine's creative abilities are being examined much more closely now than before; to such an extent that the second half of the twentieth century may well be remembered, in the domain of Lafontainian literary studies, as the age of the great awakening. This rather lofty designation, while failing to do justice to a few pre-1950 pioneers in the field, is fundamentally accurate. Despite the impressive efforts of a growing number of enlightened scholars, however, many secrets of La Fontaine's art remain to be discovered.

LIFE

Jean de La Fontaine was born, probably on 8 July 1621, in the small town of Château-

Thierry, in northern France between Paris and Rheims. His father, Charles, was a game and forest warden, exercising duties that would also occupy some of Jean's time as an adult for about twenty years. The future poet's mother, Françoise Pidoux, came from a distinguished family of Poitou that had counted in its ranks royal counselors and physicians. Jean was his parents' first child; a second son, Claude, was born in 1623. (His mother, widowed from her first marriage, also had a daughter.)

Jean may have attended school for several years in his hometown, but proof is lacking. Around 1635 he probably went to Paris to further his education and may have become acquainted at that time with Antoine Furetière (1619–1688), who was to gain recognition as a novelist, satirist, and lexicographer.

In 1641 Jean entered a seminary of the Oratoire congregation, in Paris, for instruction in the priesthood. The next year, after only eighteen months of theological training, he abandoned his studies and returned to Château-Thierry. Unlike his brother, Claude, whose clerical calling was to be permanent, Jean was already establishing a lifelong pattern, seldom interrupted, of short-term undertakings in several domains.

The 1640's must have been a very important period in Jean's literary apprenticeship, but almost no evidence of the shaping of his authorial mind during this formative decade has survived that is more than anecdotal or hypothetical. Historians would welcome reliable information about his association in the mid-1640's with a circle of aspiring writers known as the *Chevaliers de la Table Ronde* (knights of the Round Table). During the same period he no doubt dabbled in law, but the extent and circumstances of this early encounter with the legal profession are largely uncertain. Though he did not follow a career in jurisprudence, his writings frequently reflect an acquaintance with legal terminology.

His marriage contract is dated 10 November 1647, but it is not known when or where the wedding took place. Jean was twenty-six and his wife, Marie Héricart, of the neighboring community of La Ferté-Milon, related to the family of the future dramatist Jean Racine, was just fourteen. By this time La Fontaine's mother had died, but how long before is unknown. Marie and Jean had only one child—a son, Charles, born in 1653. Virtually nothing can be ascertained about the quality of their marriage, and speculations would serve no purpose. It is documented that in 1658, after the death of Jean's father, they signed an agreement for the legal separation of their individual properties; but this decision was prompted by the need to lessen their financial woes and probably offers no clues to their attitudes toward each other. They lived together sporadically until about 1671, after which they separated permanently.

In 1652 Jean had acquired the title of "maître particulier triennal des eaux et forêts," a post that was purchased and involved the duties of a forest and game warden. It was combined six years later with two similar offices inherited from his father. These functions, carried out in the area of Château-Thierry and providing a modest and irregular income, gave the budding writer opportunities to observe natural phenomena intimately. The geography, botany, and zoology of La Fontaine's literary works, however, were to be largely generalized, subjectively drawn, or fanciful.

La Fontaine's first published work, *L'Eunuque* (The Eunuch), a five-act verse comedy, appeared in 1654. It is based on a play by the Roman author Terence. Although La Fontaine's artistic skills would improve immensely as he gained experience, this initial effort established a basic principle of his literary practice: like most of his contemporaries, he would seek to be original not in subject matter but in manner, in form and tone and style rather than in theme. The topics he would choose had already been explored (often countless times through the ages since antiquity), but he would find a sufficient challenge in the delicate problem of making the traditional both new and better.

L'Eunuque did not prove to be successful, but before long La Fontaine was to display more promise—while enjoying good fortune on a social level. In 1658 he presented his first important work, the poem *Adonis* (inspired by Ovid's *Metamorphoses*), to the finance minister Nicolas Fouquet, who became the author's patron, encouraging his literary efforts with monetary rewards until 1661. This date marks the disgrace of Fouquet, the year when, having misappropriated public funds for his own benefit, he was arrested, an event leading to his condemnation and imprisonment at Pignerol, where he would spend the rest of his life. Fouquet's successor, the increasingly powerful Jean Baptiste Colbert, helped to overthrow him. Some commentators on La Fontaine have contended that the *Fables* contain many strong echoes of the Fouquet-Colbert controversy. *Le songe de Vaux* (The Dream of Vaux), a work in verse and prose in celebration of Fouquet's magnificent château, Vaux-le-Vicomte, which La Fontaine was in the process of writing at the time of his protector's downfall, was never completed. It was at Vaux that, in August 1661, La Fontaine witnessed a performance of Molière's *comédie-ballet* entitled *Les fâcheux* (The Nuisances), later composing for his good friend François Maucroix these lines about the playwright whose brilliant Parisian career had begun just two years earlier:

> Cet écrivain par sa manière
> Charme à présent toute la Cour.
> De la façon que son nom court,
> Il doit être par delà Rome:
> J'en suis ravi, car c'est mon homme.
> (Oeuvres diverses, p. 525)

By his manner this writer is now charming the entire court. From the way his name is traveling it must be beyond Rome. I'm delighted about that, for he's my man.

As in so many other cases, the possible nature and extent of La Fontaine's relations with Molière are shrouded in mystery. At the very least, the strong affinity of spirit suggested in the above passage (particularly their common interest in exposing human foibles with wit and good-natured satiric strokes) is evident in many of their works.

In 1663 La Fontaine, either voluntarily or under compulsion, accompanied his wife's uncle, Jacques Jannart, on a journey to exile in Limoges, where the latter was apparently dispatched, as Philip A. Wadsworth tells us, "so that Fouquet would be deprived of his legal assistance." Never again would La Fontaine embark on a long trip. Henceforth his world would be encompassed mainly by Paris, Château-Thierry, and Rheims. But this trip, which lasted no more than a few months, produced a fascinating legacy: *Relation d'un voyage de Paris en Limousin* (Account of a Journey from Paris to Limousin, an Ancient French Province), six letters to his wife (dated 25 August to 19 September 1663; others may have been lost) in which his maturing narrative and descriptive skills are visible.

By early 1664 La Fontaine was back in Paris, for on 14 January of that year he applied for a *privilège* (license) to publish the volume of verse tales *Nouvelles en vers tirées de Boccace et de l'Arioste* (Tales in Verse Drawn from Boccaccio and Ariosto, 1665). During the next decade he would publish several volumes of *Contes et nouvelles*, though he would live to regret his association with a genre often labeled libidinous: two years before his death, at the time of his "conversion" (return to the Catholic faith of his childhood), he publicly renounced his paternity of the tales. These poems had pleased many of La Fontaine's contemporaries and found occasional admirers in the intervening centuries, but not until the publication of a milestone study by John C. Lapp, *The Esthetics of Negligence*, did anyone write an entire book on the *contes*. In the preface Lapp helps to explain why these tales have been included in the ongoing surge of Lafon-tainian criticism:

For they were unique in their time, or in any time. Nothing like them had been seen before the first slim volume appeared in 1664, and none of La Fontaine's imitators ever succeeded in approaching their enchanting combination of wit, eroticism, lyricism and charm. At first glance they seem less original than the *fables;* there is more direct imitation; there is almost no profundity; the formula appears simple: a licen-tious tale, usually by Boccaccio, is put into verse, usually decasyllabic. But one has only to read Boccaccio or the other sources to be struck by the difference.

If the appearance of his first tales heralded the presence of a significant poet, it did not make La Fontaine wealthy. His father's debts were to remain a burden for many years; in 1676 he would even sell the family home in Château-Thierry in order to settle with credi-tors. Not many options existed for people of his middle-class background and profes-sion—the literary trade; his duties as game and forest warden were part-time occupations. Like others in his position, he sought wealthy sympathizers. (The huge commercial suc-cesses realized by many authors today would have amazed him.) With Fouquet's support gone, he turned (in 1664) to Marguerite de Lorraine, the dowager duchesse d'Orléans, widow of Gaston d'Orléans (whose brother had been Louis XIII); La Fontaine joined her entourage in the Luxembourg palace as *gentil-homme servant,* a post paying little and re-quiring little work (he would retain it until the death of the duchess in 1672). Not long after this patroness died, the poet gained the protection of Marguerite Hessein, Madame de La Sablière, who lived in Paris apart from her husband. For nearly twenty years she provided La Fontaine with lodging (first in her town-house on the rue Neuve-des-Petits-Champs, then, after 1680, near her home on the rue Saint-Honoré) and in general satisfied his basic material needs, but it appears quite cer-tain that they were never lovers. On the other hand, in her salon La Fontaine gained access to a distinguished society of *littérateurs,* sci-entists, and philosophers. Furthermore, his protectresses helped secure for him the leisure needed to develop his poetic craft.

This process had already borne mature fruit in 1668 with the publication of the first six books of the *Fables.* The collection was dedi-cated to the dauphin, the six-year-old son of Louis XIV; the final book of the *Fables,* pub-lished in 1694 (book 12 in modern editions), was dedicated to the king's grandson, the twelve-year-old duc de Bourgogne. Books 7 to 11, which appeared from 1678 to 1679, were addressed to an adult, the monarch's longtime mistress, Madame de Montespan.

The 1668 collection was heavily influenced by the Aesopic tradition, although La Fontaine always enriched the material of his sources (insofar as these can be determined). Accord-ing to Wadsworth, La Fontaine "pillaged Phaedrus more completely and more system-atically than any other poet who ever brought him inspiration," but the problem of La Fon-taine's possible sources is immensely compli-cated because many of his topics had been treated by numerous authors, whose work had in turn been popularized by various transla-tors and adapters.

The poems in books 7 to 11 tend to be longer and more philosophical than those published a decade earlier. As for the poems of 1694, they are a heterogeneous mix ranging from simple Aesopic pieces to fully developed tales. Many critics have acknowledged the merits of the last fable in this collection, "Le juge arbitre, l'hospitalier, et le solitaire" (The Judge-Arbitrator, the Hospitaler, and the Re-cluse: 12.29), which is indeed an elegant val-edictory; but some critics have too readily dis-missed book 12 as representing, in the aggregate, a decline in the author's poetic powers.

La Fontaine's most prolific years as a writer, the 1660's and 1670's, were the richest dec-ades of what is often termed the classical period of French literature. These were the golden Parisian years of Molière (until his premature death in 1673). This was the era of Racine's great secular tragedies (only the religious dramas *Esther* and *Athalie* were composed later) and of the last plays of his aging rival, Pierre Corneille. This was the age of the moralist François de La Rochefoucauld and of the lawgiver of Parnassus, Nicolas Boileau, satirist and popularizer of an array of literary precepts (most of which dated from antiquity), whose *Art poétique* (1674) discussed numerous minor genres (as well as tragedy, epic, and comedy) but omitted consideration of the fable (both in generic terms and in regard to La Fontaine's emerging redefinition of the traditionally didactic apologue). Perhaps literary historians will one day uncover a satisfactory explanation for this uncharacteristic silence on the part of Boileau, who was almost always a remarkably astute judge of the authorial talents of his contemporaries. Finally (to conclude an abridged list of writers contributing to the significant literary production of this fecund twenty-year span), Madame de La Fayette's novel of psychological analysis, *La princesse de Clèves*, was published in 1678. Thus La Fontaine's most enthusiastically acclaimed writings reached the public in eminent company.

It is important, however, to resist the temptation of imagining a school or close band of authors meeting regularly to discuss their manuscripts, agreeing on acceptable rules of composition, and encouraging each other to produce a succession of masterpieces. Although certain preoccupations do persist from pen to pen in these early years of the personal reign of the Sun King, Louis XIV, the writers mentioned above are usually more interesting for their differences than for their similarities. Anyone approaching this literary epoch for the first time would be well advised to refrain from learning a list of so-called classical traits ostensibly linking Molière, La Fontaine, and Racine. Attempts to itemize the collective features of French classicism, unless elaborated

and qualified, have a tendency to obscure the fact that genius, whatever its origin, is individual, idiosyncratic. It follows that the La Fontaine emerging from this essay will be characterized mainly by his particularity.

The final fifteen years of La Fontaine's life can be summarized quite rapidly. A few of the works composed in this period will be cited in other contexts. In 1684 La Fontaine entered the Académie Française (a society of forty "immortals" that still exists); his election was briefly delayed by the king, who desired that his own candidate (and personal historiographer), Boileau, be admitted first. La Fontaine raised his voice during the celebrated quarrel on ancients and moderns (the end-of-century polemic over the relative literary merits of antiquity and contemporary France). He voted to dismiss from the Academy his former friend Furetière, whose dictionary of the French language (1690) preceded the Academy's by four years. In 1693, after the death of Madame de La Sablière, La Fontaine resided in the Paris home of a high judicial court magistrate and his wife, Monsieur and Madame d'Hervart; there, on 13 April 1695, the poet was to die, having fallen gravely ill while returning from an assembly of the Académie Française. Pious thoughts appear to have occupied much of his time in the waning years. Though fleeting signs of authorial brilliance had appeared in the twilight of his career, the days of literary glory for which he would be chiefly remembered were now far behind.

LITERARY VIEWS

In a literary life spanning four decades, perhaps longer (the report that he may have written one of his fables as early as 1647 seems apocryphal), La Fontaine's compositional habits revealed a characteristic restlessness. He tried his hand at a spectrum of genres, themes, and styles. "Diversity is my motto," he declared in a tale first published in 1674 (*Contes et nouvelles*, p. 310). As Pierre Clarac has noted in *La Fontaine par lui-même,* "Il n'y a pas de voie qu'il n'ait tentée" (There is no path he didn't try). Although theatrical modes perpetually fascinated him, he never achieved renown as a dramatist. In a century whose novelistic output was prodigious, he managed to contribute a novel of his own, *Les amours de Psyché et de Cupidon* (The Passions of Psyche and Cupid, 1669), a work mixing verse with prose and at least as interesting for the conversations of a group of four friends as for the story indicated in the title.

A related principle of Lafontainian composition is brevity. In order to maintain a sense of diversity, La Fontaine had to change pace frequently, which meant keeping his works relatively short. Though authorial statements in literary contexts do not necessarily convey deeply held personal views, La Fontaine's published works generally conform to an attitude expressed in the epilogue to the *Fables* of 1668:

> *Les longs Ouvrages me font peur.*
> *Loin d'épusier une matière,*
> *On n'en doit prendre que la fleur.*
> (*Fables choisies mises en vers,*
> p. 172)

Long works frighten me. Far from exhausting a subject, one must only take its flower.

Similarly, in the so-called *deuxième recueil* (second collection), the *Fables* of 1678–1679, La Fontaine interrupts the development of the "Discours à Monsieur le duc de La Rochefoucauld" by stating:

> *Mais les ouvrages les plus courts*
> *Sont toujours les meilleurs. En cela j'ai pour*
> * guides*
> *Tous les maîtres de l'art, et tiens qu'il faut laisser*
> *Dans les plus beaux sujets quelque chose à*
> * penser:*
> *Ainsi ce discours doit cesser.*
> (*Fables* 10.14)

But the shortest works are always the best. In that I have as guides all the masters of the art, and I maintain that in the most beautiful subjects it is necessary to leave something to think about: Thus this discourse must end.

The passing years did not alter his attitude about the importance of conciseness, for in 1689 he included the following lines in an epistle to the prince de Conti:

> *J'aime mieux garder avec soin*
> *La loi que l'on se doit prescrire*
> *D'être court, et ne pas tout dire.*
> (*Oeuvres diverses,* p. 711)

I prefer to keep with care the law that one must prescribe for oneself: to be brief and not to say everything.

Although La Fontaine had read and enjoyed the multivolume novels that were popular in France in the decades prior to 1660, his own aesthetic (whatever the genre) joined that of novelists publishing after that date, whose works tended to be considerably shorter than those of their predecessors.

To be sure, brevity in itself is only one stone in the edifice of art. Clearly it is in vain that any author worries about the length of his compositions unless he has something worthwhile to write. What La Fontaine would eventually write was uniquely his own, but he was a voracious reader who, throughout his career as an author, would draw upon a vast and eclectic literary heritage. An accomplished Latinist, and familiar, at least through translations, with much of Greek literature, he acknowledged such ancient masters as Terence, Horace, Homer, and Vergil in a 1687 epistle to Pierre-Daniel Huet, bishop of Soissons (the "Epître à Huet," in *Oeuvres diverses,* pp. 647–649). Later in the same work we find further testimony to the breadth of his inspiration:

> *Je chéris l'Arioste et j'estime le Tasse;*
> *Plein de Machiavel, entêté de Boccace,*

J'en parle si souvent qu'on en est étourdi;
J'en lis qui sont du Nord, et qui sont du Midi.

I cherish Ariosto and esteem Tasso; filled with Machiavelli, obstinate about Boccaccio, I speak of them so often that people are dazed by it; I read some who come from the north and some from the south.

Such eclecticism should, in La Fontaine's opinion, be accompanied by discernment: "Non qu'il ne faille un choix dans leurs plus beaux ouvrages" (Not that we needn't make a choice in their loveliest works). In the "Epître à Huet," a key document in the quarrel on ancients and moderns, La Fontaine, while paying homage to the giants of the past, alludes to the popularity of the early-seventeenth-century pastoral novelist Honoré d'Urfé and recognizes as well the talents of the poets François de Malherbe and Honorat de Bueil de Racan. Likewise, in a December 1687 letter to the writer Charles de Saint-Denis de Saint-Évremond, La Fontaine acknowledged (*Oeuvres diverses*, p. 674) that three of his French masters were the buoyant François Rabelais and the poets Clément Marot and Vincent Voiture. He might well have mentioned Michel de Montaigne, too, for the Renaissance essayist was a kindred spirit. As Wadsworth writes, "Both authors have a strong feeling for the diversity of men and customs, both are believers in moderation and tolerance, both have an epicurean concern for their own pleasure and comfort, both combat whatever is irrational, both teach a restrained idealism tempered by common sense." Yet Montaigne's name figures only once (and even then in an incidental context) in the writings of La Fontaine. The thorny problem of determining sources for La Fontaine's works is illustrated by his affinities with Montaigne. Wadsworth continues: "The similarity between them seems to arise less from La Fontaine's awareness of his predecessor than from a parallelism of their culture and temperament." In any event, a more critical issue for readers of La Fontaine than the author's possible models is

that of his artistic handling of the vast reservoir of raw materials (from his varied readings, from lived memories, from reminiscences divulged by his many acquaintances) coexisting in his fertile mind.

In another important passage from the "Epître à Huet" (*Oeuvres diverses*, p. 648), La Fontaine addresses the artistic problem of imitating one's models. He criticizes those who imitate Vergil slavishly (the principle would of course be valid for other literary sources as well) and stresses his own independence from those whom he credits as being his masters:

Quelques imitateurs, sot bétail, je l'avoue,
Suivent en vrais moutons le pasteur de Mantoue:
J'en use d'autre sorte; et, me laissant guider,
Souvent à marcher seul j'ose me hasarder.
On me verra toujours pratiquer cet usage;
Mon imitation n'est point un esclavage:
Je ne prends que l'idée, et les tours, et les lois,
Que nos maîtres suivaient eux-mêmes autrefois.

Some imitators, stupid livestock, I avow, follow the shepherd of Mantua like real sheep. I make use of him in another way; and, letting myself be guided, often I dare to walk alone. One will always see me practice this custom; my imitation is not at all a bondage; I take only the idea, the devices, and the laws that our masters themselves followed in times past.

The comparison of blindly emulative writers with mindless mutton underscores La Fontaine's impatience with those whose ambition is no greater than to troop along well-trod paths. He will allow his own models to guide him, but never to the point of outright domination. Without ruling out direct borrowings, if he happens upon a passage suitable for placement among his own verses, he will try to confer on the appropriated extract the stamp of his own aesthetic personality: "Je l'y transporte, et veux qu'il n'ait rien d'affecté, / Tâchant de rendre mien cet air d'antiquité" (I transport it there and want it to have nothing affected, attempting to make my own this air of antiquity).

The need to create distinguishing marks was an important consideration when La Fontaine began writing fables. As he noted in the preface to the 1668 collection, since everyone was already familiar with the subjects being treated in these poems, "je ne ferais rien si je ne les rendais nouvelles par quelques traits qui en relevassent le goût" (I would be doing nothing if I didn't make them new by some traits which enhance their flavor: *Fables choisies*, p. 7). Finely attuned to his contemporaries' taste ("C'est ce qu'on demande aujourd'hui: on veut de la nouveauté et de la gaieté"—This is what people ask for today: they want novelty and gaiety: p. 7), La Fontaine was determined to modernize the fable by casting it in a lighter, more cheerful, less dogmatic form ("Je n'appelle pas gaieté ce qui excite le rire; mais un certain charme, un air agréable qu'on peut donner à toutes sortes de sujets, même les plus sérieux"—I call gaiety not that which arouses laughter, but a certain charm, an agreeable air that one can give to all sorts of subjects, even the most serious: pp. 7–8). These observations reveal an original attitude toward a traditionally didactic genre and help to situate La Fontaine with regard to a basic tenet of French classicism: the dual aim of instructing and pleasing one's audience.

This double preoccupation had a long history, being traceable at least as far back as the Roman poet Horace, whose well-known formula *utile dulci*—"the useful with the agreeable"—neatly capsulizes the two goals for which authors were to strive. This is not the place to explore fully the implications of such a complex and ambiguous phrase: various definitions applicable to *utile* alone could easily occupy many pages. For the present purposes it will suffice to indicate that in the case of French classicism, as in many others, literary practice did not turn out to be the handmaiden of theory, for art does not usually behave that way. As Henri Peyre has remarked in *Qu'est-ce que le classicisme?* concerning the authors of La Fontaine's generation in France, "Nos classiques sont des psychologues et des ar-tistes avant tout, des moralistes parfois, mais seulement par surcroît" (Our classical writers are psychologists and artists above all, moralists at times, but only incidentally). In his own theoretical declarations as well as in his works of imagination, La Fontaine tends to confirm this generalization.

Again, in his view the supreme arbiter in this matter is the taste of the poet's contemporaries: "On ne considère en France que ce qui plaît: c'est la grande règle, et pour ainsi dire la seule" (In France one considers only that which pleases: that is the great rule, and so to speak the only one: preface to 1668 *Fables choisies*, p. 10). The next year, in his preface to the novel *Psyché*, he conveyed virtually the same idea: "Mon principal but est toujours de plaire: pour en venir là, je considère le goût du siècle" (My principal goal is always to please: to reach it, I consider the taste of the century: *Oeuvres diverses*, p. 123). This is not to say that La Fontaine totally ignored the instructional element of the fable, which throughout its long history had been central. In the poetic tribute to the dauphin preceding the 1668 collection, he straightforwardly asserts, "Je me sers d'Animaux pour instruire les Hommes" (I use Animals to instruct Men: *Fables choisies*, p. 31). Fully aware of the objective of the Aesopic fable, he avows that he too tries to attain it:

Quant au principal but qu'Esope se propose,
　J'y tombe au moins mal que je puis,
Enfin si dans ces Vers je ne plais et n'instruis,
Il ne tient pas à moi, c'est toujours quelque chose.
(*Fables choisies* 5.1)

As for the principal goal that Aesop proposes for himself, I light upon it in the least bad manner of which I am capable. Finally, if in these verses I do not please and instruct, it's not my fault; that is always something.

Mindful, however, of the sterility of the conventional apologue, La Fontaine recognizes the need to decorate any lesson:

JEAN DE LA FONTAINE

Une Morale nue apporte de l'ennui;
Le conte fait passer le précepte avec lui.
En ces sortes de feinte il faut instruire et plaire,
Et conter pour conter me semble peu d'affaire.

(*Fables choisies* 6.1)

A naked moral brings boredom; the story makes the precept pass along with it. In these types of feints it is necessary to instruct and to please, and storytelling for its own sake seems to me a small venture.

Such views are not absolute but relate to the genre being discussed. La Fontaine perceives a different set of guidelines for the tale, noting in his preface to the first volume of *Contes* that "ce n'est ni le vrai ni le vraisemblable qui font la beauté et la grâce de ces choses-ci; c'est seulement la manière de les conter" (it is neither the true nor the verisimilar that makes the beauty and grace of these things; it is only the manner of narrating them: *Contes et nouvelles*, p. 5).

Pronouncements aside, "plaire" consistently overshadows "instruire" as a key to La Fontaine's literary art. Although it would be worthwhile to show how he succeeds in pleasing his readers aesthetically in such varied works as *Adonis,* the *Contes, Psyché,* or the short dramatic piece *Clymène* (1671), it seems best to introduce nonspecialists to La Fontaine's art by concentrating on the *Fables,* which posterity has considered to be his primary claim to fame.

THE FABLES: A LITERARY KALEIDOSCOPE

The fabulist's famous description of his *Fables* as "Une ample Comédie à cent actes divers, / Et dont la scène est l'Univers" (an ample comedy in a hundred varied acts, and whose stage is the universe: 5.1) is a convenient avenue to these poetic texts. The term "Comédie" underscores the central importance of the poet's humorous vision; it likewise draws attention to his well-developed sense of drama. The reference to a hundred-act play emphasizes the multiple aspects of the author's inspiration, whereas the vastness of his laughter-oriented perspective is highlighted by the mention of the universe.

One advantage La Fontaine enjoyed by writing fables and tales was his freedom from strict rules of composition, such as those prescribed for the classical tragedy and for fixed poetic forms like the sonnet. In the *Contes* as well as in the *Fables* he was a skillful composer of *vers libres.* Lafontainian free verse is not to be confused with the much more liberated poetic forms that writers have been creating since the second half of the nineteenth century (for example, in America, Walt Whitman; in France, Arthur Rimbaud and Jules Laforgue). The *vers libres* of La Fontaine involve unpredictable patterns of rhymes and meters, but his poems do rhyme and their metrical arrangements, if often irregular, are by no means revolutionary. Two meters are predominant: the octosyllabic and the alexandrine (twelve syllables).

Let us begin by considering some of the effects obtained from his two favorite kinds of poetic lines. (It should be noted that in French poetry the mute *e* within a line is pronounced if it precedes an audible consonant or an aspirate *h.* Thus, one counts twelve syllables in the line "En toute chose il faut considérer la fin" (3.5): the mute *e* of "toute," followed by a consonant, is pronounced, but the mute *e* of *chose,* preceding a vowel, is silent).

The French alexandrine, employed with success by authors as different as Pierre de Ronsard and Racine, Molière and Alfred de Musset, Charles Baudelaire and Paul Valéry, serves La Fontaine well in the *Fables.* It is a line length well suited to a wide variety of tones and topics. In an early poem (1.16), the fabulist uses alexandrines to draw the portrait of a pitiable woodcutter:

Un pauvre Bûcheron tout couvert de ramée,
Sous le faix du fagot aussi bien que des ans

81

Gémissant et courbé marchait à pas pesants,
Et tâchait de gagner sa chaumine enfumée.

A poor woodcutter all covered with green boughs, under the weight of the faggot as well as of years, groaning and bowed, walked with heavy steps and tried to reach his smoke-darkened thatched cottage.

The twelve-syllable line can function equally well to express La Fontaine's aphoristic voice:

Il faut, autant qu'on peut, obliger tout le monde:
On a souvent besoin d'un plus petit que soi.

(2.11)

It is necessary, as much as possible, to oblige everyone: one often needs somebody smaller than oneself.

In a similar vein, La Fontaine admonishes his readers:

Il ne se faut jamais moquer des misérables:
Car qui peut s'assurer d'être toujours heureux?

(5.17)

One must never make fun of those who are unfortunate, for who can be assured of always being happy?

Notwithstanding the alexandrine's traditional (though not exclusive) role as a more or less solemn or serious meter, La Fontaine can easily adapt it to satisfy the demands of his comic muse. Note, for instance, how he describes the shattering of a milkmaid's dreams along with the jar of milk that falls from her head: "Le lait tombe; adieu veau, vache, cochon, couvée" (The milk falls; good-bye calf, cow, pig, brood: 7.9); or how he pokes fun at the ignorant "Rat de peu de cervelle" (Rat with little gray matter) who absurdly confuses molehills with mountains—

Voilà les Apennins, et voici le Caucase:
La moindre taupinée était mont à ses yeux.

(8.9)

There are the Apennines, and here is the Caucasus: the least molehill was a mountain in his eyes.

The poet likewise uses alexandrines to introduce a slow-witted turtle who foolishly insists on traveling:

Une Tortue était, à la tête légère,
Qui, lasse de son trou, voulut voir le pays,
Volontiers on fait cas d'une terre étrangère:
Volontiers gens boiteux haïssent le logis.

(10.2)

There was a light-headed tortoise who, tired of her hole, wanted to see the country. Willingly people have a high opinion of a foreign land; with pleasure lame folks despise home.

The octosyllabic line also lends itself well to humorous effects. The opening lines from "Le curé et le mort" (The Parish Priest and the Dead Man: 7.10) display parallel structures masking the basic opposition of the two title characters:

Un mort s'en allait tristement
S'emparer de son dernier gîte;
Un Curé s'en allait gaiement
Enterrer ce mort au plus vite.

A dead man went away sadly to take hold of his last resting place; a priest went away merrily to bury that dead man as quickly as possible.

The octosyllable, like the alexandrine, can be summoned to transmit a lesson (though obviously the full meaning of any moral in the *Fables* depends on its context; thus the quotation given below illustrates a use of meter but is not meant to suggest that these lines contain the poem's entire import):

Ne forçons point notre talent,
Nous ne ferions rien avec grâce:
Jamais un lourdaud, quoi qu'il fasse,
Ne saurait passer pour galant.

(4.5)

Let's not force our talent; we would do nothing gracefully. Never could a dullard, whatever he might do, pass for a fine gentleman.

Some of the most interesting metric schemes in the *Fables* involve combinations of line lengths. La Fontaine concludes one of his early poems, "La Grenouille qui se veut faire aussi grosse que le boeuf" (The Frog Who Wants to Make Herself as Big as the Ox: 1.3), by using a descending syllabic pattern to mirror the envious frog's exploding demise—"La chétive pécore / S'enfla si bien qu'elle creva" (The puny creature swelled so much that she burst)—and perhaps to suggest the deflation of vain ambitions, moving from alexandrines (the first two lines quoted below) to a decasyllable and then to an octosyllable:

> *Le monde est plein de gens qui ne sont pas plus*
>   *sages:*
> *Tout Bourgeois veut bâtir comme les grands*
>   *Seigneurs,*
>   *Tout petit Prince a des Ambassadeurs,*
>   *Tout Marquis veut avoir des Pages.*

The world is filled with people who are no wiser: every bourgeois wants to build like the great noblemen, every little prince has ambassadors, every marquis wants to have page boys.

In the climactic lines of "Le chêne et le roseau" (The Oak and the Reed: 1.22) the poet employs octosyllables and alexandrines to narrate the ironic reversal whereby the feeble reed, and not the mighty oak, survives the north wind's fury:

>   *L'Arbre tient bon; le Roseau plie.*
>   *Le vent redouble ses efforts,*
>   *Et fait si bien qu'il déracine*
> *Celui de qui la tête au Ciel était voisine,*
> *Et dont les pieds touchaient à l'Empire des Morts.*

The tree stands fast; the reed bends. The wind redoubles its efforts, and does so well that it uproots the one whose head was the sky's neighbor, and whose feet touched the empire of the dead.

La Fontaine was willing to experiment with less common meters, including *vers impairs* (poetic lines containing an uneven number of syllables). Here, in "Le pot de terre et le pot de fer" (The Earthen Pot and the Iron Pot: 5.2), we find the two incompatible vessels embarking on a heptasyllabic (seven-syllable) journey that, for the earthen pot, will have unfortunate consequences:

>   *Mes gens s'en vont à trois pieds,*
>   *Clopin-clopant comme ils peuvent,*
>   *L'un contre l'autre jetés*
>   *Au moindre hoquet qu'ils treuvent.*

My men depart on three feet, hobbling along as they can, one flung against the other at the least jolt they find.

Heptasyllables combine with alexandrines in these initial lines of "Les Grenouilles qui demandent un roi" (The Frogs Who Ask for a King: 3.4):

>   *Les Grenouilles, se lassant*
>   *De l'état Démocratique,*
>   *Par leurs clameurs firent tant*
> *Que Jupin les soumit au pouvoir Monarchique.*
> *Il leur tomba du Ciel un Roi tout pacifique.*

The frogs, growing weary of the democratic state, by their outcries accomplished so much that Jupiter subjected them to the monarchic power. From the sky there fell to them a very pacific king.

This peaceable monarch turns out to be a joist, whose placidity is merely the start of the frogs' troubles, which are related in a metric festival with octosyllables presently joining the other two meters.

These illustrations have only hinted at the depth and breadth of La Fontaine's prosodic talent. Even an overview of the versification of the *Fables* must also include some remarks about their rhyme schemes.

Until the second half of the nineteenth century, poems in French tended to rhyme in conformity with one of these patterns (which might be combined in a single work): *rimes plates,* aabb, the standard arrangement in classical theater; *rimes croisées,* abab; or *rimes embrassées,* abba. Even today, in an age of wide-ranging prosodic experimentation, these same patterns are put to use, though no doubt much less frequently than in the past. In reading the *Fables* one easily locates passages containing each of these rhyme schemes, though rarely will any one of them be used throughout an entire poem. See, for example, however, "Le satyre et le passant" (The Satyr and the Passerby), which is composed of seven heptasyllabic quatrains entirely in *rimes croisées.* Here are isolated examples of each of the three basic rhyming patterns:

> Le roi des animaux se mit un jour en tête
> De giboyer. Il célébrait sa fête.
> Le gibier du Lion, ce ne sont pas moineaux,
> Mais beaux et bons Sangliers, Daims et Cerfs
> bons et beaux.

> (2.19)

One day the king of animals made up his mind to go hunting. He was celebrating his birthday. The game of the lion is not sparrows, but rather fine and good wild boars, good and fine bucks and stags.

> Il ne faut jamais dire aux gens:
> Ecoutez un bon mot, oyez une merveille.
> Savez-vous si les écoutants
> En feront une estime à la vôtre pareille?

> (11.9)

One must never say to people: Listen to a witticism, hear a marvel. Do you know whether the listeners will hold it in esteem similar to yours?

> Aucun chemin de fleurs ne conduit à la
> gloire.
> Je n'en veux pour témoin qu'Hercule et ses
> travaux.
> Ce dieu n'a guère de rivaux:
> J'en vois peu dans la Fable, encor moins dans
> l'Histoire.

> (10.13)

No path of flowers leads to glory. In witness of that I want only Hercules and his labors. That god has scarcely any rivals: I see few of them in mythology, still fewer in history.

What makes La Fontaine's rhyming practice original is his development, from poem to poem, of a seemingly inexhaustible stock of new combinations. Such unexpected patterns as those that follow seem to have been invented not in order to promote novelty for its own sake but so as to cast each fable in an appropriate prosodic mold.

In the first ten lines of "Le petit poisson et le pêcheur" (The Little Fish and the Fisherman: 5.3), within a metric arrangement combining octosyllables and alexandrines, the poet devises the following rhyme scheme: ababccdccd. Thus the three basic types of rhyming patterns are all utilized, with rhyme *c* serving in this respect a double function:

> Petit poisson deviendra grand,
> Pourvu que Dieu lui prête vie.
> Mais le lâcher en attendant,
> Je tiens pour moi que c'est folie;
> Car de la rattraper il n'est pas trop certain.
> Un Carpeau qui n'était encore que fretin
> Fut pris par un Pêcheur au bord d'une rivière.
> Tout fait nombre, dit l'homme en voyant son
> butin;
> Voilà commencement de chère et de festin:
> Mettons-le en notre gibecière.

A little fish will become big provided that God lends him life. But it is foolish, in my opinion, to let it go while waiting, because catching it again is not a cinch. A young carp who was as yet no more than a small fry was caught by a fisherman on the bank of a river. "Everything counts," said the man upon seeing his booty; "there's the start of fare and feast; let's put him in our game pouch."

A different strategy enlisting the three standard rhyme types is found in the first twelve lines of "La querelle des chiens et des chats, et celle des chats et des souris" (The Quarrel of the Dogs and the Cats, and the One Between the Cats and the Mice: 12.8):

La Discorde a toujours régné dans l'Univers;
Notre monde en fournit mille exemples divers:
Chez nous cette Déesse a plus d'un Tributaire.
   Commençons par les Eléments:
Vous serex étonnés de voir qu'à tous moments
   Ils seront appointés contraire.
   Outre ces quatre potentats,
   Combien d'êtres de tous états
   Se font une guerre éternelle!
Autrefois un logis plein de Chiens et de Chats,
Par cent Arrêts rendus en forme solennelle,
   Vit terminer tous leurs débats.

Discord has always reigned in the universe; our world furnishes a thousand varied examples: where we live this goddess has more than one tributary. Let's begin with the elements. You will be astonished to see that every moment they will be in contention. In addition to these four potentates, how many beings of all estates wage with each other an eternal war! Once upon a time a dwelling full of dogs and cats, by a hundred decrees expressed in solemn form, saw all their debates terminated.

Here is the above pattern converted to letters: *aabccbddeded.* As a matter of fact, the *a* and *b* rhymes (Univers/divers; Tributaire/contraire) are identical aurally, but they are technically differentiated because the latter pair is a feminine rhyme (one ending in mute *e*, sometimes followed by -*s* or by -*nt*) whereas the former pair is masculine (the designation used for *all* other rhymes in French). In the last lines of this passage an interesting counterpoint is created by the tension between rhyme and line length: the *e* rhymes end verses of eight and twelve syllables whereas the *d* rhymes end verses of twelve and eight syllables. The words ending in -*ats* participate in two patterns: they are structured as *rimes plates* (potentats/états) or *croisées* (Chats/débats).

Finally (these observations are far from being exhaustive), La Fontaine occasionally makes capital of the *rime plate* by placing the echoing word in a very short line. This technique appears at the beginning of the first fable of all, "Le cigale et la fourmi" (The Cicada and the Ant: 1.1), when the poet describes the summertime performance of the singing cicada:

   La Cigale, ayant chanté
     Tout l'Eté,
   Se trouva fort dépourvue
   Quand la bise fut venue.

The cicada, having sung all summer, found herself quite destitute when the icy wind had come.

The trisyllabic "Tout l'Eté" highlights the expansiveness of the cicada's temporarily carefree manner (she sang all summer long, or, as has also been suggested, she celebrated or sang the praises of the entire summer). In his excellent book *The Style of La Fontaine's "Fables,"* Jean Dominique Biard briefly discusses four other passages similar in structure, if not in effect, to the one from "Là cigale et la fourmi" mentioned above. In the following *rime en écho* from "La grenouille et le rat" (The Frog and the Rat: 4.11), Biard contends, "the irony comes from the contrast between the serious and learned tone of the first line and the ludicrous restriction implied in the second":

Et le gouvernement de la chose publique
   Aquatique.

And the government of the public aquatic property.

In another fable, "La montagne qui accouche" (The Mountain That Gives Birth: 5.10), the poet compares the mountain that, anticlimactically, gives birth to a mouse with a pompous author whose claim about the literary splendors he will offer—"Je chanterai la guerre / Que firent les Titans au Maître du tonnerre" (I shall sing the war that the Titans waged against the Master of Thunder)—proves to be vastly overblown:

> C'est promettre beaucoup: mais qu'en sort-il souvent?
> Du vent.

That's promising a lot, but what often comes out of it? Wind.

A different kind of ironic emphasis is achieved in the following lines from "Les animaux malades de la peste" (The Animals Sick with the Plague: 7.1), in which the lion, having just admitted that in order to satisfy his "appétits gloutons" (gluttonous appetites) he has devoured many sheep, adds:

> "Même il m'est arrivé quelquefois de manger
> Le Berger."

"Sometimes I have even eaten the shepherd."

The rhyme reinforces the unexpected image of the shepherd as a source of food, but critics are not in agreement as to whether the lion's admission springs from pride or from shame.

A final example of *rime en écho* occurs in "Le trésor et les deux hommes" (The Treasure and the Two Men: 9.16), in which a man who had hidden his fortune discovers that it is missing:

> L'homme au trésor arrive, et trouve son argent
> Absent.

The man with the treasure arrives and finds his money absent.

As Biard has pointed out, the scene's anticlimactic nature is emphasized not only by the two-syllable rhyming line but also "by the combination of the incompatible terms *trouve, absent,* which expresses the disappointment of the man's expectation admirably." As these comments imply, in the *Fables* (as in any collection of poetry) prosodic elements never exist in a vacuum. Although it can be instructive to analyze La Fontaine's inventive approach to problems of meter and rhyme, it is important to remain aware that he was not a mere versifier. His adept manipulation of prosody, though interesting in its own right, functions above all as a means to various aesthetic ends. One of these is the vivid and infinitely varied portrayal of characters throughout the *Fables.*

LA FONTAINE'S MAGICAL MENAGERIE

The universe of the *Fables* is an enchanted realm where all kinds of creatures—not only people but also animals, miscellaneous deities, even plants and pots—come to life and are endowed with human habits and speech. At the outset it must be stressed that in the *Fables* (or in any literary work) every personage, however presented, is a linguistic entity having no existence at all beyond the text. This must seem self-evident, but failure to recognize a fundamental distinction between literary reality and the reality of our world (the latter being of course controlled by laws of space, time, and biology) has led some critics to insist on too strict a categorization. (Someone has calculated that 35.48 percent of all appearances by personages in the *Fables* involve animals.) To be sure, La Fontaine, a first-rate creative writer, is a mediocre zoologist (scholars for many years have shown how nonhuman creatures in the *Fables* differ from their real-life counterparts). More important, even the so-called human characters find their destiny governed by the poem they inhabit; their status cannot be altered by extraliterary analogies, so that comparisons between, for example, social structures found in the *Fables* and a historical hierarchy, such as that of seventeenth-century France, are not useful. On the other hand, the words La Fontaine employs are inevitably more than groupings of nonsense syllables. Every word enters the poem retaining its customary semantic weight, but it always gains connotative associations generated by the context in which it appears. Thus, when La Fontaine depicts the adventures of a swallow, pigeon, or parrot, without conveying information of potential interest to an ornithologist he invites his readers to incorporate into their interpretation his direct allusions to material birds; at the same time, the poet confers new attributes on his magical birds by presenting them in situations they could never confront outside literature.How does this creative process operate?

La Fontaine's animals often bear titles normally associated with people: we encounter a portly whale named "Dame Baleine" (Dame Whale), a fox and a stork titled "compère le Renard" and "commère la Cicogne" (terms of neighborliness or comradeship), one rat known as dean ("Monsieur le Doyen") and another called sire, a pig who acquires the dignity of a Portuguese nobleman ("Dom Pourceau"), and a leopard presented as a sultan. Sometimes the poet bestows on his animals a kind of counterfeit grandeur, along with personification, by associating them with classical models. For instance, a wolf refers to himself as a pupil of the Greek physician Hippocrates (5.8), thereby evoking centuries of medical tradition. Similarly, a mountain bear is compared to the Corinthian hero Bellerophon (8.10); however, instead of performing such noble deeds as slaying the Chimera, the bear accidentally murders his human friend, a lover of gardens, by smashing his head with a stone intended to drive away a bothersome fly.

From time to time the poet humanizes his characters by using common names of animals as the root of invented place names. For example, he imagines that some rats inhabit a city called "Ratopolis" (7.3), which puts his humble rodents in a context recalling the city-states of ancient Greece. Two other imaginary domains with similarly humanizing qualities are "Eléphantide" and "Rinocère" (12.21).

Some animals in the *Fables* are humanized partly by their precisely identified possessions. In the well-known poem about the urban rat and the country rat (1.9), the city dweller serves a feast to his rural companion on a Turkish carpet. In "La cour du lion" (The Lion's Court: 7.6), His Majesty the lion invites his subjects to visit his leonine "Louvre." The fabulist, after having dignified the scene by prompting us to picture an impressive building beside the Seine, punctuates the allusion with irony by exclaiming, "Quel Louvre! un vrai charnier, dont l'odeur se porta / D'abord au nez des gens" (What a Louvre! a real charnel house, whose odor immediately reached the noses of the folk [i.e., guests]). Related to this incongruous identification of a lion's den with a symbol of human architectural skill is the remark that this leonine monarch was a relative of Caligula, the bizarre Roman emperor: "Ce Monseigneur du Lion-là / Fut parent de Caligula." Worthy of Caligula (who, after the death of his sister, sentenced to death not only courtiers who failed to cry but also those who shed tears, on the ground that it was wrong to express grief for someone destined to become a goddess), the lion reveals himself to be a capriciously brutal monarch: he punishes not only a bear who plugged his nose to escape the odor but also a monkey who praised the lion for being severe and who even had something favorable to say about the bad smell of the lion's court.

Such strategies (ironic juxtapositions of basically unrelated terms) employed for comic effect are very common in the *Fables*. After a wolf accuses a fox of theft, each party argues his side of the case before a monkey-judge (2.3). The narrator pointedly merges human and animal planes when he comments in passing: "Thémis n'avait point travaillé, / De mémoire de Singe, à fait plus embrouillé" (Themis had not, for as long as a monkey could recall, toiled on such a complicated affair). While the image of the solemn upholder of laws, armed with a pair of scales, is still fresh in the reader's mind, the poet inserts an additional thrust of humor by declaring that the monkey-magistrate "suait en son lit de Justice" (was sweating on his justice bench).

When a lion has decided to go out on a hunting expedition (2.19), the idea occurs to him to have a donkey bray so as to force his intended victims to abandon their hiding places. In explaining this plan, La Fontaine notes that the lion "se servit du ministère / De l'Ane à la voix de Stentor" (made use of the services of the ass with a stentorian voice). The proper noun in this passage, like the modern English adjective *stentorian*, echoes the name of the noisy Greek herald immortalized in the *Iliad*, an inescapably humorous reference given the context. And the comic humanization of the ass is further intensified by the poet's mention of the donkey's "ministère"—his services, but also, in a more specialized sense, his ministry.

A more elaborate example of merging human and animal levels is "L'Hirondelle et les petits oiseaux" (The Swallow and the Little Birds: 1.82), in which the little birds are warned by the swallow, a well-traveled and learned creature, that before long a peasant she has seen working in a field will design traps to kill or capture them. The swallow is not believed. The small birds call her "Prophète de malheur, babillarde" (Prophetess of misfortune, chatterbox). At this point alert readers of the poem will note that the situation being described is somewhat analogous to that of another individual blessed with the gift of prophecy whose predictions were never heeded: Cassandra, daughter of Priam, king of Troy. Lest we fail to recognize the parallel, La Fontaine remarks near the end of the poem that the little birds, tired of hearing the swallow speak, "Se mirent à jaser aussi confusément/Que faisaient les Troyens quand la pauvre Cassandre/Ouvrait la bouche seulement" (Began to babble as confusedly as did the Trojans when poor Cassandra merely opened her mouth).

We would not need this direct reference in order to comprehend the parallel being suggested between the action in the fable and human reality, but the mention of Cassandra and the residents of Troy enriches the poem by permitting us to place the situation of the birds in a legendary perspective. At the same time, of course, the allusion to the ignored Trojan prophetess contributes an element of comedy to the fable, for we are surprised and amused to find these birds elevated (even incidentally) to the majesty of antiquity. Though we may react with the delight of unanticipated discovery to such parallels, we will consistently misread the *Fables* if we approach them with an anthropocentric bias, for these poems, accepted on their own terms, do not necessarily assume that human beings are superior (intellectually, physically, or ethically) to beasts.

In "L'Homme et la couleuvre" (The Man and the Snake: 10.1), when the narrator, discussing the two title characters, refers to "l'animal pervers" (the depraved animal), he quickly clarifies: "C'est le serpent que je veux dire, / Et non l'homme: on pourrait aisément s'y tromper" (It's the serpent I mean, and not the man: one could easily be mistaken about it); and, indeed, the unfolding action of the fable will amply demonstrate that in the situation described the human character has no peer for perversity. In "Le loup et les bergers" (The Wolf and the Shepherds: 10.5), the wolf, ironically portrayed as "rempli d'humanité" (filled with humanity)—if such creatures exist in the world, the speaker adds parenthetically—first resolves to become, against his nature, a vegetarian: "Et bien, ne mangeons plus de chose ayant eu vie; / Paissons l'herbe, broutons; mourons de faim plutôt" (Well, now, let's no longer eat anything that has been alive; let's graze on grass, let's browse; let's die of hunger instead). Such a fate would no doubt be preferable, in his view, to a life of being despised by everyone. Upon seeing some shepherds feasting on spit-cooked lamb, however, he realizes that it would be absurd to reform his own conduct. And the narrator, addressing a human audience, openly sides with the wolf:

Ce Loup avait raison. Est-il dit qu'on nous voie
  Faire festin de toute proie,
Manger les animaux, et nous les réduirons
Aux mets de l'âge d'or autant que nous pourrons?
  Ils n'auront ni croc ni marmite?

That wolf was right. Is it said that we are seen making a banquet of every prey, eating animals, and we will reduce them to dishes of the golden age [that is, a vegetarian diet] as much as we are able? They will have neither meat hook nor cooking pot?

In a summary recalling the famous, though deceptive, initial line of "Le loup et l'agneau" (The Wolf and the Lamb: 1.10)—"La raison du plus fort est toujours la meilleure" (The reason of the strongest is always the best)— the narrator suggests that right and wrong, far from being absolute concepts, are determined in relation to power structures:

Bergers, bergers, le loup n'a tort
Que quand il n'est pas le plus fort:
Voulez-vous qu'il vive en ermite?

Shepherds, shepherds, the wolf is wrong only when he is not the strongest. Do you want him to live as a hermit?

And in "Les compagnons d'Ulysse" (Ulysses' Companions: 12.1), each of the former humans who was metamorphosed by a powerful potion into an animal chants in turn "Je ne veux point changer d'état" (I do not want to change my condition), and makes a reasonable case for continuing to live as a lion or bear or wolf.

In the *Fables* a character's presumed species is not relevant in itself as a standard of moral or intellectual judgment. Personages conceived as humans are as likely to be targets of the fabulist's wry laughter or gentle satire as those belonging to other (and ostensibly inferior) orders. La Fontaine is essentially a comic artist whose eye is constantly alert for characters of every type (or stripe) with a ca-

pacity to entertain. Before considering some comic strategies La Fontaine utilizes when depicting human personages, let us take a close look at the situation of a spider and a swallow.

"L'Araignée et l'hirondelle" (10.6) explores several issues raised in other poems placed with it in this fascinating set of fifteen fables. The tale of the spider and the swallow opens with the spider's ten-line complaint:

O Jupiter, qui sus de ton cerveau,
Par un secret d'accouchement nouveau,
Tirer Pallas, jadis mon ennemie,
Entends ma plainte une fois en ta vie.
Progné me vient enlever lex morceaux;
Caracolant, frisant l'air et les eaux,
Elle me prend mes mouches à ma porte:
Miennes je puis les dire; et mon réseau
En serait plein sans ce maudit oiseau:
Je l'ai tissu de matière assez forte.

O Jupiter, you who were able, by means of a new childbirth secret, to pull out of your head [literally, brain] Pallas, formerly my enemy, hear my complaint for once in your life. Procne comes to steal my morsels [of food]; capering, skimming the air and the waters, she takes my flies from me at my doorway. Mine I can call them; and my web would be full of them were it not for this damned bird: I have woven it with sufficiently strong material.

On the prosodic level this passage stands out from the rest of the poem because it is composed entirely of decasyllabic meter, a relatively uncommon line length in the *Fables*. The remaining nineteen verses contain, typically, a mixture of alexandrines and octosyllables. The technique of presentation here differs from that found in any of the five poems preceding this one in book 10. Elsewhere the fabulist began with dramatic action ("Un Homme vit une Couleuvre"—A man saw a snake, fable 1), by providing background information (on the cormorant's preying habits, fable 3) or by revealing a salient personality trait (the light head of the turtle, fable 2; the preoccupation of the "Pinsemaille," or coin-pinching miser, fable 4; the notion, cited earlier, of a wolf filled with humanity, fable 5). Here, on the other hand, the ironist's chosen victim starts by speaking for herself.

At first we do not know who is addressing us. Familiar with the workings of Lafontainian wit, we correctly assume that the sublime oratorical tone of the opening apostrophe to Jupiter will soon relinquish the stage. The identity of the speaker is approached allusively: steeped in mythology, she recites the strange legendary birth of Pallas Athena (or Minerva), who is described as her former enemy because Pallas, jealous of Arachne's skill in weaving and embroidery, turned her into a spider (see *Fables*, p. 520, n. 3). Clearly the making of cobwebs can be seen as a fitting application of her talents in adversity. Even more indirectly, the text may hint at the character's identity by structural means: the winding syntax of the initial four-line sequence brings to mind the intricate network of threads spun by spiders.

This loquacious spider continues to express herself in elevated style, rejecting the second common noun of the poem's title to call her tormentor Progné (Procne), a girl from Thrace who, like her sister Philomèle (Philomela), was changed by the gods into a bird. Abruptly the speaker abandons the mock-epic mode with the explosive present participle "caracolant" (gamboling, capering): the vision of a frolicking, mischievous swallow erases the stately mythological imagery of the opening lines. This reversal is underscored three lines later when Progné is called "ce maudit oiseau" (this damned bird).

Additional identifying details are the speaker's references to her flies and to her "réseau" (web or network). As Margaret Guiton has indicated, in these lines the spider makes ample use of possessives: mes, ma, miennes, mon. The creature insists on declaring aloud what is purportedly hers. Yet ultimately she will be shown to possess nothing at all. Guiton theo-

rizes that "La Fontaine's satire is here aimed against the loser, not the winner, in what seems an extremely pertinent, though premature, criticism of the theory of property developed by Locke in his essay on civil government (1690)." The motif of a treacherous enclosure, a basic prop in book 10, is evoked here in one of its forms, but the spider has found it futile to construct her cobweb of sturdy materials; her scheming proves to be less effective than that of the cormorant in fable 3.

Having allowed the spider a hundred syllables in which to air her grievances, the narrator intrudes with a harsh judgment:

> Ainsi, d'un discours insolent,
> Se plaignait l'Araignée autrefois tapissière,
> Et qui, lors étant filandière,
> Prétendait enlacer tout insecte volant.

Thus, with an insolent discourse, complained the spider who was formerly a tapestry worker, and who, then being a spinner, claimed the right to entwine every flying insect.

The fabric of versification in this passage suggests the artistry of cobweb making. Lines of eight and twelve syllables alternate; each rhyming pair links lines of differing lengths in a *rime embrassée* pattern (the *abba* distribution mirrors the fatal entwining in which the spider customarily clasps her victims). By juxtaposing and opposing "tapissière" (tapestry worker) and "filandière" (spinner), the author both intermingles and distinguishes human and arachnid references. Before her metamorphosis, the spider (as the woman Arachne) was a tapestry worker. In her new state, instead of weaving she spins. And La Fontaine is also offering a fascinating example of what David Lee Rubin has termed "implicit comparison." This "filandière" is more than merely a spinner. The covert analogy is evident in the only other appearances of the noun "filandière," both in the plural, in the *Fables*

(5.6 and 12.5). The spinning sisters ("soeurs filandières") twice mentioned by the fabulist are the three Fates (Parcae); like them, the spider controls the destiny of any creature that ventures into her net (this analogy breaks down if one compares the spider's activities with the specific functions of the various Parcae). The movement of fable 2 in book 10 is inverted here: whereas the two ducks persuade a (land or water) reptile to fly (to her detriment), the spider aspires to root to the earth all naturally airborne insects. But the realization of such ambitious and greedy plans is effectively frustrated:

La soeur de Philomèle, attentive à sa proie,
Malgré le bestion happait mouches dans l'air,
Pour ses petits, pour elle, impitoyable joie,
Que ses enfants gloutons, d'un bec toujours
     ouvert,
D'un ton demi-formé, bégayante couvée,
Demandaient par des cris encor mal entendus.

Philomela's sister, attentive to her prey, despite the tiny beast, snatched flies in the air for her little ones, for herself—unrelenting joy [in procuring food], which her gluttonous children, with a beak always open, with a half-formed tone, stammering brood, requested by cries still poorly heard.

The inequality of the fight is underlined by the linguistic disparity between the elegant periphrasis "Philomela's sister" and the crisp deflating term "bestion" (tiny beast). The former echoes the allusion to Progné; the latter is an outsider's droll view of the spider, in sharp contrast with her self-assessment. In the earlier "La goutte et l'araignée" (The Gout and the Spider: 3.8), La Fontaine had also employed this noun in speaking of a spider: "Le pauvre Bestion tous les jours déménage" (The poor little beast moves to a new residence every day). La Fontaine's well-read contemporaries may have judged the term to be particularly comic in its deprecatory effect because Noël du Fail, in the sixteenth century, had used the phrase "bestions domestiques" to describe fleas and lice. Though the swallow dominates the action and is discussed by both the spider and the narrator in elevated language, she is nonetheless a source of comedy as well.

The scene could have become tragic under the gaze of a more sober poet (one can imagine a five-act drama entitled *The Abduction of Arachne*), but the situation in which these characters find themselves is marvelously witty in the sense proposed by Odette de Mourgues in *La Fontaine: "Fables"*—"Wit, in poetry, implies the poet's faculty of seeing and expressing the discrepancy between the images he uses or the statements he makes, and reality." In her stimulating discussion of wit in "Le rat et l'huître" (The Rat and the Oyster: 8.9), de Mourgues comments on the poem's tone: "La Fontaine endows his hero with a mock dignity through the use of poetic diction and at the same time reminds you all the time that he is a rat"; this remark likewise elucidates the fabulist's manner in "L'Araignée et l'hirondelle." Philomela's sister this bird might be, but her behavior scarcely suggests her human origin, since on a shopping trip she "snatched flies in the air" ("happait mouches dans l'air"). The verb "happer" is used elsewhere in the *Fables* to produce a similarly jocular effect: for instance, the activity of a clever dog (8.7) or that of a hawk (12.12). As is so often the case in the *Fables*, the merging of animal and human levels heightens the comic impact.

The outcome of the rivalry in "L'Araignée et l'hirondelle" is neatly suggested by two outwardly similar but in fact very different verbal constructions. When the spider says of the swallow, "Elle me prend mes mouches à ma porte" (She takes my flies from me at my doorway), her words brim with a sense of ownership and territorial imperative. But when the narrator gives his account (quoted above) of the bird's unchecked plundering, he discards the futile possessive ("mes mouches" being shortened to "mouches") and implies that the bird preempts the disputed prey even before the doomed creatures can reach the spider's threshold: she catches them "in the air" rather than "in the doorway" of the spider.

The swallow merrily gathers flies "Pour ses petits, pour elle" (For her little ones, for herself): the repeated preposition "pour" is an insistent reminder that the spider's declaration of her property rights is a mere fantasy. The description of the bird's offspring can be read as a caricature of the spider's personality. She laments the lack of a "réseau plein," or filled web (her appetite could obviously accommodate a large supply of food); their hunger is vividly detailed ("gluttonous," "with a beak always open"). However silver-tongued the spider's entreaty to Jupiter, she is as pitiful and helpless as the "stammering brood" of tiny swallows, and (given the lack of an Olympian response) her passionate appeal seems to have been no better communicated than the "cries still poorly heard" of the little birds. Ironically, despite their powerlessness they will at least be provided with something to eat.

The next five lines disclose the spider's fate:

> La pauvre Aragne n'ayant plus
> Que la tête et les pieds, artisans superflus,
>   Se vit elle-même enlevée.
> L'Hirondelle, en passant, emporta toile, et tout,
>   Et l'animal pendant au bout.

The poor spider, no longer having anything but head and feet, superfluous artisans, saw herself abducted. The swallow, passing by, carried away cobweb and everything, and the animal hanging at the end.

The poet varies his presentation by referring to the spider by the archaic "Aragne," and he reveals that deprivation has taken a heavy toll: the starving spider has withered to such an extent that she has been reduced to a pathetic stick figure with extremities but no stomach;

her head and feet are called "superfluous artisans" because, confronted with a superior adversary, they are useless to procure nourishment. The noun "artisans" is doubly metonymic: it describes parts of the spider's body but stands as well for the little artisan-beast herself (whose craft is—or until now has been—spinning) and also for her former incarnation (Arachne the talented weaver). The reflexive pronoun highlights the spider's passivity: "[elle] *se vit* elle-même enlevée" ([she] *saw herself* abducted). She was a mute and unstruggling spectator of her own abduction.

The flight of the spider and swallow bears a curious relationship with that of the ducks and turtle in fable 2. In one case there is swift coercion; in the other, hard-sell persuasion. Both victims dangle helplessly; one falls to her death, whereas the other is transported to an uncertain end. The narrator blames the turtle for her demise: "Son indiscrétion de sa perte fut cause" (Her indiscretion caused her ruin). On the other hand, though the poet has chided the spider for her "insolent discourses," he ends the fable by suggesting that she is finally not responsible for her misfortune, but that instead she has become the quarry of circumstances beyond her control:

> Jupin pour chaque état mit deux tables au monde.
> L'adroit, le vigilant, et le fort sont assis
>   A la première; et les petits
>   Mangent leur reste à la seconde.

Jupiter for each estate put two tables in the world. The dexterous, the vigilant, and the strong are seated at the first; and the weak eat their scraps at the second.

La Fontaine has changed strikingly the import of his source, the fourth Latin fable of the sixteenth-century Italian humanist Abstemius. To recount briefly the action of this story (see *Fables choisies*, p. 520, n. 1): Angry because a swallow has been stealing her flies, a spider sets a cobweb trap in an effort to snare the bird. The latter, flying past, sweeps away both the spinner and the ineffectual net. The spider, hanging in midair and realizing she is about to die, audibly recognizes why she is being punished (her ambition had been too bold). Abstemius concludes with a concise lesson: "By this fable we are warned not to undertake any enterprise above our powers."

Our fabulist has radically transformed the narrative material of his model. The spider in the French version does not even contemplate the gradiose project engineered by her predecessor. La Fontaine's thread spinner becomes the object of our amusement not through excessive ambition but because, thanks to an ironic shift of curcumstances, her words turn out to be far removed from the reality of her situation: the hunter becomes the prey. Her defeat is ultimately shown to be an instance of the unfolding of a natural law whereby creatures like her ("les petits": the weak in body and mind, in word and deed) inevitably lose out to those who are shrewd or alert or strong. The spider's opening plea is demonstrably pointless because Jupiter is detached from her plight, having placed two tables in the world so that the imperfect participants in the earthly drama may fight for survival as best they can.

One might contend that the final four lines of this poem are detrimental to the unity of tone and effect, for the image of a doomed spider dangling from the end of her web is a fitting (and nicely understated) exit for a character whose tangible claims of natural right have been reduced to a single thread—all that prevents her from sharing the turtle's bursting farewell.

The spider's foolish, ill-omened sense of possessiveness allies her with a parade of Lafontainian misers, characters whose comic potential fascinated the fabulist throughout his career. The following six poems, spanning the three principal stages of the *Fables* (the books published in 1668, 1678–1679, and 1694), reveal a wide range of poetic structures, narrative devices, and humorous techniques em-

ployed to develop the theme of avarice: "L'Avare qui a perdu son trésor" (The Miser Who Lost His Treasure: 4.20), "La poule aux oeufs d'or" (The Hen of the Golden Eggs: 5.13), "Le loup et le chasseur" (The Wolf and the Hunter: 8.27), "Le trésor et les deux hommes" (The Treasure and the Two Men: 9.16), "L'Enfouisseur et son compère" (The Burier and His Crony: 10.4), and "Du thésauriseur et du singe" (Of the Hoarder and the Monkey: 12.3).

In view of La Fontaine's ironic outlook, his flair for dramatic situations, his fondness for unexpected reversals, and his insistence on the wisdom of moderation in human conduct, it seems natural to find him eager to expose the follies of characters whose untempered cupidity prohibits them from enjoying a full and peaceful life. If pleasure depends on the expenditure of wealth and on freedom from the obsession for possessions, the rapacious hoarder must be among the least happy of mortals. Yet a close examination of the six poems mentioned above would show that not all of La Fontaine's insatiably acquisitive characters consider themselves miserable. The overgreedy may derive immense delight from contemplating and counting their wealth, but the poet as narrative persona chides such conduct as unproductive: money stripped of its economic function loses all meaning. La Fontaine imagines an array of spoilers whose similarity consists in their success in performing deeds that, perhaps unintentionally, thwart a miser. Never content to repeat himself, the fabulist is constantly inventive in undercutting his greedy or covetous characters. A concrete illustration from the last of the six poems will reveal some of the means whereby the poet can succeed in devaluing a miser's obsession.

The monkey in "Du thésauriseur et du singe," a foil whose pleasure springs partly from a spirit of malice but also from the childlike joy of playing, has no desire to spend his master's hoarded fortune. Neither the monkey nor the hoarder is interested in benefiting from the economic potential of the treasure, but the simian spoiler profits from the coins by treating them as toys and thus making impossible an accurate audit; "Jetait quelque Doublon toujours par la fenêtre, / Et rendait le compte imparfait" (He would always throw some coin—a doublon—out the window, making the calculation imperfect). This resourceful monkey invents a game that allows him to capitalize on his natural surroundings (he lives on an island): "Un beau jour dom Bertrand se mit dans la pensée / D'en faire un sacrifice au liquide manoir" (One fine day dom Bertrand had the idea to sacrifice some of it to the watery deep). The following passage demonstrates how, late in his career, La Fontaine remained a perceptive artist with an eye for fresh details and an ear for uncommon harmonies:

Un jour donc l'animal, qui ne songeait qu'à nuire,
Détachait du monceau, tantôt quelque Doublon,
 Un Jacobus, un Ducaton,
 Et puis quelque Noble à la rose;
Eprouvait son adresse et sa force à jeter
Ces morceaux de métal qui se font souhaiter
 Par les humains sur toute chose.

So one day the animal, who thought only about doing harm, detached from the pile now a doublon, a jacobus, a ducaton, and then a rose-decorated noble; he tested his skill and his strength by throwing these bits of metal that humans desire above all else.

One may be surprised to learn that the monkey's single aim was to be hurtful; what appeared to be a simple game (though with disturbing results for the miser) has turned out to be an injurious offensive. Yet the monkey's antics remain, on another level, an individual contest of skills: the flinging of coins affords him an opportunity to measure his dexterity and muscle power. Here the poet describes the money itself more precisely than in the other poems about misers cited earlier. Although he paints a vivid picture of amassed riches by specifying the kinds of coins that attracted the

monkey's attention, from the animal's perspective these dazzling signs of opulence are not currency at all; far from serving as a medium of exchange, they are simply so many "bits of metal" useful for procuring entertainment and perpetrating a little mischief. After building the suspense, La Fontaine brings the monkey's game abruptly to an end without having the animal punished or disclosing how the master reacted upon catching his vexatious pet in action:

S'il n'avait entendu son Compteur à la fin
 Mettre la clef dans la serrure,
Les Ducats auraient tous pris le même chemin,
 Et couru la même aventure;
Il les aurait fait tous voler jusqu'au dernier
Dans le gouffre enrichi par maint et maint
 naufrage.

If he hadn't finally heard his counter put the key in the lock, the ducats would all have taken the same road and would have pursued the same fortune; he would have made all of them fly, right down to the last one, into the abyss enriched by many a shipwreck.

It is significant that the "hoarder" of the title, subsequently called a "miser," is finally labeled a "counter": he is still defined by his obsession. Thus it is clear that the playfully malicious primate has had limited success as a spoiler, reducing the size of his master's fortune but neither driving him to despair nor causing him to reform. Rather than dwelling on the relationship between the two antagonists, the poet broadens the import of their adventure in the final two lines by stating, in allusion to the great pile of money now partly dispersed, "Dieu veuille préserver maint et maint Financier / Qui n'en fait pas meilleur usage" (May God preserve many a financier who doesn't put it to better use).

These lines put us in the presence of an author performing the role of lesson giver. Though the functions of lesson giver and spoiler are in some respects analogous, the lesson giver in these poems on avarice, unlike the spoiler, is always conscious of a didactic dimension. The spoiler may be heedless of the miser's nature, totally unconcerned with teaching. But the lesson giver, while his role is subordinated to other elements (apologue being consistently subordinated to art in the *Fables*) and may indeed be detached from the main action altogether, has formed judgments about avarice and insists on sharing his views with the reader. In all six poems the narrator comments in various ways on the meaning of the fable as he perceives it. Each reader is obliged to take into account this authorial function, but it would always be a mistake to reduce the import of any fable to its overt lesson. Sometimes, as in "Les compagnons d'Ulysse" (Ulysses' Companions: 12.1), the ostensible message runs counter to the thrust of the anecdote; sometimes, as in "Le loup et le chien" (The Wolf and the Dog: 1.5), the moral is unspoken, and, despite the apparent didactic intent, its absence can give rise to alternate interpretations.

Aspects of the narrative role of La Fontaine, an observer of character who comments as he reports, are apparent in two fables that deal with widows (memory misers). La Fontaine's treatment of the topic of separation through death is foreign to the deep anguish of loss experienced in real life and evokes Elder Olsen's contention that it is not the subject in itself that distinguishes tragedy from comedy: "It is not the events by themselves which are matter for gravity or levity; it is the view taken of them."

In "La jeune veuve" (The Young Widow: 6.21) the narrator opens by disclosing a law of human nature to which the incident related in the poem will conform:

> La perte d'un époux ne va point sans soupirs.
> On fait beaucoup de bruit, et puis on se console.
> Sur les ailes du Temps la tristesse s'envole;
>   Le Temps ramène les plaisirs.

The loss of a husband does not occur without sighs. One makes a lot of noise and then one gets over it. On the wings of time sadness flies away; time brings back pleasures.

He proceeds to draw with care the portrait of a young widow who, aided by her sensible father, ultimately realizes that life must continue. La Fontaine treats the same topic much more elaborately in "La matrone d'Ephèse" (The Matron of Ephesus: 12.26), which is based on a short passage from Petronius' *Satyricon*. The story has attracted authors from antiquity to the twentieth century. (The tale has resurfaced in our era as *A Phoenix Too Frequent*, an entertaining one-act free-verse play by the British dramatist Christopher Fry first produced onstage in 1946.) La Fontaine's 196-line rendition of the story (by contrast, "La jeune veuve" has only forty-eight lines) is often listed among the *Contes*, having first been published with the *Poème du Quinquina et autres ouvrages en vers* (1682) before appearing in the 1694 edition of the *Fables*.

The themes of Petronius' version are central concerns of La Fontaine's as well: feminine fickleness unmasked; the futility and predictable ephemerality of unbridled grief; unexpected resourcefulness in times of greatest need; and, above all, the magnetic pull exerted upon the living by forces of life. But La Fontaine, never a slavish imitator of his sources, uses the Latin account as a springboard for original artistic development. The matron's tale in the *Satyricon* undoubtedly appealed to the French poet's Epicurean taste, but the poem's real meaning is contained by the manner in which the fabulist exercises his alert ironic sensibility. Here as elsewhere, the joy of reading La Fontaine lies in the journey: the road may be well traveled and its destination already known, but the scenery to be encountered on the way, landscapes overlooked before or merely glimpsed in passing, will make this and succeeding trips worthwhile.

La Fontaine's version of the timeless Petronian story may be divided for reference into the following sections (the anecdote itself is framed by authorial commentary—

a ten-line introduction and a twenty-line conclusion):

1. There lives in Ephesus a woman who is morally beyond reproach (11–22)
2. Severely distressed by the death of her husband, she remains with the corpse and desires to die as well (23–58)
3. Unmoved even by the entreaties of her devoted slave girl ("esclave"), she chooses to expire from starvation (59–80)
4. Not far away a soldier is on duty watching the body of a hanged thief (81–94)
5. Having discovered the two women, the soldier speaks to them about the value of living and obtains their permission to bring his supper to the tomb (95–123)
6. The slave girl attempts to convince her mistress that it is pointless to hasten the moment of one's death, and the widow listens with interest (123–142)
7. The matron and the soldier fall in love (143–164)
8. A thief makes off with the corpse that the soldier had been appointed to guard, and the latter does not know how to deal with his predicament (165–170)
9. The slave girl offers a solution: nobody will notice if the husband's corpse is substituted for the stolen one—and her mistress agrees to this expedient, whereupon the tale proper abruptly ends (171–177)

This outline calls attention to several elements of ironic structure: the appearance of conjugal fidelity discarded in a shift of loyalties; the discrepancy between station and wisdom (in the poem's terms, the slave girl is more perspicacious than her mistress); the dialectic of enslavement (the so-called "esclave" is instrumental in freeing the matron from the bondage of excessive sorrow); the bizarre body-watching parallel (matron and spouse, soldier and thief); the reversal of roles (having been replaced by the soldier in the widow's heart, the dead husband fills in for the pilfered criminal). How does La Fontaine in his narrative pose react to this unusual situation?

At the beginning of the poem the narrator, acknowledging that the story of the matron has already been told numerous times, anticipates the objections of critics who will question the need for yet another telling. What new traits will he manage to bestow on the characters? To respond to such carpers would be an endless affair, so the poet will simply let his verses speak for themselves. At the very outset the reader, presumably familiar with the basic plot line in Petronius, is prepared for an outcome similar to that found in the Latin model. The reader's reaction to each strand of the narrative will thus be conditioned by a confident expectation that in the end life on earth will be buoyantly affirmed. The challenge will be to determine how successfully the fabulist, ignoring the false issues raised by the doubters, has recast a shopworn story in a new and worthy form.

Though he appears to be praising her, La Fontaine in his narrative stance makes fun of the matron, a bit gently, from the start. He describes her as "Une dame en sagesse et vertus sans égale" (A lady matchless in wisdom and virtues), who, having discovered how to "raffiner sur l'amour conjugale" (be punctilious in conjugal love), had become so famous for her chastity that "Chaque mère à sa bru l'alleguait pour patron;/Chaque époux la prônait à sa femme chérie" (Each mother cited her as a model to her daughter-in-law; each husband extolled her to his dear wife). The most prominent feature of this accolade is its vagueness. How the woman's exceptional qualities were summoned into action is barely adumbrated. The verb "raffiner" suggests the lack of moderation soon to be revealed as her main personality trait. Whatever may have been her other virtues, the conjugal love that brought her great renown seems to have been noteworthy chiefly for its negative side: "Il n'était bruit que d'elle et de sa chasteté" (There was a fuss only about her and her chastity). This tribute to her chastity is undercut by its hyperbolic thrust; infidelity must indeed have been the norm in the matron's society if other Ephesians talked of nothing but her lack of extramarital escapades. Fear of the horns of cuckoldry must have been rampant.

The storyteller conveys his attitude more overtly by having "femme chérie" rhyme with "prudoterie" when he says of the matron, "D'elle descendent ceux de la prudoterie, / Antique et célèbre maison" (From her descend those of "prudotery," an ancient and famous lineage). The funny term "pruderie" had been invented by Molière, first appearing in his prose comedy *George Dandin* (1668), and the words "prude" and "pruderie" were themselves neologisms in La Fontaine's time. Although Furetière indicates in his *Dictionnaire universel* (1690) that "prude" need not have negative connotations (in the first instance he defines the word in relation to wisdom and modesty), he goes on to underscore its frequent pejorative quality. The echo of "pruderie" in our poem creates a somewhat disparaging touch, to which La Fontaine, following Molière, adds a humorously paradoxical evocation of "coquetterie" and "galanterie," the former having been introduced into the French language in the mid-seventeenth century and thus lending itself to comic spinoffs. The value judgment carried by "prudoterie" seems evident: the term conveys a sense of excessive modesty, an overweening delicacy in moral matters, with a hint of dormant coquettishness lurking behind a prim, abstemious facade. Having thus created ironic distance between the matron and the reader, the poet can proceed to tell her story from a stance of amused detachment.

Between the initial lines of the poem and the conclusion, La Fontaine as self-conscious commentator will remain largely in the background, only rarely raising his authorial voice (when, for instance, he says, "Je ne le trouve pas étrange"—[I don't find it odd] in reacting to how the widow has been transformed by stages from mourner into lover). In relating the matron's tale he has for the most part allowed the events to move forward under their own ironic momentum. Now, in the final twenty lines of the poem (beginning with the second hemistich of line 177), the fabulist considers the story's import. The first part of this concluding passage sweepingly indicts women for their inconstancy:

> O volages femelles!
> La femme est toujours femme; il en est qui sont
> belles,
> Il en est qui ne le sont pas.
> S'il en était d'assez fidèles,
> Elles auraient assez d'appas.

O fickle females! Women are always women; there are some who are beautiful, some who are not. If there were some sufficiently faithful, they would have enough charms.

Though such observations could conceivably be cited in support of La Fontaine's alleged misogyny, the tone of these lines is out of harmony with that of the main action and stands out in awkward relief from the narrator's subsequent comments. La Fontaine the fabulist is most devastating and artistically effective when his attacks are subtle or playfully oblique. Here, lumbering toward his target, he seems to be striking uncharacteristically with a cannon in broad daylight. Or does he? Surely the poet does not expect that male readers will use evidence gleaned from "La matrone d'Ephèse" as a pretext for condemning women as innately fickle. Besides, this lament on fickleness is structurally anomalous because the widow's rejection of new love would have run counter to the logical thrust of the narrative.

At this point the poet suddenly shifts emphasis, addressing the prudes among his readers, whom he warns: "vous vous devez défier de vos forces. / Ne vous vantez de rien" (you must mistrust your powers. Don't boast about anything). The firmness of a person's resolve does not guarantee success, either in resistance to an offensive or in completion of an enterprise:

> Si votre intention
> Est de résister aux amorces,
> La nôtre est bonne aussi; mais l'exécution
> Nous trompe également; témoin cette Matrone.

If you prudes are intent on resisting the bait of masculine advances, we men have good intentions too; but the execution of our plans deceives us equally [neither men nor women achieve the desired results]; witness this matron [whose tale proves the point].

Though the poet continues to generalize the meaning of the tale, he now appears to be excusing the widow's behavior, suggesting that she wanted to remain faithful to her deceased spouse but that the prospect of the soldier's affection was irresistible. Though the matron had seemed a model wife, the ironist, contemplating the fuller framework he has constructed, can look at her with amusement:

> Et n'en déplaise au bon Pétrone,
> Ce n'était pas un fait tellement merveilleux
> Qu'il en dût proposer l'exemple à nos neveux.

And may it not displease the good Petronius, but it wasn't such a wonderful fact that he should propose the example of it to our nephews.

It is as if even the Roman author who created the matron had been deceived by all the acclaim showered on her.

La Fontaine goes on to refine his judgment of the Ephesian woman:

> Cette veuve n'eut tort qu'au bruit qu'on lui vit faire;
> Qu'au dessein de mourir, mal conçu, mal formé;
> Car de mettre au patibulaire,
> Le corps d'un mari tant aimé,
> Ce n'était pas peut-être une si grande affaire.
> Cela lui sauvait l'autre; et tout considéré,
> Mieux vaut goujat debout qu'Empereur enterré.

This widow was wrong only in the noise that she was seen making, only in the plan to die, badly conceived, badly formed; for putting on the gibbet the corpse of a husband so dearly loved was perhaps not such a great matter. That saved the other man for her; and everything considered, a bumpkin erect is worth more than an emperor interred.

In these seven concluding verses La Fontaine, leaving behind the issue of inconstancy, effectively summarizes the main features of the matron's situation:

1. Grief is acceptable only if expressed with restraint and for an appropriate length of time
2. Any act that denies life or detracts from it is to be judged reprehensible
3. Human actions should be carried out in accordance with the logic of circumstances, not on the basis of an abstract, universal moral code
4. Social distinctions are of limited relevance

The memorable final line, "Mieux vaut goujat debout qu'Empereur enterré" (A bumpkin erect is worth more than an emperor interred), forcefully condenses the poem's controlling life-death antithesis by assuming the viewpoint of the survivor: even a "goujat" (defined by Furetière as an individual of humble estate, though not the "lout" of modern usage) who is alive remains a better bargain than a monarch underground. This richly suggestive alexandrine deserves further examination. The two figures, one prone and the other standing, are positioned so as to trace the lines of the gibbet—the poem's main stage prop. The images of powerless ruler and strong commoner may symbolize the ironic circumstances in which the matron is swayed by her social inferiors. The figure of "goujat" can be seen to represent the dead husband as well as the fortunate soldier: the latter is alive and unpunished for neglecting orders only because the former is also erect, albeit at the end of a rope. The emperor of the matron's tearful devotion has become a mere bumpkin at the mercy of the guard's pressing needs. Thus the last line of this poem succinctly summarizes the balance achieved in the development of a venerable theme from a novel perspective.

CONCLUSION

Seventeenth-century France is not as distant, intellectually and emotionally, as might be supposed. The most gifted authors of that era, including La Fontaine, have not lost their relevance. Just as they were able to entertain and impassion their contemporaries, they remain capable, in their best works, of moving, amusing, and charming a receptive modern audience.

Although La Fontaine was a talented writer of prose as well as verse, it is primarily as a poet that he has endured. He knew his craft very well, to be sure, but mere technical competence (which is shared after all by a beautiful sonnet, a witty fable, and a greeting-card verse) could not have guaranteed the survival of his poems. Why, beyond the surface indications, is it appropriate to declare that La Fontaine wrote not simply verse but poetry? If, as the American poet Howard Nemerov has proposed, "poetry is getting something right in language," then I think we can be reasonably confident that poetry is an unmistakable Lafontainian commodity. I doubt that anyone, including Nemerov, would claim that this fragmentary definition is adequately comprehensive; yet, in reading La Fontaine at his finest, I often have the strong impression that I am experiencing poetry precisely because the author, in his inimitable way, has managed to get something right, forcefully and economically and gracefully, in language. And at his most successful, he has created poetry that reveals itself (to quote La Fontaine out of context) as "un monde toujours beau, / Toujours divers, toujours nouveau" (a world always lovely, always changing, always new: *Fables* 9.2), a richly orchestrated body of work that we have only begun to penetrate.

Selected Bibliography

FIRST EDITIONS

L'Eunuque, comédie. Paris, 1654.

Contes et nouvelles en vers. Paris, 1655.

Nouvelles en vers tirées de Boccace et de l'Arioste. Paris, 1665. Includes two tales by La Fontaine, "Le cocu battu et content" (The Cuckold Beaten and Happy) and "Joconde," and Saint-Évremond's "La matrone d'Ephèse" (The Matron of Ephesus).

Contes et nouvelles en vers. Deuxième partie. Paris, 1666.

Fables chosies mises en vers. Paris, 1668. Modern books 1–6.

Les amours de Psyché et de Cupidon. Paris, 1669. The volume also includes *Adonis.*

Contes et nouvelles en vers. Troisième partie. Paris, 1671.

Fables nouvelles et autres poésies de M. de La Fontaine. Paris, 1671. Contains eight new fables that also appear in the 1678–1679 edition, below.

Poème de la captivité de saint Malc. Paris, 1673.

Nouveaux contes de Monsieur de La Fontaine. Mons, 1674.

Fables choisies mises en vers. 4 vols. Paris, 1678–1679. Modern books 1–6, 7–11.

Poème du Quinquina et autres ouvrages en vers. Paris, 1682. Includes "La matrone de'Ephèse," "Belphégor," "Galatée," and "Daphné."

Fables choisies. Paris, 1694. Modern book 12.

MODERN EDITIONS

Fables. Edited by René Radouant. New ed. Paris, 1929.

Oeuvres diverses. Edited by Pierre Clarac. Paris, 1958. Vol. 2 of the Pléiade edition of the *Oeuvres completes* (see under Collected Editions, below). The standard, and the source of the quotations in this essay.

Contes et nouvelles en vers. Edited by Georges Couton. Paris, 1961. Classiques Garnier edition, one of the standards; one of the sources of quotations in this essay.

Fables choisies mises en vers. Edited by Georges Couton. Paris, 1962. Classiques Garnier edition, one of the standards; one of the sources of quotations in this essay.

Fables. Edited by Pierre Michel and Maurice Martin. 2 vols. Paris, 1964.

COLLECTED EDITIONS

Oeuvres complètes de J. de La Fontaine. Edited by C.-A. Walckenaer. 18 vols. Paris, 1820–1823. Republished with more extensive annotations in 1822–1823.

————. Edited by Henri Régnier. 11 vols. Paris, 1883–1893.

Oeuvres complètes. 2 vols. Paris, 1954, 1958. Pléiade edition. Vol. 1, edited by René Groos and Jacques Schiffrin, contains the *Fables* and the *Contes et nouvelles,* and is considered a standard; vol. 2, edited by Pierre Clarac, contains the *Oeuvres diverses.*

TRANSLATIONS

A Hundred Fables from La Fontaine. Translated by Philip Wayne. Garden City, N.Y., 1961.

The Fables of La Fontaine. Translated by Marianne Moore. New York, 1964.

Fables. Translated by Sir Edward Marsh. New York, 1966. Everyman's Library edition.

Selected Fables and Tales. Translated by Marie Ponsot. New York, 1966.

La Fontaine: Selected Fables. Translated by James Michie. New York, 1979.

Some Tales of La Fontaine. Translated by C. H. Sisson. Manchester, 1979.

BIOGRAPHICAL AND CRITICAL STUDIES

Baudin, Émile. *La philosophie morale des ''Fables'' de La Fontaine.* Neuchâtel, 1951.

Biard, Jean Dominique. *The Style of La Fontaine's ''Fables.''* New York, 1966.

Blavier-Paquot, Simone. *La Fontaine: Vues sur l'art du moraliste dans les ''Fables'' de 1668.* Paris, 1961.

Bornecque, Pierre. *La Fontaine fabuliste.* Paris, 1973.

Bray, René. *Les fables de La Fontaine.* Paris, 1929. Reprinted 1946.

Clarac, Pierre. *La Fontaine.* New ed. Paris, 1959.

————. *La Fontaine par lui-même.* Paris, 1961.

Collinet, Jean-Pierre. *Le monde littéraire de La Fontaine.* Paris, 1970.

Couton, Georges. *La poétique de La Fontaine.* Paris, 1957.

————. *La politique de La Fontaine.* Paris, 1959.

Gohin, Ferdinand. *L'Art de La Fontaine dans ses ''Fables.''* Paris, 1929.

————. *La Fontaine, études et recherches.* Paris, 1937.

Guiton, Margaret. *La Fontaine: Poet and Counterpoet.* New Brunswick, N.J., 1961.

Jasinski, René. *La Fontaine et le premier recueil des ''Fables.''* 2 vols. Paris, 1965–66.

Kohn, Renée. *Le goût de La Fontaine.* Paris, 1962.

Lapp, John C. *The Esthetics of Negligence: La Fontaine's ''Contes.''* Cambridge, 1971.

Michaut, Gustave. *La Fontaine.* 2 vols. Paris, 1929.

Moreau, Pierre. *Thèmes et variations dans le premier recueil des ''Fables'' de La Fontaine.* Paris, 1960.

Mourgues, Odette de. *La Fontaine: ''Fables.''* London, 1960.

————. *O muse, fuyante proie: Essai sur la poésie de La Fontaine.* Paris, 1962.

Olsen, Elder. *The Theory of Comedy.* Bloomington, Ind., 1968.

Peyre, Henri. *Qu'est-ce que le classicisme?* Revised ed. Paris, 1971.

Richard, Noël. *La Fontaine et les ''Fables'' du deuxième recueil.* Paris, 1972.

Roche, Louis. *La vie de Jean de La Fontaine.* Paris, 1913.

Rubin, David Lee. *Higher, Hidden Order: Design and Meaning in the Odes of Malherbe.* Chapel Hill, N.C., 1972.

————. ''Introduction.'' *L'Esprit créatur* 21, no. 4:7 (Winter 1981).

Tyler, J. Allen, ed. *A Concordance to the ''Fables'' and ''Tales'' of Jean de La Fontaine.* Ithaca, N.Y., 1974.

Wadsworth, Philip A. *Young La Fontaine: A Study of His Artistic Growth in His Early Poetry and First ''Fables.''* Evanston, Ill., 1952.

RICHARD DANNER

MOLIÈRE
(1622–1673)

VOLTAIRE SAID THAT Molière was a great philosopher disguised as a farceur. But perhaps his dramatic genius, like William Shakespeare's, was double in another sense: infinitely creative and markedly entrepreneurial. In *Le bourgeois gentilhomme*, Molière presents both versions of his career in a conversation between a dancing master and a music master. The dancing master speaks as a man of genius whose work has found an appropriate audience at court: "There *is* no joy like that of working for people who have a feeling for the fine points of one's art, who can appreciate the beauties of a work and repay all one's trouble by praise which is really discerning" (1.1). The music master's response hints at Molière the actor, director, and manager of the premier comic company in France under the patronage of Louis XIV: "Praise alone doesn't keep a man going. One needs something more substantial than that, and, to my mind, there's no praise to beat the sort you can put in your pocket."

Molière's brilliant and busy life is given to easy summary, partly because it breaks into such neat periods: his youth, education, and first theatrical venture in Paris; his long apprenticeship in the provinces as a strolling player and writer of farce; his successful return to Paris as an actor, dramatist, and theatrical manager. But much of what constitutes the extraordinary texture of Molière's life comes from a reserve of experience so varied that a mere biographical brief does it little justice. Perhaps only the range of material in his plays reveals Molière's keen understanding of bourgeois aspirations and idiosyncrasies, his nuanced comprehension of provincial life, his shrewd ability to enjoy the many rewards of the court of Louis XIV while escaping most of its follies. The record that follows serves only to introduce a comic dramatist whose genius is fully cultivated in the memorable body of his work.

Jean-Baptiste Poquelin was baptized on 15 January 1622. Molière is the stage name he adopted twenty-one years later, when he first began to act (and, by all accounts, he acted badly). He was the eldest son of Jean Poquelin, a bourgeois craftsman who nine years after his son's birth became the official upholsterer by royal appointment to the king, an office that Molière would himself hold by inheritance for several years before renouncing it. Molière's mother died when he was ten, at which time his father took a wife many years his junior. The Poquelin household, with its penurious domestic head and its new, young wife, undoubtedly provided Molière with material that he would later absorb into the classically comic structure of his plays.

As a youth, Jean-Baptiste spent a good many days marveling at the troupes of foreign and local players who performed on the streets, near the bridges, and at the makeshift theaters of Paris. That was part of the young man's education, but his father, aspiring bourgeois that he was, made sure his son received ample formal schooling at one of the best educational institutions in the city, the Jesuit College of Clermont, later called the Collège Louis-le-Grand. Jean-Baptiste's fellow students at Clermont included such aristocratic scions as Armand de Bourbon, prince de Conti, a cousin of the future Louis XIV and future patron of Molière's theatrical troupe in Languedoc in the 1650's. The curriculum at Clermont was rigorous, emphasizing Greek and Latin, and the young Jean-Baptiste took special delight in his readings of classical Roman comedy. Two of Molière's greatest works, *Amphitryon* and *L'Avare (The Miser)*, are direct adaptations of Plautus, the famous Roman imitator of Greek New Comedy.

After his studies at Clermont, Molière may have participated intermittently in a special course of instruction commissioned by the wealthy father of one of his young friends and given by the great materialist philosopher Pierre Gassendi. Cyrano de Bergerac may also have attended the course, but that question is still debated. Whatever the case, strains of Gassendi's materialism and neo-Epicureanism, based on balancing the claims of reason with the demands of the senses, appear prominently in several of Molière's plays, especially *Don Juan* and *Les femmes savantes (The Learned Ladies)*. And Éliante's well-known speech on the effects of love in *Le misanthrope* is taken from a section of Lucretius' *De rerum natura*, a long materialist poem that Molière had begun to translate at the time legend has him studying with Gassendi.

We know very little about what Molière was doing in the early 1640's after his years at Clermont. The Gassendi legend shares time and space with a notion that Molière was preparing for a career in law, a career it soon became clear he would not pursue. What we do know with some certainty is that his father's office of royal upholsterer, having reverted

to him several years before, provided the young man with the credentials to travel to Narbonne in 1642 as a member of the entourage of Louis XIII. On his travels he was joined by an actress, Madeleine Béjart, whom he had met earlier in Paris. His liaison with her continued through 1643, during which time Molière became acquainted with Madeleine's entire family of roving players. At twenty-one Molière officially renounced his position as *valet de chambre tapissier*, received a 630-livre inheritance due him from the time of his mother's death, and joined the Béjarts in a theatrical venture called "The Illustrious Theater." They set up in a hall called Mestayers' Tennis-Court on the left bank of the Seine, just outside the walls of Paris.

The company struggled for two years, playing tragedies and comedies to audiences so small that in 1645 the enterprise collapsed under the weight of increasing debts. Molière was arrested for bankruptcy, had bail posted to give him time to straighten out his affairs, and casually left Paris with Madeleine Béjart early in 1646. Molière's father later underwrote some of his son's debts in a gesture of generosity that was repaid by Molière many years later with the loan of considerable sums to his aging father.

Molière's life as an actor in the provinces was a twelve-year apprenticeship in several crafts: acting, writing, staging. Whatever knowledge of classical comedy he possessed from his years at Clermont was buttressed by a practical experience with the intricately paced and riotously staged Italian farces that made up so much of the repertoire of his strolling company. His earliest efforts at original playwriting, *La jalousie du barbouillé (The Jealousy of Smut-Face)* and *Le médecin volant (The Flying Physician)*, derive from the adaptations of Italian imbroglio farce, a hectic but not entirely disreputable art.

The tradition of farce extends back to its parent forms, Greek and Roman comedy; but the word itself means things "stuffed in," and comes from the secular and comic interludes that were stuffed in or inserted during the intermissions of medieval miracle and mystery plays performed in town or cathedral squares. The evolution of these interludes into fuller comic and dramatic structures marked the early Renaissance, and their refinement in the stylized Italian commedia dell'arte troupes of the later Renaissance provided Molière with a mature tradition of comic farce upon which he could draw.

Farce employs a run of stock characters (master, servants, fools, braggarts, cuckolds, mistresses, young wives) and an array of characteristic plots (deceiving schemes, mistaken identities, double crosses, domestic betrayals—the usual comic imbroglios). If there are overt elements of farce in all of Molière's early work, there are vestigial elements even in his most sophisticated later comedies. In the important revelation scene of *Tartuffe*, for example, Orgon spends a good part of an entire act under a table onstage, watching his spiritual adviser try to seduce his wife. To see any of Molière's comedies in performance is to realize the results of his apprenticeship in the timing, plotting, staging, and general excitation so central to farce and to the French comic tradition.

Molière's career took a turn for the better in 1653, when he and the Béjarts performed at the provincial court of the prince de Conti at Languedoc. The prince, Molière's younger schoolmate from Clermont, gave his patronage to the troupe until 1656, when he turned to Jansenism (a puritanical branch of Catholicism) and abandoned his interest in the theater. (This would not be Molière's last brush with Jansenism, as we shall see when we reach the controversy surrounding the production of *Tartuffe* in 1664.) During the period of the prince de Conti's patronage, Molière began to develop and expand the farces that have come down as the earliest of his work whose performance can be dated: *L'Étourdi (The Blunderer)* in 1653, and *Le dépit amoureux (The Love Tiff)* in 1656.

Molière's troupe was soon well enough known to seek the patronage in Paris of the king's brother, the duc d'Orléans. In October 1658 they performed Pierre Corneille's *Nicomèdes* and Molière's own short farce *Le docteur amoureux (The Doctor in Love)* for Louis XIV at the Louvre. The king was better pleased with Molière's comedy than with Corneille's tragedy, and he arranged for the troupe to perform under the name of his brother at the Hôtel du Petit Bourbon. Molière's players alternated there for a year with the famous Italian troupe of Scaramouche.

It was at the Petit Bourbon in 1659 that Molière's company performed his first great comedy, *Les précieuses ridicules (The Ridiculous Précieuses)*, a parodic representation of the forced and artificial language of bourgeois young women aping the practices of what they understood, or thought they understood, as the *précieuse* tradition at the great learned salons of Catherine de Vivonne de Savelli, marquise de Rambouillet, and of Madeleine de Scudéry. Although Molière insisted that his work portrayed only a bastardized version of overrefined *précieuse* behavior, the scorn heaped on the imitators of the tradition could only reflect ill on the great Parisian originals. Since the king's court was not always at one with the learned, aristocratic salons, Molière's *Les précieuses ridicules* was an enormous success for him and his company at his royally patronized theater.

In 1660 the Hôtel du Petit Bourbon was torn down, and Molière and his troupe were accorded the privilege of transferring in 1661 to the renovated theater at the Palais Royal. They remained under the patronage of the king's brother until 1665, when Louis XIV took over support of the company with monies from his own revenues. Detailed provisions were made for the actors, including profit sharing, pensions, and insurance. The king's generosity to Molière and Molière's generosity to his players are matters of documentary record.

In 1662 Molière married Armande Béjart, a coquettish twenty at the time and either the sister or daughter of his first mistress, Madeleine Béjart. The Béjart family did everything in their power to render the circumstances of Armande's birth mysterious. In the critical controversy of 1662 surrounding Molière's first five-act comedy in verse, *L'École des femmes (The School for Wives)*, in which an older man has designs on his young ward, the circumstances of whose birth are as mysterious as Armande Béjart's, Molière's enemies charged him, among other things, with incest. Armande, to make matters worse (or better for Molière's enemies), was distinctly footloose and free with her fancies.

The marriage took its immediate toll on Molière, who might have said of Armande, as Arnolphe complains in *The School for Wives*, "There's no intriguer [un diable en intrigue] like an intelligent woman" (3.3), or as Philinte notes of Célimène in *The Misanthrope*, "[Her] coquetry and love of scandal seem to accord so closely with the manners of the age" (1.1). Paul Scarron, the great burlesque poet of the period, wrote a parodic will in which he bequeathed "to Molière, cuckoldom," which suggests what Molière's contemporaries thought of his marriage—and probably what he thought too. Molière may have had good reason to believe that the infidelities of his wife (real or imagined) were, as they are in *Amphitryon*, matters of destiny over which mere mortals have little control.

In one way or another, Molière's marriage, sometimes overtly and sometimes covertly, added degrees of emotion, frustration, and, finally, hard-won humanity to the deepening tone and texture of the great plays written in the mid-1660's. In *Le bourgeois gentilhomme*, Dorimène says of marriage what might well be graven on the hearts of all who enter into it: "Many good qualities are needed, on both sides, if people are to live happily together, and even the most reasonable people in the world often find it hard to make a success of it" (3.15). The French includes a key phrase in terms of the nature of comedy, "composer une union," because union or marriage is the natural end of comic action.

In Molière's more equivocal and difficult plays *Don Juan*, *The Misanthrope*, and *Amphitryon*, the trials of marriage or sexual relations, like the trials of comedy, fall somewhere between agony and resignation. For example, it is tempting to see in Alceste and in Amphitryon versions of a jealousy that Molière himself must have suffered in no small degree. And it is equally tempting to see in Don Juan and Jupiter an equal but opposite reaction to jealousy, an indulgence of libertine desire that represents a wish on Molière's part to act in a defiant and aloof manner, a manner comparable with what he thought was his wife's treatment of him.

Miserable in his marriage, which was ruptured for four years until a reunion in 1670, and increasingly ill, Molière continued to write, produce, and act in plays at the Palais Royal and at Versailles through the 1660's and early 1670's. His troupe performed in various farcical entertainments, fêtes, pastorals, and ballets, partly at the dictates of the court, and in a series of masterful comedies, at Molière's own dictates, that achieved for him a fame and notoriety far surpassing his early reputation as a farceur.

In 1664 Molière produced a three-act version of *Tartuffe* for an entertainment at Versailles; it raised such a stir among the Jansenists and Jesuits in Paris that the king, even though he admired the play, forced it off the boards at the Palais Royal until 1669. A few months later the censors began hacking away at Molière's *Don Juan* because several of its scenes were deemed blasphemous.

Controversy followed Molière right up to the day of his death, when church officials refused him burial. He died on 17 February 1673 after a performance of *Le malade imaginaire (The Imaginary Invalid)*, in which, as a desperately ill man, he played the lead role of a hypochondriac. The irony, we can be sure, was not lost on him. Because of the earlier charges against Molière of "libertinage" and atheism, or because of his still disreputable profession as an actor, whose mortal remains might offend hallowed ground, the parish of Saint Eustache refused to allow Molière to be buried in the local cemetery. Nicolas Boileau records in his *Seventh Epistle* that Molière was finally buried in a "piece of land obtained by supplication," a statement that supports the legend that Louis XIV, upon the petition of Armande Béjart, influenced the archbishop of Paris, who had final say in the matter, to allow the burial.

A better, but less probable, version of the story has Louis XIV asking church officials to what depth the ground at Saint Joseph's cemetery in the parish of Saint Eustache was consecrated. When told four feet, Louis suggested they bury Molière at six. More likely, the archbishop simply relented and allowed burial in order to avoid a sense of public outrage that was building to riotous proportions. Molière left the world in as agitated a manner as he lived in it.

MOLIÈRE AND COMIC FORM

In *The Imaginary Invalid*, Molière's last play, Argan, the hypochondriac played by Molière as actor, complains to his brother that a certain dramatist in Paris named Molière has too little respect for the medical profession and, furthermore, should not on any account subject professional men to abuse. Argan's brother, Béralde, responds: "What could he do better than put on the stage men of all professions? Princes and kings are put on the stage every day and they aren't of less consquence than doctors" (3.3).

A comic playwright has only the professions of recognizable men and women as his available subjects. Princes and kings belong to another genre—tragedy or heroic tragedy—and Molière was first and foremost a comedian. Of his thirty or more plays only one is nominally a tragedy: a little-played, Corneille-like heroic venture called *Don Garcie de Navarre ou le prince jaloux* (*Don Garcia of Navarre; or, The Jealous Prince*, 1661). All the rest, with the exception of *Psyche*, a tragic ballet, are comic in theme and structure. Though some of his more renowned plays strain at the binding contours of comic form, even these, in one way or another, pay homage to the comic conventions that Molière's genius elaborates, alters, and surpasses.

The word "comedy" derives from a Greek compound: *kome* (village) and *doidos* (singer). Thus comedy is something of the village voice, the song of a town singer at public *komoi* or celebratory revels. The comic mode is inclusive of as much of the social order as can be represented on stage. What we recognize today as comic action derives from the outlandish civic ribaldries of Greek Old Comedy refined into the more standard social plotting of Greek New Comedy, adapted and continued by the Romans.

At the heart of the comic process is an antithetical pairing of forces that sets the town or the family temporarily at odds. The pairings in comic action are predictable enough: master–slave, parent–child, husband–wife. These pairings reflect a potential disparity between figures of authorized law and figures of presumed obedience. In the comic action the disruption of social harmony results from too severe a split between principles of order and principles of release. Of course these principles are quite literally embodied in the principals of the dramatic action, in characters who "act" by authority or rebel by instinct.

Even in a contemporary example, the antithetical comic promptings of law and nature hold to form, and reveal themselves in the names of the principals involved. A movie of the 1970's called *The Paper Chase* opposes a professor of law named Kingsfield against a young student named Hart, who is in love with Kingsfield's daughter. Authority is set against Hart's desire. The antithetical forces in comedy each possess a sort of will, a legal will on the one hand and an instinctive will on the other. In Molière's *The Imaginary Invalid*, Argan threatens to cut his daughter, Angélique, out of his will if she refuses his plans for her marriage. Her response is a typical exercise of natural will when she says of her father: "Let him do what he likes with his wealth, so long as he doesn't dispose of my heart" (1.8).

Opposing wills remain at odds in comedy until reconciled at the end of the action in a gesture of union, usually a marriage, a feast, a dance, or all three together. The final *komos*, or revel, is a reauthorization of the social order, which in the meantime has been stretched, been rendered more flexible. But the initial comic complication consists in drawing the battle lines between law and nature. In *The Learned Ladies*, Molière has the domineering mother, Philaminte, provide a full review of comic opposition in speaking of her daughter, Henriette: "I shall soon show her to whose orders the laws of reason subject her wishes, and who is to rule, her mother or her father, mind or body, form or matter" (4.1). Earlier, the neo-Epicurean Henriette had recognized the comic rift and had wished that her lover could bring his impulsive soul more in line with her mother's law: "She is the one who rules and what she has decided becomes absolute law. I wish, I must confess, you had a nature [une âme] more disposed to please her" (1.3).

The excess of authoritarian will without modification tends to produce an imbalance that expresses itself in natural resistance. And matters are even worse when the authoritarian forces in comedy exert their will not merely to control their children but also to advance their own selfish desires. In *The Imaginary Invalid*, Argan sees the advantages for a hypochondriac such as himself in having a doctor for a son-in-law, ridiculous though that doctor be. "The idea," he says, "is, brother, for me to have the sort of son-in-law I'm in need of" (3.3). Béralde counters with a more "natural" response: "But that's no concern of

your daughter's." The forces of authority are even more hypocritical when they supposedly represent the conserving powers of tradition. Argan's second wife, Béline, abuses her stepdaughter, Angélique, because "clever and well brought up daughters like you scorn to submit to their father's wishes. Things were different at one time" (2.6).

The comic dilemma is set by unrestrained authority and unchecked nature. Young lovers may know few bounds in the expression of their love, but when an authority figure like the tyrannical Harpagon in Molière's *The Miser* has his will thwarted and his money stolen, he thinks it appropriate that a magistrate order the hanging of everyone in town. In *Tartuffe* the natural urges of Mariane seem temporarily subdued by parental law ("I confess that a father's authority is such that I have never had the temptation to say anything") until Dorine points out that an excess of parental law is a travesty of nature: "A daughter must do as her father tells her even if he wants her to marry a monkey" (2.3). But it also occurs to Dorine that lovers in comic action are often irresponsible because they are overly impulsive, almost madly so: "The truth is all lovers are a bit touched [bien fous]" (2.4). Shakespeare had reached the same conclusion in the forest scenes of *A Midsummer Night's Dream*. In Molière's *The Learned Ladies*, Henriette confesses that love seems mad because there is no rhyme or reason to it: "This amorous ardor which springs up in the heart is not, as is well known, an effect of merit; caprice has a share in it, and when someone pleases us, we are often at a loss to say why he does" (5.1).

Extremes of nature can grow as sinister, on occasion, as the extremes of law. Don Juan's nature in the play bearing his name is both excessive and destructive. He is more license or licentiousness than liberality. He is nature gone awry, and his very excess of nature makes him impervious to law: "I must have freedom in love, as you know. I cannot resign myself to confining my heart within four walls. I have often told you that my natural propensity is to follow my fancy wherever it may lead. My heart belongs to all womankind'' (3.5). Of course, what he cannot get, he is prepared to take.

For the comic action to have a chance to resolve, law and nature must be drawn into the same orbit. It may take time, as Dorine says in *Tartuffe:* "If we can only gain time we may set everything right" (2.4). Until things can be set right, the split between order and instinct or law and nature can be so grave as to contain a potential for tragedy, as in Shakespeare's *Romeo and Juliet* or even Molière's *Amphitryon,* where the comic resolution is satisfactory for Jupiter but appalling for the married pair Alcmène and Amphitryon.

But the comic breach cannot be final and still sustain the ethos of comedy, which insists on the greater reconciliatory powers of social and personal bonds. For example, in *The Imaginary Invalid,* when Argan threatens to put his daughter in a convent should she continue to disobey him, the servant Toinette says: "You won't have the heart to do it" (vous n'aurez pas ce coeur-là: 1.5). Here parental law is abridged by the metaphorical constituency of parental heart. In making a place for natural bonds in society, comic law essentially makes a place for the action of the heart.

The society must go on—its younger, more natural forces cannot be stifled forever. This is one reason the *senex iratus,* or irritable old man, in comedy is so often a figure of disgust. His will murders nature or at least defiles it. There is a marvelous example of such willful sterility in *The Miser* when Harpagon confuses the loss of his money first with the loss of his life and then with the loss of his natural desire: "I'm murdered! They've cut my throat; they've taken my money! . . . Oh dear, my dear, darling money, my beloved, they've taken you away from me and now you are gone I have lost my strength" (4.7). Earlier in the play even Harpagon realizes that for figures of law to play at nature is something of a joke. He feels especially uneasy when he ponders mar-

rying the young girl with whom his son is in love: "The girl is young, as you know, and young people generally prefer those of their own age [leur semblables] and don't fancy other society" (2.5). Harpagon is wrong about many things, but he is right about this one. When Frosine presents the prospect of marrying Harpagon to the young Marianne, she sees its issue as death, a perversion of the usual idea of marriage as ensuring the preservation of life through progeny: "I agree that Harpagon isn't what you would choose if you wanted a pleasant sort of death" (3.4).

Clearly, in comedy, law as lust without heart is associated with the death of nature and, consequently, with the end of life. This is a notion put forward in a different context by Célimène in *The Misanthrope* when she complains to the hypocritical and aging prude Arsinoé that at the age of twenty, one need not abandon one's libido. It is not yet the season for prudery, which makes the desperation of things coming to an end more important than the vitality of things just beginning. Because the *senex iratus* and the prude are anti-life, they are often excluded from the celebration that ends most comedies. Such seems to be the case with Harpagon in *The Miser,* who in the midst of everyone's goodwill still worries about who will pay for the marriage festivities, protesting to the very last that it will not be he.

To admit or allow for comic unity and reintegration, it is essential that there be characters who, for reasons that become obvious in the action, are willing to cross lines, so to speak, and expand the territory of comic exchange. Thus, a younger pair of lovers often will gain older allies in their cause against the legal or parental world. Usually an aunt, an uncle, a friend of the parent, or a servant in the household will perform this role; but on occasion the lovers gain an ally by pitting one parent against the other. This occurs in Molière's *The Learned Ladies,* in *Le bourgeois gentilhomme,* and, for other reasons, in *Tartuffe* (when Orgon's wife realizes that the man her husband has selected to marry their daughter really prefers to exercise his desires upon more dangerous game: herself). In an opposite or blocking comic action, the figures of authority will often enlist those who ought to be on the side of nature to serve the cause of restrictive law. The motive here is financial or libidinous gain. For example, the young man Trissotin in *The Learned Ladies* serves the tyrannical mother's cause in blocking the love of Henriette and Clitandre only because he thinks there is a fortune in it for him.

The recruiting of divergent characters for divergent ends in comedy results in a crossover pattern in which allies and blocking figures maneuver for advantage either to serve law or to suppress nature. There is an interesting variation of this pattern in *The Miser* when Harpagon pretends to assume an ally role while in reality effecting a blocking one. He temporarily accedes to his son's wishes in order to find out more about his desires. Harpagon says: "No, I'm not so unreasonable as you think. I have no wish to make you marry a girl against your will. . . . No, no! There's no happiness in marriage without love" (4.3). Harpagon has learned to mimic the argument of comic nature in betraying its force. As a mock ally the upholder of law employs the rhetoric of liberality to block the design of nature.

Allies and blocking figures in comedy are usually recognizable comic types known, at least from the time of the Renaissance, as humor characters. The psychology of the period defined character types in accord with the manner in which blood was thought to flow through the body: phlegmatically, cholerically, sanguinely, and biliously. Argan, Molière's hypochondriac in *The Imaginary Invalid,* is so bilious, for example, that he asks his young wife to examine the extracts of his daily enema for signs of bile. She suggests that Argan's doctors nose around in these affairs, since they are paid for it and she is not. In another instance of temperament defining comic type, the uxorious husband in *The Learned La-*

dies protests that he can be only a weak ally in his daughter's cause against her mother because his humor is too sanguine for any strong exertion of will. The humor types of Renaissance comedy are refinements, based on a primitive and metaphoric psychology, of broader Greek classifications of the comic *alazon,* or strong-willed imposter, and the comic *eiron,* or self-deprecating victim. The *alazon* invariably serves the cause of law; the *eiron,* of nature. It is testimony to Molière's comic genius and economy that in a play such as *Tartuffe* he can make its leading figure both an *alazon* (in that he is an imposter) and an *eiron* (in that he is a self-flagellating hypocrite).

When allies and blocking characters, *eirons* and *alazons,* have played themselves out, the comic action generally effects its union, usually a marriage union. Marriage, of course, is the legalization of nature, the licensing of impulse. Its institution implies legal progeny, so that the conserving nature of comedy encourages the replenishment of the social order. Molière would follow this pattern regularly, often ratifying it by ending his plays with the way cleared for marriage through the drawing of the marriage contract, as occurs in *The Miser* and *Le bourgeois gentilhomme.* On the other hand, whenever Molière undermines the notion of marriage in his plays, he frustrates the notion of comic union and continuity. It is no coincidence that when he approaches what might be called a tragic action in works such as *Don Juan, The Misanthrope,* and *Amphitryon,* he comes closest to either violating the marriage bond or subverting its social significance.

The most cynical notion of dramatic violation, as opposed to comic union, occurs in *Don Juan.* Molière begins the action with a parody of comic reconciliation. Don Juan rejects his mistress and executes her father, thus breaking the bonds of both nature and law. At the end of the play, the parodic strain returns, only to turn against Don Juan. The father (now metamorphosed into stone), instead of "giving" consent, assists in the damnation of his daughter's violator. The comic revel becomes an inverted feast, or *komos*, much like a Black Mass, where the celebratory act turns into a dinner for the creatures of hell at the gaping mouth of the gate of hell.

The frustration of comic inclusion is equally telling in *Amphitryon*, in which the leading comic couple is reduced to silence at the spectacle of Jupiter's usurping lust. Jupiter argues that the victims in the play make a comic action out of tragic circumstances by recognizing that a "stock" husband and a comic lover ought to remain separate. But the victims, Amphitryon and Alcmène, are already reconciled as married lovers, and there is no reason for them to disorder their union for a complication that need not exist. Only Jupiter, by counterfeiting the lover in the body of the husband, wills disorder and disunion. For Alcmène the doubling action (Jupiter disguised as Amphitryon) is a form of generic confusion. She chooses not to see her husband and her lover as separate, because in her mind they are not. Jupiter asserts his right as a god to breach nature and law at the expense of mortals, upon whom he exercises both his pleasure and his cruelty. He reserves the right to mix dramatic genres because he has the power to "act" in whatever way he wants: "When one has the good fortune to hold high rank, whatever one does is well and good; and things change their names according to what one happens to be" (Prologue).

Some of Molière's contemporaries saw in the treatment of Jupiter a sly reference to the activities of Louis XIV, the Sun King, in which case the final words of *Amphitryon*, spoken by Sosie, the *eiron* servant played by Molière, have a protective resonance: "It is always best in these matters to say nothing" (3.10). But in these words Molière also qualifies comic structure. To understand their full import, one must recognize in Sosie's careful isolationism the counterpoint to the inclusiveness of comic participation. Molière knows how to take comic form to its limits, always expanding the boundaries of conventional restraint.

TARTUFFE

Molière first produced *Tartuffe* in a three-act version to be performed for a fête, "The Pleasures of the Enchanted Isle," at Versailles in 1664. Almost immediately the play aroused the ire of the more sensitive purveyors of moral and religious piety. The Jesuits and Jansenists, rival wings of the Catholic church in France, were each convinced that *Tartuffe* was meant to represent their hypocrisies. Of course Molière soon began employing the generic name "Tartuffes" for his pious enemies, as if the censors of his play had taken upon themselves the bearing of its despicable hero. He rewrote the play, expanded it to five acts, changed its name, changed the conception and costuming of its master hypocrite, Tartuffe, and met with no more luck in getting the work permanently remounted. The king, though he would have liked to do so, could not let it be performed at the Palais Royal under its original title, *Le tartuffe*, until 1669, when the cause célèbre finally died down.

In the preface to the 1669 version of the play, Molière comments upon what is perhaps his most memorable and controversial subject as a dramatist, hypocrisy. He claims that all those he had previously depicted in his comedies, from noblemen to doctors, admitted amusement at their portrayal, but "the hypocrites would not stand for a joke." Molière is artfully disingenuous here. He knows enough about hypocrisy to be sure that its dissimulating mechanisms are precisely those that do not allow the hypocrite to laugh at his own expense. Instead, the general unease and discomfort caused by *Tartuffe* reveal the potency of hypocrisy in society as the prime self-regarding impulse behind so many of the dealings of men and women. Hypocrisy is a form of what François de La Rochefoucauld called *amour propre*, or self-love, in his famous *Réflexions;* and it is very difficult to isolate because it is close to the soul and under the skin of virtually the entire human race.

In the preface to *Tartuffe*, Molière admits

that there were more general reasons for the initial reaction to the play, reasons having to do with the way a dramatist, in offering to cure society of its ills, succeeds only in releasing its poisons. Molière acknowledges a complaint against dramatic representation from the time of Plato's *Republic:* "I am aware that there are people who are so squeamish that they cannot bear any sort of play whatsoever: they say that the better the play [les plus honnêtes] the more harm it does." The phrase in French containing the word "honnête" (sincere) is well chosen, because the seventeenth-century "honnête homme," who appears in other of Molière's plays, represents the moral antithesis of the hypocrite. We will see, though, that the opposition is not so simple for Molière in plays such as *Don Juan* and *The Misanthrope.* It is all too easy for sincerity and hypocrisy to cross over or merge into each other. Molière's Don Juan explains to his servant Sganarelle:

> The role of a man of principle is the best of all parts to play, for the professional hypocrite enjoys remarkable advantages. Hypocrisy is an art, the practice of which always commands respect, and though people may see through it they dare say nothing against it. All other vices of mankind are exposed to censure and anyone may attack them with impunity. Hypocrisy alone is privileged. It stills the voice of criticism and enjoys a sovereign immunity. Humbug binds together in close fellowship all those who practice it, and whoever attacks one brings down the whole pack upon him. Moreover, men whom one knows to be acting in good faith, men of integrity, are always taken in by the humbugs and caught in their snares, and blindly lend their support to men who only ape their virtues. How many men have I seen contrive to repair the disorders of their youth in this way, making religion a cloak under which they continued to live as wickedly as they pleased!
>
> (5.2)

Don Juan articulates the notion central to Molière's *Tartuffe,* the inverse trust gained by an artful failure to reveal the truth. Hypocrisy is protective not only because it deceives, but also because it is designed to gain allies from among those who have things to hide. If the whole of Don Juan's speech looks back upon *Tartuffe,* its first observations look forward to Alceste of *The Misanthrope,* who plays at the public "role of a man of principle" because his private desires are stymied. Don Juan's speech implies that the hypocrite naturally assumes the most honorable of guises, but there is also the more subtle implication (and it comes through in the French: "le meilleur de tous les personnages qu'on puisse jouer") that the role of the man of principle may be one role among many others played at the same time. Even sincerity is something of a guise.

Sganarelle says in utter desperation, after hearing his master on the subject of hypocrisy: "You only needed to turn hypocrite to become the complete villain" (5.2). When Don Juan decides to feign hypocrisy, he does so because it is exactly the guise that will secure his bond to the rest of mankind:

> So, if by any chance I am discovered, the whole fraternity will make my cause their own and defend me against every criticism. By this means I shall contrive to do whatever I choose with impunity. I shall set up as a censor of the behavior of others, condemn everyone, and hold a good opinion of no one, myself alone excepted.
>
> (5.2)

Obviously, Molière, at the time of the writing of *Don Juan,* was still smarting from his enemies' reaction to *Tartuffe.* Don Juan, for his own bizarre reasons and for Molière's vengeful ones, reduces himself to everything horrific in Tartuffe and in *Tartuffe's* censors, and everything self-righteous in the future Alceste. But whereas Don Juan feigns hypocrisy as a genius of inimical arts, and whereas Alceste is a hypocrite in spite of himself, tortured by emotions he can barely define, Tartuffe is still the grandest hypocrite of all, absolutely beyond moral reclaim.

It is one thing, then, to suggest that Molière

is simply against hypocrisy, and quite another to look at his representation of the complicated status of hypocrisy in the social order. Hypocrisy implicates its victims in the schemes of its promulgators because under its spell all lose the vital ability to distinguish between authenticity and disguise. In this sense Tartuffe's hypocrisy becomes him both in that it fits him in gesture, speech, and bearing, and in that it substitutes for any genuine being he might have once possessed. Hypocrisy is everything for Tartuffe because he is nothing without it. Like Shakespeare's Iago, Tartuffe is clever enough to know what he does, but the avidity with which he practices his art has rendered him powerless to sift through its consequences.

Molière realizes the extensive and entrapping powers of hypocrisy, and therefore prepares for the introduction of his archetypal hypocrite, Tartuffe, well in advance of his actual appearance on stage. What is more, Tartuffe himself, because his piety allows him to feign self-deprecation, speaks truth most of the time in the play, almost as if what he represents is so odious that Molière cannot bear to hear him lie about it. Generally, Tartuffe's hypocrisy does not derive from what he says, but from what he has carefully led several key figures in the household to believe he feels. Orgon and Orgon's mother, for example, seem undisturbed by Tartuffe's admitted frailties because he conveys the false impression that he remains as genuinely worried about his sins as they *ought* to be.

If some members of Orgon's family are gulled by Tartuffe, others are not. The very first scene in the play counters Madame Pernelle's observation that Tartuffe is a good man with Damis' remark that he is a hypocritical bigot, a usurper of domestic authority. Dorine follows with a brief history of Tartuffe's impoverished arrival on the premises and his gradual displacement of Orgon as master of the household. It was customary at the time, in the provinces more than in Paris, for wealthy bourgeois families to equip themselves with a lay religious figure known as a director of conscience. This is what Tartuffe seems to be, although the Jansenists in Paris saw his tactics as a domestic allegory for their own political maneuvering.

When Tartuffe finally enters in act 3, he provides the audience with testimony on the corrupt nature of his character. He is doubly outrageous because part of his act is to acknowledge the open violation of one of the oldest social bonds in human history, the guest-host relation. Tartuffe has designs not only on Orgon's estate, but also on his wife. His hypocrisy cuts across the comic bonds of law and nature. Dorine, the servant who is the *eiron* counter to Tartuffe's *alazon*, sees from the beginning that the violation is both economic and sexual: "I wouldn't trust myself with him without good security [un bon garant]" (1.1). Dorine's intuition and her metaphor set the strategy of the play. In violating the guest-host bond, Tartuffe attacks the comic family at its core. Dorine says of Orgon's relation to Tartuffe: "He addresses him as brother and holds him a hundred times dearer than wife or mother, daughter or son" (1.2). What is more, Orgon behaves thus under the guise of a piety thematically undermined by the more reasonable and modest practice recommended by his brother-in-law, Cléante, whose intent is to see things clearly and to separate truth from falsity. For these efforts Orgon calls his brother-in-law an atheist (precisely the charge that both the Jesuits and the Jansenists raised against the Cartesian rationalists of the period).

At our first introduction to Orgon, putative head of the household, he feels false sympathy at the litany of Tartuffe's vitality as opposed to his wife's physical indisposition. Health and illness are thus confused—which, of course, is the state of affairs in the house. Orgon's wife is, among other things, sick of her husband's relationship with Tartuffe. A good deal of the action in the rest of the play is designed to make Orgon see what is ill and well with him—that is, to make a man who refuses to see in an intellectual and metaphysical sense see in a literal one. Hence Orgon is later deposited under a table to watch hypocrisy in action.

When Tartuffe first enters, he is all gesture and device. From his behavior onstage we can imagine his previous tactics. He has made himself believable by directing abuse against the part of his nature that seems to defy his piety. His performance suggests concern; his behavior reveals rampant lust. In his initial remarks he tells his servant, Laurent, to put away his hair shirt and scourge, an order that conveys the impression that he has just been doing penance offstage for the same sins he is about to display onstage. His libido is always active. Tartuffe next tells Dorine to cover her bosom, because such sights give rise to sinful thoughts. As an expert in covering up, he speaks the truth. Dorine tells him that flesh seems to make quite an impression on him ("vos sens fait grande impression": 3.2), a deeper impression, no doubt, than the lashes of his scourge.

A bit later, when Tartuffe first exchanges words with Elmire, Orgon's wife, he claims he is not less manly for being devout (3.3). What he means, of course, is that he is hypocritically devout and libidinously manly. Or, to put it another way, he is devoted to his lust. And he makes scant effort to disguise that fact. Elmire and her son, Damis, witness Tartuffe's first sexual advances, and transmit the information to Orgon. Tartuffe's response is extraordinary. He calls himself a guilty wretch steeped in iniquity, a villain, and then says outright: "Everyone takes me for a good man, but the truth is I am good for nothing" (3.6). He knows that he has trained Orgon to pay no attention to the literal protestations of his frailties. Tartuffe addresses his gull thus: "Ah, if only you knew how much it grieves me to see them try to blacken me in my brother's esteem" (3.7). It does indeed grieve him to have others blacken his name, but he has just admitted that it deserves blackening. To Orgon the grief is more relevant than the guilt.

Only in the first scene of the next act does Tartuffe make one of the few palpably untrue statements in the play. He says to the clear-thinking Cléante: "People who know me will not suspect me of self-interest. Worldly wealth makes little appeal to me" (4.1). In the presence of Cléante, Tartuffe is reduced to the indignity of having to lie outright. But even here his language betrays him into a kind of truth, the truth of double entendre. He says to Cléante that he must leave: "It is now half past three, sir. Certain pious obligations [devoir] require my presence upstairs without delay" (4.1). Given Tartuffe's sexual obsession, his statement is neither completely false nor completely innocent. Tartuffe knows just how far he can go when dealing with Orgon's household. In the early encounter with Elmire, he argues that a hypocrite is a perfect lover because he cannot reveal his conquests and sustain his hypocrisy. This is an insider's version of what Don Juan later says about hypocrisy from the outside. For Tartuffe and Don Juan, the manifestation of piety covers the indulgences of sex.

In the second encounter between Tartuffe and Elmire, Elmire begins by telling Tartuffe that she has a secret to tell him. The balance of hypocrisy shifts only when Elmire appeals to Tartuffe's nature, a nature that thrives on hiding things or keeping secrets. The only appropriate antidote to hypocrisy is to ape its tactics, to go into hiding in order to seek things out. Thus characters in the play are placed behind curtains or partitions or under tables. And items are hidden in boxes or secreted out of the house. Elmire has to prepare a suspicious Tartuffe in a way similar to Molière's preparation of the audience for a hypocritical Tartuffe. When she offers herself to him, Tartuffe quite rightly doubts that he deserves her. He demands proof: "I believe nothing until you give me proofs tangible enough to satisfy my passion" (4.5).

The irony is supreme because the proof of his passion is also the proof of his hypocrisy, which have been the same all along. It is now

Tartuffe who is victimized (if only temporarily). When asked how his so often invoked "heaven" will look upon his intended performance, Tartuffe reveals that he has secret ways of appeasing religion. But there are more things under the table, so to speak, than even he knows. Orgon has been observing, insofar as he is capable, all that has been transpiring. The comic action at this point has put Tartuffe in as much jeopardy as those allied against him have power. What Elmire does not know is that while she works to trap Tartuffe, Tartuffe has already been working to trap Orgon. He has the deed of gift for Orgon's house as well as compromising papers of one of Orgon's friends. Again, the hypocrite violates everyone's bonds of trust. Tartuffe can afford to extend himself in his sexual usurpation because he has already effected his economic one.

The second denouement, and Tartuffe's downfall, comes only after the hypocrite tries to carry his case to the king, a mistake because, as vice-regent of divine authority on earth, the king has the power to see right through him. This may be part and parcel of Molière's habit of flattering Louis XIV—as in Dorine's outraged remark that Tartuffe would dare cloak "his villainies with the mantle of all that we most revere" (5.7)—but the greater implication is that hypocrisy is so difficult to control that it requires recourse to the highest law of the realm to stop it. A mere comic society, whatever it may know, cannot regroup fast enough or decisively enough to overwhelm what Tartuffe represents. For every character named Tartuffe there are, as Molière knew and any French dictionary shows, thousands of tartuffes.

DON JUAN

At the time of his 1669 petition to the king on behalf of his *Tartuffe*, Molière reflects on remarks made about him by the papal legate:

> I myself am no less diabolical: I am a fiend in human shape, an atheist [libertin], a blas-

phemer, deserving of exemplary punishment. It is not enough that the flames should expiate my offense publicly; that would be letting me off too cheaply: the charitable zeal of this worthy, godfearing man is not content to stop there: he would deny me God's mercy itself and demands in the most absolute terms that I should be damned to all eternity.

It seems as if Molière, under siege for years because of *Tartuffe*, had by 1669 identified himself with the hero of the play he wrote just after the original *Tartuffe* controversy, *Don Juan*. Critics usually argue that Alceste of *The Misanthrope* is the one character in his plays with whom Molière most closely identifies, partly because the frustration Alceste experiences at the hands of his younger, coquettish mistress is a frustration that Molière undoubtedly experienced at the hands of his younger, coquettish wife. But it is intriguing to see in the mythic hero of *Don Juan* a more complex projection of Molière's defiance of the world and his frustration with love. Alceste suffers the pangs of jealous outrage because Célimène's love is, for the most part, undifferentiating. Don Juan is the hero under social siege who transcends even the debilitations of jealousy by reclaiming universal desire as a desperate cure for restrictive love: "I cannot refuse love to what I find lovable, and so, when a beautiful face is asking for love, if I had ten thousand hearts I would freely bestow every one of them" (1.2). The premise, of course, is that the rake or libertine hero counters the possibility of jealousy by limiting the range of its agonies: "The whole pleasure lies in the fact that love isn't lasting" (1.2), says Don Juan. But liberality is also a form of revenge.

The central question of the play is to what extent Molière condemns the proclivities of Don Juan. And to what degree does this drama, with its almost farcical subplots, represent a kind of fearlessness that takes on a greater tragic stature than any other action represented in Molière's plays? For Molière it is possible to question a man's actions yet admire the integrity of his bearing. Though Don Juan is capable of all sorts of aberrations, he is incapable of betraying that which he holds central to his nature. One of the key scenes of the play, quickly suppressed after the first performance, has Don Juan engaging a beggar and trying to tempt him, with a gold piece, to blaspheme against God. The poor man says he would rather starve, and Don Juan gives him the gold piece anyway, for humanity's sake. What Don Juan really tests here is not his own urge to force blasphemy, but the beggar's willingness to adhere to principles *he* identifies as crucial. At the conclusion of this scene, Don Juan turns and witnesses one man attacked by three others. Without recourse to details, he says, "That isn't fair odds [la partie est trop inégale]. I can't allow that!" (3.2). Sganarelle claims that his master is mad for rushing into danger, but he isn't simply going after danger—he is outraged at the odds and determined to make them less one-sided. His fearlessness in the face of cause for fear conforms to the notion of tragic engagement defined so pointedly by Friedrich Nietzsche two centuries later as the "temerity of penetration, the hankering for the enemy, the worthwhile enemy, so as to prove what it means to fear something." Don Juan's bearing and integrity, no matter what faces him, mean as much to his character as piety does to the beggar.

If *Don Juan* comes close to defining tragic dimension for Molière, the play also turns on matters that were of considerable intellectual importance to him. Don Juan's servant, Sganarelle, begins the play with a paean to the pleasures of tobacco. This seemingly insignificant bit of stage business brings to the fore one of the key issues in seventeenth-century philosophy: whether the senses or reason holds primary sway in human motivation and behavior. Sganarelle's position is neo-Epicurean (after the Greek materialist philosopher Epicurus); he holds that even what we think of as rational operations are determined by sensate experience. It is not so much that a premium is placed on sensual indulgence in the materialist philosophy—though that is an element of Epicureanism in its extreme phases—but that there are material phenomena outside the consciousness of man that enter consciousness only through the senses. Even pure cognition, for materialists, is sensibly formed. One can see, and Molière obviously saw, the relevance of the materialist philosophy for the Don Juan myth, in which the usual moral and religious implications of the legend can be expanded to include the materialist argument against the dictates of all that seems reasonable.

Molière's friend the satirist Nicolas Boileau writes of these matters in his *Eighth Satire*, a work imitated and adapted by the famous English libertine John Wilmot, earl of Rochester. In his *Satyr Against Reason and Mankind*, Rochester mocks the fool who would count on reason over and above what he calls the "certain instinct" of libertinism:

> The senses are too gross; and he'll contrive
> A sixth, to contradict the other five:
> And before certain instinct, will prefer
> Reason, which fifty times for one does err—
> Reason, an *ignis fatuus* in the mind,
> Which leaves the light of nature, sense, behind.
> Pathless, and dangerous, wand'ring ways it
>   takes,
> Through error's fenny bogs and thorny brakes.
>
> (8–15)

The libertine position is a skeptical critique of pure reason; and Molière, though less extreme than many, shared skeptical views with some of the great philosophic and moral voices of the times, not necessarily all libertines, but all materialists: Gassendi, Charles de Saint Évremond, La Rochefoucauld. Molière questions the basis upon which the powers of the mind were said to exert complete control over the individual and communal senses of experience. He does so directly in *Don Juan*, and again in his later comedy *The Learned Ladies*. Armande, an overly reasonable young savant in the comedy, demands of her former suitor, Clitandre: "Could you not keep your thoughts of me clear and disentangled from the commerce of the senses?" (4.2). Armande is a Cartesian rationalist: "It is to the mind alone that all transports are directed, and one never notices that one has a body." The skeptical, Epicurean Clitandre responds: "Madame, I perceive, with your leave, that I have a body as well as a soul. I feel that it sticks too closely to the latter to leave it aside; I do not know the art of these separations."

The essence of the materialist-rationalist debate touches explicitly on the conflict in comic form between the dictates of law (reason) and nature (the senses). As Henriette says to her sister, Armande, in *The Learned Ladies:* "Thus differing in our goals, we shall both imitate our mother; you as regards the soul and noble aspirations; I, as regards the senses and the grosser pleasures; you, in the works of the enlightened mind; I, sister, in those that pertain to material things" (1.1). Intellectually, Molière would wish to effect a compromise between reason and the senses in the same way comic form effects a compromise between law and nature. To do so, he introduces the middle term between reason and the senses, the more moderate and moderating "common sense." Common sense is that collective sense to which even materialists pay "rational" homage. Rochester writes in his *Satyr Against Reason and Mankind:*

Thus, whilst against false reasoning I inveigh,
I own right reason, which I would obey:
That reason which distinguishes by sense
And gives us rules of good and ill from thence,
That bounds desires with a reforming will
To keep 'em more in vigor, not to kill.
Your reason hinders, mine helps to enjoy,
Renewing appetites yours would destroy.
(98–105)

In Molière's *The Learned Ladies,* common sense is found at the court of Louis XIV over and against the pure reason of the learned sa-lons of Paris. This is part flattery, no doubt, but the object of Molière's praise does not change the substance of its notion. Clitandre says the court "has the common sense [sens commun] to evaluate everything, that good taste may be formed there, and that the knowledge of the world which is there displayed is worth all the obscure learning of pedantry" (4.3). When, in *Don Juan,* the don tells Sganarelle that his skepticism allows him only to believe in such minimal abstractions as "two and two make four, Sganarelle, and . . . two fours are eight" (3.1), Sganarelle replies that his common sense leads him to a theological argument from design: "With my own common sense and using my own judgment I can see things better than books, and I know very well that this world we see around us didn't spring up of its own accord overnight—like a mushroom!" This is not a position Molière would disavow.

Once the bond of common sense is broken, either the mind or the body runs to excess. Self-sufficient rationality is as debilitating for Molière as wanton sensuality is. Thus the extreme libertinage of Don Juan is ambiguous. Molière's intellectual and comic instincts tell him to approach compromise at all costs; his skeptical and tragic instincts tell him to present extremes and carry them to their inevitable ends. Don Juan *is* an extreme fated for a bad end. That much is certain from the legend. He is an exaggerated materialist, skeptic, and libertine. He opposes all systems and codes of behavior that do not conform to his needs, sexual and otherwise. What sort of creature is he? Sganarelle poses this very issue to Gusman early in the play: "You still don't understand what sort of man Don Juan is" (1.1). Sganarelle tells half the story when he says:

In my master, Don Juan, you see the biggest scoundrel that ever cumbered the earth, a madman, a cur, a devil, a Turk, a heretic who believes neither in Heaven, Hell, nor werewolf: he lives like an animal, like a swine of an Epicurean, a veritable Sardanapalus, shutting his ears to every Christian remonstrance, and turning to ridicule everything we believe in.

Sganarelle's catalog (with the possible exception of "werewolf") is a record of blasphemy that touches on virtually every rationalist-moralist European belief or ethic. Of course, when he says that Don Juan lives like an animal, he does not mean his master is un-aristocratic in birth and bearing—he means that he lives by strict appeal to his senses and appetites. What Sganarelle does not see in Don Juan, though, is a figure whose behavior, though boundlessly immoral, is extraordinarily courageous, even in the face of things he comes to learn are greater than himself. It would kill him to display any lack of courage, and in fact his one and only expression of fear in the play *does* kill him.

The most intriguing moments of the action occur when the fearless Don Juan comes up against those very mysteries of life and death that his skepticism rejects—mysteries that in the legend and in the play seem particularly focused on exacting revenge from Don Juan. When he and Sganarelle meet the statue of Dona Elvire's father, so recently slain by Don Juan, Sganarelle is beside himself with fear. The don says, "Come on! I'll show you what a coward you are. Watch me! Would your Excellency the Commander care to take supper with me?" (3.5). In humoring Sganarelle, Don Juan naturalizes the supernatural. Then, of all things, he sees the statue nod assent. The skeptic, believing only what his senses tell him to believe, is astounded: "Come on. Let us get out of here!" (The French is even more abrupt: "Allons, sortons d'ici!") These are not words of fear but of irritation, as if his eyes have shown him that inexplicable things can affront his dignity. Sganarelle says: "So much for your freethinkers who won't believe in anything" (3.5). What becomes fascinating in Don Juan's subsequent behavior is that even though he has seen something that ought to

force belief (and hasty repentance, if he has any idea of salvation), he instead openly courts, as a matter of principle, that which comes to damn him.

Earlier, near the beginning of the play, Sganarelle had ironically associated his master with the fate Don Juan would ultimately serve: "I would sooner serve the Devil himself. He's made me witness to so many horrible things that I wish he was—I don't know where" (1.1). Don Juan as libertine is a veritable devil on earth, and he has only to meet his rival (and double) at the conclusion of the play, in the very place Sganarelle sensed but could not articulate at the beginning—that is, in hell itself.

Several important scenes intervene, though, before Don Juan's grand finale. First a tailor comes to collect his bill, and Don Juan's reaction proves that the statue scene has not rendered him unfit, so to speak, to deal with the fripperies of life. The farcical nature of this scene masks the more revealing point that Don Juan takes great pains to avoid an earthly debt after it has become clear that he has a much greater eternal debt to pay. Next Don Luis, Don Juan's father, arrives, and mouths the proper platitudes about filial and family honor. Having dispensed with the bourgeois ethic of the tailor, Don Juan faces the aristocratic ethic of noblesse oblige. All this simply reinforces his notion that any sort of repentance at this point, at least so far as he is concerned, would be a worse hypocrisy than libertinism.

Later it occurs to Don Juan to feign conversion in order to increase the range of his libertinism; but before he does so, even Dona Elvire comes to plead with him for the salvation of his soul: "Do not deny me your salvation" (4.6). Although Don Juan, having just had a brief chat with a stone replica of her dead father, must have some idea of what that dead man's daughter is talking about, her plea only stimulates him to ask her to stay the night, so that he may once more enjoy the pleasure of her company. He may not be long for the world, but he surely knows how to entertain himself before he is forced to leave it.

When the statue comes to dinner (and by this time Molière has forced the skeptical don into a corner by counterpointing naturalistic and supernatural representation), Don Juan continues to brave it out. He asks his musicians to play (4.6). In a similar scene from Mozart's *Don Giovanni*, the players perform an aria from another Mozart opera—which is to say that Don Giovanni literally faces the music of the composer whose music damns him. But Molière's Don Juan is given little time for such witty interludes. The statue has come only to proffer an invitation of his own for the next evening. Don Juan accepts, and it is at this point in the action that he makes his gesture of feigned, hypocritical conversion.

Unlike Tartuffe, whose putative reason for hypocrisy allows him to commit sins under the cloak of piety, Don Juan had not previously required such an excuse. It seems to matter little what kind of excuses he sets up for the future. More likely, Don Juan responds in his famous speech on hypocrisy to the need for judgment before he is, in fact, judged. He takes damnation into his own hands because he feels comfortable only when matters are in his own hands. A real conversion on his part would argue his need for grace; a feigned conversion simply increases his offense against divine justice. He adds blasphemy to his already damned state. It is almost as if Don Juan struggles to insult an order the existence of which he has just begun to intuit, because he knows that it is very much part of his fate to be judged badly. To be condemned for things he has done is not enough—he has to add things he has not yet done and, in any event, probably will not have time to do. It could be argued that his behavior in these last scenes suggests more self-disgust than courage. This is indeed possible; but if Don Juan is disgusted with his own sensate experience, he is also disgusted with the world in which that experience takes place. If he is to depart from earth, he will go with a contemptuous gesture that apes the vice that most of mankind practices.

In the last scene Don Juan faces the specter of Death: "Nothing can frighten me. I will test with my sword whether it be flesh or spirit" (5.5). He still poses the skeptic's question, and he learns what he would rather not know—it is spirit. For the materialist the spiritual is literally death. But Don Juan still persists, saying to Death: "No, come what may it shall never be said that I am the repenting sort" (5.5). The statue of the commander enters while Don Juan continues to worry over his earthly reputation. In a Dantesque gesture reminiscent of another, more fortunate descent to hell, the statue leads Don Juan by the hand, making what is mysterious rather "touching."

It is only at the point of being swallowed up that Don Juan utters words of fear: "Oh God!" (O Ciel!: 5.6). No matter what one's courage, death is humbling. His final utterance is ironic less because of his unbelief than because of what he is now forced to believe: "What is happening to me? Unseen fires consume me. I cannot bear it. My body is aflame—ah. . . ." For Don Juan, who believes only what he sees, the mystery of damnation remains unseen until the beginning of the end; and, of course, for the materialist it is fitting that he should feel the pain of what during his life he would not acknowledge existed: an afterlife.

THE MISANTHROPE

In *The Misanthrope*, Molière sets up a different dilemma for his hero than he had for the hero of *Don Juan*. Don Juan tries to reduce mystery to earthly dimension; Alceste tries to expand frustration to cosmic disorder. Alceste's inflationary tactics begin early. In reaction to Philinte's overly refined, flattering politesse, Alceste says that if he "ever had had the misfortune to do such a thing [flatter unashamedly] I'd go and hang myself on the spot in sheer disgust" (1.1). The balanced and balancing ethos of the play is concentrated in Philinte's response: "Well, personally, I don't see that it's a hanging matter." Philinte's irony touches on the central issue in the play: appropriateness, an issue crucial to the social, generic, and judgmental contexts of *The Misanthrope.*

Alceste is set up in the play to argue for a series of inappropriate reactions, especially given his disinclination to put what he articulates into practice. Philinte's view is one of ready, perhaps too ready, accommodation: "There *are* times when it's well to conceal what one really feels" (1.1), a position repeated in another of Molière's comedies, *The Miser,* by Valère when speaking about the issue of flattery: "Such methods may impair one's integrity [sincerité], but if one has need of people one must accommodate oneself to them, and if there is no other way of gaining their support, well then, the blame lies less with the flatterers than with those who want to be flattered" (1.1). Valère's words have a ring of shrewd authenticity about them. Molière knows, as Philinte puts it to Alceste, that railing endlessly against "defects inseparable from human nature" (1.1) makes one look as ridiculous as the defects one rails against. Men of too severe principles become versions of the very excesses they abhor. Alceste, for example, in the midst of insisting that Philinte make distinctions among people because esteem bestowed on everyone ceases to have meaning for anyone, refuses to make distinctions himself: "I mean to fling my gauntlet in the face of the whole human race" (1.1). Philinte asks if there are any exceptions, and Alceste responds: "No. It's universal. I hate all mankind."

But Alceste's inability to separate his verbal protestations from his socially trained reflexes becomes clear in the very next scene, when the courtier Oronte arrives and asks whether Alceste would mind his proferred friendship. Alceste answers: "Not in the least but I'm very much surprised. I wasn't expecting such an honor" (1.2). Alceste has done exactly what he said he would not do—his answer is a refined verbal politesse. To be sure, his words drip with irony; but since Oronte has not been involved in the previous conversation, he has no way of reading Alceste's tone. Irony unrecognized becomes a form of flattery, flattery for which Alceste has just said he was prepared to hang himself. Irony is hidden meaning, after all, a concealed and compromised meaning— exactly what Philinte had advised in the previous scene. Although Alceste does erupt against Oronte later, whatever *will* happen cannot interdict what Alceste originally wished to do, that is, to avoid outright rudeness through the appropriate delicacy of social exchange.

We can assume that Alceste's behavior has recently come to some sort of head, and even now, under duress, he is none too prepared to practice the unbridled sincerity he has been preaching. Even after he is goaded by Oronte into an "honest" commentary on the foolish sonnet, Alceste is confused in his motives for responding. His penchant for plain speaking here has more to do with his own wish that the fickle Célimène, to whom Oronte's sonnet is addressed, would speak plainly to Alceste (at least plainly enough to choose him once and for all) than it has to do with Oronte's execrable poetry. Bad as the sonnet is, it is worse in signaling Alceste that Célimène, instead of singling him out, has spread herself thin. Not having been singled out, Alceste therefore lashes out.

As an indication of his desire that love will turn simpler for him, as opposed to the ornate and proliferative qualities of love in Oronte's sonnet, he offers an older ballad about truth in the packaging of love as an antidote to Oronte's poem. But he also suspects that his rival's sonnet is symbolic not merely of what Célimène receives, but also of what she inspires. Célimène prefers the ornateness of variety to the simplicity of fidelity. She is, as Alceste himself admits, a young widow with faults (1.1). As a widow she is both financially secure with jointure and not exactly virgin territory. She sees no reason to be a prude at twenty, as she says to her fading enemy Arsinoé, echoing Dorine's marvelous speech in *Tartuffe* about the veteran prude who "resolves to renounce the world which is slipping away from her and conceal the fading of her charms beneath an elaborate pretense of high principles" (1.1).

A prude is a rhetorically aged version of a coquette, and Célimène refuses to hurry time. She says to Arsinoé: "I don't say that I shan't follow your example one day—there's no saying what one will come to in the course of years but you must agree that twenty is not the age for being prim" (3.4). Because she values the present so, she refuses to narrow any of her choices; because she amuses so, she refuses really to love. At the end of the play, Célimène has the decency to apologize to Alceste for what she has done to him; but she will not make the grander and, for her, more absurd gesture of running off with him. She is a social creature, ornate in her very being and made for the world.

In *The Misanthrope*, Alceste wastes very little time backing himself into a corner—a corner of the stage, of the salon, and of Célimène's heart. Though again and again he protests his readiness to clear out of the salon world, his language betrays his need to stay. In his general opinion of the world, he tells Philinte that he will not budge from his position; he is "determined not to move a single step" (résolut de n'en pas faire un pas: 1.1). And yet he always insists to Célimène, in seeming opposition to his rootedness, that he is about to leave: "I'm going" (2.3). She says: "Stay." He: "Why should I?" She: "*Do* stay." He: "I can't." She: "But I want you to. . . ." He: "No. It's impossible." She: "Very well then. Go! Be off!" Célimène has a way of taunting Alceste, who is still unmoved, a few moments later: "Haven't you gone?" (2.4).

Alceste's dilemma here and throughout the play is that his uncompromising nature is already compromised. He will not move intellectually because he is too moved by love. His exaggerated righteousness is born of frustration, and he is bound to the world he despises by a passion for a woman who helps define that world. He tries from the beginning to keep his general views on society, for which commentators like Jean Jacques Rousseau so revere him, separate from his agonizing personal confusion; but he is trapped by extreme positions that damn him as much as they damn others.

Célimène, of course, has him figured out: "You are becoming jealous of the whole universe" (2.1), she says. Alceste replies: "Because the whole universe enjoys your favors." Later Célimène says: "You are mad when you are in these jealous fits" (4.3), implying that he has had them prior to the day's action. His jealousy is as paranoid as it is bilious: "But what assurance have I that you aren't perhaps saying just as much to others at the same time?" (2.1). Of course she is, though until the end he blames everyone but Célimène for her behavior, which only proves that he has as little insight into her as he has into himself.

Even when Alceste thinks that the force of his own character produces honesty in others, he is not only wrong but almost cruel in so thinking. For example, he treats Éliante, who really loves him, very differently from the honorable ways of which he was so enamored in the ballad he recited earlier, and differently from the noble and heroic fashion in which Éliante portrays *him*. Alceste asks Éliante to help him take revenge on Célimène, and when she asks: "I avenge you? How?" (4.2), he responds with incredible insensitivity: "By accepting my love. Take it, Madam! Take the heart she has betrayed. That's how I can punish her."

Such heartlessness, meaning or unmeaning, is a symptom of petulance almost hypocritical in its effrontry. And Alceste, because he shies away from what really motivates him, is close to hypocrisy throughout the play, whether he wishes such a severe charge placed upon his head or not. He hypocritically forces martyrdom upon himself when he loses his legal suit, a suit that structurally parallels his suit for the hand of Célimène: "I'll accept it. Bitterly as the verdict may wrong me I'm far from wanting to see it squashed. It shows all too plainly how right may be abused" (5.1). Clearly, Célimène is on his mind more than the suit, and he makes a self-righteous virtue of what necessity has dealt him.

If Éliante represents an element of Alceste's delusion, the avowed hypocrite of the play, Arsinoé, represents an element of his self-righteousness. There is a nice symmetry here: Both Éliante and Arsinoé are in love with Alceste, the one openly, as befits her nature, the other secretly, as befits hers. Appropriately, it is the false-dealing Arsinoé who tells Alceste of Célimène's promiscuity, and the false-dealing Alceste who tells Arsinoé that his honest vision of the world does not extend to hearing the truth about Célimène: "You might in charity have refrained from putting such thoughts into my head" (3.5). Arsinoé, a hypocrite like Tartuffe, makes sure to tell the truth; and Alceste, a man of principle, lives something of a lie. His talk of forthrightness is belied by his reluctance to know, just as his talk of departure is belied by his reluctance to leave. Of course, we must admit that whereas Tartuffe's hypocrisy stems from a corrupted nature, Alceste's and even Arsinoé's stems from a disappointed heart.

What makes *The Misanthrope* one of Molière's problematic plays—perhaps the most problematic—is that it focuses not only on Alceste's frustration but also on how that frustration rearranges the structural anatomy of comedy. Molière in this play merely teases his audience with the possibility of comic union and equilibrium by providing a ghost relationship for Philinte and Éliante somewhat in the background. But if the play, in effect, leaves comedy behind, it fails, like Alceste, to fulfill its approach to tragedy. It is precisely the am-

biguous positioning between generic forms that produces the discordant energies of *The Misanthrope.* Alceste, of course, would see the play as a tragedy with himself as its tragic victim, and this is the view that many critics, Rousseau primary among them, would take.

But earlier Philinte had analyzed the matter more accurately when he pointed out that Alceste was a laughingstock around town—literally, in French, that he "donne la comédie" (1.1). What Alceste thinks of as tragic is really a form of bombast, a parody of the tragic diction of Molière's older contemporary Corneille and his younger contemporary Jean Racine. Alceste's defeats at law and love make him a suppliant at the door of universal disorder. Éliante asks him why he is upset, and he responds like one of Corneille's overwrought heroes: "Something beyond mortal experience! A calamity more overwhelming than anything within the order of nature! It's all up! My love—I don't know how to say it" (4.2). And when asked by Célimène, shortly afterward, what makes him look so somber, his response is Racinian: "That all the horrors the mind can conceive are nothing in comparison with your perfidy" (4.3).

Alceste's talent is less for speaking plainly about the human condition than for speaking hysterically about his own. He is a town crier in every sense of the word. He spews forth against comic, not tragic, complications, against flatterers, against poems, against coquettes, against those who have nothing better to do than pique him. As Alexander Pope said of himself, Alceste tortures butterflies upon the rack. Perhaps his rantings and ravings give us the sense of other, larger worlds: the jackal lair of the civil courts or the jungle of society beyond the salon in general, or even the metaphoric world of Alceste's long-planned exile in a desert land uncontaminated by mankind (by which Alceste means the provinces).

But Alceste would cut a sorry figure as a provincial desert rat or an aristocratic Robinson Crusoe. The tragicomic Alceste parodies his own call to exile by refusing to stray too far from the easy recall of Célimène. The only world for which Alceste is equipped he is ill content to live in. That remains both his philosophic and his generic dilemma throughout the play. As a parody of the tragic hero, his rage is "too wild" (trop sauvage: 1.1), suggesting Alceste's rhetorical incivility in comparison with the controlled urbanity of society. He resists the usual comic compromises between rudeness and tact, tirade and flattery, isolation and involvement. And, significantly, Alceste ends where comedy begins, with the threat of separation.

What enables Molière to undermine comedy in *The Misanthrope* while mocking the tragic posture is the use of a literary strategy present in many of his plays and abundant in this one: satire. His principal figures, Alceste and Célimène, are both, after a fashion, satirists. Alceste is the typical satiric railer whose model is the classical misanthrope extending as far back as the Greek poet Archilochus, who, disappointed in love, wrote such vicious dithyrambic attacks directed against his lover and her father that both were said to have hanged themselves in humiliation. If Alceste is the satirist as foul-mouthed outcast, then Célimène answers to the more refined Roman notion of satire as *satura* or *satura lanx,* a well-filled dish. Satire is cognate with appropriate words for Célimène, "satiated" and "satisfied." She is indeed the satiric hostess, serving up her exquisitely roasted absent guests for the delectation of her present ones.

But Molière does not stop here. While his characters cast satiric looks at the world in which they live and the figures who people it, Molière turns his own satiric attack against his satirists. We have already observed how he compromises Alceste. He does the same, in a different way, with Célimène. Her talents are *only* those of satiric rhetoric. She is long on wit and short on compassion or understanding. In the extraordinary scene in which she demolishes the hypocrisy of Arsinoé, she reveals the moral emptiness of her own rhetorical world: "I believe there's nothing people can't contrive to praise or condemn and find justification for doing so" (3.4). There are no principles at work here, merely performances. Célimène's world falls apart not only when her series of satiric portraits goes awry, but also when she is forced to make her private correspondence public. It is difficult for those she has victimized to accept that she is as mean-spirited within as without.

The problem in representing two judgmental characters and asking for judgment to be cast upon them in turn is that Molière asks for the condemnation of characters who, though flawed, are among the most dominating and brilliant creations to have graced the comic stage. This is what so confused Rousseau in regard to Alceste, and so infuriated him against Molière in the name of *The Misanthrope*'s hero. But perhaps the effort of judgment is rendered somewhat easier when we realize that the entire play trains us for it. Every scene is a judicial contest of sorts. We come upon verbal disputes, poetry contests, lawsuits, witnesses, affidavits, edicts, ultimatums, verdicts, and appeals. The central episodes of the play are all adversary: Alceste versus Philinte, Oronte versus Alceste, Célimène versus Arsinoé, Alceste versus Célimène, Célimène versus her entire salon.

Although Molière resolves some of these adversary proceedings, the court is still out on others. The evidence is never complete for those of Molière's comedies that transcend the resolute structures of conventional comic form. Philinte's compromising soul may answer to those in the world able to accommodate others, but those whose frustrations and longings are more complex must appeal to a dramatic court willing to make greater allowances for the gifted and the idiosyncratic. When *The Misanthrope* is nearly over and, as Shakespeare's Juliet says, the motion is ended, Molière still leaves open the contingent possibility that things may change for his hero, and perhaps even for his heroine. This is the final gesture of a comedian with unsurpassed confidence in the suppleness of his comic imagination.

Selected Bibliography

INDIVIDUAL PLAYS AND DATES OF FIRST PERFORMANCES

La jalousi du barbouillé (The Jealousy of Smut-Face). Date unknown.

Le médecin volant (The Flying Physician). Date unknown.

L'Étourdi (The Blunderer). 1653.

Le depit amoureux (The Love Tiff). 1656.

Le docteur amoureux (The Doctor in Love). 1658.

Les précieuses ridicules (The Ridiculous Précieuses). 1659.

Sganarelle ou le cocu imaginaire (Sganarelle; or, The Imaginary Cuckold). 1660.

Don Garcie de Navarre ou le prince jaloux (Don Garcia of Navarre; or, The Jealous Prince). 1661.

L'École des maris (The School for Husbands). 1661.

Les fâcheux (The Bores). 1661.

L'École des femmes (The School for Wives). 1662.

La critique de l'école des femmes (The Critique of the School for Wives). 1663.

L'Impromptu de Versailles (The Versailles Impromptu). 1663.

Le marriage forcé (The Forced Marriage). 1664.

Les plaisirs d'île enchantée (The Pleasures of the Enchanted Isle). 1664.

La princesse d'Élide (The Princess of Elis). 1664.

Le Tartuffe ou l'imposteur (Tartuffe; or, The Imposter). 1664.

L'Amour médecin (Love Is the Best Medicine). 1665.

Don Juan ou le festin de pierre (Don Juan; or, The Feast of Stone). 1665.

Le médecin malgré lui (The Doctor in Spite of Himself). 1666.

Mélicerte, comédie pastorale héroïque (Mélicerte, a Heroic-Comic Pastoral). 1666.

Le misanthrope (The Misanthrope). 1666.

Pastorale comique (Comic Pastoral). 1666.

Le Sicilien ou l'amour peintre (The Sicilian; or, Love as a Painter). 1667.

Amphitryon. 1668.

L'Avare (The Miser). 1668.

George Dandin ou le mari confondu (George Dandin; or, The Abashed Husband). 1668.

Monsieur de Pourceaugnac (Mister de Pourceaugnac). 1668.

Les amants magnifiques (The Magnificent Lovers). 1670.

Le bourgeois gentilhomme (The Bourgeois Gentleman). 1670.

Les fourberies de Scapin (The Rascalities of Scapin). 1670.

La comtesse d'Escarbagnas (The Countess of Escarbagnas). 1671.

Psyche, Tragédie-Ballet (Psyche, a Tragedy-Ballet). 1671.

Les femmes savantes (The Learned Ladies). 1672.

Le malade imaginaire (The Imaginary Invalid). 1673.

COLLECTED EDITIONS

Oeuvres complètes. Edited by René Bray. 8 vols. Paris, 1935–1952.

————. Edited by Gustave Michaut. 11 vols. Paris, 1949.

————. Edited by Eugene Despois and Paul Mesnard. 13 vols. Paris, 1873–1900. Repr. London, 1959. Collection des grands écrivains de la France.

————. Edited by Georges Couton. 2 vols. Paris, 1971. The new Pléiade edition.

TRANSLATIONS

For the sake of accuracy and for ease of access, I have used John Wood's Penguin Classics translations of the plays: *Molière: The Misanthrope and Other Plays* (Harmondsworth, 1959) and *Molière: The Miser and Other Plays* (Harmondsworth, 1962). These volumes contain the following plays that I have cited in the body of the text: *The Misanthrope, Tartuffe, The Imaginary Invalid, The Miser, The Would-Be Gentleman* (cited as *Le bourgeois gentilhomme*), and *Don Juan.* In addition, I have used Renée Waldinger's translation of *The Learned Ladies* (Great Neck, N.Y., 1957), and my own translations of short sentences and phrases from other plays in Molière's canon.

BIOGRAPHICAL STUDIES AND DOCUMENTARY MATERIAL

Bray, René. *Molière, homme de théâtre.* Paris, 1954.

Fernández, Ramón. *La vie de Molière.* Paris, 1929. Translated by Wilson Follet as *Molière, the Man Seen Through the Plays.* New York, 1958.

Grimarest, Jean Léonor le Gallois de. *La vie de Monsieur Molière*, edited by George Mongrédien. Paris, 1955. Originally published 1705.

Jasinkski, René. *Molière, l'homme et l'oeuvre.* Paris, 1969.

Jurgens, Madeleine, and Elizabeth Maxfield-Miller. *Cent ans de recherches sur Molière, sur sa famille et sur les comédiens de sa troupe.* Paris, 1963.

La Grange, Charles Varlet, sieur de. *Le régistre de La Grange*, edited by Bert E. Young and Grace P. Young. 2 vols. Geneva, 1947.

Meyer, Jean. *Molière.* Paris, 1963.

Michaut, Gustave. *La jeunesse de Molière; Les débuts de Molière á Paris; Les luttes de Molière.* 3 vols. Paris, 1921–1925. Notes for a fourth volume are included in Michaut's edition of *Oeuvres complètes.* Paris, 1949.

Mongrédien, Georges. *La vie privée de Molière.* Paris, 1950.

————. *Recueil des textes et des documents du XVIIᵉ siècle relatifs á Molière.* 2 vols. Paris, 1965.

Palmer, John. *Molière.* New York, 1930.

Simon, Alfred. *Molière par lui-même.* Paris, 1957.

CRITICAL, HISTORICAL, AND INTELLECTUAL STUDIES

Adam, Antoine. *Histoire de la littérature française au XVIIᵉ siécle.* Paris, 1953. Vol. 3, pp. 207–408.

Brody, Jules. "*Don Juan* and *Le Misanthrope*, or the Esthetics of Individualism in Molière." *PMLA* 84: 559–576 (1969).

Bénichou, Paul. "Molière." In *Morales du Grand Siécle.* Paris, 1948. Pp. 156–218.

Cairncross, John. *Molière bourgeois et libertin.* Paris, 1964.

DiBattista, Maria. "*The Misanthrope.*" In *Homer to Brecht: The European Epic and Dramatic Traditions*, edited by Michael Seidel and Edward Mendelson. New Haven, Conn., 1977. Pp. 255–272.

Elliott, Robert C. "The Satirist Satirized: Studies of the Great Misanthropes." In *The Power of Satire: Magic, Ritual, Art.* Princeton, N.J., 1960. Pp. 130–222.

Frye, Northrop. "The Mythos of Spring: Comedy." In *Anatomy of Criticism.* Princeton, N.J., 1957. Pp. 163–186.

Gossman, Lionel. *Men and Masks: A Study of Molière.* Baltimore, 1963.

Gross, Nathan. *From Gesture to Idea: Esthetics and Ethics in Molière's Comedy.* New York, 1982.

Guicharnaud, Jacques. *Molière, une aventure théâtrale.* Paris, 1963.

————, ed. *Molière: A Collection of Critical Essays.* Englewood Cliffs, N.J., 1964.

Howard, W. D., and Merlin Thomas, eds. *Molière, Stage and Study.* Oxford, 1973.

Hubert, Judd D. *Molière and the Comedy of Intellect.* Berkeley and Los Angeles, 1962.

Johnson, Roger, Jr., Editha S. Neumann, and Guy T. Trail, eds. *Molière and the Commonwealth of Letters: Patrimony and Posterity.* Jackson, Miss., 1975.

Knutson, Harold C. *Molière, an Archetypal Approach.* Toronto, 1976.

Lancaster, Henry Carlington. "The Period of Molière." In *A History of French Dramatic Literature in the Seventeenth Century*, 2nd ed. Baltimore, 1952. Part 3.

Lawrence, F. L. *Molière, the Comedy of Unreason.* Tulane Studies in Romance Language and Literature, no. 2. New Orleans, 1968.

"Molière." *Revue de l'histoire littéraire de la France* 72: 769–1093 (1972). A special issue of articles and essays.

Moore, Will G. *Molière, a New Criticism.* Oxford, 1949. Reissued with a postscript, New York, 1962.

BIBLIOGRAPHIES

Saintonge, Paul, and Robert W. Christ. *Fifty Years of Molière Studies: A Bibliography, 1892–1941.* Baltimore, 1942.

Saintonge, Paul. "Molière." In *A Critical Bibliography of French Literature.* Vol. 3: The Seventeenth Century, edited by Nathan Edelman. Syracuse, N.Y., 1961.

————. "Thirty Years of Molière Studies." In *Molière and the Commonwealth of Letters: Patrimony and Posterity*, edited by Roger Johnson, Jr., et al. Jackson, Miss., 1975. Pp. 747–826.

MICHAEL SEIDEL

BLAISE PASCAL
(1623–1662)

PASCAL BELONGS IN any collection of European writers or indeed of world writers, for such is his stature. "He is a giant, a conqueror of minds," said Voltaire, in spite of the fact that he was unsympathetic to Pascal, except as a writer. He judged the *Lettres provinciales* to be the first prose work of genius in French; he dated the fixing of the French language from that collection of letters. But, as Voltaire knew, Pascal did not think of himself mainly as a writer or literary figure, and we would do well to look elsewhere for what is essential in his achievement. He was above all a seeker after truth; his life is a series of encounters with it; his writing, in all its artistry and brilliance, flowed from the obligation he felt to use and communicate what he had found; and there came a time when living his truth was more important to him than putting it into words.

LIFE AND CAREER

Blaise Pascal was born on 19 June 1623 in Clermont-Ferrand, about 240 miles south of Paris in what was then the province of Auvergne. His father, Étienne Pascal, was a judge in the royal tax court. His position was important, as the court had jurisdiction over the whole of central France. He belonged to the influential class of civil servants and magistrates known as the noblesse de robe. Pascal's mother, née Antoinette Begon, was of bourgeois origins; her father was a merchant in Clermont. Two other children were born to them: Gilberte, three years older than Blaise, and Jacqueline, two years younger. Little is known of Pascal's first years. His mother died in 1626, and five years later Étienne Pascal, a man of serious intellectual interests and, it would seem, some social ambitions, gave up his work at Clermont and took his family to Paris.

There, with a moderate fortune to ensure his independence, he began to cultivate his interests, one of which was the education of his children. For Blaise, a frail child with great curiosity, he provided at first informal lessons and explanations arising out of daily life. His plan was to move later to training in the classical languages, then to mathematics. Religious teaching was not to be neglected, but Étienne Pascal took as a principle that matters of reason and matters of faith were quite separate. This distinction, which he made clear to his children, is, as we shall see, one of the keys to understanding his son's life and career.

Noting that the boy had a precocious aptitude for mathematics, his father tried to keep it in check until the language training could be finished. To early questions Blaise asked about geometry, he answered that it treated figures and the proportions among them. With that to go on, the boy invented at the age of twelve his own vocabulary for dealing with figures and began to construct demonstrations about them. One day his father asked what he was doing and learned that Blaise had reached the point of trying to demonstrate what was in fact the thirty-second proposition in Euclid's *Elements of Geometry*, that the sum of the angles in a triangle is equal to two right angles.

Étienne Pascal was one of the original members of a circle of mathematicians and physicists known as the Académie Mersenne, named for its founder, Marin Mersenne, who has been described as "the secretary general of science in Europe" at the time. Thanks to Mersenne's travels, correspondence, and contacts, the circle knew and discussed the work of Descartes, Fermat, Hobbes, Galileo, Torricelli, and others. Blaise made such rapid progress in mathematics that his father soon began to take him along to the meetings of the Académie. At sixteen he started a treatise on conic sections. Though not completed, it very probably included the substance of a remarkable one-page *Essay pour les coniques* (Essay on Conic Sections) that Pascal published in 1640.

During this time the Pascal family was gradually widening its relations to include something of the world of the aristocracy and even of the court. There were visits to their friends' salons, those centers of polite social life, where conversation about poetry, music, books, and even science was one of the principal activities. Jacqueline Pascal attracted considerable attention by her talent for writing verse. Richelieu knew and thought highly of Étienne Pascal and his children.

In the autumn of 1639 Étienne Pascal was sent by Richelieu to Rouen as the royal commissioner for the imposition and collection of taxes. For the next nine years he carried out this difficult assignment with distinction. The family's stay in the capital city of Normandy was a time of change and development for them. Gilberte was married in 1641 to a cousin, Florin Périer; and they established themselves in Clermont-Ferrand.

Corneille, whose tragicomedy *Le Cid* had made dramatic history in 1637, lived in Rouen. He became a friend of the family and took an interest in Jacqueline's continuing poetic efforts. Blaise served as an assistant to his father, helping especially with the long and complicated tax calculations. Out of this work came the idea for his arithmetical machine, a portable device with a mechanism of gears and dials that, when activated by a stylus, did addition, subtraction, multiplication, and division. This apparatus, clearly lacking a mind but capable of something like mental activity, was the subject of much discussion in Paris; it brought to Pascal, then in his early twenties, a measure of fame that he obviously enjoyed. In 1645 he obtained a royal privilege, rather like a patent, entitling him to produce the machine and protecting his rights from imitators. He hoped to make his fortune from it, but assembling it in quantity turned out to be too difficult and costly. At least seven of the machines are still in existence.

In 1646 Pascal became interested in an experiment that had been performed with mercury by Torricelli, a pupil of Galileo. Torricelli found that a tube closed at one end and filled with mercury, when turned upside down and immersed in a bowl containing more mercury, does not empty itself completely. Since nature was commonly said to abhor a vacuum, what could be in the space at the top (the closed end) of the tube? And why did the mercury stay at a certain height in the tube instead of flowing out into the bowl? Pascal repeated Torricelli's experiment and went on to invent many other versions of it, using various tubes, containers, and liquids. Thus began his intense concern with the branch of physics known as hydrostatics, the study of liquids in equilibrium. Although the full significance of his work was to become clear only later, he described his experiments in *Expériences nouvelles touchant le vide* (New Experiments Concerning the Vacuum), published in 1647.

While Pascal was developing his reasoning in mathematics and physics, a decisive event took place on the side of faith, the other end of the opposition that often seemed to preside over his life and creative activity. In January 1646 Étienne Pascal injured his hip in a fall. The Deschamps brothers, two gentlemen whose calling it was to do works of charity and to care for the sick, came to live for three months in the Pascal household. They were Jansenists. Their example, their ideas, and the books they read changed the lives of the whole family.

Jansenists were followers of Cornelis Jansen (1585–1638), a Dutch theologian and the bishop of Ypres. In his *Augustinus* (published posthumously in 1640) Jansen expounds from his point of view the teachings of Saint Augustine on free will, grace, and predestination. He is pessimistic as regards human nature; he emphasizes original sin and its corrupting effects; he rejects the more optimistic views of the contemporary Jesuit theologians. To be a Christian has always involved both dependence on God and, at the same time, some difficult-to-define degree of free cooperation with him in the work of salvation. Jansen, following Saint Augustine, stresses the former, the Jesuits the latter. He sees every person as placed between God and the world, and in his fallen state as all but fatally attracted to the world's goods and pleasures. A conversion based on God-given grace and faith is called for, a radical reorientation that affects every aspect of one's being and doing.

Introduced to this doctrine by the Deschamps brothers, Pascal was strongly affected by it. He underwent (at the age of twenty-three) what is usually called his "first conversion." By his example and efforts, Jacqueline was converted; the children then converted their father; and later that year Gilberte and her husband were won over during a visit to Rouen. (Conversion means here, of course, the deepening or renewal of a preexisting faith; the Pascal family had always practiced Catholicism.)

Pascal's health had never been good. In 1647 it took a serious turn for the worse. He suffered from headaches, stomach pains, and paralysis of the legs. The doctors in Rouen brought about a partial recovery, but toward the middle of the year, accompanied by Jacqueline, he returned to Paris for further treatment.

During the next four years Pascal actively pursued the lines of research already begun on conic sections in mathematics and on problems of the vacuum in physics. The *Expériences nouvelles touchant le vide* stirred Père Noël, eminent rector of the Collège de Clermont in Paris, to compose a letter refuting Pascal's position and returning in the light of scholastic philosophy to the idea of nature's horror of a vacuum. In an answering letter that refuted the refutation and in other related correspondence, Pascal vigorously defended his approach, which was mathematical and experimental rather than speculative and metaphysical. An experiment conceived by Pascal and carried out by his brother-in-law on the Puy de Dôme, a mountain near Clermont-Ferrand, finally settled the question by explaining in a purely mechanical way the behavior of the mercury in Torricelli's experiment: the weights of two liquids—a column of mercury and a column of air (Pascal considered air a liquid)—were balancing each other, and as one went up or down the mountain, the variations in air pressure were correlated with changes in the height of the mercury. This widely discussed experiment was a triumph for Pascal. It stimulated him to investigate further the laws and applications of hydrostatics, which he formulated in a treatise that did not, however, appear until 1663.

These writings show signs of a passionate interest in science and a thirst for recognition and fame. At times the tone seems out of keeping with what one would have expected after his conversion experience. But Pascal apparently believed that holding science and faith in separate spheres was enough; he did not yet see the former as an obstacle to progress in the latter. Besides, there is evidence that he was reading and thinking about religion during this period. On returning to Paris both he and Jacqueline established contact with the convent of Port-Royal, center of Jansenism in France; indeed, Jacqueline soon wished to become a nun there. Pascal also wrote some remarkable letters to Gilberte on religious subjects, two in 1648 and another in 1651. They bear witness to intense personal meditations on the theme of the visible world taken as signifying or prefiguring an invisible, spiritual domain, on grace and the discipline required for it to be constantly renewed, and on the necessity of accepting the will and providence of God—this last written after his father's death. (Étienne Pascal had returned to Paris in 1648.)

Jacqueline went ahead with her project of entering Port-Royal, which she realized in 1652 in spite of opposition from Pascal, though at last he relented. This event left Pascal in a state of relative independence, and in the next two years (1652–1654) he spent much time in the company of the duc de Roannez, a friend from childhood. Of a very noble family, Roannez had fought in Flanders and was a favorite at the court; he had been made a field marshal at the age of twenty-two. Among others in the duke's entourage Pascal became acquainted with the chevalier de Méré, who exemplified the seventeenth-century ideal of the *honnête homme*, the gentleman who embodies politeness, amiability, moral distinction, and culture without pedantry. He also came to know Damien Mitton, a wealthy man of the world with a skeptical temperament and a taste for gambling. It seems clear that through these associations and others of the same sort Pascal came to understand characters and attitudes to which he had paid little attention before. He must have been struck by the concern for distractions and by the absence of strong religious commitment that he saw about him, and by the fact that his abilities as a mathematician and as a scientist had to be subordinated in social life to an ideal that prized general rather than special excellence.

In 1654 Pascal's activities and attitudes reached a critical juncture. This was a time of social and intellectual success combined, however, with a growing sense of detachment, of spiritual emptiness. In a memorandum written in that year and offered to the group of mathematicians and scientists with whom he had long been associated, Pascal listed the treatises and researches that he had completed to that point. They bore on many problems of arithmetic and geometry, on the calculus of probabilities (a science invented by Pascal and Fermat), on the vacuum, on a method of linear perspective in drawing, on other subjects not indicated in detail; and at the end Pascal added a mention of the arithmetical machine. He obviously enjoyed compiling this list, which was full of novelties and extraordinary in its variety.

Yet during this same year Pascal was turning away from the world and felt increasingly a distaste for all who were caught up in it. But nothing was replacing it; in his detachment from it he was not drawn to God. We know from letters written by Jacqueline to Gilberte that such was his state of mind in September. Two months later there occurred a great renewal of fervor and commitment. On the night of 23 November 1654, from half past ten to half past midnight, Pascal had an ecstatic experience in which he was certain that God was present with him—the biblical God of Abraham, Isaac, and Jacob, not the abstract God of the philosophers. Out of the mixture of joy, exaltation, humility, and contrition he felt on this occasion came a new submission to Jesus Christ. (He wrote down a telegraphic record of what happened that night and thereafter wore it as a reminder in the lining of his coat. No one knew of the existence of this record until it was found at the time of his death.) At last the emptiness was filled, and a new period in Pascal's life began.

There followed a stay at Port-Royal, where Pascal put himself under the spiritual guidance of Antoine Singlin, confessor at the convent. But in the succeeding months he did not adopt an ascetic life. He retained his contacts with the duc de Roannez and in fact converted him. Then late in 1655 Antoine Arnauld, one of the leaders at Port-Royal, was accused of heresy by Jesuits in the theological faculty of the Sorbonne; Pascal came to his defense and to that of the Jansenist cause. He composed, with help from Arnauld and Pierre Nicole, another Jansenist, the series *Lettres provinciales* (*Provincial Letters*). Published anonymously from January 1656 to March 1657, these attacks on Jesuit doctrines and moral theology were enormously successful; as examples of polemic writing they have rarely if ever been equaled.

In March 1656, soon after the fourth letter appeared, Marguerite Périer, Pascal's niece, was cured of an abscess on her eye, thought to be incurable, when a thorn venerated as a relic of Christ's crown was applied to it. The cure occurred in the Paris house of Port-Royal, and after an investigation by competent authorities, it was declared miraculous. Pascal, his family, and his friends interpreted this as a sign of divine favor. As the controversy between the Jansenists and the Jesuits wore on, they drew much encouragement from it.

The period 1656 to 1658 was in some ways the most fruitful time in Pascal's life. In addition to composing the *Provinciales* (and some related brief documents on Jesuit moral theory), he accumulated most of the notes for a defense of the Christian religion that we know as the *Pensées*. These are the works for which he is best known. But several other important texts and fragments date from this period. He wrote nine letters of spiritual advice to Charlotte de Roannez, the duke's sister, who was considering a religious vocation. He began a work on grace, which has come down to us in a series of about fifteen fragments; the doctrine is difficult and strictly Jansenist, but Pascal tries to smooth out its technicalities for his intended readers. He started a textbook on geometry for the schools at Port-Royal; all that remains of that project—it seems—are two important drafts of prefaces. He took up with

some mathematical friends a set of problems in the geometry of curves, and in particular the one known as the "roulette," or cycloid: the curve described by a point on the circumference of a wheel as it turns on a flat surface. To distract himself one evening from a severe toothache, Pascal turned his attention to some questions concerning the properties and measurements of these curves. After a period of great concentration the problems were solved, and the toothache had disappeared. The duc de Roannez suggested the idea of a contest challenging other mathematicians in Europe to solve the problems. He saw this as an opportunity to show, for the benefit of religion, that someone who knew perfectly the capabilities of reason could also be a critic of reason and a person of strong religious belief. Pascal adopted the idea, and the contest was launched; but it led to a tangle of complaints and disputes. He finally published his results, which included some major discoveries. However, it must be said that the vanity, harshness, condescension, and even self-promotion that he showed in the conduct of the contest did him little credit, and it is doubtful that the project did much for the cause of religion.

In the last four years of his life (1659–1662) Pascal's health was so impaired that he could do no work requiring sustained attention. It improved slightly from time to time, but for the most part he remained in a pitiably weak state. With the onset of this serious illness (the exact nature of which has never been determined) he underwent another conversion or—more precisely—another degree of conversion. He spent his days praying, reading the Bible, offering devotions, and doing works of charity. Personal and social contacts were limited to family and very close friends. He helped the poor by contributions; he sometimes visited them; he invited them to stay with him.

In 1661 he was involved for the last time in theological controversy. New pressure had been put on the Port-Royalists and others to sign a condemnation of certain doctrines attributed to Jansen. Jacqueline Pascal finally signed the statement against her conscience. (Her health was so affected by the strains of the controversy that she died early in October of that year.) Blaise found himself in disagreement with his friends Arnauld and Nicole, who sought a way of signing with restrictions so as not to compromise their principles. Pascal was adamant: no such device was acceptable, for he thought the church was about to deny the ancient doctrine of efficacious grace. Since his attitude gained no support from his friends, he withdrew from all further controversy.

At the end of June 1662 his health had deteriorated to such a point that Gilberte cared for him in her Paris lodgings. He saw his confessor often, but did not take communion because the doctors refused to believe that the end was near. On the night of 17 August his state worsened, the priest was called, and he received communion with great feeling. Afterward he said, ''May God never abandon me!'' Those were his last words. He died on 19 August, at one in the morning. He was thirty-nine.

WORKS IN MATHEMATICS AND PHYSICS

Pascal had a passion for truth. He wanted to find it, grasp it fully, and share it. But he came to see that it was not single. There were, he concluded, three kinds of certain knowledge, and each kind had a typical way of formulating and justifying its truth.

Arithmetic and geometry make up the first class of science for Pascal; he thinks of them as "abstract," since they deal with quantities apart from the things in which they may be embodied. His works include about forty texts (mostly short, consisting of a few pages) in this area. He called them "traités" (treatises) when he had brought them to their most elaborate and technical form, but he often composed them or left them in the form of notes, letters, narratives, or discourses. In arithmetic

what interested him especially were the properties of numbers, the formation and interrelations of number series, and the uses of the arithmetical triangle (a diagrammatic way of displaying number series). In geometry he studied the generation, properties, and measurements of a variety of curved lines and figures, such as conic sections, figures drawn on cylinders, and, of course, cycloid curves.

We cannot here go into the details of these works, but it is not difficult to recover the logic behind Pascal's approach to the problems treated in them. The two texts that he composed, apparently for Port-Royal, on the subject of the "esprit géométrique" (roughly, the spirit of geometry) give a lucid—though somewhat rambling—account of his procedure. His argument is historically interesting, since it exemplifies in a pure way the seventeenth-century tendency to promote geometry to the status of the one science among all human inquiries that arrives at truly convincing demonstrations. Quite apart from that, however, it is impossible to understand certain essential aspects of the *Provinciales* and the *Pensées* unless one has a clear idea of geometrical method as Pascal conceives it.

In the opening paragraph of *De l'esprit géométrique* (The Spirit of Geometry) Pascal makes an important distinction: "One can have three principal aims in the study of the truth: one, to discover it when one seeks it; another, to demonstrate it when one possesses it; and the last, to distinguish it from error when one examines it."[1] In the following paragraphs he stresses and analyzes the second of those objectives, though he adds that if one can demonstrate the truth, one has the means of separating it from error. For if one can state a truth and justify it adequately, one can evaluate by inspection rival statements and evidence.

Then comes a crucial step. Pascal turns to

[1]Pascal, *Oeuvres complètes*, edited by L. Lafuma (Paris, 1963), p. 348. All quotations in this essay are taken from this edition. The page number is in parentheses at the end of each quoted passage.

geometry for his model of demonstrative procedure. He makes his reasons for doing so quite clear. The first has to do with terms: in geometry we always know what our words mean, either because their definitions are made explicit as they are introduced or because they refer to realities that we grasp intuitively ("time" and "space," for example; to try to define them—and words like them—only obscures their meanings). The second has to do with statements: every proposition that the geometrician advances is either self-evident or derived from something self-evident. The third is that the geometrician takes care to arrange his demonstrations in a sequence so as to form a chain of truths and their justifications. Everything is in its place, and that place follows from what precedes it and opens the way to what comes after it.

This ideal, though sought hitherto only by mathematicians, can be generalized; and it is essential to recognize that Pascal is proposing—with an enthusiasm that reminds us of Descartes and his *Discourse on Method*—that all serious inquiries and discussions should be conceived in the spirit or mind-set of geometry and should embody the features of its method.

As a matter of fact, apart from the idea of extending the uses of geometrical thinking, Pascal already understands the science of geometry itself as having a narrow or a broad subject matter. Narrowly defined, it treats of plane and solid figures, and it is contrasted with arithmetic, where the subject matter is numbers rather than figures or spaces. Broadly defined, it includes not only those two sciences, but also physics or mechanics, which is the study of bodies and their motions. And so geometry in this latter sense is a comprehensive inquiry into problems of number, space, movement, and time. (Time is needed and implied in any description of movement.)

As we see, the discussion is moving away from its original topic, which was geometrical demonstration. But Pascal wants to lay before us the implications of geometry for understanding the nature and status of man. First he draws our attention to the fact that these four realities—movement, time, space, number—have an extraordinary property in common. Each of them can be increased or diminished without limit. For any number that we conceive, however large it may be, there is always another that is larger; and similarly, however small it may be, there is always a number or a fraction that is smaller. However fast or slow a movement may be, there is always a faster or slower movement, and so on, ad infinitum. We can make statements of the same kind about spaces and time intervals. And so the essential and defining characteristics of natural objects and quantities are subject to what might be called the law of the double infinite. Everything in nature—including man—lies on a scale between the infinitely large and the infinitely small; and everything in nature—including man—is, as a result, paradoxical: referred to the infinitely small it is large, even colossal, but referred to the infinitely large it is small and approaches nothingness. Thus one learns to see one's true value and, as Pascal says, to "engage in reflections that are more valuable than all the rest of geometry" (355).

Pascal has told us, then, that the art of demonstration is nothing more or less than a generalized version of geometrical method, with its definitions, axioms, and linear sequences of propositions. But he is rarely content to demonstrate truth; he looks forward to communicating it to someone else. The second half of *De l'esprit géométrique* takes up the "art of persuasion." It is soon apparent that this art merely adapts the technique of geometry to a situation involving another person. The first task of the persuader is to locate in the mind or will of the person to be persuaded a suitable basis—some stable belief or object of desire—on which the process of reasoning may build. If, for example, the proposition to be conveyed can be attached in the mind to an axiom—such as "the whole is greater than any of its parts"—or in the will to a common desire—such as the wish of every person to attain happiness—the persuader can bring into play, from that point on, his two rules of defining everything and proving everything, and they must necessarily have their effect. Pascal, like many of his contemporaries, abandons two traditional and once highly esteemed arts. He explicitly dismisses logic, because the rules of the syllogism are, he thinks, so natural that we cannot not know them; and by implication he dispenses with rhetoric (the usual name for the art of persuasion), no doubt because in neither Aristotle's nor Cicero's formulation of it do we find anything like reliance on geometrical devices.

Pascal follows the axiomatic method to perfection in the mathematical works. The treatise he composed on the arithmetical triangle consists of a series of definitions, then a set of nineteen consequences, with six "avertissements," or comments, attached to particular points in the argument. The extant portion of the treatise on conic sections is presented even more formally: there are six numbered definitions, fourteen corollaries, and nine "scholia," or consequences.

A modified version of this approach appears in Pascal's work on problems of the vacuum and the equilibrium of liquids. Here we meet the second kind of science that fascinated him: the investigation of natural phenomena (instead of the study of abstract quality). With the change of subject matter comes a change of method. He keeps mathematics insofar as it makes precise measurement possible and supplies a model of exposition, but he adds the new element of experimentation. Pascal, like Galileo, Torricelli, and even Descartes at times, saw that common experience did not suffice if one wished to achieve a mathematical physics (as we have come to call it); it needed to be supplemented by special experience gained through controlled observation. He showed much inventiveness in devising ways of proving and illustrating his conclusions, the most famous being the experiment carried out on the Puy de Dôme.

It was a great victory for Pascal, and one that he clearly savored. In concluding his description of the experiment he stresses that he has corrected a false proposition accepted everywhere by common men and by the multitude of philosophers: namely, that nature is full, that it is a plenum, that it cannot tolerate an empty space. The widespread and long-standing error is, he says, testimony to the insidious power of human imagination, which makes up causes and explanations when the real ones are not known; and he is sure that there are many such fallacies that need to be cleared away. One senses behind the text someone who would willingly work at the task.

However, Pascal's thought and attitudes were evolving on the spiritual as well as the intellectual level. At first he seems to have kept the two separate. With the passing of time he began to feel a conflict between the levels as bases of vocations. Finally, in 1654, after months of soul-searching, he reached a resolution of the tension in the mystical experience of 23 November. In the record of that event he wrote, looking toward the future, "Oubli du monde et de tout hormis Dieu" (Forgetting of the world and of everything except God).

THE PROVINCIALES: *LETTERS ON GRACE, MORALITY, AND THE JESUITS*

As mentioned earlier, late in 1655 and early in 1656 Arnauld, who lived and worked at Port-Royal, came under attack in the Sorbonne for views he had expressed in two letters on the subject of holy communion. He prepared a reply, but Nicole and others at Port-Royal thought it would be ineffective because of its difficult presentation and style. Pascal, who was at the convent on a visit, was asked to see what he could do. The result was the first of the *Provinciales*. His friends liked it and had it published clandestinely. It created a sensation; it was read and discussed privately, in salons and at court. This episode created a demand for more letters, and Pascal complied, producing them at intervals between 1656 and 1657 until there were eighteen in all.

How can the prodigious effect of this work be explained? In part by the marvelous variety of tones, styles, and technical devices that Pascal brought into play. In part by the way in which he made sense out of a tangled contemporary situation that his readers knew about but did not understand. And finally by the fact that he threw brilliant light on a perennial problem to which few of us can be indifferent.

Let us try to see what is at stake. The main issue concerns human freedom and its role in a moral perspective that includes the Judeo-Christian God. Thus the issue involves two freedoms, two initiatives, two beings, and, above all, the question of how their designs may be coordinated, in view of the fact that one of the beings is omniscient and omnipotent. The question is as old as Christianity; indeed, in one form or another, as old as humankind.

Humankind desires final happiness or beatitude, but the catastrophe of original sin has left us in an altered, weakened state; we cannot effectively choose and will that end without help from God, that is, without grace, which has become particularly accessible through the redemptive life and passion of Jesus Christ. Theologians generally agree in asserting both the reality of human freedom and the necessity of grace, but as they develop their views, they diverge.

One may, for example, emphasize the corruption of human nature and the dependence of humankind on God; this leads to a conception of grace that is "efficacious," that always has its effect (coming from God to a creature aware of his weakness and need, it could not be otherwise). Or, one may stress the relative worthiness of human nature and posit something less than corruption—a wound, perhaps, that may be healed: this leads to a conception of grace that is "sufficient"; it is present, but it does not always have its effect, for man may freely accept or reject the divine initiative.

The second of those possibilities was elaborated into a doctrine by a sixteenth-century Spanish Jesuit, Molina (1535–1600). His theology was spread by the Jesuits, many of whom were established by the middle of the seventeenth century in French educational and religious life. On the other hand, the first of the possibilities had been developed into a doctrine by Saint Augustine (354–430), in opposition to a heretical movement led by Pelagius. As it happened, both the sixteenth and seventeenth centuries saw in France a widespread renewal of interest in Saint Augustine and his works. Since it was possible to argue that the views of Molina and the Jesuits resembled the condemned teachings of Pelagius, the stage was set for the reenactment of an ancient controversy.

It is fascinating to watch Pascal move into this situation and dominate it from start to finish. He knows exactly what he wants to do: to refute his opponents, to gain their assent to his position, or, failing that, to reduce them to silence. As the means with which to ferret out and expose error, he uses the truth. But the kind of truth involved is not mathematical or scientific. In works belonging to those categories, his arguments consist of proofs based on reasoning or on a combination of reasoning and observation; here the starting points are matters of faith; and the principles are assumed to be true on the basis of authority. Since the greatest authority of all is God, and he has spoken in the Bible, the Bible assumes a central role in the discussion, as a repository of authoritative statements. Church fathers, church councils, and popes may be appealed to as well, but with the understanding that the value and force of what they have said derives ultimately from Scripture and from the original source of authority.

Here an analogy suggests itself. Theological terms and principles thus conceived function like the vocabulary, statements, and sequences of geometry. It seems to me that the inner logic of the *Provinciales* owes much to Pascal's geometrical habit of mind, though of course he does not apply it arbitrarily. Provided the point is not carried too far, one may say something similar regarding the external outline of the work. The letters fall into three groups according to the main subjects treated: grace (letters 1–4); the moral maxims of the Jesuits (letters 5–16); and grace again (letters 17–18), but now more precisely as entering into a system of doctrine. These divisions correspond to the three main topics mentioned or developed in *De l'esprit géométrique:* defining terms, asserting propositions, and arranging demonstrations in their proper order.

Pascal restates what he takes to be orthodox views in something akin to that quasi-geometrical framework, and he shows that one cannot fit the views and behavior of the Jesuits into it. In the first four letters the opposition between the two sides appears to be summed up in two adjectives, since grace is "efficacious" or "sufficient." To Pascal the issue is real: efficacious grace always works, whereas sufficient grace does not: it is in fact *in*sufficient, since it requires validation by human will to be effective. To substitute sufficient grace for efficacious grace is to fly in the face of a long tradition that goes back to Saint Augustine and to the Bible. The Jesuits have not bothered to do what comes before everything else in such a discussion: clarify the meaning of crucial terms. But this violation of an elementary principle of logic is not an accident. Behind it lies what really concerns his opponents. They have agreed among themselves on a plot to discredit Arnauld, who is a threat to their Society; they are using theological formulas as slogans and rallying points rather than as means of getting at the truth.

This conclusion leads Pascal into an investigation that fills letters 5 through 16. What kind of spiritual advice are the Jesuits giving in the exercise of their priestly duties? As the seventeenth century sees the problem of Christian conduct, everyone needs a spiritual adviser or confessor, whose vocation it is to furnish guidance regarding things done or to be done: were they or would they be sinful? Pascal is now working, it will be noted, on a lower level of generality than before. The question of man's freedom and nature versus God's freedom and grace has given way to the question of deeds, intentions, and circumstances. This change of context brings with it a change of focus from terms and their definitions to precepts and stated rules of conduct. It also involves the art of applying those rules in particular situations, a process known as casuistry. To assist confessors and directors, books of casuistry had long been available, and there was a new vogue of them in the late sixteenth and early seventeenth centuries. They cataloged sins, discussed them, and suggested advice and penances. Since the Jesuits made much use of them, it was natural for Pascal, in undertaking to judge their moral theology, to turn to treatises written by some of their celebrated casuists.

As one might expect from his model of demonstration, Pascal examines the origins of the principles they advance. He soon finds a flaw in their procedure. Instead of attaching their reasons as immediately as possible to a traditional authority, such as a church father, whose views would have the status of axioms, the casuists consider themselves authorities. Their habit, and they pride themselves on it, is to make up their own rules about cases and classes of cases. That is the first way in which they are aberrant: their moral reasoning is cut off from truly authoritative sources.

That is not all. As the more famous casuists have published their treatises and catalogs, sometimes agreeing and sometimes disagreeing with each other, there has grown up a loosely organized system of principles that is full of ambiguities and contradictions. Pascal is never comfortable in such a situation. Oppositions must be exposed, treated somehow, and if possible resolved; otherwise there is no knowing where the truth lies. He is struck by the fact that some casuists tend toward strictness, others toward laxity. As he (or the inquisitor he imagines as passing from Jesuit father to Jesuit father with his questions) discovers, this paradox is no problem at all; indeed it is an advantage. How? Because with precepts of both kinds at his disposition, the priest may adjust his counsel to the wishes of the penitent, or even offer him the option of a strict or an easy solution to his case. And so, as the Jesuit says, there are principles for everyone and the contradictions are a source of strength and universal appeal. The difficulties for Pascal's inquisitor are more numerous even than the difference between strict and lax approaches would indicate, and all the more vexing in that the maxims proposed are, technically speaking, "probable opinions," that is, "justifiable opinions," and that they have in fact been justified. The fathers have developed ways of reconciling contradictions when they wish to do so, by such means as making fine distinctions in the meanings of words or by appealing to the uniqueness of the situations to which the maxims must be adjusted.

To back up his points Pascal often cites, translates, or paraphrases passages from writings of the casuists; and he knows how to choose telling examples of the way they reason. For instance, in the sixth letter he takes up the subject of probable opinions. By resorting to them the Jesuits have found ways of easing restrictions on priests. The question is asked whether a priest may celebrate mass on the same day that he committed a very serious crime (Pascal's euphemism for sexual intercourse with a woman). The answer is no, in the opinion of Villalobos; it is yes, according to Sanctius, and without any sin. Father Bauny, in whose treatise the discussion appears, takes the judgment of Sanctius as a safe and sure opinion. But what of the church laws that exclude such a priest from the altar? The Jesuit father who is explaining all this to Pascal's fictive inquisitor replies that according to Cellot and Reginaldus, "one must not follow in matters of morality the ancient fathers but the new casuists." The inquirer insists, mentioning church law again. His informant cites Filiutius, in whose opinion "the laws of the church lose their force when they are not observed." Moderns know better than the ancients what is now necessary for the church. If we are severe in excluding priests from celebrating mass, there will be less glory for God; and one might say with Cellot that there would not be too many priests if all men, women, inanimate bodies, and brute animals were made priests for the saying of masses.

Another example occurs in the seventh letter, which deals with the direction of intention, a resource almost as important in Jesuit casuistry as probable opinions. The idea is that, where one cannot prevent an act that should be avoided, one may be able to purify the intention; if done with a right intention an otherwise sinful act may be condoned. Pascal has his inquirer bring up the subject of homicide. To relax on that would seem difficult, since one of the Ten Commandments forbids it. However, in a dazzling display the Jesuit informant appeals to Reginaldus, Lessius, Escobar, Mendoza, Hurtado, Diana, Layman, Sánchez, Molina, Sa, Henríquez, Azor, Baldelle, Tannerus, Lamy, and Caramuel in order to establish the cases in which killing may be permitted—if the intention is pure. Suppose, for example, that one has been challenged to a duel on a point of honor. One may appear at the assigned place, not with the aim of fighting a duel but merely of defending oneself, should that be necessary; and if self-defense leads to the death of the challenger, no sin has been committed. Other possible situations in which one may kill, provided one does not do so in a spirit of hate or revenge: a false accusation (one may kill the accuser, his witnesses, and the judge who supports them), a slap, an accusation of lying, a piece of gossip. With the same proviso, priests and religious are free to kill in order to defend their property or their order. Caramuel solves a pertinent problem: may Jesuits kill Jansenists? No, he says, because they cannot by their attacks harm the Society of Jesus; on the contrary, they are causing it to be more highly esteemed than before, though that is not their intention.

The last two letters return to the discussion of grace, this time in connection with five propositions that had been allegedly extracted from Jansen's *Augustinus*. In 1653 Pope Innocent X declared them to be heretical. The sense of the propositions is that the accomplishment of God's commandments to men is not possible without his grace and that the operation of grace cannot be resisted; these views deny human freedom and subject humans to both a natural and a supernatural determinism. In defending the Jansenist position, Pascal introduces a distinction between a question of faith and a question of fact. Are the propositions heretical? And then, are they as a matter of fact found in the *Augustinus*? He answers yes to the first question, but no to the second. It has not been shown, Pascal argues, that the propositions are in Jansen or represent the "sense of Jansen." And so the pope judged unerringly in condemning the propositions, but he was mistaken in attributing them to Jansen. His infallibility does not extend to matters of fact, which cannot be settled by an appeal to authority.

This important distinction and its consequences are easily related to the two kinds of reasoning that Pascal has used before. The process of deciding whether the five propositions are consistent with the beliefs of true faith suggests the image of the mathematical model, of the orderly arrangement of parts that must fit, that must not contradict each other. On the other hand, the approach to the question of fact suggests the inductive model that Pascal favors in his physical treatises. Of the three sources of knowledge that he recognizes—sense, reason, and authority—the first two suffice when we wish to determine what is the case. If the heretical propositions are present in Jansen's work and in so many words, as has been asserted, it ought to be possible to see them there. Discovering them in the *Augustinus* would be, from the point of view of logic, very much like discovering in

nature that a column of mercury and a column of air move into an equilibrium.

Letter 18 is rich in themes and developments that are essential in Pascal's thought. It draws on and sums up much that has gone before, but also begins to make explicit some new things that are destined to grow in importance. One should note that letters 17 and 18 are addressed to Père Annat, Louis XIV's confessor and a leader among the Jesuits. Up to and including the seventeenth letter Pascal states the opposition between the two points of view in such pure terms that no solution seems possible, unless the Jesuits surrender and recant. However, Annat wrote a reply to the seventeenth letter in which he said that the view of Jansen regarding grace and free will was the same as that of Calvin (and, of course, as heretical as that of Calvin). This rapprochement suggests to Pascal a completely new way of conceiving the whole controversy. He now constructs an argument based on three fundamental terms instead of two. Calvin and Molina (the Jesuits' hero) emerge as occupying two extreme positions. Their affirmations present two unbalanced views, whereas the doctrine of Saint Augustine offers a synthesis, a balance that saves the elements of truth contained in each of the others without falling into the excess of either. Pascal presents Saint Augustine as defending human nature against the Calvinist thesis of radical corruption (which distorts, as a result, the notion of grace), and as defending grace against the Molinist thesis of a merely sufficient grace (which distorts, as a result, human nature and its powers). The position of Saint Augustine assumes the others insofar as in their partial ways they point to the whole truth of the matter, which is: that the will of man (Pascal always uses "l'homme" and "les hommes"—man and men—in the inclusive sense) is free; that when by the grace of God man becomes fully aware of God as Goodness and Truth personified, his will chooses God as its goal; that in so choosing, the will acts necessarily but freely; that it could reject grace, but at that stage of spiritual insight it never does.

It is interesting to see Pascal engage in reconciling opposites in this rather abrupt attempt to bring the polemic with the Jesuits to an end. He often adopts a tactic like this in the *Pensées.* In his hands it is much more than an individual's logical device. It becomes a broad intellectual method, a fruitful way of asking and answering the most important questions regarding nature, humankind, and God. It takes its place alongside the geometrical and experimental habits of thought that we have already noted; and, indeed, in many respects it can be said finally to outrank and include the other two. In still another way this letter contains a forecast of what is to come in the *Pensées.* Pascal's (or Saint Augustine's) way of defining the proper relation between humankind and God and of analyzing the working of grace actually sets the outlines of a religious conversion. Without such a pattern Pascal could never have written the *Pensées,* for the single most important aim in the fragments is to produce a turning away from the world toward God that is typically Augustinian.

The form of presentation that Pascal selected for the *Provinciales* follows closely from his aim, which is rhetorical rather than literary or aesthetic: he addresses an audience about something important in order to clarify difficulties and to affect attitudes. That he was a master at exploiting the possibilities in the rhetorical situation is shown by the phenomenal success of the letters when they appeared and by the appeal they have had for readers ever since. Anyone coming to them for the first time, provided he has a slight acquaintance with the history of the Jesuits and Jansenists, finds himself quickly drawn into the issues, the arguments, and the passions of the controversy, which seems scarcely dated at all. We never have a sense of letdown; on finishing one letter we look forward to the next. Even for Pascal the project seems to have had a life of its own. At several points he hints that

the series is about to end, but some new question or external event propels him and us onward.

It is only on reflection and rereading that one appreciates the astonishing diversity of means Pascal drew on to achieve his effects. Actually he wrote the *Provinciales* not in one form but in an evolving series of forms, each deriving from an insight into a particular aspect of his task and what that required for treatment. I find in the letters four basic situations or frameworks: (1) an unnamed observer-inquirer reports to a friend in the country (a "provincial") on the disputes at the Sorbonne and on his conversations with several theologians; (2) the same, except the observer talks with only one theologian; (3) the unnamed writer addresses letters (11–16) directly to the Jesuit fathers as a group; and (4) the writer addresses two letters (17–18) to one Jesuit, Père Annat. Each framework leads smoothly into the next; and each has its peculiar advantage: the first for showing— through dialogue—inconsistencies, intrigues, and unworthy motives behind pious facades; the second for arriving at a coherent view of Jesuit moral theory and practice; the third for the anonymous author to defend himself against Jesuit attackers who have been reading his letters and reacting to them publicly; the fourth for proving (Pascal, at least, thought it proved) to Annat that he—one of the principals on the Jesuit side of the dispute—had made written statements that refuted the charges of heresy against the Jansenists.

Each letter in this one-sided correspondence assumes two audiences: the person or persons to whom it is addressed, and Pascal's readers, who are allowed, by the fact of publication, to follow matters being said in private or at least within a fiction of privacy. As the addressees change, as the topics change in consequence, the role that readers are to play changes also. From spectators amused by the antics of some theologians and relieved to learn that the Sorbonne disputes are largely verbal, they are called upon to become moralists as they read about the devices of the casuists, and finally they must act as members of something like a jury, since they have before them evidence for judgments on the question of Jesuit immorality and on the accusation of heresy brought against Arnauld and the Jansenists. And Pascal or, rather, the character he assumes (for he never reveals his identity) develops in a parallel way. At first the detached inquirer with an eye for comic details, he becomes more and more incensed by what he hears and at the end of the tenth letter explodes in indignation; then he formally confronts his opponents and accusers; and at the last he engages in exchanges with Annat that give the effect of being face-to-face.

"Unbroken eloquence is boring," writes Pascal in the *Pensées:* the *Provinciales* show how he avoided that pitfall. They unfold on many levels; and he controls the shadings of tone and varieties of expression needed to encompass them. He is capable of many degrees of irony, seriousness, ridicule, logical analysis, and emotion. His sentences can be short and aphoristic or long, periodic, and cumulative. His transitions are in place but not obtrusive. His sense of the order to be followed in exposition is truly remarkable; he arranges his arguments—as though they were incidents—into logical plots that have beginnings, complications, and surprising, sometimes disconcerting, dénouements.

This is in fact one of the hallmarks of Pascal's way of thinking and writing. His sister Gilberte tells us that when Étienne Pascal taught young Blaise, he sought always to keep him "above his work" and free of absorption in details. The lesson was well learned. In the *Provinciales,* as in the mathematical and physical treatises, we find him approaching every intellectual problem from a certain altitude. Of course he cares a great deal about the texture of what he writes, but he works that out in the light of a leading idea and a clearly seen structure.

Elsewhere in the *Pensées* we read, "True eloquence scorns or disdains eloquence"—of the academic sort, that is. Pascal has no patience with the copiousness and the stylistic ornamentation favored by the admirers of Cicero. His rhetoric has its roots, as we have seen, in geometry rather than in oratory. But whether we study it in the light of the geometrical ideal (that includes in Pascal's case a theory of assent, how the reason and will cooperate in persuasion) or in terms borrowed from a sophisticated traditional textbook like Quintilian's *Institutes of Oratory* (one inevitably discovers in the *Provinciales* many of the devices defined and cataloged by Quintilian), the fact remains that the technical features of Pascal's rhetoric do not finally account for its power. All of the technique comes alive because it is at the service of his extraordinarily quick intelligence and his passion for truth and justice.

THE PENSÉES: FRAGMENTS ON THE CONDITION AND DESTINY OF MAN

The work for which Pascal is best known, one that has had from the first a profound influence on both readers and writers, is the *Pensées.* In them he leaves behind natural science and theological quarrels in order to tell us the truth about man. They are extraordinarily accessible. One can open them at almost any point and find something to admire or remember or disagree with (Pascal does not leave his reader indifferent). But it is still a good idea to keep certain general points in mind as one takes them up.

First, the title: it is not Pascal's. It was given by a group of editors to a collection of extracts from his papers that appeared posthumously in 1670. Pascal had intended to write an apology for the Christian religion, something that would, he hoped, have a good effect on the indifference, skepticism, and hostility toward religion that he found widespread in the upper levels of seventeenth-century French society. From clues he gives in the texts it seems that he meant to cast the work in the form of a series of letters or dialogues. He had seen in the *Provinciales* what he could do along those lines. But he never finished the project, and what we know as his "thoughts" is a collection of about a thousand jottings, notes, reflections, and developments written in preparation for the final task of composition. Thus, although the title indicates the fragmentary nature of the work, it does not suggest the mosaiclike unity that emerges from these bits and pieces when they are studied with attention to Pascal's mental habits and expressed aims.

Second, it is useful to note that Pascal's reflections gravitate toward certain polar ideas. Starting out from the center of an imaginary circle, Pascal often moves along a line of thought concerning humankind in general and the human condition, apart from particular circumstances. At other times, moving at a right angle to the preceding line, he turns to humankind in its social existence: that is, vis-à-vis the categories and conventions of society. Again, he may start out along a line that leads to an encounter of humankind with nature, which is full of surprises for human powers of knowledge. Finally, Pascal turns again and again in the direction of the hidden God, the "Dieu caché," who as author and end of humankind is an object of intense attention. These four directions form a sort of compass that helps us discern and follow the shifts in Pascal's thought as we go from fragment to fragment (or even through one particular fragment).

A third point takes us immediately into analysis of the *Pensées.* Pascal obviously thinks that he is there engaged in constructing proofs. But we must be careful to distinguish between proving and demonstrating. For him, to demonstrate means to think in the manner of geometry; he knows that here such discourse is neither possible (because of the subject matter) nor suitable (because of the reader he has in mind). Instead of a single line of reasoning he offers a large collection of more or less distinct proofs that converge and by that

convergence establish the validity of the conclusion. Early in the first section, which he entitled "Ordre," he indicates that he has two propositions in mind: "that nature—human nature—is corrupt, by nature itself," and "that there is a Redeemer or Repairer of nature, by Scripture." In other words, the proofs for the first proposition will be drawn from a study of human nature as it is, as it shows itself to a candid observer. Only later will Pascal turn to the Bible, when warrant for the second proposition will be presented. Some have criticized him for this choice of strategy, saying that his apology is off-center, and that he should have started with "And God so loved the world that he gave his only begotten son . . . ," that is, with more emphasis on God and Christ, less on humankind. In my view he has chosen his way of beginning so as not to alienate his reader; he wants to lay a natural basis for a coming supernatural structure. When the indifferent or skeptical reader has seen himself as a paradoxical being whose makeup and needs cannot be understood or satisfied by natural means, his attention will be fully engaged and he will listen more readily to what religion has to say.

The next two groups of fragments, entitled "Vanité" and "Misère," show man in his present state of uncertainty and wretchedness. He wants to know the truth, but his powers betray him: his senses are often unreliable; his reason is weak—even when it is not deceived by the senses; and, above all, that "mistress of error," the imagination, substitutes its version of reality for things as they are. The greatest philosopher in the world, Pascal says, if he is standing on a plank above a precipice, will not listen to his reason telling him that he is safe; the plank may be of ample width, but his imagination will prevail. Pascal adds that there are many who cannot even think of such a thing without turning pale and breaking into a sweat. Imagination seems to be a faculty designed expressly for leading us into error.

Pascal turns to life in society and administers another disillusioning lesson. What we would like to think of as fixed and universal principles of goodness and justice vary everywhere: "Three degrees of latitude overturn all of jurisprudence, a meridian determines what is true. . . . It is an amusing sort of justice when its bounds are set by a river; true on this side of the Pyrenees, false on the other" (60).[2] This justice is irrational as well, for theft, incest, the murder of children—and parents—have been considered just in some societies. Actually justice has nothing to do with reason or right. The social order has its origin in usurpation, acts of violence that become acceptable and binding through the power of custom.

Our aspirations toward the true, the good, and the just are bound to be frustrated; and the more or less conscious recognition of this fact explains our taste for all kinds of divertissements, those distractions that keep us from thinking about our essential condition, which is "inconstancy, chagrin, anxiety" (24). Then suddenly Pascal reverses the direction of the argument. The awareness of our plight is an indication of privilege and special dignity. Trees, animals, the physical universe have no such knowledge. Pascal introduces a striking image: "Man is a reed, the weakest in nature, but he is a thinking reed" (200). There is, therefore, greatness in knowing that one is wretched: "It is the wretchedness of a great lord, of a dispossessed king" (116).

In such paradoxes Pascal believed that he had effective means of arousing curiosity and stimulating thought in a reader he assumed to be unfavorably inclined. They start him on a search for further enlightenment and above all for an explanation of the contrarieties of human nature. Eventually they require him to leave the level of common experience on which the apology begins. Pascal appears to have envisaged, as part of his plan, one or more dialogues with some moral philosophers. Although these encounters are not worked out in the *Pensées*, the arguments are summed up at several points. These technical thinkers divide into two groups, Stoics or dogmatists and Epicureans or skeptics. The former exalt man, magnify his capacity for self-control, and assert that he can know God by natural means and then bring his will into conformity with the divine will. The latter depreciate man's powers of knowing and will, and in morality set their sights much lower than their opponents do. The two "sects" of professional moralists tend to make of man respectively an angel or a beast—which is to say that in their opposition to each other they merely restate without solving it the basic problem of human misery and grandeur.

Pascal presents this as a contest, even a war, between the two parties. Everyone must choose a side: the camp of the dogmatists or that of the Pyrrhonian skeptics. There is no escape: whoever suspends judgment and tries to assume a neutral position will be a member par excellence of the latter group. The ensuing oscillation between arguments that stress radical doubt and those that affirm principles ("sentiments") whose certainty is imposed by nature rises to a climax in a famous passage: "What a chimera man is! How novel, how monstrous, how chaotic, how full of contradictions, how prodigious! Judge of all things, feeble earthworm, repository of truth, sink of uncertainty and error, glory and refuse of the universe!" (131).

Attempts to understand and explain the enigma in natural terms must fail. Addressing his reader directly, Pascal comes to the heart of the matter: "Know that man transcends man infinitely. Hear from your master your true condition. . . . Listen to God." We learn then that we have an idea of happiness but are unable to attain it, and have an image of truth but possess mainly falsehood. It is manifest, concludes Pascal, that we existed once in a degree of perfection from which we have fallen. In other words, the enigma is explained by the

[2]All quotations from the *Pensées* are followed by a number in parentheses that indicates not the page number but the fragment number in the Lafuma edition of the *Oeuvres complètes*.

mystery of original sin. As incomprehensible as it is, as shocking as it is to our human sense of justice, that sin with its consequences forces itself on our minds, for "man is more inconceivable without this mystery than this mystery is inconceivable to man" (131).

Whereas the aim of an apologist is by nature practical, this solution may seem to have a dry, theoretical ring to it. It makes possible, however, the transition to the third level of discussion in the *Pensées*. Pascal has moved his reader from common experience and its paradoxes to philosophical experience and its controversies; now he rises to the level of religious experience and the reconciliations that it proposes. Early in the *Pensées* (in the first group of fragments, entitled "Ordre") he says he wants to show that the Christian religion is (1) "vénérable," worthy of respect, because it understands man; (2) "aimable," desirable, because it offers him the promise of the true good, and (3) "vraie," true, because it has marks of truth setting it apart from other religions. These adjectives and the reasons supporting them give us in a succinct form the program for what he says on this third level of the argument. When he takes up the sin of Adam as a principle of explanation, he is obviously at the stage of his plan where Christianity is shown to be venerable in that it knows and has known all along what humans are like and it can explain their present dispossessed state. In what follows it will be clear that he is dealing with the other adjectives and with topics suggested by them; it will not be necessary, I think, to refer specifically to them.

I should like now to analyze in some detail the much-discussed argument of the wager, or "pari." Here matters take a distinctly practical turn, as Pascal treats at some length (five pages) the approaches to faith. Recourse to faith would be unnecessary if God were accessible to natural reason. Differing on this point from Descartes and others in a long tradition, Pascal says emphatically that the existence of God cannot be demonstrated, nor can his na-

ture be known, by the natural operations of our powers. This is so because the precondition of any knowledge is a "proportion" between the knower and the known. A finite knower is capable of knowing the existence and nature of a finite object, because he—like the object known—has a finite existence and nature. But the existence and nature of God are infinite, without limits of any kind. Hence the situation is one of "disproportion" and lack of "rapport" between the human knower and the divine person to be known. The problem resembles the one that arises when man faces out on the two infinites of nature—its unlimited vastness and its unlimited divisibility into smaller and smaller particles: in neither direction is man capable of overcoming the disproportion.

But by faith, says Pascal, man can at least know the existence of God, though knowledge of his nature is reserved for the next life and beatitude. That said, the center of attention shifts to the attitudes that reason may take with regard to faith. Two possibilities come into view: (1) Reason may reject faith as unacceptable; and Pascal's answer (much of the rest of the fragment is cast in dialogue) is that reason is incompetent to make such a judgment. (2) Then reason ought simply to refrain from judging; and Pascal's answer is that the suspension of judgment is a judgment, and a negative one at that. (One recalls his refusal to allow a third position between the dogmatists and the Pyrrhonians.)

It is just here that the wager and its terms and imagery emerge: "God is or he is not. To which view shall we be inclined? . . . at the far end of this infinite distance a game is being played in which heads or tails will turn up. How will you wager?" (418). The interlocutor tries once more to avoid a decision and to stay out of the game. Pascal presses on: the choice is not whether to wager ("You are embarked": willy-nilly on board; in the game) but which way to wager—for or against the existence of God. The argument focuses on the self-interest of the interlocutor: "Let us weigh the gain and loss if you take heads, that God exists . . . if you win, you win everything; and if you lose, you do not lose anything." "That is admirable. Yes, I must wager, but I am perhaps wagering too much."

To deal with that hesitation Pascal engages in a detailed and at times confusing analysis of what is risked, the odds, and the possible rewards. It seems to me that the complexity and force of the argument derive in large part from the fact that Pascal superimposes on the bet a double a fortiori argument. Regarding the odds, he defines two possibilities: (1) one chance of winning vs. one chance of losing; and (2) one chance of winning vs. an infinite number of chances of losing. The a fortiori reasoning here is that it would be attractive to wager if the odds were as indicated in (2), but actually they are as indicated in (1); and so one would be even more attracted to the wager (if you would do it when the odds are relatively unfavorable, you will surely do it when they are quite favorable). Regarding the possible rewards, again Pascal defines two alternatives: (1) one might win two or three lives—a finite amount of life—and (2) one might win "an infinity of life that is infinitely happy." The a fortiori reasoning here is that one would want to bet if the reward were two or three lives, but the possibility before one is in fact that of eternal and infinitely happy life; and so one would be even more attracted to the wager (if you would do it for the lesser reward, you will surely do it for the greater).

Now if we draw into a single statement all the data in the situation, we have something like the following: to bet one life for two or three lives when the odds are one chance of winning out of an infinite number of losing chances would be worth doing, but the wager is much more appealing than that, since one is betting one life for eternal and unlimited happiness when the odds are even—one chance of winning and one chance of losing. Or, to pick up Pascal's words, "And thus our proposition has infinite weight when there is the finite to risk in a game where there are

equal chances of winning or losing, and the prize to win is finite" (418).

Although the interlocutor admits the force of what has been said, he remains perplexed: "my hands are tied, my lips are sealed, I am obliged to wager and I am not free, I am held fast and I am made in such a way that I cannot believe." All that is true, comes the answer, but the point is that this inability to believe comes from the passions: "Since reason inclines you to believe and you cannot, work then not at convincing yourself by more proofs of God but by the diminution of your passions." By passions Pascal means all the desires that attach us to the goods and pleasures of the world. They present a new kind of obstacle to faith. Moral rather than intellectual, it will not respond to reasoning, at least not directly. The solution must be sought in the formation of a new moral state, a new habit of desire, to go along with the new habit of mind that comes from accepting the wager. Now, one acquires a new habit by repeated acts, and that is exactly what Pascal recommends. Act as if you had the habit you want; others have preceded you in this journey; start out as they did: "They behaved as if they believed, taking holy water, having masses said, and so on. That will make you believe and will make you more receptive." Pascal said literally and with a vivid image, "That will make you like an animal," by which he appears to mean: you will act without thinking, mechanically, as animals do.

In one of his closing remarks Pascal goes so far as to say that his partner in this little dialogue will finally realize that he has bet on something certain and infinite for which he has given nothing. It is useful to keep in mind that Pascal uses the words "Infini rien" (Infinite nothing) as a title at the beginning of the fragment; and four lines later he writes, "the finite is annihilated in the presence of the infinite and becomes pure nothingness." The title and the principle explain still another a fortiori argument that is built into the wager, one that applies to what is risked—the way of life of the wagerer. In the presence of the infinite that finite existence is relativized to the vanishing point. The argument then runs as follows: if you are willing to give up something finite for an infinite gain, you will surely be willing to give up nothing for it!

Several things should be kept in mind as one ponders fragment 418. One is that Pascal did not include it in the ensemble of fragments he classified under chapter headings, and that suggests some reservations about it on his part. The virtuosity and complexity of the reasoning, the use of the language of gambling, and the bald appeal to the self-interest of the interlocutor have disturbed some commentators. (Voltaire, for example, found the text "puerile" and "indecent.") It may be pointed out that the wager is obviously designed to get and hold the attention of a particular character—a skeptic who enjoys gambling (Pascal knew such people); there is no reason to suppose that this presentation is intended for everyone. In the second place the wager comes at a particular point in a spiritual itinerary. To accept it does not mean that one has reached the summit of religious experience or commitment. Later on, when the seeker has made more progress, he will see the significance of the argument as only a means to a further end.

Whatever one's judgment of the fragment may be, the fact remains that in it Pascal reveals some absolutely fundamental points about his understanding of the dynamics of religious conversion: (1) The mission of the apologist is not to bring about faith—that must be a gift from God—but to remove obstacles to faith. (2) The obstacles are of two sorts: those connected with the reason and those centering in the powers of desire. (3) Reason and desire tend to go their own separate ways, along their natural lines of operation. (4) The task of the apologist is to reorient them away from their uncoordinated concerns with the self and with the world; and to do this in such a fashion that the innate tendencies to seek the true and the good are turned in the direc-

tion of the True and the Good (God combines both). (5) In order to effect this change, the apologist will suit his means to the obstacle in question, offering reasons to the reason and proposing a habit to the heart. (6) When the two tendencies are directed to the same object (and thus harmonized), the reader is in a posture that invites the inspiration of faith.

Pascal writes in fragment 808 that there are three "moyens de croire," means or ways that lead to belief: reason, custom (or habit), and inspiration. As apologist he addresses himself directly to the first, indirectly to the second (since all he can do is to explain how habituation occurs), and the third is up to God. He continues, with beautiful concision:

> Christianity, which alone has reason, does not admit as its true children those who believe without inspiration. It is not that it excludes reason and habit, quite the contrary, but we must open our minds to the proofs, confirm ourselves in them through habit, while offering ourselves through humiliations to inspiration, which alone can produce the real and salutary effect. Lest the Cross of Christ be emptied of its power.
>
> (1 Corinthians)

In the light of the inferences that one may draw from the fragment on the wager and in the light of the text just quoted, the effect of confusion that one feels at first as one moves through an edition of the *Pensées* is lessened. The lack of continuity becomes less disconcerting, and the hundreds of fragments begin to present themselves as variations—some elaborate, some succinct as telegrams—on a tightly connected set of basic themes.

Pascal promised at the outset of the *Pensées* to show two things: that human nature is corrupt, by evidence drawn from human nature itself; and that there is a Redeemer, by evidence drawn from Scripture. Reacting to the demonstration laid before him in the wager, the imagined interlocutor asks a question that leads to reflection on the second of these propositions: "Is there any way to see the underside, the hidden part of the game?" "Yes, Scripture and the rest, etc.," Pascal replies.

Pascal as an interpreter of the Bible is a large subject. In this essay I should like to approach it in terms of something already apparent. Pascal's favorite mode of thinking in the *Pensées* is dialectical. Important problems always present themselves to his mind as antitheses, and he deals with these oppositions, contrarieties, and contradictions in two ways: by developing them and making them more striking, and by introducing some comprehensive term that unifies them, thus working through what might be called the negative and positive phases of his method.

Human nature furnishes an excellent example. It appears to him as made up of contrasting aspects, with concupiscence and wretchedness on one side and pride or illusory greatness on the other. In dozens of fragments he draws our attention to one or the other of these—or to both simultaneously—until we feel puzzled and uncomfortable. We want to know why it is thus with man and what can be done about it. At that point Pascal introduces the mystery of original sin, a principle that makes the contradictions intelligible and gives a certain unity to a being otherwise inexplicably divided against itself. Of course, he has an even more decisive positive principle: God. When human pride and concupiscence (the contradictory pulls upward and downward) are directed away from creatures—from the self and the world—toward God, the argument moves onto a plane where a resolution may be found. In the effective presence of God, pride and concupiscence are transformed into their positive counterparts, humility and penitence, and the tension disappears. Or again, note what happens when Pascal discusses external nature. It presents itself to him as an endless scale of beings and collections of beings that extend from the infinitely small of submicroscopic particles to the infinitely large of the stellar universe. He locates man somewhere in the middle of this scale as a knower curious about the extremes of na-

ture, but forever excluded from any knowledge of them, for they are out of proportion to him. He cannot know with certainty even what he finds in the medium-sized masses that surround him, for really to know the near middle requires a grasp of the distant extremes. This negative situation is resolved, however: "These extremities touch and join by dint of moving in opposite directions, and meet in God and in God alone" (199). Thus, in some sense, God is both infinitely large and infinitely small, as he is both revealed and hidden, just and merciful—and in Christ, human and divine.

When Pascal takes up the Bible, it falls at once into two opposed parts, Old and New Testament. The Jews, sole custodians of the sacred book for centuries, defend the Old Testament; to the Christians that is only the beginning, and without the New Testament the account is fatally incomplete. Clearly this discontinuity must be resolved. The absence of a true link between the testaments would entail the breakdown of Pascal's whole undertaking, for on that supposition he has no Christian, that is, Messiah-centered, religion to defend. The Old Testament abounds in testimonies to the weakness and corruption of human nature and to the need for some superhuman redemption of the race—that much of his case is supported by the Bible; but what if the prophecies were never fulfilled?

Pascal takes this to be essentially a problem of interpretation, and he is quite aware of the exegetical principles he intends to bring into play: "Every author has a sense in which all contradictory passages agree or he makes no sense at all. One cannot say that of Scripture and the prophets: they are certainly too sensible. We must therefore look for a sense that reconciles all the contradictions" (257). There he indicates his strategy. Here is his tactical rule: "Two errors: (1) to take everything literally, (2) to take everything spiritually" (252). In other words, since the text cannot be changed, modify and adapt the sense. Pascal does not see himself as introducing these rules from the outside: since the texts themselves hint or speak of hidden senses, parts of the Bible may be thought of as enciphered messages. Nor does he think he is the first to do the deciphering. That was done by Christ and the Apostles: "They removed the seal. They rent the veil and revealed the spirit" (260). They taught us, continues Pascal, summarizing the main themes of the Old Testament and their figurative meaning, that the true enemies of man are internal—the passions—and not external; that there would be two comings, one in lowliness and not in triumph, and the second in glory to exalt the humble; and that the Christ would be both man and God: "Thus the true sense is not that of the Jews, but in Christ all contradictions are reconciled" (257). This way of proving that the prophecies were accomplished and that the New Testament is the culmination of the Old relies on the familiar negative and positive devices of Pascalian dialectic. There is, however, an interesting novelty. The process of reconciliation requires that the reworking of the original terms so as to give positive counterparts be carried out only on the Old Testament passages; to Pascal it would be unthinkable to take the New Testament figuratively.

There is a great deal of evidence in the Pensées that Pascal had in mind a definite itinerary for his reader. As I have suggested, it would start from indifference (if not actual hostility) to religion, and it would pass through a series of stages and insights: the recognition of the vanity of human doings and aspirations; the perception of human dignity as implied in the knowledge of self and of nature; astonishment at the contradictions of human nature, followed by understanding as the sense of original sin imposes itself; the development of a positive mental attitude toward faith; the addition of moral discipline to bring the passions under control; and continuing enlightenment from Scripture. The task Pascal set for himself is broad, varied, and ambitious. He approached it with confidence, but from the outset he was aware of its final limitation. It could never give faith; it could only prepare the way for the unpredictable working of inspiration, the third means to belief. Unless and until that came, all that preceded—though it might be supported by proofs—could not be certain.

Pascal refers directly to inspiration several times in the Pensées, but nowhere do we get a better grasp of what the term meant for him than in the Mémorial, the documents that record his experience of 23 November 1654. On the original paper (Pascal later wrapped it in a piece of parchment on which he had copied the text of the original) he wrote, after the date and times, the word "feu" (fire). There follow twenty-six lines of phrases and words related to what happened, including some short quotations from the Bible.

In its ecstatic aspect the experience seems to have been marked by an awareness of the presence of God, the "God of Abraham, Isaac, and Jacob, not of the philosophers and scholars." There are two references to the "God of Jesus Christ" as well as four mentions of Jesus Christ alone. In a period of complete forgetfulness of the world, Pascal somehow knew God and received from him a communication. His reaction to what happened is described as certainty—heartfelt and immediate certainty—joy, and peace. But he undergoes moments of distress and anxiety, as he recalls that he had separated himself from God and had crucified Christ; twice he prays that he may never be separated from them again. He has an intuition of what eternal life is: to know God and the one sent by God, Jesus Christ. The text ends with expressions of resolve for the future: total renunciation, total submission to Christ and to his spiritual director. There is a sentence in fragment 449 in which Pascal seems almost to be writing a commentary on his experience:

But the God of Abraham, the God of Isaac, the God of Jacob, the God of the Christians is a God of love and consolation: he is a God who fills the soul and heart of those whom he possesses; he is a God who makes them inwardly aware of their wretchedness and his infinite mercy; who unites himself with them in the depths of their soul; who fills it with humility, joy, confidence, and love; who makes them incapable of having any other end but him.

UNIFYING ELEMENTS IN PASCAL'S THOUGHT

If one desires, in conclusion, a general view of Pascal's intellectual and artistic discoveries, I can think of no better place to turn than to the opening of fragment 308: "The infinite distance between bodies and minds symbolizes the infinitely more infinite distance between minds and charity, for charity is supernatural." In this one sentence Pascal reveals the scope and content of his universe. He sees three orders of reality: bodies, minds, charity; the three are utterly different, separated by unbridgeable distances, but they have figurative or analogical relations to each other. After distinguishing them radically, even violently, Pascal still wants to hold them together; in fact they arrange themselves along a scale. A diversity of beings or states asserting themselves in a universe marked by discontinuity, analogy, and hierarchy: such seems to be the synoptic view at which Pascal finally arrived.

The metaphysical sense of the distinction is completed by its moral implications. Pascal makes them explicit in three symmetrically constructed sentences: "All the splendor of worldly greatness has no luster for those engaged in the pursuits of the mind. The greatness of intellectual people is invisible to kings, rich men, captains, who are all great in a carnal sense. The greatness of wisdom, which is nothing if it does not come from God, is invisible to carnal or intellectual people. They are three orders, differing in kind." People may be classified according to the plane on which their interests and activities center, and those living on a lower level cannot grasp the values and achievements proper to those who live on the plane or planes above them. What great minds do (Pascal mentions Archimedes) is invisible to kings and captains; and the greatness of saints and of Jesus Christ eludes those who inhabit the two lower orders.

Thus the notion of the three orders allows Pascal to establish three main classes of people according to their determining trait or tendency. But he can take a further step with it, since no one is merely body or mind or spirit. The schematism applies in toto to everyone individually: every one of us has by nature the three aspects, and every one of us is a theater in which these tendencies work out their interrelationships. Their proper order is found in the hierarchy that Pascal assumes. Since we cannot suppress the lower orders, the perfection both of body and of mind must consist in being subordinated to the order above it. Now we can see at a glance the itinerary that Pascal was proposing to his reader in the *Pensées*. Like a rising line it ascends through each of the lower domains, ordering partial truths and goods as it goes, until it reaches the top order, which is open to grace.

To the three realities—corporeal, intellectual, and spiritual—correspond three powers of knowing: sense, mind (or reason), and heart. The mind, when it works in its most characteristic domain, that of quantity and geometry, adopts a procedure that is axiomatic, propositional, and linear. It can also turn down to the level of bodies and engage in another though closely related kind of discourse, as it measures and correlates natural phenomena. The heart, aided by reason but having its proper reasons ("Le coeur a ses raisons que la raison ne connaît point": 423), is at once the target and the source of an art of persuasion that regulates the use of language in apologetic and other rhetorical situations; it starts and ends in insights and immediate feelings. The reasons of the heart constitute the devices and principles of a dialectic that moves easily from level to level. For example, Pascal can be sure in his heart of the truth of notions such as space and number; then, descending, he arrives at the level of mind, where these two concepts are elaborated into geometry and arithmetic; he may then continue downward to the plane of bodies, where they are applied to data obtained in experiments. Or, in morality, by a movement in the opposite direction, his thought may be directed upward; then the contradictions found in the opinions and actions of carnal men lead him to the causes behind those effects: pride and concupiscence, perceived on the level of mind; but the true explanation is to be found only on the level of the heart and in the story of Adam's sin. Perhaps one should make explicit the fourth order or degree, that of the transcendent God, who is the beginning and end of all the rest. In the face of all that is scattered, unfinished, and fragmentary in Pascal's works it is useful to note such patterns and movements that draw the various lines of his thought into a single, coherent perspective.

CONTINUING INTEREST IN PASCAL

Pascal's diverse achievements rank in quality with the best work done in his century, a time when intellectual and artistic genius was present and active in many fields. His mathematical work bears comparison with that of Descartes and Fermat. His understanding of the experimental method and his inventive applications of it to the behavior of liquids remind us of Galileo's pioneering experiments with solids and their motions. Living in a period when the theater was beginning to dominate literature, he has, like Molière, a satirical eye, a talent for dialogue, and a dramatic imagination; like Racine, he sees a strong probability of tragedy in the contradictions of the human mind and heart. He came to believe that the only science *for* man was the science *of* man; and the great moralists, La Rochefoucauld and La Bruyère, seem to us to be working in his shadow as they compose reflections and portraits. As an apologist for the Christian religion he surpasses all of his contemporaries. He argues not only from a wide range of common human experience but also from moral philosophy, from the opposed tenets of the Stoic and Epicurean schools, both influential in the seventeenth century and both transcended in Pascal's treatment. In theology he takes his stand upon the Jansenist strain of Augustinianism, and there, if the themes are not new, the manner of elaboration and expression is unmistakably his own. "Let it not be said," he remarks in fragment 696, "that I have said nothing new; the disposition of the material is new; in playing tennis both players use the same ball, but one places it better."

With the passage of time Pascal's mathematical and physical works have blended into the history of science; they now have relatively few readers apart from specialists. But the *Provinciales* have always been read, if only as models of style and form in controversy; and every age has encountered the Pascal of the *Pensées* and communed with him in its way. For almost two centuries his image was fixed by the first edition of 1670, which consisted unfortunately of no more than a selection from the total corpus of fragments; and furthermore the editors had not hesitated to amend those texts. Still, the *Pensées* were never ignored. Apparently Voltaire found them an irritant difficult to dispose of. In 1729 and again in 1777 he expressed his judgment. He called Pascal "a sublime misanthrope" and summed up his view as follows: "He was a geometrician and he was eloquent; the combination of those two merits was rare then; but to them he did not add true philosophy," that is to say, the deistic philosophy of the Enlightenment. D'Alembert, the encyclopedist, choosing his words carefully, as if a censor were looking over his shoulder, wrote that Pascal was a "universal and sublime genius whose talents could not be regretted enough by philosophy, if religion had not profited from them."

The religious renaissance that was an essential part of romanticism brought with it a new appreciation of Pascal. In fact the nineteenth century is studded with the names of eminent readers and admirers of Pascal. In 1802 Chateaubriand composed a glowing tribute that was tinged with awe as he summarized all that Pascal accomplished in his thirty-nine years; he concluded by calling him "cet effrayant génie" (this frightening genius). Sainte-Beuve, measurer of men and talents, saw in Pascal the perfection of a human understanding that is set off against the universe, aware of both its dignity and its fragility; and it must search until it finds the only key: faith, "Dieu sensible au coeur" (God perceived by the heart). In Germany Schleiermacher said that Pascal was the most profound of all French thinkers. At the end of the century (1897) Renouvier asserted that "Pascal has become an author of our time." In 1919 Valéry saluted in Pascal one of the greatest minds that ever lived, but reproached him for "sewing papers in his pockets [a reference to the *Mémorial*] when the time was ripe to give France the glory of the infinitesimal calculus." Unamuno recognized in Pascal the Spaniard's tragic sense of life; he alleged that "we Spaniards understand perfectly and no doubt better than the French what Pascal meant in saying, 'Il faut s'abêtir.'" By this phrase, which occurs near the end of the fragment on the "pari," Pascal enjoins the unbeliever to humble himself and, specifically, to add to the proofs of reason the disipline of habitual devotions.

Recent years have seen the emergence of a Pascal whose dialectical way of thinking makes of him a precursor of Hegel and Marx, and a stop on the way to the socialist revolution; there have been also the more plausible interpretations of the existentialists (who find it easy to connect their themes of anxiety and commitment with the vocabulary and ideas of Pascal) and of the linguistically based structuralists (whose analytical tools sometimes lead to insights into his habit of language that are otherwise difficult to come by).

A universal author is in part what he is and in part what he is said to be. A striking thing for us about the Pascal of the *Pensées* is that for so long the objective element in that equation—what he is—has been obscured and, until recent years, subject to serious misunderstanding. For more than a century and a half he was a prisoner of the 1670 edition of the *Pensées* as augmented and reworked by various editors. The task of freeing him from the limits imposed by that edition has occupied scholars ever since 1842, when Victor Cousin called for a return to the manuscripts and for a complete and accurate edition. In response to that appeal they have addressed themselves in turn to the corpus of fragments as bound in the *Recueil original,* then to the first and finally to the second of the so-called *Copies,* all of which are preserved in the Bibliothèque Nationale in Paris. As a result of their labors (especially in the last thirty years) we are in a better position than any preceding generation of readers to distinguish the different lines of thought in the fragments, to understand the apologetic project to which the majority of them belong, to appreciate the varying degrees of elaboration that Pascal attained in composing them, and to relate them to the rest of his works. The problem with the *Pensées* has always been twofold: to recover and decipher as many texts as possible, and to put them in an intelligible order. The collection now appears essentially complete; and the problem of order, which for so long seemed to depend on the principles and preferences of editors, has in great measure disappeared. There is good reason to think that the two *Copies* indicate the state of Pascal's papers at the time of his death, and that the second of the two reproduces the way in which Pascal himself had classified and ordered them.

He can now, therefore, make himself understood more clearly and fully than ever before, and we as readers have a renewed stimulus to seek him on his own terrain in the *Pensées* and to attempt an adequate account of this unfinished masterpiece. In so doing we shall find ourselves linked in our fashion to something that is at the center of Pascal's achievement: an unyielding effort to honor the truth—in mathematics and physics, by demonstrating it; in religion, by preparing himself to receive it, by separating it from error, by undertaking to spread it, and, in his last days, by striving to exemplify it totally in his life.

Selected Bibliography

EDITIONS OF INDIVIDUALS WORKS

Traité de l'équilibre des liqueurs et de la pesanteur de la masse d'air. Edited by J. Payen. Paris, 1963. Excerpts.

Les provinciales, ou les lettres écrites par Louis de Montalte à un provincial de ses amis et aux RR. PP. Jésuites. Edited by Louis Cognet. Paris, 1965. Recommended.

Pensées de M. Pascal sur la religion, et sur quelques autres sujets. Edited by Georges Couton and Jean Jehasse. Saint-Étienne, 1972. Reprint of first edition of 1670.

Pensées. Edited by P. Sellier. Paris, 1976. Follows the Second Copy as closer than the First Copy to Pascal's intentions. Highly recommended.

COLLECTED EDITIONS

Oeuvres. Edited by Léon Brunschvicg. 14 vols. Paris, 1908–1921. Monumental critical edition. The *Pensées* are put in logical order.

Oeuvres complètes. Edited by Jacques Chevalier. Paris, 1954. Readable one-volume edition. The *Pensées* are ordered according to the plan proposed by Filleau de la Chaise, whose *Discours sur les "Pensées" de M. Pascal* (1672) is reprinted in the notes.

————. Edited by L. Lafuma. Paris, 1963. Less readable than the Chevalier edition, but more up to date in scholarship. Presents the *Pensées* in order of the First Copy of the manuscripts. Recommended.

————. Edited by Jean Mesnard. 2 vols. Bruges, 1964–1970. Includes documents and works to 1654; appears to be replacing the Brunschvicg edition as the standard.

TRANSLATIONS

The Physical Treatises of Pascal: The Equilibrium of Liquids and the Weight of the Mass of the Air. Translated by I. H. B. Spiers and A. G. H. Spiers. New York, 1937. Reprinted 1969. Introduction and notes by Frederick Barry.

Pensées; The Provincial Letters. Translated by W. F. Trotter (*Pensées*) and Thomas M'Crie (*The Provincial Letters*). New York, 1941. The *Pensées* are given in the order and numbering of the Brunschvicg edition.

Great Shorter Works of Pascal. Translated and introduced by Émile Cailliet and J. C. Blankenagel. Philidelphia, 1948.

"Pascal." In *Great Books of the Western World*, edited by R. M. Hutchins and M. J. Adler. Vol. 33. Chicago, 1952. Contains the M'Crie translation of the *Provincial Letters*, the Trotter translation of the *Pensées* (in the Brunschvicg ordering), and selections from the Richard Scofield translation of the scientific writings. Handy collection for readers of Pascal in translation.

Pensées. Translated by A. J. Krailsheimer. London, 1966. Recommended. Follows the order and numbering of the Lafuma edition.

BIOGRAPHICAL AND CRITICAL STUDIES

Béguin, A. *Pascal par lui-même: Images et textes.* Paris, 1967.

Broome, J. H. *Pascal.* New York, 1966.

Costabel, P., et al. *L'Oeuvre scientifique de Pascal.* Paris, 1965.

Croquette, Bernard. *Pascal et Montaigne: Étude des réminiscences des "Essais" dans l'oeuvre de Pascal.* Geneva, 1974.

Davidson, Hugh M. *The Origins of Certainty: Means and Meanings in Pascal's "Pensées."* Chicago, 1979.

Gounelle, A. *La Bible selon Pascal.* Paris, 1970.

Guenancia, P. *Du vide à Dieu: Essai sur la physique de Pascal.* Paris, 1976.

Le Guern, Michel. *Pascal et Descartes.* Paris, 1971.

Mesnard, J. *Pascal.* Paris, 1967. Highly recommended.

—————. *Les "Pensées" de Pascal.* Paris, 1976. Highly recommended.

Miel, J. *Pascal and Theology.* Baltimore, 1969.

Mortimer, Ernest. *Blaise Pascal: The Life and Work of a Realist.* London, 1959.

Pol, E. *Approches pascaliennes.* Gembloux, 1970.

Rex, W. *Pascal's "Provincial Letters": An Introduction.* London, 1977.

Sellier, P. *Pascal et Saint Augustin.* Paris, 1970.

Taton, R. "Pascal." In *Dictionary of Scientific Biography,* edited by Charles C. Gillispie. Vol. 10, pp. 330–342. New York, 1974. Clear and authoritative article.

Topliss, Patricia. *The Rhetoric of Pascal.* Leicester, 1966.

HUGH M. DAVIDSON

JACQUES BÉNIGNE BOSSUET
(1627–1704)

A S A STUDENT of theology at the Collège de Navarre in Paris, the young Bossuet made the acquaintance of his father's old friend the marquis de Feuquières, governor of Verdun and military general of Metz. Feuquières was fond of boasting of his young protégé's speaking ability and claimed that the lad could give an extemporaneous talk on any given religious subject, without notes or references, that would surpass anything the average priest could deliver from the Sunday pulpit. Feuquières's proposition was of such novelty as to appeal to the Hôtel de Rambouillet, one of the most brilliant literary salons of the day. Thus the young theological student was summarily fetched and asked to preach before an assembly of the most fashionable and literary—if not the most pious—congregation upon a sacred subject, selected for him with no devout end but simply as a dramatic curiosity. Bossuet's eloquence was well-received and soon after he gave an improvisation at the Hôtel de Vendôme, at the bidding of the bishop of Lisieux. This time the youth confronted, in a more suitable manner, a select audience of bishops; and instead of a flood of exaggerated, empty compliments, Monseigneur Phillippe Cospéan (Cospeau), doctor at the Sorbonne, gave Bossuet much profitable advice about how to conduct himself in society and took him under his wing.

What is interesting about these curious episodes is that they foreshadow the success Bossuet would have throughout his life both in satisfying the expectations of court patrons—not so much by his words as by his rhetorical, at times theatrical, skill—and in edifying devout members of the clergy more interested in his message, notwithstanding that they, too, were impressed by this same power of rhetoric. It would seem, even though he was still a youth, that the fulfillment of these two aspirations—pleasing the court and guiding Christian devotion—characterizes Bossuet's public career and points to all that was to come.

THE EARLY YEARS

Jacques Bénigne Bossuet was born on 27 September 1627, son of a prominent lawyer and member of the Parlement of Dijon. He was the seventh child and the fifth son of ten. Burgundians were known as matter-of-fact people with strong wills and hearty appetites. Two epigrams, one French and one Latin, punning on the name Bossuet, illustrate the soberness and obstinacy as well as the wiliness of this family of staunch Catholics: "Bois bossu est bon" (Crooked wood is good) and "Bos suetus aratro" (The ox ploughs steadily along).

Young Jacques received the tonsure at the age of eight from Sébastien Zamet, bishop of Langres, a family relation. This tonsure was not the sign of a minor order; it simply enabled him to receive benefices at a later date.

Indeed, on 20 November 1640 he was nominated to be canon of Metz. This wise investment by a prudent father qualified him to acquire the revenues of the canonry and involved no religious obligations.

In 1642 Bossuet went from the Collège des Godrans, a Jesuit school, to the Collège de Navarre, one of the annexes of the University of Paris. It has been remarked that Bossuet had a "precocious vocation" for the priesthood, due in part to the love of learning he manifested at an early age. In January 1648 he received his degree. His thesis, "Existence and Attributes of God and the Immortality of the Soul," was dedicated to and presented before Louis de Bourbon, prince de Condé, former governor of Burgundy and a patron of the Bossuet family. The most celebrated soldier of his day, the Grand Condé attended the ceremony surrounded by his military suite.

It should not be assumed that for Bossuet the priesthood was merely a career laid out for him. Like all young men on the verge of making such a formidable commitment, Bossuet had his moments of doubt concerning his vocation. A turning point was reached soon after his graduation from college. He was making a retreat in preparation for the subdeaconship when he experienced a spiritual moment much like Blaise Pascal's "night of fire." He weighed the instability of human affairs against the promise of eternity and, in an articulate piece of writing—the "Méditations sur la brièveté de la vie" ("Meditations on the Brevity of Life")—recorded his anguish and his resolutions. It was a milestone and showed that, at that time, the greatest conflict in his life was the one taking place within himself.

Bossuet was ordained as subdeacon at Langres in 1648 and twelve months later as deacon at Metz. In order to obtain the license it was necessary to defend three theses, the last being "la sorbonnique," defended, as the name indicates, at the Sorbonne. Bossuet ran the risk of rejection when he faced the doctors on 9 November 1650, not for want of learning, but for being involved in one of those inter-college feuds traditional in Paris. The prior of the Sorbonne presided, and it was customary to address him as "dignissime domine prior" (most dignified lord prior). Following the instructions of Nicolas Cornet, the "grand maître de Navarre," Bossuet used the term "doctissime" (most learned) in lieu of "dignissime." The prior stopped the session at once, and a dispute broke out among the doctors of the Sorbonne and those of Navarre. The squabble was not settled until the parlement stepped in; it was agreed that Bossuet had acted under instructions, and his thesis was eventually accepted. He was third on the list of successful candidates. At the head was Armand de Rancé, godson of Cardinal Richelieu, who became a lifelong friend of Bossuet. The second was none other than the prior whom Bossuet had slighted. Irony and controversy appear side by side in many of the significant affairs of Bossuet's life. He managed to side-step any further obstacles and was ordained on 18 March 1652. On 16 May of that year he received his doctorate and was ready to exercise his calling.

The teaching at the Collège de Navarre seems to have been thorough but unenterprising. Scholasticism had lost its hold, and there was a movement away from medieval thought back to the teachings of the church fathers. Linked to this study of the fathers was the growing attraction of historical research. One of the lecturers at the college, Jean de Launoy, dared to question the truth of some of the legends of the saints and the authenticity of documents that had long been thought genuine. This novel scientific treatment of historical evidence was to have considerable influence on Bossuet's studies; from this method he learned the importance of going back to original sources and of basing arguments on authoritative proof.

The emphasis on the fathers had another consequence. Bossuet noted at that time that Nicolas Cornet esteemed Saint Augustine as "the most enlightened, and most profound of the doctors of the Church." It was to Augustine that Bossuet turned again and again throughout his life. Although Bossuet was devoted to learning, he did not become a bookish recluse. He made a point of contacting other scholars in Paris and of acquainting himself with intellectual society through a relative, François, clerk of the council of state. It has also been suggested that Bossuet made the rounds at the theater and in fashionable circles with his friends Rancé and Michel Le Tellier, but it is not likely that these excursions were anything more than ordinary divertissements for a healthy young man.

From an examination of these early years, it is apparent that Bossuet possessed a vigorous mind, logical, precise, and with an instinctive dislike of the vague, doubtful, and morbid. He was an essentially good man with enough ingenuousness to be taken in by the wiles of self-seekers like his two nephews, Louis and the abbé Jacques-Bénigne, who exploited his fame. He had no liking for coteries or fashions, still less for anything eccentric or newfangled.

One can only think that Bossuet was painting himself in the "Panégyrique de Saint-Bernard" (Panegyric on Saint Bernard), as he portrays the young saint's impatience and inner conflict in a highly personal tone:

> Should I describe to you what a young man of twenty-two is like—his ardor, his impatience, the impetuousness of his desires? Such strength, such vigor, such hot-bloodedness, like mulled wine, does not allow for anything stale or moderate. . . . This verdant youth is violently agitated by all the passions: luxury, infatuation, ambition, and the vanity of outward things exercise their empire without resistance. Everything is done impulsively. How can discipline and love of solitude be acquired at an age that takes pleasure only in restlessness and disorder and never in composed and ordered action? . . . We see everything according to our dispositions in such a way that youth seems to be formed only for joy and pleasure; everyone laughs with it, all applaud. Youth has had no traffic with the evils of the world, nor with the difficulties that will arrive soon enough. Because of this, youth cannot imagine that there is disgrace and disgust in store for it. How strong and vigorous is youth! It banishes fear and tends its sails to the wind, full blown with the hope that swells and guides them.
>
> (Oraisons funèbres et panégyriques, Velat ed., p. 296)

Here, at an early age, we have Bossuet estimating life before entering into it. He had an almost judicial rationality that caused him to pass sentence on ideas. His lyrical effusion enhanced this evaluative tendency by considering its opposite effect. This combination of capacities is a major trademark of his style.

Bossuet's readings of the works of Pierre Bérulle, founder of the French Oratory, and of Saint Augustine, and above all his meeting with Saint Vincent de Paul, add the finishing touches to the portrait of this worthy and dedicated priest about to begin his public ministry.

THE PASSAGE INTO MATURITY

Before his ordination Bossuet spent ten days in retreat at Saint-Lazare under the direction of Saint Vincent de Paul. It may have been Nicolas Cornet who brought the two together, but Sébastien Zamet, another friend of "Monsieur Vincent," also supported Bossuet's work. It was probably soon after Bossuet became a deacon that he began to attend the "Conférences des mardis" (Tuesday Conferences) at which priests and those studying for orders met under Vincent's direction for instruction and discussion.

Vincent promulgated a doctrine of "une parole simple, évangelique et directe" (simple speech, evangelical and direct). He was strongly opposed to "clever" sermons. From the fragments of Bossuet's early sermons that have survived, it seems that at first they were highly theological, like those of many young priests fresh from seminary. Under Vincent's influence Bossuet strove to deliver his message in language that ordinary folk could understand. Bossuet began to sign his letters "prêtre indigne" (unworthy priest) and he cultivated the "charitable initiatives" suggested by John Chrysostom, the great church father. But although the influence of Saint Vincent de Paul was direct and personal, and although Bossuet as a pastoral bishop never lost his respect for the "eminent dignity of the poor," Bossuet was never a popular preacher. A popular audience would have forced him to restrain his natural eloquence, his sense of style, and his imaginative power. So it was that he sought out the great congregations of the fashionable world who filled famous churches to hear him preach.

After his ordination, Bossuet departed for Metz to assume his duties as canon, despite a position at the Collège de Navarre offered him by Nicolas Cornet. It seems likely that Bossuet wanted to join his parents, who had settled there in 1638. After fourteen years, it must have been a pleasure to enjoy family life again.

Metz was an outpost of France in the independent duchy of Lorraine. During the Thirty Years' War, Lorraine was hotly contested, and the peasantry had been reduced to destitution. The fortified town of Metz was the refuge of a mixed population with a high percentage of Protestants and Jews. Bossuet lived at Metz for four years. He had already made a name for himself as a preacher, and some scraps of his Metz sermons have been preserved. One theme occurs frequently—the duty of all Christians to help the poor and needy. This theme came partly from his association with Saint Vincent de Paul, but no sensitive man, let alone a priest, could have shut his eyes to the poverty that surrounded him. While Louis XIV pursued glory, misery stalked the land, and help for the poor came mainly from the church.

One example of Bossuet's appeals for charity is his sermon preached on the feast of Saint Francis of Assisi in October 1652:

No, no, you rich people—it is not only for you that God makes the sun to rise, and sends rain on the earth, and provides such a variety of crops; the poor have their share in these things as much as you. It is true that God has not given them any property, but He grants them their sustenance out of your riches. It is not that He could not support them in any other way, He under whose governance the very beasts of the field do not lack food; nor is His arm shortened, nor His treasure spent, but He wishes you to have the glory of helping your fellow men. Indeed, what a glory that is, O Christians, if you would only realize it! So, far from despising the poor you should respect them, and think of them as human beings entrusted to your care by God.
(Velat ed., p. 270)

It can be seen from this passage that Bossuet expressed himself with a certain sentimental sincerity.

In 1653 the French parlement was besieged by rebel troops who had collaborated with the Spanish army. Condé, who deserted the royal army after Anne of Austria, the queen regent, had Louis XIV crowned, led this revolt, which was called the Fronde of the Princes because the princes of royal blood had demanded an end to the civil war. During the seige of Metz, Condé's representative demanded a high ransom for the town, and Bossuet was chosen as a member of a delegation to negotiate terms. When the negotiations failed, Bossuet insisted on seeing Condé himself. Bossuet, of course, could be loyal only to the king, and Condé was a traitor. The encounter was successful in that a smaller ransom was exacted. Perhaps Condé had some qualms when he met this representative of a Burgundian family that he had always respected.

During his years at Metz Bossuet was faced with the problem of trying to convert Protestants and Jews. Saint Vincent de Paul's general disposition toward Protestants was far more ecumenical than that of most hard-line Catholic ecclesiastics; he treated them with "a loyal charity." The effect on Bossuet was to make the unity of the church the major theme of his apostolic teaching throughout his life; it dominated his writing and preaching. The friendly relations established by Bossuet's father with Paul Ferry, the elderly and greatly respected Huguenot pastor, paved the way for conversations with other leading Huguenots.

In 1654 Ferry published a catechism for the members of the reformed religion. His idea, put forth in the traditional sermon on Holy Saturday, was that salvation could no longer be obtained by Roman Catholics as of 1543, when the Roman church erred in its doctrine of justification. Prior to this pronouncement, most Protestant ministers decreed that salvation was possible, though difficult, through the sacrament of confession. Thus Ferry's stand was more militant.

Bossuet analyzed the controversy in his *Refutation of the Catechism of Paul Ferry* (1654), which he dedicated to the governor of Metz, marshal Charles de Schomberg, a devout Catholic and friend of the Bossuet family. This was his first published work. In the *Refutation* he points out, as he also does in later writings, that the church's doctrine had not been altered in 1543 and that the church had always conformed to tradition. He states that the beliefs of the church had been abused by loyalist Protestants who were merely resorting to phantoms.

Bossuet was making his first experiment in a new kind of polemic. Both Catholics and reformers had lost themselves in interminable disputes on trifling points with little bearing on the issues that had originally divided them. The *Refutation* was too slight a production to have wide effect, but Protestant theologians, who at first did not take his new approach seriously, were forced by it to deal with fundamental differences in beliefs; ordinary folk could grasp what Bossuet had to say, and they began to ask questions. Throughout his life, Bossuet's relations with reformers were consistent: he respected their learning and insisted on keeping the argument on a high level and in civilized terms. The personal vilification that had marred so much of the contro-

versy was absent from his writings. To one Protestant he wrote:

> You believe a part of what I believe, and I cannot regard as false a belief you share with me; but I maintain it is necessary to accept not only part but all that I believe, because all that I believe has been revealed by God, and it is not enough to believe only part of what God has revealed.
>
> (Ernest E. Reynolds, *Bossuet*, p. 34)

He made many converts in Metz, both Protestants and Jews, and long after he left the town he did what he could to help those who, on account of their change of faith, were in difficulties.

Through study of apostolic writings, Bossuet came up against the Jewish question; that is, how best to assess the position of Jews with respect to their historical transformation. At this time the Society for the Propagation of the Faith was founded at Metz by a woman named Clerginet to welcome converted Jews into the Catholic movement and teach the catechism. Bossuet came to know the erudite Jewish community and was instrumental in leading its most prominent members, the Veil brothers, into Catholicism. Through them, Bossuet familiarized himself with the Talmud and began a more realistic study of the Bible. He was neither supple nor subtle in his dealings with Protestants and Jews; his success derived from a rationalistic vigor that was both passionate and clearheaded.

In July 1656 Bossuet went to Paris to carry out his duties as doctor of the Sorbonne—attending defenses, assessing theses, and preaching. He renewed his contacts with other scholars. The absence of learned society in Metz was probably one reason for his gradual withdrawal from the town. The years 1660 and 1661 mark the opening of a new phase in Bossuet's life. His mother's death in 1660 loosened his ties to home. Saint Vincent de Paul died in the same year, followed by Nicolas Cornet two years later. His influence at the Sorbonne steadily increased. He was in demand as a preacher and as director of conferences in monasteries and convents.

Nevertheless, he continued to preach in his parish and divided his time equally between Paris and Metz. After the death of his father in 1667, Bossuet severed his connections with Metz. Furthermore, a new stage in French history was opening. Cardinal Mazarin died in March 1661. The marriage of Louis XIV to Maria Theresa of Spain had confirmed the treaty made with that country. It was the beginning of the most absolute monarchy Europe has ever known.

THE KINGLY PATTERN

Soon after his arrival in Paris on 17 October 1642, Bossuet had watched the funeral cortège of Richelieu and, less than six months later, that of Louis XIII. Despite Mazarin's power as first minister and Anne of Austria's influence, rival groups were taking up positions, and the Parlement of Paris was becoming restive. The first Fronde—an insurrection against the crown—broke out in Paris in January 1649, and on the last day of that month Charles I of England was beheaded. The civil turmoil must have strengthened Bossuet's conviction that peace could be maintained only under a strong king.

Bossuet spent seven years at Metz as archdeacon of the chapter. He was then called upon to preach in Paris, where his six "stations" (Lent or Advent sermons) and funeral orations enhanced his reputation. In 1670 he was made bishop of Condom, in southwest France, though he never resided there. A few months later Louis XIV chose him from a list of one hundred candidates to tutor the dauphin. It was a difficult task lasting eleven years, and Bossuet performed it with more zeal than pleasure, more credit than personal satisfaction.

In 1681 he was given the bishopric of Meaux, an unassuming see but one near Versailles. He devoted himself to his episcopal duties with the earnestness he applied to everything he undertook. He supervised the administration of his diocese, controlled the seminary, presided over meetings of the trustees, prepared a catechism, and busied himself with the poor.

Meanwhile, he remained one of the most prominent official orators, always at the service of the court on ceremonial occasions. He was the guide, philosopher, and friend of the church of France and, in a way, of the king. Louis certainly respected Bossuet, but it is difficult to say whether he liked him. As Charles Augustin Sainte-Beuve so aptly put it: "They understood each other."

Bossuet's character and the quality of his faith led him to identify with the accepted order of things, which seemed to justify his own way of life. He strove not merely to adhere to a view of the world that embraced the principle of monarchy by divine right, but even to defend and consolidate that view. Nevertheless, he knew the dangers and limitations of the system, and when royal absolutism ran the risk of compromising through pride the established order of God, Bossuet intervened with the objective of preventing a split between the two kinds of authorities—divine and human—that govern the world.

In the Middle Ages the monarch was at no time sovereign. The pope was the universal lawgiver, not only in matters of faith but in business and politics as well. As late as the early seventeenth century, Pope Paul V insisted that the doge of the Venetian Republic had no right to arrest a canon on the charge of flagrant immorality. When the canon was arrested, the pope laid Venice under an interdict and excommunicated the doge and the senate. However, the Venetian government answered that it was founded on divine right. In the end the pope gave way; the reign of the pope as king of kings was over. The church ceased to have universal dominion and was held to be supreme only within its own domain.

The problem for Bossuet and many other clerics was a growing uncertainty as to what that domain was. Until the Renaissance, a priest was a divinely commissioned agent and a prince, a divinely tolerated power. But by the sixteenth century, Philip Melanchthon, a friend of Martin Luther's, had denied that the church could make laws binding the conscience of providential rulers. Out of this view developed the much misunderstood but essentially modern doctrine of the divine right of kings. In its original historic setting, this doctrine was a way of asserting that the civil authority, embodied in the king, derived its power not from the pope as God's viceroy on earth, but by direct appointment from God himself.

Everything we know about Bossuet places him squarely in a Catholic and patriotic context. In his *Politique tirée des propres paroles de l'Écriture Sainte* (Politics Derived from the Very Words of Holy Scripture), written for the dauphin and updated for publication in the 1690's, Bossuet made a definite break with the tradition of Robert Bellarmine and Francisco Suárez, which undermined the doctrine of kingship by divine right. Bossuet refined the doctrine (3.2):

> A king's throne is not the throne of a man, but the throne of God Himself. . . . Royal Power is sacred: God raises up kings as His ministers and reigns through them over nations. . . . Obedience to princes is therefore an obligation of religion and conscience. . . . One should not consider how princely authority was established; it is sufficient that it exists and governs. . . . An inherent holiness exists in the character of a king, and no crime can efface it.
>
> (*Oeuvres complètes*, Lachat ed., vol. 23, p. 533)

As the dauphin's instructor he pointed out the defects of popes and kings; in particular he condemned Charles IX and the slaughter of Protestants on Saint Bartholemew's Day. He proposed as a model Louis IX, who, according to Bossuet, performed his duties as a king in a Christian way. These ideas had been with Bossuet for some time. On Palm Sunday 1662, in the presence of all the court, he boldly preached to Louis XIV on the "duty of kings":

> How great the wrong if kings seek pleasures that God forbids; if they turn against Him the powers He commits to them; if they break the laws that they are bound to maintain. This is the great overwhelming danger of the great ones of the earth. They are bound to combat their passions like other men; but beyond all other men they are bound to resist their own power. . . . No man is fit to exercise power save he who is most reticent in using it. . . . Sire, be faithful to God and do not hinder the great things He has in store for you by your sins.
>
> (*Oeuvres oratoires*, Lebarq ed., vol. 4, p. 264)

Much of Bossuet's conception of the social state is derived from Saint Augustine's outline of the society of man in *The City of God* (12.27). Social organization should conduct man to his ultimate end, which is God. The best form of government is an absolute monarchy; however, all forms of government that have endured appeared to him to be legitimate and respectable. The king does not derive his power from the people and is not accountable to them; he must submit to reason and to God. Authority is not the will of the sovereign leader but the reason and will of God represented in him. In this way, argues Augustine, the security of the people is guaranteed. Whether power is invested in a king, in an aristocracy, or in the people, Bossuet insists that unless it is sustained by reason and God's will, it will degenerate into tyranny. Hence heresy is treason to society and the state as well as to the church.

Another probable source of Bossuet's thought is Thomas Aquinas' "Treatise on the Divine Government" (in *Summa theologica*), which attempts to prove that "the natural necessity of things," that is, the order of the universe, demonstrates the government of Divine Providence.

In the funeral oration on Henrietta Maria, the queen consort of England's Charles I, Bossuet dramatizes this view:

157

When Almighty God has chosen someone to be the instrument of his designs, no one can divert Him from His course: or else He enchains, blinds, or vanquishes all who are capable of resistance.

(*Oraisons funèbres et panégyriques,* Velat ed., p. 120)

In his sermons and elegies Bossuet included references to Louis's conduct and, in the final analysis, it must be said that he praised the king far more than he admonished him. In the funeral oration on Le Tellier, he refers to Louis as "the miracle of our times" and compares him to Constantine, Theodosius, and Charlemagne. In the elegy for Maria Theresa, Bossuet addresses the king directly:

Monseigneur, open your eyes and witness this great gathering! If only I could help you dry your tears . . . by making you see, in the midst of this glorious congregation, a mother so cherished and so admired.

(Velat ed., p. 125)

He stresses divine selection in the family of rulers:

In His eternal council God has prepared the first families who are the source of nations, and in all nations the dominant qualities that bring fortune to the throne.

He concludes with an apostrophe to Louis:

Louis is the rampart of religion; it is in the name of religion that he offers us his military arms, so feared and respected on land and on sea.

In its simplest form, Bossuet's vision of political loyalty can be reduced to the truism that the gentry need a king as much as the king needs the gentry. It must be admitted that Niccolò Machiavelli's influence on Bossuet sometimes extended to unacknowledged quotation; the Florentine had long been known to constitutional monarchists and their retinues.

Louis XIV understood, as Bossuet did, that the existence of rival sects cannot but dispose man against an unquestioning acceptance of the authority of the church. One thinks of the pertinent Latin epigraph that was an accepted principle in Europe at that time: "Cujus regio, ejus religio" (The crown decides the religion of the state). When the Reformation was an accomplished fact, men looked out upon the world and no longer saw a single Catholic apostolic church as the visible embodiment of God's government. However, when Louis XIV revoked the Edict of Nantes in 1685, there were some who thought that the tide had suddenly turned against the Protestants. It should be remembered that the revocation was not a new policy but the culmination of a series of actions over a long period of time. Between 1661 and 1685 no fewer than one hundred declarations or regulations were issued to restrict exercise of the Protestant religion. This steady pressure made many Huguenots renounce their faith, but many of those were Huguenots by birth—not by conviction—and indifferent to religious principles. It is surprising that church authorities should have thought that such lax Huguenots would make strong Catholics.

Bossuet was more intolerant in theory than in practice. He hailed the revocation as the "pious edict that will give the deathblow to heresy." In the elegy for Le Tellier he claims that his predecessors could not see that this long-lasting heresy would be overthrown. He states that the "wandering sheep have returned to the fold and our churches are too small to hold them"; and that "their pretended pastors have deserted them without waiting for the decrees, only too glad to make the order of banishment an excuse for leaving the country."

Even during periods of relative toleration, French Huguenots were regarded as serious obstacles to the growth of royal power. Many were deprived of their civil rights and they were constantly compelled to abjure their faith. When the Edict of Nantes was revoked, more than 500,000 Protestant subjects were driven out of France, to carry their industry, wealth, and skill to other countries. With our knowledge of this infamous treatment, we are today repelled by such exultation as Bossuet's.

Bossuet's reference to "pretended pastors" was unworthy of him; he had known and won the respect of such men as Paul Ferry and Jean Claude. Perhaps Bossuet would not have spoken these words had he known of the atrocities taking place outside his own province. Nor could he foresee what was to happen to those pastors who remained in France. Bossuet was among the bishops who rejected violence as a means of converting Protestants. He stated publicly that it was wrong to force recent "reuniteds"—converts from Protestantism—to receive communion and assist at mass; he claimed that in his diocese he attempted to treat them with tact and to instruct them with gentleness—without much success, it must be admitted. Elsewhere the dragoons were far more effective.

Bossuet's position prompts us to be wary in our criticism of what may appear to us to be a dreadful and repugnant measure—but which, in the eyes of his contemporaries, seemed politically wise and justifiable on religious grounds.

THE SERMONS

Late into the seventeenth century the pervasive Protestant emphasis on the Bible as a book requiring literary analysis fostered, in Catholic circles, theories of biblical aesthetics concerned with the lyrical expression of spiritual truth. In keeping with this tradition, Bossuet developed an oratorical style whose guiding principle was the representation of truth as embodied in the Scripture.

Saint Augustine, reacting against the elaborate dialectic and verbal display of Roman rhetoricians, had sought to found Christian oratory on more solid ground—on truth rather than on probabilities. According to Augustine, the Christian orator is "the commentator and teacher of the Sacred Scriptures."

Augustine's book *De doctrina christiana (On Christian Doctrine)* examines the ties that bound educated Christians to the culture of their age. He states that culture, as a product of society, is a natural extension of the fact of language. In the same way, religion was a specific product of the need to communicate. What interested Augustine was the spoken word, the speech of God committed to a book, "an eloquence teaching salvation, perfectly adjusted to stir the hearts of all learners" (book 7, epistle 55). Thus, in an age when culture was thought of in terms of the understanding of a classical text, the Bible became the basis for a Christian culture. Bossuet's sermons embody the traditional Augustinian concept of Christian eloquence and its connection to the Bible.

Bossuet always spoke "ore rotundo" (with soaring elegance). For him, preaching was a continuation of the mystery that the priest celebrates at the altar. By about 1660 pulpit oratory in France was at the height of its success, though it was not entirely free from obvious defects such as affectation, bad taste, and a superficial gloss of erudition. Even the best preachers did not escape these faults.

Bossuet, for example, referring to the fall of great empires, which he regarded as proof of the intervention of Providence, mentioned those of "Bacchus and Hercules—renowned conquerors of the Indies and the East." He compared the blood of Christ with the blood that Catiline forced his fellow conspirators to drink. On another occasion, when calling to mind the tortures suffered by Saint Gorgonius, he spoke of the "foul effluvia emanating from the fat from his roasting body." These extravagances may have resulted from the haste in which he composed. Close textual scrutiny reveals that these sermons were, for the most part, rich in style and sound in doctrine. Great skill went into their composition: the general arrangement, the setting out of facts, the realism of the imagery, and the melodious assortment of words.

Various styles emerged, each with its own idiosyncrasies. The seventeenth century, it must be remembered, bore witness to a long, inconclusive battle over the place of profane rhetoric in religious persuasion. Although Bossuet claimed that he was not interested in "forming a style," his deliberate choice of expressiveness over formal or classical syntax suggests a predilection for the "baroque," as we now call it.

Literary style, like human personality, is admittedly a compound exceedingly difficult to analyze. Even when its more obvious characteristics are made clear, there still remains an elusive element that leaves the analyst with the unpleasant sensation of not having reached the heart of the matter. Nevertheless Bossuet's obvious characteristics are an extensive use of figurative language; a robust oratory style often known as "cursus," that is, rapidity, flow, progress; various Latinisms; and concreteness.

Bossuet's discursive prose was not as rawboned as the so-called Attic style of Justus Lipsius, Montaigne, or Francis Bacon. As mentioned earlier, he did not employ the "plain style" recommended by Saint Vincent de Paul; nor did he pretend to the worldly wisdom or the private morality of the ancient Stoics, of a Tacitus or a Machiavelli. Despite the fact that the "Ars Historica," or body of rhetorical principles that guided all French men of letters who wished to create literary images of the past, pervaded almost every aspect of Bossuet's culture, he maintained a close affiliation with the precepts of Christian eloquence established by Augustine. The fruit of rhetoric was in teaching men to know themselves and, by means of this knowledge, to rise up to the knowledge of God. This is the essence of the work he composed for the dauphin, *La traité de la connaissance de Dieu et de soi-même*

(Treatise on the Knowledge of God and of Oneself).

The majority of Bossuet's sermons were written during the years 1660–1670, at the height of his renown as a preacher. Certainly the most famous of them date from that period. In general he disdained complacency, suavity, emptiness, and ease. In avoiding these characteristics, he sometimes obtained contorted or obscure effects, which he did not always regard as faults. He preferred the forms that expressed the energy and labor of minds seeking the truth to the forms that expressed a contented sense of the enjoyment and possession of it. In short the "motions" of souls, not their states of rest, had become his preeminent theme. For this reason the scriptural text that served as the "point of departure" for each sermon was often transformed into a lyrical motif.

It was customary to begin with an exordium of two parts separated by the "Ave Maria," which was pronounced by an assistant. The first part, or "avant-propros" (which preceded the prayer), was usually shaped by Bossuet to arouse attention. After the Ave Maria Bossuet usually presented his subject and commented on it in clearly marked subdivisions (divisios). The central part was traditionally divided into two or three "points," or moral observations: two points would normally form a thesis/antithesis; three points would form a progression of accumulated evidence. The peroration drew the conclusion from the premises. In order to avoid too brief an ending, Bossuet often added concluding elements of consolation and hope.

One of the early sermons that have come down to us is "Le sermon sur la loi de Dieu" ("Sermon Concerning God's Law"), written in 1653. In this work Bossuet, at the age of twenty-six, reveals the manner in which he organizes his thoughts. He describes with a Pascalian fervor the agitation of the human mind tossed about from error to error; then a rule emerges from which comes repose and equilibrium. The following passage is from the first point, or thesis, of his argument:

Finally after much doubting, here is the conclusion that I have reached: I am cast in profound ignorance as if I have been exposed in a world where I know not what to do; all I have learned of it is tainted with so many kinds of errors that my soul dwells in continuous uncertainty, as if the only light to guide it is its own; and, in spite of this uncertainty, I am forced to make a long and perilous journey.

The powerful and persuasive metaphor of the journey of darkness intensifies the plight of man's troubled mind. In the next point, or antithesis, Bossuet defines, with classical fullness, the controlling principle of God's harmony and order:

The rule of reason is the rule of God Himself; indeed, when human reason selects its movements according to the will of its God, that marvelous ordering is the result—that honest disposition—that balanced moderation—that seasoned equilibrium between two extremes—which provides the soul with all its wondrous beauty.

Bossuet's images are often prolonged into allegories that weave in and out through the whole of a sermon. The vivid beauty of his conventional imagery did not go unnoticed; nor did the swelling cadences so typical of his grand style. The repetitions, the enumerations, the gradations, the beautiful effects of balance, the sonorous harmonies—these qualities suggest that a measure of theatricality was needed to get through to his listeners. Witness this climactic passage from "Le sermon pour la préparation à la mort" ("Sermon Concerning Preparation for Death"):

The vanities of the world would so easily seduce us if death were not so readily staring them in the face. All such temptations have passed me by; they curl around me like wisps of smoke because I am prepared to go where all things are.

Almighty God, Eternal God, Resplendent God— I rejoice in your power, in your immortality, in your joyfulness! When will I see you?—Oh essence who is the absence of all essence!

Effective oratory allows for each word to be governed by a particular idea. The structural cohesion of Bossuet's sermons creates emphasis as much as balance; in fact, the symmetry is enhanced by sensational incidents or personal candor. Nevertheless, inflated style is itself a kind of euphemism. Ciceronian principles had become part of the structure of Bossuet's thought. He knew when to take liberties with precepts, and he knew how to be natural. Compared to other orators of his time, Bossuet seems eminently more lucid, despite the numerous incidents of overblown language. This lucidity may be due to his sincerity. When there is a gap between one's real and one's declared aims, one turns, as it were, instinctively to long words and exhausted idioms. For present purposes it is sufficient to say that he created just such a credibility gap in some of his funeral orations. But as we shall see, the reasons for this are fairly complex. As for the sermons, Bossuet's sincerity has never been questioned. John Donne's remark is appropriate: "Eloquence is not our net . . . only the Gospel is" (*Sermons* 2. 307).

One of Bossuet's biographers remarked that the only contemporary writer Bossuet read and admired was Jean-Louis Guez de Balzac, a powerful rhetorician known as a writer of terse prose. Bossuet stated that in Balzac's writing there were very few thoughts but that he was a master of the art of giving a multitude of forms to a simple idea. It is not surprising that Bossuet would hold this to be a just ideal.

In a commemorative service in the chapel at the Louvre during Lent of 1662, Bossuet delivered his "Sermon sur la mort" ("Sermon on Death"), which is considered by some critics to be his masterpiece in this genre. Insisting on the vanity of earthly delights, Bossuet reproaches man for never measuring himself by his casket, which alone gives the exact dimensions. He repeats the themes of other sermons and reminds his audience that death proves the existence of Divine Providence in marking the passage from terrestrial disorder to the order of eternity.

Bossuet was also combating the circulation of libertine notions, in the manner of Montaigne, Pierre Gassendi, and La Mothe le Vayer, which assimilated man and the animals under the pretext that they all return to nothing. Bossuet's first point treats the familiar theme of "nothingness." In his second point, he demonstrates with logical precision that man is superior to nature, independent of his faith or the quality of his religious life.

The remarkable passage that follows, from the central part of the text, underscores the contradictions inherent in human conduct. Bossuet overwhelms his somewhat frivolous audience; he placates them, sides with them, and ultimately forces them to submit to the vigor of his logic and to the ardor of his imperatives:

> Dare I crave permission to open a grave before the court, and will not such fastidious eyes be averted from so gloomy a subject? . . . Strange weakness of human nature that death is never really present to it, although presented on every side and in every shape. . . . When their fellows die, men are in great haste to bury the inevitable thought of death, as to bury those that are dead. Yet among all earthly passions, one of the strongest is the craving for knowledge, and thanks to that craving, men exhaust themselves in striving to read the secrets of nature. . . . You may marvel that I bid you gaze on death that you may learn what is life; but look into the tomb, and confess that there is no truer interpretation, no more fruitful mirror of man's course. . . . O Eternal King of Ages. . . . all that has a limit is as nothing; for when that limit is reached one final instant causes it to be as though it had never been. . . . Heap up what you will of honor, riches, pleasures; what matters it, since the faint fluttering grasp of death will overthrow all your pomp in an instant, as though it were but a

child's house of cards. . . . Everything speaks to us of death. Nature herself, as though well-nigh envious of the gift she gave us, is forever reminding us that the little heap of mattered clay she lends us is ours but for a brief season; that she will soon reclaim it—it is not to remain long in the same hands, she needs it for other forms. This spiritual renewal of the human race, the ever-rising generation who shove us aside and assert their turn, warns us how, even as we see one generation pass, another will see us pass, and they likewise do the same. My God, what we are! If I look before me, how fearful the infinity where I am not! If I look backward, how vast the space where equally I am not! And what a mere speck I fill in this boundless abyss of time! Nothing! . . . It is not even the compass of your whole life that separates you from this nothingness— it is never more than one brief moment.

One can only guess how such words might have fallen on the cold pride, the hard indifference, the resolute self-seeking of many who surrounded the monarch to whom such burning words were uttered.

In this sermon Bossuet displays a dramatic talent for entering into the mode of thought of those whom he is pillorying. But we must not let this ability to adopt a persona deceive us. For Bossuet, a sermon was not a manuscript prepared for a publisher; it was a mode of proclaiming a documented truth.

Of the five or six hundred sermons Bossuet delivered, a scant two hundred remain. In most of them he denounces the folly of splendor, sensual pleasures, pride, and hardness of heart. He handles invective and innuendo with a precision that is admired today. French critics praise his "exactness of expression." The passages cited above contain numerous examples of "bonus sensus," that exquisite judgment in a literary form that could appeal alike to Counter-Reformationists like François Louvois or Archbishop Harlay and to moderate sectarians like the Huguenot pastors already mentioned.

In intention, in the inner meaning of his message, Bossuet was at variance with many of the popular creeds of his day. He rejected the idea of attaining salvation by placating God. In his sermons he taught that salvation was a condition of the soul reached only by some kind of self-discipline. "Disciplina" is derived from the word "discere" (to learn). To those who wanted salvation cheap, there was very little comfort to be had from a teacher like Bossuet.

THE FUNERAL ORATIONS

Bossuet conceived of the funeral oration primarily as a sermon in which the life of the deceased is used to illustrate a lesson. He usually chose a biblical text that clearly demonstrated the theme of his oration. In his exordium, he explained the theme more fully. Then followed details from the life of the person being eulogized, nearly always presented in two contrasting parts: for example, Joseph François Bourgoing as priest and Bourgoing as head of the Oratory; Nicolas Cornet as "treasure," but a "hidden treasure"; Henrietta of France in prosperity and in adversity; the aberrations of Anne de Gonzague and her atonement. Finally, Bossuet closed with a peroration in which he exhorted his listeners to profit by the lesson to be drawn from the life he had just related.

The other famous orators of Bossuet's time were Valentin Fléchier (1632–1710), who gave the funeral elegy for Henri Turenne; Jean Baptiste Massillon (1663–1742), who preached the funeral oration for Louis XIV with its often cited dramatic introduction; and Louis Bourdaloue (1632–1704), whom Madame de Sévigné called "the great Pan." Bourdaloue was Bossuet's rival for consummate perfection of the genre; but there was something sinister about the strident tone he adopted and his fire-and-brimstone style.

Bossuet's first oration was given at Metz in 1655 in memory of Yolande de Monterby, abbess of the convent of Sainte-Marie. In a con-

ventional tone he praises the humility of the abbess' character and reminds his audience that a "glorious eternity" is affixed to even the shortest life.

In the elegy spoken for Henri de Gornay at Metz in 1658, Bossuet's tone is noticeably more sumptuous than in the 1655 oration. The theme is death, the great equalizer. He likens the human condition to running water, flowing irresistibly toward the finality of death. He used this same metaphor, from the second book of Samuel (14.14), in the funeral oration on Henrietta of England. Bossuet's language, though not haughty, certainly contains a large measure of self-righteousness. He claims that death will "crush underfoot human arrogance and stifle the imaginary grandeurs that cause ambitious people to assume that they are above everyone else." Bossuet's message was far from comforting, but he had that special perception that put him in tune with his listeners. His concluding remarks are, for all intents and purposes, denunciatory, but he never abandons the sense of form and ear for rhythm that are essential for an effective orator:

> All men start off in life with the same disadvantages. With the progress of age, the years push them against one another like floating timber; their lives roll and descend toward death by their own natural gravity. Finally, after making a little bit of noise, like gurgling streams—some more than others—they are all lumped together in the infinite waste of nothingness. There are no longer any kings, or princes, or captains; nor any other kind of weighty title that might separate men from one another. There is only defilement and decay; worms, ashes and the dust that unites us.

The funeral oration delivered at Metz in 1662 for Bourgoing is less inflammatory in tone and has for its ends a different purpose: to reconstruct historic events and examine their consequences. In this oration Bossuet takes a close look at the Gallican church and emphasizes the importance of Pierre Bérulle and Bourgoing in creating and sustaining the ideals of Gallicanism.

Bossuet begins with a disclaimer. He states how difficult it is to add anything to such an illustrious and model life. Then he takes a potshot at the Vatican while praising Pierre Bérulle's merits and virtues: "The dignity of this great man, to which I dare say the purple of the Roman cloth added nothing, made the Gallican church shine with the purest and most sublime light of Christianity and ecclesiastical life."

Gallicanism was a cast of mind common among the French clergy and quite distinct from questions of doctrine. There were, moreover, degrees in this tendency toward moral particularism and ecclesiastical chauvinism, and they could be recognized in the cassock worn by the bishops: the deeper the blue, the more closely the wearer inclined toward Gallican ideas. Saint-Simon speaks of the "blue patches" of bishops, and Hyacinthe Rigaud's celebrated portrait of Bossuet in the Louvre shows him dressed in a violet cassock with a definite tinge of blue.

The bulk of the Bourgoing oration is flat and unappealing, although Bossuet's metaphors continue to be rich and striking. He concludes by citing what Augustine called "the flowers of elocution," ornaments of the Christian orator (*De doctrina christiana*, book 4).

One would expect a great deal of sentimentality in the funeral oration on Nicolas Cornet in 1663. However, Bossuet, always the opportunist, uses the occasion to point out that fanatical Jansenists and the prevaricators among the Jesuits both represent extreme positions and that the true man of God should "walk the middle way." The most powerful passages are those in which he rebukes the lax morality of Jesuits and decries the overly austere doctrines of Jansenists.

The funeral oration on the queen-mother was conferred on François Faure, bishop of Amiens. It is reported that he handled it badly. Bossuet gave his elegy in the presence of the king thirteen days after her death. It was ac-

tually a sermon for the feast of the Purification on 2 February 1666, in the royal chapel at Sainte-Germaine-en-Laye. (Voltaire mistakenly remarked in *Le siècle de Louis XIV* that Bossuet had been commissioned to deliver the queen's formal oration.)

This elegy is, for the most part, a long-drawn-out lesson in piety, packed with a recounting of historical events. Its many highly charged phrases of excessive flattery fall just short of obsequiousness, since there is, purportedly, a lesson behind it all. In general the tone is lofty and sonorous, punctuated with short exclamatory phrases in the following manner: "Oh illustrious life! Oh glorious and eternally memorable life! Oh life so short and so soon precipitated! . . . Oh how we are nothing; and power and opulence but names that deceive us!"

Bossuet does not always avoid platitudes, and his admonitions tend to approach hysteria. He seems to have aimed at striking the fear of God into his congregation. However, it must be remembered that the court in the first half of the reign of the Sun King was appallingly licentious. Louis himself, with unrestrained carnality, set the pace. It took a certain courage for a priest to attack the vices that flourished around the throne.

The elegy given in 1669 for Henrietta Maria of France, daughter of Henry IV and wife of Charles I of England, was the first that Bossuet submitted for publication. This carefully developed oration reads like a historic treatise meant to be sung. In *Le siècle de Louis XIV* (1751) Voltaire noted this innovation in style: "He applied the art of oratory to history itself, a literary form that would seem incapable of admitting it. . . . The lofty vigor with which he describes the manners and customs, the government, the rise and fall of monarchs, is astonishing."

Bossuet proceeds, as usual, by antithesis. He condemns the "emptiness of pomp and ceremony" and then concludes with paragraphs of strangely contrasting moods. After stating that the "days of blindness have run their course and it is time now for the light to return'' (a reference to the repression of Catholics in England), he signals out Henrietta Maria as a scapegoat whose suffering was beyond description:

> Who is able to express her heartfelt sorrow? Who could record her distress? No, my friends, Jeremiah himself, who alone was capable of converting his calamities into exquisite lamentations, could never have endured her pains.

Bossuet's closing words, albeit gloomy and contrite, describe an almost mystical state of Christian austerity:

> Just as Christianity was born on the cross, it is misfortune that fortifies it. . . . Thus, when misery opens our eyes, we relive with bitterness all our transgressions and limitations.

A great deal of psychological truth was rendered affable by the vigor of sincerity in Bossuet's pleasing voice on that November day in the chapel at Chaillot.

In 1670 the sudden death at the age of twenty-six of Henrietta of England, duchesse d'Orléans and wife of Louis XIV's brother, filled the court with consternation, for there was suspicion that she had been poisoned. Bossuet, the great conciliator, kept clear of political issues and used the well-known line ''Vanity of vanities, all is vanity!'' (Ecclesiastes 1) to introduce his theme.

This is one of Bossuet's orations often cited as a model of the form. The limpid style, the grandeur of the cadence, and the diversity and appropriateness of the metaphors make it an immensely appealing work. He employs a detailed series of juxtaposed phrases, all leading up to the recitation of the central idea:

> After all we have come to see, we now realize that health is but a name; life but a dream; glory but an illusion; social graces and pleasures but dangerous amusements: all is vain in us except the suspended judgment with which we scorn and despise all that we are.

Bossuet then takes up the theme of derision and mockery, and extends it into the theological domain:

> Am I not speaking the truth? Man, whom God has made in His own image, is he not but a shadow? That which Jesus sought on earth, was it not this great nothingness?

Bossuet's language becomes excessively morose, as he creates an atmosphere to house his ideas. His gratuitous remarks, his personal entreaties, and his identification with suffering humanity are props for this great design. His use of the editorial ''we'' is most effective in these closing words:

> Let us now change our manner of speech; let us no longer say that death suddenly cut short one of the most exemplary lives we have seen, or a story that had such a noble beginning; let us say that it simply put an end to the greatest dangers that have ever accosted a Christian soul.

When the king's wife, Maria Theresa, died on 1 September 1683, Bossuet was asked to deliver the funeral oration. In this elegy he refers to Maria Theresa as a ''humiliated soul''—an apt description. Yet because Bossuet never openly reprimands Louis for the suffering he caused her by his infidelities, his final declaration that ''faith alone remains victorious'' has a hollow sound.

Bossuet's performance on this occasion, and on others already mentioned, suggests that he was caught in a double bind. He recognized that he had a sacred duty to obey his conscience, and yet he was forced, in order to maintain any influence at all, more or less to ignore the king's caprices. He cannot be blamed for failing to serve two masters, but it is interesting to note the ways in which sincere language makes its concessions to discretion; hackneyed words and vacant phrases are more often than not the result.

Bossuet's elegy in 1685 for Anne de Gonzague, the princess palatine, contains an explicit warning against "that subtle poison—libertinism." He points out that the princess was a self-centered crowd pleaser at court but miserably unhappy just the same. She repented and, through God's intercession, led a devout life. In recounting the life of this troubled lady, Bossuet found grist for his mill.

The oration on Michel Le Tellier (1686) is much like the one on Nicolas Cornet except that on this occasion Bossuet had no political platform to erect. In a somewhat exaggerated tone he states that Le Tellier was "an example of true wisdom" and that he had been "predestined by God to be an example of justice." This is a curious phrase, coming as it does from the pen of the same man whose *Histoire des variations des églises protestantes* (*History of the Variations in the Protestant Churches*) attempts to give the lie to Calvin's notions of predestination.

In March 1687 Bossuet delivered the funeral oration for his old patron, Louis de Bourbon, prince de Condé. He begins by proclaiming that it is God who makes warriors and conquerors. He epitomizes Condé as the great Christian hero and compares him to Judas Maccabaeus. This comparison is a pretext because in the end Bossuet subordinates everything else to the instruction of his audience. What strikes one most is the verbal splendor with which "glory" is contrasted with "nothingness":

> Look at the unfortunate destiny of these men whom God has chosen to be the ornaments of their century . . . these columns of glory that carry to the heavens the magnificent testimony of our nothingness. . . . Mourn then for these feeble remains of human life; mourn for the sad immortality that we assign to our heroes. . . . The true victory, which places the entire world beneath our feet, is our faith.

In this speech, praise and lament for the merely human pull strongly against the moral lesson that human greatness is nothing without piety.

It is clear that we cannot expect Bossuet's funeral orations to contain straightforward history or biography. In the funeral oration on Henrietta Maria of France, he admits that he is no historian:

> These are not human anecdotes upon which I meditate. I am not a historian who can trace for you the secrets of cabinet meetings, the sequence of battles, or the personal interests of rival sects: I must go beyond man to make every human creature tremble before God's judgment.

Nevertheless the historical and biographical aspects of these eulogies are considerable: the lives of his heroes allow him to evoke the battle of Rocroi and other victories of Condé, to draw a parallel between Turenne and Condé as commanders, to recount the English civil wars and the two Frondes, to praise Le Tellier's work as chancellor, and to mention the revocation of the Edict of Nantes.

The main themes of the orations are death and providence. The duty of priests charged with delivering a funeral oration, says Bossuet in his earliest essay in the genre, is "to make their congregation contemplate the common condition of all mortals in order that the thought of death give them a saintly distaste for the present life, and that human vanity blush and fluster in regarding the fatal term that Divine Providence has in store of its deceitful expectations."

This duty he never omitted. The universality of death, which renders all men equal and annihilates all human achievement, is stressed time and time again. But there is another side to the bleak description of the human condition. God constantly watches over humanity, and in everything that befalls man, His Providence is at work. It is God who sends conquerors, distributes talents, ordains victories. Providence is no less concerned with the fate of individuals than with the destinies of nations. It was God, Bossuet tells us, who caused the English civil wars—in order that Henrietta Maria might become a Catholic.

JACQUES BÉNIGNE BOSSUET

Bossuet is one of the masters of French prose. Narrative, portraits, historical tableaux, indignation, exhortation, pathos—all varieties of prose writing and of tone are present in his sermons and elegies. Although the mixture of short and long phrases marks his style, it is perhaps as the master of the solemn complex sentence that the reader remembers him. The following example is from the oration on Henrietta Maria of France:

> When the angel of the Lord let the smoke rise from the shaft of the abyss, as if from a furnace, to darken the sun—as the *Book of the Apocalypse* tells us; that is to say, when error and heresy rose up; and when, in order to stamp out blasphemy and stir up His priests and His people, God allowed men's minds to be seduced, so that haughty souls were deceived and manifold anxiety, untamed curiosity, and the spirit of revolt were let loose upon the land; yes, when He permitted this, in His profound wisdom He set the limits that He wished to impose on the unfortunate progress of error and on the sorrows of His church.

This is a masterly sentence. Two subordinate clauses, the second repeating and expanding the ideas in the first, balance the main clause, and the entire sentence is constructed with rhythmic groups—nouns and infinitives in pairs, but with three linked nouns at the end of the second clause for the sake of variety and to mark the end of the first half of the sentence.

As we have seen, Bossuet's mood varied. He could be in turn solemn, realistic, lyrical, poetic, didactic, and occasionally familiar. What refined art lay in the balanced development of his argument and in that "dome-like sentence" of which Paul Valéry writes, rising by stages, each one awakening more deep-toned reverberations, then descending in flowing accents until it reaches the deliberately sought words that bring it to a close in perfect harmony—a powerfully abrupt closure, the whispering echo of a lingering dirge.

THE GALLICAN CHURCH

The Pragmatic Sanction of Bourges (1438) and the Concordat of Francis I (1516) established the right of French kings to appoint bishops and abbots, to determine their income, and to regulate all benefices in a diocese between the death of its bishop and the installation of his successor.

As an extension of these historic decisions, Gallicanism attempted to maintain certain liberties—never clearly defined—on behalf of the French church with respect to Vatican influence. Gallican prestige developed in proportion to the growth of royal power. A large number of Jansenists, whose hostility to the pope arose out of their hatred of the Jesuits, were Gallicans. "Scratch a Gallican, and beneath you will find a Jansenist," was a popular saying.

By family tradition and doctrinal training, Bossuet was a Gallican: firm in his resolution concerning the apostolic mission of bishops and far from according to the pope any kind of personal infallibility. However, he was ready to make the concessions necessary to avoid a rupture with Rome and to safeguard Roman authority, generally thought to be indispensable for the conservation of unity.

In 1663 the Sorbonne issued six articles confirming the Gallican position. In February 1673 Louis XIV issued a declaration affirming the "regalia" as inalienable. The regalia was the right, mentioned above, by which the king took possession of the revenues of vacant sees. In 1678, in response to this declaration, Pope Innocent XI excommunicated the archbishop of Toulouse for deposing an anti-Gallican bishop.

The king called a general assembly of the clergy. Bossuet was accorded a high-ranking position and was asked to give the opening discourse. Using moderate language, Bossuet resisted the efforts of the partisans of total autonomy for the French church to win him over. In March 1682 the assembly reaffirmed the six articles and drew up the famous four articles—clearly injurious to the pope—that almost divorced the French church from Rome.

Scholars are uncertain about the part that Bossuet played in drawing up these articles. Some say that he collaborated as an editor; others say he rewrote them using more docile terms. Perhaps he supervised their translation into Latin, as one critic contends. In any event, Bossuet was certainly an active participant. The affair dragged on for years, and Louis XIV was secretly excommunicated by Innocent XI on 16 November 1687. Louis eventually conceded, the pope died, and France and the Vatican resumed the delicate balance of a standoff.

Bossuet expressed his feelings on the matter in a letter to Cardinal d'Estrées in December 1681:

> It was absolutely necessary that I should speak of the liberties of the Gallican church. I set two points before myself: one, to do this without any loss to the true greatness of the Holy See; the other, to explain those privileges from a bishop's point of view—not a magistrate's.

Bossuet did not consider the regalia gravely important. In his mind, it was one of those practical problems that could be settled by discussion and compromise. His inaugural address is considered a masterpiece of literature, an important theological statement, and an impressive appeal for moderation.

The entire sermon was a vindication of the unity of the church. Twenty years earlier he had declared in his funeral oration on Bourgoing:

> All the graces of the Church, all the power of the Holy Spirit, are in unity; unity is its treasure and its life—loss of unity is its certain death.

It was this conviction that gave power to this address and helped turn the thoughts of his congregation from secondary problems to the larger issues involved.

THE DRAMA OF DESTINY

Renewal of Christian faith in Europe brought with it the revival of ideas that had disappeared during the Renaissance. One such idea—the progress of humanity—stood out amid the shifting winds and currents of doctrine in the Reformation.

The thinkers of the Renaissance were less inclined than their medieval predecessors to see history as the ascent of the human race. What they saw behind them were the peaks of classical antiquity, representing the summits of human reason. These thinkers assumed the existence of a closed culture in which there were limits to human achievement.

Christianity, with its transition from the Old Testament to the New, provided a meaning for history and a grand purpose toward which the whole of creation moved. Bossuet, among others, believed in the idea of a progressive development of history that would see its highest moment in the Christian state.

The Discours sur l'histoire universelle (Discourse on Universal History), originally written for the king's son, was being printed at the time Bossuet was made bishop of Meaux in 1681. During the two centuries after his death nearly two hundred editions were published. It is a work for which Bossuet had great affection. He said that the idea of such a history had been in his mind since his youth, and as an old man he enjoyed listening to passages being read aloud to him.

The purpose of the book was indicated in the subtitle: "To Explain the Progress of Religion and the Vicissitudes of Empires." Bossuet had set out to write a synthesis in which faith and history would sustain one another, with history being the stronger element. In Bossuet's view all history was the manifestation of Divine Providence. The nineteenth-century philosopher Auguste Comte wrote in his Positive Philosophy (1830–1842):

> Bossuet was unquestionably the first who proposed to survey, from a lofty point of view, the

whole past of society. . . . The spirit of universality, so thoroughly appreciated, and, under the circumstances, so wonderfully sustained, will always preserve this admirable composition as a model, suggesting the true result of historical analysis; the rational coordination of the great series of human events, according to a single design.

Bossuet expressed his philosophy of history in the opening chapter, "General Plan of this Work":

He who has not learned from history to distinguish different ages will represent men under the law of Nature or under written law as they are under the law of the Gospel; he will speak of France during the upheavals of the civil wars as being as powerful as at the time of Louis XIV, when, united under that great king, France alone triumphs over all Europe.

In sum, Bossuet is saying to his pupil that he will become lost in the particularities of history, ignorant of the meanings of the great events and their place in the larger design, unless he has a panorama of the whole in condensed form:

Such a condensation . . . will afford you a grand view. . . . You will see how empires succeeded one another and how religion, in its different states, maintains its stability from the beginning of the world to our time.

The book is divided into three parts. The first describes twelve "epochs," as he called them. Bossuet was trying to establish certain historical moments marked by a great event to which he could relate the rest:

That is what we call an "epoch," from a Greek word meaning "to stop," because we stop there in order to consider all that has happened.

These epochs form a chronology, and the twelve stages can be classified by names: Adam, Noah, Abraham, Moses, Troy, Solomon, Romulus, Cyrus, Scipio, Jesus, Constantine, and Charlemagne.

Part two of the *Discourse*, entitled "The Continuity of Religion," is a history of the Jews from the creation to the victory of the church and includes a long chapter on the teaching of Christ. In a revised edition of 1700, Bossuet extended this part in order to refute the Dutch philosopher Baruch Spinoza's denial of the inspiration of the Bible and to criticize Richard Simon's attack on the Mosaic tradition put forth in his *Critical History of the Old Testament* (1678).

"The Empires," the final part of the book, is a series of astute reflections on the historical changes of the great empires of the past. The following passage, taken from the second chapter of this section, conveys the style and flavor of the work:

This spectacle will be more useful and interesting if you reflect not only upon the rise and fall of empires but also upon the causes of their progress and decadence. . . . For the God who caused the universe to be linked together and who, though all-powerful in Himself, willed, for the sake of order, that the parts of the great whole be dependent on one another—the same God also willed that the course of human affairs should have its own continuity and proportions. . . . The true science of history is uncovering for each age the hidden tendencies that have prepared the way for great changes and the important combination of circumstances that have brought them about.

The striking aspect of the *Discourse* is the essentially modern framework of Bossuet's thought, even though its lineal descent from the early efforts at universal history by Eusebius, Tertullian, and Augustine is evident. Both Eusebius and Tertullian formulated conceptions of the Christian empire's place in the scheme of history, but it is in Augustine's *City of God* that the idea of a universal social bond, of a unified humanity, attained its first and richest expression. In this work many of the essential elements of the idea of progress are present: the unfolding, cumulative advancement of mankind; the idea of time as a unilinear flow; the belief in the necessary character of history and in the inevitablity of some future end or objective.

These influences are significant if we wish to understand how Bossuet, troubled by René Descartes's suggestion that all events in the world—given an initial push by God—could be explained as mechanically following the laws of nature, conceived of every episode in history as part of a divine plan. In the conclusion of the *Discourse* he makes the following observation:

> Do not speak of chance or hazard; such words only conceal our ignorance. What seems chance to our faltering opinions is part of a design conceived in the mind of the eternal. . . . All moves toward the same end, and it is for want of grasping the whole that we imagine the presence of chance and irregularity in particular events.

The explanation of facts by their apparent causes does not exhaust the fertility of their substance. Bossuet emphatically informs us that the history of empires manifests the action of Divine Providence. In his *History of France* (vols. 1–6, 1833–1846; vols. 7–18, 1855–1867), Jules Michelet declares that these same events represented the gradual ascension of democracy—the preparation for the French Revolution. The question at stake is not that of the particular interpretation of the historian, but that of the exactness of the report. Bossuet respected facts and did not bend them to suit his own purposes.

The meaning of the Latin word "providentia" is "foresight." In Bossuet's "Sermon Concerning the Good Will and Severity of the Lord," he examines what he sees as the two aspects of providence—"mercy" and "justice"—in light of both the Old and New Testament, and he states that these aspects "reigned side by side, each supported by the other."

Thus we see that religious considerations of this kind were for Bossuet integral components of historical reality. His fusion of the Christian legacy inherited from the church fathers with the humanist motifs of civic morality give a distinctly modern cast to his providential structure of history.

Soon after he completed the *Discourse*, Bossuet began to assemble the materials for a new project. During the next seven years he appealed to many correspondents for information and for copies of documents and records. He had access to the royal archives, where he could consult the records of the national synods of the Huguenots. The result of his research, *History of the Variations in the Protestant Churches,* was published in May 1688.

The main thesis of the book is that the history of Protestantism demonstrates that the exercise of private judgment as to the meaning of Scripture leads not to universal dogma, but to schism and heresy. The true church cannot change, because it is infallible. The Reform movement, on the other hand, which had existed for only a century and a half, was already divided into a multitude of different sects. It offered the spectacle of a faith in perpetual evolution, lacking in the authority that is the abiding principle of Catholicism.

Much of the book is a denunciation of heretics, those who hold a "particular" opinion in matters of faith. The following remarks are from the preface:

> The perverseness of heretics is a great and instructing spectacle to the humble of heart. . . . The property of a heretic is to be wedded to his own conceits: the property of the Catholic is to prefer the general opinion of the whole Church to his own. . . . In the midst of so many disputes and complications, the Catholic truth, like a beautiful sun piercing heavy clouds, will everywhere display its luster.

The main text is divided into fifteen books. The first two deal with Luther; Bossuet's study, in fact, is based largely on Luther's Latin works and on the correspondence of

Erasmus. Melanchthon, a moderate theologian, is the subject of the next three books. Bossuet's treatment did much to rehabilitate Melanchthon in the Protestant world, where he had been overshadowed by Luther. Book 7 is devoted to the Reformation in England and book 8 to the Diet of Worms. The next book is devoted to Calvin, who is treated far less sympathetically than Luther. In book 10 Bossuet returns to England and the Elizabethan religious settlement. Books 11, 12, 13, and 14 treat minor heretical sects. The last book is an extended account of the Catholic faith and is a treatise in itself. The closing remarks reveal a far-reaching apologetic:

> These variations, the history of which we have now finished, enable us to see the reformed religion for what it is—a kingdom divided against itself. While the Catholic church, unalterably attached to established doctrines in which not the least variation can be shown since the origin of Christianity, reveals herself as a church built on a rock, confident in herself, resolute in her principles, and guided by a Spirit that never deceives.

It should be noted that Bossuet's evident desire to understand the personalities of the reformers in no way modified his condemnation of their teaching. Many Protestants were not in the least perturbed at the picture he had painted of their variations; they took pride in this tribute to the freedom of man's inquiry into the nature of religion. However, the *Variations* undoubtedly brought many Protestants to reconsider the basis of their beliefs and to concentrate on the principles that distinguished them from the Catholics.

Many critics praised Bossuet's objective attitude toward persons, as distinct from doctrines. Indeed the work is in general so reasonable and fair-minded that one might be tempted to overlook the tirades against Protestantism that Bossuet reserved for the pulpit. The following passage is from the funeral oration on Henrietta Maria of France:

> Countless Anabaptist sects have issued from this foul source [the Reformation], and their ideas, joined to those of the Calvinists, have given rise to other independents, whose impudence is boundless. Among them we have the Quakers, fanatics who think that all their reveries are inspired, and those who are called Seekers because seventeen hundred years after the coming of Christ they still haven't found religion, and refuse to give up the search.

Notwithstanding such invective, and despite the fact that Bossuet left little margin in his historical studies for the unexpected and the contingent, his underlying conception that the entire history of mankind is an expression of Divine Will serves to recall one of the first modern examples of what would become the distinct and independent genre of world history.

THE DEEPER CONFLICT

The eminent French critic Paul Hazard has pointed out that the year 1690 marked the debut of the crisis in European consciousness from which emerged the philosophy of the Enlightenment, the French Revolution, and many of the principles of thought that characterize the modern world.

At this time it seemed as if Bossuet had won all his battles; the king had been won over and the Huguenots were clearly nonplussed by his *Variations.* Suddenly Bossuet saw the conclusions that unscrupulous men might draw from the philosophy of Descartes, and he prophetically exclaimed in a letter to François Lamy: "I see a great combat smoldering within the Church. More than one heresy will spring from the misunderstood principles of Cartesian philosophy."

He was also disturbed by Nicolas Malebranche, the Oratorian metaphysician, whom he suspected of wishing to reduce ethics to a mere question of order and thus eliminate the spirit of penance. He considered that, even if the aims of Malebranche were justifiable, his disciples were plunging headlong into heresy. It can now be appreciated why Bossuet was becoming seriously perturbed by the tendencies of new philosophical ideas. The tradition of the church, he felt, was being attacked from without and from within, and even at the Sorbonne there was a failure to recognize the dangers.

Bossuet's adversaries were numerous and powerful. The influence of freethinkers appeared to be spreading: Bernard Fontanelle had been elected to the French Academy, and Thomas Hobbes, Pierre Bayle, and Spinoza were striking terrible blows at the edifice of faith. The absurd pride of incredulity and the irony of the skeptics seemed as seditious as they were shameful. In his youth Bossuet had written a handbook for Protestants called the *Exposition de la foi catholique* (*Exposition of the Catholic Doctrine*), which had stirred many consciences; but by 1690 respect for him had diminished. Pierre Jurieu, a banished Huguenot, published a statement to the effect that Bossuet had "nine children and several concubines."

An examination of Bossuet's dispute with Madame Guyon over the merits of quietism (a form of mysticism that taught that fulfillment of the spiritual life on earth is achieved by continuous passive contemplation) indicates that he did not realize the wave of Spanish and Flemish mysticism that had cut across the century was at full strength in 1690. Bossuet claimed that the freethinkers owed their success to the quietists, who seized every opportunity to "turn piety into hypocrisy and to deride everything pertaining to the Church." When Bossuet lent the weight of his authority to crush not only Madame Guyon, but François Fénelon, his own friend and disciple, he failed to see that in condemning mysticism outright he was depriving the Christian experience of a precious stone in its crown; the effect was to reduce it to a kind of emaciated dogmatism. It was this lack of understanding, as well as his taste for austerity in religion,

that caused him to be too lenient toward Jansenism, which was really more dangerous than quietism. This leniency was noticeable in the Quesnel affair.

In 1671 Pasquier Quesnel, director of the Paris Oratory, published a book entitled *Moral Reflections on the New Testament*. With subsequent editions the book became more Jansenist in tone, and the opponents of Jansenism began a campaign against him. Bossuet's *Justification of the "Moral Reflections"* was an attempted warning to Quesnel that he should delete anything from his book that might be deemed suspect. Quesnel absolutely refused to make the corrections suggested by Bossuet, and the *Moral Reflections* was ultimately condemned by the Holy See in 1708, after fourteen years of discussion. Quesnel then republished his *Reflections* very much enlarged and rendered all the more discreditable by the fact that the work was prefaced by Bossuet's *Justification*, which had never been published before. The result was a violent outburst against the Jansenists. Finally Pope Clement XI, pressed by Louis XIV, promulgated the bull "Unigenitus" in September of 1713.

Bossuet's quarrel with Fénelon was a long series of misunderstandings. In July 1696 Bossuet wrote a second *Instruction sur les états d'oraison* (*Instruction on the States of Prayer*) and sent the manuscript to Fénelon, seeking his approval. Ever since Bossuet's repudiation of Madame Guyon, Fénelon had suspected Bossuet's intentions, and he neither read nor approved the work. Then he wrote, at top speed, his *Explanation of the Maxims of the Saints on the Inner Life* and published it one month before Bossuet's work. Bossuet was furious and appealed to the king. The two books became a matter of widespread discussion as lively as the furor over Port-Royal.*

Bossuet and Fénelon wrote numerous pamphlets denouncing one another. Cardinal

*Toward the end of the seventeenth century, the abbey of Port-Royal, once known for its teachings of piety and reform of discipline, and as a prime center of Jansenism, suffered intense persecution and was closed.

Grente has described it as "a magnificent contest lasting ten years; the indignant Bossuet riding full tilt against his adversary, and Fénelon parrying swiftly and brilliantly and assuming, with devastating elegance, an air of injured innocence." The dispute reached a climax with the publication of Bossuet's *Relation sur le quiétism (Aspects of Quietism)* in 1698, a veritable lampoon equal in literary quality to Pascal's *Provincial Letters.* By an appeal to the pope, Fénelon angered Louis XIV, who ordered him to leave the court and remain at Cambrai, where he was archbishop. Finally Pope Innocent XII signed a condemnation—mild in tone—of Fénelon's book. Fénelon's submission brought the affair to a close.

In these arguments Bossuet seems to have misconceived the function of the moralist. One wonders if he really fancied that he was standing upon the rock of eternal truth. He did not grasp that the modern world is more chaotic than the minds of orthodox thinkers, for whom the problem of religion was to find a way of reinforcing sanctions that appeared to be falling away. Bossuet suffered the fate of many polemicists: in his younger days he was confident that his opponents would see reason, forgetting that these opponents nourished the same illusions about him.

In 1694 the Theatine priest Père Caffaro wrote an introduction for an edition of the plays of Edmé Boursault, a popular dramatist. Bossuet was so angry at the idea of a priest commending the work of a playwright that he wrote a long letter of protest, which he later elaborated and published under the title *Maximes et réflexions sur la comédie (Maxims and Reflections on the Theater).* In this work he raged against the theater, insulted Molière, and included the plays of Pierre Corneille and Jean Racine in his condemnation of "Byzantine spectacles." Bossuet saw a direct connection between the stage and relaxed morality. Pascal, too, regarded the influence of the theater as pernicious, and declared, "All great distractions are dangerous to the Christian life,

but of all those which the world has invented, there is none more dangerous than the theater."

Because Bossuet perceived the changes taking place in human affairs as a kind of temporary corruption, he set himself the task of chastising the rebels and refuting their beliefs. He failed to comprehend how deep and inexorable was the dissolution of the ancestral order.

The great figures of the new epoch were the heirs and disciples of Bérulle, Saint Jean-Baptiste de la Salle, and Saint Vincent de Paul, but they were not destined to raise aloft the Christian standard with the spiritual upsurge of these men. The great century was drawing to a close as the Age of Faith gave way to the Age of Reason. In the eyes of history this was no smooth transition.

THE CRUCIBLE OF FAITH

Aside from embroilment in controversy, the 1690's saw the formation of Bossuet's finest spiritual tracts. His piety and spiritual enrichment are best expressed in the *Meditations on the Gospels* and the *Elevations on the Mysteries* (both written 1695, published 1709). The *Elevations* represent familiar expositions of passages from Holy Scripture, intended to aid the clergy in their meditations.

The *Treatise on Concupiscence* (written 1694, published 1731) is a deeply personal work that represents the extreme point of Bossuet's antiworldliness. Originally a study of the Gospel of John, this work is a series of spiritual exercises in the tradition of Saint Ignatius Loyola.

The *Treatise on the Knowledge of God and of Oneself* was found among Fénelon's papers and originally attributed to him. Published in 1722, it is presumed that Bossuet lent it to him when Fénelon was tutoring Louis XIV's grandson.

In this connection might be included Bossuet's correspondence with the German philosopher Gottfried von Leibniz concerning the unification of the Protestant and Catholic churches. Leibniz dreamed of rebuilding Europe through the creation of a Christian republic. He proposed the membership of all Christians in an invisible church founded on charity and faith, although membership in a visible church would be maintained by private selection. In his conception of faith, Leibniz claimed liberty of thought; Bossuet stood for complete adherence to the doctrines of the church. The correspondence, which went on for many years, indicates that no effective compromise was possible between these two incompatible systems of thought.

It might ultimately be said that Bossuet's fundamentalism was a protest against the attenuations that his contemporaries found it necessary to make. However, he was correct in thinking that one cannot have a faith of which the only foundation is the desire to believe. Bossuet always exhibited the confidence that the truly devout display. He never subcribed to the god of impersonal reality or to the indefinite god of skeptics, mystics, and agents of unbelief. Furthermore he never leaned on oversimplification in an age of self-indulgence in such matters. In all his works, he sought to communicate his belief in a coherent, sacred, and familiar body of knowledge.

Bossuet's prolific writings and the number of memorable men and women whose lives were interwoven with his own present a rich field of historical interest; but it is difficult to separate the ephemeral from the permanent. His attitude toward kingship is no longer tenable, although his *Politics* remains a valuable exposition of ideas widely held in his century. His defense of the Gallican church is now of interest only as a phase in ecclesiastical history, and even his views of the papacy were dismissed at the Vatican Council of 1870. His narrative of historical events has been superseded by later research, but his interpretation cannot be brushed to one side; no adequate alternative has been suggested in the many discussions on the meaning of progress in history. His main work concerned the truths of revealed religion, and, to the believer, these are not subject to change or fashion.

Sainte-Beuve said that the cult of Bossuet is one of France's religions. Faith was the central fact of his character and of his life. Such a faith was not born of personal cognition but of profound allegiance to authority. Behind everything he did lay an intensely rich experience of humanity; in consequence, he was the most solid and the most well-balanced of the Christian thinkers of his day.

Bossuet died eleven years before Louis XIV, on 11 April 1704; thus he did not witness the decay that marred the end of the reign. The epithet given him by Fénelon—the Eagle of Meaux—describes him perfectly in his steadfastness, in the manner in which he soared to the heights of eloquence and in which he attacked his opponents.

Bossuet represented one of those vast pillars of established order that stood in a time of kings and courts. His art and his convictions were never conveyed through simple means. He lived in an age that would not tolerate such concessions. Although Bossuet was by and large the most typical representative of his era, many writers after his time—citing the vitality of his commitment—have claimed him as one of their own.

Selected Bibliography

Separately published translations of individual works by Bossuet are not widely available, except as indicated under Individual Editions below. The reader may find some works translated in either anthologies or critical studies of Bossuet.

INDIVIDUAL EDITIONS

Discours sur l'histoire universelle. Edited by Jacques Truchet. Paris, 1966. Translated by Elborg Foster as *Discourses on Universal History.* Chicago, 1976.

Élévations sur les mystères. Edited by Maturin Dréano. Paris, 1962.

Maximes et réflexions sur la comédie. In *L'Église et le théâtre.* Edited by Charles Urbain and Eugène Lévesque. Paris, 1930.

Méditations sur l'Évangile. Edited by Maturin Dréano. Paris, 1966. Translated by Lucille Franchère as *Meditations on the Gospels.* Chicago, 1962.

Platon et Aristote: Notes de lecture. Edited by Thérèse Goyet. Paris, 1964.

Politique tirée des propres paroles de l'Écriture Sainte. Edited by Jacques LeBrun. Geneva, 1967.

Traité de la concupiscence. Edited by Charles Urbain and Eugène Lévesque. Paris, 1930.

Trois sermons du Carême de Minimes. In *Annales de l'est,* no. 28, edited by Jacques LeBrun. Nancy, 1965.

COLLECTED AND SELECTED EDITIONS

Oeuvres. Edited by Bernard Velat. Paris, 1936.

Oeuvres choisies. Edited by Jean Calvet. Paris, 1824.

Oeuvres complètes. Edited by F. Lachat. 31 vols. Paris, 1862–1866.

Oeuvres oratoires. Edited by Joseph Lebarq. 6 vols. Paris, 1892.

──────. Edited by Charles Urbain and Eugène Lévesque. 7 vols. Paris, 1914–1926.

Oraisons funèbres. Edited by Jacques Truchet. Paris, 1961.

Oraisons funèbres et panégyriques. Edited by Bernard Velat. 2 vols. Paris, 1951.

LETTERS

Correspondance. Edited by Charles Urbain and Eugène Lévesque. 15 vols. Paris, 1909–1926.

BIOGRAPHICAL AND CRITICAL STUDIES

Bayley, Peter. *French Pulpit Oratory.* Cambridge, 1980.

Calvet, Jean. *Bossuet.* Paris, 1968.

──────. *La littérature religieuse de St. François de Sales à Fénelon.* Paris, 1956.

Daniel-Rops, Henri. *The Church in the Seventeenth Century.* Translated by J. J. Buckingham. New York, 1963.

Dargan, Edwin Charles. *A History of Preaching.* Vol. 2. Grand Rapids, Mich., 1970.

Durant, Will and Ariel. *The Story of Civilization: The Age of Louis XIV.* Vol. 8. New York, 1963.

Gaquère, François. *Les suprêmes appels de Bossuet à l'unité chrétienne.* Paris, 1969.

Goyet, Thérèse. *L'Humanisme de Bossuet.* 2 vols. Paris, 1965.

Grente, Cardinal Georges. *Dictionnaire des lettres françaises.* 4 vols. Paris, 1951–1964.

Hazard, Paul. *La crise de la conscience européene (1680–1715).* 2 vols. Paris, 1968. Originally published in 1935. Translated by James Lewis May as *The European Mind, 1680–1715.* Cleveland, 1963.

Lanson, Gustave. *Bossuet.* In *European Political Thought,* edited by J. P. Mayer. New York, 1979. Reprint of 1894 edition.

LeBrun, Jacques. *Bossuet.* Paris, 1970.

──────. *Les opuscules spirituels de Bossuet: Recherches sur la tradition nancéeienne.* Nancy, 1970.

──────. *La spiritualité de Bossuet.* Paris, 1972.

Martimort, Aimé Georges. *Le gallicanisme.* Paris, 1973.

──────. *Le gallicanisme de Bossuet.* Paris, 1953.

Martin, Victor. *Les origines du gallicanisme.* Paris, 1939.

Nisbet, Robert. *History of the Idea of Progress.* New York, 1980.

Orcibal, J. *Louis XIV et les Protestants.* Paris, 1951.

Perry, Elisabeth Israels. *From Theology to History: French Religious Controversy and the Revocation of the Edict of Nantes. The International Archives of the History of Ideas,* no. 67. The Hague, 1973.

Reynolds, Ernest E. *Bossuet.* New York, 1963.

Terstegge, Georgiana. *Providence as ''Idée-Maîtresse'' in the Works of Bossuet: Theme and Stylistic Motif.* Washington, D.C., 1948.

Treasure, Geoffery. *Seventeenth-Century France.* London, 1966.

Truchet, Jacques. *Bossuet panégyriste.* Paris, 1962.

──────. *Politique de Bossuet: Textes choisis.* Paris, 1966.

──────. *La prédication de Bossuet: Étude des thèmes.* Paris, 1960.

Urbain, Charles, and Eugène Lévesque, eds., *Les dernières années de Bossuet.* 2 vols. Paris, 1929. Edited version of the *Mémoires et journal* of François Ledieu, Bossuet's secretary.

──────. *Revue Bossuet.* Vols. 1–5. 1890–1904. Reprinted Geneva, 1968.

ROBERT J. FRAIL

NICOLAS BOILEAU-DESPRÉAUX

(1636–1711)

LIFE AND WORKS

NICOLAS BOILEAU-DESPRÉAUX was born in Paris on 1 November 1636, the year that witnessed the smashing success of Corneille's trend-setting tragicomedy *Le Cid* and the publication of Descartes's *Discours de la méthode (Discourse on Method)*. This conjuncture of dates is of more than coincidental import, for historical assessments of Boileau's role in the development of the so-called French classical literature do not always take proper or realistic account of the fact that he and his work grew to intellectual maturity in a context and an age pervaded by the spirit of experiment and invention and dominated by a salon and court culture that was committed above all to secularization and modernization of the powerful but still academically oriented heritage of humanism.

As the fifteenth child of a rather well-to-do clerk in the Parlement of Paris, Boileau received the kind of privileged education that was customary in his social class. Although his family did have some vague noble pretensions, these were never properly validated legally, and from the beginning to the end of his career Boileau was to live the life of a more than commonly prosperous upper-middle-class gentleman of letters.

As late as fifty years ago, Boileau's biographers attached importance to the fact that he had lost his mother at the age of eighteen months and was raised, so it was assumed, in the absence of female tenderness and human warmth. In the somewhat romantic and sentimental criticism of yesteryear, this deprived childhood was often identified as the source of Boileau's alleged coldness, aggressiveness, satiric bent, and acerbic wit. All the hard evidence points, however, in the direction of a full and pleasant family life, surrounded by numerous siblings and all held together in substantial harmony by their concerned and conscientious father, Gilles, who saw to it that his male children, at any rate, received the very best start in life. In the case of Nicolas, this meant a fine, rigorous classical education at the prominent schools of Harcourt and Beauvais. Between 1643 and 1652 Boileau acquired a firm grasp of Greek and Latin languages and literatures, more than a passing good knowledge of Italian, and an excellent grounding in church history and theology. He was in fact tonsured in 1646, but showed no interest in the ecclesiastical career that some members of his family seemed to have in mind for him. His brother Jacques, just one year older, was to elect that option and accede eventually to a professorship in theology at the Sorbonne. Another brother, Jérôme, followed the example of their father and pursued a rewarding career in the parlement and courts of Paris. Nicolas too was drawn to this alternative and after the requisite years of study (1652–1656) was duly admitted to the bar. It is not known whether or not he actually practiced, but his legal career was extremely short-lived. For in 1657 his father died, leaving him an income generous enough to allow him at the age of twenty-one to give up the law and all other thoughts of gainful employment and devote the rest of his days to literature.

Even as a schoolboy this had been Boileau's deep temptation and, as events were to prove, his governing direction. He is known to have read extensively during those formative years and took normal adolescent delight in the modish, lengthy novels of love and adventure by Gautier de La Calprenède and Madeleine de Scudéry. With the encouragement of his teachers he had tried his hand at writing poetry while still a secondary-school student and even undertook a tragedy in verse that has not been preserved. Boileau's first sustained, professional literary effort took place in the early and middle 1660's. During this period he composed the first nine of his twelve satires, modeled in part on Horace and Juvenal but unmistakably modern in conception and content.

Boileau's chief innovation was to use satire as an instrument of literary criticism, although the word "criticism" in this connection may be a bit benevolent. As there will be occasion to observe later, Boileau's criticisms seldom rise above the level of playful and witty invective. Boileau jolted his contemporaries and is still remembered today as the very first poet-critic in French literature to frame highly personal, peremptory literary judgments on living writers whom he did not hesitate to call by name. Boileau rose to immediate notoriety, which finally turned to lasting fame, by expressing in vivid and explicit terms his own irrepressible impatience with mediocrity, in an age that tended to regard literature as a more or less amusing but unimportant pastime. Boileau attracted wide attention to himself by behaving as if it were, on the contrary, a sacred occupation. The reception accorded to the *Satires* was astonishing both in the scale of its success and in the

passions that it generated. Boileau's victims, with their sympathizers and henchmen, did him the favor of replying to his attacks, a strategy that helped put him even more prominently before the public eye. Pirated editions of the *Satires* began to appear in France and Holland. The publication in Rouen in 1666 of what Boileau called a "monstrous" edition compelled him to bring out during the course of that same year an authorized version. By the late 1660's his reputation as a poet, critic, and polemicist was firmly established.

In 1670 he began to publish a series of *épîtres*, retracing in this respect as well the itinerary already mapped out before him by Horace. Boileau's verse epistles, however, are no more than satires in disguise; they exhibit the same rebellious wit, the same youthful irreverence for the literature and literary taste of the preceding generation.

Boileau's principal target in his satirical writings was Jean Chapelain, a poet, scholar, and critic who is remembered today only by professional students of French literature but who in his time enjoyed extraordinary prestige and power. Chapelain was not only a founding and ranking member of the Académie Française, but more specifically was chief consultant to the crown in the matter of pensions to be distributed to writers, historians, and scholars. Chapelain was far from dull or stupid; he was, nevertheless, a weak individual who, although he probably knew better, allowed himself to be identified as a tool of the old guard and a symbol of academicism. Chapelain's most unforgettable and unforgivable blunder was to have yielded to the pressures of Corneille's envious critics and to have issued over his own signature the Académie's stodgy, retrograde, insensitive indictment of the greatest box-office success of his century, *Le Cid*. With such credits as that to his name and as keeper of the royal pension lists—from which the young and unknown, a certain Nicolas Boileau among them, were ritually excluded—Chapelain was indeed fair game. As author of *La pucelle* (The Maiden, 1656), a tedious epic poem based on the life of Joan of Arc, Chapelain was open to substantive criticisms of another kind, especially since his ponderous verse style was reminiscent of another era. It took no great powers of imagination, no real torturing of the facts to identify Chapelain as the incarnation of a tired, self-serving literary establishment.

Boileau hated mediocrity and knew a loser when he saw one, but he also had a passion for quality coupled with an incredible capacity for picking winners. Accordingly, at the same time that he was bringing down Chapelain, he was heaping generous praise on Molière (*satire* 2, 1663) long before it was fashionable to do so. It was Boileau once again who defended Jean de La Fontaine against his detractors (*Dissertation sur joconde*, 1669). He was also among the first in France along with Molière to recognize the genius of Racine and the only critic of note to have supported the author of *Phèdre* against his rivals (*épître* 7, 1677). In short, Boileau had the shrewdness, conviction, taste, and, above all, talent required to set himself up as the champion of youth, vitality, elegance, and quality in an age of unprecedented political, social, and cultural expansion—and in a Paris that was then and remains to this day the hub of European, if not international, literary life. It would be entirely accurate to identify Boileau as the very first of a long line of men of letters—among them Voltaire, Victor Hugo, Émile Zola, and Roland Barthes—who were to build dazzling careers on the ruins of smug, effete, and vulnerable literary and cultural establishments. In terms that today have become automatic and familiar, Boileau could be described as the arch-agent of the new criticism and poetry with respect to what we would call traditional criticism and poetry.

The definitive triumph of the new over the old can be dated with precision: it took place in 1674, the year of Chapelain's death, the same year that saw the publication of Boileau's *Oeuvres diverses.* Nor is this a coincidence. Chapelain's power and influence had

enabled him for years to prevent Boileau's publisher from securing the indispensable *privilège,* or royal imprimatur. With Chapelain's demise, all opposition crumbled; permission to go to press was immediately forthcoming, and Boileau's claim to fame assured.

The *Oeuvres diverses* of 1674 contained, in addition to the first nine satires and four of the epistles, the first four cantos of his mock-heroic poem, *Le lutrin,* in four cantos (two more were published in the 1683 edition) and, of crucial importance in the history of Boileau's reputation, the long-awaited *Art poétique.* Also of major significance in the development of European critical thought was the inclusion, in the 1674 edition, of Boileau's translation of the anonymous treatise *On the Sublime,* then attributed to the third-century Greek rhetorician Cassius Longinus. It was in fact through the French version that the highly influential "Longinus"—in Jonathan Swift's words, "translated from Boileau's translation" (*On Poetry: A Rhapsody* 1.261)—became known in England.

From the beginnings of French literary historiography in the middle of the eighteenth century until the late 1920's, Boileau's *Art poétique* was read as a manifesto of French classical doctrine, as a handbook of rules that he was supposed to have formulated in the name of the school of 1660—Molière, La Fontaine, Racine, and himself—aimed at certain refractory, insufficiently "classical" contemporaries. The *Art poétique* was once thought to have played, in fact, the same defining role in the rise of French classicism as Hugo's *Préface de Cromwell* did in the triumph of romanticism. In reality the *Art poétique* added nothing to critical theory that had not been known and readily accessible fifty or a hundred years earlier. More impressive and original than the precepts and definitions that Boileau had the knack of framing in unforgettable alexandrine couplets was his insistence on the role of intensity and passion in the aesthetic experience. It was this very preoccupation, moreover, that had also motivated his long interest in the Greek treatise *On the Sublime.* If Boileau valued purity of form and diction—and there can be no doubt that he did—it was not out of any picayune or superstitious concern for correctness; rather, he viewed careful attention to the details of composition and style as a means of purging the work of all blemishes that might lessen (that is, interfere with, disrupt) its emotional impact.

Boileau enjoyed the greatest literary and personal success that a man in the seventeenth century could know. Very early in his career he caught the notice of Louis XIV and was to benefit throughout the years from substantial royal pensions. The king is reported always to have taken special pleasure in having Boileau read to him. In 1677 Boileau was appointed jointly with his good friend Racine to the highly prestigious post of royal historiographer. The chronicle of Louis's reign and military campaigns at which both poets worked devotedly for many years was destroyed by fire when only partially completed. Owing in large measure to Boileau's poor health, it was not resumed.

Just one years after his election to the Académie Française in 1684, Boileau took up residence at Auteuil, now a fashionable suburb of Paris but then considered the country. There in semiretirement he received the most celebrated writers and ecclesiastics of the time. Auteuil soon became an essential pilgrimage for aspiring young poets and distinguished travelers from abroad. Joseph Addison has left an enlightening account of one such sojourn at Auteuil. In a letter to Bishop Hough sent from Marseilles in December 1700, Addison recorded the elements of a style and personality that have not always come through even to the most practiced readers of Boileau's critical writings:

I had the honor to be introduced to Mr. Boileau, who is now retouching his works and putting them out in a new edition. He is old and deaf, but talks incomparably well in his own calling. He heartily hates an ill poet and puts himself in a passion when he talks of anyone that has not a high respect for the ancients. I don't know whether there is more of old age or truth in his censure on the French authors, but he wonderfully cries down their present writers and extols his former contemporaries very much, especially his two intimate friends Arnaud and Racine. . . .

(*Letters of Joseph Addison*, Graham ed., pp. 25–26)

The final consecration of Boileau's fame was guaranteed by Claude Brossette, a young lawyer from Lyons, who played Boswell to the aging poet during his later years. Brossette's annotated edition of Boileau's *Oeuvres* appeared in 1716. The exaggerated reminiscences gathered and canonized by Brossette are largely responsible for the inaccuracies and myths that have accompanied Boileau's fame down to the present century. The naive scribe of a particularly vain old man, Brossette made Boileau seem like the Legislator of Parnassus who had put down single-handedly the literary heresies of the older generation.

Most of Boileau's writings during the Auteuil period were polemical in nature. In January 1687 Charles Perrault read to the Académie a poem, *Le siècle de Louis XIV*, claiming the cultural superiority of modern France to ancient Greece and Rome. In reply Boileau wrote the *Réflexions critiques sur Longin*, which with much humor and irony detailed Perrault's often incredible ignorance. With *épître* 12 (1698) Boileau lashed out at religious casuistry, as Pascal had before him, lampooning with characteristic verve the opinion attributed to some Jesuits that love of God is not prerequisite to grace. In this epistle Boileau shows a close familiarity with a large body of rather abstruse theological writing. It also provides evidence as to Boileau's sympathies with the Jansenist party in the course of a quarrel that led to the eventual destruction of the abbey of Port-Royal des Champs by Louis XIV's soldiers. The controversy that prompted *épître* 12 grew so hot that Louis XIV felt obliged to prohibit publication of a renewed attack by Boileau in *satire* 12 (1705–1711), which appeared posthumously in 1713.

During the late eighteenth century Boileau's reputation began to wane, and it suffered greatly during the romantic period. Just the same, until quite recently Boileau's *Satires* and *Art poétique* were widely read in French secondary schools. Since 1968, however, a series of reforms, with emphasis on relevance, have reduced sharply the role of the classics in the scheme of national education. Not only Boileau but Corneille and Racine also are on the way to becoming objects of almost antiquarian curiosity.

The *Art poétique* was translated into English during the Augustan period and won particular praise from John Dryden and Alexander Pope, the English writer who most closely approaches Boileau in tone and style. Pope's *Essay on Criticism* owes perhaps as much to the *Art poétique* as Boileau's work owes to Horace's.

Boileau died in Paris on 13 March 1711. In 1800 his remains were transferred from the Sainte-Chapelle to the Musée des Monuments Français, and from there nine years later to the church of Saint-Germain-des-Prés.

THE POET AND HIS CRAFT

In the eyes of his contemporaries Boileau was a poet, and from their point of view that is perhaps all he was. Three years before its publication, the *Art poétique* was already known and appreciated, not only as a literary success, but as a first-rate poem. "Monsieur B. Despréaux has composed . . . an art of poetry," Pierre Richelet wrote in 1671, "*but* it is in verse" (*La versification française*, p. 13). The word "but" must be understood here in all its adversative force, because for Richelet an art of poetry in verse was an extraordinary event. He goes on to stress this unusual formal aspect: "We have never seen anything from this rare spirit in a better or more lively style than the verses of his *Poétique*."

Two years later, Boileau's readings in society circles elicited similar reactions: "I dined yesterday at the Gourvilles," Mme. de Sévigné confided to her daughter, "along with M. le Duc, M. de La Rochefoucauld, Mme. de Thianges, Mme. de La Fayette, Mme. de Coulanges, the abbé Têtu, M. de Marsillac, and Guilleragues. You were remembered and toasted. Then we heard the *Poétique* of Despréaux, which is a masterpiece." At the end of the same letter, she reiterates her enthusiasm: "Despréaux's poetry will delight you" (15 December 1673). And her admiration for this work was apparently shared. The following month she wrote once again to her daughter: "I went to lunch on Saturday at M. de Pomponne's, as I mentioned to you. He sat there until five o'clock charmed, enraptured, thrilled by the perfection of Despréaux's verse in the *Poétique;* D'Hacqueville was there; we spoke two or three times of the pleasure it would give me to have you hear him read" (15 January 1674).

It is often true, especially in factual matters, that contemporaries are mistaken, that in many respects they are even less well informed than we are. It is also true that in aesthetic matters, their enthusiasms and aversions may involve passing fashions, that their literary judgments may reflect individual fancies, personal biases, or partisan viewpoints. Thus, we need not attribute to Mme. de Sévigné's raptures or to the hyperbole in her report of Pomponne's reaction any absolute meaning or any special historical value. The delight that they took in hearing Boileau recite his poetry may well be no more than the expression of a taste and sensibility that belong to another era. Their comments, however, imply and overlay an attitude as widespread today as in their time: that the experience of literary form, in this case, poetic form, is an activity and a pleasure that is autonomous and is precious independently of any other consideration. This conception of poetry

poetry as form is especially worthy of our notice in the present instance, since it coincides exactly with Boileau's own conception of himself as a writer.

Whether out of modesty or self-satisfaction, Boileau said very little in any open or direct way about his own vocation as a poet. But even the few remarks that he has left us on this subject have not received all the attention that they deserve. With respect to his *Ode on the Taking of Namur,* for example, Boileau made a practical observation that has been the object of a ridicule almost as complete as the contempt in which the poem itself is usually held. He wrote to Racine:

> I have tried some rather novel things here. I have even gone so far as to speak of the white feather that the king wears in his hat. But, in my opinion, to create new forms of expression in poetry, we have to deal with subjects that haven't yet been treated in poetry.
>
> (4 June 1693, *Lettres à Racine,* p. 50)*

It may seem surprising to hear the grand old man of Auteuil, at the height of his fame, boast of such a trivial accomplishment. And yet, however insignificant the actual occasion may appear, Boileau's comment on Louis XIV's feather points up two tendencies that, when considered in and by themselves, are both important and revealing: a conscious striving for originality and, along with it, an implicit declaration of priorities. It would appear on the face of things that Boileau was preoccupied with virtuosity to such an extent that he was all but indifferent to his subject matter. But there is far more at stake here than mere pride in overcoming obstacles. In a letter of 29 April 1965 to Maucroix, he states explicitly that there is an impressive disparity between the banality of content and the richness of language that can more than justify these

*All citations are to Boileau's text in *Oeuvres complètes,* 7 vols., edited by Charles-H. Boudhors (Paris, 1934–1943). Translations of the text are by Ruth Sussman and Jules Brody.

ostensibly pointless concerns. The poetic quality that Boileau was aiming for in the Namur ode is the same one that he attributes to the incomparable Malherbe:

> He is especially good, in my opinion, at saying the little things, and it is in this respect that he most resembles the ancients, whom I admire particularly for that reason. The drier the subject, the more difficult it is to treat in verse, the more striking it becomes when it is expressed nobly, and with that special elegance that defines true poetry.

Boileau goes on to tell Maucroix that it was just this "striking" relationship between antithetical qualities that their mutual friend La Fontaine especially appreciated in Boileau's lines on the transfer to France of the Venetian lace industry:

> *Et nos voisins frustrés de ces tributs serviles,*
> *Que payait à leur art le luxe de nos villes.*
> (*épître* 1.141–142)

And our neighbors, deprived of this servile tribute Which their craft received from the wealth of our cities.

This couplet might seem a trivial accomplishment. And yet, Boileau insists,

> Vergil and Horace are divine in this regard and so is Homer. They are the exact opposites of our own latter-day poets, who speak only of vague things that others have spoken of before them, and for which pat expressions already exist. . . . As for myself, I don't know whether I have succeeded or not, but when I write poetry, I always try to say something that has never been said before in our language.
>
> (29 April 1695, *Lettres à Racine,* p. 114)

Boileau differs radically, then, from those poets—the vast majority, in his opinion—who are content to trade in clichés, those "whose expressions are common coin." He, on the contrary, sets for himself the arduous task of going after new expressions, the kind difficult to come by: "I have more or less finished the ode on Namur," he wrote to Racine, "except for a few lines in which I haven't quite caught the expression that I am looking for" (3 June 1693, p. 47). The idea, or rather the image, of writing as a linguistic quest both personal and solitary had already served thirty years earlier as the theme of Boileau's *satire* 2 addressed to Molière: "Enseigne-moi, Molière, où tu trouves la rime" (Teach me, Molière, where you find your rhymes). Although in less explicit fashion, Boileau attributes to other considerations of pure form a somewhat unexpected, slightly exaggerated prestige. "This is a work," he told Racine concerning *satire* 10, "that is killing me by the enormous number of transitions—which constitute, in my opinion, the most difficult achievement in poetry" (7 October 1692, p. 43). This concept of poetry as an essentially verbal undertaking reflects, in fact, the same artisanlike bias as Mallarmé's famous remark "It is not with ideas . . . that poetry is written, but with words" (reported by Paul Valéry, *Oeuvres* 1.1324, Pléiade ed.).

At times Boileau's interest in form approaches pure hedonism; that is to say, pleasure derived from virtuosity, from the playful and witty uses of language. Thanks to this penchant for verbal play, Boileau was able to shift from one moral position to its opposite simply for his own amusement and that of his readers. Here, for example, is what this allegedly crabby, misogynistic old bachelor had to say on the subject of his friend Brossette's impending marriage:

> Let's talk now about your marriage. In my opinion you could not be taking a more judicious step. Although I composed, *animi gratia* [for the fun of it], a satire against evil women, I am nevertheless in agreement with Alcippus, and I believe, as he does, that "it's easy to be happy in the blessed married state/Provided you have chosen an appropriate cellmate." Poets must not be taken literally. Today they celebrate bachelorhood, tomorrow they rave about marriage. Today man is the dumbest of all creatures; tomorrow he

is the only one capable of justice and for that reason is the image of God.
> (5 July 1705, *Lettres à Brossette*, p. 97)

This passage is not the first time, moreover, that we hear Boileau denouncing the dangers of literalism. Concerning certain erudite commentators on the ancients, Boileau answered Brossette's queries simply by quoting twice, with contempt, this verse of Terence (*Andria* 17): "Faciunt nae intelligendo ut nihil intelligant" (They understand so much that they understand nothing: 29 December 1701 and 9 April 1702, pp. 46, 50). When it came to his own work, Boileau took a more aggressive stance with Brossette: "In all your letters for some time now you have been critizing my poetry in a way that borders on pedantry. . . . You have consistently been far too carping and rigid" (2 August 1793, pp. 66–67). On one occasion Brossette accused Boileau of having committed a grammatical error in the verse "De Styx et d'Achéron peindre les noirs torrents" (Of Styx and Acheron depict the murky floods: *Art poétique* 3.285). His criticism elicited the following reply from Boileau:

> If you want to know my opinion, your ear in the present instance may be a bit prosaic; a true poet would never find fault with this line, because "de Styx et d'Achéron" flows much more smoothly than "du Styx et de l'Achéron.". . . But these niceties are mysteries that Apollo teaches only to those who are true initiates in his art.
> (7 January 1709, pp. 119–120)

Boileau was to direct essentially the same reproach at another literal-minded critic who had taken it upon himself to decry the boldness of Racine's famous hyperbole "Le flot qui l'apporta recule épouvanté" (The wave that brought it in recoiled aghast: *Phèdre* 5.6, Cairncross trans., 1524). This image, Boileau insists, "would be acceptable even in prose if it were framed by a 'so to speak' or a 'if I may say,'" but such justifications "are rarely tolerated in poetry, where they would be flat and weak, because poetry carries its own justification with it'' (*Réflexions critiques* 11, pp. 179–180). Boileau's comments on ostensibly minor details of style and language often reveal to what extent he viewed the writing of poetry as an autonomous and privileged activity. In translating a verse of Pindar, Charles Perrault, his archadversary in the Quarrel of the Ancients and Moderns, had displaced one word, thereby eliminating an image; in the original, Boileau points out, there is ''a very lovely figure of speech, whereas in the translation, since the figure is lacking, the poetic effect has been destroyed'' (*Réflexions critiques* 8, p. 102).

This collection of random observations surely does not invite any radical new conclusions concerning Boileau's ideas on poetry, but it does point to the existence of a rather unique literary sensibility. Whenever Boileau is faced with concrete problems of expression, composition, rhythm, and imagery, he argues, criticizes others, and defends his own poetic practice with the authority and self-confidence of a man who believes himself possessed of a gift denied to ordinary mortals. His sensitivity to linguistic nuance is so keen, at any rate, that a single image or preposition, even one syllable more or less, is enough to crown or to damn a difficult and perilous enterprise.

It would be far less urgent for us to define or defend Boileau's very special sense of poetic vocation if it were not for a tendency, easily as old as romanticism, that leads readers to equate nondramatic poetry with mere lyricism; certain postromantic critics would even go so far as to deny any poetic potential to the didactic forms and genres that Boileau practiced. It is true that even his detractors make the ritual genuflections—more out of superstition and conscience than conviction—before Boileau's craftsmanship, precision, cleverness, richness of rhymes, knack for picturesque detail, and many dense, finely chiseled maxims. But there is a long and stubborn tradition of opinion on Boileau that is neatly summed up in this epigram by Joseph Joubert: ''Boileau. A great poet, but in semipoetry.''

Of course, if the storehouse of French literature were overcrowded to the point where a choice had to be made between the *Art poétique* and the *Fleurs du mal*, most critics would agree to remove Boileau in order to make room for Baudelaire. If a choice had to be made, however, between *épître* 9 and Lamartine's *Le lac*, between *satire* 9 and Hugo's *À Villequier*, there would be more than ample room for discussion. And yet that is not really the question either, because in Boileau's mind poetry was an absolute. It could exist or not exist, but never by halves. For Boileau this distinction was fundamental. In fact, no critic before him—and perhaps none after—emphasized as strenuously as he did the totally irreconcilable differences between these activities: to write verse and to write poetry.

THE CRITIC AS POET

The rare attempts to approach Boileau's writing through the study of his particular uses of language have been few and far between. In 1938 Leo Spitzer in his *Stilstudien* put forth some interesting views on Boileau's repetitions (toujours, jamais, à nos yeux, grossier, fertile, plaire, among other words), showing how they accumulate and converge to produce the image of an oracular mentality endowed with infallible judgment, an intellectual personality who aspired to play the same role in literature as did the court in the realm of taste or the king in the realm of politics. Elton B. O. Borgerhoff (see bibliography), taking another route, stresses what he so perceptively sees as Boileau's ''duplicity,'' that penchant for evasive ambiguity which the second and ninth satires exemplify so well. Borgerhoff's analyses reveal a playful Boileau, a conscious and clever manipulator of roles and of words, a stager of comic dialogues, a poet who systematically blurs the contours of his thought by continually pointing out its personal and provisional nature. Boileau's elaborated and sustained duplicity assumes the dimensions of a figure of thought, which, unlike immediately recognizable figures of style, is diffused throughout his poems in such a way as to perform a structural function. Nathan Edelman (see bibliography), who was very much impressed with Borgerhoff's contribution, undertook to show how the meaning and the essence of Boileau's aesthetic are reflected in a series of recurrent images of movement–repose, waking–sleeping, and tension–relaxation. His invaluable 1974 study shows that Boileau's thought is a poet's thought, inseparable from the texture of his language. From Edelman's vantage point we can see beyond the rules and the doctrine, and share in Boileau's vision of literary success as an affective victory over a reader who is always ready to escape the boredom of bad writing through flight or sleep.

By their insistence on the poetic properties of Boileau's writing, the clearly ahistorical approaches of Borgerhoff and Edelman open up the possibility of restoring Boileau to his true place in history. We have known for a long time that Boileau's ideas about literature were absolutely commonplace. Boileau criticism has, in fact, become a long series of demolitions. For more than fifty years literary historians have been unanimous in denying to the erstwhile Legislator of Parnassus any originality as a theoretician or any importance as a critic. His "doctrine" was a mirage, merely the sum total of what people had been saying about literature for over a generation; his influence on his contemporaries proved to be a myth manufactured out of whole cloth by an enormous ego rendered even more arrogant by an uninterrupted notoriety and prolonged success. The difficulty for today's reader is that Boileau has still not recovered from the effects of the radical demythification to which he has been subjected. Having denounced the errors, having exploded the fictions, we are now faced with the task of replacing them with truths;

what remains to be done now is to raise up from the ruins of the old thinker-theoretician Boileau the Boileau who really existed. Celebrated too long for all the wrong reasons, Boileau still awaits his true niche in history.

All that remains of the Boileau discredited by modern scholarship and by inevitable changes in taste is the nonideological aspect of his work, which is to say the work itself: the words, verses, images, rhythms, and rhymes of which it is actually composed. There also remain the incredible prestige that his work enjoyed, the admiration that it aroused among his contemporaries, and the pleasure—amply documented—that they took in reading it. Finally, there remains the exalted opinion—also well-documented—in which Boileau himself held his own achievement.

The elements that made the historical Boileau what he was would no doubt make of him if he were alive today the kind of vibrant, public personality who would host a highly successful literary and intellectual talk show on television. This comparison is both true to life and very much to Boileau's credit. For the historical Boileau was exactly that: a man of impact and influence, an opinion maker, a trend setter, a provocative critic, one who knew how to get around, a readable, entertaining success-hungry writer who wanted the literature of his time to be, above all else, "modern," relevant, accessible, enjoyable. And yet, despite this popular bent, his constant concerns were supremely serious. In publicly decrying and denouncing what he considered cheap and inauthentic writing, he hoped, and to a large extent managed, to make himself the legitimate spokesman for culture and, one might even say, the consecrated high priest of poetry.

In *satire* 9 (1667–1668), Boileau marshals all his poetic "duplicity" to get a lively debate going between a fictitious Self, the alleged enemy of satire, and an Other—his Esprit—also fictitious, who is satire's devoted, incurable practitioner. At a certain point in their give-and-take, the Self, who is fighting a losing battle, gives up out of weariness and reluctantly wishes his alter ego all the success in the world:

> . . . je veux que le sort, par un heureux caprice
> Fasse de vos écrits prospérer la malice,
> Et qu'enfin votre livre, aille au gré de vos voeux,
> Faire siffler Cotin, chez nos derniers neveux.
>
> (79–82)

> . . . I hope that Fate, by some happy caprice,
> Will cause your malicious writings to prosper,
> And that your book, in keeping with your wishes,
> Will make Cotin the laughing-stock of our most
> remote descendants.

These few lines devoted to Charles Cotin (1604–1682), a minor poet now largely forgotten, may be described or classified as literary criticism only to the extent that they convey a summary value judgment: Cotin deserves to be booed. In the present instance, however, one scarcely has the right to use the word "judgment." We are dealing here, at best, with opinion; at worst, with invective, perhaps insult, even slander. What is more, the verb "siffler" (literally, to whistle or hiss), with the low-class aura that surrounds it, is not likely to lend much dignity to the judgment that it recapitulates. Boileau's purpose, presumably, is not, then, to convert Cotin's admirers, if in fact Cotin really had any, to his own point of view. It is rather surprising, moreover, that Boileau bothers to surround this quite peremptory criticism of Cotin with such an arsenal of rhetorical weapons. For the three lines that are used to set off "faire siffler Cotin" appear to have a much greater literary complexity than the remark itself. Or are they in fact a part of it?

The Self finally consents to the satirical project of the Other, but unwillingly, grudgingly. In the opinion of Boileau's wise, circumspect, just, and reasonable Self, this kind of judgment, prompted as it is by the sheer malice and impertinence of an incorrigible satirist, will be able to capture the public ear only if some caprice, some quirk of fate, helps the Other to implement and impose his essentially unjust and perverse designs. Such a situation, so the Self implies, comes close to moral scandal, since in a rational, well-ordered world, "malice" should simply not "prosper."

The function of this indignant Self, then, is to bring out the arbitrariness of the Other's judgments, to take exception to his personal, willful bias, and to condemn his injustice. In short, into the Self's indictment of the Other, Boileau incorporates a selection of the criticisms that his own satires provoked from the very day of their appearance and that they continued to arouse among his victims and his detractors for the remainder of his career. Thus a fact drawn from the actual reception of Boileau's *Satires* becomes the subject of a new poem; the scandal created by his early forays against the literary establishment of his day is skillfully dramatized and purposefully perpetuated by an author avid for notoriety. It further serves him as a pretext for exploiting a dialectical relationship between his work and his public, and as a way of magnifying his role as the opponent of sham and the friend of truth in an allegedly corrupt literary world ruled by the Cotins and other poetasters.

The argument put forth by the Self, whose apparent purpose is to condemn the excesses of satire, really functions to set off in brilliant relief a particularly low-down, subjective kind of criticism. The ostensible adversary of the Other argues eloquently against malicious criticism, but in the end, of course, he himself operates as his opponent's spokesman. Having said everything he can think of to discourage the Other from expressing himself so freely, he finally bows out of the fray, battle weary in the face of the Other's visceral need to ridicule his fellow poets, a need that the Self has tried valiantly but unsuccessfully to temper—"Je veux qu'enfin votre livre aille" (All right, what's the use, let your book take off). Once liberated, the book of the uncontrollable satirist, propelled forward by an accumulated, pent-up energy too long repressed, soars through the ages to accomplish its mission in a far-off distant future: "Faire siffler Cotin, chez nos derniers neveux." (Let Cotin be booed by our remotest descendants).

Outside of the context that the poet has so cleverly constructed around it, this line, banal in itself, might pass unnoticed. As the culmination of the development that precedes it, however, it takes on rich overtones. Coming as it does at the end of a rhetorical blast-off, this insignificant judgment on a still more insignificant author assumes bizarre proportions. At the end of the first hemistich in line 82, where this archetype of the contemptible author is finally named, the literary fortunes of Cotin—what the Germans so nicely call his "Nachleben"—are determined forever. In the space of six short syllables, the judgment and its practical consequences—"Faire siffler Cotin"—have been established. At the end of the following six syllables Cotin's crime and its punishment have been telescoped in time, consecrated for all eternity. With the hemistich "chez nos derniers neveux," Cotin is ensconced in an endless future, consigned forever to his irrevocable destiny. A moment's reflection tells us just how adroitly Boileau has contrived to endow his subjective opinion of Cotin with all the authority of an objective fact, a fact as "natural" as the uninterrupted flow of time or the continuous propagation of the human race. Through a poetic—lexical, syntactical, grammatical, and metrical—strategy, a completely personal opinion is elevated instantaneously to the status of an eternal truth. The twelve syllables "Faire siffler Cotin, chez nos derniers neveux" in the last analysis propose two "truths" of equal weight, two complementary constants: the incorrigibility of bad poetry on the one hand, and, on the other, the immutability of good taste.

These four lines from Boileau's *satire* 9 are built on an absolute ideological void. They tell us nothing new about Boileau's literary ideas, and still less about the literary value of Cotin. Their interest, then, resides neither in their content nor in the way in which this content

is expressed. Like any authentically "poetic" message—in the etymological sense of the word (from the Greek verb *poiein* = to do, to make)—this passage is more performative than informative; it concentrates our attention primarily on what it *does*, on the verbal construction that is its essence. By the efficacious organization of their language, these lines conceal the subjectivity of an arbitrary opinion behind the outward appearance of an objective truth. Boileau's procedure here is at the same time original and typical. It consists in removing literary criticism, associated through long custom in his reader's mind with reflection and proof, from the sphere of discursive argument to the nondiscursive domain of image—a domain from which all discussion, all ideological activity, is automatically excluded. Thus Boileau's critical stance as illustrated here breaks all traditional links with analysis and reasoning; it abandons all ideological ambitions and sets itself up, instead, as an independent object of contemplation.

It is worth noting that the images of the satirist's book as the model of unchanging good taste and of Cotin as the paragon of mediocre poetry are not the kinds of images that we grasp immediately. These are not striking figures of style that impress us or create a vivid mental picture through their precision or color or evocative power. Boileau presents us rather with figures of thought sketched lightly in pencil rather than painted with broad strokes of the brush, and the reader gradually becomes aware of these images and their meaning.

In Boileau's own vocabulary the act of penetrating a text is called "rentrer dans une idée" (getting into an idea: October 1692, *Lettres à Racine*, p. 63). To the extent that Boileau succeeds in involving us in his poetic strategy, he plants in us the desire not only to learn what he is saying but to understand what he is doing, by living out through our reading the verbal experience of his idea.

As a practical problem, the art of getting

into an idea must presuppose, if not an immediate connivance, at least an honest understanding between poet and public, a common denominator between the activity of the writer and that of his reader. The factor that has contributed most to distorting our critical perspective on Boileau is the disproportion between our expectations as readers and the real possibilities for literary experience inherent in his work. What we expect of him rarely takes into account what he may have been expecting of us. And yet Boileau's intentions with respect to his reader are perfectly clear and reasonable. By his explicit views on his craft, and by the forms that he practiced, he invites us to read him with the same openness to verbal experience and sensitivity to stylistic effects that presided over the elaboration of his own work. Any reading of Boileau that does not recognize the preeminence of the nondiscursive and figurative modes constitutes a fundamental deviation from proper method, which consists of trying to explain authors, not on the basis of their supposed intentions, but on the basis of the linguistic acts that they have actually performed.

For the reader who really wants to come to grips with Boileau's writing, to confront him on his own territory, a first obstacle is the apparently intermittent or erratic nature of his talent. Reading him, even with the greatest sympathy, one is easily dazzled by the most visible and brilliant feature of his style: his numerous and memorable aphorisms. And in this respect Boileau does in fact run the risk of falling victim to his own verbal facility. It is extremely difficult to resist the impact of these dense and chiseled maxims; it is difficult to resist the temptation to separate them from their contexts as just so many oases of wit, art, and verve that punctuate an otherwise prosaic desert. It remains to be seen whether Boileau's elegant maxims are no more than the expression of common wisdom or whether they might perhaps indicate, within his work as a whole, deeper aesthetic and poetic preoccupations.

"Il n'est point de degrés du médiocre au pire" (There are no degrees between middling and bad: *Art poétique* 4.32). This is the quintessential Boileau, the perfectionist insisting on quality:

Il n'est point de degrés du médiocre au pire;
Qui dit froid écrivain dit détestable auteur.
Boyer est à Pinchêne égal pour le lecteur;
On ne lit guère plus Rampale et Ménardière,
Que Magnon, Du Souhait, Corbin et La Morlière.
Un fou du moins fait rire, et peut nous égayer;
Mais un froid écrivain ne sait rien qu'ennuyer.
J'aime mieux Bergerac et sa burlesque audace
Que ces vers où Motin se morfond et nous glace.

(4.32–40)

Be a mason, if that is your talent,
An estimable worker in a useful art,
Rather than a commonplace writer and a poetic
  hack.
In all other arts there are different degrees,
One can occupy the second rank with honor;
But in the dangerous art of rhyming and writing
There are no degrees between middling and bad;
When we say "frigid writer" we mean detestable
  author.
For the reader, Boyer is just like Pinchêne;
We no more read Rampale and Ménardière,
Than we do Magnon, Du Souhait, Corbin and La
  Morlière.
A fool at least makes us laugh and can cheer us
  up;
But a frigid writer can't do anything but bore us.
I prefer Bergerac and his burlesque daring
To the verse of Motin which depresses and chills
  us.

(4.26–40)

When read as a unit, this passage develops organically around two complementary polarities. In one, the "art dangereux" (31) of the poet is opposed both to the "art nécessaire" of the mason and to "tout autre art" (27, 29) without exception. And in the other polarity, within the unique and exclusive art of poetry, a group of "froids écrivains" is opposed to an unnamed poetic elite. With respect to the privileged status of poetry, all the other arts can be grouped together under a common rubric of inferiority. Similarly, in contrast to those poets who are really worthy of the name, the others, bunched together pell-mell in a veritable avalanche of proper names (34–36), are related to one another by a common bond of mediocrity, already implicit in the initial uses of the words "commun" and "vulgaire" (28). These writers constitute the "pecus," the herd, the *profanum vulgus* (common herd) in Horace's term, which a spirit bent on distinction sets at a distance that is as much aesthetic as it is social.

These polarities, furthermore, are absolutely without nuance: "Boyer est à Pinchêne égal pour le lecteur" (34); "On ne lit guère plus . . . que" (35–36); " . . . ne sait rien qu'ennuyer" (38). Thus, the two polarities "art poétique–tout autre art" and "froid écrivain–bon poète" relay and reinforce each other, and converge to evoke the image of an irreducible, unbridgeable gap. And it is precisely this suggestion of a spatial figure, fleshed out and broadened by the rhymed couple "degrés différents–seconds rangs" (29–30) that lends prominence to the much-quoted maxim "Il n'est point de degrés du médiocre au pire." As critical "thinking," the passage before us is of meager interest. As a poetic structure, however, it *does* more than it *says.*

"For Boileau," in the words of Nathan Edelman, "the only possibilities open to the poet are signal success or utter failure. There is no in between." Boileau's critical attitudes have this much in common with both his stylistic habits and his satiric vision: they all trace their origins to the same nuclear hyperbole. From whatever angle we may approach his work, whatever aspect of his literary activity we may want to consider, it is not ideas as such that we encounter, but rather ideas in contrast and conflict, mutually exclusive values, hyperbolically polarized positions. Under closer inspection, moreover, hyperbole is not simply a rhetorical device or strategic weapon in Boileau's hands; the constant presence of this figure of speech throughout his work

bears witness rather to a deep mode of sensibility, a chronic state of mind. If Boileau's judgments so often sound authoritarian or dogmatic, it is because they are the direct expression of a hyperbolic attitude and an intransigent credo: literature is a business of all or nothing, always or never.

The very first couplet of the *Art poétique* lays out a scheme of binary opposition that runs through the poem to the end:

> C'est en vain qu'au Parnasse un téméraire auteur
> Pense de l'art des vers atteindre la hauteur.

> A foolhardy dabbler in the poetic art
> Aims in vain for the heights of Parnassus.

The rich homophony of the rhyme "auteur/hauteur" transcends its mere prosodic function and turns a critical commonplace into a hyperbolic figure:

> S'il "ne" sent "point" du Ciel l'influence secrète,
> Si son astre en naissant "ne" l'a formé poète
> Dans son génie étroit il est toujours "captif."
> (3–5)

> If he doesn't feel the secret influence of Heaven,
> If his star did not make him a poet at his birth,
> He remains enslaved to his tiny talent.

Boileau's negations and exclusions, acting in concert with a vocabulary of altitude (ciel, astre), underscore the auteur/hauteur identity in such a way as to give special emphasis to the word "toujours."

In *satire* 9 Boileau had already made use of this same image of altitude to illustrate his personal vision of the topography of the republic of letters. All the many judgments contained in that early poem build on the same hyperbolic polarity that underlies the severe warning that Boileau addresses to the Other, his satiric spirit:

> Qui vous a pu souffler une si folle audace?
> Phébus a-t-il pour vous aplani le Parnasse?
> Et ne savez-vous pas, que sur ce mont sacré,
> Qui ne vole au sommet tombe au plus bas degré,

Et qu'à moins d'être au rang d'Horace ou de
Voiture,
On rampe dans la fange avec l'abbé de Pure?

(23–28)

Who could have inspired you with such mad
audacity?
Did Phoebus level Parnassus for you?
And don't you know that on this holy mount,
If you don't soar to the highest peak
You will fall to the lowest valley,
And that if you're not on the level of Horace or
Voiture,
You will crawl in the mud with the Abbé de Pure?

The entire interest of this passage lies in its poetic impact, which grows progressively stronger as Boileau exhausts the creative possibilities inherent in the altitude/platitude polarity, and in so doing develops and sustains an image of irreconciliable extremities, of an unbridgeable gap between good and bad, sublime and ridiculous. Both within the verse lines (sommet/bas degré; Voiture/Pure) and from one end of the passage to the other (au plus bas/au rang d'Horace; vole/rampe), the choice of each word and each sound is calculated to contribute to a cumulative convergence of antitheses. Boileau's procedure here is typical: He persuades us to share his opinions and attitudes by making us partners in his carefully worked out verbal game, a game so thoroughly sustained that he compels us to accept as logical evidence the essentially philological comparison between the pair of proper names (Voiture/Pure) that closes the passage and hammers home its point.

Thirty years later Boileau was to express the same idea more directly and graphically in a letter criticizing an opinion of the actor Baron. He takes exception to the fact that Baron

puts the poor poets so close to Apollo. The poetic riffraff of whom he speaks lives at the foot of Mount Parnassus, in its swamplands, where it crawls about with the frogs and the abbé de P[ure], but Apollo lives at the summit with the Muses and with Corneille, Racine, Molière, etc. No shoddy author has ever made it to the top.

(3 January 1700, *Lettres à Racine*,
pp. 131–132)

There are, says Boileau, two alternatives: to fly or to crawl, with no middle ground possible. The common run of poets, those who will never rise to the heights of their art, constantly swing back and forth between equal but opposite evils:

Souvent la peur d'un mal nous conduit dans un
pire.
Un vers était trop faible, et vous le rendez dur;
J'évite d'être long, et je deviens obscur;
L'un n'est point trop fardé, mais sa Muse est trop
nue;
L'autre a peur de ramper, il se perd dans la nue.

(*Art poétique* 1.64–68)

Often the fear of one evil leads us into a greater
one.
A line was too weak and you make it too strong;
For fear of being overlong, I become obscure;
This poet is not too gaudy, but his Muse is too
naked;
Another, for fear of crawling, gets lost in the
clouds.

The archetypal evil is platitude, flatness, as in the case of the poet who falls far below the style of the eclogue:

Ses vers plats et grossiers dépouillés d'agrément
Toujours baisent la terre, et rampent tristement.

(2.19–20)

His flat and vulgar verses, devoid of charm,
Always kiss the ground and crawl sadly along.

The poet "abject en son langage" (with abject clownish style: 17) whom Boileau has in mind here was presumably trying to avoid an error antithetical to the one that he finally committed. For grandiloquence is just as much out of place in the eclogue as is colloquial language:

NICOLAS BOILEAU-DESPRÉAUX

Son tour simple et naïf n'a rien de fastueux,
Et n'aime point l'orgueil d'un vers présomptueux.
Il faut que sa douceur flatte, chatouille, éveille,
Et jamais de grands mots n'épouvante l'oreille.

(2.7–10)

Its simple and natural style shuns pomposity,
And it spurns the arrogance of a presumptuous
    verse.
Its sweetness must caress, excite, enliven,
And never assail our ears with big words.

The problem evoked here is the same one faced by another poet who, for fear of crawling on the ground, gets lost in the clouds: "L'autre a peur de ramper, il se perd dans la nue" (Another, for fear of crawling, gets lost in the clouds). The trick is to strike a certain note, touch a precise point—ill-defined because no doubt undefinable—a point whose coordinates are known intuitively to the author of the *Art poétique*, and will be perceived instantly by the kind of exigent, sophisticated public to whom authentic literary works are addressed.

The way in which Boileau localizes this delicate point is typical of his method, in that he explains to his reader what he has in mind not in terms of a theory or a doctrine but in a consciously nondiscursive form, that is to say, poetically:

Entre ces deux excès la route est difficile.
Suivez, pour la trouver, Théocrite et Virgile.
Que leurs tendres écrits, par les Grâces dictés,
Ne quittent point vos mains, jour et nuit
    feuilletés.
Seuls dans leurs doctes vers ils pourront vous
    apprendre,
Par quel art sans bassesse un auteur peut
    descendre . . .

(2.25–30)

Between these two extremes the path is difficult.
To find it, follow Theocritus and Vergil.
May their tender writings, dictated by the Graces,
Never leave your hands; read them day and night.
They alone, with their polished verses, will be
    able to teach you

By what art an author can lower his tone without
    lowering himself . . .

Here, at a crucial juncture where the highest literary quality is at stake, Boileau undertakes, in Marie de Gournay's expression, to "speak about poetry poetically" (*L'ombre*, 1626, p. 972). He knows that he is dealing here with a nuance whose subtlety borders on paradox, with a rare capacity that he was one day to attribute to himself:

. . . polir un écrit
Qui dit sans s'avilir les plus petites choses. . . .
(épître 11.48–49)

. . . to polish a work
Which can say the smallest things without
    trivializing itself. . . .

This was a quality that he admired in Horace and that his insensitive friend Brossette had to have explained to him:

No man was ever less careless than Horace, and you most certainly mistook for carelessness certain expressions that in order to convey the naiveté of Nature he seems purposely to have framed in a lower style but that have an elegance that is worth more at times than all the pomp in Juvenal.
(6 December 1707, *Lettres à Brossette*, p. 111)

Boileau's critical strategy is extremely subtle indeed: it does not consist in locating a middle ground situated between two known extremes, but rather in reconciling contraries that appear irreconcilable, in making concrete, at the level of language, a seemingly ineffable poetic essence. An analogous ideal is implicit in the two lines that introduce his remarks on the burlesque:

Quoi que vous écriviez, évitez la bassesse.
Le style le moins noble a pourtant sa noblesse.
(Art poétique 1.79–80)

Whatever you write, avoid baseness.
The least noble style still has its nobility.

This paradoxical "nobility," which has no more to do with the grand style than it does with vulgarity, is precisely the one that Boileau admires in Theocritus and Vergil. It can be learned only by example, because like all poetic essences it is internal and secret. And the only way in which Boileau attempts to evoke this quality is by creating for his reader a poetic structure—analogous in its kind to the ineffable poetic nobility that he has set as his ideal. In the single line "Par quel art sans bassesse un auteur peut descendre," he suggests, by means of a calculated density of form, that his observation on the eclogue had been concerned all along with a level of literary performance that eludes factual or discursive description. But the verse line before us does not begin to function and to signify poetically until we become aware that it is completely void of a describable intellectual content. Rather than explain to us what he means, Boileau asks us to probe a construction, to study its geometric workmanship, to experience it in all of its aspects—semantic, linguistic, rhythmic, structural—to perceive and experience it as linguistic playfulness. The words "bassesse" (lowness, degradation) and "descendre" (descend, decline) relate to each other through their antithetical position within the line, and at the same time they continually conflict and collide with each other as they float between their literal and metaphoric meanings. When we allow Boileau's words to work on us in all their complexity and power, we see that we are dealing with a paradoxical descent that constitutes not a degradation but an ascension. There is a special art, then, that manages to "lower" the tone of a poem (descendre), without causing a simultaneous decline in beauty or dignity (bassesse).

As an idea, the opposition "sans bassesse/peut descendre" presents the reader with a logical absurdity, or, at the very least, a semantic problem to be resolved. The reader fulfills his participatory function and enters into the poet's idea by letting the word "art" resonate with all its associations and accumulated overtones ("la route est difficile" . . . "par les Grâces dictés" . . . "leurs doctes vers"). By bringing to the text the implicit but unmentioned notion of "mystery" and by keeping that notion in his mind, the reader penetrates and actualizes Boileau's poetic strategy. As a paradoxical structure, which can be embraced and perceived only through a conscious and conscientious act of decoding, the line in question does not simply present Boileau's idea, it *re*-presents it, by becoming the figure of that idea. Thus the work of reunification and comprehension is accomplished by the reader, who has become the poet's accomplice in his verbal craft. If this had been a discursive text, with a clear message, all this work of deciphering would have been done by the writer for the reader. Once again, by refusing to *describe* his thought at the surface of the text, by preferring to *inscribe* it in a figure, Boileau raises critical comment to the level of poetry.

An enormous distance separates Boileau, the all-too-well-known literary critic who explains his ideas through the medium of language, from this other, too-little-known Boileau, the poet of criticism, who implies in his language—who quite literally "folds" into it, encloses within its structures—an attitude toward the literary text that he invites his reader to explore from within. The narrator in Marcel Proust's *A la recherche du temps perdu* observes that Hugo, in his early poems, "is still thinking, instead of being content, like nature, with provoking thought in others." This observation, which goes far beyond the case of Hugo, defines perfectly the kind of poetic efficacy that Boileau, through his uses of language and his manipulation of his verse line, claimed for his art. How many of his alexandrines seem to have been conceived for the sole purpose of "provoking thought"? One need only lift a few typical examples out of their context in order to see at a glance the extent to which Boileau was trying to set in motion—through studied contrasts, reverberations of sense or sound, paranomasia, patterning, redundancy—a mental activity geared to integrating contradictory quantities and qualities:

> *Et toujours mécontent de ce qu'il vient de*
> *faire,*
> *Il plait à tout le monde, et ne saurait se plaire.*
> (satire 2.93–94)

And always discontent with what he has just done.
He pleases everyone but cannot please himself.

> *Chacun veut en sagesse ériger sa folie.*
> (4.50)

We all want to pass off our madness for wisdom.

> *Pour honorer les morts, font mourir les vivants.*
> (6.26)

To honor the dead, they kill the living.

> *Je ne puis bien parler, et ne saurais me taire.*
> (7.90)

I cannot speak well, yet I cannot shut up.

> *De choquer un auteur qui choque le bon sens;*
> *De railler d'un plaisant qui ne sait pas nous*
> *plaire;*
> (9.170–171)

To shock an author who shocks our reason;
To ridicule a joker who can't amuse us.

> *Grand Roi, cesse de vaincre, ou je cesse d'écrire.*
> (épître 8.1)

Great king, stop conquering or I will stop writing.

Simple antitheses? To be sure. But is antithesis ever simple? On the contrary, and by definition, it is double, adversative. Its essential function is to point up whatever may be doubtful, problematical, or illusory behind the facade of apparent unity or simplicity. To whatever purpose it may be used, antithesis serves to present in an ironic light contradictions or duplicities that are far from obvious.

By forcing words, concepts, and sometimes simple sounds to bounce off one another or to bend back upon themselves, this elementary rhetorical device exploits its potential for clarity by making readers sensitive to the depths of obscurity that the elements contained within its structure may actually conceal. On the scale at which Boileau practiced antithesis, it can hardly be considered a simple stylistic device or effect. Like hyperbole, antithesis, in Boileau's hands, assumes the power of a sign and opens the way to the exploration of primordial aesthetic questions.

THE LOVER OF LITERATURE

In one of his very early and little-known works, *Le dialogue des héros de roman* (1665), Boileau has recourse to a metaphor that seems banal but that plays a prominent role in his critical vocabulary. In this satiric piece Boileau describes Joan of Arc, the heroine of Jean Chapelain's *La pucelle*, in terms of the emotional impact of her character on the reader: "Truly, she does not preach tenderness. She is all hard and dry, and I would think that she is more likely to chill the soul than to fill it with love" (p. 46). In the language of this metaphor, poetic success is equated with arousing strong feelings in the reader, whereas poetic failure leaves him, as it were, anesthetized.

For Boileau poetry is always a kind of "love affair." At the very beginning of the *Art poétique*, he deplores the temptation to "prendre pour génie une amour de rimer"(confuse a love of rhyming with genius: 10). Some poets, he claims, never manage to inspire love in their readers, for the excellent reason that they are infatuated with themselves:

> *Mais souvent un esprit qui se flatte et qui s'aime,*
> *Méconnait son génie, et s'ignore soi-même.*
> (1.19–20)

But often a poet who flatters and loves himself,
Overestimates his talent and ignores his limitations.

Souvent, sans y penser, un écrivain qui s'aime,
Forme tous ses héros semblables à soi-méme.

(3.127–128)

Often, without knowing it, an author who
   loves himself
Makes all his characters in his own image.

Boileau knew well, as Valéry was to say, that "enthusiasm is not a writerly state of mind" (*Oeuvres* 1.1205, Pléiade ed.). The enthusiast in love with his own thoughts and with himself stops exactly at the point where poetry and aesthetics begin; he is unable to communicate to his reader the emotion that he feels. Boileau's use of this self-erotic imagery emphasizes the conflict between the poet's self-love and his metaphoric quest for the love of others:

Voulez-vous du public mériter les amours?
Sans cesse en écrivant variez vos discours.
Un style trop égal et toujours uniforme,
En vain brille à nos yeux, il faut qu'il nous
   endorme.
On lit peu ces auteurs nés pour nous ennuyer,
Qui toujours sur un ton semblent psalmodier.

(1.69–74)

Do you wish to win public approval?
When you write always vary your discourse.
A monotonous, uniform style
Will not dazzle our eyes, it will put us to sleep.
We avoid those authors who have a knack for
   boring us,
Who always seem to sing the same old song.

On the other hand, the virtuoso poet, who boasts a mastery of all styles and shades of feeling, is assured of success:

Son livre aimé du ciel et chéri des lecteurs,
Est souvent chez Barbin entouré d'acheteurs.

(1.77–78)

His works, beloved of Heaven and cherished by
   readers,
Are often surrounded by customers in Barbin's
   bookshop.

This kind of language might pass unnoticed if the emotional arousal implicit in "mériter les amours" (as in 1.69) were not precisely counterbalanced by the words "endorme" and "ennuyer." In other words it is the contextual function of the erotic metaphor rather than its surface meaning that attracts the careful reader's attention. In the same way that Boileau uses various versions of the altitude/platitude polarity, he defines aesthetic experience here in terms of another set of hyperbolic extremities: a sudden, vigorous awakening, with all the resonances implicit in the word "amours," is opposed to the deep sleep in which the reader, who is overwhelmed by boredom and fatigue, seeks refuge. From this comes Boileau's personal refusal to share the fate of the many effusive lovers who, in the vapid idiom of the day, write circumstantial amorous verse that is devoid of any real passion:

Faudra-t-il de sens froid, et sans être amoureux,
Pour quelque Iris en l'air faire le langoureux;
Lui prodiguer les noms de Soleil et d'Aurore,
Et toujours bien mangeant mourir par métaphore?
Je laisse aux doucereux ce langage affété,
Où s'endort un esprit de mollesse hébété.

(satire 9.261–266)

Must they, coldbloodedly, lovelessly,
For some imaginery Iris go into a swoon,
Shower her with epithets like Sun and Dawn,
And although they are well fed, metaphorically
   starve to death?
I leave this affected language to the sweet talkers,
They lull us into lethargy and put us to sleep.

Boileau's aesthetic attitudes reflect the preoccupations of his age, which after the long interruption of romanticism were espoused once again by the postsymbolists. Boileau advocated, as have the best poets since Baudelaire and Mallarmé, a poetry of effects rather than a poetry of intention. But he, unlike a necessarily more sophisticated modern critic defined these effects, in metaphorical terms.

He had no system or doctrine, nor did he advance any particular theory of language or of genres; rather, he took as his starting point the obvious, universally recognized power of certain concrete words rooted in the experience, lived or imagined, of every *homo sentiens*. Boileau's conception of the function of literature is often expressed by means of a pair of antithetically hyperbolic metaphors that underlie his critical judgments and characterize the poets whom he extols or condemns—metaphors that incorporate the inner substance of the very notion of aesthetics, in the etymological and concrete sense of the word (from the Greek verb *aisthanomai*, to feel). In Boileau's view the failure or the success of a poetic work must be recognized by its ability to communicate feelings, to make the reader experience an emotion analogous to the ones felt by people in love.

In bucolic poetry, for example, Boileau wishes us to share his feeling of what it should be rather than to judge it according to some abstract definition:

Telle qu'une bergère, au plus beau jour de fête,
De superbes rubis ne charge point sa tête,
Et sans mêler à l'or l'éclat des diamants,
Cueille en un champ voisin ses plus beaux
  ornements.
Telle, aimable en son air, mais humble dans son
  style,
Doit éclater sans pompe une élégante idylle:
Son tour simple et naïf n'a rien de fastueux,
Et n'aime point l'orgueil d'un vers présomptueux.
Il faut que sa douceur flatte, chatouille, éveille;
Et jamais de grands mots n'épouvante l'oreille.
                                        (Art poétique 2.1–10)

Just as a shepherdess, on a festive occasion,
Won't load down her head with superb rubies,
And rather than add the glitter of diamonds to
  gold,
Gathers her loveliest jewels in the nearby fields,
In the same way, with pleasant tone but humble
  style,
The elegant idyll should modestly shine forth.
Its simple and natural style shuns pomposity,

And it spurns the arogance of a presumptuous
  verse.
Its sweetness must caress, excite, enliven,
And never assail our ears with big words.

The *élégante idylle* inspires feelings of affection similar to those that one might experience in the presence of an unadorned but seductive shepherdess.

The unusually long discussion that Boileau devotes to the elegy points up the disparity between a poetic form whose very subject is love and the indifference that most of its practitioners evoke in their readers:

Elle peint des amants la joie, et la tristesse,
Flatte, menace, irrite, apaise une maîtresse:
Mais pour bien exprimer ces caprices heureux,
C'est peu d'être poète, il faut être amoureux.
                                        (2.41–44)

And it describes the joys and torments of lovers,
It caresses, threatens, irks, appeases a mistress:
But in order to express these happy caprices,
It's not enough to be a poet, you have to be in
  love.

These lines on the effects of the elegy are informed by the same notion of aesthetic experience that underlies Boileau's judgment, as recorded by Brossette, on the poetry of Quinault: "He told me that in his operas Quinault had written very prettily of love and tenderness, but that his words were not those of a lover, that is, he did not speak as nature should" ("Mémoires," in *Correspondance Boileau-Brossette*, Laverdet ed., p. 535). Doubtless Boileau did not require of a librettist that he be in love. These words suggest, rather, that in Boileau's judgment, Quinault had failed to arouse in the reader the sentiments appropriate to the passions that he was trying to express.

It is impossible and, in reality, unimportant to know whether Boileau considered actual sincerity in love to be a vital factor in his indictment of bad elegiac poets. He insists, rather, on the transparency of the artifices they employ, on the all-too-obvious gap between the stylistic and rhetorical machinery that they bring to bear and the meager effects that they manage to produce in their readers:

Je hais ces vains auteurs, dont la Muse forcée,
M'entretient de ses feux toujours froide et glacée,
Qui s'affligent par art, et fous de sens rassis
S'érigent, pour rimer, en amoureux transis.
Leurs transports les plus doux ne sont que phrases
    vaines.
Ils ne savent jamais que se charger de chaînes,
Que bénir leur martyre, adorer leur prison,
Et faire quereller les sens et la raison.
Ce n'était pas jadis, sur ce ton ridicule
Qu'Amour dictait les vers que soupirait Tibulle,
Ou que du tendre Ovide animant les doux sons,
Il donnait de son art les charmantes leçons.
Il faut que le coeur seul parle dans l'élégie.

                         (2.45–57)

I hate those vacuous authors, whose cramped
    Muse
Always frigid and glacial, speak to me of passion's
    fire.
Artistically afflicted and rationally insane,
They become forlorn lovers for literary purposes.
Their sweetest transports are but empty phrases.
All they know how to do is put on shackles,
Bless their martyrdom, adore their prison,
And stage debates between passion and reason.
It was not this way, not in this ridiculous vein,
That Cupid dictated Tibullus' sighing verses;
This is not how the tender Ovid with his sweet
    sounds,
Taught his delightful lessons in the art of love.
In the elegy the heart alone must speak.

The ironic oppositions that Boileau stresses here are familiar: the poet who wants us to appreciate his love finally succeeds only in arousing our animosity. The antithetical expressions "feux"/"froide et glacée," "sens rassis"/"amoureux transis"), along with the exhaustive list of conventional tortures ("chaînes," "martyre," "prison," and so on) and stock phrases used in so-called love poetry, prepare us for a final application of the

erotic metaphor. Only in the ancient elegiacs does the reader find the quasi-magical effects that he has a right to expect—effects that seem to have their origins not in human technique but in divine intervention: "Amour dictait les vers que soupirait Tibulle" (Cupid dictated Tibullus' sighing verse); see also "les tendres écrits" of Theocritus and Vergil "par les Grâces dictés" (dictated by the Graces). Similarly, the "charmantes leçons" of Ovid ("charmant" in its strong sense of the Latin *carmen*—incantation, enchantment) intensify, by extending the metaphor on which this entire passage is based, the vision of aesthetic experience that Boileau sets up here as a model. Boileau's entire aesthetic can be reduced to a sustained opposition between a "froid écrivain," frigid writer, a "détestable auteur," detestable author (*Art poétique* 4. 33), who, by definition, cannot be loved and who leaves us cold, and a poet who has the gift of entrancing us, whose work gives off a captivating emotional warmth.

Boileau's criteria for judging the elegy are identical to those on which he bases his commentaries on the noble genres of tragedy and epic. Inevitably, irresistibly, he returns to the same metaphorical equation: aesthetic experience equals amorous experience. For Boileau, the reader is an *amateur*, in the primary sense of the word; the *Art poétique* is a kind of literary *ars amatoria*.

In tragedy, to cite one of the most striking examples, above and beyond the few commonplace observations that he was obliged to lay out, Boileau highlights and elaborates a rare kind of excitation that is the real aim of the genre, and, in his personal aesthetic perspective, its raison d'être. Boileau's discussion of tragedy takes as its starting point the paradoxical view of *mimesis* that he found in Aristotle's *Poetics* (1448b): although we recoil at the sight of certain objects—ferocious animals, human corpses—we somehow are able to find enjoyment in verbal or graphic images, or imitations, of them. The third canto of the *Art poétique* begins thus:

NICOLAS BOILEAU-DESPRÉAUX

Il n'est point de serpent, ni de monstre odieux,
Qui par l'art imité, ne puisse plaire aux yeux.
D'un pinceau délicat l'artifice agréable
Du plus affreux object fait un objet aimable.

(1–4)

There is no serpent, no monster so odious,
That it cannot please the eye when reproduced
   in art.
The delightful skill of a deft painter
Can transform a hateful object into an object of
   affection.

Like Aristotle, Boileau marvels at the magical art—"l'artifice agréable"—thanks to which the tragic poet "du plus affreux objet fait un objet aimable." In the antithesis "affreux objet/objet aimable," Boileau celebrates, in a different but equally intense register, the same Eros that he had acclaimed in the verses of Tibullus dictated by Cupid and in the "charmantes leçons" of Ovid. The "charmes" of tragedy, however, are far more intense:

Ainsi, pour nous charmer, la Tragédie en pleurs
D'Oedipe tout sanglant fit parler les douleurs. . . .

(3.5–6)

Thus for our enchantment, tragedy in tears
Gave voice to the sufferings of gory Oedipus. . . .

The "charm" that emanates from this "objet aimable" is intimately associated in Boileau's mind with effects that can be described only in terms of the heat of passion:

Que dans tous vos discours la passion émue
Aille chercher le coeur, l'échauffe, et le remue.
Si d'un beau mouvement l'agréable fureur
Souvent ne nous remplit d'une douce "terreur,"
Ou n'excite en notre âme une "pitié"
   charmante,
En vain vous étalez une scène savante:
Vos froids raisonnements ne feront qu'attiédir
Un spectateur toujours paresseux d'applaudir,
Et qui des vains efforts de votre rhétorique,
Justement fatigué, s'endort ou vous critique.

(3.15–24)

In everything you write moving passion
Must seek out the heart, warm it and stir it.
If the pleasing fury of strong feeling
Does not often fill us with a sweet *terror*,
Or instill in our soul a beguiling *pity*,
Your learned stagecraft will be useless:
Your frigid arguments will only chill
The spectator, who is always reluctant to
   applaud.
Faced with the empty gestures of your rhetoric,
Understandably weary, he will doze off or
   censure you.

In order to "échauffer" and "remuer," both equivalent synonyms for "émouvoir," in order to make us feel the "agréable fureur" characteristic of tragic excitement, the poet, according to the traditional theory of the genre, must inspire in us a "sweet terror"; he must instill in our souls a "seductive pity." By printing "terreur" and "pitié" in italics, moreover, Boileau is alerting the educated reader to the fact that he fully endorses, that he is taking pains to elaborate for a French audience, the noted Aristotelian theory of emotional catharsis. In the terms of Boileau's erotic metaphor, however, this deep, affective experience stands in constant jeopardy. The pitfall to be avoided is "refroidissement," the cooling-off inevitably produced by "froids raisonnements," by those tepid verses that are technically adequate but lacking in emotivity. The major risk, and the cardinal sin, is to desensitize, to anesthetize a reader who is hungry for a vitalizing experience, an experience whose symbol in Boileau's vocabulary is the vigilance of love, whose nemesis is the refuge of sleep.

The image of anesthetic slumber runs throughout Boileau's critical writings like a leitmotiv. Frigidity in poetry has the same soporific effect on Boileau as the "eloquence" of a dull preacher—"Peut-on si bien prêcher qu'il ne dorme au sermon" (However well he preaches, he still puts me to sleep: *satire 9*. 126)—or as a scholarly paper that he once had to suffer through at a session of the Academy of Medals: "The meeting began with the reading of a very learned but rather tedious work, which lulled us into a very scholarly boredom; but later on, however, we heard another, much more enjoyable, which really held our attention. . . . I didn't see another mouth open up into a yawn" (23 August 1702, *Lettres à Racine*, p. 134).

This anecdote, while of no intrinsic importance, reflects the same aesthetic attitude that Boileau had exploited so brilliantly in the Battle of the Books scene in his *Lutrin* (1674). On that famous day, thousands of volumes came out of a long oblivion to take up once again their soporific functions:

O, que d'écrits obscurs, de livres ignorés
Furent en ce grand jour de la poudre tirés!
　　　　　. . .
D'un Pinchêne "in quarto" Dodillon étourdi
A longtemps le teint pâle, et le coeur affadi.
Au plus fort du combat le chapelain Garagne,
Vers le sommet du front atteint d'un
　　Charlemagne,
(Des vers de ce poème effet prodigieux!)
Tout prêt à s'endormir bâille et ferme les yeux,
A plus d'un combattant la Clélie est fatale.
　　　　　(5.151–153; 163–169)

O, how many obscure writings, forgotten books
Were on that great day rescued from of the dust!
　　　　　. . .
Dodillon, dazed by a Pinchêne "in Quarto,"
For a long time was pale; his heart grew faint.
At the height of the battle, chaplain Garagne,
Struck on the top of the brow by a *Charlemagne*,
(Such is the wondrous effect of the verses in that
　　poem!)
On the verge of slumber, yawns and closes his
　　eyes.
To more than one warrior the *Clélie* proves fatal.

But this burlesque scene is nothing more than the systematic reprise of an image of sleep, closely bordering on death, which Boileau had already used to similar advantage in a satire:

Quel démon vous irrite et vous porte à médire?
Un livre vous déplait. Qui vous force à le lire?
Laissez mourir un fat dans son obscurité.
Un auteur ne peut-il pourrir en sûreté?
　　　　　. . .

Quel mal cela fait-il? Ceux qui sont morts sont
　morts.
Le tombeau contre vous ne peut-il les défendre?
Et qu'ont fait tant d'auteurs, pour remuer leur
　cendre?
　　　　　(satire 9.87–90; 94–96)

What demon eggs you on and makes you speak ill
　of people?
So you don't like a book. Who forces you to read
　it?
Let fools die in their obscurity.
Can't an author rot in peace?
　　　　　. . .
What harm does he do? The dead are dead.
Can't even the grave protect them from you?
What have all those writers done, that you should
　stir up their ashes?

If Boileau insists on reviving, in the *Lutrin* and elsewhere, the names of authors and books consigned to oblivion years before, it is because they represent for him, in the same way as bad love poetry—"Où s'endort un esprit de mollesse hébêté" (*Lutrin*, 266)—the denial of authentic aesthetic experience. It is as an aesthete that the author of the *Satires* and of the *Art poétique* rebels against a literature that, instead of arousing feelings of love in the reader, bores him, as it were, to death. In contrast to such writings, produced by authors whose inspiration has been petrified, whose souls are in cold storage (see *Lutrin* 226: "pétrifié," "glacé"), we have the marvelous Corneille, who overcomes all obstacles, and who wins the love of his public as irresistibly as the exemplary lovers who thrill us in his plays:

En vain contre le Cid un ministre se ligue:
Tout Paris pour Chimène a les yeux de Rodrigue.
L'Académie en corps a beau le censurer,
Le public révolté s'obstine à l'admirer.
　　　　　(satire 9.231–234)

In vain does a minister plot against *Le Cid*:
All Paris views Chimène with the eyes of
　Rodrigue.
The Academy may censure it unanimously,
But the public revolts and persists in admiring
　it.

Boileau extolled the same magical power in Racine, who possessed "l'art d'enchanter les coeurs et l'esprit" and won "tous les coeurs."

> *Que tu sais bien, Racine, à l'aide d'un acteur,*
> *Emouvoir, étonner, ravir un spectateur!*
> (7.1–2)

How well you manage, Racine, with the help of
  an actor,
To move, to stun, to ravish a spectator!

It is this power of seduction and emotional upheaval that differentiates Corneille and Racine from a poet like Godeau, who is "fort estimable" but who lacks that vital spark:

> One could say about him what Longinus said about Hyperides, that he is always sober, he has nothing that stirs or excites us. In a word, he lacks that force of style and that vivacity of expression that people look for in works of literature and that makes them endure. I don't know whether he will be remembered by posterity, but in order for that to happen, he would first have to be resurrected, since you might say that he is already dead, now that no one at all ever reads him anymore.
> (29 April 1695, *Lettres à Racine*, p. 113)

This reflection reproduces identically a passage from Boileau's own translation of Longinus' *On the Sublime* (*Traité du sublime*, pp. 107–108), which served earlier as the basis for his lines on tragedy quoted above:

> *Que dans tous vos discours la passions émue*
> *Aille chercher le coeur, l'échauffe, et le remue.*
> (*Art poétique* 3.15–16)

Boileau is nothing if not consistent. His "thought" has all the simplicity and force of an obsession. In any genre, at whatever stage of his long career that we may choose to sound out his views on aesthetic experience, his reply will always be given in the terms of the same erotic metaphor: the task of the poet is to make his work irresistible, to practice that quasi-magical seduction that the Greeks called *psychagogia*, leading the soul as if by enchantment.

When it comes to epic poetry, Boileau looks for the same hypnotic quality that he stresses in his treatment of the secondary genres and tragedy. "Là, pour nous enchanter, tout est mis en usage" (There, to enthrall us, every effect is utilized: 3.163). His predilection for the pagan myths also has an aesthetic justification: the heroic adventures related by Homer and Vergil produce in the reader, in the same way as Racinian tragedy, those emotional reactions that in his eyes constitute the only valid criteria for poetic success:

> *C'est là ce qui surprend, frappe, saisit, attache:*
> *Sans tous ces ornements le vers tombe en*
> *langueur,*
> *La poésie est morte, ou rampe sans vigueur:*
> *Le poète n'est plus qu'un orateur timide,*
> *Qu'un froid historien d'une fable insipide.*
> (3.188–192)

Those are the things that surprise, strike, seize,
  attract us:
Without all those adornments the verse turns
  languid,
The poetry dies or limply crawls along:
The poet becomes a mere timid orator,
Or the cold reporter of a pallid tale.

In contrast to those "auteurs toujours froids et mélancoliques (dull authors always stiff and stale: 292), the Homeric poems—"Une heureuse chaleur anime ses discours (A happy warmth he everywhere may boast: 301)—conquer the hearts of his readers in an almost miraculous way:

> *On dirait que pour plaire, instruit par la Nature,*
> *Homère ait à Vénus dérobé sa ceinture.*
> (3.295–296)

You would swear that Homer, schooled by nature
  in the art of pleasing,
Had stolen Venus' sash away from her.

In all of Boileau's writings, there is no more explicit or more powerful example either of the erotic metaphor that underlies his artistic vision or of the radically poetic character of his critical method. In this couplet in praise of Homer, which aims at describing an apogee of aesthetic experience, the allusion to Venus' sash associates the heights of poetic effectiveness with the magic of Greek fable. In this sash, so we read in Homer's text, "are figured all beguilements, and loveliness is figured upon it, and passion of sex is there, and the whispered endearment that steals the heart away from the thoughtful" (*Iliad* 14.215–217, Lattimore trans.). In a great poet the counterpart to this sash would be a magical power analogous in his domain to the charms of Aphrodite in hers: a prodigious ability to bind, to attach, to subjugate the reader metaphorically. The lines that follow and develop the initial couplet consider an ability in Homer so miraculous that his poem seems almost to have written itself:

Son livre est d'agréments un fertile trésor.
Tout ce qu'il a touché se convertit en or.
Tout reçoit dans ses mains une nouvelle grâce.
Partout il divertit, et jamais il ne lasse.
(3.297–300)

His works are a treasure-chest of pleasures.
Everything he touches turns to gold,
In his hands everything assumes an added grace,
He always pleases us, never becomes tiresome.

The Homeric miracle brings together with the secrets of the goddess of love a king of poetic Midas touch. It is as if the human mind had played no role at all in the composition of his work:

Son sujet de soi-même et s'arrange et s'explique:
Tout, sans faire d'apprêts, s'y prépare aisément.
Chaque vers, chaque mot court à l'événement.
(3.304–306)

His subject by itself develops and unfolds:
Everything, without plan, works out with perfect ease.
Each line, each word falls neatly into place.

This passage on Homer leaves us with two overall impressions. An accumulation of reflexive verbs ("s'arrange," "s'explique," "s'y prépare," all contrasted with the artifice denoted by "apprêts"), reinforced by the alliterative *s* in line 304, sketches in the image of a process of composition that is both sui generis and suo motu—an image of spontaneous creation that illustrates and elaborates the theme of natural inspiration ("instruit par la nature") with which the passage began. There is a parallel accumulation of "tout" (298–299, 305; and in line 300, "partout" in antithesis with "jamais") and the twice-repeated "chaque" of line 306; and this accumulation expresses and emphasizes the permanence of the bond and the totality of the conquest produced by Homer's poetic magic. The imperative in the final couplet is almost superfluous:

Aimez donc ses écrits, mais d'une amour sincère,
C'est avoir profité que de savoir s'y plaire.
(3.307–308)

You must then love his works, but with a love that is sincere,
To know how to enjoy them is a boon in itself.

This "aimez donc," reinforced by "d'une amour sincère," which concludes the panegyric of Homer, brings us to the final "s'y plaire" of line 308, which echoes in its turn the initial "pour plaire" of line 295. This passage, with its almost geometric architecture, brings together a vast repertory of code words, ingeniously deployed so as to make both visible and tangible an ideal erotic bond between author and reader. In the terms of Boileau's poetic argument, Homer's work is a fiction that nevertheless betrays no trace of artifice. Although it is the product of the human mind, the *Iliad* gives the illusion of having written itself through a kind of spontaneous generation. In a word, it exercises on us an emotional hold so strong that we begin to view it as the exact opposite of what in fact it really is; that is, as a product not of art but of nature. For in reading Homer, Boileau suggests, we are made to feel the kind of truth and immediacy that we normally associate with the most direct and profound experiences of life itself.

The example of the aesthetic triumph of Homer, "instruit par la Nature" (295), raises certain questions concerning the use of the word "nature" both in Boileau's literary judgments and in the body of critical writing associated with the emergence of French classicism. Similar questions will have to be asked concerning the twin notion of "truth," which in Boileau's vocabulary and in that of his age is inseparable from the concept of "nature." The "naturalness" and the aesthetic "truth" that Boileau singled out in the *Art poétique* as Homer's special qualities adhere to the same premises that underlie his indictment of falseness in *épître* 9 (1675), a poem devoted to the rhetoric of encomiastic writing. The "truth" of a "beautiful" encomium is conceived of there, with the simplicity of an equation, as producing the same kind of erotic effect as the Homeric fictions: "Rien n'est beau que le *Vrai*. Le Vrai seul *est* aimable" (Nothing is beautiful but the Truth. Only Truth can be loved: 43). In reading this verse, it is essential to stress the words "vrai" and "aimable," which correspond to each other by their antithetical positioning at the ends of the hemistichs and which in this way mutually define each other. As Boileau is careful to specify in the following lines, however, this "vrai" has nothing to do with philosophic or moral abstraction:

> *Il doit régner partout, et même dans la fable:*
> *De toute fiction l'adroite fausseté*
> *Ne tend qu'à faire aux yeux briller la vérité.*
> (*épître* 9.44–46)

It should reign everywhere, even in fable:
The clever falseness of every fiction
Aims only at making the light of truth glow
  before our eyes.

We are dealing here with the paradoxical "vérité" of aesthetic seduction, which Boileau found in the artifices of fiction and which he congratulates himself for having realized in his own poetry:

> *Sais-tu pourquoi mes vers sont lus dans les*
>   *provinces?*
> *Sont recherchés du peuple, et reçus chez les*
>   *princes?*
> *Ce n'est pas que leurs sons agréables, nombreux,*
> *Soient toujours à l'oreille également heureux:*
> *Qu'en plus d'un lieu le sens n'y gêne la mesure,*
> *Et qu'un mot quelquefois n'y brave la césure.*
> *Mais c'est qu'en eux le vrai du mensonge*
>   *vainqueur*
> *Partout se montre aux yeux et va saisir le coeur.*
> (9.47–54)

Do you know why my verses are read in the
  provinces?
Why they are sought out by the public, and
  received among kings?
It is not that their pleasant, harmonious sounds
Always strike the ear with equal grace.
Nor that meaning doesn't occasionally interfere
  with the rhythm,
Nor that a word now and then doesn't violate the
  caesura.
But it's because truth in my writings always
  conquers falsehood,
Stands out for all to see and grips the reader's
  heart.

This truth that shines forth and dazzles the eyes with its brilliance is an aesthetic truth; its function is not to prove or to persuade, but to arouse strong feelings. It is "aimable." The visual imagery that runs throughout this epistle echoes, in fact, with slight variations, the conventional image of love—personified by Cupid with his arrows—that reaches to the heart by penetrating through the gateway of the eyes (see "Tout Paris pour Chimène a les yeux de Rodrigue": *satire* 9.232).

Truth, for Boileau, designates a symbolic quality. It is not simply a word endowed with one or several meanings; it is a poetic figure with multiple resonances that can be comprehended only contextually. In *épître* 6 (1677) truth is defined by comparison with "sots discours," with a "satire fade" and an "insipide boutade'' (68–70)—by comparison with all that factitious literature, lacking in color and spice, condemned by the friend of the truth, defender of good taste. At the heart of the truth-falsehood polarity, just as with the several other polarities native to Boileau's way of thinking, it is the presence or the absence of a strong affective element that determines his judgments:

> Le faux est toujours fade, ennuyeux, languissant:
> Mais la Nature est vraie, et d'abord on la sent;
> C'est elle seule en tout qu'on admire et qu'on aime.
> Un esprit né chagrin plaît par son chagrin même.
>
> (9.85–88)

Falseness is always dull, boring, languid:
But Nature is true and we sense it instantly;
It is Nature alone that we admire and love.
A naturally glum person pleases us by his glumness.

From the point of view of their actual content, Boileau's reflections on Truth and Nature constitute a vast tautology: the Beautiful = the True = that which pleases = Nature = the True = that which pleases. As nondiscursive linguistic symbols, these very general terms take on a luminous specificity as soon as we consider, not how they function in propositions, but rather the role that they play in oppositions. Nature and Truth in Boileau connote internal aesthetic absolutes, which reveal their presence only through the feelings that they produce. And these feelings, in turn, may be verified through their resemblance to the real affective experiences in everyone's daily life. The feeling aroused by the True, for example, is reminiscent of the immediate and irresistible sympathy that we experience, for example, when we encounter the simplicity of a small child:

> La simplicité plaît, sans étude et sans art.
> Tout charme en un enfant . . .
>
> (9. 81–82)

Simplicity pleases, without effort and without art. Everything that a child does is delightful.

This manifestation of the True is radically different from our perceptions of all other feelings; the False, for example: "Le faux est toujours fade, ennuyeux, languissant'' (85). This opposition is formal and invariable. Such is its force and immediacy, in Boileau's view, that no confusion is ever possible.

Endowed with a deeply dialectical mind, Boileau is able to celebrate the True only by denouncing the False: false nobility (satire 5), false praise (épître 9), falsity as incarnated in verbal equivocation (satire 12), and, in the aesthetic domain, throughout the corpus of his work, the falseness of mediocre poets. The instinctive gesture of this friend of truth in the face of unauthenticity is to back away from and to reject those who fall short of his ideal. Faced with a horde of "froids écrivains,'' who chill his soul instead of kindling love in his heart, Boileau cannot refrain from taking flight. And, from the summit of the citadel of truth where he finds refuge, he thunders, accuses, ridicules, and denounces. With that confident, authoritarian voice that he has come to be known for, this praeceptor Franciae, this self-proclaimed guardian of an aesthetic vision denied to the profanum vulgus, arrogantly peals off his litany of imperatives. "Aimez'' and "fuyez,'' his characteristic recommendations, mark the two poles of his literary sensibility.

The language of love in Boileau assumes the same peremptory tone and expresses the same depth of conviction that we find in his frequent use of "seul,'' "toujours,'' and "jamais.'' Indeed, his simplest traits of style express a love of literature that explains better than any theory or doctrine the extraordinary energy and aggressiveness that he brought to the craft of criticism. Because it operates at such a rudimentary level of expression, Boileau's erotic vocabulary must be taken as pure and concrete testimony to the literary passion that motivated him. His constant recourse to the erotic metaphor was, all in all, his personal way of saying what Descartes had said thirty years earlier with respect to his own first intellectual occupations: "I had a high opinion of oratory, but I was in love with poetry" (*Discourse on Method*, part 1).

CONCLUSION

"An idea," according to Joubert, "is the result and the spirit (the pure essence) of an infinite number of thoughts" (*Journal intime*, 19 February 1808). It is only in this Platonic sense of the word that one would be justified in crediting Boileau with any real "ideas," because, essentially, he had only one: a visionary idea, an almost physical and palpable idea of the distance between the pleasurable and the boring, the lively and the deadly, the impassioned and the frigid. It is in this sense that Boileau may be called a "poet of distance" (Beugnot, "Boileau et la distance critique"; see bibliography). In its figurative dimension, distance implies separation and rejection; it brings to mind gestures of dismissal, expulsion, and banishment. This poet of distance, whose ambition as a critic was to drive out of the republic of letters an entire class of writers whom he considered unworthy of residing there, is also the poet of refusal. The notion of distance encompasses at one and the same time the artistic "hauteur" (elevation) that constituted Boileau's ideal and that other "hauteur" (haughtiness), part and parcel of the first, that elicited the unanimous complaints of both his adversaries and his victims— whom he dealt with, it is true, as if he were looking down his nose at them from some incredibly exalted eminence.

It is also in terms of stern distance and arch superiority that we must understand the so-called dogmatism of this Boileau who is always right, whose adversaries are always wrong. It is the dogmatism of a satirist who holds himself apart from and above the contemptible masses whom he makes the target of his exultant ridicule. As Beugnot has shrewdly pointed out, satire itself, at least in the way that Boileau practiced it, must be defined as "a poetry of distance." For satire is not merely a single element in his work, or an individual genre that Boileau happened to use among others; it is rather the essence of the work itself. In other writers satire may be nothing more than a literary form, whereas in Boileau, this poetry of distance, refusal, and rejection manifests a quality of mind. It is true that Boileau sometimes simply adopts the traditional posture of the satirist, poking fun at this one or the other. But more often, satire functions in his writing as the sign of a sustained intellectual outlook and a vision of the world, of a need to denounce disparity and deviance wherever he may find them.

Boileau's criticism is to a great extent what the French call a criticism of faults, a negative criticism that centers on deficiencies, on perceptions of the difference between what is and what could or should be. His most elementary habits of style bear the mark and reveal the extent of this point of view. His two favorite devices, hyperbole and antithesis, are in effect the direct and limpid expression of this way of looking at things. Hyperbole is a natural vehicle for criticism that divides phenomena into bipolar entities (high/low, sublime/ridiculous, passionate/frigid, and so on) irreconcilably separate from one another. Antithesis, on the other hand, brings mutually exclusive concepts close together syntactically, and in so doing points up, through the spatial proximity of the words, the qualitative distance between the things that they represent, which, although similar in appearance, are actually far from alike: "La raison dit Virgile et la rime Quinault."

The critical mission that Boileau took upon himself—and this is at one and the same time a stylistic, biographical, and historical fact— consisted essentially in accomplishing a task of separation, purification, and classification, with the eventual aim of forcing his reader to share his personal literary reactions and judgments concerning the enormous qualitative gap that he perceived between the Vergils and the Quinaults. It should be noted, in this connection, that the proper names in Boileau's criticism often have a synecdochic function; for rather than simply designate individual identities—Homère–Voiture–Racine and Cotin–Quinault–Pradon—they represent two disparate levels of artistic accomplishment, two qualities of aesthetic experience, between which no common ground can possibly exist. His urge is to build a dividing wall between two territories, to separate writers into two distinct classes—one on the heights of Parnassus, the other bogged down below in the mire. This urge carries within it a functional definition of the very notions of classical and classicism. In this hierarchical vision of literary art, the true poet, the classical author, is the one who breaks away from the crowd of frigid writers, who rises above the common herd, who distinguishes himself from the vulgar through the extraordinary class of his writings, who, in the construction of national literary traditions, is deemed fit to constitute a class apart. At the same time topographical and political, Boileau's language expresses the same fundamental idea that underlies the first definition of classicism in Western literature: the author who can serve as a model, according to Aulus Gellius (2nd century A.D.), must be a "member of the illustrious cohort of ancient orators or poets; by this I mean a writer who is a *classicus,* an *assiduus,* not a proletarian" (*Attic Nights* 9.8.15). Boileau's criticism, and the elaborate stylistic apparatus that lends it its unity of tone and vision, testify to a purpose that is at once simple and ambitious: to point up the distance between the pretensions of poets and their realizations, between an all but general mediocrity and a unique, superior, exalted, and sublime class that alone is capable of satisfying his exigent aesthetic criteria. This is the real sense of the adventure that was his career as poet-critic; as Beugnot said, "an adventure in the course of which . . . he often confesses his disappoint-

ment at not finding in literary works the resonances that he had hoped for, resonances that, in his estimation, defined literary pleasure, as the abolition of all distance."

Selected Bibliography

EDITIONS

Oeuvres. 2 vols. Paris, 1713. First posthumous edition. Includes some previously unpublished material.

—————. Edited by Claude Brossette. 2 vols. Geneva, 1716. Contains Brossette's commentary based largely on materials gathered in conversations with Boileau.

Oeuvres complètes. Edited by Charles-H. Boudhors. 7 vols. Paris, 1934–1943. First really complete critical edition with elaborate notes, variants, and commentaries; did much to renew interest in Boileau and to revitalize the study of his work. Includes the *Lettres à Racine, Lettres à Brossette,* and *Réflexions critiques.*

—————. Edited by Antoine Adam and Françoise Escal. Paris, 1966. Pléiade edition. More up-to-date than the Boudhors edition; handy because it is in one volume; contains a useful index of names.

Oeuvres diverses. Paris, 1674. Contains *Satires* 1–9, *Epîtres* 1–4, *Le lutrin, L'Art poétique,* and *Traité du sublime.*

—————. Paris, 1701. New, enlarged edition. Boileau's "favorite" edition; the last one revised by him personally.

TRANSLATIONS

The Art of Poetry. Translated by Sir William Soame, revised by John Dryden. London, 1683. Included in the 1712 translation. Reprinted in Dryden's *Poetical Works,* edited by G. R. Noyes. Boston, 1950.

Selected Criticism. Edited and translated by Ernest Dilworth. Indianapolis, 1965. Contains a prose version of the *Art poétique* and Boileau's prefaces both to his translation of Longinus and to the 1701 edition.

The Works of Monsieur Boileau, Made English by Several Hands. 2 vols. London, 1712.

NICOLAS BOILEAU-DESPRÉAUX

BACKGROUND AND CRITICAL STUDIES

Beugnot, Bernard. "Boileau et la distance critique." *Études françaises* 5:195–206 (1969).

————. "Boileau, une esthétique de la lumière." *Studi Francesi* 44:229–237 (1971).

————, and Roger Zuber. *Boileau: Visages anciens, visages nouveaux, 1665–1970.* Montreal, 1973.

Borgerhoff, Elton B. O. "Qu'est-ce que le sublime, où entre le sublime?" In his *Freedom of French Classicism.* Princeton, N.J., 1950. Pp. 200–212.

————. "Boileau: Satirist *Animi Gratia.*" *Romanic Review* 43:241–255 (1952).

————. "'Mannerism' and 'Baroque': A Simple Plea." *Comparative Literature* 5:323–331 (1953).

Bray, René. *Boileau, l'homme et l'oeuvre.* Paris, 1942.

Brody, Jules. *Boileau and Longinus.* Geneva, 1958.

Clarac, Pierre. *Boileau.* Paris, 1964.

Clark, Alexander F. B. *Boileau and the French Classical Critics in England (1660–1830).* Paris, 1925.

Edelman, Nathan. "*L'Art poétique:* 'Longtemps plaire et jamais ne lasser.'" In *The Eye of the Beholder,* edited by Jules Brody. Baltimore, 1974. Pp. 142–153.

Lanson, Gustave. *Boileau.* Paris, 1892.

Mason, H. A. "Hommage à M. Despréaux: Some Reflections on the Possibility of Literary Study." *Cambridge Quarterly* 3:51–71 (1967–1968).

Pocock, Gordon. *Boileau and the Nature of French Classicism.* Cambridge, 1980.

Tiefenbrun, Susan. "Boileau and His Friendly Enemy: A Poetics of Satiric Criticism." *Modern Language Notes* 91:672–697 (1976).

White, Julian E. *Nicolas Boileau.* New York, 1969. With substantial bibliography.

BIBLIOGRAPHY

Magne, Émile. *Bibliographie générale des oeuvres de Nicolas Boileau-Despréaux.* 2 vols. Paris, 1929. Complete listing of editions and translations up to 1928. Indispensable for history and chronology of early editions. Detailed index.

JULES BRODY (Translated by Ruth Sussman)

JEAN RACINE
(1639–1699)

THE PLAYS OF Jean Racine are commonly contrasted with those of his older rival Pierre Corneille. In Corneille, we are told, the passions are dominated by the will; in Racine the will is baffled and humiliated by obsessive passions. The formulation is too simple, but it is a good starting point. Although the passions do not always win in Racine, they are all that matter; there is no life without them. A number of his characters do indeed stubbornly refuse the promptings of their desire, but their refusal brings them no glory, as similar refusals do to the heroes of Corneille. It simply empties their existence of meaning. "It is no longer a question of living," a Roman emperor says in Racine's *Bérénice* (1670), as he renounces all hope of sharing his throne with his love, "but a question of ruling." His reign without Bérénice will be merely "a long banishment," the career of a ghost.

More often Racine's characters wish to resist their passions but cannot, because their will is not so much defeated as disloyal, eager to give in. This is what Raymond Picard has called the "consent of the character." Oreste and Hermione, in *Andromaque* (1667); Néron, in *Britannicus* (1669); Phèdre, in *Phèdre* (1677): all embrace their temptations or obsessions as if they were a doom—and *make* them into a doom the process. It is true that Phèdre puts up more of a fight than the others, hates her own passion with a furious loathing; but the pattern is the same. She cannot want what she wants, the will itself is infected, and the stage is cleared for the ravages of bewildered desire. We may add that these plays, which were written to be performed at court as well as in theaters and which are marked by an extraordinary decorum of language and sparseness of physical action, conjure up again and again vivid intimations of extreme violence. Cities are sacked, heroes march about besmeared with the blood of their victims, a young man is dragged to his death by runaway horses, a woman is devoured by savage dogs. These visitations, never seen, only remembered or reported by the characters themselves, have the effect of nightmares, images of the heart's own violence. (A troubled queen, in *Athalie* [1691], does dream of her mother's grisly end.) The formality of Racine's diction serves not to distance all this damage but to make it seem inevitable, the irresistible consequence of a force that haunts and will finally ruin this ordered world. Racine, thinking of his *Bérénice* and contradicting Aristotle, whom he had studied closely and translated, said that corpses and blood were not necessary in a tragedy. But *Bérénice* is the only one of his tragedies not to conclude in a death or an execution or a human sacrifice. In *Bajazet* (1672), the play that followed *Bérénice,* all three main characters are killed off: two murders and a suicide.

LIFE

Racine was a poet and scholar as well as a playwright. He wrote Latin verse in his youth, and psalms, odes, and epigrams in French all his life. He annotated Homer and Pindar, and translated Plato's *Symposium.* He was a courtier and a member of the Académie Française, and from 1677 was the king's historian, following and recording the military campaigns of Louis XIV.

He was born in 1639, one year later than the king he was to serve and amuse. His mother died when he was thirteen months old, his father two years later. The orphan was brought up by his grandmother and educated at Port-Royal, the severe religious community of which he later wrote a history. His first published work was an ode celebrating the marriage, in 1660, of Louis XIV to Maria Theresa of Spain.

Racine studied theology for a time in the hope of gaining ecclesiastical preference through his uncle, a canon at Uzès, in the south of France. This scheme came to nought, and Racine in any case had his eye on a livelier and more literary career. He returned to Paris, met Molière, and began to move in theatrical circles, receiving regular scoldings for his worldliness from his aunt, a nun at Port-Royal. His first play, *La thébaïde, ou les frères ennemis* (The Thebaid), a grim exploration of the mortal rivalry between the sons of Oedipus, was performed by Molière's troupe in 1664. A year later he wrote a rather tepid play about Alexander the Great, which he withdrew from Molière's theater after two weeks of performances ostensibly on the grounds that Molière's actors were not up to tragedy and were not getting the rhythms of the verse right. Relations between the two men were cool ever after. Corneille meanwhile, on the basis of Racine's *Alexandre le grand* (performed 1665), decided that the young writer had a talent for poetry but not for tragedy and suggested he take up another genre. Corneille was doubly wrong, since Racine, one of the world's great tragic poets, is a great poet *only* in his tragedies—although Corneille can certainly be forgiven for not seeing this in *Alexandre.* Racine was merely competent in his

nondramatic verse, and although his one comedy, *Les plaideurs* (The Litigants, 1668), is lively and skillful and has remained popular in France, it would not alone have gained him a large place in literary history.

Andromaque, performed for the king and his court in 1667, was an enormous success. Contemporaries compared its acclaim to that of Corneille's *Le Cid* in 1637. It was clear that the representative of another generation had arrived. The fame of the play was sufficient to get it parodied in a piece put on by Molière, and *Les plaideurs,* based on Aristophanes' *The Wasps,* was an answer to this attack as well as a satire of the contemporary rage for litigation. The chief case tried in the play is that of a dog that has stolen a capon. Racine then wrote six tragedies, of which at least three (the first two and the last in the following list) are masterpieces: *Britannicus, Bérénice, Bajazet, Mithridate* (1673), *Iphigénie* (1674), and *Phèdre.*

In 1677 Racine married Catherine de Romanet, a sensible woman of good family; was named, with his friend Nicolas Boileau, historian to the king; and abandoned the theater, apparently for the sort of moral reasons his aunt at Port-Royal had urged on him much earlier. A great deal has been written about Racine's "silence" in these years, and about his "conversion" back to the austere values that presided over his youth. Raymond Picard, on the other hand, one of the most noted of Racine scholars, bluntly says it is "obvious" that Racine gave up the theater because he had become the king's historian and not that he became the king's historian *after* he had given up the theater on religious grounds. That would have been, Picard says, a "remarkable coincidence." We cannot pursue the question here, but we may safely say that if there is less sanctity in all this than the legend proposes, there is perhaps a little more than Picard allows. Racine certainly moved closer to Port-Royal in his later years; he wished to be buried there, and was. His preface to *Phèdre* plainly indicates a desire to be reconciled with his old mentors and their successors. Whereas he had said before *Phèdre* that the chief rule in tragedy is "to please and to move" the public—a courtier's version of Aristotle's *Poetics*—he now thought the theater should be "a school of virtue," as much devoted to "instruction" as to entertainment. This argument no doubt was meant to reflect retroactively on the plays already written, to salvage them for mortality rather than to suggest a program, since it did not persuade Racine himself to keep writing for the theater.

He was tempted out of his retirement from drama, however, when Madame de Maintenon asked him to write a religious play for the girls at the aristocratic school of Saint-Cyr. For them he wrote *Esther* (1689) and then *Athalie,* his last dramatic work and one of his greatest, a powerful portrayal of angry righteousness triumphing over confused wrong. An old tradition, denied by modern scholarship, has it that Racine fell from favor with the king toward the end of the decade and was much troubled by his disgrace, which must have been extremely mild if it existed at all, since he still attended court. He developed an abcess of the liver, which was treated too late, and died 21 April 1699. In 1709 Port-Royal was dissolved on the king's orders, and two years later Racine's body was moved to the Church of Saint Étienne-du-Mont in Paris and buried near that of Pascal.

Louis Racine, the playwright's second son (and seventh child), composed a pious but informative memoir of his father in which the ambitious courtier and man of letters fades before the sensitive and melancholy worldling who found his way back to the bosom of the church. Jean Racine was "born tender-hearted," Louis says, "all feeling and all heart." A contemporary insisted, however, that the poet was given to "bitter mockery," and certainly his letters and polemical writings suggest a sharp tongue. We have only to think of the preface to *Alexandre,* with its picture of ignorant critics in the audience, hoping to prove by shaking their heads and making grimaces that they have studied Artistotle in depth. These traits are not contradictory, of course; a person may be sentimental *and* bitter. In fact we know very little about Racine's character, and the evidence leaves plenty of room for interpretation. Louis reports, for example, that his father told his oldest son that the slightest criticism of his work caused him more sorrow than any amount of praise could give him pleasure. Louis sees in the remark a reason for not writing plays, a judgment against the folly of temporal temptations. But we may well see in it a frank confession of prickly authorial vanity, particularly since the context suggests that the trouble with the theater, for Racine, was not its frivolity but the impossibility of arriving at an ideal excellence: "and when one considers, however well one has done one's work, that one could have done it better, and how far one is from perfection, one often loses heart."

Louis's most extravagant claim for his father is that he had no personal experience of the amorous passions he inflicted on so many of his characters. This flatly contradicts fairly well authenticated assertions of Racine's liaisons with at least two famous actresses, to say nothing of rumors that credit him with more than one illegitimate child. And yet it is possible that Louis caught a piece of the truth, in a way he cannot have intended. His father, Louis says, "had never been the slave of love, which perhaps because of the very tenderness of his heart he regarded as more dangerous for him than for others." It is unlikely that Racine avoided love in the literal sense of Louis's claim. It chimes with everything we know about him that he should have held back from profound engagements, should really never have been love's slave, committed to that obliteration of self in passion that marks the world of his plays. The plays explore extremes of feeling that Racine may have feared rather than felt.

But this is highly hypothetical, and the same must be said for Lucien Goldmann's guess that Racine, haunted by a sense that he had betrayed the teachings of Port-Royal, represented in his plays a rejection of the world he was not disposed to practice in reality. The advantage of such theories is that in spite of their fragility, they do suggest something of the intricacy of the links between an artist's life and work.

Racine's relations with Port-Royal are indeed as hard to fathom as his character and his emotional life. In 1666 a phrase in a polemic that Port-Royal was conducting against contemporary apocalyptic writing caught Racine's eye. A novelist or a playwright, he read, was "a public poisoner, not of bodies but of souls," and should regard himself as guilty of "an infinite number of spiritual homicides." In a brilliant, if superficial, letter Racine defended literature against such lofty strictures. Literature, he said, was neither moral nor immoral, it was innocent: "There are things that are not holy, and that yet are innocent." Further, saintly people should not meddle in secular competitions: "Look, sir, you must content yourself with the distribution of places in the other world; do not arrange the rewards of this one."

There were replies and counterreplies, although Racine was persuaded not to publish his further efforts on the subject. Nothing in his tone suggests a seriously troubled conscience hiding in the glitter of the arguments. On the other hand it is hard to see why Racine, for a phrase that concerned him only in the most general way, would launch such an onslaught on his old masters. It is as if any attack on literature, at least from that quarter, were an attack on him, and perhaps that is what he felt. He needed, we may think, to free himself from the demands of Port-Royal in order to pursue his worldly career, just as he later needed to return to Port-Royal in order to fortify himself against the solicitations of society. In his preface to *Esther* Racine speaks of the value of a "detachment from the world in the midst of the world itself." No such detachment was his, in the midst of the world or apart from it. But it seems likely that he admired it all the more for that reason. His ad-

miration made him touchy when young and repentant when older.

But these religious and moral issues are not exactly central to the plays. They are *present* in the plays, flickering in certain images and aspects of character and turns of plot. A renegade priest in *Athalie,* for example, continues to believe in the God he has deserted and hopes to bury his remorse in a material victory over that God's representatives. He speaks of leaving the temple for the court. Note that this priest, in Racine's source, was not a renegade. But it is false to suggest that Racine's tragedies are dominated by religious anguish and a rejection of the world. They are dominated by problems of power, both political and sexual.

INDIVIDUAL WORKS

Andromaque, Racine's first major work, is set in the aftermath of the fall of Troy. Andromaque, Hector's widow, is now the prisoner of Pyrrhus, son of Achilles. Oreste, son of Agamemnon, arrives in Pyrrhus' kingdom with a message from the Greeks, who are anxious that Troy should not rise again and want Pyrrhus to hand over to them the young son of Hector and Andromaque. Even this bald description of the play's opening situation makes clear that it concerns the children of heroes and the survivors of wars, that the past throws a long shadow, that the future is threatened.

There is a word that recurs with eloquent frequency in all of Racine's theater; "reste" (remainder), what is left when almost everything is gone. Astyanax, child of Hector and Andromaque, is the "remainder of so many kings buried beneath Troy." Bajazet is the "remainder" of his line. Junie in *Britannicus* and Aricie in *Phèdre* are the sole "remainders" of their respective families. Esther is an orphan. The child Joas, in *Athalie,* is an orphan and heir to a kingdom, the "precious remainder" of the house of David. Joas, like Astyanax, has been saved from a massacre; the boys in both plays represent an inheritance at risk and a chance of continuity amid ruin. "Think," a character says in *Athalie*, "that all Israel resides in this child." It is significant that in both *Andromaque* and *Athalie* the boy is saved, and the forces that menace his life are repulsed.

These forces, however, especially in *Andromaque*, are not the expected ones. Astyanax's danger stems not from the Greeks but from the turbulent personal passions that have taken over the political stage. Hermione, the daughter of Menelaus and Helen, is betrothed to Pyrrhus but has been neglected by him since he has succumbed to the attractions of his noble captive, Andromaque, who in turn maintains a stubborn fidelity to her dead husband. Hermione, in a casual phrase, suggests that it is she who has brought Astyanax to the Greeks' attention. Meanwhile Oreste, the Greeks' ambassador, has long been in love with Hermione and hopes to use his mission to gain her favor. Pyrrhus thinks he can blackmail Andromaque into accepting him by offering to sacrifice her son to the Greeks. All of these characters, except Andromaque, are entirely at the mercy of the shifting moods dictated by their unhappy passions. Hermione at last persuades Oreste to murder Pyrrhus, only to accuse Oreste, once the deed is done, of recklessly taking her at her word. Hermione commits suicide over the corpse of Pyrrhus, and Oreste sinks into madness, conflating, in an extraordinary moment of psychological horror, a phantasmagoric vision of Hermione with the Furies. Andromaque, who had planned to marry Pyrrhus and kill herself immediately afterward, saves her child and receives the kingdom.

It is this play, more than any other, that has created the impression that Racine's characters, unlike those of Corneille, are sealed off from history, locked in a vacuum where only stormy and imperious private emotions speak. It is certainly true that the protagonists of *Andromaque* use the public world of history for their private designs. But this has the effect of politicizing love itself, which becomes a matter of siege and conquest and slavery. Of course, military metaphors for sexual affairs have always been common. But in seventeenth-century France, where the adventures of the heart were a more or less official topic, these metaphors were highly formalized, aspects of an elaborate courtesy as well as of courtship. In Racine's *Alexandre*, for example, the conquering hero is "defeated" by the woman he loves and becomes her "captive." This is simply a moderately witty use of a convention.

In *Andromaque* the metaphors go further. Oreste says he is Hermione's "slave," caught in her "irons," dragging her "chain." This is still the language of amorous compliment. But Andromaque is literally a captive in Pyrrhus' kingdom, and Pyrrhus himself takes the issue beyond that of elegant paradox. Hermione, he thinks, is a prisoner because he does not love her; his love for Andromaque cancels her captivity. Conquest and servitude, with the memory of Troy so close and so vivid, are no longer comfortable figures of speech but awkward intimations of a genuine continuity between the worlds of love and war. If Pyrrhus were simply to "burn" with love for Andromaque, the formula would be conventional enough. What he says is that he burns, in his passion, with more fires than he lighted in the sacking of Troy, and the boldness of his phrase abolishes all courtesy and makes his love a form of world-historical violence.

Even so, the phrase chiefly concerns Pyrrhus' love; it relegates Troy to the plane of antecedent and allusion. The complaint against Racine is that this is history's regular fate in his plays. Two answers must be made. One is that the characters of *Andromaque* are conscious of their defection from a wider universe. Oreste thinks of his fame as "more important" than his love for Hermione; it is merely less compelling. Pyrrhus imagines, erroneously, that he has overcome his humiliating passion. Hermione, suddenly anxious that Pyrrhus should know that she is the author of his death, sends her companion to tell him he is being sacrificed to her hatred and not to the enmity of the Greeks. The world beyond the passions is not ignored by the play— the survival of Astyanax is a sign of that. But most of the characters do not inhabit that world. We see this in their insistent, helpless references to it, their bids to reproduce it within the interplay of their feelings. Pyrrhus, Hermione, and Oreste all speak of calling down the Greeks to make "a second Troy" in Epirus. They struggle not only with their passions but with the illustrious historical patterns they cannot forget and cannot seriously repeat. All they can do is pretend to burn Troy again and again.

The second answer to the complaint is that *Andromaque* is the only play by Racine in which the historical world is so thoroughly dwarfed by the passions. In *Bérénice* two lovers separate forever for the sake of the Roman Empire. In *Bajazet* and *Mithridate* love and politics are inextricably entangled. *Iphigénie* explores a conflict between the demands of history and the demands of the family. *Britannicus* takes certain of the implications of *Andromaque* to their opposite extreme: politics and passion are the same for Néron in that play, not because he makes the first serve the second, but because his only passion is endless power, a realm where he cannot be denied. He falls in love with the innocent Junie in part because she embodies a limit. Pyrrhus must conquer Andromaque because he loves her; Néron loves Junie because he must conquer her if his power is to have any meaning.

In *Esther* and *Athalie* biblical history is animated but not diminished by personal feeling. *Phèdre* is a special case, because the world of the play, far from conflicting with the characters' desires, looks like a massive mirror for them. The monster that terrifies Hyppolite's horses and thereby indirectly causes his death seems to have emerged less from the local sea than from some dark domain of strangled and offended love. Yet the characters themselves do not see the world as a fig-

ure for the way they feel, as they do in *Andromaque.*

We can say generally, then, that history for Racine is present *in* the passions of his characters rather than apart from them. And it is clear that history cannot be absent from a universe in which love is most often an exercise of power, and power so frequently seeks to collect sexual dues. In the plays after *Andromaque* the characters do not exploit history; they suffer it and make it, demoralized by the interaction between intimate feeling and sweeping dynastic ambition.

Britannicus is the portrait of a historical and legendary monster: Nero—Néron in the French spelling. But the monster is barely at the start of his career; no major infamy disgraces him as yet. He is a "monstre naissant," as Racine says, a monster in the process of being born; and indeed the subject of the play is the monster's birth in two linked senses. Néron *becomes* Néron, embarks here on his reign of murder and menace; and he breaks free of his domineering mother, Agrippine. One of the play's cruelest ironies is that Néron, who rules Rome because of the crimes and conspiracies his mother orchestrated on his behalf, can assert his personal liberty only through further crimes, this time directed against the party his mother is supporting.

For Agrippine favors the marriage of Britannicus and Junie, who love each other. If Néron consents, she feels she will regain something of her visibly waning power. Néron does consent, and Agrippine is joyful. "It is enough," she says. "I spoke, and everything changed." In fact nothing has changed. Néron, who earlier had abducted Junie and fallen in love with her, or rather with her purity and helplessness, now, in spite of his promise to Agrippine and after a few lukewarm hesitations in the name of virtue, decides on Britannicus' death. Britannicus dies poisoned, Agrippine violently curses her son, Junie escapes to the temple of the Vestal Virgins, and Narcisse, Néron's accomplice and evil spirit, is killed by the crowd as he attempts to pursue her into the sanctuary. We last see Néron not on stage but in a description: alone with his conscience and his future, he is murmuring Junie's name, walking aimlessly up and down, his uncertain eyes downturned, avoiding the potential reproaches of heaven. Burrhus, Néron's ex-tutor, closes the play by piously wishing that the murder of Britannicus will be the last of Néron's crimes. On the contrary. As we and history know, it is the first; he is just beginning.

The tragedy, as Racine says in his preface, is as much about Agrippine as it is about Britannicus or Néron. She is a daunting, unforgettable figure, imperious and witty. He can be the father of his people if he likes, she says of Néron, but let him remember that she is his mother. She treats her son as subject, not as emperor; tells him to approach and sit down; dismisses him when an interview is over. And yet she is powerless when Néron is not in her presence, and his wily silence is more than a match for her commanding eloquence. When the play opens she is waiting in vain outside Neron's rooms, and she does not see him face to face until the fourth act.

As wife of Domitian, then of Claudius, Agrippine has had power—enough to make her son emperor. As a mother, she is merely a piece of the past. Néron finds the present in Junie; in the play's most famous scene (act 2, scene 6) he makes her talk to her lover while he hides and watches and listens. A single word of love, he has told Junie, means Britannicus' death; "You should have no secret languages for me;/I shall hear the looks that you think are mute." Junie nevertheless gives the most transparent of hints about what is happening, but Britannicus, who is not quick of understanding, misses them all. Only Néron catches the point and derives added pleasure from his rival's failure to see how much he is loved. He promises himself great joy from driving Britannicus further toward despair, and constructs for himself a "charming picture" of the poor fellow's sorrow.

Is Néron in love with Junie? He says he

idolizes her, and his own surprise at his feelings is evidence of a certain sincerity. His love began a moment ago, he says (2.2) in one of those brilliant expansions and contractions of time so remarkable in Racine, and will last a lifetime. But Néron's love is indistinguishable from his appetite, as a wonderful dialogue with Burrhus makes clear. Burrhus asks Néron to give up his love for Junie, saying Nero has not seriously tried to resist it. This is undoubtedly true, but Burrhus' next remark shows how little he understands the passions: "One does not love, my lord, if one does not wish to love." And yet again, he is right about Néron, who does not wish not to wish, and whose love therefore is an expression of power rather than an overwhelming emotion. Néron speaks like a lover—love, he says to Burrhus, does not resemble statesmanship, it is "une autre science" (another form of knowledge)— but he behaves like a tyrant discovering the possibilities of unhampered caprice. Burrhus is not deceived; when alone, he speaks not of Néron's love but of his revealed ferocity.

Bérénice is in one sense the least Racinian of Racine's plays, since it shows profound passions being sacrificed to a rather abstract sense of duty. Titus, emperor of Rome, has long been in love with Bérénice, queen of Palestine, but cannot marry her because of Rome's deep-rooted hatred for royalty of all kinds, and because he himself is anxious not to imitate Néron, the model of a tyrant consulting only his own pleasures and not his country's weal. An attractive tradition, not much credited these days, has it that Henrietta of England, duchess of Orléans, proposed the subject to both Corneille and Racine, so that a duel of tragedies by the age's two masters would result. Whatever we think of this notion, it remains true that both playwrights had works on the same subject performed in November 1670 (Corneille's play is called *Tite et Bérénice*) and that *Bérénice* is Racine's attempt to invade his rival's moral realm. When Racine's characters sacrifice themselves in his other plays, their motives are usually more personal than the claims of empire.

Yet *Bérénice*, in the simplicity of its action, is often thought to represent the quintessential Racine, tragedian of the inner life. Racine himself encouraged this view by insisting on it so eloquently in his preface. Almost nothing happens in the play. Titus' father is dead, and Titus is now emperor. Bérénice expects him to marry her; he realizes that he cannot; has difficulty in telling her; does tell her; she accepts his decision, after horrible mental struggles. The greatness of the play lies in the painful contrast between the violence of the feelings involved and the stately, almost religious calm with which the characters refuse all temptations to sudden action—although it is true that both Titus and Bérénice threaten to commit suicide.

Titus is the play's weakness. It is hard for us to see his Roman (Cornelian) destiny binding him so closely. Indeed, some critics have suggested that he does not love Bérénice, that Rome is an excuse. The thrust of the play seems to be the reverse. He does love her, but genuinely believes he cannot marry her. His abandonment of his love, her magnificent acquiescence in his sorry reasons, are among the most moving moments in literature. The way they are portrayed is perfect. *Why* they must occur is not so clear. Titus appears to have sacrificed both himself and Bérénice to a faulty sense of politics and to an exaggerated desire to be on the right side in the history books. That he is afraid of what others will think seems to make him a little short of stature for a tragedy. This is one of the rare moments when Racine's life may have constricted his work: such a fear could not have seemed trivial to a serious courtier.

Phèdre is the most famous and most often performed of Racine's plays. It was also Racine's own favorite. "He was always convinced," his son Louis said, "that if he had written anything perfect, it was *Phèdre*." Some critics have found the language of the play more expansive than that of the others,

and many people, including Racine himself, have been taken with the moral tone of the work, with the heroine's disapproval of her own destructive love. What gives *Phèdre* its particular strength, though, is the resonance of the classical myths it invokes and relies on, notably those of the Minotaur and the amorous adventures of Theseus (Thésée). All of Racine's plays are subtle and eloquent. *Phèdre* is subtle and eloquent and creates an impression of range and depth that non-French readers and viewers are apt to find lacking in Racine. It is an ideal place to begin an acquaintance with this author.

Phèdre, wife of Thésée, is ill, apparently dying. Thésée is absent, and Hippolyte, his son from an earlier marriage, is troubled not only by his father's failure to return but also by his love for Aricie, his father's captive and enemy. Phèdre's illness, we learn, is the result of a smothered passion for her stepson. Her love, she says, is no longer a hidden fire in her veins, but Venus personified claiming her prey. Rumors of Thésée's death give Phèdre a faint hope that her love may cease to be illicit, but then news reaches her of Hippolyte's affection for Aricie, who loves him in return. Meanwhile Thésée appears, and Phèdre, in a panic of jealousy and remorse, allows her companion to accuse Hippolyte of the love he does not feel for her. Thésée, outraged, calls on his protector, Neptune, to avenge his honor. In response Neptune produces a terrifying sea monster, which so startles the horses of Hippolyte's chariot that they bolt and drag him to his death. Phèdre then confesses the truth, takes poison, and dies.

The play is colored by attitudes and images suggesting a sexuality that lurches from excessive license to excessive restraint. Thésée, for example, is famous for his sexual exploits, which include deserting Ariadne, Phèdre's sister, who had helped him escape from the Cretan labyrinth. Hippolyte, on the other hand, is a prude, ashamed of his feelings for Aricie, less concerned about caring for his father's enemy than about being in love at all.

214

In Racine's model, Euripides' *Hippolytus*, the young man was devoted to Artemis, a virgin goddess fiercely hostile to love. Racine has humanized him by giving him a love Hippolyte himself thinks of as a weakness, but has left him all his fear and suspicion of emotions. Phèdre is a virtuous woman driven by a passion she cannot dominate. Speaking to Hippolyte, she begins a description of her husband that keeps turning into an evocation of Hippolyte himself and a declaration of love. Sexuality is a kind of family curse for Phèdre—her mother is Pasiphae, who was also mother of the Minotaur—and her mention of Venus is not a casual piece of rhetoric. The passion is Phèdre's own, and the responsibility for her actions is hers too, but the overwhelming force of the feeling does indeed seem a doom, a mark of the goddess' special attention.

The gods of Racine, as Raymond Picard has said, ordinarily represent human limitation: they are names for the points where our will abdicates or our comprehension ends. But in *Phèdre* the gods are active; they are parcels of energy abroad in the world. Venus persecutes Phèdre: "her crime," Racine says in his preface, "is a punishment from the gods rather than a movement of her will." He means not that she is innocent, but that she has been given more than her share of temptation. Neptune grants Thésée's misguided wish and kills his son—as if a god could not know when to do a favor and when to refuse one. None of this makes *Phèdre* a religious play in the strict sense, but we cannot convert these gods into psychological phenomena. They are metaphors not for states of mind, but for consequences the mind cannot see. The simplest way of putting it is to say that the gods embody the vicious whims of fortune, all those emotions and outcomes that we do not choose and that often look like a mockery of our best intentions.

This interpretation needs to be taken a little further, if only because of the monster sent by Neptune. The play is full of monsters, apart from this final one. Thésée is a famous killer of monsters; Hippolyte says his mother, an Amazon, is not a monster; Aricie calls Phèdre a monster, and Phèdre calls herself one; both Phèdre and Thésée call Hippolyte a monster. There is an elementary irony here that the characters themselves do not miss: monstrous passions lurk unslain in the palace of Thésée the monster-slayer. More subtle and more suggestive, though, is the constant linking of these monsters to troubled sexuality.

The concept of the monstrous usually implies a natural order that has been transgressed. In *Phèdre*, however, nature seems to be behind the transgressions, an avid accomplice. Phèdre is a monster because she is in love, Hippolyte because he is accused of the same passion. Thésée's monster-hunting excursions are repeatedly connected to his sexual adventures, which Hippolyte rather priggishly calls "the unworthy half of such a handsome story" (1.1). At the time of his rumored death, Thésée is in the dungeons of a tyrant of Epirus, waiting to be fed to the tyrant's pet monsters. He manages to feed the tyrant to his own creatures, but he got into this scrape in the first place through helping a friend to abduct, or try to abduct, the tyrant's wife. The Minotaur, mentioned more than once in the play, was killed by Thésée but was also the fruit of Phèdre's mother's transgression, the sign of Venus' hatred of the family. What all this suggests is that disorderly love, like the sleep of reason, breeds monsters. Love is carelessly offered and casually withdrawn, cruelly repressed, reluctantly acknowledged, bestowed on indifferent hearts; under these conditions it becomes a monster. It is out of this world of deformity, seeking but not finding normality, that the spectacular beast of Neptune arises, a mixture of bull, dragon, and giant snake—sexuality itself as it appears to the horrified eyes of virtue. It is worth noting that Hippolyte kills this monster, but then dies when his horse bolts, dashing him to pieces, staining the rocks with blood, so that his whole body, Racine says, was a single wound. Virtue, we may say, first wins and then is broken by another aspect of the insubordinate self. In Phèdre's case virtue is broken earlier, with the confession of her love, but she gains nothing and ends in an irretrievable disgrace that echoes Hippolyte's physical disfigurement. There is no escape from the prison of sex, except, it seems, for Thésée, whose very immorality provides him with a form of immunity.

Athalie, Racine's last play, was drawn, like *Esther*, from the Bible. At first sight these two works seem extremely remote from the Greek, Roman, and Oriental preoccupations of the earlier tragedies. It is true that *Athalie* especially is marked by a double vision of doom and salvation that is not at all characteristic of the classical world (if we make a partial exception for Vergil). A priest in *Athalie* falls into a trance and prophesies: he sees the destruction of Jewish Jerusalem but also the new Jerusalem of Christianity. Zion will fall, a chorus sings, and Zion will rise to the skies. Similarly, although the pious child Joas is crowned, a "happy end" to a perilous plot, the play is full of intimations that Joas later, as king, will give in to the bloodthirsty traditions of his family—this is Athalie's curse on him, and it is his own fear. In his preface Racine mentions that the historical Joas, after thirty years of just rule, ordered the murder of the high priest, son of his own protector. Such ambivalences are not confined to Christianity, of course. But they are characteristic of that religion of paradox, in which a crucified God represents a promise of eternal life.

Yet *Athalie* has a great deal in common with Racine's earlier works. Joas, as we saw before, is a version of Astyanax, the threatened inheritor. But he is also, like Néron, a "monstre naissant," or rather a monster-to-be, a noble king shadowed by an ugly future. Athalie's curse on him echoes Agrippine's curse on Néron. Athalie herself resembles Pyrrhus in a number of ways. She is a violent, passionate, unrepentant ruler, but she is not evil, not immune to milder human feeling.

Like Pyrrhus, who protects Astyanax, she feels some tenderness toward a vulnerable child, even though that child has been stalking her dreams. Driven by fear, doubt, sympathy, greed, she loses her political balance and enters the temple where Joad, the high priest, has hidden young Joas, who is to become Athalie's successor. She recognizes that her reign is over, and a group of Levites lead her out to her execution. "God of the Jews," she cries before she goes, "you carry the day." And this victory of God, far from seeming to restore order to a violent and erring world, seems merely tactical and temporary. Athalie is trapped in the temple by a verbal quibble and a rumor—she came for the boy *and* the treasure said to be hoarded by the Jews, but the boy *is* the treasure—and by the high priest's having hidden weapons in the supposedly defenseless holy place. One of Racine's very rare stage directions indicates that at the moment of Athalie's confrontation with Joad and Joas, the back of the theater is to open, revealing a pack of armed Levites. The trick has something of the dark irony of Neptune's gift of an avenging monster to Thésée, or indeed of the ending of *Andromaque*, where the heroine receives the kingdom but the only winners appear to be despair and ungovernable resentment.

The God of the Jews is also, for Racine, the Christian God, and we must not attribute skepticism to him. Nevertheless the flow of feeling in *Athalie* makes God's justice seem harsh and overeager. Athalie seeking a peace of mind she has lost—"Cette paix que je cherche, et qui me fuit toujours!" (2.3)—joins the company of Racine's hunted and troubled heroes and heroines, and although her opponent, Joad, is a spectacular, saintly figure, he is also furious and unbending. His cause is the right one, but he and the God he serves seem as fierce and irrational as the cruel divinities of Greece. It is not too much, perhaps, to see in this confrontation of the bad but human queen with the good but rigid priest a symbol of the essential conflict that animates Racine's theater. His characters in general do not occupy a middle ground, as Racine, following Aristotle, suggested the characters of tragedy should: neither good nor bad in excess. They are not, that is, merely human. They are human to a fault; their fault is their humanity. A merciless logic judges and destroys them, but we remember their sufferings rather than their sins.

THEATRICAL CONVENTIONS AND THE THEORY OF TRAGEDY

The theatrical conventions of Racine's France required a strict adherence to the classical theory of the three unities: those of action, time, and place. A play was to tell a single story whose events occurred within twenty-four hours or less and whose location remained substantially the same. Another room in the palace where the play began would be permitted, for example, but not a shift to another city. As Boileau put it: "Let a single complete deed, in one day, in one place, keep the theater filled till the end of the play."

Verisimilitude was the argument usually advanced for observing these rules: they were thought to guarantee a certain plausibility. If we are to be rigorous about such matters, it is not more plausible that the affairs of ten hours should be compressed into two than that those of several years should be bundled into the same span. Verisimilitude, in seventeenth-century France, as in other ages and countries, was a convention, an agreement between authors and public as to what was proper. Racine's audience accepted the conversion of a day into two or three hours, but would have been shocked by longer lapses of time on the stage. It is true that liberties occasionally had to be taken with sources, if the rules were to survive. Thus Racine, in *Mithridate*, conflates twenty-six historical years into a single dramatic day.

It is a mistake, though, to think of these rules as hurdles for Racine. It is customary to praise the ease and grace with which he

obeyed them, but even that perspective is slightly askew. The rules for Racine were more an opportunity than anything else, an enhancement of the concentration that is the mark of his art. Molière, consulted about some early verse of Racine, preferred an awkward but natural turn of phrase to a more correct form. "Art itself," he is supposed to have said, "must teach us our freedom from the rules of art." By the same principle, art must teach us what the rules of art are for, even when we choose to follow them scrupulously, as Racine did.

Racine interpreted the unity of action to mean that a tragedy should examine a moment of extreme crisis. His plays always open on a new occurrence or access of information. Of course something of the kind happens in all stories, or there would be no stories at all. But affairs are not always so desperate in other stories, and the characters are not always surprised. Many critics have noted how frequently the phrase "for the last time" echoes through Racine's work: the action always hovers on the edge of some ultimate determination. What is not so frequently noted is the extraordinary pressure exerted in these plays by new or altered facts.

Phèdre, for example, could not know in advance how much difference her confessing her love would make: a whole chain of horrors arises from her simply answering, with great reluctance, her companion's question about what is wrong with her. Titus, in *Bérénice*, knows that his father will die sooner or later, that he will then become emperor, and that his love for the queen of Palestine will cause trouble for him in Rome on that day. He knows all that, but he does not know how he will feel when that day comes, when he *is* the emperor, and this is the day he and Bérénice live through in the course of the tragedy. Néron, in *Britannicus*, has Junie abducted, is startled to find himself in love with his victim, and spends a sleepless night reviewing the image she presented, weeping, disheveled, when his soldiers brought her in. "I was in

217

love," he says in a particularly refined and cruel line (2.2), "even with the tears I made her shed."

This surprise of the characters comes not from the blindness of their passion, but from their lack of preparation for the realities that follow the arrangements they have imagined. They live in worlds colored by their wishes. *Bajazet* is an excellent instance. The hero is in love with Atalide but is at the mercy of Roxane, favorite mistress of his brother, Sultan Amurat. In order to save her lover's life, Atalide courts Roxane on his behalf. Roxane responds to these advances and is ready to free Bajazet from captivity and join his rebellion, but only if he loves her. Bajazet himself cannot keep up the pretense. Roxane orders the execution of both Bajazet and Atalide, but Amurat, it turns out, has anticipated her and sentenced her to death, along with Bajazet, as a recompense for their projected betrayal of him. Atalide, alone, sees that her scheme has brought only ruin and kills herself. Yet what can Atalide and Bajazet really have expected? How could Bajazet have contented Roxane and remained free to love Atalide? Atalide indeed is startled by her own jealousy when the time comes for Bajazet to simulate his love for Roxane. How could these pathetic stratagems have done anything but buy a little time? These lovers, like Titus, consulted only their hopes and were destroyed by the actual realities of the feelings they thought they could manipulate. (Titus had the good—or bad—fortune to be destroyed morally rather than physically.)

The unity of action is thus intimately linked to the unity of time. It is because these stories are nearing their end, hurried on by the incursion of new, unmanageable material, that time is so short for the characters. It is not that the time and the action follow the rules; the protagonists are so close to their final fates that the rules cannot but apply. The principle, it seems, is not verisimilitude, whatever Racine himself says on the subject, but intensi-fication, a tightening of the tragic screw. The unity of place serves the same effect. There is no need to go anywhere else; there is nowhere else. Everything happens here, on this stage, in this setting, or is reported here in such a way as to make it seem more vivid than if we had actually witnessed it in performance. Hippolyte's horrible death, for example, described by his tutor, could not be staged realistically or could scarcely be filmed without bathos. Even if staged in a stylized manner, it would be less disturbing than it is in Racine's version, with the alarming precision of its gory detail: bloodstained rocks, dripping bushes, and red, smoking grass.

Racine himself speaks frequently of the "simplicity" of his plays. His ideal, he implies in his preface to *Alexandre,* is "a simple action . . . sustained only by the interests, feelings, and passions of the characters." In his preface to *Bérénice* he speaks of "a simple action, sustained by the violence of the passions, the beauty of the feelings, and the elegance of the expression." He also speaks of the "marvelous simplicity" that delighted the ancient world, and rebukes people who think simplicity is the sign of a lack of inventiveness. "They don't realize that on the contrary the whole art of invention consists of making something from nothing." "Nothing" in *Bérénice,* as we have seen, means a minimum of physical action and a threat of violence rather than the actual thing. The play is packed with feelings and implications. Racine's declarations, therefore, need to be treated with care. They help us to understand the purity of narrative line that he sought for his tragedies and his stringent sense of artistic economy. But we must remember that these are *polemical* declarations, strategic attacks on the complications of Corneille and other writers. It would be a serious error to assume without qualification that Racine's plays are simple. Racine's "simplifications," as Odette de Mourgues says in her lucid study, lead to "a very subtle and complex treatment" of the reality that has been simplified—"stylized" is de Mourgues's word. Simplicity in Racine is a question of sharpness of focus and exclusion of material he finds irrelevant. There is no reduction of difficulty, no refusal of the problematic.

Indeed Racine's simplicity goes hand in hand with the violence he so regularly depicts. In the sentence quoted above, the simplicity of an action and the violence of the passions are named in immediate sequence, and Racine speaks earlier in the same preface of the violence of the passions in the story of Bérénice as making it especially appropriate for the theater. In his later moralizing mood he was capable of suggesting that he portrayed passions only in the hope of showing the disorder they cause, but in the preface to Athalie he returns to his former position, and sees "trouble," "disturbance," as a value in a tragedy. His plays are designed to portray a deeply troubled world in an atmosphere of extreme formal calm, and a great part of the pleasure to be had from Racine's work stems from this contrast.

To be sure, all tragedy is often thought of as opposing the order of art to the discord of reality. We suffer with Hamlet and Lear, but we enjoy the plays because their form sets these sorrows at a distance and the form itself constitutes a victory of the spirit over mean and unruly matter. This view of tragedy is more than debatable, but even if accepted, it leaves a number of distinctions to be made. The victory of form in Shakespeare, for example, is implicit; we do not perceive it unless we think rather theoretically about Shakespeare's art. Form in Racine, however, is everywhere, unmistakable, the most visible aspect of every play. This visible form indeed is a barrier for some readers and spectators, who tend to confuse the formal with the stilted and the empty. There is a special pathos, then, in the clash between the perfect manners of Racine's characters and the terrible confusion of their lives. Racine himself writes, in the preface to Bérénice, that a "majestic sadness" makes up the

whole pleasure of tragedy. The phrase is grand enough and vague enough to mean many things. But at the very least it does connect formality with sorrow. The plays suggest, finally, not the triumph of art over chaos but the helplessness of decorum in the face of violent passion. Nothing can save these characters, neither their own style nor Racine's art, and the tragic stage, in the place of deceitful consolation, offers a beautiful and despairing fidelity to the truth of this predicament.

But tragedy, of course, is not simply disaster, whether palliated or merely witnessed by art. It is a particular relation of character to situation, perhaps an exaltation of failure, as Roland Barthes suggests, but failure of an especially calculated kind. Why can't Hamlet avenge his father, or Lear believe Cordelia? Why can't Oedipus discover his identity without simultaneously uncovering his implication in incest and murder? It is almost as if we need to reverse Aristotle's doctrine of the tragic flaw: these heroes suffer for their faults, but they inhabit universes that appear to have been constructed with these very faults in mind. Who but Hamlet would have found Hamlet's plight so intricately impossible? This is not to say that the heroes of tragedy are victims or puppets, merely that their situations, in relation to their characters, are intolerable—and are not tolerated. Hence the catastrophe.

In Racine the privileged form of the intolerable is the love that cannot be shared—either because it is not returned or because other obstacles intervene. This is intolerable and tragic rather than unfortunate, because the love itself is terminal, unchangeable, a demand as imperious as any other form of destiny. Andromaque, for example, is faced with the exacerbation of moral conflict so frequent in tragedy: she cannot save her son, it seems, without betraying Hector, which she cannot do. But Oreste, Hermione, and Pyrrhus in the same play, and Titus, Bérénice, Eriphile, and Phèdre in others, all face double impossibilities of a similarly implacable nature: they cannot rescind their love, and they cannot live with it. Tragedy appears when highly conscious creatures are caught in such balanced traps.

Apart from the three unities, as codified by French poets and theorists, there is one other suggestion in Aristotle's *Poetics* that Racine took up with exceptional enthusiasm. It concerns the composition of the cast of characters rather than any particular figure. Tragic actions, Aristotle says, can involve conflicts between people who are friends, enemies, or neither the one nor the other. If an enemy kills an enemy, he continues, we do not feel pity; and we do not feel much pity for the deaths of those who are neither friends nor enemies. The events the poet must seek, Aristotle says in Racine's translation, are those that take place between people linked by blood (or friendship): "as for example when a brother either kills or is ready to kill his brother, a son his father, a mother her son, or a son his mother."

The story of Oedipus, of which Aristotle is no doubt thinking, shows a son killing his father and marrying his mother; and Oedipus' sons kill each other. Racine in his first play, *La thébaïde*, which portrays the struggles of these sons, follows Aristotle's prescription to the letter and seems generally to have been attracted by the notion of intimate hatred. Jocaste, Oedipus' mother and widow, and mother of these quarreling sons, says to one of them in *La thébaïde:* "All that is needed is that you should cease to hate your brother." It sounds easy, but nothing is more difficult, since this hatred is synonymous with both brothers' lives, and will end only with their deaths. "They seemed united in the excess of their hatred," a character says of their last battle, "and on the point of slaughtering each other, they appeared to be friends."

In later plays Racine does not pursue the prescription so literally, but remains thoroughly faithful to the principle. Jean Giraudoux saw Racine as the author of a "theater of

incest." *Britannicus* concerns the attempt of Néron to free himself from his mother's dominion and her attempts to hang on to her power over him. Pyrrhus, in *Andromaque,* wants to marry the woman whose husband was killed by his father. Phèdre, in a sense, wants to put herself in Jocaste's place and become the lover of her husband's son. Athalie does not shrink from killing her own children to preserve her position or, as she puts it, to avenge her parents on her posterity. Agamemnon, in *Iphigénie,* is asked to sacrifice his daughter so that the gods will grant the Greeks a good wind for Troy. Two brothers are rivals in *Mithridate,* and for good measure they are the rivals of their father too, suitors of his wife-to-be. Shadowy father-figures haunt virtually all the plays, from the legacy of Oedipus in *La thébaïde* to Hector's tomb in *Andromaque;* from the memory of Domitian and Claudius in *Britannicus* to the invisible Judaic God of *Athalie.*

All this material seems to invite psychoanalysis, and indeed Charles Mauron has written an extremely interesting psychoanalytic interpretation of Racine. But it seems that the family relations of Racine's embattled characters are mainly yet another reflection of his concern for intensity and concentration. The intimacy of these rabid conflicts brings out a certain horror implicit in human affairs: killing your brother or your children is an extreme form of killing, different in degree but not in kind, a form of pinnacle, just as incest may be seen as an exaggeration rather than a perversion of love.

STYLE

The firm focusing of the plot is an important aspect of Racine's formal discipline. There are secondary characters in his plays, but they are confidants, companions to the principal figures, their sounding boards and sometimes their agents. There are no extraneous characters, no gratuitous turns in the narrative, no subplots. Everything serves to heighten the dominant emotions.

But Racine's most striking formal achievement lies in his language, since it is his language that makes him a major poet as well as playwright. His plays, apart from the choruses of *Esther* and *Athalie*, are cast in the twelve-syllable lines called alexandrines, which ordinarily contain a pause—the caesura—after the sixth syllable. The alexandrines rhyme in couplets, a pair of masculine rhymes (ending in a sounded syllable) alternating with a pair of feminine rhymes (ending in a mute one). *Andromaque*, for example, begins with the following lines spoken by Oreste:

Oui, puisque je retrouve un ami si fidèle,
Ma fortune va prendre une face nouvelle;
Et déja son courroux semble s'être adouci
Depuis qu'elle a pris soin de nous rejoindre ici.
Qui l'eût dit, qu'un rivage à mes voeux si funeste
Presenterait d'abord Pylade aux yeux d'Oreste;
Qu'après plus de six mois que je t'avais perdu,
A la cour de Pyrrhus tu me serais rendu?

Yes, since I meet again so faithful a friend, my fortune is going to assume a new face; and already its anger seems to have softened, since it has taken the trouble to reunite us here. Who would have said that such an inauspicious shore would at first offer Pylade to Oreste's eyes; that after having lost you for six months, I would find you again at the court of Pyrrhus?

The play ends with these words of Pylade, Oreste's friend:

Il perd le sentiment. Amis, le temps nous presse;
Ménageons les moments que ce transport nous
   laisse.
Sauvons-le. Nos efforts deviendraient impuissants
S'il reprenait ici sa rage avec ses sens.

He is losing consciousness. Friends, time is short; let us use the moments left us by this attack. We must save him. Our efforts would be fruitless if his madness resumed when he came to his senses.

Feminine and masculine rhymes have followed each other regularly throughout, as they normally do in French classical drama.

This sort of performance is not as difficult in French as it would be in English, since most Romance languages offer an abundance of rhymes. The vocabulary of Racine and his contemporaries is limited and largely conventional; the verse rings changes on a relatively small stock of figures and phrases. The rhyme "funeste/Oreste," for example, which appears in the first quotation above, recurs seven more times in *Andromaque*. The name Andromaque is rhymed three times with "attaque." In the same play "vie" (life) rhymes with "envie," "convie," "suivie," "servie," "furie," "sacrifie," and "asservie" (envy, invite, followed, served, fury, sacrifice, subordinated); and "Grèce" (Greece) rhymes with "promesse," "faiblesse," "maîtresse," "cesse," "princesse" (twice), and "tendresse" (three times) (promise, weakness, mistress, ceasing, princess, tenderness). We should not praise Racine for doing what any competent hack could do; his relation to the contemporary rules of verse is much the same as his relation to the three unities. Boileau is said to have taught Racine to "rhyme with difficulty," that is, to resist the easy line. The beauty of Racine's verse lies in the play of precisely expressed thought against a constriction that is scarcely felt, and in a musical repertory that commands all the resources of poetic language, from delicate alliteration to the secrets of syntax, and from shifts of rhythm to the clash of contrasting tenses.

Oreste, arriving in Epirus, asks Pylade to tell him what is happening in Pyrrhus' court and heart, "dans sa cour, dans son coeur" (1.1). The words, apart from making a slant rhyme, have different genders, and their sequence has the effect of a quiet change of key. Hermione, reproaching Pyrrhus for his desertion of her, memorably says, "Je t'aimais inconstant; qu'aurais-je fait fidèle?" The break in the alexandrine supports the balanced logic of her claim, and the f's of the final words underline the remarkable ellipsis taking place: "I loved you (when you were) inconstant; what would I have done (if you had been) faithful?" The wonderful rhetoric also conceals a pathetic illusion. How could she have loved him more than she does, since she is ready to have him killed and then die of grief herself? She might have loved him less.

Titus, in *Bérénice*, speaks of his love, Bérénice, as

Tout ce qui de mon coeur fut l'unique désir,
Tout ce que j'aimerai jusqu'au dernier soupir.

(3.1)

Everything that was my heart's sole desire, everything I shall love till my last sigh.

The past tense of the first line and the future tense of the second effectively cancel out the present, as de Mourgues has noted. Titus has no life except in memory or in painful anticipation of Bérénice's perpetual absence.

But Racine's poetic gifts are most clearly seen in his set pieces, those nights of violence scattered throughout his plays. In the following passage Andromaque, speaking to her confidante, evokes her first sight of Pyrrhus during the sack of Troy:

Songe, songe, Céphise, à cette nuit cruelle
Qui fut pour tout un peuple une nuit éternelle;
Figure-toi Pyrrhus, les yeux étincelants,
Entrant à la lueur de nos palais brûlants,
Sur tous mes frères morts se faisant un passage,
Et, de sang tout couvert, échauffant le carnage;
Songe aux cris des vainqueurs, songe aux cris des
*   mourants,*
Dans la flamme étouffés, sous le fer expirants;
Peins-toi dans ces horreurs Andromaque éperdue:
Voilà comme Pyrrhus vint s'offir à ma vue.

(997–1006)

Think, think, Céphise, of that cruel night that was an eternal night for a whole people; imagine Pyrrhus, with shining eyes, appearing in the light of our burning palaces, making his way

over my dead brothers, and, covered with blood, stirring up the carnage; think of the victors' cries, think of the cries of the dying, stifled in flames or put to the sword; picture Andromaque distraught among these horrors: that is how Pyrrhus first appeared to me.

This is not the place to make a detailed analysis of these lines, but we may note the masterful architecture of the sentence, with its repeated instructions to the listener (think, think; imagine; think, think; picture); the sense of Pyrrhus in his violent element, shining eyes amid the burning palaces: the meticulous antitheses (flames/sword, the victors/the dying); and the subtle modulation of the first line of the passage, with its almost caressing tones ("Songe, songe, Céphise") giving way to the sudden shrillness of the eek-sound in "nuit cruelle." It is tempting to believe that Andromaque finds a certain attraction in these horrors, that there is a subdued excitement in her portrait. But this is perhaps to transfer to her the feelings of women in other plays by Racine. Eriphile, for example, in *Iphigénie*, is certainly in love with her captor's violence, and the same seems to be true of Cléofile in *Alexandre*.

Athalie, in one of the most celebrated moments in Racine's theater, sees her mother in a dream:

C'était pendant l'horreur d'une profonde nuit;
Ma mère Jézabel devant moi s'est montrée,
Comme au jour de sa mort pompeusement parée,
Ses malheurs n'avaient point abattu sa fierté;
Même elle avait encor cet éclat emprunté
Dont elle eut soin de peindre et d'orner son
*   visage,*
Pour réparer des ans l'irréparable outrage:
"Tremble, m'a-t-elle dit, fille digne de moi;
"Le cruel Dieu des Juifs l'emporte aussi sur toi.
"Je te plains de tomber dans ses mains
*   redoutables,*
"Ma fille." En achevant ces mots épouvantables,
Son ombre vers mon lit a paru se baisser;
Et moi je lui tendais les mains pour l'embrasser;

Mais je n'ai plus trouvé qu'un horrible mélange
D'os et de chairs meurtris, et traînés dans la
*   fange,*
Des lambeaux pleins de sang, et des membres
*   affreux*
Que des chiens dévorants se disputaient entre eux.
                                    (490–506)

It was during the horror of the depths of night; my mother Jezabel appeared before me, impressively arrayed as she was on the day of her death, her misfortunes had not brought down her pride; she even had still that borrowed brightness with which she had taken care to paint and adorn her face, in order to repair the irreparable damage of the years: "Tremble," she said, "my deserving daughter; the cruel God of the Jews has the better of you too. I pity you for falling into his fearful hands, my daughter." As she uttered these frightful words, her shadow seemed to bend toward my bed; and I stretched out my hands to embrace her; but I found only a horrible mixture of bones and broken flesh, and, dragging in the mud, blood-covered remnants and hideous limbs, which ravenous dogs were quarreling about among themselves.

The first of the quoted lines has a remarkable simplicity, to use Racine's word. The horror is almost abstract, and the night is merely deep. Yet "during the horror" has an especially chilling effect, achieved, it seems, by a form of syntactical switch on the phrases we might have expected: during a night of deepest horror, during a deep and horrible night, and so on. Jezabel in her finery and makeup, still fighting time although she is dead, is carefully contrasted with her own dismembered and dispersed corpse, the handiwork of the cruel God whose power she now acknowledges. The force of the feeling is enhanced by the fact that this Old Testament heathen appears to be half-quoting the Epistle to the Hebrews: "It is a terrible thing to fall into the hands of the living God." Her speech stops abruptly at the beginning of a line, thereby displacing the caesura. It is as if she were interrupted by her next incarnation, or as if there were, after all, nothing of importance she could say to her daugher. We see here, finally, that this verse form, as used by Racine, is a magnificent narrative instrument, a perfect vehicle for story and suspense.

Racine's imagery has already been mentioned in connection with the monsters in *Phèdre* and the military metaphors in *Andromaque*. Its ingredients are familiar, part of the common store of the century. Racine's characteristic touch is to lend an edge or a sense of complexity to a fairly threadbare formula. It may be worth watching what he does, in *Phèdre*, with the notions of light and purity.

Phèdre's love is described as a poison and a fever—a slight variation on the rather trite contemporary metaphor of love as a fire or a burning or a flame. Consequently she avoids the heat of the sun and seeks the shade. But the shade suggests to her the forests where Hippolyte hunts, and it thereby feeds the fever again. The shade is also the silence in which she hides her passion. At the beginning of the play she emerges into the light, is dazzled, and announces that she is now seeing the sun for the last time. Prompted by her companion, she then confesses her secret. The sunlight is shared knowledge, but it is purity as well, the clear day stained by these feelings that have crept out of the darkness. Phèdre's last words proclaim that her death will give back to the soiled day the purity her life had taken from it; and Hippolyte says the day is not purer than the depths of his heart ("Le jour n'est pas plus pur que le fond de mon coeur": 4.2). More than this, Phèdre's lineage situates her uncomfortably between day and night. The sun is her ancestor; her grandfather is Minos, judge of the underworld. The suggestion is that neither darkness nor light can help her, neither heaven nor hell, neither speech nor silence; and that the demand for purity, which is as much Phèdre's own as that of anyone else, is a pitiless posture, as glaring and indiscriminate as the sun.

PSYCHOLOGY

Racine is often praised as a master of psychology. The reference is not to his already mentioned fondness for situations that now suggest psychoanalysis, but to the quality of his scrutiny of the mind and the emotions. Racine's theater is "psychological" in the sense that it places its principal actions in the characters themselves rather than in their relations with each other. Strictly speaking, they have no relations, they have only needs. They kill each other, die for each other, without leaving an essential, confining solitude. They cannot, most of them, escape into a realm of shared experience. Racine's plays thus belong to a powerful French tradition that includes the essays of Michel de Montaigne and the novels of Madame de La Fayette, Choderlos de Laclos, Benjamin Constant, Stendhal, and Marcel Proust. These works specialize in introspection and analysis, in a lucidity that captures the most elusive shades of thought and feeling. But they are not psychoanalytical, or even psychological, in the sense that they search for unconscious motives or drives. These motives and drives are there, part of the personality displayed in the fiction or the essay. But these works customarily concentrate on consciousness, with all its lures and delusions and excesses of plausibility.

This is a second meaning of Racine's "psychology": he understands the interruptions of consciousness, all the forces that conspire to defeat the best, as well as the worst, intentions. We think of him as a psychologist because he knows so much about the shadier habits of the mind, especially the self-deceiving mind. His theater is largely one of desperate error—but the errors are subtle and insidious, as we see in two forms of crucial mistake that recur again and again in the plays.

The first crucial mistake is the recourse to a logic impeccable in everything except its premise, which is disfigured or fabricated by longing. "How easily love believes what it wishes to believe," Atalide says in *Bajazet*, and this is standard practice in Racine. Some of his most famous lines reflect the cruel irony of this situation. Bérénice, afraid she is about to be abandoned by Titus, decides his current coldness stems from jealousy of Antiochus, who is also in love with her. She is much heartened by this thought, almost happy. "If Titus is jealous," she says, "Titus is in love." The deduction is reasonable, but yields only a pathetic misconstruction. Titus is not jealous of Antiochus; the idea has not crossed his mind. He *is* in love with Bérénice, as it happens, but that does not help, cannot stave off their final separation. Similarly Hermione, in *Andromaque*, caught by one of the oscillations of Pyrrhus' feelings—he has decided to marry Hermione in order to teach Andromaque a lesson—chooses to believe that his decision means he loves her. "Il n'est point ennemi de lui-même" (He is not his own enemy: 3.3) she thinks, if he is marrying her; it is because that is what he wants. Nothing could be further from the truth, and Hermione has unwillingly offered a perfect negative definition of Pyrrhus. He *is* his own enemy; in imagining he is not, Hermione has created not only a premise but an entire character shaped by her desire. In another example, Roxane, seeing Bajazet embarrassed in her presence, interprets his awkwardness as a mark of timid passion. "I thought," she says, "I caught a glimpse of his tenderness in his confusion." The principle is not wrong: tenderness is often shy. It is just that Bajazet is troubled not by his love but by his honor, which dislikes the deception he is practicing on Roxane. Finally, Britannicus decides that Néron, who in fact is about to have him poisoned, wants to be his friend. He is not treacherous, Britannicus says; either he hates openly or he gives up his hatred. The point, once again, is the *premise*—a pure guess, informed by nothing but Britannicus' hope. Junie warns him not to judge Néron's heart by his own.

The other form of mistake that recurs a

great deal in these plays is complementary to the first kind. Just as many characters argue from passion, so many others fail to see that passion itself is an argument to end all discussions, with a weight quite different from that of gratitude, for example, or self-interest, or fame. All kinds of characters who ought to know better, like Agrippine and Atalide, do not recognize or do not remember that love and the hankering for power, when they are serious, easily eclipse all other claims on the attention. Roxane, in this instance, is more clearsighted than those who would deceive her. "What does it matter," she says, "that he owes us both the scepter and his life? Do benefits received weigh the same as love in a person's heart?"

These mistakes mirror each other, then, and help us to understand the workings of Racine's universe. Either the truth is not seen because passion gets in the way, or passion's extravagant authority and unique status are denied or ignored. Passion, the force that moves and often kills these creatures, is consistently out of focus. Racine's characters are among the most lucid in literature, and yet they are blind too, unable to see the fundamental features of their ruined lives. Their characteristic stance is to imagine they have conquered the passion that is about to break them.

Examples of Racine's acuity in matters of psychology could be multiplied almost indefinitely. Among the instances already noted for other reasons, we may think of Néron's interest in Junie's tears, Titus' failure to anticipate the reality of his father's death, Oreste's final perception of Hermione as a snake-trailing Fury. Other justly celebrated moments are represented by Hermione's cry to Oreste, when he informs her that he has killed Pyrrhus, as she instructed him—"What have you done? Why murder him? What has he done? By what right? Who told you?" (5.3)—and by Hippolyte's reluctant confession of love to Aricie. The very beauty of Hippolyte's lines, with

their images of self-neglect and obsessive desire, suggests how little he enjoys his passion, and how little his resistance to it has availed:

Depuis près de six mois, honteux, désespéré,
Portant partout le trait dont je suis déchiré,
Contre vous, contre moi, vainement je m'éprouve:
Présente, je vous fuis; absente, je vous trouve;
Dans le fond des forêts votre image me suit;
La lumière du jour, les ombres de la nuit,
Tout retrace à mes yeux les charmes que j'évite;
Tout vous livre à l'envi le rebelle Hippolyte.
Moi-même, pour tout fruit de mes soins superflus,
Maintenant je me cherche, et ne me trouve plus;
Mon arc, mes javelots, mon char, tout
   m'importune;
Je ne me souviens plus des leçons de Neptune:
Mes seuls gémissements font retentir les bois,
Et mes coursiers oisifs ont oublié ma voix.
               (*Phèdre* 2.2.539–552)

For almost six months, desperate and ashamed, everywhere bearing the dart that wounds me, in vain I try my strength against you, against myself: in your presence, I flee; in your absence, I find you; your image pursues me in the depths of the woods; the light of day, the shadows of night, everything recalls the attractions I seek to escape; everything puts the once rebellious Hippolyte at your mercy. The only result of my fruitless efforts is that I seek myself now, and am not to be found; my bow, my spears, my chariot, everything irritates me; I no longer remember the lessons of Neptune: only my groans echo through the woods, and my idle chargers have forgotten my voice.

THEATER AND COURT

Racine was an assiduous and skillful courtier, and it would be absurd to see him in any simple sense as a critic of his society. Nevertheless, the picture of life at court that emerges from his plays is worth attending to.

There is no court in *Andromaque*. Nominally the action takes place at the court of Pyrrhus, but this is merely a location for the clash of passions, not a social space or structure. Everything changes in *Britannicus* and the later works. Junie has not lived at court until her abduction by Néron but quickly grasps the principles of hypocrisy and expediency that rule there. Change is common at court, she says, and "in this court, such a distance separates what is said from what is thought." The scene in which Néron spies on her encounter with Britannicus is an instance of Néron's cruelty and voyeurism, of course. It is also, as Charles Mauron suggested, a figure for the theater and its public: no less than Néron, although no doubt our motives are kinder, we are eavesdropping on troubled lives. But the scene also serves as an emblem for the customs of a court: the curtains have ears and eyes; privacy is an illusion, or simply unthinkable. In *Bérénice* Titus explicitly identifies the court as Néron's world, a region of pure sycophancy, and contrasts it with Rome, which means history and destiny. Racine himself, in a preface to *Bajazet*, described the seraglio of a Turkish sultan as a court, a closed universe of seething rivalry; and the importance of rumors and accusations in Racine's theater is relevant here. Kings are said to be dead in several plays; battles are reported as lost; grotesque slurs are cast. Characters act fatally on this false information. More than this, rumors are carefully spread: Mithridate insists that he owes his life to the reports of his death he has scattered about. Truth in these plays is not absent or relative as it is, say, in Luigi Pirandello. But it is extraordinarily elusive, constantly altered or refused or covered over. This is the political equivalent of filtering the truth through personal wishes, although the motive here is doubtless not passion but prudence, the necessary caution of people who live in the proximity of power.

We may add here Racine's expertise on the subject of fear. He knows not only what it means, but how it is used. Néron says he is tired of being loved as emperor, he wants to be feared, and Agrippine realizes that her hold on him will last only as long as he fears her. "I should soon be afraid of him," she says, "if he were no longer afraid of me." Sultan Amurat, in *Bajazet*, is united to his janissaries by a similar bond: "Since he is constantly afraid of them, they are always afraid of him." Mithridate, we are told, has killed two of his sons simply because of his suspicions of them. Another of Racine's shrewd insights awaits us here: "The more miserable he is, the more he is to be feared." *Mithridate*, we may note in passing, was Louis XIV's favorite among Racine's plays. A line in *Athalie*, admittedly spoken by the evil turncoat Mathan, suggests that kings need only their own fear as a justification for any action: "Dès qu'on leur est suspect, on n'est plus innocent" (As soon as they suspect you, you are no longer innocent: 2.5).

Racine's public, including the king, probably saw these negative images of the court as proper and convincing but locally inapplicable. Nothing is more common, in our century as in that of Louis XIV, than the comfortable condemnation of habits we do not recognize as our own. Nevertheless it is also true that Racine's public was quick to spot topical allusions or to imagine it had spotted them. The persecuted Jews of *Esther*, for example, were taken to represent the hounded Huguenots of France. This whole question needs further investigation, not so much at the level of Racine's intentions as at that of resemblances between patterns in the plays and the order of contemporary events. What is clear is that the values of Racine's theater and the actual, if not professed, values of Louis XIV's world were distinctly at odds. Racine's heroes seek their own wholeness beyond compromise, even if they rarely find it. There is no sign that anyone much at court sought such authenticity, and the Jansenists were always in trouble because they were so intransigent. It is slightly too neat, perhaps, to see Racine as caught perfectly between two realms, as Lucien Goldmann does: "A serious Jansenist would not have *written* tragedies and conversely, a man who was integrated into the world . . . would not have written *tragedies*."

226

We do well to remember, as de Mourgues prompts us to, that "Jansenism itself may well be no more than the most conspicuous expression of a split between religious life and earthly values which turned the seventeenth century into a two-truth world." Perhaps we should also remember that the seventeenth century in France was a period of conflict, an age of civil strife and foreign war, as well as religious division, and we shall not go wrong if we choose to see in Racine's work not a criticism of his time or a resistance to it, but a mark of the time itself, a universe of grief and contradiction, where particular moral impossibilities stand out with a clarity that political life, with its battery of techniques of survival, cannot afford. Phèdre, for example, appears to be punished for her uncontrollable desire. But the play also represents the incompatibility of urgent desire of any kind and the domain of marriage and compromise and accommodation usually described as reality. Reality judges Phèdre, but she judges reality and finds it wanting. Or rather, we may so judge on her behalf, since she plainly accepts reality's verdict. Both verdicts are part of the play: a two-truth world, although not quite in the sense that de Mourgues intends.

REPUTATION

Racine is in many ways the most perfectly French of French authors, an epitome of the nation's traditional finesse and clarity. French schoolchildren know dozens of Racine's lines by heart, and an appreciation of Racine is often seen as something like an oath of loyalty. Racine is almost too respectable to be enjoyed, and performances of his plays are frequently crippled by the piety of actors and directors. He does not have the range of Shakespeare and does not invite theatrical experiment as Shakespeare does. The romantics even attacked Racine's verse. Victor Hugo insisted that Racine was a figure "of the second or third rank" and found the lines already quoted from Phèdre ("Mon arc, mes javelots, mon char, tout m'importune") "empty and pompous." But Racine's current standing is high, partly because modern poets and critics have understood that classicism and romanticism represent alternating movements of a culture rather than consecutive stages of a progressive history. We cannot outgrow Racine, and Stéphane Mallarmé and Paul Valéry, among the moderns, have been as classical as he was.

For all the differences between them, Racine is the French Shakespeare, a master who is mingled in all assessments of the national literature. In spite of Hugo's charges and the aura of dullness that inevitably surrounds national monuments, Racine's reputation has never been seriously shaken. He brought the French theater to a pitch of perfection that has never been surpassed or even equaled. His greatness perhaps lies, as Roland Barthes suggested, less in his specific virtues and gifts, which are many, than in the extraordinary flexibility of his mind and his apparently rigid art. He speaks with unchanged authority and persuasion to age after changing age.

Selected Bibliography

FIRST PERFORMANCES OF INDIVIDUAL PLAYS

Le thébaïde, ou les frères ennemis. 1664.
Alexandre le grand. 1665.
Andromaque. 1667.
Les plaideurs. 1668.
Britannicus. 1669.
Bérénice. 1670.
Bajazet. 1672.
Mithridate. 1673.
Iphigénie. 1674.
Phèdre. 1677.
Esther. 1689.
Athalie. 1691.

COLLECTED EDITIONS

Oeuvres. Paris, 1962. Senil edition. Preface by Pierre Clarac.

Oeuvres complètes. 2 vols. Paris, 1940–1952. Pléiade edition. Vol. 1 edited by Edmond Pilon and René Goos; vol. 2 by Raymond Picard.

Théâtre complet. Paris, 1960. Garnier edition. Preface and notes by Maurice Rat.

TRANSLATIONS

Andromache. Britannicus. Bérénice. Translated and introduced by John Cairncross. Baltimore, 1967.

Five Plays. Translated by Kenneth Muir. New York, 1960. Contains Andromache, Britannicus, Bérénice, Phaedra, and Athalie.

Iphigenia. Phaedra. Athaliah. Translated and introduced by John Cairncross. Baltimore, 1964.

Phaedra and Figaro. New York, 1961. Phaedra translated by Robert Lowell.

Phèdre. Translated by R. C. Knight. Austin, Tex., 1972.

————. Translated by Margaret Rawlings. New York, 1962.

Three Plays: Andromache, Britannicus, and Phaedra. Translated by George Dillon. Chicago, 1961.

BACKGROUND AND CRITICAL STUDIES

Barthes, Roland. On Racine. New York, 1964.

Bersani, Leo. A Future for Astyanax. Boston, 1976.

France, Peter. Racine's Rhetoric. Oxford, 1965.

Giraudoux, Jean. Racine. Cambridge, 1938. English translation. French version in Nouvelle revue française 8:733–756 (1929).

Goldmann, Lucien. The Hidden God: A Study of Tragic Vision in the "Pensées" of Pascal and the Tragedies of Racine. London and New York, 1964.

Hubert, Judd D. Essai d'exégèse racinienne. Paris, 1956.

Knight, R. C. Racine et la Grèce. Paris, 1950.

Maulnier, T. Racine. Paris, 1936.

Mauron, Charles. L'Inconscient dans l'oeuvre et la vie de Racine. Paris, 1969.

Mourgues, Odette de. Racine, or the Triumph of Relevance. London, 1967.

Picard, Raymond. La carrière de Jean Racine. Paris, 1956 and 1961.

Pommier, Jean. Aspects de Racine. Paris, 1954.

Racine, Louis. Mémoires sur la vie de Jean Racine. Lausanne and Geneva, 1747.

Vinaver, Eugène. Racine et la poésie tragique. Paris, 1951.

Weinberg, Bernard. The Art of Jean Racine. Chicago, 1963.

MICHAEL WOOD

JEAN DE LA BRUYÈRE
(1645–1696)

AMONG THE GREAT moralists of French classicism, Jean de La Bruyère stands out in the originality of his method, the broad range of his observation, and the unique perfection of his style. Published in 1688, eighteen years after Blaise Pascal's *Pensées* and thirty-three years before Montesquieu's *Lettres persanes, Les caractères ou les moeurs de ce siècle* constitute in many ways a bridge between the literary tradition of the seventeenth century and the genres and concerns of the Enlightenment.

The aim of the moralists was to analyze and portray the human condition and psychology in their most universal and timeless aspects. La Bruyère shared their purpose and probed the recurrent weaknesses and drives, but he also perceived that one of the essential constants of human nature is change. He therefore expanded the moralist's field of inquiry to include the interactions among social, economic, and political institutions, and through his study of the mechanics of change he showed how human nature shapes these structures and is in turn shaped by them. To achieve a more comprehensive view than that of the other moralists, he multiplied angles of vision and moved his focus from the innermost drama of passions to superficial mannerisms and gestures, from the individual to social groups. He taught us how to pierce the surfaces with which people confront each other and how to recognize the psychological drives behind apparently trivial details of individual and collective behavior.

The scope of the *Caractères* embraces all levels of human interactions in their myriad manifestations, and in an endless variety of characters and settings, from the coarseness of the glutton to the subtle hypocrisy of the plenipotentiary engaged in diplomatic negotiations. Unlike other moralists, he included in his observation physical objects such as clothes, food, carriages, and houses to bring out the part they play in human experience and their symbolic meaning in human relationships. He depicted the social classes and institutions of the ancien régime as a case study of human society and viewed the intellectual and artistic achievements of his time as a moment in the history of civilization. The lasting value of the *Caractères* resides in the universal human truths they convey and to an even greater extent in the richness and permanent validity of a method for the scrutiny of individual and collective behavior, for a historical and genetic examination of contemporary social structures—from fashion and fads to values, to scientific theories, to the structure of institutions. The hundreds of human types and situations sketched with lucidity and wit act as so many little lenses that bring greater clarity and sharpness to the way we perceive ourselves and the world.

Jean de La Bruyère had the opportunity to

observe at close range the social classes and the milieus that he portrayed. His family and early career placed him among the wealthy bourgeois, among lawyers and financiers. As a member of the Condé household he had ample occasion to scrutinize the courtiers and the great. As a writer and an elected member of the Académie Française he interacted with contemporary authors and critics.

He was born in Paris on 16 August 1645, into a well-established bourgeois family whose records reached back over four generations to 1571, when the first Jean de La Bruyère was a wealthy apothecary who became involved in politics as one of the founders of the Holy League (1576) against the Protestants. His father, Louis de La Bruyère, was controller-general of finances at the town hall, and his mother, Elisabeth Hamonyn, was the daughter of a prosecutor at the Châtelet courthouse. His paternal uncle, Jean, was a financier who amassed a considerable fortune, acquired the honorary title of royal secretary, and upon his death in 1671 left an inheritance that assured the material comfort of the family. After an early education received from the Oratorians, a religious order known for its teachers and scholars, La Bruyère studied law; and at the age of twenty he passed the certifying examinations at the University of Orléans. It is not known how active he was in the legal profession.

He came into contact with the world of tax collectors in 1673 when he purchased the position of treasurer at the bureau of finances at Caen. This type of office, which had also been held by Jean Racine, was a lucrative sinecure that carried with it the nobiliary title of écuyer (esquire). He kept the position for thirteen years, but after his installation he never returned to Caen for meetings with the other treasurers. He continued to live with his brothers in Paris and to enjoy the freedom to write and meditate that he was to praise in the Caractères. In spite of sentimental attachments echoed in his lyrical passages on tenderness and love, La Bruyère never married.

He wrote that philosophy helps a man to bear the wife he has or to live without one.

It is not clear why in 1684, at the age of thirty-nine, La Bruyère renounced his independence to become part of the princely household of the Condé. Upon the recommendation of his friend Jacques Bénigne Bossuet he was hired to tutor the sixteen-year-old duke, Louis de Bourbon, in history, geography, and French institutions. He was disappointed at having to share the task of educating the lazy and recalcitrant duke with two Jesuits and another tutor. The lessons were supervised by the duke's grandfather, the prince de Condé. La Bruyère lived with his pupil at Chantilly and accompanied him to court at Versailles, Paris, Chambord, and Fontainebleau. The duke's education came to an end upon the death of his grandfather in 1686, but La Bruyère remained at the house of Condé in the post of secretary and librarian.

While he had admired the prince de Condé, whom he portrayed in the Caractères under the name Émile, the prince's son Henri-Jules de Bourbon and his grandson Louis offered sources for unfavorable descriptions of the great. According to the testimony of Saint-Simon, the new masters were brutal, tyrannical, and stingy. The personal humiliations that La Bruyère suffered at their hands found expression in comments on the ingratitude of princes toward their servants. Perhaps his most effective revenge was the remark that the great are fortunate to employ men who are superior to them. La Bruyère had few friends among the courtiers who at times ridiculed him, but he was portrayed by Saint-Simon and others as a refined man of good company, unpedantic and free of ambition—a philosopher who wished to live peacefully with his carefully selected books and friends. He was elected to the Académie Française in 1693, after two unsuccessful candidacies. The story of his election may well be seen as an episode in the quarrel of the ancients and moderns, in which La Bruyère, along with his friends Bossuet, Racine, and Nicolas Boileau-Despréaux took the side of the ancients. He died of an attack of apoplexy at Versailles in 1696.

La Bruyère published his work anonymously in Paris, in 1688, under the title *Les caractères de Théophraste traduits du grec, avec les caractères ou les moeurs de ce siècle.* The volume contained the *Discours sur Théophraste,* followed by a translation of the Greek portraits (pp. 53–149), and La Bruyère's *Caractères,* consisting of 420 original entries (pp. 151–360). The book had an enormous success and was reprinted twice in the same year. A fourth edition came out in 1689 with 344 additional entries, which almost doubled the size of the volume. La Bruyère continued to expand the work in each successive edition, with 158 additions in 1690, 72 in 1691, 83 in 1692, 44 in 1694. In their final form of 1694, the *Caractères* contained 1,120 entries. Some of the new material expands or elaborates existing themes, but there are also clusters of entries that introduce new subjects. While the first edition consisted mostly of maxims and observations, portraits became more numerous after 1689. Many keys were published that claimed to identify the models of the portraits, but most of them were hypothetical and all were disavowed by the author as contrary to his typological intentions.

The author explains in the preface to the *Caractères* that the variety of length and form of his entries is adapted to the nature of his thought. The entries vary in length from one line to several pages, with most in the range of a paragraph between three and fifteen lines long. La Bruyère referred to them at different times as characters, remarks, and reflections. The various traditional genres represented are the *maxim,* a brief and ingenious statement of a general truth; the *observation* (or reflection) in which the maxim is accompanied by an illustration or commentary; the *portrait;* the *dialogue;* the short *moral* (or philosophical) *essay;* and occasionally the *anecdote* (or narration). Often several forms are combined in a single entry, so that maxims are joined with portraits, short portraits are incorporated into

reflections, and dramatic dialogues appear in portraits and reflections. La Bruyère's immediate predecessors were Theophrastus for the portrait, François de La Rochefoucauld for the maxim, and Blaise Pascal for the reflection.

It has been noted that La Bruyère was not the first to offer to the public the *Characters* of Theophrastus, the fourth-century-B.C. Greek philosopher and disciple of Aristotle; it had been translated into Latin in the sixteenth century and published several times in England and France. The *Characters* is a collection of twenty-eight moral portraits intended to illustrate a variety of vices, such as flattery, dissimulation, impertinence, ostentation, avarice, cowardice, and pride. Each begins with a definition of the particular weakness, and then proceeds to describe a series of behavioral traits associated with it. Portraits in the Theophrastian tradition had also been written by Exeter Joseph Hall, John Earle, Louis Dumoulin, and Father Lemoyne. La Bruyère's translation is based on the Latin version of Isaac Casaubon, and parts of the *Discours sur Théophraste* follow Casaubon's commentary.

In spite of the borrowings, the *Discours* is a highly original and daring text in which, within the context of a discussion of Theophrastus, La Bruyère introduces the method and themes of his own work. He points out that he shares with the Greek moralist the aim to improve men by showing them their weaknesses and vanity in contrast with goodness and strength. Their common method is to make people look at each other and draw instruction from contemporary images. La Bruyère notes, however, that he will give greater importance to psychological analysis and employ a more flexible form akin to Theophrastian proverbs and the proverbs of Solomon. He did, in fact, diversify the portrait and used it along with other genres in the *Caractères.* Yet there are many similarities in the method of description and in the subjects treated. Theophrastus and La Bruyère analyze dissimulation, frivolous speech, sycophancy, dishonesty, avarice, insulting manners, vanity, ostentation, and pride. Both enumerate the gestures and speech patterns that result from particular moral traits. Both make frequent use of truncated dialogue and indirect discourse. Both portray the character in action viewed from the outside like an actor on the stage.

While La Bruyère placed himself in the tradition of Theophrastus and the proverbs of Solomon, he stressed the differences that distinguished him from his contemporaries. Pascal sought to convert people to Christianity and La Rochefoucauld tended to oversimplify human motivation by reducing it to a single principle.

Studies of sources, notably those of Maurice Lange and René Jasinski, have revealed that La Bruyère based his analysis of man on his readings of ancient and modern authors as well as on direct observation. Among moralists and philosophers, those who influenced him most were Michel de Montaigne, René Descartes, La Rochefoucauld, Pascal, Baltasar Gracián, and Baldesar Castiglione. Numerous affinities have also been pointed out between La Bruyère's attack on social classes and institutions and that of writers like Jean de La Fontaine, Molière, Boileau, and of contemporary preachers such as Bossuet, Louis Bourdaloue, and the abbé Lejeune. But comparisons with the sources indicate that whenever La Bruyère borrowed an idea or theme he transformed it into an original adaptation by his own method and vision.

In the *Discours sur Théophraste,* La Bruyère introduces the main subjects of his social and political criticism by portraying three societies: contemporary France, a primitive community, and Athens. In the description of France he lashes out against the absurd sale of judgeships; the honors bestowed on tax collectors, gamblers, and debauchees; the emptiness and frivolity of city life; the disorder and deficiencies of urban environment, the lack of safety, the bad administration. These contemporary vices and corrupt values are next con-trasted to the moral ideal of a society of primitive men. In this social setting is found true greatness free from vanity, luxury, and ambition; here man is honored for his strength and virtue rather than for his pension and position. Clothes are simple, diet is healthy, pleasures are innocent, and peace reigns in families and among neighbors. In the image of Athens, La Bruyère emphasizes the positive political values of freedom, republican government, and equality; the cleanliness and comfort of the city; the meaningful nature of public gatherings; the perfection of arts and sciences; the politeness of manners and language. This composite picture of three moments of civilization outlines the elements that will be examined in the *Caractères,* and it announces the emphasis on the changing nature of society, the attention to physical environment, and the method of contrasting the negative aspects of reality with a positive ideal.

Ever since the publication of the *Caractères* there have been those who claimed that the work lacks organization. Yet the author affirmed in a 1694 addition to the preface that there were definite reasons behind the sequence of chapters and remarks. In the preface to his *Discours de reception à l'Académie Française* (Acceptance Speech to the French Academy, 1693) he argued against critics that it is ridiculous ever to assume that a thoughtful writer is not able to connect his ideas and provide transitions. Studies of the overall plan of the *Caractères* and of the structure of individual chapters indicate that La Bruyère did in fact devote considerable attention to composition. He divided his material into sixteen chapters, each devoted to a different aspect of human existence, with its particular set of psychological resources, social relationships, and circumstances. While no single idea explains the overall sequence of chapters, there are connections between contiguous units and a thematic progression that justify their arrangement.

It has been observed that one of the principles behind the organization of chapters is the Cartesian rule of proceeding from the simplest subjects to the most complex. The first ten chapters progress from problems of the individual to those of social groups, classes, and the state. A similar arrangement appeared later in Montesquieu's *Lettres persanes*.

The first chapter of the *Caractères* examines the contribution an individual can make through artistic creativity. The next deals with the general subject of personal merit and achievement. It is followed by "Of Women," which analyzes the particular form of attainments open to women and the inseparable theme of physical attraction between the sexes. "Of the Heart" complements the subject with a discussion of pure love, friendship, and other noble emotions. "Of Society and Conversation" places the individual in the broader social arena and considers the ways in which he establishes a superficial presence in the world through manners and speech. The next six chapters study his relationships with the economic, social, and political structures. While in the first four units man is seen as an active agent using his personal, intellectual, and moral resources, in the next six he interacts with situations that weigh upon him. The title "Of Gifts of Fortune" introduces the outside forces to which man is subject. First among these is wealth, examined in its effect on social structure and on individual destiny. It is followed by two social environments, each with its particular conditions and demands: the town and the court. Finally, two aspects of the power structure are examined: the great and the sovereign. The progression from the nouveaux-riches to the bourgeoisie, the nobility, courtiers, princes, and the monarch obviously follows the social hierarchy.

In "Of Man" La Bruyère returns his attention to the individual for an analysis of the enduring aspects of human nature and condition. The four chapters that follow, "Of Judgments," "Of Fashion," "Of Certain Usages," and "Of the Pulpit," study how the endless inconstancy and arbitrariness of man's opinions, feelings, tastes, and affections shape the nature and evolution of civilization. The word "esprit" (wit, mind) appears symmetrically in the titles of the first and the last chapters. The work begins with artistic creativity and ends with the paradoxical weakness and strength of human intelligence in pursuit of religious, metaphysical, and scientific truth.

The overall plan of the chapters is reflected on a small scale in the group of remarks on childhood ("Of Man," entries 50–59). The sequence of themes is: the vices of children ("Of Man"), their joys ("Of the Heart"), differentiation of character ("Of Personal Merit," "Of Society and Conversation"), ability to rise above fortune ("Of Gifts of Fortune," "Of the Court"), relation to authority and superiors ("Of the Great"), attitude toward duty and pleasure and the strict ritual of games ("Of the Town"), perception of greatness ("Of the Great"), government ("Of the Sovereign or of the State"), judgment ("Of Judgments"), and perception of justice ("Of Certain Usages").

Another indication of La Bruyère's attention to composition is found in the concluding remarks of chapters, which often function as transitions from one chapter to the next and provide a clue to the contrast or continuity between them. For instance, "Of Works of the Mind" ends with the theme of the writer's merit and looks forward to the future when the same thoughts will be repeated by others. The first remark of the next chapter raises the general problem of the worth of personal achievement in the light of posterity. The story of Émire at the end of "Of Women" illustrates the fatality of passions that destroy friendship: Émire's devotion to her girl friend Euphrosine ends when she falls in love with Euphrosine's suitor, and subsequently becomes ravaged by jealousy. "Of the Heart" begins with friendship as the privilege of superior souls. The last entry in "Of the Town" contrasts the bourgeoisie with the high nobility who are the subject of the next two chapters. "Of the Great" concludes by pointing out the danger of speaking against the powerful, and the next chapter begins with the need to submit to the regime. The penultimate remark in "Of Man" states the inconstancy of human opinions, feelings, tastes, and affections, which will be the themes of the four chapters to follow. The concept of human smallness connects "Of Judgments" with "Of Fashion." The decay in the forms of discourse provides the link between "Of Certain Usages" and "Of the Pulpit."

The role assigned to the first remark in each chapter is of primary importance in the internal organization of chapters. Each one introduces the themes, the method, and the tone of the chapter, and some present the characteristic antithesis of the subject. The themes are highlighted by sentences and by key words within those sentences. The thematic pattern of the opening statement frequently announces that of the entire chapter. For instance, in "Of Fashion" the first part of the remark deals with fashion in general and the second with fashionable piety; the chapter will be similarly divided between the two themes. In "Of Gifts of Fortune," the sequence of themes—the power of money, the injustice of property distribution, the psychology of the wealthy, and comparisons to others—is repeated in the subsequent arrangement of subjects. As noted by André Stegmann, Jasinski, Alain Niderst, and others, the entries within chapters are organized into clusters with thematic unity. The remarks in a group complement each other as they discuss or illustrate various aspects of a social phenomenon or different manifestations of a moral trait. Thus, each remark is part of a larger development and acquires its full meaning only in this context. Transitional remarks appear between the groups. The concluding entries of chapters frequently summarize the author's point of view.

The order of the chapters, their titles, and the opening remarks were established in 1688 and remained unchanged in subsequent editions in spite of the expansion of the work.

The only variations are the title "Of the Sovereign or of the State," a paragraph added to the first remark in "Of the Town," and a change of wording in "Of the Great." Numerous additions were made at the ends of chapters that improved the transitions and cohesion between adjoining units.

La Bruyère's style has been greatly admired for its variety and precision and its perfect adaptation of vocabulary, rhythm, and syntax to theme. His language differs from that of other classical authors in its broad range of concrete and technical vocabulary. He uses an abundance of rhetorical devices to make the form of the sentence correspond exactly to the reality portrayed. In his type of discourse, meaning is conveyed not only by the referential value of words but also by structural and syntactical relationships between terms.

The *Caractères* opens with a discussion of writers and literature that is also an introduction to the work itself. The title of the chapter, "Of Works of the Mind," suggests that literature will be considered from the point of view of the creative process. The first remark introduces the major theme and La Bruyère's attitude toward contemporary literary doctrines:

> Everything has been said and one comes too late after seven thousand years during which men have thought. On the subject of morals and manners the most beautiful and the best has been gathered; one can only glean after the ancients and the able among the moderns.

The statement is in part the sincere expression of the challenge that La Bruyère set out to meet by writing an original work on morals. But it is above all the repetition of a critical cliché that had already been satirized by other authors of the time. The same discouraging voice is heard again at the beginning of the last remark of the chapter, where we read, "Horace or Despréaux has said it before you." La Bruyère replies that he may nonetheless think and write as his own the truths that others have thought before and will think after him. His half-earnest repetition of a common critical stance announces the independent position that he will assume toward the generally accepted literary tenets of the time. As an introduction to the entire work, the opening remark places the *Caractères* within the context of the totality of the cultural tradition; the author will take into account everything that has been written on morals by the ancients and the moderns.

As in other opening remarks, the individual terms used in the paragraph announce the themes of the chapter: the element of time, or the relation of the writer to his age; saying and thinking, or the connection of content to form; the criteria of the good and the beautiful; the ancients and the moderns; the talented or the men of genius; and the particular problems of writing about manners and morals. The subjects are treated in the following sequence: the problems of the beginning writer (entries 1–5), mediocrity and perfection in art (6–15), literary criticism (16–28), freedom from rules (29–36), women writers and sixteenth-century authors (37–46), theater (47–54), style and content (55–58), genius and inferior minds (59–64), La Bruyère's own aims and solutions (65–69).

In the first section La Bruyère mentions the skill and painstaking effort required to produce a book and the difficulties of having one's first work accepted by the public. He announces his own determination to think and write well independently of the taste and opinions of others.

On the subject of judging the quality of a work of art, the moralist declares that there exists a point of perfection that can be discerned by the few who have good taste. Contrary to general opinion, he maintains that it is possible to argue about taste and to distinguish the good from the bad. To stress the equal importance of form and content, he points out that extraordinary deeds of history are enhanced by the way they are told. He attributes the superiority of such great writers of the past as Moses, Homer, Vergil, and Horace

to their clarity of expression and originality of images. But at the same time he insists that superior style is useless without a meaningful message. Faithful to the classical doctrine of imitation and clearly taking the side of the ancients in the quarrel of ancients and moderns, La Bruyère states that the way to achieve perfection of form is to imitate the ancients. A remark on the unjustified criticism of the ancients serves as a transition to the next subject.

The cluster of remarks on criticism is an example of a carefully organized sequence. The group begins with the positive idea that writers should seek out and welcome constructive criticism. The development progresses through increasingly more spurious opinions voiced by critics ever less familiar with the work: from those who have studied it closely, to those who have not read it at all. The first type of criticism discussed is self-criticism. In this connection, La Bruyère offers original insights into the reasons for the artist's dissatisfaction with his creation. An important cause of frustration is the belief in the *mot propre*. The writer knows that for every thought there is only one expression that conveys it correctly, but he is not always able to find it. Authors who create through inspiration are more subject to self-criticism because the forms that appear best to them vary with their moods. Moreover, the same judgment and talent that allow the writer to produce great works make him critical of what he has written. The better and more intelligent the author, the more modest and demanding he is about his work. The criticism exercised by others may be marred by jealousy, passion, indifference, the pleasure of disparagement, the hesitation to express independent judgment. Some critics disfigure what they read; others don't read at all; still others know only what is written by their clique or by themselves.

La Bruyère upholds the general classical tenets of clarity, simplicity, naturalness, and adaptation of form to content, but he advocates freedom from more specific rules and recommends experimentation with style. A work judged irregular by contemporary criteria can be beautiful, he maintains, and will be vindicated by the public against the critics if it lifts up the spirit and inspires noble emotions.

Among the remarks on sixteenth- and early-seventeenth-century authors and their effect on style, he places a comment on the contribution of female writers. He credits women with introducing emotion into literature and attributes to them a talent for style and cohesion of narrative. But his confidence in women's ability to produce great literature is qualified by reservations on their capacity to write with precision.

After contrasting men of genius with those of inferior talent such as imitators, translators, and literary critics, La Bruyère places himself among the inspired writers who cannot be imitated. In the concluding remarks he takes up again, and in the same sequence, the major themes of the chapter as they apply to his own works: satire, style, perfection, criticism, and content. He declares himself limited in the subject of satire because, born a Christian and a Frenchman, he found that the great themes were forbidden and could only be touched upon. He defends the use of new expressions and syntactical innovation. With confidence in the judgment of posterity he states that he will seek perfection rather than conformity to contemporary taste, discern what is ridiculous and where it is found, and portray it in order to please and to instruct.

The chapter "Of Personal Merit" examines the effect of exceptional talents and virtue on human achievement and aspirations. The subject is studied from the point of view of the individual who ponders how talent will affect his existence: "What man, endowed with the most rare talents and the most excellent merit, can fail to be convinced of his uselessness, when he considers that at his death he leaves a world which does not feel his loss, and in which so many people are found to replace him?"

The remark introduces the themes of the chapter: exceptional qualities, usefulness of talent, the place and renown they bring in the world, and the uniqueness of extraordinary men. Morover, the question, which contains its own pessimistic answer, suggests that the outstanding individual is discouraged by his own superior perception: merit itself brings humility and awareness of its limitations.

The first part of the chapter considers the various obstacles to achieving success through merit (2–9), ways of using one's talents to make a contribution to society (10–12), the relationship of merit to modesty (13–17), and the need to place people in appropriate positions (18). The second part examines various types of merit and of exceptional men: virtue (19–20), outstanding qualities (21–25), substitutes for merit (26–28), types of greatness (29–35), false appearances (36–42), the self-destructive character of merit (43–44).

In the first group of remarks La Bruyère elaborates the various reasons why extraordinary gifts do not necessarily bring success and renown: the element of chance, the difficulty of succeeding on one's own without supporters and intrigue, the lack of opportunity, the failure to discern and to use talent, and the supreme obstacle of death. Life ends when one has barely begun one's work.

The ideal situation, in which an individual succeeds through education and merit, is contrasted with the tragicomedy of competitive striving for the protection of the great. As it often does in the *Caractères,* the description of social conditions leads to a lesson in renunciation and withdrawal. The moralist suggests that the best way to use one's talents is to withdraw to a private life of meditation, reading, and conversation.

The man of merit is modest and never satisfied with his accomplishments because his imagination always makes him aspire to higher achievements. He must rely on his talents because modesty makes it difficult for him to court the great. He is motivated from within and finds satisfaction not in winning public praise but in doing his duty.

Among the various types of greatness, La Bruyère has special praise for the good man and, in the tradition of Montaigne, for the many-sided individual like Socrates. He points out further how both merit and lack of real worth can sometimes hide under deceptive appearances. For instance, intelligent men may appear naive in conversation while less able men give the impression of ability through glib speech and by repeating the thoughts of others. In the absence of exceptional talents, people seek to distinguish themselves through clothes, carriages, titles, and high positions.

The conclusion, added in 1689, returns to the basic question of the ambition of outstanding men and their outlook on worldly success. The wise man aspires beyond money, position, and favor to the glory of being recognized for his virtue. But this type of honor is not granted by society and he must do without it. Moreover, the most lofty ambitions are tragic because the highest form of virtue consists in suffering and giving one's life for others.

From the general theme of what can be accomplished through outstanding talent and virtue, the moralist proceeds to the question of what constitutes the merit of a woman. "Of Women" is a chapter on the relations between the sexes and on the controversial subject of feminine strengths and weaknesses. The scope and special emphasis of the chapter are introduced in the opening remark:

> Men and women rarely agree on what constitutes the merit of a woman. Their interests are too different. Women do not please each other by the same charms by which they please men. A thousand manners, which kindle great passions in men, evoke aversion and dislike between women.

La Bruyère examines the differences and the relations between the sexes, the qualities of women, the controversy about their merit and their efforts to please. Through numerous comparisons between men and women he shows their different interests and ways of looking at each other. He discusses passions and the manners that kindle desire. There are also comments on the way women judge each other and on the sources of dislike between them.

The strengths and weaknesses of women are considered in the first part of the chapter: the merit of women and their efforts to please (2–9), the way men view women (10–15), the dissolute conduct of women (16–26), women's selection of men (27–34), piety (35–45), other forms of hypocrisy (46–48), the education of women (49), the antipathy between women (50–58). The second part focuses on the relations between the sexes: the interests of young women in marriage (59–62), their subjective judgment of men (63–65), male and female expressions of love (66–72), marriage (73–80), the fatality of passion (81).

The treatment of women is satirical, with the overwhelming majority of remarks critical of their weaknesses. Yet the picture of vices and ridiculous traits is contrasted frequently enough with images of virtue and chastity for us to assume that the censure was not intended as a comprehensive commentary on the nature of women. The second remark contrasts the artificial and the natural greatness of women. The former consists of a dazzling and superficial wit and of gestures such as the way a woman moves her eyes, carries her head, and walks. The simple and natural greatness stems from the heart and lies in a solid and quiet merit accompanied by virtues and modesty.

Extremely critical of artificial manners, adornments, and cosmetics, La Bruyère points out that by their use women may please themselves and other women, but they do not attract men. The section progresses chronologically from youth to old age. The logical sequel is a group of remarks on the male reaction to feminine beauty. It begins with the admiration of the beautiful face and voice of the woman one loves and ends with the resistance elicited in men by feminine capriciousness.

In the remarks on dissolute behavior, La Bruyère distinguishes various types of women such as the coquette, the *femme galante*, the unfaithful, the weak, and the treacherous, and he points out the vices and passions that motivate their behavior. The *femme galante* wants to be loved, seeks to bind, and moves successively from one relationship to the next; she is dominated by a desire for pleasure, and her behavior stems from a weakness of the heart or a flaw of temperament. The coquette, on the other hand, wishes to be admired and to please; she amuses herself with several men at the same time; she is motivated by vanity and levity, and her coquetry is a defect of the mind. The worst type of woman, La Bruyère notes, is a combination of the two.

Strongly opposed to the role that the directors and confessors played in women's lives, he portrays piety as a passion or as a replacement in old age for the passions of youth.

Education was a key issue in the controversies of the time about the nature of women. Feminists like Poullain de la Barre argued that the weaknesses of women were due to their lack of instruction and to the vain and subservient roles imposed upon them. Women would be equal to men if they received the same education. La Bruyère inverts the argument when he insists that women's lack of learning is caused by weakness of temperament, laziness of mind, concern with appearance, poor concentration, and a natural dislike for subjects that demand intellectual effort. Their talents are for manual work and for the details of domesticity. Since no edict, statute, or law prevents women from reading and learning, he argues, they are themselves to blame for their ignorance. Whatever La Bruyère may have thought about the intellect of women, the statement is too exaggerated not to be tinged with irony. His intent was to satirize the paradoxical positions that, then as now, were adopted in polemics about the equality of the sexes. He points out, moreover,

that a learned woman has no opportunity to apply her knowledge and is regarded as no more than a useless curiosity. He shows, in conclusion, that the question of whether learning is compatible with virtue is a corollary of the view that women do not study because of their natural weaknesses.

Marriage receives a poor rating from La Bruyère. Few women, he writes, are perfect enough to prevent their husbands from wishing at least once a day that they were single. He portrays an unfaithful wife and spouses who live like strangers under one roof, but men are given part of the blame for the infidelity of their wives. A husband who is moody, stingy, sloppy, impolite, cold, rude, and taciturn can hardly expect to compete with an elegant, attentive, generous, and accommodating lover. The final remark in the 1688 edition asks if a way could not be found to be loved by one's wife.

The concluding narrative added in 1689 summarizes and illustrates the general view of the chapter that the overriding interest of women is love. It is an uncontrollable passion, more intense in women than in men, stronger than friendship and more compelling than principles. While "Of Women" examines primarily physical love and its effects, the next chapter portrays the spiritual aspects of love.

"Of the Heart" deals with the privileged emotional states of friendship and love (1–40, 55–58), generosity (41–54), freedom (59–61), happiness (62–65), revenge (66–70), rationality (71–81), surroundings (82), emulation (83), and renunciation (84–85). The subject is introduced by the first remark: "There is a profound pleasure in pure friendship which cannot be attained by those who are born average." The syntax of the sentence, composed of an affirmative and a negative clause, announces the pattern of the chapter. The first clause states the existence of noble impulses and the profound pleasure they provide; the second, however, declares that these feelings are not universally accessible and that obstacles to attaining them are inherent in the nature of man. All men are not equal in their sensibility and their capacity for pure and disinterested emotion. The movement of the chapter is between affirmation and negation. With regard to each emotion, La Bruyère first describes its positive aspects and then points out its fragility, its inconstancy, and the psychological obstacles to its fulfillment. The assertive tone of the sentence suggests that the author portrays feelings that he has experienced himself. The term "heart" is used in the general sense of spontaneous instincts, impulses, and affections.

The first group of remarks brings out the irrationality of love through a comparison with friendship (2–10). The analysis of love follows the various stages of its evolution: the beginning (11–16), the plenitude (17–23), the decline (24–30), the end (31–34), and the aftermath (35–40). Love, La Bruyère observes, is the source of intense happiness, but, marred by inconstancy, jealousy, and misunderstanding, it does not last. Its end is as involuntary as its beginning. The way to recover from the loss of a lover is to try not to think about one's passion. Friendship also has its reversals, as friends may become enemies and enemies turn into friends.

There is another source of delight in the freedom of pursuing one's whims that is contrary to the servitude of working for advancement. But some people are so impatient to achieve their goals and strive so hard that success does not compensate for their efforts. Others are so ardent and anxious in the pursuit of their ambitions that they fail to do what is necessary to attain them, and the fulfillment of desires either does not come at all or comes too late to bring the greatest satisfaction. Moments of extreme happiness are part of human experience, but in the course of a long life they add up to only a few months.

At the other extreme from friendship, La Bruyère points to feelings of hostility, hatred, and revenge, which may also bring intense gratification. But the downfall of the men we hate does not come at a time when we are able to rejoice; resentment does not last; and laziness prevents us from seeking revenge. Furthermore, although it would be satisfying to be governed always by reason, one's own or that of another, this ideal state cannot be achieved because throughout his life man is dominated by passions stronger than the mind.

Prefiguring the romantic communion with nature, La Bruyère finds delight in the affinity one experiences with certain sites: he observes that surroundings affect the state of mind, feelings, and mood. The chapter concludes in a Cornelian manner with a celebration of the highest forms of altruism and sacrifice. It is a sweet revenge, the moralist declares, to excel over those who make us envy their goodness, and the deepest pleasures of love can be surpassed by the satisfaction of virtuous resignation. Strength does not lie in avoiding love as a weakness but rather in transcending it on a higher plane.

For La Bruyère the world is a stage and society a jungle of competitive striving. From an examination of the inner sphere of passions and emotions he proceeds to a survey of the roles man must play, the various settings, and the forces with which he has to contend.

The chapter "Of Society and Conversation" studies the various forms of social interaction through speech and manners. The first remark introduces the general subject of the image that the individual presents to the world: "A flat character is one that has none." An individual defines himself even in the absence of distinctive traits. Everything characterizes man, both his qualities and his deficiencies, what he does and what he fails to do. The fundamental fact of social existence is that he cannot escape playing a role and being judged; he is opaque to others even if he wants to be transparent. The disparaging tone of the sentence suggests the human tendency to criticize and the author's own deprecating attitude toward contemporary conversation. The absence of character announces the theme of boredom and lack of communication. The classification prefigures the subsequent categorization of speakers.

The second remark contrasts the fool, whose role it is to importune, with the man of sense, who discerns whether he pleases or bores and knows how to disappear the moment before his presence becomes excessive. The rest of the chapter similarly contrasts the wrong and the right type of communication. The essential criterion is appropriateness or adaptation to time, place, and public.

After distinguishing several categories of speakers (2–4), La Bruyère discusses the foolish roles they play (5–14), the art of conversation (15–19), efforts to replace deeds by words (20–22), verbal aggression (23–29), manners (30–37), quarrels (38–50), mockery (51–62), forms of useless discourse (63–75), tone of speech (76–78), keeping secrets (79–81), other forms of communication (82), and withdrawal (83).

Common everyday conversation is judged by La Bruyère for the most part as boring, vain, childish, and useless. The subjects he mentions are universal: false news reports, vague opinions on government, the interests of rulers, and expressions of good intentions. People talk in proverbs and about themselves, their illnesses, their headaches, and insomnia. Yet the moralist concludes that one must bear all kinds of speakers and their useless discourse, for it is a lesser evil than the alternative of perpetual silence. In the section on people who talk not to convey meaning but to create an image of themselves, each remark is a dramatic scene that portrays the speaker's act and the reaction of the audience. The actor is satisfied with his performance and does not realize that he fails to convince his suffering listeners, who feel pity or contempt for him. In most of the scenes the author involves himself or the reader in the role of listener.

The examination of the wrong types of speech is followed by a contrasting section on the art of conversation. The subject for the transition is provided by people who try so hard to talk well that what they say is correct but boring. The aim of conversation, according to La Bruyère, should be not to show one's wit but to give others the opportunity to please and to be applauded. He views conversation as an art that should follow the rules of moderation, truth, reason, good judgment, and adaptation to the situation and feelings of the listener. For instance, it is wrong to boast of excellent health before the sick or of happiness before the unfortunate.

The moralist views polite manners and speech as essential to social intercourse. Though civility is not always an indication of good inner disposition, it at least gives its outward appearance. The spirit of politeness demands the same consideration for others and appropriateness as conversation: it should take into account their aspirations, feelings, and tastes. Good character requires tolerance of the bad character of others.

He finds that many types of discourse are useless because of their form or content. Into this category fall ineffective consolation, unheeded advice, preciosity, and pedantry. In most conversations, moreover, people do not listen, do not seek the truth, and think only about what they are going to say next. Finally, there are means of communication more effective than words. In a scene of courtship, an old man fails to achieve through verbal persuasion what a young man obtains merely through his presence. The conclusion of the chapter is in line with others that offer the solution of withdrawal and retirement: in order not to be bored or annoyed, it is wise occasionally to avoid people. The old man's futile boasting about his wealth connects this chapter to the next, which considers the power of money.

The chapter "Of the Gifts of Fortune" studies the effect of wealth on individual character and destiny, on the structure of society, and on personal relationships. It is the first of the chapters that, along with universal truths, gives prominence to criticism of contemporary social and political institutions. La Bruyère attacks the extremes of poverty and wealth, the means by which fortunes are acquired, and the blurring of the traditional class structure. The opening statement outlines the themes of the chapter:

> A man of great wealth can eat side dishes, have his walls and alcoves painted, enjoy a palace in the country and another in town, have a large retinue, place a duke in his family and make his son a great nobleman: this is just and in his power; but it belongs perhaps to others to live satisfied.

The sentence is divided into two parts that state what the wealthy can and cannot do, the power of money and its limitations. The actions of the rich man are arranged in an ascending order that mirrors the stages of his rise in society. He can eat fine food, he can have men work for him and transform the inside of his home, he can expand in space, he has control over horses and servants, he has power over the nobility that he can place in his family, and he can overcome class distinctions by making a nobleman of his son. These are the various aspects of the power of the rich that will be elaborated in the chapter. The ironic comment that what the rich can do is just and in their jurisdiction introduces the theme of the injustice of the acquisition, distribution, and power of wealth. It also reflects the public acquiescence, submission, and suspension of judgment with regard to the rich. The observation that it belongs to others to live happily announces the motif of the unhappiness brought to the rich man by his greed, anxiety, and impending ruin. The verb "belongs" suggests that contentment cannot be owned or acquired by money like other possessions. Finally, the wealthy man is compared to others who have moral superiority over him. The first clause is considerably longer than the second as the rich man crowds

out the poor. He is the active subject of a clause, while the others are passive: their happiness is without the striving and social climbing of the rich. The first part of the sentence is a satirical commentary on the power of the wealthy; the second, qualified by "perhaps," is a meditation on the human value of wealth.

The following thematic groups may be distinguished in the chapter: wealth and station in life (2–11), the financier and the *philosophe*, the moral and physical sacrifices for money (12–14), social ascent (15–23), injustice and immorality in the acquisition and distribution of wealth (24–35), talent and making money (36–38), wealth and happiness (39–41), making money through fraud (42–46), wealth and poverty (47–49), the passions of the rich (50–51), the rich and men of merit (52–57), the destructive effect of wealth on human relations (58–70), gambling (71–76), the rise and fall of the rich (77–81), their lack of tranquillity (82), comparison of the rich with the poor (83).

The first way in which wealth gives power to the rich man and promotes his rise in society is by influencing people's perception of him. The man may be ugly, short, and stupid, but if he has money he is respected and encouraged to believe in his talents. Moreover, money determines the choice of profession, makes possible marriage with the nobility, and allows the acquisition of noble status so that sons become ashamed of their fathers. La Bruyère deplores the transfer of noble names, lands, and castles to sons of peasants. Money affects even the place an individual occupies in his church and the attention he receives from the clergy.

The moralist brings out the injustice of the distribution of wealth by portraying the immoral methods by which it is acquired, the misery and suffering of the oppressed, and the greed and corruption of the tax collectors. Behind the brilliance and splendor of their fortunes hide the filth and squalor of the kitchen.

Insatiable greed makes them seek out ever new objects of taxation. La Bruyère identifies opulence with dishonesty and views business activity as one of continuous cheating and fraud. He lashes out against ecclesiastical benefices enjoyed at the expense of starving families. With strong indignation, he contrasts the heartbreaking deprivation of the poor with the wanton luxury and waste of the rich.

On the relation of wealth to happiness, he points out that money does not bring great satisfaction because it rarely coincides with youth. Moreover, the rich do not enjoy the fruits of their own labor, but acquire and build for posterity. They find no peace or tranquillity because they either labor furiously to amass a fortune or regret not having done everything possible to that end. Greed is a tyrannical passion that does not abandon them till death. Furthermore, money corrupts and destroys the closest human ties. Sordid men pursuing interest and gain are neither parents, friends, citizens, nor Christians. Friendships are broken and unnatural marriages contracted for money. The coveting of inheritance mars the natural relationships between parents and children. Often the rich do not enjoy the palaces they build because they ruin themselves in the process.

The wealthy are compared to the thinkers, to the poor, and to men of merit. The unapproachable manners of the financier busy with his forms and files are contrasted with the relaxed familiarity of the *philosophe,* who is superior by nature of his intellectual pursuits. The rich have paid a high price for their wealth in loss of tranquillity, health, honor, and conscience. They should not be envied by those who, like the author, would not accept the sacrifice. Furthermore, the position of the tax collectors has no permanence and they often inspire compassion at the ruinous end of their careers.

The rich are not much happier than the poor because while the latter suffer total deprivation, the former are irritated by the least frustration of their desires. La Bruyère stresses the idea that wealth is relative and depends upon how much one spends. A wealthy man is poor if his expenses exceed his income, and a great fortune is often close to ruin. While the ambitious and the greedy are poor because of their immoderate desires, the wise man is wealthy because he moderates his needs. The superiority of others is brought out again through a comparison of the rich and the man of merit, with whom the author identifies. There is an irrational tendency, he observes, to respect or disdain people according to their wealth and position rather than merit and virtue. The wealthy have no regard for intellectual achievements, but posterity honors the writers and forgets the tax collectors. The present favors the wealthy, but the future belongs to the virtuous and the able. The concluding double portrait of Giton and Phédon compares the rich and the poor in their appearance, gestures, speech, and manner, and the place they occupy in a group. The study is a transition to the next chapter, where money is seen as one of the factors that influence one's position in a group. It has been pointed out that in the two portraits the rich man dominates in the physical space he occupies but the poor man has moral superiority.

The chapters "Of the Town" and "Of the Court" portray two different social environments that represent two aspects of human relationships. Each has its own set of conditions, motivations, and behavior. The town is the city of Paris; it is any town. It is a man-made artificial environment in which men congregate and live in close quarters to each other; it is an enclosure; it is the counterpart of the country and of the court. The chapter is the study of man's need to belong to a group through participation in the social ritual. It examines how groups are formed, how they maintain their solidarity, and the superficial roles people play to belong, to be accepted, or to appear to be part of the group. While in "Of Society and Conversation" the actor relates to his audience through speech and manners,

242

in "Of the Town" the stage is broadened and the interaction takes place through gestures, appearance, and the material symbols of status.

The opening scene defines the ritual and the nature of the relationships:

People in Paris give themselves, without talking, a very precise public appointment every evening on the Cours or in the Tuileries, in order to look each other in the face and to criticize each other.

They cannot do without the very persons whom they dislike and whom they mock.

They wait for each other in the public avenues; they parade in front of each other: carriages, horses, liveries, coats of arms, nothing escapes the eye, everything is curiously and maliciously observed; and according to greater or lesser retinue persons are respected or disdained.

Thus, people need to congregate and to participate in the public ritual, which is carried out at a fixed hour and place. They feel constrained to be part of a group with the very people they dislike. Between the actors there is a superficial visual confrontation followed by mutual judgment and disapproval. The social situation is propelled by the conflicting forces of attraction and repulsion. The third paragraph, included in 1692 and the only addition La Bruyère made to any opening remark, stresses the reciprocity of the relationship and the peremptory nature of the encounters within a moving social scene. It also adds the display of material props to indicate wealth or class. While in the first scene people judge each other face to face, in the second they view each other at a greater distance and respect or disdain each other according to external signs of status. The Parisian scene announces that group behavior will be studied with reference to contemporary society.

In subsequent remarks, La Bruyère examines further public rituals (2–3), social sets

(4), occupational groups and social classes (5–11), lives wasted on participation in public ritual (12–13), rituals associated with women and marriage (14–20); and he contrasts the artificial world of the town with the country (21), the ostentation of the bourgeois with the simplicity of their ancestors (22).

The second remark, added in 1690, points out that there are also natural reasons such as climate and sexuality behind public gatherings. In hot weather, La Bruyère reports, women are seen walking on the bank where the Seine merges with the Marne and where men can be watched coming in and out of the water. The ladies do not walk there before or after the season. The indirect form of the concluding sentence suggests the discretion surrounding the ritual, and the confluence of the two rivers a natural merger. In other meeting places women congregate to show their clothes and establish their presence on the stage. What is important is to be seen and to participate. Speech itself becomes an object of vision as the women talk not to say anything, but to be seen speaking.

La Bruyère examines further the behavior that gives cohesion to the various groups into which the town society is divided and the roles people play to appear to belong to a given group. He portrays social sets that, like swarms of flies, congregate and disband without reason. They are held together by mutual approval of members and contempt for outsiders. Their speech, reinforced by laughter, is a meaningless activity that serves only to maintain group solidarity and to exclude the stranger. He also shows how the occupational groups such as magistrates and attorneys, as well as the intermediate group of barristers, compete and disagree over their boundaries. He points out how one group may try to imitate the behavior of another and the various roles people play in different settings. A magistrate, for instance, looks and behaves differently when he is at court or in town. The moralist portrays the efforts people make to give the illusion of status or higher social class.

Some bourgeois are described as lengthening their retinues of servants and horses to participate in the race for status. Others display coats of arms and imitate the behavior of the nobility; they go hunting without knowing how to shoot, give parties, and speak of large expenses. The magistrates allow their status-seeking leisure roles to overshadow the gravity of their occupations. Still others ruin themselves by imitating princes in their clothes and carriages, only to become the laughing-stocks of the town. Tragically, some of them play the ruinous role in obscurity before an audience no larger than their neighborhood. As the roles in "Of Society and Conversation" were intended to give the impression of personal quality, in this chapter they are aimed at creating the illusion of status.

Two satirical portraits show men for whom participation in public ceremony, seeing and being seen, constitutes the sole aim of a wasted existence. Among the rituals associated with marriage, the moralist criticizes the exchange of expensive wedding gifts, the squandering of the dowry on the marriage ceremony and on furnishings, and the theatrical practice of displaying the bride in her bed for several days after the wedding.

A comparison of the town with the country shows how this man-made environment limits the vision of its members. Ignorant of nature and contemptuous of country occupations, they cannot conceive of a society free of town functions and relationships. They have become prisoners of an artificial world that they cannot transcend even in their imagination. Another comparison of the bourgeois with their ancestors shows how participation in the empty social ritual leads to ruinous ostentation, creates artificial needs, obliterates external class differences, spoils family relationships, and stands in the way of natural activity. Unlike their ancestors, the bourgeois are too lazy to walk.

The town is an absurd theater where people play empty and wasteful roles in order to be identified with a group. The court, on the other hand, is a turbulent, cruel, and corrupt stage where men compete for the high stakes of position, power, and fortune that depend on the favor of those on top of the hierarchy. The chapter "Of the Court" is a study of the impact on human behavior of an authoritarian structure in which advancement depends on personal relationships with the individual in a superior position. The court of Louis XIV was the epitome of this type of situation, but similar relationships continue to prevail in organizations and institutions where patronage and favoritism operate under the veneer of rationalized norms.

The introductory remark states the corruption and the complexity of the human relationships engendered by this type of environment: "The most honorable reproach, in a sense, that one can make to a man is to tell him that he does not know the court: all kinds of virtue are implied in this one word." The oxymoron "honorable reproach" suggests the general paradox of the court situation, which manifests itself in the courtier's behavior, in the unpredictability of success, in the surface joy and hidden misery, in the artistic splendor and moral squalor. Moreover, the court values are false: what is a reproach from the point of view of the court is actually praise. The court is a complex environment that requires a thorough and intimate knowledge if it is to be mastered. It is also in the light of close acquaintance that the author, a courtier himself, will study the court. Its language is devious, and one must know the court relationships to understand it. Being a courtier involves a wide range of passions and vices; the chapter will examine the psychology of courtiers and the corruption incurred in learning the ways of the court. Furthermore, in the court situation each man is alone, dependent on what is said to him, and subject to rejection and failure. The indirect form of the introductory sentence implies the atmosphere of dissimulation in which speech is carefully premeditated and a word has many meanings. Just as the opening statement is at the same time an interpretation of language and a moral judgment, so the author will assume the role of interpreter and judge.

The second remark explains what knowledge of the court means and examines the falsehood, the complexity, the corruption, and the paradox. A man who understands the court, La Bruyère explains, has premeditated control of body language, remains mysterious, hides his hostilities, disguises his passions, acts and speaks against his feelings. Paradoxically, the courtier's corruption and falsehood do not necessarily lead to success and may be as useless as frankness, sincerity, and virtue.

The organization of the chapter alternates groups of remarks on three major themes: the courtier's actions and behavior, his psychology and passions, the unpredictability of success and its effect on the psychology of the courtier and on the public view of him. The picture is abstract and does not give precise references to the hierarchy and conditions of the court of Louis XIV. Yet it must be seen as a political statement on a situation that the tyrant had created to keep the nobility in check. La Bruyère's attack on the courtiers and the great was daring, to be sure, but had its roots in the policies of the Sun King.

The court environment is portrayed as a constantly changing, unstable, kaleidoscopic world that requires continuous attention and appears admirable only from a distance. Observed at close range, it reveals the universal humiliation, the discomfort of life spent on the margin of things while trying to get in, the harshness of men beneath the politeness, the equivalence of the good and the bad. The moralist explains that people come to court out of vanity, greed, and the desire to dominate outside the court, even at the cost of being slaves inside.

A characteristic sequence that examines in succession the courtier's psychology, his efforts, and their results is found in remarks 13–34. Manners at court are shown to be a mixture of haughtiness and abasement, important airs without true authority, and claims of noble lineage, real or fictitious (13–21). Self-interest is the motivation that dominates the totality of behavior, thought, judgment, and human relations (22–30). Public regard for a man depends entirely and solely on his position in favor and authority. There is no recognition of merit or virtue without high office. Yet power is easier to achieve than to retain, and sometimes the same faults that allow men to rise cause them to fall (31–34).

La Bruyère perceives that people hide their ambitions and their efforts in order to avoid the shame of being refused or to give the appearance of having been selected on the basis of their merit alone. In an ideal situation, on the contrary, one would train for a high post and ask openly for the opportunity to serve the state.

The original conclusion of 1688 reiterates the anguish and corruption involved in obtaining greatness at court and suggests retirement as the way to avoid them. Later editions point out, however, that the court embodies the highest aesthetic achievement of man and therefore cannot be disdained without contempt for the entire civilization. Looking ahead toward the future, La Bruyère predicts the universality of the court situation and the lasting relevance of his analysis. The world, he writes, is a stage on which the actors change but the play remains the same.

The chapter "Of the Great" is the most direct attack on the contemporary authority structure, for it challenges the very foundations of hereditary rank and class privilege. The central idea is that the nobility have no moral or intellectual superiority to justify their status. The first remark summarizes the argument and brings out the polemical unity of the chapter:

> The prejudice of the people in favor of the great is so blind, and the infatuation with their gestures, their faces, their tone of voice, and their manners so general, that if they took it upon themselves to be good they would become objects of idolatry.

In an earlier version of this remark, found in the first copies of the 1688 edition, the word "princes" appeared instead of the "great" and idolatry was qualified as "the only danger to be feared in this reign."

The general theme is the relation between the people and the great. Princes and high nobility are the beneficiaries of an irrationally favorable public opinion unjustified not only because they are not good but also because of their mindless unconcern and indifference: they do not even think of being good. Their manners and appearance do not correspond to moral worth. The system is so irrational that if the great were truly deserving it would become even more extreme. The word "idolatry" attacks the worship of the king as a divinity and also implies the identification of a spiritual reality with a physical being: the embodiment of the concept of authority in a person. The use of the term "favor" immediately after the chapter on the court, where everyone depends on the favor of the great, suggests a certain reciprocity by which the power of the nobility depends in turn on the blind prejudice of the people. The structure of the sentence, composed of three clauses on the public exaltation of the great and one implied statement on their deficiencies, reflects the situation in which the true nature of the great is submerged in the swell of public admiration. It also announces the author's method, which will be to praise and to deflate.

The chapter alternates three themes: the nature of the great, their manners and morals; the public attitude toward them; and comparisons between the great and the people. Three sequences may be distinguished in the general plan: the viciousness and ingratitude of the great (2–13), the unjustified prejudice in their favor (14–22), comparison with the people (23–25); the morals and manners of the great (26–33), their public image and how they are affected by it (34–46), the equality of men (47); the manners of the great (48–50), how to cope with the great (51–52), their equality with the people (53). The concluding remarks are on how the great judge and are judged (54–56).

The first sequence brings out their lack of generosity and ingratitude toward servants, who surpass them in virtue and intelligence. They are proud of their accomplishments as builders of palaces and gardens but have no interest in helping men. Objects of undeserved praise, they believe that they are endowed by birth with outstanding talents, when in fact their only uncontested superiority lies in estates and long lines of ancestors. In a remark added in 1690 La Bruyère points out that the people not only admire the great, but also hate them for the evil they do, holding them responsible for their own obscurity, poverty, and misfortune. The comparison of noblemen with the rising bourgeoisie shows that their actual authority and functions no longer correspond to their rank. While the great, ignorant and negligent of their own affairs and those of the state, let themselves be impoverished and dominated by their stewards, the bourgeoisie, educated and knowledgeable, take over the positions of authority. Comparing the deeds, morals, and education of the nobility with those of the people, La Bruyère openly expresses his preference for the people.

The second sequence reiterates condemnation of the selfishness of the great, points out that they owe their reputations to public comments made by intelligent servants, and recalls the Christian concept of human equality.

The third sequence begins with a description of the hypocritical and theatrical manners of the great and of their imitators. On the question of the attitude to adopt with regard to the powerful, La Bruyère advises not to court them and not to depend on them for one's fortune. In the last comparison, he equates the great with the people, arguing that beneath differences of birth, dignities, and manners, they have the same weaknesses, passions, and family quarrels. The conclusion asserts the difficulty of speaking about the powerful: to praise them is flattery, to criticize them is dangerous while they are alive and cowardly when they are dead. In his treatment of the high nobility, La Bruyère took revenge for the humiliation he suffered as a tutor in one such household, and the chapter ends appropriately with the words "they are dead."

The discussion of the great makes it clear that La Bruyère did not approve of the system of hereditary privilege. If he deplored the rise of the wealthy into the ranks of the nobility and the blurring of traditional class distinctions, it was not because he believed that the existing order should be preserved, but because he was equally critical of an authority structure based on money acquired through oppression and fraud. The only greatness he recognized was that of talent, service, and virtue. He regarded as justified the rise of the bourgeoisie through education, ability, and service to the state.

He expresses his ideas on government and on the absolute monarchy of Louis XIV in the next chapter, "Of the Sovereign or of the State." The opening statement, a lesson in political relativism, skepticism, and pragmatism, conveys his attitude and method of treating the subject:

> When one surveys all forms of government, without prejudice for one's own country, one does not know which to choose: there is in each of them the least good and the least bad. The most reasonable and safest course to take is to consider the government under which one is born as the best of all and to submit to it.

The remark distinguishes two approaches to the problem of government: objective reasoning about political systems in general and pragmatic thought about the concrete situation of the system under which one lives. The first leads to the skeptical conclusion that no form of government is perfect and that political good and evil are subject to weighing and compromise. But while abstract thought fails to reveal what is best, it is possible to ascertain in a concrete situation what is safest and

most reasonable. In contrast with the unbiased view of the first sentence, the total bias of the second appears to be an abdication of reason. Yet the hyperbolic phrase "the best of all," antithetical to the objectivity of examining "all" systems, is an ironic exaggeration that suggests critical judgment is abandoned only on the surface. The author's method will be to criticize the contemporary regime within the context of an ironic panegyric. The submission isolated at the end of the paragraph is simply a response to necessity without logical connection to the preceding reasoning. La Bruyère's practical conservatism is analogous to that of Montaigne, Descartes, and Pascal. He did not consider monarchy the best system of government, but portrayed it in its ideal form while at the same time pointing out its dangers. Openly challenging the doctrine of absolute power, he maintained that sovereignty does not stem from God, but rests on the reciprocal obligations between the monarch and his subjects. The repetition of the term "prejudice," which appears at the beginning of the preceding chapter, implies that hereditary monarchy rests on the same irrational assumptions as the system of class privilege.

The plan of the chapter parallels that of the opening paragraph. The first part discusses government in general and types of political evil: wrong methods of government (2–4), autonomy of the people (5–6), types of political evil and compromise (7–8), war (9–11), the art of diplomacy (12); the second part deals with monarchy and the regime of Louis XIV: the personal situation of the monarch (13–16), the favorite (17–20), the ministers (21–23), the power and duties of the king (24–35).

In three remarks on wrong methods of governing, La Bruyère vigorously condemns government that applies capital punishment to maintain or strengthen itself, criticizes the use of festivals and spectacles, which leads to despotism by absorbing the attention of the people, and observes that under despotism, patriotism is replaced by self-interest, glory, and service to the prince. The following comments are a reminder that though the people may be willing to give up rights and privileges at one time, they may resist at another, and their turbulence is uncontrollable.

The discussion of various types of evil illustrates the pragmatic weighing and compromise necessary to ascertain "the least bad" in government. There are evils that are tolerated to prevent greater ones, and institutions evil in their origin but good in practice; evils that could be corrected only by dangerous innovations, others too shameful to uncover; major evils that prevent a multitude of small ones. There are evils that oppress the individual but serve the public good; evils to families that are necessary to the state. Finally, there are evils that sap the foundations of empires and change the face of the earth.

La Bruyère strongly denounces the evil of war and satirizes the tolerance, interest, and enthusiasm that people show for battles. As an alternative to armed conflict, he depicts the art of diplomacy in an unusually perceptive and universally valid portrait of the gestures, manners, speech, scheming, and hypocrisy of a diplomat engaged in negotiations and forming alliances.

In the discussion of government priorities, the criticism of the policies of Louis XIV is couched in praise. La Bruyère portrays the military victories and glory of the king and the international power of France, but he rejects the pursuit of these goals as useless to the welfare of the people. What the subjects need, he observes, is freedom from oppression and poverty; personal safety; order and cleanliness in cities; protection against abuses by the nobility; education and physical well-being fostered by commerce, industry, and agriculture. The implication is that the king has sacrificed human lives and the good of the state for his personal glory and foreign adventures.

Comments on the role of the ideal prince are followed by a daring attack on the doctrine of absolutism. The king is by definition the father of his people, and his interest should coincide with that of the state. There are recip-rocal obligations between the prince and his subjects. Neither absolute master of the property of his subjects nor arbiter of lives, the monarch himself is subject to the law in the enforcement of justice.

The duties of the prince toward his people are represented in an idyllic image of a shepherd attentive to his flock, but the ostentation and luxury of Louis XIV are condemned in the picture of the shepherd and his dog dressed in silk and gold. Always in the form of praise mixed with warning, the king is reminded of the responsibility attached to his authority. His high office brings the happiness of being able to do good to multitudes, but also the danger of doing harm. Repeating the initial statement of relativism, La Bruyère places on rulers the responsibility of choosing policies most appropriate to the times and circumstances. The concluding panegyric, filled with conventional praise, was included by the author as a protective device. Yet it is also an appropriate ending for the chapter, as it summarizes once again the duties of the prince. La Bruyère praises the Sun King for his real accomplishments and, ironically, for the things he failed to achieve: it was obvious to any reader that Louis XIV did not alleviate the plight of the people, did not reduce taxes, and did not turn his court and his kingdom into one united family.

Unlike earlier chapters that focus on human nature as it manifests itself in social interactions, the chapter "Of Man" is a psychological study with emphasis on the inner life of the individual. La Bruyère discusses the problems involved in analyzing human nature and the question of what is natural in mankind. He views the human being confronting problems inherent in his moral and physical constitution, such as illness, old age, and death. The major themes and method are introduced in the first remark:

Let us not be angry at men when we see their harshness, their ingratitude, their injustice, their pride, egotism and forgetfulness of others: they are made this way, it is their nature; we must bear it like the stone that falls or the flames that rise.

The author explains that an objective study of man is difficult because he himself is human and prone to anger. He will isolate the enduring natural drives of man and the psychological laws that are as fixed and inevitable as the physical laws of nature. The movement of the falling stone and the rising fire suggests the inevitable change; the opposite directions foreshadow the contradictory tendencies of body and soul, passions and reason.

The chapter covers a wide range of subjects: inconstancy (2–6), vices reflected in offensive behavior (7–10), human nature and environment (11–18), happiness (19–23), dishonesty (24–28), desires (29–33), time and death (34–47), the stages of life (48–49), childhood (50–59), errors (60–62), vanity and need for approval (63–78), empathy and compassion (79–82), self-image (83–84), emulation, jealousy, and envy (85), intelligence (86–92), effect of success on personality (93–96), evolution of character (97–99), amusements and vanity (100–104), old age (105–120), portraits of selfishness (121–125), ferocity of man to man (126–129), contempt and self-image (130–131), philosophy (132–136), setting goals and psychological obstacles to achieving them (137–143), affectation (144–146), human contradictions (147–154), complexity of the subject (155–158).

La Bruyère considers human nature a composite of inborn and acquired tendencies. It is difficult to define what is natural, he maintains, because the morals, manners, and character of most men are a product of conditioning. The study of man is complicated further by his inconstancy and diversity. Surprising as the statement may appear in the *Caractères*, the author affirms that men have no characters—or at least none that are consistent and sustained.

Psychological evolution and the way in which man confronts aging and death are major themes of the chapter. The moralist offers a variety of insights into the incongruity between self-destructive behavior and the desire to prolong life, the misuse of time and the unawareness of its passing, the contradiction between the fear of old age and the hope of attaining it. The section on the stages of life begins with the obstacles that each presents to the use of reason and continues with a perceptive analysis of the psychology of childhood, variations on irrational motivation, and a study of old age.

In another series of remarks the moralist points out that reactions to success and misfortune depend on inner disposition. For instance, the fact that happiness is rare and achievement demands effort makes man distrust easy success and diminishes his satisfaction. Fulfilled desire does not bring the anticipated pleasure because one already wishes for something better. Conversely, one finds unexpected fortitude in misfortune, and little things can be consolation for a great loss. Rejecting the stoic view of man as unrealistic, he recognizes, however, the value of philosophy for mitigating the impact of external circumstances.

The gallery of vices portrayed in this chapter includes primarily those that divide and alienate men from each other. La Bruyère explains that incivility is the effect of several vices: vanity, irresponsibility, laziness, instability, stupidity, absentmindedness, contempt for others, or jealousy, and our reaction to insulting manners depends on the weaknesses or passions we perceive to be their cause. The long portrait of Ménalque is an inventory of the many ways in which man shows his absentmindedness and indifference to others. In a footnote applicable to many of the portraits, La Bruyère explains that the picture is not that of one character but a collection of the various manifestations of the moral trait. Their list is so long that everyone can recognize himself in one of the facets of the composite mirror.

Another series of five portraits illustrates

the various forms of selfishness. Gnathon lives only for himself. Cliton, the glutton gourmet, lives to eat and eats to the very moment of his death. Ruffin is the portrait of jovial indifference, even to the loss of his son. N**, forgetful of his approaching death, keeps building and planning for his future. Antagoras, the lawyer, continues to be involved in every court case until he dies. The portraits are followed by examples of human cruelty, such as the dehumanizing poverty men inflict upon the peasants whose labor feeds them (128).

In a final comment on his method, La Bruyère states that he has limited his analysis only to the most common vices of mankind and to those that lend themselves to instructive satire. Anticipating the subject of the following chapters, he concludes that in view of the falsehood of human thoughts, feelings, tastes, and affections, it is better for man to be changeable than obstinate.

In "Of Judgment" La Bruyère analyzes the uncertain nature of human opinion, the reasons for the uncertainty, and its effect on human behavior. The problem is stated in the opening remark: "Nothing resembles strong persuasion more than wrong infatuation: from there stem parties, intrigues, and heresies." Thus, people judge subjectively, cling with equal fervor to right and wrong beliefs; it is impossible to distinguish truth from falsehood on the basis of human opinions. Three points of view appear in the sentence: that of the correctly persuaded, that of the wrongly infatuated, and that of an outside observer who cannot distinguish between the two because of their resemblance. Therefore, uncertainty stems as much from the deceptive appearance of the object judged as from the subjectivity of the judges. The word "nothing" in the strong position at the beginning of the paragraph suggests that no judgment of human psychology and motivation is fully reliable. The repetition of the term "infatuation," which appears in the first remark of the chapter on the great, indicates that this one

will continue to explore irrational public opinion and its social consequences. The second part of the sentence states the result of strongly held beliefs on the level of action. The mood is one of pessimism and exasperation with the absurdly contradictory human race.

After three remarks on the inconstancy of opinion and the effect of habit (2–4), La Bruyère examines opinion on conduct (5–11), art (12–16), science and literature (17–21), foreigners (22–24), character (25–55), merit (56–73), warriors and politicians (74–78), justice (79–82), education (83–85), contradictions of public opinion (86–99), subjective experience of time (100–108), subjectivity of happiness (109–110), subjective reaction to satire (111), public opinion on projects (112–117), war and the presumption of human superiority (118–119).

The elements of deceptive appearance, subjectivity of the observer, and effect of opinion on action are considered in the first group of remarks on the judgment of others. A man's success gives the unreliable appearance of merit. On the other hand, people are reluctant to judge independently and are affected in their opinions by jealousy and dislike of each other. Since men are inclined to error and ridicule, it is best not to model one's conduct on the example of others.

Public prejudice against learning and literature is revealed by the failure to reward scholars and writers. Men of learning are assumed to lack manners and be unfit for public office. Authors may be flattered and encouraged to write, but they are not adequately paid for their work.

Anticipating Montesquieu's satirical treatment of the subject, La Bruyère points out that chauvinistic pride makes people regard those of other cultures as barbarians incapable of reason.

The section on judgment of character begins with the unreliable appearance that the individual presents to the world, and continues with remarks on methods of judging, results of prejudice, and definitions of terms. It is difficult to assess a man because his manners often do not correspond to his character, and few people behave naturally. Therefore, no man should be judged at first sight, and few are capable of discerning his inner being. Physiognomy is not a guide for judging people but only a basis for conjecture; the reaction to physical traits is relative to what one knows about the individual. For instance, a man recognized for his merit and intelligence is never found ugly.

Turning to results, La Bruyère notes that strongly held opinions about character may prove embarrassing because human behavior is inconsistent. Furthermore, a man in power who is influenced by slanderers and flatterers is a danger to the public and to himself. The section ends appropriately with the recommendation that the Cartesian rule of accepting only the most clearly perceived truth be applied to the appraisal of character.

In remarks on education, La Bruyère points out that it is excessive to believe that good training can change everything, but it is also a great error to espouse the opposite opinion, which results in neglect of education. Schooling is useful even if it can improve the child only superficially.

A variety of examples illustrates the contradictory, arbitrary, and unpredictable nature of public opinion. For instance, to be accused of a crime is almost as bad as to be convicted, because acquittal does not always exonerate the man in the public's mind. An individual who does not speak is presumed to be more intelligent than he is. A new convert is exalted while a lifelong believer is forgotten. If an individual does not obtain a prize, people wonder why, and they ask the same question when he gets it. La Bruyère notes that if his own observations are contradictory at times it is because human judgments are inconsistent.

Extending his analysis to every domain of knowledge, he observes that opinions vary even on questions of fact and scientific truth. Theories are subject to modification occa-

sioned by new discoveries or by change in method, as different weight is given at various times to observation and abstract reasoning. Consequently, what is considered true in science at one time is error at another, and opinions on matters of the greatest certainty may be overturned in less than twenty years.

The relativity of the perception of time is examined by La Bruyère in connection with its use. Time, he observes, is always found insufficient by those who waste it on futile occupations or on thinking about actions instead of acting. In judging how to spend time, public opinion fails to recognize that the most important pursuits are health, tranquillity, and freedom. The notion of freedom does not imply inactivity, but the free choice of work and exercise. In a sweeping and prophetic statement on human history, La Bruyère shows how contemporary civilization must be evaluated within the perspective of time. The historical past is relatively short in comparison with the expanse of time that the world is still to endure, and civilization is still in its infancy. Yet what has been accomplished in the relatively short period since the patriarchs allows one to predict the immensity of what will be learned and the vast changes and revolutions that will occur in the centuries to come.

The belief in man's superiority over animals, invalidated by the ferocity of contemporary politics and wars, is the final example of subjective opinion offered by La Bruyère. In defense of his own book, the moralist tells readers that the reaction to satire is subjective and that they are offended by what he says only to the extent that they identify with the objects of criticism.

La Bruyère's satirical outlook in the chapter "Of Fashion" is conveyed by the opening remark:

A foolish thing and one that betrays our small-mindedness is the subjection to fashion when it extends to taste, way of living, health and conscience. Game is out of fashion and, therefore, insipid; it would be a sin against fashion to heal from fever by bleeding. Similarly, for some time it was no longer fashionable to die by Théotime; his tender exhortations no longer saved anyone but the people, and Théotime beheld his successor.

The moralist does not object to the phenomenon of fashion, trivial though it may be, but to the fact that its tyranny extends to the totality of life expressed by the verbs to live, to heal, to die, to save. The second sentence criticizes the turning of religion into a thing of fashion. The antithetical terms to heal and to die, to sin and to save, suggest that, paradoxically, religion has been reduced to a fashion and fashion elevated to a religion. The most important aspect of religious observance has become to follow a fashionable preacher, while true religious values, such as salvation, have been relegated to the people. Théotime has been identified as the preacher Jacques Sachot (d. 1686), and his successor as Louis Bourdaloue. The statement on Théotime introduces in addition the general theme of men in fashion. Théotime lost his popularity for no valid reason since he was still able to save souls and there had been no interruption in his activity; popularity with the public is an ephemeral state with an abrupt end. Just as the last clause added abruptly at the end of the paragraph has no logical connection to what precedes it, so the public in its fickleness creates a line of succession without rational justification. The precise reference to contemporary style and to the career of Théotime suggests that the discussion of religion in particular will focus on the reign of Louis XIV.

The chapter is organized in the same way as the paragraph. The first half deals with fashion in general: fashionable hobbies (2), duels (3), fashionable men (4–10), fashion in clothing (11–15); the second half is a satire on the fashionable piety at the court of Louis XIV (16–30); the conclusion comments on the passing nature of all human attachments (31).

The four domains of fashion discussed by La Bruyère—hobbies, dueling, men in vogue, and dress—serve to illustrate three aspects of the phenomenon: tyranny, irrational criteria, and instability. The first extreme example of subjection to fashion is the absurd and obsessive passion for collecting useless rare objects or skills. Among the victims La Bruyère portrays are an amateur gardener who lives solely for his tulips; a coin collector; a bibliophile whose library is an accumulation of fine leather bindings; a linguist who studies only the most exotic languages; and a bird lover whose life is totally absorbed in feeding and cleaning up after thousands of specimens. Dueling is another foolish and tyrannical fashion that deprives men of their right to live.

The fashion in dress is noted for an instability that reveals the fickleness and inconstancy of men. In a short period of time, the same proportions once considered beautiful and decorative become ridiculous. Such reverses tyrannize a woman's life and destroy her tranquillity. The moralist believes that while excessive attention to style is a sign of foolishness, it is also unwise to ignore fashion. A philosopher lets himself be dressed by his tailor; a man's inordinate concern with fashionable dress is a sign of effeminacy.

The second part of the chapter is a satire on the religious piety that became fashionable at court during the latter part of the reign of Louis XIV. The essence of the criticism is contained in the remark that a pious man is one who, under an atheist king, would be an atheist. The word "piety" used in the text and explained in seven footnotes to mean "false piety" mirrors the hypocrisy of courtiers and emphasizes the difficulty, dramatized by Molière in *Tartuffe*, of distinguishing between the true and the false.

The conclusion of the chapter joins the theme of fashion, in the most general sense of the word, with that of Christian ethics. It is a lyrical meditation on the passing of time and all the frivolous human values that depend on it: fashion, greatness, favor, wealth, power, authority, independence, pleasure, and joy. Only virtue, so little in vogue, survives into eternity.

In "Of Certain Usages" La Bruyère examines the evolution of social, religious, and cultural institutions through customs and practices often contrary to the original principle and purpose of the institution. He shows that new procedures are brought about by need, passion, selfishness, or circumstances, but sometimes the vagaries of usage are mysterious and inexplicable. The first remark introduces the theme by indicating how the concept of nobility has evolved through practices incongruous with its original principle:

> Some people do not have the means to become noble.
> Others would have become noble if they had obtained a six-month delay from their creditors.
> Still others go to bed commoners and rise noblemen.
> How many noblemen whose fathers and older siblings are commoners!

Each of the four sentences points out a way in which established structures are altered or remain unchanged. Some changes cannot happen; others depend on fortuitous circumstances of time, money, self-interest, and passion. Still others take place suddenly and mysteriously, or, as the footnote reference to retired magistrates suggests, through an arbitrary rule. Some are falsely assumed to have happened. The overall result is a massive transformation in the nature of the institution. The reasons for stability or failure, mentioned in the first two sentences, appear to be better known than those for change or success. The key idea of the remark and of the entire chapter is the discrepancy between principle and practice.

Evolution through usage is examined in the context of a wide range of activities and institutions: nobility (1–15), priests, churches, and sacraments (16–26), ministering to the dying (27–28), placing girls in convents (29–

32), marriage (33–36), usury (37), corruption of public officials (38–40), judges and court procedures (41–55), wills (56–60), class privilege (61–62), hygiene and medicine (63–68), magic and astrology (69–70), the study of languages and texts (71–72), diet, clothing, war, vocabulary, and poetry (73).

The remarks on the nobility show for the most part how claims to noble status are made on false pretenses, and how the misrepresentations are supported by illogical legal procedures. Within this context, La Bruyère ironically declares himself to be a direct descendant of Geoffroy de La Bruyère, who took part in the Third Crusade (14).

The church is another institution in which he found astonishing discrepancies between original principle and current customs and practices that developed through laziness and greed. Certain usages associated with death are caused by unreasonable reactions; among them are the exhortations necessary to make a man accept the last rites, and the intervention of a director needed to reconcile parents with a dying daughter. Financial exigencies lie behind the practice of placing girls in convents according to the financial status of their family rather than their vocation. Some of the customs connected with marriage, such as the marriage of convenience, are explained by necessity; but others, like the shame attached to being seen in public with one's wife, are inexplicable. Greed has caused the incongruity between the long-established practice of usury and its condemnation by theologians.

A long section criticizes the discrepancies between the idea of justice and judicial procedures: the slowness of the courts, the hampering of legal eloquence, the deferments of trials, the solicitation of the judges' favor, the special severity of some magistrates toward personal friends. La Bruyère also found incongruity between the serious responsibilities and the dissolute conduct of judges, between the gravity of their functions and the lack of apprenticeship, and, of course, between the duties of magistrates and their corruption. He denounces the use of torture as an invention that leads to the condemnation of innocents who happen to be weak and to the acquittal of robust criminals.

La Bruyère's recommendations on the learning of languages and literature are as timely now as they were in his day. He deplored the fact that teaching of foreign languages to children at an early age had been abandoned and that the study of texts had been replaced by the reading of commentaries. The shortest, most reliable, and most pleasant way to understand a text, he maintains, is to read it on one's own. It was laziness that encouraged critics to fill libraries with explanations and to drown the original work under the weight of commentaries. But laziness defeated its own purpose as it multiplied the amount of reading and research.

In conclusion, La Bruyère reiterates the arbitrary nature of customs related to eating, dress, and combat, and he demonstrates that the evolution of vocabulary through usage is often mysterious and inexplicable.

The entire chapter "Of the Pulpit" is a series of variations on a single theme—the contrast between what religious oratory is and what it should be:

> Christian discourse has become a spectacle. The evangelical sadness which is the very soul of it is no longer noticeable: it is replaced by good appearance, well-modulated voice, regular gestures, choice of expressions, and long enumerations. People no longer listen seriously to the holy word: it is an entertainment among a thousand others; it is a game in which there are rivalry and persons who bet on the competitors.

The categorical statement of fact is followed by two sentences that explain the two aspects of the transformation. The first occurred in the discourse and behavior of the preacher whose feeling has been replaced by visual appeal, form, and quantity. The second is found in the reactions of the audience: the sermon is no longer regarded as a unique type of message, but as one of many amusements and a competitive game. The organization of the chapter is again similar to that of the opening paragraph. It deals with the content and form of sermons (2–8), the reactions of the audience (9–12), the worldly ambitions of preachers (13–23), the talent for preaching (24–26), the evaluation of sermons (27–28), and homiletic art (29–30).

The first section is a series of antithetical statements on current pulpit oratory compared with the ideal Christian instruction. La Bruyère reproaches the fashionable preachers of the time for their excessive concern with form, which manifests itself in the use of profane quotations, allusions, rhetorical devices, careful partitions, wit, and flowery style instead of simple and inspired explanations of the Gospel. He blames them for aiming to win approval rather than to convert the audience.

The remarks on the reactions of the public show that the sermons do not serve the purpose of the pulpit. They are judged as oratorical exercises and not according to the emotional impact they produce. People listen with pleasure and admiration but are not converted. The artistic portrayals of sin fail to make it hideous.

For the preachers, the pulpit is a means of gaining advancement and benefices. Funeral orations are included in this section as one of the ways in which the ecclesiastics flatter the great. Comparing religious oratory with courtroom eloquence, La Bruyère observes that the former is a more difficult art because it deals with familiar subjects, well-established principles, simple ethics, and known conclusions. Its success, therefore, depends on the strong convictions of the speaker. The final message is that the preacher should follow the classical rules of unity of theme, naturalness, and adaptation of form to content, and, above all, should persuade and move the audience by his own enthusiasm.

In the preface to the *Discours de réception à l'Académie Française* La Bruyère assigns special importance to the chapter "Of Freethinkers" within the plan of the *Caractères.* He states that the first fifteen chapters, which show the falsehood and absurdity of human passions and worldly concerns that separate man from God, are a preparation for the concluding one, which attacks atheism, brings forth proofs of the existence of God, and defends Divine Providence against the insults of the libertines. Few readers were convinced, however, by this plan, modeled on Pascal's *Pensées* and put forth as an afterthought only after seven editions of the *Caractères* had already appeared. The preface is a polemical text in which La Bruyère defends his work against critics, and the statement of an overall apologetic intent is a defensive ploy against accusations of impiety. The author himself had written in the *Discours sur Théophraste* that he did not share Pascal's religious purpose.

Though the chapter does not have the key role attributed to it in the preface, the fact remains that it is unique by virtue of its content and its place at the end of the *Caractères.* "Of Freethinkers" is the most serious and philosophical chapter of the entire work. With religion as its unifying theme, it broadens the scope of the *Caractères* to include new scientific, psychological, metaphysical, and social perspectives that were to become the major concerns of the Enlightenment. There is no reason to doubt the sincerity of La Bruyère's religious conviction expressed in the text, but a question arises about what type of religion he defends. The chapter presents a forceful and effective demonstration of the existence of God, but it is not an apology for the Christian religion. Precise references to Christianity are few and the arguments relatively weak and indirect.

The title "Des esprits forts" can be taken both in its figurative meaning of "freethinkers" and in the literal sense of "strong minds." The chapter explores both themes and brings out the complexity of what constitutes intellectual weakness and strength. The title also suggests that religion will be studied

through man: his need for religious faith, his attitude toward it, and his reasoning about it.

The opening remark consists of four rhetorical questions on the effect of religion on the mind. The interrogative form is a polemical way of addressing unbelievers, but also introduces the entire subject of religion as problematic. The first question is whether there is real strength in free thought. Do freethinkers know that they are called "strong-minded" ironically? The next two questions point to the existential anguish experienced without faith: "What greater weakness than to be uncertain about the principle of one's existence, life, senses, knowledge, and about their end? What greater discouragement than to doubt if the soul is not material like a stone and a reptile, and subject to corruption like these vile creatures?" The three questions are balanced symmetrically by the fourth, which affirms the greatness and strength derived from accepting the idea of God. The problems enumerated in the opening paragraph will be the major themes of the chapter: the origin of being, of life, of the senses, and of knowledge; the distinction between spirit and matter; the incorruptibility and immortality of the soul; the solutions offered by the idea of a creator and a final cause. The chapter is organized in the same way as the paragraph. The first part deals with the weaknesses of free thought and the second with the answers provided by religion.

The first group of remarks is a study in the psychology of religion and of free thought in particular. Religious belief is shown to depend on character traits such as docility, impressionability, moral strength, and worldliness. The freethinker is the strong, independent man who may be considered weak only insofar as lack of religion is found to be a weakness. Other factors stem from the environment. For instance, exposure to many different cults through travel leads some people to give up their faith. La Bruyère thus foreshadows the eighteenth-century comparatist argument that the diversity of religious ceremonies and beliefs makes it difficult to choose among them. Some independent spirits become freethinkers because they shun the majority opinion, others because of servile imitation of their masters. Religious belief is also physically determined: in illness, the moralist notes, a man abandons his concubine and embraces God; bad health reverses the attitude toward God as automatically as that toward a concubine. Disbelief may be further motivated by vice or a desire for freedom from religious sanctions. La Bruyère doubts the existence of atheists who have rejected faith on the basis of clear reasoning and convincing arguments. What is considered atheism, he observes, is in fact no more than indifference.

The moralist begins his demonstration of the existence of God with proofs drawn from psychological need: the impossibility of proving that there is no God; the feeling that there is a God and the natural tendency to believe; the desire for divine justice in the face of human inequity. These arguments foreshadow Jean Jacques Rousseau's sentimental deism and Montesquieu's assertion that faith in a creator is a natural law.

After discussing the weakness of the atheist position, La Bruyère also points out those of the religious camp: futile theological speculation, intolerance, lack of conviction, disputes, and, worst of all, hypocrisy. His insights into the subjective nature of religious experience prefigure Gustave Flaubert's analysis in *Un coeur simple* (*A Simple Heart*, 1877). Though on the surface, La Bruyère observes, an entire nation may have one faith, in reality every individual adapts the religion to his own mind and feelings so that each one has his own (25).

Christianity is the subject of only five remarks. The first two praise the wisdom and the knowledge of the church fathers. The third argues, without mentioning the name of Jesus, that if we believe the accounts of the life of Caesar, we should also have faith in a book that is divinely inspired and has been jealously guarded for almost two thousand years

(20–22). Another contention is that the success of Christian missionaries in the Orient proves the truth of their message. The main argument, reminiscent of Pascal, is based on the perfection of the Christian doctrine: its mysteries, its coherence, and its ethics. This proof, however, is expressed in an ambiguous and indirect manner. La Bruyère's proposition is that if the religion is false, it is the best snare that anyone could imagine. He concludes that he would rather deny the existence of God than reconcile him with this fraud. But since he cannot be an atheist, he is necessarily drawn back to his religion. The central idea seems to be that the fundamental element in religion is a belief in God that results from the inability to espouse atheism. It is not religion that teaches God; it is faith in God that leads to religion (34).

The most philosophical part of the chapter is organized around three proofs of the existence of God: the Pascalian bet (31–35), Cartesian dualism (36–42), and the order of creation (43–46). While the arguments fit into the religious polemic of the chapter, they also serve as a pretext for bringing into the work major philosophical and scientific developments of the time. It is here that the horizon of the *Caractères* expands to embrace the universe.

The Pascalian argument is adapted within the framework of a meditation on life and death. At the beginning La Bruyère states the need to choose between the conflicting values of this world and the next. At the end he echoes Pascal's "bet" that if religion is false, a monk or a virtuous man loses only sixty years of life, while if it is true, the wicked man guarantees for himself an eternity of suffering. But between the two remarks La Bruyère recognizes—and, unlike Pascal, does not condemn—man's passionate attachment to life. He admits that if one were given the choice to die or to live forever, it would be a difficult decision to make, in spite of the anguish and hardships of living.

The discussion of the nature and immortality of the soul is derived from Descartes. La Bruyère repeats the Cartesian argument that the thinking element in man must come from a superior spiritual being: "I think, therefore God exists." He maintains that matter cannot produce thought and that the soul or the thinking part of man can exist independently of sensory perceptions.

The subsequent arguments are those of the order, the immensity, and the mystery of the macrocosm and of microscopic life. La Bruyère reviews the latest astronomical discoveries on interstellar distances, the countless number of stars, and the regularity of their movements. He describes the wealth and the complexity of life revealed by the microscope. He confronts the idea that the universe has been created for man with the possibility of life on other planets, but rejects this latest hypothesis on the grounds that other beings have not yet been observed. After the survey of the new perspectives opened by science he points out the many mysteries that still remain. For instance, man cannot create life; he cannot control the weather; he understands the order and the effects of nature; but he does not comprehend the causes, the underlying principles, of phenomena such as vision.

The concluding remarks return to the problems of society viewed within the broad framework of the problem of evil, man's place in the universe, divine justice, and Providence. Two ideas are stressed in the discussion of the problem of evil. The first is the infinite smallness of man in duration and space compared to the eternity and immensity of God. The second is the definition of justice as a conformity to reason and the eternal truth only. The knowledge of this truth is identified with God.

Turning his attention to what is just in the social order, La Bruyère maintains that some degree of inequality in the distribution of wealth is necessary to stimulate labor and to preserve subordination and cooperation among men. He views the economic structure as the basis for the social hierarchy and political organization. Need makes the poor serve, obey, invent, work, cultivate, and perfect, while the rich enjoy, nourish, help, protect, and govern. The fabric of society is held together by their mutual dependence. But while moderate inequality is beneficial and may be considered as the effect of Providence, La Bruyère condemns the existing social order with the extreme disproportion of poverty and wealth as unjust and established by force: "The extremes are faulty and stem from men: all compensation is just, and comes from God."

Thus the *Caractères* conclude in the spirit of Jean Jacques Rousseau, who would write later that all things are good coming from the Creator, and everything degenerates in the hands of man. The injustice of the inequality established by the law of the strongest prefigures Rousseau's analysis of the origin of inequality. The chapter "Of Freethinkers" appears as a prophetic bridge thrown to the next century and a connecting link between the seventeenth-century moralists and the eighteenth-century *philosophes*. The title itself announces the importance of free thought in the Enlightenment. The chapter foreshadows the importance of science; the exploration of the nature of thought and of the relation of sense perceptions to knowledge; the debates on the problem of evil, free choice, and determinism; and the foundations of the social order. La Bruyère's discussion of the eternal idea of justice was continued by Montesquieu in the *Lettres persanes* (1721) and in *De l'esprit des lois* (1748).

By his criticism of the contemporary society La Bruyère was a precursor of the *philosophes*. The direct influence of the *Caractères* on the *Lettres persanes* appears in portraits such as those of the visitor (letter 87) and the know-it-all (72), in subjects of religious criticism such as theological speculation on the attributes of God (69) and the lack of religious conviction (75), in the satire on women, marriage, gambling, the inconstancy of fashions and fortunes, the idolatrous worship of the king, and the intolerance toward foreign cultures. La Bruyère's insistence on naturalness and his exaltation of the patriarchal way of life anticipates the ''Story of the Troglodytes'' in Montesquieu's *Lettres persanes* (letters 11–14) and the primitivism of Jean Jacques Rousseau.

The tradition of the maxim was short-lived after La Bruyère and continued in the eighteenth century only by Luc de Clapiers de Vauvenargues and Sébastien Chamfort. The technique of the portrait, however, had a lasting influence; it was incorporated into memoirs like those of Claude Henri de Rouvroy, duc de Saint-Simon, and into the novel. Social types and characters in the works of Alain René Lesage have been traced back to La Bruyère, along with aspects of the realism of Honoré de Balzac and Émile Zola. He was admired by Flaubert and Proust, who recognized their debt to him; the Goncourt brothers saw him as a model to follow. His characters and themes were used in the eighteenth-century theater of Lesage, Jean François Régnard, Philippe Destouches, and Nivelle de la Chaussée. His influence extended to Joseph Addison, Richard Steele, and William Makepeace Thackeray in England; Alessandro Manzoni in Italy; and Mariano José de Larra in Spain.

It has been said that of all the seventeenth-century writers, La Bruyère is the one who would be least surprised if he were to return to the world today. He would find the financiers, the courtiers, the diplomats; hero-worship, image-making, unreliable public opinion, fashion, idle conversation, ambition, vice, war. He would recognize his method of observation and analysis in modern books on social psychology. He wrote at the end of his work that he would be astonished if people did not like the *Caractères* and he would be no less astonished if they did.

The *Dialogues sur le quiétisme* (*Dialogues on Quietism*, 1699) are a posthumously published work attributed to La Bruyère even though they were left unfinished and considerably altered and expanded by their editor,

the abbé Elies Dupin. The last two of the nine dialogues were written entirely by Dupin, and it is not known how much he contributed to the others. Quietism is a form of Christian mysticism first expounded by Miguel de Molinos (1627–1696), a Spanish priest residing in Rome whose writings were condemned by Pope Innocent XI in 1687. The doctrine was propagated in France by Madame Jeanne Marie Guyon and associated, not too justly, with the archbishop Fénelon. After gaining some popularity at court, it was opposed by La Bruyère's anti-quietist friend Bossuet. The essence of quietism is the practice of passive contemplation and total self-abandonment to the will of God. To achieve the mystical state the quietist must resist all tendency to premeditated thought and action.

Intended to aid Bossuet in his controversy with Fénelon, the *Dialogues* are a satire on quietism, written in the tradition of Pascal's *Provincial Letters*, in which Jansenism is defended through a satirical attack on the Jesuit doctrines. The polemical method adopted by La Bruyère is to give a greatly exaggerated account of the quietist doctrine and to refute it by its moral consequences. The personae are a spiritual director, a twenty-eight-year-old penitent, and her brother-in-law, a Sorbonne theologian. While the discussions between the director and the theologian are lengthy and monotonous, the conversations between the director and the penitent have the dramatic quality, humor, and irony associated with La Bruyère's style. The dialogues discuss the principal tenets of quietism regarding prayer, the concept of God, the undesirability of actions that may be attributed to one's own will, and the essential union. They also bring out the differences between the doctrine and orthodox Catholic teachings. La Bruyère's main argument holds that the abandonment of will required to achieve a union with God results in total indifference to good and evil, virtue and sin, and carries with it dispensation from religious obligations. The most humorous and effective passages are those in which the director's precepts contradict the moral principles and religious duties that the penitent has been taught since childhood. For instance, it is difficult for her to understand that she should resist the inclination to give alms to the poor. She is shocked to learn that she need not go to mass or be chaste. She finds it extremely hard to create the mental void necessary for quietist prayer, but she does at times achieve what she calls the state of inactivity and "perfect stupidity." When in the eighteenth century the authors of the *Encyclopédie* sought to ridicule quietism, they quoted from the *Dialogues* of La Bruyère.

In his survey of the literary production under the reign of Louis XIV, Voltaire called the *Caractères* a book unique in its genre and admirable for its original, concise, rapid, nervous, and picturesque use of language; he predicted that, since the work comprises things for all places and all times, it would never be forgotten. The *Caractères* do in fact epitomize the universality, lucidity, and perfection of form of French classicism. They stand out by their comprehensive and balanced view of man. La Bruyère portrayed human weaknesses and vices, but he also pointed out the potential for transcending them. He traced the path to greatness through altruism and abnegation, but lucidly showed the sacrifice of personal happiness on the way. His vision embraced the most noble impulses, the sublime moments as well as the triviality of everyday existence. The human relationships he analyzed range from superficial encounters to the deepest emotional attachments. He studied all aspects and stages of love, friendship, and all degrees of antagonism, from absurd quarrels to rivalry and hatred. He observed man confronting his inner being in solitude, and he portrayed him on the stage of the world. To the frustration of social involvement he offered the antidote of detachment and withdrawal. He provided the tools for understanding individual motivation as well as the vagaries of collective opinion and behavior. The varied, witty, and delightful style of the *Caractères* assures the permanence of their composite picture of mankind presented by the 1,120 miniature masterpieces.

Selected Bibliography

EDITIONS

Les caractères de Théophraste traduits du grec, avec les caractères ou les moeurs de ce siècle. Paris, 1688.

Discours prononcé dans l'Académie Française, par M. de La Bruyère, le lundy quinzième juin 1693, jour de sa réception. Paris, 1693.

Dialogues posthumes du sieur de La Bruyère sur le quiétisme [continués et publiés par Louis Ellies Du Pin]. Paris, 1699.

Oeuvres de La Bruyère. Edited by G. Servois. 3 vols. Paris, 1865–1878.

Oeuvres complètes. Edited by Julien Benda. Paris, 1951.

Les caractères de Théophraste traduits du grec avec les caractères ou les moeurs de ce siècle. Edited by Robert Garapon. Paris, 1962.

Les caractères. Edited by Jean-Pierre Kaminker. 2 vols. Paris, 1971. Excerpts.

Les caractères ou les moeurs de ce siècle. Edited by Pierre Kuentz. Paris, 1976. Excerpts.

TRANSLATIONS

Characters. Translated by Henri Van Laun. London, 1963.

The Characters. Translated by Jean Stewart. Baltimore, 1970.

CRITICAL STUDIES

Allaire, Étienne. *La Bruyère dans la Maison de Condé.* 2 vols. Paris, 1886. Reprinted Geneva, 1970.

Barthes, Roland. *Essais critiques.* Paris, 1964. Pp. 221–237.

Brody, Jules. *Du style à la pensée: Trois études sur les "Caractères" de La Bruyère.* Lexington, Ky., 1980.

Doubrovsky, Serge. "Lecture de La Bruyère." *Poétique* 2:195–201 (1970).

Eustis, Alvin, ed. "Actes de Berkeley." In *Papers on French Seventeenth-Century Literature,* edited by Wolfgang Leiner. Vol. 8, no. 15, 2 (1981).

Gallas, K. R. "La composition interne du chapitre 'Des ouvrages de l'esprit.'" *Neophilologus* 3: 253–260 (1918).

Garapon, Robert. *"Les caractères" de La Bruyère.* Paris, 1978.

Goyet, Thérèse. "La composition d'ensemble du livre de La Bruyère." *Information littéraire* 7:1–9 (1955).

Guggenheim, Michel. "L'Homme sous le regard d'autrui ou le monde de La Bruyère." *PMLA* 81: 535–539 (1966).

Hankiss, Jean. "Inspiration géométrique dans les *Caractères* de La Bruyère." *Neophilologus* 36: 65–75 (1952).

Harth, Erica. "Classical Disproportion: La Bruyère's *Caractères.*" *Esprit créateur* 15:189–210 (1975).

Hellegouarc'h, Jacqueline. *La phrase dans les "Caractères" de La Bruyère.* Paris, 1975.

Horowitz, Louise K. "La Bruyère: The Limits of Characterization." *French Forum* 1:127–138 (1976).

————. *Love and Language: A Study of the Classical Moralist Writers.* Columbus, Ohio, 1977. Pp. 145–160.

Hudon, L. "La Bruyère et Montaigne." *Studi francesi* 6:208–224 (1962).

Jasinski, René. *Deux accès à La Bruyère.* Paris, 1971.

Kirsch, Doris. *La Bruyère ou le style cruel.* Montreal, 1977.

Knox, Edward C. *Jean de la Bruyère.* New York, 1973.

Koppisch, Michael S. "The Ambiguity of Social Status in La Bruyère's *Caractères.*" *Esprit créateur* 15:221–230 (1975).

————. *The Dissolution of Character: Changing Perspectives in La Bruyère's "Caractères."* Lexington, Ky., 1981.

Lange, Maurice. *La Bruyère, critique des conditions et des institutions sociales.* Paris, 1909. Reprinted Geneva, 1970.

Laubriet, Pierre. "À propos des *Caractères:* ordre ou fantaisie." *Revue d'histoire littéraire de la France* 67:502–517 (1967).

Linkhorn, Renée. "Le point de vue négatif chez La Bruyère." *Romance Notes* 18:214–220 (1977).

Marmier, Jean. "Le sens du mouvement chez La Bruyère." *Lettres romanes* 21:223–237 (1967).

Michaut, Gustave. *La Bruyère.* Paris, 1936. Reprinted Geneva, 1970.

Mourgues, Odette de. *Two French Moralists: La Rochefoucauld and La Bruyère.* Cambridge, 1978.

Navarre, Octave. "Théophraste et La Bruyère." *Revue des études grecques* 27:384–440 (1914).

Niderst, Alain. "'Du mérite personnel': Remarques sur la composition d'un chapitre des *Caractères* de la Bruyère." In *Approches des Lumières.* Paris, 1974. Pp. 333–344.

Richard, Pierre. *La Bruyère et ses "Caractères."* Paris, 1965.

Sainte-Beuve, C.-A. *Portraits littéraires.* Paris, 1843. Vol. 1, pp. 389–413.

Stegmann, André. *"Les caractères" de La Bruyère.* Paris, 1972.

Taine, Hippolyte. *Nouveaux essais de critique et d'histoire.* Paris, 1880. Pp. 35–50.

Truchet, Jacques. "Place et signification du chapitre 'De la chaire.'" *Information littéraire* 17:93–101 (1965).

Van Delft, Louis. *La Bruyère moraliste.* Geneva, 1971.

————. *Le moraliste classique: Essai de définition et de typologie.* Geneva, 1982.

Wadsworth, Ph. A. "La Bruyère Against the Libertines." *Romanic Review* 38:226–233 (1947).

PAULINE KRA

FRANÇOIS DE SALIGNAC DE LA MOTHE-FÉNELON

(1651–1715)

THE LIFE AND works of François de Salignac de la Mothe-Fénelon were so enmeshed in the labyrinthine coils of seventeenth-century theology and French ecclesiastical history, and his reputation had so suffered from the political biases of nineteenth-century academic criticism, that it took a heroic effort on the part of Henri Brémond to produce the *Apologie pour Fénelon* (1907). Since then, interest in him has been renewed but much of the literature on Fénelon has remained contentious or defensive. Father François Varillon, for instance, still finds it of paramount importance to demonstrate Fénelon's orthodoxy. One may well wonder whether an author who has made such a slight impression on literary history that he requires perpetual apology can be intrinsically important, and whether an author so bound up in the national and religious controversies of his time can be sufficiently universal to justify the considerable effort necessary to extricate him from his historical matrix.

The test of an author is in the reading of his works and not in their popularity. Few famous authors may be as little read as Fénelon, and fewer still known by such unrepresentative works. He was a churchman—eventually the prince archbishop of Cambrai—who wrote

very little that can be called belles lettres apart from a pedagogic historical novel, some short dialogues and fables, and a letter to the Académie regarding the French language and the writers of his time. A substantial part of his output was controversial or polemical, works intended to make an immediate impression on a narrow reading public. They would not, therefore, be supposed to retain much appeal for a general audience centuries later, however skillfully they may have been written.

Most of the pieces that Fénelon produced in a long and active career are the occasional papers of a conscientious churchman—a manual of piety, episcopal mandates, letters of spiritual counsel and direction, innumerable sermons (most of which are unfortunately lost or were never committed to paper), and treatises and letters relating to theological controversies. It is not in this sort of writing that we now look for great literature, although in Fénelon's time and for at least the next hundred years, clergymen with a similar or even narrower range were much admired in literary circles. Fénelon was so negligent in publishing his circumstantial writings that an important treatise was first published as late as 1930, and it would not be at all surprising if

261

additional manuscripts were identified in the Saint-Sulpice library in Paris, where a very great number of letters and documents of biographical interest have been recently discovered, or if other pieces of correspondence were found almost anywhere. There is no modern edition of his works, and the best nineteenth-century edition is quite incomplete and makes no attempt to date the works that it reproduces. The chronology of most of the sermons and the dates of composition of several major works are still conjectural despite the intensified research since Brémond's *Apologie.* Fortunately, a modern, scholarly edition of the correspondence is now nearly complete; it has permitted new precision in Fénelon's biography and will require minor revisions in the standard studies of his work.

Even the literary critics have contributed to the obfuscation that surrounds Fénelon. French academic critics used to suffer from the compulsion to produce neat, binary comparisons for all occasions. It was, and remains, a French sport, like bicycle racing, to compare the national greats, Pierre Corneille and Jean Racine, Voltaire and Jean Jacques Rousseau, the bishops Fénelon and Jacques Bénigne de Bossuet; the less the pairs have in common the better the occasion they furnish for ingenuity and brilliant rhetorical strokes. These critics, almost to a man, sacrificed the subtle, scrupulous Fénelon to the thundering, affirmative, sumptuous Bossuet, his older colleague and erstwhile friend and patron, although they could hardly have known Fénelon's works very well; and these same critics damned him by comparison for religious and political heresies to which our time may be much more sympathetic. If we no longer insist upon defending fallen imperial glories, and if we are willing to find the finely expressed torment of a subtle soul as interesting as clarion calls of orthodoxy, or even more so, we may be disposed to appreciate Fénelon.

Apart from his literary qualities, which once identified, need no apology at all, a study of Fénelon is rewarding because it affords the occasion to glimpse a fascinating chapter of European religious history, one with implications outside the domain of Catholic theology. Some authors in the literary canon, like John Milton, may carry us into the wilderness of dissenting and peculiar sects, while others, such as Pierre Bayle and Bossuet, may submerge us in the thickets of controversial theology, and still others may initiate us into the triumphs and pitfalls of the profoundest scholarship. A study of Fénelon draws us, even against our will, into the pure religious quest and experience. Like Martin Luther, Blaise Pascal, Saint Theresa, and Saint John of the Cross, Fénelon belongs in the history of religious consciousness. There is also a substantial body of religious poetry in the French seventeenth century, notably by Claude Hopil and François Malaval, that bears comparison with Fénelon in its reflection of profound religious experiences, but it is not read much today. Among French writers in that class he and Pascal are the only ones to have survived the narrowing of the canon, the only ones who still figure in the literary manuals.

Fénelon is a particularly useful author because he was both a religious seeker and a director of novices toward the mysteries of the religious experience. Adepts tend to express themselves in a hermetic code that, even when it can be deciphered, may not transmit its immediacy to the reader. Fénelon was a worldly bishop whose profession and inclination led him to translate, without vulgarizing or trivializing, spiritual experience into worldly terms that his penitents and friends could understand. We need only retranslate him—not only out of his fluent and fluid French but out of the very special terms and circumstances created by the social, political, and theological ethos of the France of Louis XIV—in order to be initiated into the intense religious experience that Fénelon sought, glimpsed, and tried to capture in words for the unilluminated.

FRANÇOIS DE SALIGNAC DE LA MOTHE-FÉNELON

LIFE

Fénelon was born on 6 August 1651, rather late in the century in one regard. He missed the generation of the 1630's, the generation of Louis XIV himself, of Racine and the other greats who distinguished his reign, the *classiques* of France who came of artistic age in the 1660's, coincidentally with their young sovereign's personal reign, which they celebrated. They were formed like him, however, in the France of cardinals Richelieu and Mazarin; and their older predecessors, Corneille and Molière, were even more firmly rooted in the France of Louis XIII. But the writers such as Fénelon and Jean de La Bruyère who were born and came of age during the ascendancy of Louis XIV, and Montesquieu and Voltaire a generation later, became implacable critics of the France of their early manhood.

Little is known about Fénelon's youth except that his first eight years were passed in the ancestral château of Fénelon overlooking the Dordogne Valley in the Périgord, southwestern France. It must have been a reassuring childhood because the pastoral Périgord is idealized in many of his later works, and his approach to education reflects an appreciation of the child as well as the assumption that learning can be an agreeable experience. He studied the arts with the Jesuits at Cahors from the age of eight until he was fourteen or fifteen. (Another account has it that he was raised by an uncle, the bishop of Sarlat.) Again, we know little that is intimate or even specific about this part of Fénelon's life, but we can reconstruct it hypothetically on the basis of what is known about the Jesuit curriculum of the period. It emphasized the study of Greek and Latin literature, suitably expurgated and moralized, in addition to philosophy and religious training. Not much science or mathematics nor oriental languages or ancient history were taught at Cahors; these were the specialties of the Oratorians' schools. Nor would Fénelon have received much in-struction in his native language; that was a specialty of Port-Royal, the school forever associated with Pascal and the Jansenists (an Augustinian Catholic sect). Though he was separated from his family during these years at Cahors, his student days must have been at least tolerable since he took away with him a love of classical letters, Greek in particular. He admired their virility, vigor, and especially their pastoral simplicity. This is not everyone's classicial corpus: his embraces the less bellicose episodes in Homer, Vergilian bucolic poetry, and Plato, the poet among philosophers. The French *classiques* with whom he is inevitably and inaptly compared were equally influenced by the Greek and Latin classics, but hardly the same ones. They explored the intense sociability of the city and the precariously poised life at court, and found their tragic inspiration in Aristotle, in the splendid rhetoric of Cicero and Seneca, and in Sophocles. In the *Maximes* of La Rochefoucauld, in Madame de La Fayette's *Princesse de Clèves*, and, above all, in Racine's plays we see the pattern of human self-delusion, cruel destiny, and finally, the consoling catharsis accompanying recognition and insight so familiar in Greek tragedy.

From Cahors, Fénelon went on to study philosophy at the Collège du Plessis of the University of Paris. Again, we have little information: in 1672 or 1673, at the age of twenty-one or twenty-two, he entered the Saint-Sulpice seminary, from which he was ordained, probably in 1675. Saint-Sulpice was then still a young and extraordinary institution, not yet the overbearing pseudo-Roman church begun in 1643 and not completed until 1788—six architects and several conflicting styles later—but a seminary situated on the square that now faces the church. At this point let us digress very briefly.

France had been shaken in the early sixteenth century by currents of religious reform. Some early reformers were Erasmians, humanists oriented toward biblical study and hostile to the many corruptions of the Renaissance church and the religious orders that still sought to remain within the church, while other reformers risked independence and eventually separated themselves from it or were anathematized by it. Political interests and the religious zealotry of the Catholics and the reformers brought France to a period of civil war, massacres, and regicide that lasted almost fifty years (1562–1610). While France fought, the Roman church excommunicated the sectarians and sought to reform its own rites and discipline, an aspect of the Counter-Reformation, a movement broader than mere reform, which would have a profound influence on arts and letters wherever it penetrated. Actually it hardly penetrated France until many years after the council of Trent (1663), which had initiated it. The Parlement of Paris was loath to accept the canons of the council for political reasons, alleging that they asserted papal authority in areas reserved for the king. Moreover, there were pious and influential Catholics (such as Fra Paolo Sarpi, the theological counselor of the Venetian republic and first historian of the council of Trent) who opposed the council's acts, claiming that they reinforced the schism of the Protestants rather than reconciling them to the church.

By 1589, the ruling Valois dynasty of France had died out and the Protestant Henry of Navarre·was obliged to assert his claim to the crown on the battlefield. After several important victories against the Catholic forces, then led by Charles de Lorraine, duc de Mayenne, Henry abjured his Protestant faith in order to claim Paris and the throne. During his reign he reestablished peace with France's neighbors and sought domestic reconciliation and economic revival. He accorded the Protestants of his kingdom the Edict of Nantes (1598), which was not a guarantee of religious toleration in a modern sense but a series of well-defined religious, political, and military privileges. Upon Henry's death—by assassination—in 1610, the regency of his widow

Marie de Médicis and the subsequent reign of their son Louis XIII finally brought the Counter-Reformation to France. Military pressures were exerted by Richelieu upon the Protestants because their political privileges were thought to compromise royal authority. Their religious privileges were continually eroded in practice and gradually rescinded in law until 1685, when Louis XIV formally revoked the edict, denied his Protestant subjects any legal status, and threatened their pastors with the gallows and the galleys. But despite such draconian repression, in the pious France of Marie de Médicis and Louis XIII (who even issued an edict, never enforced, expelling all Jews from his realm) there were already pensions for Protestants who converted and institutions for education in the Catholic faith of Protestant children who were, or could be, separated from their parents. There were polemics, some scholarly, many merely bombastic, and debates between Catholics and Protestants, the most famous of which, between the cardinal Jacques Davy Du Perron and the minister Philippe Duplessis-Mornay in 1600, actually preceded this period.

The early seventeenth century in France was also a period of genuine Catholic spiritual revival and institutional reform. Led by the Benedictines, various monastic communities returned, after many lapses and irregularities, to their vows of obedience and chastity, and to strict application of the rules of their orders. The Benedictines in particular underwent a "great reform" and rededicated themselves to historical scholarship. Dom Jean Mabillon and Dom Bernard de Montfaucon of the abbey of Saint-Germain des Prés in Paris invented in the late seventeenth century the discipline of paleography and established the chronology of medieval Europe. New religious orders such as the Visitandines under the inspiration of Saint Chantal, and the Lazarists under that of Saint Vincent de Paul, were founded. The Oratory (founded by Saint Philip Neri in Italy) was established in France by Pierre de Bérulle to encourage the spiritual renewal of the clergy by creating suitable schools for the young and seminaries for future priests, while the Jesuit order, dedicated in other ways to a renewal of the church, became very active in France. Somewhat later Jean-Jacques Olier (1608–1657) founded the Compagnie de Saint-Sulpice (1642) as a seminary to train dedicated priests, rather than ecclesiastical scholars, who attended the universities.

The religious life that accompanied so much institutional ferment manifested itself in the Jansenist movement led by the abbés de Saint-Cyran and Antoine Arnauld, in a circle of mystics around Madame Acarie (Beata Marie de l'Incarnation, 1566–1618) and Benet of Canfield, and in a distinctive French "school of spirituality" inspired by Saint François de Sales and exemplified by de Bérulle and by Charles de Condren, Bérulle's successor as superior of the Congregation of the Oratory, and later by Olier at Saint-Sulpice. These great men had already passed from the scene when Fénelon entered the seminary, although he did study with Louis Tronson (1622–1700), Olier's disciple and successor. Fénelon's version of the mystical quest would not quite be theirs, as we shall see, and before he became involved in the disputes regarding quietism he had not yet, by his own testimony, read any of the mystics, although his education under Tronson has been described as "premystical" and should have disposed him toward a pursuit of intense religious experience as the highest level of Christian life. Bossuet, in contrast, was educated in a different milieu, the University of Paris, and oriented toward dogmatic theology and historical scholarship; he showed little knowledge of the mystical tradition of the church when he first engaged in controversy with Fénelon, or particular esteem for the religious experience in itself. He has been described by Varillon as a great simplifier of doctrine. All dogmatic questions are clearly and definitely decided. Fénelon too was a doctor of theology, but his natural idiom was the subtle study of the religious conscience, in the abstract and in the particular cases of the penitents he directed. This is the religious counterpart of the so-called psychological analysis so prominent in the French *moralistes*, the seventeenth-century writers like La Rochefoucauld, La Bruyère, La Fontaine, and sometimes even Pascal who described the manners, mores, and motives of their contemporaries with rare perception and hardly a trace of normative prescription. To regard Fénelon's preoccupation with the religious experience and relative neglect of dogmatic theology as a religious version of French *moralisme* is not inconsistent with Paul Hazard's discussion of Fénelon's anti-intellectualism and Madame Guyon's illuminations as Catholic counterparts of the pietism that was arising in Halle, Germany, at that time and that would become very influential in eighteenth-century German life. Different religious traditions and spiritual exigencies can produce analogous tendencies. In any event it was inevitable that Bossuet's more institutional and intellectual construction of the religious life and thought would oppose Fénelon's emphasis on the private "voie intérieure" (the inward way, which we take to mean, in contemporary terms, religious experience) in the tradition of the mystics of the generation of Olier and Bérulle.

The young abbé Fénelon served the parish of Saint-Sulpice—a notoriously lower-class and indocile parish when Olier assumed responsibility for it in 1642, and probably still a difficult one in the 1660's—for three years, teaching, preaching, and hearing the confessions of its poor and humble denizens. None of the sermons of this period has been preserved. In 1678 he was appointed superior of a penitential institution for the shelter and reeducation of Nouvelles Catholiques, Protestant girls and women who wished to convert to Catholicism. The majority were girls, often very young children, who had been removed from the custody of their Calvinist parents by royal decrees or private abduction. O. Douen has shown that before Fénelon's appointment and throughout the seventeenth and eighteenth centuries, the Nouvelles Catholiques of the rue Sainte Anne in Paris and similar houses in other parts of the city and in the provinces were prisons for Protestant girls and women, as many as two hundred at a time in the rue Sainte Anne, where the most recalcitrant of them were subject to harsh, even violent treatment and, in the last resort, to imprisonment under such brutal conditions that several are known to have been driven mad. Accepting appointment as superior of such an institution implies support of its goals—Fénelon was never apologetic about the rights of orthodoxy in France nor of the effort to reunite the church on its own, post-Tridentine terms—and responsibility for, if not active participation in, its deplorable methods. Jean Orcibal (*Correspondence*, vol. 1, ch. 4) offers a legal if not a moral defense of the young Fénelon. In fact he had very little responsibility for the conduct of the Nouvelles Catholiques and was rarely present except to deliver occasional sermons and to perform the conversions that were induced by the sisters who directed the house. The institution itself depended on the king, who administered it through his *procureur général*, François de Harlay, and his *lieutenant de police*, La Reynie.

We do not know much more about Fénelon's conduct on the "missions" to convert Protestants in Saintonge and Poitou after the revocation of the Edict of Nantes. Again, participation in the missions shows what was never in doubt: he accepted the objective of destroying French Protestantism. He preferred guile and persuasion to cruelty in circumstances where other missionaries enlisted the aid of the royal dragoons, but the means he did employ are still shocking to a modern conscience. He wrote that those in authority should support the campaign against the Protestants, that Christian persuasion should be joined to vigilance against deserters from the faith against whom draconian punishments ("la rigueur des peines") should be imposed, and that the Huguenots' avenues of escape

along the Bordeaux coast should be more effectively guarded and blocked. He complained about the leniency of former Protestants in the army who were charged with converting the Huguenots, and urged engaging a Protestant of dubious reputation to write against and discredit Pierre Jurieu, a leader of the exile community in Amsterdam. In an ambiguous passage he seems to have approved the dragging in the dust of the cadavers of persons who had refused the sacraments. Tolerance was always a pejorative word in his vocabulary. Yet, by the cruel standards of his time, Fénelon was moderate and even charitable.

The literary product of these years is slender. Upon Bossuet's request he undertook in 1687 a refutation of Nicolas Malebranche's *Traité sur la nature et la grâce* (*Treatise on Nature and Grace*, 1680). That he was then far from an expert in philosophy is revealed by a request to the marquis d'Allemans to explain to him Malebranche's quite traditional terminology (see Adam, p. 160, n. 2). In the same year he wrote a *Traité de l'éducation des filles* (*Treatise on the Education of Girls*) as a guide to the duchesse de Beauvilliers (one of the daughters of Colbert, the finance minister), with whose family he had long been and was to remain very closely connected. This is a famous document in the history of education, though hardly for its advanced feminism. Ely Carcassonne has astutely remarked in *Fénelon: L'Homme et l'oeuvre* that Fénelon was proposing an education for girls' future duties in the France of Louis XIV, not for intellectual disciplines and professional advancement, which were unthinkable for women at the time. A girl's education was not to be too intellectual nor too scholarly, but it was to be moral and religious in the best sense: an acquisition of a love of the good and an appreciation of the beauty and solemnity of church rites, all proposed in their most positive and attractive forms, according to the conciliatory tradition of humanistic Christianity. What may be most innovative is the idea of educating a person, a young person at that, with a particular nature and future role, rather than stuffing a head or disciplining a mind or inculcating a doctrine.

The most curious and revelatory document of this period is a letter (9 October 1687?) addressed to Bossuet from Sarlat (*Correspondence*, Orcibal ed., no. 22) in which the young abbé Fénelon dreams of undertaking a mission to Greece in order to liberate from Islamic domination the churches where Saint Paul had preached and the land that Socrates had trod. A burning imagination bears him lightly beyond French borders and beyond the present, a soul seeking escape from its mundane circumscription yet still restrained by modesty and prudence, and casting its escape in the language, and according to the ideals, of his church.

Toward the end of October 1688 Fénelon met Madame Jeanne Marie Bouvière de la Mothe-Guyon, a woman who had already acquired a reputation for spiritual gifts and pretensions. It is usually said that he immediately fell under her influence, but that is an exaggeration. His contact with her stimulated an articulation of tendencies that had been inchoate in his religious life. The letters to Madame Guyon offer nearly the only confessions of his inner life that have survived. They recount the affliction of spiritual aridity. Neither his assent to all the articles of the Catholic faith nor his unreserved submission to the church, the practice of its rites, and the exercise of the ethical duties it prescribed brought him spiritual confidence or satisfaction:

> At any event I believe that God is never so much in me as when He is most deeply hidden there. As soon as He grants me some slight hint, I abandon myself to it without reserve. Beyond that, there is only a drying up of my soul to the point of agony. Ordinarily I feel neither pain nor intense consolation. All my emotions are blunted. I feel only a languor which resembles a slow fever. In this state one weakens every day; nothing hurts very much, but nothing pleases either. I can hardly pray except when walking about, or when I am in my coach. As soon as I settle in one spot my imagination and my senses become very uneasy. I am however persuaded that my exterior aridity is much greater than my interior aridity.
>
> (*Correspondence* no. 76, 26 July 1689)

Even beyond normal faith and the works demanded by the church, there were in Fénelon's day certain methods of prayer and devotion aimed at producing higher levels of concentration and communication. There had always been practical methods of intensifying or even inducing the religious experience among the initiates and persons possessing spiritual gifts. Fasts and flagellation, asceticism and seclusion had served this function in Catholicism, while other religious traditions have also practiced dance, chants, and even the ingestion of hallucinogenic substances for the same purpose. The Counter-Reformation had begun to preach spiritual perfection and religious experience more democratically—literacy was more common than in the great age of faith, so that churches were designed (the so-called Jesuit style) to permit worshipers to follow the texts of the service, and the bishops' quarrels about the intricacies of dogma and the secrets of spirituality, once committed to print, could no longer be immured within clerical society—and created a desire among many Christians without the spiritual gift for recipes, guides, and methods that would permit them too to realize the aspirations aroused within them.

Aldous Huxley's two fine studies of the religious conscience in the age of Richelieu, *Grey Eminence* (1941) and *The Devils of Loudon* (1952), describe and interpret several of the newer (for the period) methods of religious concentration and prayer. One method, indebted to Saint Ignatius of Loyola and his *Spiritual Exercises*, proposed a concentration of the mind upon a succession of religious ideas (moments in the life of Jesus or aspects of his being), visualizing them and then spiritualizing them; what is called "baroque piety"; frequent, discursive self-examinations; and, more generally, a direction of the will by these and other exercises to induce religious experiences. Other methods prescribed by Benet of Canfeld and elaborated on by the Capucin François Le Clerc du Tremblay, Richelieu's famous diplomat known as Father Joseph of Paris, required a suppression of the self, that notorious impediment to religious vision, by an annihilation by spiritualization in the consciousness of the good works performed and religious obligations discharged by the worldly self. (Father Joseph even tried to annihilate the evil that he accomplished daily in the service of the state in order to maintain his spiritual equilibrium.) Pre-seventeenth-century spiritual methods, especially those of the Franciscans, tended to be less technological and more flexible, better adapted to an individual's talents and more tolerant of his weaknesses, less willful and more open to whatever form the religious vision might assume in a seeker.

Madame Guyon was neither a theologian nor an intellectual. On the contrary, her inexpertise and naiveté were occasionally embarrassing to Fénelon, who defended her but not the letter of her texts. Her *Moyen court* (*Short Method*, 1685) proposed a kind of religious antitechnology that harked back to the less formal and willful Franciscan methods in the background of Olier's Saint-Sulpice seminary. Jejune or profound, she described a luxuriant religious experience, even to the point of claiming to have received visions and prophecies. In the expression of Father Varillon, she brought back trophies from her religious explorations, proofs of the existence of a strange and occasionally accessible reality, which reassured the pilgrim soul in Fénelon that the object of his quest was attainable; and she proposed a method for reaching it that was antithetical to those with which he was familiar.

The term "quietism" is always associated, correctly or not, with Madame Guyon, and from her, by a transitive application, to Fénelon. Strictly speaking, one should refer to Molinosism, the doctrine of Michel Molinos (1628–1696). His *Spiritual Guide* (1675) taught an easy manner of attaining and sustaining a state of contemplation that would be accompanied by a passive abandonment of oneself into the hands of God. While the treatise has no logical plan, it has a logic of sentiment that is still more effective. And its sentiment revolves around two tendencies, one toward absolute passivity and the other toward quietistic contemplation. He insists upon a contemplation of pure faith and the annihilation of self in the good pleasure of God; in one bound he transports his disciples beyond the stations of the purgative and illuminative life into regions of a unity with God.

Molinos' teachings were at first sympathetically received, but in 1682, Iñigo Caracceolo, archbishop of Naples, denounced them as heretical and designated them as "quietism." Under pressure from Louis XIV (Antoine Adam cites a letter of 1 April 1685 in which the secretary of state for foreign affairs mentions assemblies of quietists "who believe that contemplation of God alone is sufficient to excuse sexual irregularities" ["les désordres des sens"]), Pope Innocent XI condemned Molinos' doctrine (*Caelestis pastor*, 1687). Molinos recanted but nevertheless ended his days in prison. Despite Louis's intervention and the pope's condemnation, quietism became known in France. Molinos was translated into French in 1688, but an alert writer like Jean de La Fontaine could discuss the doctrines even before that, in 1687. Finding her inspiration in Saint Francis de Sales and in a *Pratique facile* (1664, also subsequently condemned) by the Marseilles poet, mystic, and scholar François Malaval, rather than in Molinos as her enemies charged, Madame Guyon had preached a doctrine "that excluded petitional prayer . . . and led to an idle contemplation" since the early 1680's, yet she enjoyed liberty and increasing influence until 1692.

Association with Madame Guyon was not yet compromising, and despite his connection with her, Fénelon was appointed in 1689 tutor to the duc de Bourgogne, Louis's grandson and presumed heir to the throne. Madame Guyon recognized the opportunity of forming a future king of France along the most evangelical lines and for the forces of her kind of piety to exert an influence on the king, one that would replace the influence exerted by such venal or political prelates as Harlay, archbishop of Paris (who died in particularly scandalous circumstances), and Maurice Le Tellier, archbishop of Rouen.

Louis de France, duc de Bourgogne (1682–1712), the object of their hopes, was a violent, willful seven-year-old when his education was entrusted to Fénelon. Fénelon took responsibility for the child's religious and moral education while leaving much specialized instruction to the abbé Claude Fleury, a sounder Greek and Latin scholar than himself as well as an experienced and, what is much rarer, successful pedagogue. By gentle means rather than by frequent beatings (normally a part of even the dauphin's education), Fénelon and Fleury humanized the royal brat. He learned his Latin decently well and became a considerate, scrupulous adult who retained respect and affection for his former tutor, even in the latter's disgrace.

In 1693 Fénelon was elected to the Académie Française; two years later he was named to the archbishopric of Cambrai (on the northern frontier of the realm), which had been annexed to France by conquest in 1677. By virtue of his consecration, Fénelon acquired the magnificent titles of prince of the Holy Roman Empire and duc de Cambrai, as well as substantial revenues (100,000 livres a year).[1] He would spend most of his time in his archdiocese, with only brief sojourns in his Versailles apartment to continue the education of the now adolescent duke. During this period Fénelon wrote the thirty-six Fables and the

seventy-nine Dialogues des morts (Dialogues of the Dead) for his royal pupil, as well as a series of biographies of ancient philosophers. The Fables were not meant to belong to the same genre as La Fontaine's, which Fénelon admired (see his Lettre à l'Académie); they are in prose, more didactic, and much less cynical. To appreciate them one must imagine the pleasure of a child in having little stories invented especially for him to illustrate the moral exhortations that royal children received from pious tutors in no smaller doses than did commoners at the hands of less exalted personages and preachers. In the Dialogues des morts Fénelon enlisted the child's imagination to further his own moral education. The Dialogues show a strain of moral realism: there are no idealized, perfect heroes nor any totally unredeemed scoundrels. Vice and virtue are mixed in varying proportions in all the examples for the child to analyze and measure, and so he learns to shun the former and pursue the latter. Still later, in 1694, Fénelon wrote for him Les aventures de Télémaque, fils d'Ulysse (The Adventures of Telemachus, Son of Ulysses), a series of illustrations of the principles of statecraft and royal duties. Fénelon published the first part anonymously in 1699, during his disgrace and exile, because there were so many manuscript copies circulating; and the second part followed shortly thereafter.

During this period of his greatest prestige and influence at court, Fénelon became the unofficial and extremely frank "directeur de conscience," or spiritual adviser, of Madame de Maintenon, Louis XIV's morganatic wife. She would copy his letters of direction into her little black book and take them to heart when they did not cut too deeply, because she took her role as the first Christian lady of the realm very seriously. Fénelon preached at Saint-Cyr, the school for daughters of the poorer aristocracy, which she had founded. Madame Guyon also preached there and provoked much enthusiasm for her version of the Catholic faith and practice—a bit too much so. In 1693 a

---

[1]The mean income of a rural French family in the period around 1700 was two hundred to three hundred livres, or between 365 and 550 dollars.

nun denounced her spiritual innovations to the superior of the Lazarists, who transmitted the complaint to Godet des Marais, bishop of Chartres. He introduced two nuns into Saint-Cyr to report on its discipline and doctrine. Madame de Maintenon was informed of the situation and, without withdrawing her confidence from Madame Guyon, advised her not to return to Saint-Cyr.

There are various accounts of Madame de Maintenon's motives in pursuing the scandal until it reached Fénelon, or in refusing to intervene. The version by Antoine Adam claims that she was afraid of being compromised as a supporter of heretics—François de Harlay, her enemy, had already taken a threatening step aimed at Fénelon—so it was better to strike first and sacrifice her friends. Another version argues that she was envious of Madame Guyon's spiritual success and resented the severe but justified spiritual criticism she received from Fénelon, so she was psychologically disposed to instigate proceedings against both on the first occasion that found them vulnerable. Still another version, by Henri Brémond and Fénelon's other apologists, has her genuinely scandalized by a verbal indiscretion on the part of the young, beautiful, and high-spirited Madame de la Maisonfort, who publicly said on one occasion that one need not agonize about anything, that it was enough to forget oneself and to refuse to consider one's own interest. Such an affront to an avid seeker of Christian perfection, especially in the mouth of a young and beautiful girl, was quite enough to provoke Madame de Maintenon, whose own Christianity has been described as fervent and sincere but very narrow-minded and somewhat crude. Still another account would have it that the girls had "ecstasies," acquired an exaggerated taste for prayer, neglected their chores, and were disobedient. Obedience to authority was supremely important in French society of the time, as the fathers in many of Molière's comedies testify.

In any event, Madame de Maintenon went to Bossuet and urged him to examine Madame Guyon's life and writings—including the *Moyen court,* her "short method" for prayer and the attainment of Christian perfection, and her *Cantique des cantiques* (1688), an interpretation of the *Song of Songs,* a classical text for all mystics—even though both books had been published with ecclesiastical approbation. For his part, Fénelon urged Madame Guyon to submit herself to his erstwhile friend's examination. The examination proceeded through the winter of 1693–1694. Bossuet gave Madame Guyon a certificate of good conduct—but he was not satisfied with the orthodoxy of her writings.

A committee of inquiry was convoked at Issy, where Tronson was spending his declining years, to identify the precise doctrine of the church regarding the inward life in the light of spiritual emphasis in Madame Guyon's teaching. Though not part of the committee—besides Tronson it included Bossuet and Antoine de Noailles, then bishop of Châlons—Fénelon found himself in the role of Madame Guyon's advocate and defender; but he agreed in advance to subscribe to whatever articles of faith and discipline the Issy conferees would issue. During the course of their deliberations Fénelon submitted several long treatises for their information: a *Mémoire sur l'état passif (Essay on the Passive State)* dealing with the *Theologia mystica* of Pseudo-Dionysius (a fifth-century Syrian); *De l'autorité de Cassien (Regarding the Authority of Cassianus),* dealing with a fifth-century account of the primitive monasticism of Egypt and the contemplation practiced by the monks (first published in 1720 and republished by Goré in 1956); and the *Gnostique de Saint Clément d'Alexandrie (The Gnosticism of Saint Clement of Alexandria,* first published by Father Dudon in 1930). In these memoirs Fénelon explains and comments on the three classical texts of early Christian mysticism. He claims that the gnosis about which Clement wrote was a secret tradition deriving from the Apostles about the mystery of God, a mystery that one must respect while in the process of discovering it, and that it can be better discovered through experience than through precept. The masters of spirituality had distinguished three "ways": the purging, the illuminating, and the unifying. It is the last of these that Fénelon identifies with Saint Clement's gnostic: God alone enlightens him, governs him, and prompts all his works; his union with God is immediate and essential. Dudon claims that both Fénelon and Bossuet, the latter in the posthumously published treatise *La tradition des nouveaux mystiques (The Tradition of the New Mystics)*, misunderstood Saint Clement quite thoroughly, yet that Fénelon's error was the grosser of the two since he read Madame Guyon's writings back into Saint Clement; as a result he discovered that Clement and Madame Guyon guaranteed each other.

The conferees of Issy finally arrived at a compromise formulation, thirty-four "articles," arid doctrinal formulas that never refer to Madame Guyon. Fénelon had a greater role in drafting the articles than Bossuet ever admitted. Like many diplomatic formulas, the articles meant different things to each signatory. While Fénelon was satisfied that the equivocations and reservations he had prevailed upon the conferees to introduce into the articles did not condemn his views, Bossuet interpreted the articles as a condemnation of the doctrine of Madame Guyon. He proceeded to elaborate on the condemnation in an *Instruction sur les états d'oraison (Instructions Regarding the Levels of Prayer)*, which he sent to Fénelon for his formal, episcopal approval. Fénelon read the first page and refused to read further because he saw that Madame Guyon was explicitly attacked and that he would have to withhold his approval. He answered Bossuet with his *Explication des maximes des saints (Explanations of the Apothegms of the Saints)*, which actually appeared in print on 25 June 1697, three months before Bossuet's *Instruction*. Bossuet was furious and condemned the *Maximes*. Even well-disposed modern critics are unhappy with the work.

Marcel Raymond calls it a rigid, agonized book composed in haste and prefers Fénelon's earlier draft, the *Explication des articles d'Issy (Explanation of the Articles of Issy*, first published in 1904), because it is more supple, less tense, and more an inquiry into the varieties of mystical experiences and the means that may be employed in the quest for them. The *Maximes* contain too much theory and too many doctrinal distinctions between the licit and the illicit in the manner and degree of the love of God. This was inevitable in any attempt to define the position of the church regarding the obligations and the limits of Catholic mysticism. We find that the *Maximes* belly their reputation and are quite interesting and impressive. Their attempt at organizing the perceptions of the more recent mystics, Saint Francis de Sales, Saint Theresa, Saint John of the Cross, regarding "le pur amour" (disinterested love of God) and its practical consequences is an intrinsically useful theological study, even if imperfect. The *Maximes* in that sense are the natural successor to the memoirs that Fénelon had prepared for the conferees of Issy regarding the doctrines of the church's earliest mystics.

Bossuet riposted with a *Relation sur le quiétisme (Account of Quietism)*, full of exaggerated charges, misunderstandings, distortions, and even a betrayal of confidences that Fénelon had offered under the seal of the confessional. Fénelon answered in a tone of injured innocence in a *Réponse à la Relation . . . (Reply to the Account . . .)* and spent the rest of the year issuing polemical tracts against Bossuet and Godet des Marais. Actually, the *Maximes* were generally well received. The public that would read such a treatise with curiosity and even an interest in its own spiritual perfection could not have been too large, yet its response was adequate for Fénelon to begin preparing an amended second edition; and so it seemed that Fénelon was winning the battle of polemics.

There was not much that Bossuet could do about the *Maximes* after having banned it in his own diocese (as was his right), since Fénelon was a fellow bishop but outranked him. To put an end to the dispute, Fénelon chose to defer his *Maximes* to the Roman curia. It was a tactical error. Bossuet induced Louis XIV to exert his influence in Rome against Fénelon, and it was considerable because of his political and military might and the possibility that he and the Gallican wing of the French church might find the courage of their convictions, reassert their *Déclaration des quatre articles* (*Declaration of the Four Articles,* 1682), which Louis had withdrawn in 1693, and separate themselves from Rome as England had done a century earlier. Even before Rome could act against the *Maximes,* Bossuet and Madame de Maintenon induced Louis to withdraw Fénelon's title of preceptor to the duc de Bourgogne, his salary, and his apartment in the palace, and to banish him to his archdiocese. This was indeed a fall from the heights of royal grace that would have devastated a courtier or a more political prelate.

Even before his fall, Fénelon spent nine months of the year in Cambrai, administering to the spiritual and institutional needs of his largely Flemish-speaking flock who lived in France and in the Spanish Netherlands, and he now continued to do so with undisputed devotion and humility. In the meantime Bossuet's Roman campaign finally bore fruit: his representatives persuaded the examining cardinals to issue a divided report recommending condemnation of only certain points in the *Maximes.* On 12 March 1699 Innocent XII issued a brief condemning certain expressions in the book, but not Fénelon himself nor the book as a whole. Fénelon accepted the condemnation of his propositions in humility and obedience and without equivocation, issuing a mandate within his archbishopric condemning his own book. Father Varillon claims that Fénelon could have done no better (Carcassonne remarks that Fénelon's act of obedience was almost superbly humiliating, a conscious and almost proud act of disappropriation, or rejection of a quality or work that one has ac-

quired or produced, and renunciation of pride and self), and that the condemnation of the *Maximes* was so narrow (injudicious language in a hastily composed book) that Fénelon's reputation need not be sullied by a suspicion of heresy. Whether or not Fénelon's orthodoxy is a necessary condition for an appreciation of his qualities as writer and thinker, Varillon's claim is supported by the fact that none of Fénelon's polemics defending the positions he had taken in the *Maximes* was ever impugned. Besides, in his defenses of Madame Guyon Fénelon recognized that the meaning of a person or a book is often imperfectly expressed in its prose; one must judge its interior meaning and general lines rather than isolated expressions. When that criterion is applied to the *Maximes* he is clearly vindicated.

Fénelon spent the last fifteen years of his life in Cambrai, doing all the things that archbishops are supposed to do. During the War of the Spanish Succession, in the last years of Louis XIV's reign, the military frontier crossed and recrossed his archdiocese so that he was obliged to receive the troops and commanders of both France and its enemies as they passed through. The devastation of his archdiocese was extreme, and biographies recount his efforts to relieve the distress of its peasants and bourgeoisie, to the limit of his financial ability. Even Louis de Saint-Simon, always hostile to Fénelon, conceded this.

Before his disgrace and "exile," in fact in the period of his greatest worldly success (1693–1694), Fénelon had written a political pamphlet that remained unpublished in his lifetime. The *Lettre à Louis XIV (Letter to Louis XIV)* is a bitter attack against the king and his politics of war, luxury, and the interests of the state as a valid excuse for any sacrifice of principles. The *Lettre* was a practical application of the principles that Fénelon was expounding in abstract in *Télémaque,* which he was then composing for the duc de Bourgogne, and they would be expressed again in the political writings of the Cambrai period. In 1711 he prepared a plan of government with the duc de Chevreuse (the *Tables de Chaulnes*) for the eventual use of the duc de Bourgogne. The next year he drew up a series of memoirs dealing with the political and economic state of the realm, which under the burdens of war was sinking into exhaustion. Whatever hopes Fénelon and his friends held of a return to influence were dashed by the death of the duc de Bourgogne in 1712. Fénelon subsequently undertook a political correspondence with Philippe, duc d'Orléans, Louis's nephew and eventual regent of the realm during Louis XV's minority. Philippe's regency was to be a notoriously dissolute period, and he himself was to dissipate his energies and dull his intellect by sexual excess, but Fénelon evidently perceived serious qualities in him that suggested he might be inclined to lead France with more modesty and prudence than his old uncle, as indeed he did.

Fénelon died in January 1715, preceding Louis XIV by nine months. On his deathbed he begged the king to permit the Compagnie de Saint-Sulpice to direct the seminary that he had founded in Cambrai. Despite his "exile" and fall from royal grace, he was the leading prelate of France, especially after the death of Bossuet in 1704; and to judge from the many editions and translations of *Télémaque* and other works, he enjoyed an imposing European reputation. The eighteenth century adopted Fénelon as a sympathetic precursor; critics of the period had a special impression of him: a sentimental, humanistic Christian, for Rousseau; an apostle of tolerance and an enemy of tyranny, for Voltaire. These were indeed aspects of the man, but they fail to portray the ascetic, orthodox prelate that he was. Nineteenth-century literary critics and some conservative Catholic writers toward the end of the century preferred Bossuet and his more "patriotic" political doctrines, while the positivist orientation of French thought was not receptive to Fénelon's strain of anti-intellectualism and questing mysticism. Raymond finds Fénelon's quest for religious experience and for God, despite his profound uncertain-

ties, singularly suited to our "post-Christian" era, an "interregnum where humanity, having collapsed upon itself, is groping in the dark in search of the limits of its own isolation." Even on the less exalted planes in which we may conceive of our lives and careers, the writings and thought of Fénelon are valuable as an extreme pole of human existence: radical denial of the ego (and hence of the inner turbulence and exterior malice and damage it provokes) without recourse to the debilitating hatred of self preached by Pascal. Examples of the "imperial self" are all too common, and history records the depredations that many of the strongest have inflicted on mankind. Examples of the more benign denials of self and a vision of what they can produce are, at the very least, a necessary corrective. They can be found in the hagiographic corpus and in this one writer.

RELIGIOUS WRITINGS

It is exaggerated but convenient to say that the great seventeenth-century French *classiques* describe man's overweaning will. Corneille's dramas deal with heroes who impose their wills on enemies and lovers alike and in whom will transcends even duty and common ethcial obligations. In his plays Racine regards the passions negatively, in the tradition of Christian psychology, but the will—the true expression of the ego—is still his subject. The novel *La princesse de Clèves* portrays passion, the illusions and suffering it induces, and, finally, recognition and illumination: the tripartite scheme of Greek tragedy. The same elements are barely disguised in many of La Fontaine's *Fables* and are explicit in La Rochefoucauld's *Maximes*, while their discovery becomes the means by which Pascal in his *Pensées* shakes the complacency of those who are worldly and prepares them for conversion. These renowned *moralistes* and psychologists did not invent the willfulness that they recorded or portrayed, and there was no lack of models from among willful kings, courtiers, and prelates before their time. Nevertheless the *classique* literature as well as French biography and portraiture of the period reflect, sometimes critically but often admiringly, a pervasive willfulness and an astonishing tendency toward haughty self-aggrandizement. Think of the iron will of Richelieu overcoming all obstacles but his own mortality, of the pretentious palace at Versailles, and of the cult of the king formed within the palace by introspective, uneasy courtiers wearing wigs that gave them a look of superhuman virility, and seeking to "distinguish themselves" (Alceste's famous desire in Moliere's *Misanthrope*) before king and court while remaining within the strict conventions of their class.

Yet many were "religious." They worshiped in splendid churches, were entertained when they were not listening to the sumptuous sermons preached by Bossuet, Bourdaloue, and other great ecclesiastical orators, and performed the duties and benefactions of devout Christians. It is not to denigrate devotions and benefactions to remark, as Fénelon did, that such behavior, when not unthinkingly routine, can reflect the will to excel and to distinguish oneself as much as profane and blasphemous conduct (for example, Molière's *Dom Juan*). The will was merely directed toward the distinction of being a perfect Christian; courtiers and intellectuals took a strange satisfaction in the punctilious observance of religious obligations and in being completely orthodox. Before his contact with Madame Guyon, Fénelon had directed his penitents toward complicated spiritual regimens of prayer and pious readings. These are methods of art and tension rather like Loyola's famous *Spiritual Exercises*. This kind of Christian life may bear good fruit because the will is diverted into approved and constructive directions. A more common form of egocentric Christianity—one hardly unique to seventeenth-century France—was the performance of prescribed works with the object of achieving personal salvation. In the terms that Fénelon

shared with Bossuet, both forms of Christian life are represented by the theological virtue hope. Hope is more than an authorized state of mind; it is, they both agreed, a Christian's obligation, and indeed it has always been accepted as a motivation for faith and obedience even though Saint Paul, and after him Fénelon, recognized the superiority of the charity that "seeketh not her own" (1 Corinthians 13:5, 13).

An alternate Christian strategy urges a self-mortification that goes beyond the humbling of oneself to seek what modern psychoanalytic jargon would designate as the death of the ego. Matthew 10:39 promises that "one who grasps at self will lose it, but one who rejects self on my account will gain it" (compare John 12:25; Mark 8:35; Luke 9:24, 17:33). Fénelon construes this as an injunction to suppress the ego ("mortification") in order to obey and to worship God unreservedly; that is, in his terms, the "pure love" of God, without the admixture of personal gain or self-interest. He carries this tradition to an extreme that, according to Father Varillon, remains within Catholic orthodoxy: he urges that one perform the will of God exclusively from motives of "pure love." This requires that one obey in a spirit of complete disinterestedness and "disappropriation"; in other words, one should not seek or anticipate any benefit, material or spiritual, from acts of obedience, nor should one experience pride or satisfaction in performing such acts. Fénelon designates this form of worship as charity, the charity "that vaunteth not itself, is not puffed up, . . . seeketh not her own" (1 Corinthians 13:4–5). Fénelon's emphasis on worship from the debris of the self is an implicit critique of the predominance of worship and obedience from the plenitude of self and will in the conscience of the France of the *classiques*, a critique that explains the enmity of Bossuet and Louis XIV.

The mystical tradition to which Fénelon attached himself had always prescribed exercises directed at the suppression of a will and self that were—to the extent that they were distinguished—recognized as impediments to a perception of the divine element within oneself and thus to an experience of unity with the all-encompassing and undifferentiated divine ambiance. Christian mysticism could not go quite so far as pagan mysticism in locating a measure of the divinity itself within man because the Christian theological tradition accepted the Jewish emphasis on the separability of the divine from the created (see Fénelon's *De la nature de l'homme*, p. 579), except the incarnation of God in Jesus. Still, the Dionysian tradition remained relatively untheological, stressing the greatness and omnipresence of the godhead without distinguishing its several hypostases (Father, Son, Holy Ghost). The doctrines of Benet of Canfield, Olier, Bérulle, and their school were more particularizing and theological in their conscious attempt to render the Dionysian tradition orthodox. Fénelon's vision of God was closer to the more authentic mystical tradition insofar as it tended to be pantheistic or at least nonparticularizing. The second part of his *Traité de l'existence de Dieu (Treatise on the Existence of God)* interrupts its arguments with rapturous "metaphysical hymns" (Raymond's expression) to the one existent being, the creator before whom all other reality recedes:

> I see being and I have seen all; I have drawn from the well; I have nearly seen you face to face. It is you yourself, for what are you but being? . . . Alas, how can this be? I who am that which is not at all, or, at most, who is an indefinite something that can neither be found nor named, and who in just a moment is no longer. I a nothing, I a shadow of being, I see Him who is; and when I name him, He Who Is, I have said all and I do not fear that I have said too little about him.
>
> I take flight toward him who is; I am no longer in myself nor myself; I become he who sees him who is; I see him, I lose myself . . . without reasoning I see the universal truth; I see, and it is my life; I see what is and no longer what is not. When will it be that I shall see what is, because I no longer have any other life than this fixed view? When shall I be, by means of this single and permanent glance, a single thing with him? When will my entire self be reduced to this single, inutterable utterance: HE IS, HE IS, HE IS? And if I add, HE WILL BE FOR EVER AND EVER, it is to address my weakness and not to express his perfection any better.

(1.84)

Father Varillon defends Fénelon against the charge of pantheism, arguing that he remained within the bounds of orthodox Catholic theism, which has its own pantheistic tendencies. Raymond, however, emphasizes the second part of the *Traité* and refuses to qualify Fénelon's pantheism. We would add that Fénelon shows a profound commitment to a God who operates upon nature through the laws of nature, in *Lettres au P. Lami, Bénédictin, sur la grâce et la prédestination* 1 (*Letters to Father Lamy, of the Order of Saint Benedict, Regarding Grace and Predestination*), and generally tends to deprecate miracles and special providential interventions. Both positions are part of a disposition toward the pantheism of Baruch Spinoza that he refutes in the first part of the *Traité*. He was not a disciple of Spinoza any more than he was of Malebranche; it is simply that there were certain directions common to their individual theisms, parallel developments rather than offshoots.

In Catholicism and outside the Christian confessions, mystics have always emphasized the rejection of self and taught techniques of suppressing or escaping a self that would otherwise interpose itself between the seeker and the internal or external element with which he wants to make intimate contact. As the famous letter to Bossuet suggests, even the young Fénelon was already a seeker of something outside France, and apparently outside himself. The next time he reveals himself as candidly, in the correspondence with Madame Guyon, he is profoundly dissatisfied with a self too dry and "discursive" (that is, intellectual), too much given to reasoning and analysis, and he desires to cast it off. Is that the reason for the emphasis on mortification found in even the pre-Guyon texts, or is it the psychological expression of a standard homiletic theme that he adopted as a matter of course and internalized? We don't pretend to answer that.

Madame Guyon was a finder. She had had the experience of a spiritual answer for her pains of casting off a measure of self and of respectability, and Fénelon evidently hoped for as much, though not necessarily for the same answer. At any rate, he writes that a suppression or dissolution of will and self would be followed by a flooding of the soul with God, an experiential phenomenon describable to the uninitiated solely in terms of analogies:

This passive state of mind regarding which the sainted mystics have said so much is not passive except in the sense that contemplation is passive, that is to say that it does not exclude calm and disinterested acts but only those that are agitated and urgently forward our own interests. The passive state is that one in which the soul, no longer loving God with an adulterated love, performs all the acts that independent and efficacious wills ordinarily perform, but tranquilly and disinterestedly. . . . This passive state does not depend upon any extraordinary inspiration. It encompasses only the peace and infinite suppleness of the soul which lets itself be moved by all the promptings of grace. A feather, when it is dry and light, as Cassianus said, is carried away by the slightest breath of wind, and that breath drives it in every direction, whereas when it is wet and heavy its proper weight renders it less mobile and less easy to lift away. When the soul loves in an interested fashion, which is less perfect, it still possesses a vestige of fear for itself which renders it less light, less supple and less mobile when the breath of the interior spirit nudges it. Water that is turbulent cannot be clear nor receive the image of neighboring objects; but still water becomes like the pure glass of a mirror. It receives the images of diverse objects without distorting or retaining any of them. The pure and tranquil soul is like that. God stamps his image upon it, and those of

all the objects which he desires to be registered upon it. Everything is stamped upon it and everything is effaced. The soul has no shape of its own and it acquires with equal ease all those which grace lends it. It is, Richard of Saint-Victor has said, like metal melted by the fire of love. It takes and relinquishes all the forms which it pleases the artisan to give it. It flows in all directions at the will of the foundryman. The man who achieves this degree [of self-renunciation] may say: I am rendered all things to all men. He is willing to be anathema to all his brothers. Nothing remains in this soul, and all is effaced within it as in the water upon which God wants to impress new images. There is nothing but pure love that can give such perfect peace and docility.

(*Explication des Maximes des Saints*, p. 200)

Nonetheless, grace cannot be compelled and need not descend, despite a successful annihilation of self. But the essential element of Fénelon's method is that it is not a technique or effort at all. One annihilates self by emptying oneself, by letting oneself go, not by tensing the will and bending it to punctilious works in order to expel the ego. The repudiation of will and of interested obedience in a century that admired authority and rewarded social conformity must have made Fénelon appear to be somewhat quixotic to his contemporaries; Louis XIV characterized him as his "most chimerical subject." Raymond argues that Fénelon's letting go and subversion of the will permitted him to achieve a certain "gaiety" in his literary work, even in his religious writings. This view is not entirely convincing, but there is a measure of impudence in the *Dialogues des morts* and a lightness and limpidity in many of Fénelon's religious metaphors.

Now we can understand why the laborious compromise of the incredibly dry and uninspiring articles of Issy broke down; it papered over a fundamental difference of approach. On one level Fénelon was putting the best—charity—at war with the good—hope. That induces the obedience and the conformity of practice and doctrine necessary to sustain a community of faith (or even a secular community when the two are as intimately connected as they were in pre-Revolutionary France). The suppression of self that is the condition for Fénelon's conception of charity atrophies the faculties that are moved by hope, so while emptying oneself to receive the grace of God and to be moved naturally and involuntarily to acts of charity, one risks a spiritual interregnum of religious and ethical indiscipline. Furthermore, the discipline of works is usually held—and Fénelon does not deny it—to be basic spiritual training for those either inept at or unprepared for mysticism, instructing the soul in obedience so that it may reach greater intensity of worship. The mystical method, especially in such vulgarizations as Madame Guyon's *Moyen court*, claims to operate directly upon the soul, circumventing the works and disciplines that pastors and bishops promote within their dioceses. Still more alarming to the conventional was the possibility that during periods of prayer ("oraison") and "contemplation"—Fénelon's (and Bossuet's) expressions for the unitive experience or at least its approaches—the would-be mystic might regard himself as beyond the obligations of Catholic discipline. Fénelon had found and emphasized this idea in Saint Clement's descriptions of the gnostic.

Fénelon assured his antagonized colleagues that the state of contemplation and ravishment by grace, which he identified as the object of Christian religious life, is at best momentary and attained by only a small elite; therefore, the freedom from discipline that it confers is too fleeting to be dangerous or even significant. He explained at length in the *Maximes* that, because God in his love of man desires his salvation, whoever has arrived at the state of pure love would still desire salvation, not for his own sake, but because such is the will of God. He would thus still observe all the ritual and practical obligations of a good Catholic at least as punctiliously from motives of pure love and obedience as he would have ob-

served them from motives of self-interest. Varillon cites chapter and verse to show that Fénelon had no dishonorable designs upon Catholic discipline, and he is doubtless right.

Bossuet was not satisfied by Fénelon's explanations. The specters of religious indiscipline and doctrinal liberty were too formidable. But the dispute regarding the *Maximes* revolved around a more serious question than that of merely defining the church's doctrine regarding a mystical experience that is, after all, rarely attained. The general disappointment that Fénelon's critics and biographers express regarding the *Maximes* derives from their feeling that once Fénelon had implicitly conceded that mysticism is a matter of experience, he ought to have accepted the consequence of his concession: that the mystical experience will inevitably assume whatever forms are possible, given a subject's personality, imagination, and religious vocabulary. The attempt to prescribe the licit forms of experience is rather like King Canute commanding the ocean to recede. It was implicit in Fénelon's recognition of the mystical experience that neither he nor Bossuet could subject it to their ecclesiastical authority, whereas the assertion of authority—of the king over the realm, of the bishops over the varied institutions and individual consciences in the French church—was at that time of fundamental importance.

Actually, we cannot find rhapsodic renderings of the mystical experience in the *Maximes*, nor much talk of the unitive experience. The object of the treatise is a delineation of the degrees of pure love of God and their subtle admixtures with baser kinds of worship and obedience. In particular Fénelon tries to determine the range of devotion, obedience, and religious experience that the church could demand of the faithful, the upper limit beyond which nothing more may be asked (though gifted individuals may transcend it) and the lower limit beneath which religious aspiration and observance are to be condemned as inadequate. (These limits are framed in pairs of "true" and "false" propositions that enclose the legitimate range and exclude on either side the excessive obligation and the insufficient commitment.) In that century of aspirants to an egocentric Christian perfection, the bishop who exceeded the upper limit and required a mystical unitive life as the norm of Catholic duty would have cast those who failed to attain it into despair, alienation, and disobedience. Sacrificing an attainable good—faith, hope, and works—to an unattainable best would have been as irresponsible as demanding too little and subordinating charity to interest and gratification.

As we read the *Maximes* we find that Fénelon tries to identify a fairly wide range of approved religious motivation between the extremes he condemns—yet Bossuet was not convinced. He was a rationalist, dogmatist, and historian. Fénelon's emphasis on the non-rational experience, on religious psychology rather than on dogma, and his lack of interest in the history of doctrine must have offended him because they were diametrically opposed to the motivations for faith and good works that he propounded so energetically. He was so unimpressed with Madame Guyon's witness that he could not have been a seeker of the unitive experience that Fénelon extolled, and he of course disapproved of the suspicion of antinomianism—antagonism to law and discipline—that clung to her and to her quietism. For all of these reasons he chose to characterize quietism by the extreme positions that Fénelon had repudiated as legitimate demands upon the faithful, and he exploited his influence with the king and the curia to seek ultimate condemnation of the *Maximes* and of their author as though they represented a major challenge to Christian life. To put Bossuet's opposition to Fénelon in perspective, one must recall that he opposed all the dispersive tendencies in the French church relative to his definition of orthodoxy: ultramontanism, Jansenism, scientific study of the Bible and of ecclesiastical history. In Paul Hazard's

expression, he dominated the French church more than he represented it.

Raymond asks why Fénelon remained a despairing, mortified seeker who perpetually approached mystical exaltation, recognized it, but barely felt it, while Madame Guyon—less learned, infinitely less intellectual, and clearly possessed of less poetic sensibility—succeeded in crossing the threshold and experiencing the joy of the mystical life. He audaciously suggests that Fénelon lacked the talent: he was by nature too dry and too lucid; he understood more than he ever felt. The great hymns of the *Traité*, the evidence of his metaphysical ecstasies, are still emotionally very chaste. For example, in the Cyprus episode in book 4 of *Télémaque*, when the young hero arrives during a festival of the goddess Venus and sees women dressing and assuming languid postures to attract men, Fénelon portrays his reaction as quite hysterical: everything about the women seems vile and despicable. Impudence and dissolution horrify him, and he must escape the temptation to sin and the emotional turbulence that accompanies it. Nothing is described in this scene; all is conceptualized. Unlike the biographies of so many great saints, that of Fénelon records no experience of profane love nor temptation to carnal passion that might have been transmuted to the spiritual domain—where love of God and God's love for his creations are almost invariably described in analogies to the strongest physical and sentimental attachments.

Another explanation that Raymond offers is that Fénelon never entirely succeeded in his own mortification; some small measure of worldly self always survived to impede his spiritual progress. Raymond cites a remarkable passage from Fénelon's correspondence:

> What I wish for you as I wish it for myself is that we would never perceive in ourselves any vestige of life without letting it be extinguished. When I attend services in the choir of the church

I see the hand of one of the chaplains holding a large candle extinguisher which puts out the candles from behind, one after another; if he does not extinguish them entirely there remains a little glowing end which lasts a long time and consumes the candle. In the same way, grace comes to extinguish the natural life but that opinionated life smokes on for a long time and consumes us with a secret fire, unless the candle extinguisher is firmly held and quenches completely, even to the least vestige of that hidden fire.

(*Oeuvres complètes*, 1848 ed., vol. 8, p. 580)

Still another explanation that Raymond offers for the failure (in his own terms) of Fénelon's spirituality is that it was extraordinarily interior and negative. Christian imagery and ceremonies are deprecated to the limit of orthodoxy as being merely propaedeutic and of limited intrinsic value, while the imagination, which they engage, actually impedes the mystic quest; the sacrifices and token offerings of petitional prayer are described in the *Maximes* as lower forms of prayer than that which demands nothing of God and worships in complete disinterest. Personal needs for absolution, mediation, and salvation such as one finds in Pascal, for example, are not profound themes in Fénelon's spirituality, although he never denies them as orthodox doctrine. Yet these are the means, models, and exercises of communication with the divine, if not yet with the godhead, of the mystics. Fénelon's attempt to circumvent them and approach the divine directly on a higher plane of renunciation of self and passive reception of omnipresent grace is precisely the opposite of casting off the ladder after one has reached the heights; it is trying to dispense with the ladder before one has mounted. The result is a melancholy Christianity, always conscious of failure and of the lack of communication with God on any plane, which results in an anguish of abandonment that endangers the ability to continue the sacrifices of self and gratification. This argument is consistent with the frequent emphasis in Fénelon's writings on Jesus, in agony on the cross, calling out, "Why hast thou abandoned me?" and explains in particular one of the strangest points in Fénelon's dispute with Bossuet. Fénelon prevailed on the conferees of Issy to add a thirty-fourth article to their document, one that specifies that if—unlikely hypothesis though it may be—a man is certain of his own damnation, he may still be capable of worshiping God in pure love. For Bossuet this meant that one could have charity without hope and was quite obnoxious. Evidently, suggests Raymond, it reflected Fénelon's desire to transcend his own despair and perception of failure.

We can extrapolate still another, only apparently contrary, explanation for the paradox of Fénelon, the unfulfilled mystic, from the argument of Huxley's *Grey Eminence:* Fénelon did not go far enough in undoing the distortion imposed on the traditional Dionysian mystical system by Benet of Canfield and his disciple Bérulle. On one plane in his personality (and in his ecclesiastical magisterium) he retained the orthodox, personalistic theology, and it tended to diffuse the pure and intense theocentrism expressed in the second part of the *Traité* (which Fénelon never published and which cannot be dated with certainty). Bérulle was able to combine theocentrism with "adherence" to the other poles of Catholic interest, the person of Jesus (Bérulle was saluted by the pope when he was elevated to the cardinalcy as "the apostle of the word incarnate") and the Virgin Mary. But Fénelon could not balance these images and particularizations with the godhead. They apparently misdirected his efforts, forcing him to employ the faculties of analysis and imagination (literally, from image) that he recognized as impediments to the unitive experience, which is neither intellectual nor figurative. Similarly, his daily discipline and works, scrupulous Catholic that he was, dissipated his concentration. The quietism of Molinos,

Malaval, and Madame Guyon may indeed have been a return to pre-Bérullian mysticism, but Fénelon did not, or could not, bring himself to go all the way back with them to the Dionysian and antinomian roots of Catholic mysticism. The bishop in Fénelon that restrained him may have been precisely the self to be mortified, but he who was so perceptive a director of others did not have the courage to recognize excessive scruple in himself.

The last two arguments are complementary. They identify in Fénelon a single fatal flaw: the lack of courage to give himself over to either a nonpersonalist, nontheological, somewhat antinomian, Dionysian mysticism, or, alternatively, to luxuriate in the promptings of "baroque" piety with its appeal to the imagination as a way station in his soul's pilgrimage. What is curious about these accusations of spiritual timidity is that Fénelon was a man of uncompromising theological and political courage and integrity, as well as the possessor of a remarkable aesthetic sensibility and the power to express it.

POLITICS

Louis XIV's reign was, as we have already noted, celebrated by the writers of his own generation and criticized by those whom it had formed. The political criticism it engendered was at first nostalgia for lost aristocratic power and preeminence (Saint-Simon and Boulainvilliers), and later, among the writers who came of age during the military and economic reverses of the end of the reign, a relatively liberal (recognizing subjects' rights and freer commerce) criticism of its most fundamental assumptions. Fénelon falls between the two camps. In certain respects his criticism was conservative when it was not actually reactionary, while much of the practical program of reform he proposed could have been accepted by all but the most radical materialists before 1789.

The other critics and would-be reformers of

Louis XIV's domestic and foreign policies among Fénelon's contemporaries were, except for Sébastien Vauban (born in 1633), of Fénelon's generation or younger. Fénelon's criticism was rooted in a thorough knowledge of the conditions of the realm, in fundamental political principles, and in a pervasive ethical disposition. The principles in themselves were not original; Antoine Adam finds them in Malebranche, while Roland Mousnier argues that they reflect those of Saint Thomas Aquinas. Like his theology, Fénelon's politics did not conform to the distinctive orthodoxy of his time, the ideology of the Sun King. This is not to say that Fénelon was a liberal in the eighteenth-century sense of the term, merely that opposites tend to meet and even to share limited areas of agreement.

Fénelon's point of departure is generally described as subjecting the state to evangelical values, but this notion requires precise definition since various theological traditions identify different values as evangelical, or apply those upon which they agree in diverse manners. Fénelon subjects the king to divine law and charges him with the obligation of seeing that it is respected; he is to accomplish this as much, or more, by example as by coercion. The church and state are two independent powers. In temporal matters the church is subject to royal law. Ecclesiastics must pay taxes on their revenues according to the uniform law of the realm. (Under the ancien régime they were exempt, but the clergy made a substantial annual gift to the king.) On the other hand the king may not interfere with the church in its exercise of moral or spiritual authority, nor with its internal administration and discipline, after the model of the Reformed church of France, which had enjoyed such independence. (This is a denial of the *régale* that Louis had extended, the right to dispose of the revenues of bishoprics during their vacancy, and even of the privileges of naming bishops and abbots that had been accorded the French monarchy in François I's concordat with the pope.) But Fénelon proposes no theory to deal with cases where church or state usurp powers that are not theirs; this may not be a reproach because such a theory is not necessary if the king is inherently subject to the church's spiritual power and the church is subject to his temporal power; each has its own means of coercion. However, the separation of church and state is not to be so strict as one might assume. In France during the ancien régime the two supported each other (and fell together during the Revolution), and Fénelon would have had them continue to lend each other assistance in order to subdue their "rebellious children."

Fénelon legitimizes the acquisition of worldly effects, but only to the extent that they aid the spiritual life and promote the works that lead to salvation, a reflection of the extremely strong ascetic disposition in Fénelon's thought. Luxuries and manufactured goods of almost any and all sorts are condemned or deprecated. The king has heavy responsibilities before God for the welfare and security of his subjects (see the *Discours pour le sacre de l'électeur de Cologne* [*Sermon on the Occasion of the Coronation of the Elector of Cologne*]) but no legitimate gratifications. Even the king must worship God from motives of pure love that require such disinterest that he may not even take satisfaction in political responsibilities adequately discharged.

In practice Fénelon's principles translated themselves into a ferocious attack on Louis XIV. He found Louis's concentration of the majesty and authority of the state in his own person, with all the license and self-indulgence that it implied, ethically abhorrent and politically destructive. His position was diametrically opposed to that of Bossuet, who propounded in his historical and political works a theory that held the king to be divinely elected, quasi-divine in his person, and entitled to almost unlimited prerogatives. The most famous expression of Fénelon's opposition to Louis and to almost all his policies, domestic, foreign, and ecclesiastical, is the *Lettre à Louis XIV*, written in 1694 or 1695,

well before Fénelon's fall from influence. No one claims that Louis ever saw the letter, although almost everyone except Mousnier thinks that it was communicated to Madame de Maintenon either as a reform project or to guide her in effecting a "conversion" of the king. Mousnier argues convincingly that both she and Louis are violently criticized in the *Lettre;* the court at Versailles (with its many amorous courtesans and political prelates), the king's desire for glory and conquest, and the concentration of power in his hands are all so explicitly condemned that had the *Lettre* ever escaped either Fénelon's or his confidants' possession, he would surely have been imprisoned in the Bastille immediately. Although Mousnier describes the *Lettre* as violent and hateful, he does exaggerate; it is a bishop's letter, respectful in its address, yet devastating in its candid criticism. Fénelon deplores the sins without rejecting the sinner and discharges his responsibility by indicating the paths of restitution and penitence. The portrayal of Idoménée in book 10 of *Télémaque* is in the same vein, a sympathetic portrait of a king whose virtues and vices appear in exaggerated perspective, because of the exposed royal stage on which they are displayed, yet without any concession to the vices themselves.

Mousnier goes further and assimilates Fénelon's criticism of Louis's reign into Saint-Simon's opposition to Louis's "bourgeois" monarchy; bourgeois in the sense that it ruled through intendants and administrators chosen more or less on merit rather than for their aristocratic rank. This seems gratuitous. Fénelon, at least in theory, supported the appointment of men of merit to the army, judiciary, and administration, even if they were not aristocrats. But while he opposed the consolidation of authority in the person of the king (in modern terms, Louis's despotism), as did Saint-Simon, the interest in restoring the political power of the aristocracy, which is primary in Saint-Simon, is secondary or even incidental in Fénelon.

FRANÇOIS DE SALIGNAC DE LA MOTHE-FÉNELON

The most curious, and the most sympathetic, of Fénelon's political heresies is his denial of the right of conquest. He abhorred the archetype of the conquering, glorious king upon which Louis modeled himself so conspicuously. (Sauveur Le Compte painted Louis as a heroic, equestrian figure in armor, haughtily surveying his troops in the "Passage du Rhin," 1672.) The distinction between just and unjust wars is a scholastic concept, and Fénelon makes the distinction on the basis of the principles of the "rights of people" (les droits des gens) and natural law, without further precision. Wars that are unjust do not confer upon the victors rights over their conquered territories and peoples; consequently the peace treaties that the victors impose are invalid. In the *Examen de Conscience* (Scrutiny of a Conscience), a kind of catechism of royal duties written for the duc de Bourgogne, Fénelon seems to protect himself from the horrors of wars of conquest by an extraordinary (for him) retreat into satire:

> They hang a poor devil who, in extreme need, stole a pistol on the highway, while they regard as a hero the man who has made a military conquest; that is to say, who has unjustly subjugated the land of a neighboring state. The usurpation of a meadow or a vineyard is regarded as an irremissible sin in the eyes of God, unless one makes restitution, while men regard as negligible the usurpation of cities and provinces! To take a field from an individual is a great sin; to take a territory from a nation is an innocent and glorious deed!
>
> (3.26)

Although he does not have a theory of international rights, Fénelon does propose mechanisms to avoid wars: the adjudication of differences between states, and conciliation, concession, and even international federation to guarantee the terms of peace treaties (*Télémaque* 9).

Fénelon did not have a strongly developed theory or even feeling of nationalism, the lat-

ter even though he was French by birth and a son of a very old aristocratic family. He was catholic in his outlook and ultramontanist by virtue of his ecclesiastical loyalty (rather than Gallican as were many of his colleagues); he was responsible for a largely Flemish archbishopric in which it could have made little practical difference to most of the inhabitants under which government they lived, and no difference at all to their religious obligations and ability to earn salvation. One would not have expected chauvinism from him and indeed Mousnier accuses him of disloyalty, of bending so far over to avoid injustice to France's enemies of the moment, during the War of the Spanish Succession, that he urged retreats and cessions of border territories and fortifications to secure peace that would have seriously sacrificed France's legitimate rights and interests. Mousnier's Fénelon is a modern, pacifist idealist. An injection of idealism and even naiveté in the practical politics of interest and glory is becoming in a bishop and is always welcome. In fact, however, Fénelon's perception of the military situation was weak. He demonstrated that Louis's pursuit of conquest and glory had brought ruin to France. The still greater disaster that he predicted did not occur because the Maréchal de Villars, of whom he disapproved, saved France from defeat at the battle of Denain in 1712.

In book 10 of *Télémaque*, Nestor examines the commerce and demography of Idoménée's realm of Salente and sets out to give it suitable laws. And in the *Tables de Chaulnes* (drawn up at the duc de Chevreuse's country estate of the same name) Fénelon and Chevreuse drafted a scheme for the reform of French government. The two plans are largely complementary but Mousnier goes too far, perhaps, in projecting all of the Salente laws on the Chaulnes reforms, as well as in attributing the latter's aristocratic bias to Fénelon. It is less pronounced in the works to which Chevreuse did not contribute. A synthesis of the two models provides for a separation of church and state subject to the limitations already mentioned; that is, the reform of taxation and judicial procedures in order to eliminate the venality and corruption that were then rampant. A reform of the army provides for the appointment of more competent and experienced officers, adequate rations, prompt payment, severe discipline (which Fénelon realized could not be imposed until the other two conditions were satisfied), and release of soldiers upon expiration of their enlistment. Still more attractive at first sight is the proposal to organize provincial representative bodies that would in turn be represented in an Estates-General to be convoked by the king periodically. He could rule only with the approval of his subjects (if not quite with their consent) and within the constraints of the prior legal traditions of the realm, and he must set the example of scrupulous adherence to strict sumptuary laws, must live at his own expense (paid by his own feudal revenues), and must maintain an absolutely minimal court. The only women at court would be those needed by the queen and the princesses, and these women would be older, respectable matrons. The lists of the nobility would be purged and the hierarchy of noble families reestablished. Commerce would not be discouraged. In fact, it would be closely supervised, but the manufacture of articles of luxury for the domestic market would be forbidden because such luxuries corrupt the population. Free trade would be encouraged under the assumption that France would have a favorable balance of trade if it exported its agricultural produce and imported relatively little from the Dutch and English. Aristocrats would be permitted to engage in wholesale trade without "dérogation," the loss of rank and its privileges. Merchants would be forbidden to join in corporations and allowed to risk only a part of their personal capital. Bankrupts would face severe criminal penalties. Only bankers would be allowed to lend at interest. The *fermiers généraux* (farmers general, or tax farmers), who paid the taxes of a province for the privilege of exacting, arbitrarily, as much as they could

from that province, would be suppressed; and royal administrators would collect taxes directly on the basis of legal and uniform criteria. Accurate accounts would be established of royal income, expenses, and debts.

Fénelon's political writings read in part, but only in part, like a *cahier de doléances*, a petition for reform drawn up in the provinces for the Estates-General of 1789. Many of the reforms he proposed would have been useful, but the fundamental economic perception is, as Mousnier has shown, quite naive. Mousnier further argues that no king subject to an Estates-General dominated by aristocrats and obliged to administer (or rather judge) his realm exclusively through aristocrats and members of the higher clergy, as Fénelon had proposed, would have been able to implement the reforms that he sought; nor could the model of "agrarian socialism" or "agrarian communism" (Mousnier's descriptions) joined to the rigid social hierarchization proposed for the imaginary Salente have been transferred to the France of the years of the War of the Spanish Succession. Mousnier wittily compares Fénelon's projects for an ideal society to the stratified, authoritarian social structure of a monastery whose rationale is, needless to say, to further and to deepen the spiritual life of all its constituents, regardless of class. To Raymond it recalls Plato's republic because of the comprehensive nature of the scheme, the philosophical underpinning, its government by the most worthy and most able (without the qualification that they be aristocrats, contrary to Mousnier's claim) for the purpose of promoting the highest (that is, spiritual) interests of the population. Fénelon does not define the rights of peoples nor those of subjects. He writes in passing that they are conferred by natural law, but he does not explain how natural law can offer a special dispensation for the aristocracy, although the ancient tradition in which their privileges are established appears to be justification enough for Fénelon. He has no theory of greater or lesser civil rights equivalent to the ones that the eighteenth-century *philosophes* developed from John Locke's contractual myth of government. Although Fénelon mentions religious tolerance—there must be a connection with the *Lettres au P. Lami* (1.1), a late theological work that analyzes the autonomy and dependence of the will very subtly and impressively—the idea remains undeveloped. It may not have gone beyond a renunciation of coercion in affairs of conscience, which he had held to be useless in any event; and he still does not suggest the recall of the Huguenots from the exile to which they were dispersed when Louis XIV revoked the Edict of Nantes.

In his politics, as in his religious writings, Fénelon had the courage to proclaim one profound heresy, but not the courage or imagination to abandon most of the structures and mores of his time. He would abandon the personification of the state in the monarch and the centralization of authority that had begun again, at the close of the wars of religion, but only to return to the aristocratic privilege and decentralization of power that had already failed. The heresy itself was attractive enough to eighteenth-century liberals—rather less so to advocates of French glory and power in his time and thereafter—and certain practical reforms coincided with what would be urged by various *philosophes*, but these similarities mask fundamental differences. Fénelon was, after all, a child of his century, or at best a transitional figure, even in his "radicalism."

TÉLÉMAQUE

Télémaque achieved great popularity almost instantly. It appeared in at least fifty-one editions before 1800 and almost innumerable ones after, and it had been translated into ten European languages by 1750. One reason is surely the then prevailing impression that it was a daring *roman à clef* in which Louis XIV, Madame de Montespan, and other great personages were thinly disguised and harshly criticized. In fact, "keys" to *Télémaque* were

published soon after it appeared; and Pierre Marivaux wrote a *Télémaque travesti*. *Télémaque* must have greater qualities than that of scandal-mongering, however, because none of the many audacious satires of Louis's reign achieved anything near its dissemination and popularity. It retained its esteem during the nineteenth century, and its place in the literary repertoire can be judged from the fact that it was long deemed a suitable and attractive book to award as a prize for high-school excellence. A reaction was inevitable and in some ways well deserved. Carcassonne describes its worthy sentiments with more approval than he can muster for its literary qualities, while Varillon, normally Fénelon's most enthusiastic apologist, finds it a faded, banal sermon. Marcel Raymond is more positive, but, like Carcassonne, he admires mainly its proposals of regional federations of states to avert war, an idea that is a legitimate precursor and inspiration of the more famous eighteenth-century projects for perpetual peace, such as those offered by the abbé de Saint-Pierre, Voltaire, and Immanuel Kant, to name a few. We shall argue that *Télémaque* is an intriguing work on its own ambitious terms, though hardly a success in comparison to its great model—how many works can rival the *Odyssey*?—or to the great modern novels; so we shall not try to justify it by its worthy sentiments.

Fénelon undertook to extend the fourth book of the *Odyssey* (which concludes Telemachus' search for his father) for the pleasure and edification of the fourteen-year-old duc de Bourgogne. Télémaque, like his royal reader, advances from naive adolescence to vigorous manhood by experiencing the moral and political diversity of his Mediterranean world and especially by learning how to recognize his own faults and weaknesses, and how to survive his triumphs. That experience and recognition permit him to appreciate the generally traditional precepts that accompany each episode. In this way he is prepared by the goddess Athena, in the guise of his elderly tutor, Mentor, with the political skills and personal qualities that he will require when the time comes to succeed his father as ruler of Ithaca. Thus *Télémaque* is fundamentally a Bildungsroman, a novel of a young man's intellectual and sentimental education, imposed upon the form of the picaresque novel inherited from the *Odyssey*. The irreverent and bawdy elements of the picaresque form would not have suited Fénelon's intentions and would surely have disgusted him. They are replaced by elements of the classical epic, which is really an entirely different literary structure, and by the rich Homeric mythology and folklore that at least suit the pretext of the novel. Its conflicting structures and intentions prevented a complete success, and a lack of confidence in novelistic portrayal (or perhaps a shrewd awareness of a lack of talent in that area) induced a heavy burden of moral exhortation and commentary. This failed, ambitious attempt is more interesting (though admittedly less satisfying) than many more adequately realized modest designs.

The *Odyssey*, into which *Télémaque* fits like an interjection, is not an epic in the same sense as the *Iliad*. It is a collection of tales and adventures, Ulysses' voyages and trials during his perilous and prolonged return from the Greek victory at Troy. By his wisdom, courage, and perseverance (and by the timely interventions of Athena) he survives and surmounts them all to return to his realm, reclaim his throne, and be reunited with his now grown son, his faithful wife, and his aged father. The theme of trial and testing, more appropriate to a mature hero like Odysseus who has already acquired precept and experience, is carried over into Télémaque's story. In the eighteenth (and last) book, Athena reveals herself and explains that the trials and suffering he endured during the search for his father were themselves the object of his voyage. André Blanc argues that this is the "way of purgation," a necessary and inherently valuable experience that must precede the "way of illumination," the theophany represented by his uncomprehending meeting with his father. It is an at-

tractive idea, a reading of Fénelon's religious schema back into the large structure of *Télémaque*, but Athena explains the very pragmatic, and exclusively moral, purposes of Télémaque's travail: the experience of suffering was necessary in order to understand others' humanity and weaknesses, while the acquisition of patience was necessary in order to rule wisely. The homecoming and reconciliation that provide the classical (and ever so satisfying) resolution of a tale of trial and suffering are suppressed as inappropriate to *Télémaque*. Homer had already, and incomparably, described Ulysses' triumphant return and touching reunion with his family. Fénelon could only paraphrase it, and he nowhere paraphrases Homer. The suitable ending for his novel would have been Télémaque's succession to his father's throne and his wise government of Ithaca, but it would have been for the duc de Bourgogne to write such an ending with his own career, had it not been cut short. More fundamentally, perhaps, Fénelon is so profoundly committed to the disappropriation of virtues, even those that must be practiced, that he could not portray the pride of accomplishment or the satisfaction of human reconciliation. That is the stuff of the great comedies, such as *A Midsummer Night's Dream*.

Whereas earlier European epics depicted a narrow range of themes, mostly the missions and battles of aristocratic heroes, all the elements consecrated by the classical epic appear in *Télémaque*: on the mythological plane Fénelon portrays councils of the gods, amorous nymphs and vengeful goddesses, and even a descent into Hades and a tour of the Elysian Fields; on the human plane he includes voyages and shipwrecks, hunts and contests of arms, song and wisdom, battles and sexual temptations. One element of the heroic tradition becomes Fénelon's real subject: the founding of cities by hero-kings and the establishment of their constitutions by philosophers and prophets like Solon and Numa. Thus Mentor gives a comprehensive constitution for Idoménée's Salente, while the fictional, heroic persona adopted as a disguise by Ulysses in book 18 is in search of a kingdom to found and to govern. That Fénelon could identify so many elements of the epic tradition testifies to the sympathy and intelligence with which he read the classics; and the fact that he transformed them into situations that could be exploited for purposes of his Christian pedagogy testifies to his ingenuity. Where the requirements of his epic took him beyond his own experience, as in combat scenes and maritime episodes, his classical models filled the gap. But even the most eloquent models were not sufficient to permit him to treat sex with the grace and casualness of the classics. Or rather he refused to imitate them (except, possibly, in the fourth book, where Venus appears to Télémaque in a dream as the temptress in a tableau of "Sacred and Profane Love") because love and sex are always negative qualities: they induce anxiety, worry, and jealousy, destroying the tranquillity that is a man's highest licit personal ambition. Classical tradition was hardly mute regarding these negative aspects of sex and love, yet Fénelon does not appear to have drawn upon its models for them, except for Phaedra, as represented by Racine, who is clearly the model for the spiritually and physically disfigured Calypso.

In itself, a transformation of the elements of classical mythology into representations of Christian theology is not original. The classical gods survived the Middle Ages in various demonic forms, but after the Renaissance, they were pressed into more varied iconographic and literary service all over Europe and were even travestied into Christian allegories, or regarded as echoes or corrupt imitations of Christian doctrine. What is so singular about Fénelon's novel is his success in re-creating the Homeric ambiance (with the addition of biblical orientalisms) on the physical, geographical, and even formal planes, while putting his Homeric tale in the service of a pedagogy quite opposed to the Homeric spirit. It is clear that Fénelon tried to write an evangelical-political epic, a coordination

rather than a subordination of classical to Christian themes. As a result he was obliged to transcend the profound anomaly of having explicitly elevated the king and his legislation and defense of the state to the preeminent dignity that politics and military participation enjoyed in Greece and Rome, while being inhibited, as an inevitable consequence of his choice of literary form and pretext, from expressing an equally strong concern for personal salvation or the value of a retreat from worldliness. The classical epic celebrates heroism and leadership in worldly affairs. Fénelon could deform it to the extent of showing how a Christian may comport himself when he must take an effective role in politics, but to force the epic to celebrate a retreat from the world would have been to vitiate or to travesty it. Besides, Fénelon was the theorist of the coordination of pure love with worldly duties, despite Bossuet's complaints about the passivity induced by quietism, and only occasionally does he celebrate the cloistered life. Thus he insists upon the theme of the king's disinterest and disappropriation in the performance of his duties—it obviously derives from the theory of pure love—as a way of reconciling the worldliness of the epic form with his version of the Christian ethic. The same opposition expresses itself in other contradictions. He is obliged to portray Homeric "simplicity" as an asceticism that is foreign to Homer. The *Odyssey* includes many scenes of aristocratic generosity and others that depict exchanges of rich and ingeniously fashioned gifts, while the great eighteenth book of the *Iliad* describes Hephaistos forging the incomparably rich shield of Achilles. Other Christian structures of thought betray the integrity of Fénelon's classical setting, not that he was really trying to forge a Homeric epic in any event. In book 3, for instance, Télémaque is spared when the royal mistress, Astarbé, substitutes for him an effeminate young man who had spurned her; this young man, like Jesus, dies an innocent's redemptive death.

In books 4 and 14 Télémaque achieves ecstatic visions. In the first, Venus represents the godhead and Télémaque recounts that

> my senses were constricted and suspended; I tasted a profound peace and joy which intoxicated my heart. All of a sudden I believed that I saw Venus who rent the clouds in her chariot drawn by two doves. She had that sparkling beauty, that vibrant youthfulness, those loving graces. . . . Smilingly she put her hand upon my shoulder and pronounced these words, "Young Greek, you are about to enter my empire; you will soon arrive at that fortunate island where pleasure, laughter, and amorous play are born under my gaze. There you will burn incense upon my altars; there you will plunge yourself in a river of delights. Open your heart to the sweetest hopes, and take care that you do not resist the most powerful of the goddesses. . . ."
>
> (Goré ed., p. 125)

From passivity to nonresistance to the flood of grace that is offered—just the itinerary that Fénelon had prescribed in his theological works for whoever would arrive at the illuminative state. This, however, is profane love, easily visualized, and thus an apt stand-in for the godhead; Fénelon immediately counters it with a more appropriate representation, the vision of sacred love in the person of Athena, whose beauty is "simple, casual, modest; everything about her was grave, vigorous, noble, full of force and majesty." She turns aside Cupid's arrow from her protégé.

The second episode clearly represents the unitive experience for which Fénelon yearned and hardly dared imagine (literally, find images for) in his formal theological treatises. Télémaque has passed through the fearful Tartarus by virtue of his own valor and, when necessary, Athena's encouragement (Fénelon's *Inferno*). Theoretically at least he has undergone a purging of his own psyche while witnessing the torments of the damned—actually, unlike Dante, he shows no compassion for the suffering of the kings whose sins might yet become his own; the little prig merely draws the correct lessons—and comes upon

the virtuous kings of antiquity in their merited bliss. The Elysian Fields are a

> happy abode of peace . . . where a pure and soft light enfolds the bodies of the just and surrounds them with its rays like a garment. That light is quite unlike the dark one which illuminates the eyes of miserable mortals and which is only shadow; it is a celestial glory rather than a light; it penetrates the thickest bodies more swiftly than the rays of the sun penetrate the purest crystal; it never blinds; on the contrary, it strengthens the eyes and brings a certain serenity to the depths of the soul. . . . An eternal youth, an endless felicity, an entirely divine glory is registered upon their features, but their joy has nothing amorous or indecent about it; it is a soft, noble, quite majestic joy; it is a sublime taste for truth and virtue which moves them. Uninterruptedly, at every moment, [they feel a joy] . . . which never escapes them; it never languishes; it is always new for them; they experience the ecstasy of intoxication without its uneasiness and obtuseness. . . . They recall with pleasure those sad but brief years when they had to resist themselves and the torrent of corrupt men in order to become good; they admire the help of the gods who led them, as though by the hand, through all those perils, toward virtue. Something indefinably divine flows ceaselessly through their hearts; it is as though a torrent of divinity unites itself to them; they see, they taste, they are happy, and they feel that they will be so eternally.
>
> (bk. 14, p. 397)

No, not quite the rapture of the thirty-third canto of the *Paradiso*. What we have is unity rather than illumination here; one recognizes mystical theory and personal desiderata ("peace," "serenity," "tranquility" rather than mystical experience). Fénelon's rapturous hymns of illumination are found in the *Treatise* where he prays in his own voice. But still, how remarkable a vision in the rationalist, rhetorical belles-lettres of seventeenth-century France.

Télémaque's prose, which Varillon finds so faded, is most extraordinary for the period. Fénelon enriches his already highly nuanced prose with elements of language and style drawn from his beloved Greek and Latin poetry. He must have expected that much of the reader's pleasure would lie in recognizing the sources of his plot, the references of his metaphors, and the originals of the elegant and figurative expressions out of which he confected his novel, while admiring how he still maintains a uniformity of style and tone all his own and bends it all to the objective of royal pedagogy. If we must now read an annotated *Télémaque* in order to identify the models in Homer, Vergil, Ovid, and Horace, then, through our own fault, two important aesthetic elements of *Télémaque,* the pleasure of recognition and the admiration of ingenuity, must always escape us. Fénelon uses epithets and indulges in long, lovely metaphors. He displays a palette of primary colors (even that is extraordinary in a period when writers refused to describe appearances) and permits himself the leisure to describe nature and human scenes at luxurious length. Here is Venus preparing to implore Jupiter to avenge the slight that Télémaque offered her when he disdained the amorous celebration of her rites on Cyprus:

> Venus appeared with all the charm that is born in her breast; her floating dress had greater magnificence than all the colors with which Iris adorns herself amidst the dark clouds when she comes to promise fearful mortals the end of a tempest and to announce the return of fair weather. Her dress was girded by that famous sash upon which all the graces appeared; the goddess's hair was knotted casually behind her head with a golden braid. All the gods were surprised by her beauty as though they had never seen it before; and their eyes were dazzled by it, just as are those of mortals when Phoebus, after a long night, comes to shine his rays.
>
> (bk. 8, p. 216)

The combination of elements of classical prosody, description by litotes (denials of negative qualifications), the effect produced in an observer, and intensive use of adjectives that are normative and nouns that have exchanged their primary, specific references for normative connotations (*éclat, charmes*), with relatively pictorial descriptions (Venus' dress floating behind her, her hair knotted behind her head with a gold braid), is distinctively Fénelonian.

Outside *Télémaque* Fénelon was still inclined to describe scenes when the circumstances permitted. In "Parrhasius et Poussin" (*Dialogues des morts* 52) he describes a Poussin landscape, figures, colors, plants, and movement, with relatively few adjectives that carry value judgments, and in "Léonard de Vinci et Poussin" (*Dialogues des morts* 53) a painting is described with still greater precision and the strategy of the relationships between the poses and expressions of the figures is sympathetically discovered, a piece of description and art criticism that would not be out of place in Denis Diderot's *Salons.* Even in Fénelon's ecclesiastical tracts the language is fluid and graceful. Raymond and Carcassonne admit that there is something not quite polished and finished in all of Fénelon's works, as though he lacked the vanity or ultimate degree of artistry to apply the finishing touches to such mundane acts as writing for his own or readers' pleasure. We suspect that the slight awkwardness and redundancy in his prose to which they must refer may derive from an unwillingness to desist from glossing poetic metaphors that explain and familiarize religious experience with the correlative theological term or qualification. The result is an impression of constant redundancy and lack of sinew. Still, in comparison with the other great prose artists of his time, Bossuet, Madame de Sévigné, and Madame de La Fayette, Fénelon's prose struck his readers as absolutely luxuriant (René Pomeau quotes Madame Roland's testimony to the sensuality of Fénelon's prose, and she is a late-eighteenth-century admirer of Rousseau), on a level with the imagination that tried to penetrate the profoundest of God's secrets, his own essence.

What is most curious about *Télémaque* are its intimations of eighteenth-century writers. The emphasis on the variety of states and the diversity of principles of government anticipates Montesquieu, who developed the same theme in the *Esprit des lois (Spirit of Laws)*. Unlike Fénelon, he did not assume that Christian ethics ought to determine the large lines of statecraft. The insistence on pastoral, agrarian simplicity as an ethical norm is a foretaste of Jean Jacques Rousseau, although his point of departure was secular rather than religious. The portrait of Télémaque as a young man with a youth's uncertainties, temptations, and shames ("la mauvaise honte") anticipates Rousseau's *Confessions*. A passage like the opening of the eighth book, which describes the earth as seen from Olympus as a little heap of mud ("un petit amas de boue"), might have come from Voltaire's *Micromégas* (ch. 7). Of course the contexts are different; Voltaire deals in a satirical change of scale while Fénelon's passage is clearly a religious proposition inspired by Psalms 2:4 ("He that sitteth in heaven laugheth, the Lord hath them in derision"): "The immortals laugh at the affairs which agitate weak mortals the most, which appear to them as though they were children's games. What men call grandeur, glory, power, subtle politics, appear to these supreme divinities to be nothing but misery and weakness." And many other isolated expressions were caught up by one eighteenth-century writer or another; after all, they were brought up on *Télémaque*.

Yet it was not enough to commit seventeenth-century heresy to become a real eighteenth-century *philosophe*. Superficially, there is much that Fénelon holds in common with the eighteenth-century critics of Louis XIV's absolutism and of Bossuet's rationalistic dogmatism. When they were of a mind to look for ancestors within the French intellectual tradition and thus for assurance and authority for their own positions, there was always something effectively progressive in Fénelon that the *philosophes* could appropri-

ate. If one does not look too closely, it is easy to share their illusion that the "chimerical" bishop was really one of their own, just a little too early and too timid. Similarly, it would have been plausible to associate Fénelon with the first (and possibly mythical) generation of 1960's flower-children. He too preached gaiety of spirit, letting go, abandoning oneself, letting the grace of God enter unimpeded to stimulate works of charity.

We have argued that these are only partial convergences of the consequences of radically different assumptions, not only in religion but in ethics as well. Obedience in religion and duty in ethics remained fundamental for Fénelon even though the motivations to induce their pursuit are no longer to be found in the ego. In the eighteenth century Bernard Mandeville and many others preached the doctrine that separate and even competing wills and interests would prove compatible and induce general social well-being, while regarding asceticism and annihilation of self as socially counterproductive. Fénelon's proposition is quite the contrary—that will and self are the basis of conflict and despotism and that their suppression is necessary for any (spiritual) amelioration of the human condition. His conception of the spiritual objective to which each person must strive of his own volition or be impelled by the state leaves as little room for individual liberty as did the religious policy of Louis XIV and Bossuet, and his definitions of civic duties are not subject to revision in the light of political reality. The century to come would have a much more pragmatic approach to liberty and social policy.

Selected Bibliography

EDITIONS

INDIVIDUAL WORKS

Les aventures de Télémaque. 2 vols. Edited by Albert Cahen. Paris, 1927. Critical, annotated edition.

——————. Edited by Jeanne-Lydie Goré. Paris, 1968.

Ecrits et lettres politiques. Edited by C. Urbain. Paris, 1920.

Explication des articles d'Issy. Edited by Albert Cherel. Paris, 1915.

Explication des maximes des saints sur la vie intérieure. Edited by Albert Cherel. Paris, 1911.

Fénelon inédit d'après les documents de Pistoie. Edited by E. Jovy. Vitry-le-François, 1917.

Fénelon métaphysicien. Edited by E. Griselle. Paris, 1904.

Fénelon. Pages nouvelles pour servir à l'étude de quiétisme avant 1694. Edited by M. Langlois. Paris, 1934.

Le gnostique de Saint Clément d'Alexandrie. Edited by Paul Dudon. Paris, 1930.

Lettre à l'Académie. Edited by Ernesta Caldarini. Geneva, 1970.

"Mémoires sur l'état passif." In Jeanne-Lydie Goré, *La notion de l'indifference chez Fénelon.* Paris, 1956.

"La nature de l'homme expliquée par les simples notions de l'être en générale." Edited by E. Griselle. In *Revue de philosophie* 4:23–50, 574–597; 5:64–89 (1904).

"Premières explications [des articles d'Issy]." In *Revue Bossuet* (1906), pp. 176–220.

"Traité sur l'autorité de Cassien." In Jeanne-Lydie Goré, *La notion de l'indifference chez Fénelon.* Paris, 1956.

COLLECTED WORKS

Oeuvres de M. François de Salignac de La Mothe-Fénelon. 9 vols. Paris, 1781–1792. Includes Querebeuf's life of Fénelon.

Oeuvres complètes de Fénelon. 35 vols. Versailles, 1820–1830.

Oeuvres de Fénelon. . . . 3 vols. Paris, 1835.

Oeuvres complètes de Fénelon. . . . 10 vols. Paris, 1848–1852. The so-called Saint-Sulpice edition.

Note: None of the above editions is complete, and all but the 1835 edition omit the *Explication des maximes des saints,* one of the few works published in Fénelon's lifetime.

Oeuvres. Edited by Jacques LeBrun. Paris, 1983. The Pléiade edition.

SELECTED WORKS

Brémond, Henri, ed. *Les plus belles pages de Fénelon.* Paris, 1930.

Varillon, S. J., François, ed. *Fénelon: Oeuvres spirituelles. Introduction et choix de textes.* Paris, 1954.

TRANSLATIONS

The most important of Fénelon's theological treatises have never been translated. To date there is no modern translation of *Télémaque.*

Dialogues on Eloquence. Translated by W. S. Howell. Princeton, 1951.

Fénelon on Education. Translated by H. C. Bernard. Cambridge, 1966.

A Guide to True Peace . . . Compiled from the Writings of Fénelon, Madame Guyon and Molinos. New York and London, 1946.

CORRESPONDENCE

Correspondance. 11 vols. Edited by A. Caron. Paris, 1827–1829. A supplement to the Versailles 1820–1830 edition.

Correspondance de Fénelon. 5 vols. to date. Edited by Jean Orcibal. Paris, 1972–1976. Correspondence, annotations, reestablished chronology, many valuable appendices.

Letters from Cambrai, Written to the Countess de Montberon. Translated by M. W. Stillman. Cornwall-on-Hudson, 1949.

Letters of Love and Counsel. Selected and translated by J. McEwen. New York, 1964.

HISTORICAL STUDIES

Adam, Antoine. *Histoire de la littérature française au XVIIe siècle.* Paris, 1949–1956. Vol. 5, ch. 5.

Armogathe, Jean Robert. *Le quietisme.* Paris, 1973.

Havens, George R. *The Age of Ideas: From Reaction to Revolution in Eighteenth-Century France.* New York, 1955. Ch. 3.

Hazard, Paul. *La crise de conscience européenne 1680–1715.* Paris and Berlin, 1934. Pp. 264–265, 398–408.

Rothkrug, Lionel. *Opposition to Louis XIV: The Political and Social Origins of the French Enlightenment.* Princeton, 1965. Pp. 249–298.

Sarafian, Kevork Avedis. *French Educational Theorists.* Los Angeles, 1933.

Tilly, Arthur. *The Decline of the Age of Louis XIV.* Cambridge, 1929. Ch. 8.

CRITICAL STUDIES

Adler, Alfred. "Fénelon's *Télémaque:* Intention and Effect." In *Studies in Philology* 55:591–602 (1958).

de la Bedoyère, Michael. *The Archbishop and the Lady.* London, 1956.

Blanc, André. "Au dernier livre du *Télémaque:* Rencontre du Père ou passage du divin." In *Revue d'histoire littéraire de la France* 5:699–706 (1980).

Brémond, Henri. *Apologie pour Fénelon.* Paris, 1910.

Carcassonne, Ely. *État présent des travaux sur Fénelon.* Paris, 1939.

————. *Fénelon: L'Homme et l'oeuvre.* Paris, 1946.

Cherel, Albert. *Fénelon au XVIIIe siècle: Son prestige, son influence.* Paris, 1917.

————. *Fénelon ou la religion du pur amour.* Paris, 1934.

Cognet, Louis. *Crépuscule des mystiques.* Tournai, 1958.

Cosentini, John W. "The Literary Art of Fénelon's *Dialogues des morts.*" In *Thought Patterns* 6:29–61 (1959).

Davis, James H., Jr. *Fénelon.* Boston, 1979.

Dédeyan, Charles. *Le "Télémaque" de Fénelon.* Paris, 1958.

Delplanque, A. *Fénelon et la doctrine de l'amour pur d'après sa correspondance avec ses principaux amis.* Lille, 1907.

————. *Fénelon et ses amis.* Gabalda, 1910.

Douen, O. *L'Intolérance de Fénelon.* Paris, 1872.

"Fénelon et le tricentenaire de sa naissance." *XVIIe siècle.* Bulletin of the Société d'étude du XVIIe siècle. Nos. 12, 13, 14 (1951–1952). See in particular essays by Gabriel Joppin and Roland Mousnier.

Goré, Jeanne-Lydie. *L'Itinéraire de Fénelon: Humanisme et spiritualité.* Paris, 1957.

Gouhier, Henri. *Fénelon philosophe.* Paris, 1977.

Griselle, E. *Fénelon: Études historiques.* Paris, 1911.

Haillant, Marguerite. *Fénelon et la prédication.* Paris, 1969.

Henk, Hellenaar. *Fénelon et les jésuites.* The Hague, 1967.

Janet, Paul. *Fénelon.* Paris, 1982.

Joppin, Gabriel. *Fénelon et la mystique du pur amour.* Paris, 1938.

Kapp, Volker. *"Télémaque" de Fénelon: La signification d'un ouvrage littéraire à la fin du siècle classique.* Études littéraires françaises 24. Paris and Tübingen, 1982.

Little, Katherine D. *François de Fénelon.* New York, 1951.

May, James L. *Fénelon: A Study.* London, 1933.

Raymond, Marcel. *Fénelon.* Paris, 1967.

Sanders, E. K. *Fénelon: His Friends and His Enemies 1651–1715.* London, 1901.

Varillon, François. *Fénelon et le pur amour.* Paris, 1957.

BERTRAM EUGENE SCHWARZBACH

GIOVANNI BATTISTA VICO
(1668–1744)

T HE LIFE OF Giovanni Battista (often referred to as Giambattista) Vico is inseparable from his masterwork, *Scienza nuova
(New Science)*, which he published in 1725,
when he was forty-seven. He had contem-
plated such a work for at least a quarter of a
century. From 1699, he tells us in his autobiography, "Vico was agitating in his mind a
theme both new and grand, to unite in one
principle all knowledge human and divine."
This search for a modern synthesis of ancient
and modern "wisdom" *(sapientia)* dominated
his thought for the remaining forty-five years
of his life. The culmination of his quest—
though not its fulfillment, which he never
quite reached—came in the first version of his
book, entitled *Principles of a New Science
Concerning the Nature of Nations, By Which
Are Recovered the Principles of Another System of the Natural Law of Nations.* Except for
the striking impact of the words "new science," reminiscent of Galileo's great work,
the book might well have been known by the
first word of Vico's title: for his purpose was
to do for the human past what Isaac Newton
had done for the physical world (in his *Principia mathematica*, 1687), that is, to fashion a
principia of history.

In this epoch-making enterprise Vico was
unwavering but not quite single-minded. He
followed a circuitous and often unmarked

course, sometimes losing his bearings, doubling back to find the right path, yet never
doubting that his instincts were sound and his
final judgments correct. In fact the pattern of
his own life, as he reconstructed it in his *Vita
(Autobiography*, 1725–1728), was congruent
in many ways with the philosophy of history
that he proposes in his *New Science*, published almost simultaneously with the *Autobiography;* and the "principles" he adopted
apply equally to his life and his works. The
first of these principles is, appropriately, to
begin at the beginning: just as a natural process has to be studied from its beginning and
a historical process followed from its source,
so an individual life, and especially the life of
a mind, had to be understood genetically. It is
a common but most un-Vichian and ultimately misleading view that tries to define Vico's thought through a static and logical analysis of the mature phase of his "new science";
for according to Vico's own axioms, nature is
nothing more than "coming into being in certain times and in certain guises," and, even
more fundamentally, "doctrines must take
their beginning from that of the matters of
which they treat." Vico's own nature cannot
be understood apart from his original character or "genius."

It was a principle of Vico's cultural history
that "Providence . . . aroused human minds
first to topics rather than to criticism." In history, as in science, the movement is from ex-

perience to reason, and so it is also with individual education. Vico began his own learning, as he did his teaching, with "topical knowledge" and the arts of language, moving only later to rational criticism and conceptualizing. In terms of his larger intellectual heritage, this meant that Vico grounded himself first in the tradition of humanist scholarship and then proceeded, through ancient, medieval, and modern philosophy, to give systematic form to his learning. "Experience plus reason equals science" is the equation of Francis Bacon's *New Organon* (1620). Vico agrees in principle, but with his humanist orientation he reformulates it as "philology plus philosophy equals the new science." To complete the formula properly, it should be added, one ought to insert the essential but imponderable factor of Providence, for Vico makes divinity both the beginning and the end of the process of human history.

"The Vico road," in James Joyce's phrase, marks a quixotic journey. It begins with the most fantastic etymological and mythological speculations—giving philosophical form to philological "topics" through "criticism"—and ends with a most elaborate system, one that displays features of both Roman jurisprudence and Euclidean, or rather Cartesian, geometry. At first glance it looks less like a road than the invention of a pedantic madman—a grotesque, rococo summa of Western learning. Later, especially to those infected with Vico's eclecticism and conceptual virtuosity, its depth may impress more than its surface, and it may appear rather as a bottomless well of disciplines not even imagined in his time—cultural anthropology, sociology of knowledge, philosophical hermeneutics, and others. In any case his work is pivotal in the history of thought, looking forward as well as backward, both richly endowed and extraordinarily seminal; and it deserves attention both more and less respectful than it has usually received: more respectful of its pattern of historical development, less respectful of the fanciful and worshipful interpretations that it has

accumulated since the days of Hegel and especially Benedetto Croce. First impressions count: it *is* a sort of latter-day version of Saint Thomas Aquinas' *Summa.* But sympathetic wishful readings should not be dismissed either: it is also a fountain of cultural insight and speculation that has survived to the present day. Still, its nature must be understood on its own original terms.

II

Vico has given us his own life story, but he has reshaped it to suit a retrospective view of his curious intellectual development. Like the *Education of Henry Adams,* the *Autobiography of Giambattista Vico* gives us a highly stylized account of a highly eccentric mind. Vico was born in Naples on 23 June 1668 (he errs by giving the year as 1670). At the age of seven (possibly, it has been suggested, while reaching for a book in his father's shop) he fell on his head and was unconscious for five hours or more. Although his doctor predicted that he would either die or sustain permanent damage, it would be unkind to suggest that this misfortune had a major impact on Vico's thought. Yet it was the first event of his life that he felt was significant enough to mention; if nothing else, it interrupted his studies and forced him to become his own teacher for some three years before returning to school. It marked his first departure from a conventional course of education, hence the first phase of his growing intellectual independence; to this extent he never fully recovered from his fall.

In the castle of Cilento at Valtolla, too, where Vico worked for nine years (1686–1695) as tutor in the household of the bishop of Ischia, Geronimo della Rocca, he continued his solitary habits of study. He continued to be an autodidact and was proud of it; his genius was as impenetrable as those of the cultures he came to study. Later he "blessed his good fortune in having no teacher whose words he had sworn by." Nor was he to have, at least for some generations, disciples who would swear by his words. He was used to being alone in his opinions, out of step with his times, and, as he put it, "a stranger in his own land."

The model for Vico's autobiography was René Descartes's vastly influential *Discourse on Method* (1637). Descartes likewise rehearsed the stages of his education in order to introduce his own system of thought. But it was a negative model for Vico: he disapproved of the invidious judgments that Descartes passed on certain disciplines, especially the humanities and the study of history, and he despised Descartes's obsession with mathematics. Vico writes in the autobiography:

> We shall not here feign what René Descartes feigned as to the method of his studies simply in order to exalt his own philosophy and mathematics and degrade all other studies included in divine and human erudition. Rather, with the candor proper to a historian, we shall narrate plainly and step by step the entire series of Vico's studies, in order that the proper and natural causes of his particular development as a man of letters may be known.
>
> (Fisch and Bergin trans., p. 113)

Vico, too, had his intellectual priorities, and they were strikingly different from those of Descartes. In particular he rejected analytical geometry, the very paradigm of Cartesian method, as "proper to minute wits": "So he gave up this study as one that chained and confined his mind . . . and in the constant reading of orators, historians, and poets his intellect took increasing delight in observing between the remotest matters ties that bound them together in some common relation." Vico's *Autobiography* was not only an introduction to his "new science," it was also virtually an anti-*Discourse on Method.*

Like Descartes, Vico began his education with the Jesuits and received a somewhat premature introduction to scholastic philosophy, especially in the logical works of Peter of Spain and Paul of Venice. Much more interesting to him was the study of law, canon as well as Roman, to which he was led by a chance attendance at a lecture at the University of Naples. From the textbook of Hermann Vulteius on civil law, Vico was led both to the medieval commentators, whose rational methods made them in his eyes "philosophers of natural equity," and the humanist critics, "whom he later perceived and considered to be pure historians of the Roman civil law." This combination of philosophical and philological methods (of logical analysis and humanist textual criticism) underlay the view of jurisprudence he was to take in *On the Study Methods of Our Time* (1709) and the more systematic reworking of the legal tradition in his *One Principle and One End of Universal Law* (1720).

As he matured, Vico gained a better appreciation of scholastic philosophy, especially in the work of Francisco Suárez; but it was above all the philosophy of law, also in its scholastic form, that guided Vico's continuing search for wisdom. On the other hand legal humanism, specifically Lorenzo Valla's philological approach to Roman law, encouraged his literary interests as a youth, first Latin and then vernacular poetry; and indeed Vico was encouraged to try his own hand at versification, his "Feelings of a Desperate Man" (1692) being his first published work. At the same time his affection for philosophy increased and, since he associated Aristotle with Cartesian naturalism, Vico settled upon Plato as his ancient philosophical ideal, especially because of the social and political orientation of Plato's idealism and his notion of an "eternal law."

After nine years of the "solitude of Valtolla," Vico returned to Naples and to another kind of solitude. Intellectually he was still isolated from the philosophic mainstream, for Cartesianism reigned, and older forms of wisdom were forgotten or scorned. Nevertheless he continued his search for encyclopedic wisdom. The next decade capped what may be regarded as the humanist phase of his career. In

1699, having made a reputation as a Latin stylist, Vico competed successfully for the professorship of rhetoric at the University of Naples; and for the rest of his life this academic chair remained his abode professionally, as Naples did physically.

Vico set down his intellectual position in a series of seven academic orations (including *On the Study Methods*) delivered between 1699 and 1708. In these platitudinous addresses Vico celebrated the value of self-knowledge through encyclopedic knowledge of the cultural past and argued for the importance of these for both human virtue and the achieving of social and political ideals. Vico's assumptions about the coherence of culture appear especially in the fifth oration, which revives the old humanist theme of Mars in the company of Minerva, that is, the parallelism of excellence in science, literature, and arms in particular nations.

The classic expression of Vico's humanist philology appears in the last of these orations, *On the Study Methods of Our Time* (delivered in 1708), a late descendant of a popular Renaissance genre celebrating the cycle of liberal arts inherited from classical antiquity. Vico himself, emphasizing the "instruments," "aids," and "institutions" of modern science, preferred to place his work in the company of Bacon's *Advancement of Learning;* but his argument that moderns were superior to the ancients is most conventional, and so is his emphasis on new arts and inventions, most notably printing. "How many new arts have been devised," he marvels in a formula that had been part of the humanist litany for generations. "How many new sciences?" Nor is there anything novel about Vico's search for a proper method, pedagogical as well as scientific, for this had been a central theme of the history of learning since the sixteenth century. What is unusual about Vico's approach is its conservatism, rejecting as he does the mathematical and naturalistic values of Cartesianism. Instead, though to be sure under cover of Baconian "memory" and empiricism,

he turns back to the old tradition of Italian philology and the humanities, at least at this early stage of development. For if reason is powerful in old age, imagination and memory (in Baconian terms) predominate in youth; and so educational method should begin with "topical" knowledge—substantive and memorized instead of formal and logical. "Young men should be taught the totality of sciences and arts," Vico writes, "and their intellectual powers should be developed to the full; thus they will become familiar with the art of argument, drawn from the *ars topica*" (the forms of argument in logic and rhetoric).

For this anti-Cartesian reversal of priorities Vico had social as well as methodological grounds, for "the greatest drawback of our educational methods," he continues, "is that we pay an excessive amount of attention to the natural sciences and not enough to ethics." The result is that one of the noblest of studies, "the science of politics, lies almost abandoned and untended." Anyone concerned with public affairs, Vico adds, "should not waste too much time, in his adolescence, on those subjects that are taught by abstract geometry." It is in this connection that Vico invokes the ideal of classical antiquity, when "all arts and disciplines were interconnected and rested in the lap of philosophy," and that he returns to his favorite theme, the excellence of jurisprudence and indeed its equivalence to wisdom itself. He observes: "Notice that the same definition served the Romans for jurisprudence and the Greeks for wisdom: the knowledge of things divine and human." This theme, which plays a central role in the first version of the "new science," leads Vico first to a historical celebration of Roman law and its political ideal and then to a parallel attack on the divisiveness of doctrinal sects, whether in law, philosophy, or religion. Instead, he suggested,

Our professors should coordinate all disciplines into a single system so as to harmonize them with our religion and with the spirit of the political form under which we live. In this way, a coherent body of learning having been established, it will be possible to teach it according to the genius of our public polity.

The first level of Vico's science of humanity, then, is a philosophy of education.

The major expression of humanist or philological thought appears in his *Most Ancient Wisdom of the Italians* (1710), a work that had a precedent in Bacon's *The Wisdom of the Ancients*. Here for the first time Vico transforms the ideal of wisdom into a cultural and historical category. His basic insight is that the primitive wisdom of the Italians might be disinterred from the early remains of the Latin language, or, put differently, that ordinary linguistic expression was a vehicle of conceptual thought. Viewed historically, this implied that the true relationship between philology and philosophy was not only a tension between them but, in a longer perspective, a development from the first to the second. This fundamental historicism links Vico both with humanists such as Jean Bodin, who assumed that poetry was the first expression of philosophy, and with romantic historians such as Barthold Niebuhr, who saw poetry as an expression of national mentality.

It is in this context that Vico formulates one of his most essential principles, which is the conviction that the "true" *(verum)* and the "made" *(factum)* were equivalent in Latin: " 'Verum' et 'Factum' reciprocantur, seu . . . convertuntur." Again, the implications of this proposition are both historical and philosophical. Historically, Vico's argument is that knowledge originates in doing and that wisdom is a product of practical experience. In discussing this theory he expresses admiration for such celebrators of prudence and realism as Niccolò Machiavelli and especially Tacitus. To demonstrate and illustrate the derivation of wisdom from experience, Vico resorts to a conjectural etymology and semantics worthy of the *Etymologies* of the ingenious Saint Isidore himself, including the derivation of *auctoritas* from the Greek

autos (self) and *Jupiter* from *jus* (law). He points out, too, that the word "cause" referred at first to a piece of business (in the sense of a legal suit) and only later to a category for understanding physical or metaphysical processes (as in Aristotle's four causes). He discusses at length the origin of the idea of nature in the word for character *(ingenium)*, and the idea of soul *(anima* for the universe, *animus* for humanity) in the word for air *(aer)*. In general Vico opened up possibilities for understanding the physiological and social basis, the "factual" basis, for philosophical terms and patterns of thought.

Philosophically, the *verum-factum* principle had even profounder consequences. For one, it was the first critical formulation of Vico's anti-Cartesian epistemology. "I think, therefore I am" was empty and meaningless to Vico, and he had nothing to do with it. By contrast (though like Descartes he drew inspiration from the scholastics) Vico declares that "the criterion of truth, the rule by which we may certainly know it, is to have made it." The wise men of ancient Rome understood what Descartes did not, namely, that "truth is simply fact, what is made." Such was the message, too, of God's "word" (here Vico associates *verum* [truth] with *verbum* [word]); for God's truth also derives from the circumstance that He is the "first maker." Human science is subject to the same conditions, and so all that man can truly know is the product of his labor: artistry and, on a higher level, conceptualization, such as mathematics. Only in concrete reflection, not in abstract skepticism, can Descartes's famous "clear and distinct ideas" arise.

In the course of this argument Vico presents another and related distinction with wide implications for his later work, this one between the true and the certain. The second of these, the certain *(certum)*, corresponds to consciousness, the first only to true knowledge. Certainty is acquired through authority, whether human testimony or divine revelation, and its opposite is the doubtful. Truth on the other hand is limited to what is made by the knower or constructed rationally, and its opposite is the false. It is in this sense that Vico interprets the old Latin phrase that "to know is to understand through causes." This formula, passing from Celsus (a Roman of the second century A.D.) into civil law, was expressed more poetically (though perhaps not more famously) in Vergil's line: "Felix, qui potuit rerum cognoscere causas" (Happy is one who understands things through their causes). In a sense this piece of ancient wisdom might be taken as the motto of the whole intellectual enterprise culminating in Vico's "new science."

The Most Ancient Wisdom of the Italians, which Croce regarded as the first phase of Vico's theory of knowledge, contains a statement of his metaphysics (anti-Aristotelian as well as anti-Cartesian). Here, somewhat obscurely and perfunctorily, Vico also seeks to establish ties between the human, natural, and divine worlds. In this work the conscious and almost uncontrollable eclecticism of Vico's method is apparent. Three of the famous "four authors" of Vico are here enshrined: Tacitus for describing man as he is, Plato for contemplating him as he should be, and Bacon for his scientific method; only Hugo Grotius remained to be added. More significant for the future, however, is the imaginative use Vico makes of etymology and mythology in his efforts to discover the nature of primitive wisdom. Besides provoking controversies at the time, this book figures prominently in the elaboration of the successive stages of Vico's science of humanity. It represents the first and most fundamental way of combining philology and philosophy according to the ancient as well as modern encyclopedic ideal.

III

The second turning point in Vico's life, even more upsetting than the fall he took almost a half-century before, was his failure in the competition to gain an appointment as professor of law at the University of Naples. His account of the experience is at once comic and pathetic. He describes his assigned lecture, delivered on 10 April 1723, as a triumph of wit, strategy, and learning. His subject was the title "On Prescriptions" in the Digest (the great collection of Roman jurisprudence made by Emperor Justinian), and he displayed both his erudition and his characteristic eclecticism by defending both the medieval "Accursians" and the humanist "Alciateans." But Vico's curious learning did not carry the day, and in view of the overreaching and rather bizarre notions he had published with an eye to this chair, the decision of the university authorities may not seem surprising. "Men of limited ideas take for law what the words expressly say," Vico set down slightly later among the axioms of his "new science"; such a sentiment was not likely to please academic minds. In any case Vico remained in his chair of rhetoric, henceforth not only isolated but without chance of professional advancement. Aside from his large family, Vico had only his "scientific" vision to sustain him; and in this second phase of his development, the vehicle of his philosophical thinking was jurisprudence.

In his dream of a systematic science of humanity, Roman law had always occupied a central place. The *Corpus Juris* assembled by Justinian in the sixth century, especially the Digest, was itself a conceptual system that claimed to be the embodiment of wisdom, indeed "true philosophy," in that it was anthropocentric and oriented toward practical as well as theoretical knowledge—that is, was a *prudentia* (practical wisdom) concerned with the art of application as well as a *scientia* (science) that claimed to understand "through causes." The position of Roman law was even more conspicuous in the *Study Methods* and *Ancient Wisdom,* but it was in the aftermath of the polemics over the latter that Vico turned seriously to the study of jurisprudence.

In the course of his work on a commissioned biography of Marshal Antonio Caraffa, Vico came across Grotius' *Law of War and Peace* and saw in it at least a partial fulfillment of his demand for a modern system of universal law that combined philology and philosophy; and so he made Grotius—"the jurisconsult of mankind," Vico called him—the last of his inspirational "four authors." The Caraffa biography itself put Vico in touch with the great legal historian Vincenzo Gravina, to whose *Origins of Law* Vico was much indebted. When to these circumstances was added the incentive provided by the opening of competition for the law professorship in 1717, the consequence was the second phase of Vico's theory of knowledge, which was the first version of what he was soon to call the "new science": this was the treatise *De universi juris uno principio et fine uno liber unum* (*One Principle and One End of Universal Law*).

In this book the characteristic Vichian pattern of unity, genetically as well as teleologically ("one principle and one end"), and his insistence on "constancy" (in contrast to the inconstancy of doctrinal sects) emerge with remarkable clarity and are argued with the most scholarly ingenuity. Axiomatic in the argument is Vico's earlier distinction between reason and authority, the judicial forms of truth and certainty, which corresponds to the distinction between natural law (*jus civile*) and the law of nations (*jus gentium*). "Jurisprudence is founded on reason and authority," declares Vico in the prologue to his *Universal Law*. "Reason proceeds from the necessity of nature, authority from the will of man. Philosophy studies the necessary causes of things, whereas history [equivalent to philology] investigates individual wills." The other basic distinction is between the public and private spheres, "civil doctrine" and "moral doctrine" in the civilian (that is, Roman law) terms adopted by Vico; and the ultimate cultural unity established by the union of these two disciplines corresponds both to the "wisdom" of law and to the "science of humanity" Vico envisions.

In the *Universal Law*, Vico repeats the observation he had made a decade earlier in the *Study Methods:* "To jurisprudence the Romans gave the same definition as the Greeks gave to wisdom, 'the knowledge of things divine and human.'" For Vico this famous formula, derived from the Roman jurist Ulpian and located in the first title of the Digest, had a threefold function. First, it provided him with a vehicle for his concept of culture, the "topical" base for his science of humanity; second, it established temporally the point of departure and destination of human history, which in a collective way recapitulated individual education; and third, it fixed Roman experience as the paradigm of historical change. This had been the case with earlier Italian humanists, including Machiavelli, but Vico characteristically transformed a philological assumption into a philosophical principle.

Remember, O Romans, you keep universal rule
  over nations
In these ways: by maintaining peace through law,
By doing justice to the lowly, by bringing down
  the haughty.
(Aeneid 5.123)

These lines of Vergil, which Vico was fond of citing, symbolized also Vico's own appropriation of Roman law. For like the Vergilian epigraph, Roman law imposed universal form on history, gave new significance to barbarous nations, and placed the most exalted constructs of civilization in critical perspective. In Vico's vision of history, in short, Rome once again ruled the world of nations and established the conditions for humanity, or rather for Vico's science of humanity.

Despite the pagan base of Vico's thought, Christian theology is never far away, at least in spirit; and a fundamental trinitarianism permeates his insistence on unity. Jurisprudence itself is threefold: philosophy, history (or philology, which was the basic science of historical reconstruction), and the art of applying law to facts. Congruent, but more essential, is the famous anthropological triad set down in the prologue: *nosse* (knowledge), *velle* (will), and *posse* (power). In God these three are one, but in human nature made in His likeness they have, since man's fall, been at odds; and this is the case as well with other homologous trinities that appear later in the areas of ethics, law, and politics. It is hardly too much to say that Vico's work on universal law—the *De Uno*, as it is often called—represents Vico's three-in-one creed transposed into every level of the human world.

Of the three parts of jurisprudence, Vico is concerned with only the first two—philosophy and history-philology; and the initial problem he discusses in the inconstancy arising from the traditional disjuncture between the philological and the philosophical aspects. Greek views of the law tended to be abstract and unhistorical, whereas Roman views were unphilosophical and authoritarian; and in the "new jurisprudence" of modern tradition a similar disparity was evident between scholastic and humanist jurists, at least until the synthesis attempted by Grotius in the seventeenth century. Vico himself admired both traditions of European law, especially the philologists—scholars like Poliziano, Guillaume Budé, Andrea Alciato, and Jacques Cujas—who tried to restore the old encyclopedic ideal in legal terms. But a modern legal science—"constant character of jurisprudence" (*constantia jurisprudentiae*) is Vico's phrase—requires a reunion of both; and Vico's own efforts to force this version of the fifth-century myth of the marriage of Mercury and philology* leads directly to his "new science."

Another requirement for a universal system of law is a correlative theory of anthropology.

This is where the *nosse-velle-posse* triad comes in, especially the first member. Knowledge is the distinguishing feature of man, the basis of his mind (*mens* is the legal term adapted by Vico); also, with the help of reason and divine illumination, knowledge is the means of understanding scientific truth through causes. The "true" represents the philosophical aspect, while on the philological side, law, which depended on human authority, had to attain the level of the "certain,'' and in this connection Vico remarks on the value of rhetoric and the arts of persuasion. The point for Vico is that, in accordance with his Platonism, philosophy demands not only the light of truth, which benefits the mind, but also the fruits of virtue (*honestas*), which improve the will, second member of the anthropological trinity. At this point we may observe also the transition from a psychological to a moral level, where the corresponding triad is prudence (practical knowledge), temperance (controlled will), and fortitude (effective action). The attainment of these qualities through human and "natural" means Vico designates, significantly, as "heroic wisdom."

After moral doctrine comes civil doctrine, after ethics the law; and Vico moves, again in Platonic fashion, from virtue to justice. The cause of the founding of society was not utility, as (the Protestant) Grotius had argued; utility was merely the occasion. The true cause, according to (the Catholic) Vico, was virtue (*honestas*). Human communities arose not from sin but from the fact that man is naturally social. This fundamental truth is the very metaphysics of jurisprudence, and on it are built the two cornerstones of the science of law, the aforesaid standard of truth (*verum*) and the aim of justice, which is equity. Here, Vico has established the basis, at least to his own satisfaction, for "natural law" understood in a modern sense.

Like his contemporary Charles de Montesquieu, Vico was deeply concerned with the "spirit of the laws" (*mens legum*, another legal term to which he gave a larger philo-

---

*In Martianus Capella's *De nuptiis Philologiae et Mercurii*, Mercury gives his bride seven maidens, each of whom declaims on the one of the seven liberal arts she represents.

sophic meaning). In this concern he builds upon another long juridical tradition, the theory of interpretation, which was divided along the familiar lines of literal versus liberal construction. Like most jurists Vico inclined to believe that the life-giving spirit is superior to the letter—"To know laws is to take not the words but their power and meaning" is the formula of Celsus that Vico took as his own—but characteristically he was more indulgent than the standards of jurists would allow. Once again Vico had recourse to his old distinction between certainty (historical and philological) and truth (philosophical). The spirit of the laws (*mens legum*, but Vico also called it *certum legum*) referred simply to the will of the legislator, which is to say authority, while the "reason of the laws" (*ratio legum*) referred to their truth and scientific status.

But the overriding pattern of Vico's interpretation of law, and hence of civilization, is neither unity nor trinity; it is a regular cultural development, an original sort of historicism that has been qualified by various interpreters of Vico as linguistic, cultural, sociological, and anthropological, but that is above all juridical. Beginning with the question posed in the second title of Justinian's Digest, "On the Origin of Law," Vico tries to probe into prehistory—"obscure," "heroic," or "fabulous" times, according to Vico—through his usual etymological conjectures. In general these primitive times constituted no golden age; rather they were filled with crime and acquisitiveness, a sort of natural anarchy that was regulated first by what Vico calls "the law of private violence." Whence the legal terms for acquisition, including *mancipatio* (*res manu captae*, "things seized by hand") and *usucapio* ("by use"); whence also the notorious paternal power (*patria potestas*) of life and death, freedom and slavery, over members of the family. Originally, Vico argues, "good" (*bonus*) meant simply "strong" (*fortis*), and early institutions were founded not on reason but on will. Testimentary succession, based on heredity (from "hero"),

was itself a legal act stemming from individual "will," Vico points out, and so was the famous principle that the prince's will is law (*quod principi placuit legis habet vigorem*). In general the link was clear, and one of the first premises of Vico's legal historicism is that "familiar or domestic authority" constitutes the "first foundation of government."

The main thrust of Vico's argument, then, is expressed by the old legal maxim that law originates in facts and develops out of customs; but his elaboration of it is much more speculative and fanciful than that of professional jurists. Out of "natural authority" and that heroic form of justice called the "law of private violence" emerges another of Vico's conceptual threesomes, a triad of protolegal categories that he designates lordship, liberty, and self-defense, and that encompasses the transition from "natural" to "civil authority." One way of looking at the process of history is as a transformation of each of these from a private into a public institution, that is, into the political concepts of eminent domain, civil liberty, and sovereignty. Corresponding to each of these, too, were the three parts of human nature—knowledge, will, and power—and the other trinities of human life, which reflect the general states of leadership, independence, and force. On the political level, Vico concludes, "All republics are born out of lordship, liberty, and self-defense."

What Vico is describing here, or rather rationalizing in historical terms, is the progression of the "law of nations" (*jus gentium*), which arose first in primitive custom (*jus naturale gentium*), then was formulated in jurisprudence (*jus naturale philosophorum*), and finally is expressed scientifically by Grotius and Vico. What the emergence of lordship, liberty, and self-defense signified in the "adolescence of the human race" was the appearance, first, of the "greater nations," which arose before the establishment of governments and laws and which appear in mythology; and second, of the "lesser nations" (such as the original Romans), which appeared later and which established the "law of public violence," that is, of war and peace. These developments were the basis of the law of nations, but it was also, as Vico argues, in one of his most striking transmutations of legal convention, the basis of the feudal stage of history. It was a common view of Roman lawyers that feudal law derives from Roman law, probably from the client-patron relationship, but Vico's historicism leads him to reverse this argument: "Roman law came from feudal" (*ex feudis*, literally "from fiefs"), Vico declares, "not feudal from Roman law." European "feudalism" was simply a recurrence of the same barbaric phenomenon at a similar stage of cultural development, and in both cases the consequence was a pattern of growth, corruption, and eventually return to barbarism.

Politically, the cycle also derives from these categories; for "out of lordship, liberty, and self-defense arose the three mature forms of republics," Vico continues. Corresponding to self-defense is aristocracy, exemplified by the Roman patriciate and ruled by good customs; lordship corresponds to monarchy, for instance the "heroic kings" in Homer and the Roman prince referred to in the ancient *lex regia;* and to liberty corresponds a democracy of free citizens. In these two versions of what Vico called the "divine circle of law" appears the first statement of Vico's famous "corso-ricorso" *(cursus-recursus)* thesis elaborated later in the *New Science*.

Vico's historicism is not merely developmental, it is genetic, and he is always seeking first sources. In these archeological endeavors he resorts again to inventive etymologies, working his way, for example, from the Greek for omen or bird *(dion)* to the Latin for gods *(dii)*, to the Greek for law *(diaion)*, and finally, with a letter added, to Platonic "justice" *(dikaion);* similarly he links Roman law with Roman gods *(jus* with Jupiter). This brings us to another dimension of Vico's view of legal and social origins: its religious (at points this is all Vico means by "divine") character. Indeed the word "religio" is related not to *ligo*

(blind) but to *lego* (read), Vico argues, hence to *lex* (a written law). "The laws of nations are everywhere part of religion," he writes. The divine law of nations *(fas gentium)* was, moreover, written in heroic language and was mythical or fabulous *(fabula* from *fas)*. Only through etymology, he believes, could philologists plumb those "heroic times" and reach the "true origin." Yet in this enterprise Vico rejects the "grammatical" approach of Valla, one of the founders of legal humanism, and turns instead to a sort of divination that transcended historical scholarship and reached indeed beyond the letter to the spirit of law. For only there was the "true origin."

The true source and supreme model of *Romanitas* (Roman spirit) was the great "image of antiquity" (as Cicero called it), the law of the Twelve Tables, Rome's first written code (*ca.* 450 B.C.); and in his analysis of this alpha and omega of civil law Vico once again was carrying on a central theme of humanist scholarship, which since the sixteenth century had tried to reconstruct this monument. In this manifestation of the "heroic wisdom" of Rome, Vico recognizes three elements. The first is the divine origin and character of primitive law, which caused the founding fathers to enshroud their handiwork in secrecy and led later jurists to style themselves (in Ulpian's phrase) as "priests of the laws." Second, and correlative to this, is the poetic character of this law, which Vico later refers to as a "serious poem" because of its mythical overtones and because traditionally it was chanted. Recalling Justinian's own remark about "the fables of early law," Vico declares that "ancient jurisprudence is poetic throughout." Third, and as a function of first two, is the extreme formalism of ancient law ("As the tongue has declared so shall it be binding," Vico liked to quote from the Twelve Tables, and "When the words fail the cause is lost"), reflecting the literalism of a preconceptual period when words had a magic power. From these elements came the conservative and almost hermetic nature of Roman law and the intimidating historical force that inspired even in the reforming Justinian, as Vico recalls, a great "reverence for antiquity." "The ways of the fathers must be preserved" is the formula Vico cites, but he was thinking as well of his famous epistemological distinction. "Ancient jurisprudence," he writes, "neglected the *verum* [truth] for the *certum* [certainty]."

In this reconstruction of the spirit of Roman law Vico brings together for the first time the main ingredients of his philosophy of history. The cultural cycle begins with a "heroic wisdom" that, however obscurely, contemplates "things" both "divine and human." The poets, who formulated this wisdom, were at once the first theologians, the first historians, and the first jurists; and out of their vision comes the next stage, the "jurisprudence of the philosophers," which moves from the *certum* (certain) of civil law toward the *verum* (true) of natural law. The coherence of this process makes it impossible for Vico to conceive of appreciable influence from other cultures in the early stages of a national history, for each of the nations had its own impenetrable character *(ingenium)*. Hence he rejects the account given in the Digest about the trip made by the *decemviri* (the ten designated legislators) to consult with the wise men of Athens before drawing up the law of the Twelve Tables. The "wisdom" of Greece was philosophy, that of Rome jurisprudence; the two were parallel but fundamentally independent. His conception of feudalism as a congruent but separate stage in all national histories is perhaps the most familiar example of Vico's theory of separate but congruent cycles. Within this framework Vico presents his impressionistic sketch of Roman legal history.

How would it all come out? After the poetic and philosophical stages comes the third part of the cycle, which was that "constant" form of jurisprudence produced by the fusion of philology (corresponding to poetry) and philosophy. So the poetic and religious mind would be reconstructed and wisdom reconstituted in historical form. Vico writes in the *Universal Law:*

> So turns the circle of divine law. As all human law begins with divine law, so, by the succession of things that we have followed, it returns to divine law. And as society was begun among men by God through that succession of the law of the major nations, common civil law, and the law of the minor nations through war, so it endures in God himself.
>
> *(Diritto universale* 1.156)

Vico's life task was to reconstruct this "circle of divine and human erudition," this higher wisdom that, he concludes, would also be a mystical reuniting of the human trinity: knowledge, will, and power.

To this almost Dantesque vision Vico devotes the second part of his *Universal Law,* called the "Constancy of Jurisprudence" (1721), which is directed against certain old-fashioned critics of the first part. From the "constancy of philosophy" (the first subsection) he moves to the "constancy of philology," and it is in that subsection finally that "the new science is essayed." In an unusually clear statement of his new scientific method Vico also reveals the extent of his debt to humanist scholarship. He explains:

> Philology is the study of speech, and it treats of words and their history, shows their origin and progress, and so determines the ages of languages, thus displaying their properties, changes, and conventions. But since the ideas of things are represented by words, philology must first treat the history of things. Whence it appears that philologists must study human governments, customs, laws, institutions, intellectual disciplines, and the mechanical arts.
>
> *(Diritto universale* 2.2.1)

If mathematics is the language of the book of nature, as Galileo taught in his "new science," philology is indispensible for anyone who hopes to read the book of humanity; from here Vico proceeds to a scheme of universal chronology. The fulfillment of this scheme in terms of historical understanding depended, Vico believed, on the union of those twin disciplines, etymology and mythology; and this in turn would begin the reunion of philology and philosophy, which Cartesians had alienated. This was the necessary precondition both of the "constancy of jurisprudence" and of its offspring, the "new science."

The remainder of Vico's *Universal Law* treats the structure and composition (*complexio*) of universal history. Although many of the terms and ideas are conventional, Vico arranges them with his irrepressible virtuosity. He makes the usual distinction between "sacred" and "profane" history but, characteristically, arranges them chronologically. Sacred history he divides into four periods: creation, the flood, Abraham, and Moses. This was in effect the time of prehistory, of sacred law. The transition to profane history begins with the rudiments of secular law, inaugurating the terrain of the "new science," which Vico here calls the "dark ages" of human history.

Vico divides profane history into five epochs. First came a theocratic period under divine authority, expressed most notably in the Mosaic law, accompanied by the development of familial institutions under paternal power. Second was the emergence of clientele and feudal arrangements out of the family. Third was the rise of aristocracy in the "major nations," including the beginnings of civil law and its protecting gods. Fourth was the corruption of the optimate order, succeeded by the rise of kingship and democracy and the transition from the "major" to the "minor" nations. Fifth was the introduction of war and imperial expansion and with these the development of the law of nations. The *complexio* of this historical panorama Vico sees best understood in terms of the Egyptian scheme of three world ages—that of the gods, that of heros, and finally that of man. With these observations Vico returns to the law of the Twelve Tables to conclude the *Universal Law.*

With the completion of this system, derivative of Roman law, the stage is set, philosophically as well as philologically, for the major phase of Vico's "new science."

IV

Reactions to the *Universal Law* were mixed. Vico received an admiring letter from Jean Leclerc, who praised his "mathematical method" and his mastery of philosophy, law, and philology. Lesser-minded critics, however, objected both to the chaotic form and to the curious and unfamiliar methods of the argument. In 1722 Vico responded in a set of published "Notes." These efforts were all directed at attaining a position on the law faculty, but Vico's eccentric and self-indulgent speculations in fact reduced his chances. In his lecture on prescription, on which he had worked the night before until five in the morning amid the conversation of friends and the cries of children, Vico tried to behave more professionally. Unexpectedly, he made no attempt to base his interpretation on his *Universal Law;* but he was so disorganized that his hour was up before he was able to discuss the most important commentator on the title. This confusing performance ended Vico's chances for professional advancement; but, fortunately for posterity, it also sent him back, with renewed vigor, to his historical and philological work.

In terms of his intellectual development, in fact, Vico was already finding a better vehicle than the law for his "new science," and was on the way, in particular, to what he would call his "discovery of the true Homer." Already in the "Notes" to his *Universal Law* he was launched into the study of the Homeric poems, to the extent indeed that in his mind they were replacing the Twelve Tables as the great monument of ancient wisdom. As he broadened his scope to encompass Greek culture, so he turned from Latin to the vernacular to formulate his "new science" as a genuinely international and intercultural discipline.

In 1725, two years after his professional hopes had been dashed and after he wrote an abortive (and now lost) essay often referred to as the "New Science in a negative form," the first version of his masterwork was published. "History does not yet have its principles," Vico had written five years earlier, but in the meantime he had gone far toward a remedy. At the same time Vico was working on his *Autobiography*, responding to a request for a contribution to a collection of autobiographies by contemporary Italian scholars; and it is not surprising that this work is largely a historical portrayal of the evolution of the "new science." "By the light of this new critical method," Vico writes in the *Autobiography*, "the origins of almost all the disciplines, whether arts or sciences, which are necessary if we are to discuss with clarity of ideas and propriety of language the natural law of nations, are discovered to be quite different from those that have previously been imagined." Then he proceeds to outline the principal features of his work. He remained dissatisfied with it, however, because it still did not achieve the synthesis of philology and philosophy he required; and five years later he recast it—suppressing scholarly "authorities" in favor of rational and geometric form—as the "Second New Science" of 1730. The third and final version appeared in 1744, the year of Vico's death.

Vico depicts "the idea of the work" by an engraving, a "Table of Civil Life," which serves as the frontispiece of the *New Science*. To describe this engraving briefly: illumination from the eye of God reflects off the breast of Lady Metaphysics down to a statue of Homer, standing on a cracked base amidst a miscellany of man-made objects including a fasces, a caduceus, a lute, Mercury's winged cap, and a tablet with letters on it. Even without Vico's help, the Platonic allegory is not hard to decipher: the divine source of knowledge is transmitted through philosophy and terminates in poetic wisdom; the cracked base, resting on an encyclopedic ground of human arts and sciences, stands for Vico's "discovery of the true Homer," with the implication that he may from there be able to retrace the illumination back to its source. It is nothing else than the "circle of divine and human erudition" suggested in the *Universal Law*, but now it takes on a more vivid coloring and richer context.

The opening sentence of the text might also be taken as a gloss on the frontispiece: "This New Science studies the common nature of nations in the light of divine providence, discovers the origins of institutions . . . and thereby establishes a system of the natural law of the nations." The pattern of cultural development is the same as he seizes upon in his *Universal Law*, that is, the three ages handed down by the Egyptians: the age of gods, characterized by divine government commanded by "auspices and oracles, which are the oldest institutions in profane history"; the age of heroes, organized by aristocracy composed of superior natures; and the age of men, organized into democracies and monarchies. Corresponding to these three ages, and indeed making them intelligible, are three languages: one mute and gestural like the Egyptian hieroglyphs, another of "heroic" emblems or images, and the last one human and conventional.

The study of languages, especially such "mother languages" as Greek and German, Vico thought, would permit unprecedented penetration into the "dark ages" and their essentially poetic and mythical wisdom. Through the understanding of Homer (to return to the frontispiece) we can rise to philosophical understanding, to form what Vico calls a "mental dictionary" by which to read the cultural histories of all of the nations.

Finally, corresponding to the three ages and three linguistic forms are three homologous kinds of jurisprudence: the first a "mystic theology," the second a "heroic jurisprudence" based on "reason of state," and the third a "natural equity" of modern civilization.

The chronological framework for this trinitarian design is presented in a foldout chart of the histories of seven major civilizations arranged in parallel columns, on which Vico gives a commentary; and then begins the "geometric" structure of which he was so proud. Under "elements" Vico sets down two premises concerning the anthropomorphic and the anthropocentric tendencies of human intelligence, that is, man's tendency to "make himself the measure of all things" and the human tendency to judge the remote and alien by the near and familiar. Among the consequences of the latter are the two "conceits" that Vico detected (on the analogy of Bacon's famous "idols"): the conceit of nations, which is their belief in their cultural superiority and antiquity; and the conceit of scholars, which is their similar tendency to overvalue their knowledge. Armed with these axioms, philosophy, which considers humans as they should be, and legislation, which considers them as they are, may join together effectively.

At this point, Vico reintroduces his old distinction between science and consciousness in order now to argue for the union, or at least cooperation, between reason and authority, that is, between philosophers and philologists. The latter investigate the nature, or genesis, of particular institutions; the former continue the analysis on a more general level in terms of the "mental language" symbolized by Lady Metaphysics. So a philologist can study the Twelve Tables and the Homeric poems as, respectively the Roman and Greek versions of the "ancient natural law of the nations," and a philosopher can raise the discussion to the "common ground of truth" uniting the entire "world of nations."

Altogether Vico set down 114 "axioms" of varying degrees of generality and plausibility, some establishing the foundations of the true and others of the certain, and many more pre-senting specific historical principles and linguistic divinations. Among the most important for Vico's dogmatic historicism the following may be mentioned:

Number 12: Common sense is judgment without reflection—[an axiom that made possible a] new art of criticism [applied to] founders of nations, who must have preceded by more than a thousand years the writers with whom criticism has so far been occupied.

Number 14: The nature of institutions is nothing but their coming into being at certain times and in certain guises.

Number 46: All barbarian histories have their beginnings in fables.

Number 64: The order of ideas must follow the order of institutions.

Number 71: Native customs, and above all that of natural liberty, do not change all at once but by degrees and over a long period of time.

Number 82: In all ancient nations we find everywhere clients and clienteles, which are best understood as vassals and fiefs.

Number 106: Doctrines must take their beginning from that of the matters of which they treat. [A rule that, Vico adds, should perhaps have been placed among the earlier, more general axioms.]

After the elements (the axioms) come the "principles" of the new science. Vico begins by asserting the presence of (as usual) three human customs in all national traditions: "all have some religion, all contract solemn marriages, all bury their dead." Forget skeptics like Pierre Bayle and travelers' tales, Vico adds; none, even outside the four "primary religions," live "without the light of God." Marriage was guaranteed by the requirements of parenthood and proved by the universality of the incest taboo, and reverence as well as more practical considerations established burial as likewise ubiquitous. Vico's principles, then, reinforce his conviction of the "divine origin" of human history in empirical as well as rational terms.

Next comes Vico's discussion of method. In order to find the first "principles of humanity" philologists have to delve into mythical and monstrous prehistory through a great effort of imagination. The past is almost as foreign a country as the future, and "what is hidden in [human] consciousness" must be uncovered by a critical version of the ancient process of divination. Through philosophy, history must be reconstructed by studying the "certain" wisdom not merely of the learned, as Grotius did, but of the whole human race. In this enterprise there are a few "philological proofs" that bring metaphysical patterns down to a historical grounding. So mythologies, heroic discourse, and etymologies are brought into agreement with human social institutions as expressed in the "mental vocabulary" provided by philosophy; truth is attained by the criticism of ancient tradition; antique monuments are restored; and all are fitted into the framework of "certain history." This is Vico's way of reuniting authority and reason, philology and philosophy.

The first target of Vico's metahistorical undertaking, the subject of book 1 of the *New Science*, is the same as that proposed in his first academic oration over a quarter of a century before, and in most writing in between, namely, wisdom. In view of his new assumptions (axioms 14 and 106 in particular) this means the "poetic wisdom" of the "dark ages." This is the period after the flood when the "giants"—mythical descendants of Noah's son—founded the nations of "gentile humanity."

It is at this point that Vico comes finally to define the seven "principal aspects of this science." Of these the first and most fundamental aspect coincides with the first rule set down earlier, that primitive men, driven by despair to "something superior to save them," sought and found religion. "So that this science becomes in this principal aspect a rational civil theology of divine providence," expressed first in the "vulgar wisdom of the

lawgivers." All the other "aspects" depend on this divine source and take their character from the "age of gods," when "Jove is full of all things."

In its second aspect the new science is also a "philosophy of authority," now a complement of rational theology as it was originally a reflection of man's fears of the gods. Again Vico makes the etymological connection between law *(jus)* and Jupiter (formerly *Jous*). Originating in property rights—since *"auctor,"* repeats Vico, certainly comes from *"autos,* meaning one's own"—"authority" is here at last reconciled with reason, as it was in Vico's "philosophical grammar"; and political and social justice is established on the grounds of human nature itself. In this way Vico prepares the ground for "an eternal natural commonwealth," a Neoplatonic republic founded truly on natural law. As the "rational civil theology" offers theological proofs, so the philosophy of authority offers philosophical ones and thus makes "clear and distinct the philological ones," thereby making philology itself a science and making human will a conscious "certitude." The substance of human experience as retrieved by philology, in other words, is given rational structure in philosophical and, ideally, political terms. This joining of the historical particular with the general and the transcendent recalls the frontispiece, showing divine illumination reaching and reflecting off its human base.

The third aspect is "a history of human ideas," which also arise out of divine comtemplation, illustrated by Vergil's remark "From Jove the muse began" (*Eclogue* 3.60). Here human language and history are raised from a particular to a general level, whence Vico's dream of a mental language, a "dictionary of mental signs" that is the philological counterpart to Gottfried von Leibniz' "universal characteristic." Whence, too, arises Vico's conception of an abstract sort of history that permits not only the divination of prehistorical phenomena and the inference of analogies between different national histories (between the Twelve Tables, for example, and the Salic law of the Franks) but also permits, the inference is, prediction of future stages. It opens the door to, but in a sense begs the question about, comparative history.

The fourth aspect, as a direct consequence, is the "philosophical criticism," which, beginning with Jupiter, "will give us a natural theogony, or generation of the gods, as it took form in the minds of the . . . theological poets." Vico suggests twelve subepochs to correspond to the twelve gods of the "greater nations" and to a "rational chronology of poetic history" before the second and third periods, the "heroic" and "vulgar," for which there is more obvious evidence. It is apparent that the new science makes no distinction, except a chronological one, between mythology and history proper.

"The fifth aspect," Vico tells us, "is an ideal eternal history traversed in time by the histories of all nations," and this philosophy of history (in a modern sense) in fact constitutes most of the substance of the *New Science*. What Vico had in mind was a sort of general cultural morphology applicable to every society and leading directly to the famous theory of cycles (*corso-ricorso*). For this reason Vico could speak of a "second" or "returned barbarism," when the Roman client-patron relationship was reincarnated in the form of European feudalism—which, significantly, was called *clientelae* by the learned feudists themselves. Vico noted that the same cycle appeared in the history of scholarship, so that just as Roman jurists lost sight of early Roman law, so the medieval feudists forgot "ancient feudal law." Only through the new science could the whole life cycle of legal wisdom, and social customs, be kept in mind.

The sixth aspect, the starting point as well as the end of Vico's quest, is the system of natural law, which he calls the "natural law of nations" both here and in the *Universal Law.* Here we can see one of the most conspicuous aspects of the "new science," though as usual

the originality consisted in a bold stroke of synthesis in contradiction to previous authorities. Disputing the assumptions of his immediate predecessors (Grotius, Samuel Pufendorf, John Selden), Vico conflates the natural law *(jus naturale)* and the law of nations *(jus gentium)*. Although one is based on reason and the other on a wide-ranging, comparative study of the positive law of many different societies, they achieve identity in the new science because of their common source in the "divine law of nations" *(jus divinum apud gentes)* and in the "common sense" of humanity. The convergence would be complete in the new science, when science and consciousness become one.

Finally, the new science reveals Vico's "principles of universal history." Out of this comes the "rational chronology" mentioned before, that is, one that begins at the beginning (*ab orbe*, not merely *ab urbe*) and is correlated with the "ideal eternal history." For failing to envisage this "metaphysical" sort of chronology Vico rebukes the great Joseph Justus Scaliger, giant of Renaissance learning and father of this particular auxiliary science, chronology. This is the ground for Vico's conception of "the uniformity of the *corso*" and for the threefold periodization for which he is perhaps most famous. According to this theory, the life cycle of individual men, through childhood, youth, and maturity, is recapitulated on the level of mankind as a whole. The pattern consists of three ages: gods, heroes, men—feeling, perception, reflection—poetry, philology, science—Homer (we may say), Scaliger, Vico.

Within "poetic wisdom," which represents the general state of mind of the first age, "poetic logic" has priority, and here Vico resumes his semiotic, semantic, and etymological speculations as the "philological proofs" of the underlying conceptual patterns. The object of his investigation is primitive consciousness, which is to say, in a sense, unconsciousness; and the discourse reflecting this primitive state of mind consists of tropes (fig-

ures of speech), especially metaphor, synech-
doche, and metonymy. (The fourth major
trope, irony, requires a more reflective state of
mind.) In the earliest age, heaven indeed (or
rather, in word) "smiled," the wind "whis-
tled," and the waves "murmured"; men spoke
and thought truly in body language. Such "poetic wisdom" Vico illustrates by the stories of
Aesop. That Aesop in fact antedated the Greek
wise men, Vico demonstrates according to his
twofold method: philologically, through the
poetic and metaphorical style of Aesop's work;
and philosophically, through the absence in
poetic wisdom of the conscious rationality of
"civil doctrine," as in "know thyself." By contrast with philosophers, the poets appealed directly to nature.

A related aspect of poetic wisdom is discussed in corollaries that Vico adds concerning language and speech. The process of
"naming" also, he finds, had its origin in nature, historically as well as etymologically;
and the first words, monosyllabic and ono-
matopoetic, not only had "natural signification" but were imitations of natural forces.
"Pa!" and so "pa-pa!," in imitation of the sky
god Jove's roars, became associated with fa-
therhood. Out of natural language, the "baby
talk of the human race," emerged first nouns,
then verbs (beginning with commands, typically monosyllabic, such as the Latin *duc, dic,
fac:* lead, say, do), and from there song and heroic verse forms, which mark the second stage
of language, the heroic and symbolic. In this
period the tendency is to allegorize and to per-
sonify, as in the identification of laws with
their makers, Solon and Romulus. In Vico's
opinion the German language was still in this
heroic phase. Then, in emergent consciousness, comes the "hewing out of topics," the
philological analogue, Vico suggests, to Bacon's inductive method. Last of all comes
"criticism" and rational understanding, left
for maturity, all of this implicit, however, in
"poetic logic."

Two other related offshoots of poetic wisdom are poetic morality and poetic economics,
likewise derived from the trinity of historical
principles. Primitive morals originate in the
context of marriage and the family, and so do
the first form of domestic economy. Marriage,
based first on a fear of divinity, produces not
only children but also piety, a certain necessary togetherness (Vico links the tutelary goddess of the institution with "yoke," that is,
Juno with *juga*), and a set of virtues valuable
for survival. Poetic economy begins in the nuclear family headed by a father who is, at once,
priest, king, and wise man; and it is the product of the need for labor and education for
preservation in time. The sense of family symbolized by burial of the dead also reinforces
claims to land, and this creates the conditions
for an extended family—extended not only in
time (*fama*, or fame, being an etymological
relative of *familia*) but also in space (as the
domestic group was increased by so-called *famuli*, refugees who became virtual slaves).

For Vico there never was a "state of nature"
in the sense of some of his contemporaries,
but there was a transition from a domestic to
a more socialized condition. This was reflected in another form of primitive wisdom,
"poetic politics," which arises when the relationship between *paterfamilias* and *famuli* becomes that of patron and clients, in effect lord
and vassals, thus generating the feudal phase
of civil society. The Roman patterns had been
anticipated by the Greeks, according to Vico's
reading of Homer, and would be repeated by
many others, including the Spanish in the
West Indies in the time of Charles V. Cultural
developments in this earliest period were still
given mythical expression, for instance in the
poetic character of the war-bringing Mars and
of Venus, who embodied honor (*honestas*), a
quality that changed from beauty to virtue in
the transition from the divine to the heroic period. "Poetic politics" was most clearly expressed, however, in the Twelve Tables,
which guaranteed paternal power and property. The corresponding constitutional form is
not monarchy, as so many scholars thought,
Bodin most conspicuously, but an aristocratic

republic of virtue formed by the paterfamilias: the *res republica,* Vico concludes, was really the *patria* (*res patria* being understood). And the first jurisprudence, he suggests in another ingenious and sometimes fanciful etymology, had as its aim "to enter into the fathers"—their hermeneutical art being to interpret (*interpatrari,* later *interpretari*). But the necessary condition of these developments is symbolized by Mars and the conflict of the gods, most notably Saturn and Jove; and the "philological proof," Vico adds, is the derivation of war (*polemos*) from city (*polis*).

A fascinating illustration of both Vico's use of mythology in his philosophy of history and his use of "philosophical criticism" to escape the anachronistic view of more literal-minded scholars is the story of Vulcan splitting with his ax the forehead of Jupiter and the subsequent emergence of Minerva. Vulcan surely signified the subordinate *famuli,* proto-plebeians, practicing servile arts and opposing the rule of the patriciate order; but despite the views of modern "philosophers," Minerva by no means stood for reason in the eyes of the "theological poets." Rather she signified the aggressive aristocracy responding to the plebeian challenge, and thus the elaboration of the paleofeudal order of the Roman republic. There were similar misconceptions about Mercury, the messenger-god who symbolized not learning but, as etymology teaches, commerce and merchants. In any case the elaboration of institutions takes place in the context of various struggles, internal and external, and myth testifies to culture in the heroic age more than do historians like Livy. The whole story is told, Vico observes, in the myth of Cadmus and in Homer's depiction of the shield of Achilles.

Poetic wisdom, which represents the substance of the first phase of cultural history, is sometimes pictured by Vico as a great tree with as many branches as there are disciplines in the encyclopedia of learning. Vico concludes his discussion of the subject with brief descriptions of several other branches of poetic wisdom: poetic physics (including physiology), cosmography, astronomy, chronology, and geography. This complex of wisdom is the first stage of what Gotthold Ephraim Lessing calls "the education of the human race," and of course it has its imperfections, among them the "conceit of nations" that arises from the almost impenetrable national spirit and traditions leading to the equally parochial "conceit of scholars." Vico also gives a pioneering analysis of the errors of anachronism, of which he recognizes four sorts, all of them violating the scheme of chronology established by philological and philosophic proofs. Only in the new science would these fallacies be overcome and the potential of poetic wisdom be fulfilled in the "circle of divine and human erudition" that is philosophic wisdom.

In the third book Vico turns to the primary vehicle of poetic wisdom and, by means of his new method, to the philological and philosophical proofs set down in book 1, that is, to the "search for" and "discovery of the true Homer." Vico's method demands first that Homer be located in place and time. Modern scholarship had not solved these puzzles, for many cities claimed to be his fatherland, and traces of many places appear in his poems. As for chronology, the *Iliad* seemed to exhibit a youthful spirit, whereas the *Odyssey* sighed with old age. Vico's solution to the problem of Homer seems implied by these judgments, which he offers as scientific proofs. His conclusion is that, although the Homeric myths indeed are monuments of the poetic wisdom of a heroic age, they were composed centuries after the Trojan wars, and, more than that, they are themselves separated by centuries, so that the impression of youth and old age had a cultural rather than a psychological origin. In short, "Homer" is a heroic and mythical confection, standing in fact for a complex tradition and two separate "treasure stores of the natural law of the nations of Greece," just as the Twelve Tables was a "serious poem" that reflected "the natural law of the nations of Rome."

Finally, in book 4, we arrive at Vico's philosophy of history in the longest perspective, which is "the course the nations run," suggested already in the *Universal Law* but here described, calibrated, and explained much more carefully. In this elaboration of the fifth aspect of the new science, the "ideal eternal history," we return also to Vico's trinitarian obsession. He reviews some dozen cultural triads that inform every level of human existence and give shape to the process of history. In analyses that are at once insightful and chaotic, sometimes perfunctory or fantastic, Vico finds three species in the categories of nature, custom, natural law, government, language, character, jurisprudence, authority, reason, and judgments; and chronologically these categories translate into the familiar three stages: divine/poetic, heroic/formal, and human/civil (or social). Though realized in the most fragmentary fashion, this historical taxonomy is the culmination of the conceptual and methodological devices formulated in the first two books of the *New Science.*

Having outlined the *corso* of nations in their recapitulation of the universal pattern, Vico turns in book 5 to their *ricorso.* After the decline of ancient civilization—involving the passage of antique wisdom through its poetic, heroic, and civil phases and its subsequent corruption—a new order was established by the divine source in the form of the Christian religion. So was inaugurated the "second barbarism," which generated another tripartite cycle of wisdom. In the new religious context myth was revived and so were "heroic" institutions such as raids, reprisals, slavery, the founding of cities, and above all feudalism and the troubles attendant on the conflicts between aristocratic patrons and upstart clients. Finally, with the humanist efforts to revive classical antiquity (at least in its "civil" phase), the European "course" moved from the heroic to the human stage; and Vico himself returns to the theme of his youth, which is the celebration of the recovery of the arts and sciences and their perfection through philosophy and method.

But the "course of nations" is still running, and Vico is of two minds about the future. He fears the "great disease of cities" and the infection of philosophy, that is, corruption by false eloquence and skepticism through the culture of the popular governments succeeding the heroic age. In his conclusion he repeats "the first incontestable principle of our science," which is that "men have themselves made this world of nations." The world of nations is not self-contained, however; its "one principle and one end" is divine providence, whose purposes are superior to the wills and even the intellects of men. Left to themselves men have no other remedy for inevitable "civil disease" except Caesarism or surrender—turning to monarchical control of all civil institutions or else becoming victims of a naturally fitter political power. There is a third possibility, however, and that is a return to the simplicity of the "first world of peoples," that is to religion. Without religion there can be no social life, declares Vico: "no shield of defense, nor means of counsel, nor basis of support, nor even a form by which they may exist in the world at all." So Vico himself retraces the "circle of divine law." "It is to be finally concluded," writes Vico, "that this science carries inseparably with it the study of piety, and that he who is not pious cannot be truly wise."

V

Vico was no doubt pious, and he had learned in some ways to be wise, but he was never happy. From the despair of his early poetry to his aged complaints about illness, failing memory, and family problems, Vico was a melancholy if not tragic figure; a difficult man, confessedly "choleric to a fault" and intolerant of criticism. Isolated in childhood, disappointed in professional life, largely unappreciated as an author (compare his nemesis Descartes), Vico found peace only in the world of his making, in the intellectual cosmos of the "new science." The later sections of his autobiography largely concern its transformations and fortunes, especially favorable reactions to it. Meanwhile, he continued to teach rhetoric and to write occasional poetry and commissioned works, including orations and epigraphs. In 1735 he was appointed royal historiographer to the king of Naples. Among his minor writings were his "Discovery of the True Dante" (1728), a study of an author who suffered similar isolation while, guided by Vergil, composing a masterpiece that culminates in a providential and trinitarian vision; his "On the Heroic Mind" (1732); and his "Idea of a Philosophical Grammar" (1740).

By 1740 Vico was almost overwhelmed by his troubles. He took pleasure in his uneducated wife, his learned daughter, Luisa, and his son Gennaro, who succeeded him in his chair of rhetoric the next year; but another son, Ignazio, seemed incorrigible and spent time in prison. Medical bills mounted, and Vico's health declined. His own *corso* seemed to be turning back on itself: he found it difficult to walk and his memory failed; he stopped reading and, according to the continuator of his autobiography, "confused the names of the most familiar things." So Vico completed his course and, "with a most perfect submission to the divine will," died peacefully on 22 January 1744.

But this was not the end of Vico in a Vichian sense: he has had an extraordinary *ricorso*, indeed a number of *ricorsi*, since his badly organized funeral ceremony and burial in the Neapolitan church of San Girolami. The afterlife of Vico has been as extraordinarily rich as it has been insufficiently understood. There were minor Vichian traditions in the eighteenth century, especially in Italy; but the first major revival was inspired by Jules Michelet, who published his translation of Vico's

Scienza Nuova in 1827, thus introducing to the world what might be regarded as the "romantic" Vico. The second and greatest *ricorso*, still going on, began with Croce's neo-Hegelian *Philosophy of Giambattista Vico*, published in 1911 and translated two years later by R. G. Collingwood. In this reincarnation Vico has become not only a relic but an icon, not only a classic but a commodity. In his own term he has become a giant (or perhaps only a hero) of the modern intellectual tradition and has spawned a new mythology. James Joyce made him a staple of literature, hence of literary criticism; Collingwood, Isaiah Berlin, and others have elucidated his work for philosophers and historians; and a host of other enthusiasts have communicated the Vichian word, however imperfectly and anachronistically (a cardinal Vichian sin) to a new world of sciences. And meanwhile the work of discovering the "true Vico" goes on.

From a twentieth-century perspective Vico is indeed a Janus-faced figure, looking back through the whole landscape of Western culture and forward through his admirers and epigones to vistas of modern and postmodern thought. According to his own autobiographical reconstruction, moreover, he recapitulated the basic pattern of the course of Western thought; reading for "topical" learning in his youth, when memory was strong; professing to substantial science (that is, jurisprudence) in his middle period, bringing philosophy and philology together; and moving on finally to a higher synthesis of the two in the "new science" of his old age. No wonder his culminating philosophical system, which incorporates all of these stages, has intrigued, baffled, obsessed, or even infuriated such a wide variety of readers in the past two and a half centuries.

Depending on one's point of view the *New Science* takes numerous forms. It can be seen as a medieval *Summa* of modern erudition, a Dantesque comedy of philological speculation, a Renaissance cornucopia of transcendental wisdom, an antirationalist system of eternal ideas, an Enlightenment encyclopedia of traditional lore, a superhuman code of universal law. More speculatively, it appears as a mythic (or perhaps mythological) reconstitution of the divine pattern in man, a prophetic vision of a comprehensive "science of humanity." All of these possibilities have been suggested, and more. "The Vico road goes round and round to meet where terms begin," James Joyce wrote.

Like *Finnegans Wake*, the *New Science* retains many of the features of a large enigma composed of small riddles and intuitions; but at least some of its themes are enduring and have left an indelible imprint on Western thought. In the first place, man is seen clearly, and even schematically, as a historical being: in almost existentialist terms he is not given his own nature, but rather makes it (not a static nature but rather a dynamic character). He makes his own world, too, and godlike, surveys his creation with a kind of understanding that no outside observer can attain. This is Vico's Promethean version of the old scholastic formula, *verum* equals *factum*, which produced a new standard of knowledge. Science, the most complete form of knowledge, is achieved most perfectly not through the mechanical processes of either induction or deduction, but rather through a self-conscious, imaginative sort of re-creation of which only the creator himself is capable. For this epistemological innovation, which bases science on reflective memory extended from autobiography to history, Vico may well be regarded as one of the founders of modern philosophical hermeneutics.

In the second place Vico proposes synchronic correlations between various sorts of human wisdom, including logic, ethics, economics, aesthetics, and politics, so that these categories are seen as changing in a similar manner through a common scheme of periodization. He further assumes that all of them are grounded on, and draw their consonance from, what Karl Marx called the material base of society. In other words Vico formulated a comprehensive theory of culture, a theory that insists on historical individuality, that is, national character. This view was worked out first in the context of Roman legal history and then more generally for all of the Western nations (the nations whose customs had themselves first been systematically recognized in the law of nations [*jus gentium*] of Roman jurisprudence). All human creations—laws, institutions, literature, art, science, and philosophy—display a common style and configuration at any given time. This conception of cultural coherence represents one of the cornerstones of Vico's so-called (and often called) historicism.

Finally, there is the famous "philosophy of history," which is the other cornerstone. Cycle and recycle (*corso* and *ricorso*) suggests some of the schematizing weaknesses of Vichianism and ultimately is perhaps less significant than the *verum-factum* notion, but the first pair undoubtedly represents the most influential of Vico's "principles of history." Drawing on humanist (indeed ancient) ideas of cultural progress from the primitive to the civilized, Vico argued with astonishing erudition and insight that every nation lives through three stages: first, myth, poetry, and unwritten custom; second, history, prose, and written law; and finally (before falling back into a "second barbarism"), philosophy, that is, ideally, the various forms of the "new science" he envisioned. The most sensitive indicator of the courses of national histories is language, and it is above all through the historical study of language—a philology combined with philosophy and raised to the level of science—that modern scholarship can reconstruct not only these individual courses but also the metahistorical trajectory of humanity as a whole. Although contemporary readers tend to see his masterwork as an early paradigm of human science, for Vico himself its ultimate expression was truly a religious vision.

Selected Bibliography

EDITIONS

COLLECTED WORKS

Opere di G. B. Vico. Edited by F. Nicolini. 8 vols. Bari, 1911–1941. The standard edition, on which other partial collections are based. See the list compiled by Michael Mooney in G. Tagliacozzo and D. Verene's edition *Giambattista Vico's Science of Humanity*, under Biographical and Critical Studies below.

INDIVIDUAL WORKS

When the year of original publication is not certain, the year of composition or first presentation is given after the title of a work. For each title the volume and page numbers are given for reference to the Nicolini edition of the *Opere*.

Affetti di un disperato. Venice, 1692. (Vol. 5, pp. 313–317).

Correspondence, written 1693–1743. (Vol. 5, pp. 137–278; vol. 8, pp. 245–253).

Six university inaugural orations (delivered 1699–1707). Naples, 1869. (Vol. 1, pp. 1–67).

De nostri temporis studiorum ratione. Naples, 1709. (Vol. 6, pp. 301–362).

De antiquissima Italorum sapientia ex linguae laitinae originibus eruenda. Naples, 1710. (Vol. 1, pp. 123–194).

De universi juris uno principio et fine uno liber unus. Naples, 1720. (Vol. 2, pp. 23–263).

De constantia jurisprudentia liber alter. Naples, 1721. (Vol. 2, pp. 265–589).

Notae in duos libros. . . . Naples, 1722. (Vol. 2, pp. 591–760). Notes on the two works immediately above; altogether these three books make up what Vico called the *Diritto universale*.

Scienza nuova prima. Naples, 1725. (Vol. 3, pp. 1–529). Vico's shortened title for the *Principi di una scienza nuova dintorno alla natura delle nazioni, per la quale si ritruovano i principi di altro sistema del diritto naturale delle genti*.

Vita di Giambiattista Vico scritta da se medesimo. Venice, 1728. (Vol. 5, pp. 3–54, 89–91). Supplement added in 1731. (Vol. 5, pp. 55–79). Commonly called the *Autobiografia*.

"Discovertà del vero Dante. . . ." 1728 or 1729. (Vol. 7, pp. 79–82).

Vici vindiciae: Notae in "Acta eruditorum. . . ." Naples, 1729. (Vol. 3, pp. 530–584). The defense of the *Scienza nuova*.

Scienza nuova seconda. Naples, 1730. 3rd ed., 1744. (Vol. 4, pp. 1–1112, 1488–1492, 1499–1506). Vico's shortened title for the *Principi di scienza nuova d'intorno alla commune natura delle nazioni*. Nicolini uses the short title for his combined version of the 1730 and 1744 editions.

"Sui diritto naturale delle genti." 1731. (Vol. 7, pp. 25–31).

De mente heroica. Naples, 1732. (Vol. 7, 3–22).

"Idea d'una grammatica filosofica," *ca.* 1740. (Vol. 7, pp. 33–37).

TRANSLATIONS

Affetti di un disperato. Translated by H. P. Adams. In *The Life and Writings of Giambattista Vico*. London, 1935. Pp. 223–226.

————. Translated by T. G. Bergin. *Forum Italicum* 2:305–309 (1968).

The Autobiography of Giambattista Vico. Translated by M. H. Fisch and T. G. Bergin. Ithaca, N.Y., 1944.

The New Science of Giambattista Vico. Translated by M. H. Fisch and T. G. Bergin. Ithaca, N.Y., 1968. Abridged ed., 1970.

"Discovery of the True Dante." Translated by Irma Brandeis. In *Discussions of the Divine Comedy*, edited by Irma Brandeis. Boston, 1961. Pp. 11–12.

"A Factual Digression on Human Genius, Sharp, Witty Remarks and Laughter." Translated by A. Illiano, J. D. Tedder, and P. Treves in *Forum Italicum* 2:310–314 (1968).

"Practice of the New Science." Translated by M. H. Fisch and T. G. Bergin. In *Giambattista Vico's Science of Humanity*, edited by G. Tagliacozzo and D. Verene. Baltimore, 1976. Pp. 451–454.

"On the Heroic Mind." Translated by Elizabeth Sewell and Anthony C. Sirignano. *Social Research* 43:886–903 (1976).

On the Study Methods of Our Time. Translated by Elio Gianturco. New York, 1965.

Selected Writings. Translated by Leon Pompa. Cambridge, 1982. Includes parts of *On Method in Contemporary Fields of Study* (same as *On the Study Methods of Our Time*, above), *On the Ancient Wisdom of the Italians*, *The First New Science*, and *The Third New Science*.

BIOGRAPHICAL AND CRITICAL STUDIES

Adams, H. P. *The Life and Writings of Giambattista Vico.* London, 1935.

Amerio, F. *Introduzione allo studio di G. B. Vico.* Turin, 1947.

Atti del Convegno internazionale sul tema: Campanella e Vico. Rome, 1969.

Auerbach, E. "Vico and Aesthetic Historicism." In *Sciences from the Drama of European Literature.* New York, 1959. Pp. 183–200.

Badaloni, N. *Introduzione a G. B. Vico.* Milan, 1961.

Baviera, G. *Vico e la storia del diritto romano.* Palermo, 1917.

Bellofiore, L. *La dottrina del diritto naturale in G. B. Vico.* Milan, 1954.

Berlin, Isaiah. *Vico and Herder.* London, 1976.

Bernardini, A., and G. Richi. *Il concetto di filologia classica.* Bari, 1947.

Bianca, G. *Il concetto di poesia in Giambattista Vico.* Messina, 1967.

Brown, Norman O. *Closing Time.* New York, 1973.

Cantelli, G. *Vico and Bayle.* Naples, 1971.

Cantone, C. *Il concetto filosofica del diritto in G. B. Vico.* Mazara, 1952.

Caponigri, A. R. *Time and Idea.* London, 1953.

Cassirer, E. "Descartes, Leibniz and Vico." In *Symbol, Myth and Culture,* edited by D. Verene. New Haven, Conn., 1979. Pp. 95–107.

Chaix-Ruy, Jean. *La formation de la penśee de G. B. Vico.* Gap, 1943.

Ciampolini, C. *La concezione del diritto naturale in G. B. Vico.* Ravenna, 1927.

Collingwood, R. G. *The Idea of History.* Oxford, 1946.

Corsano, A. *G. B. Vico.* Bari, 1956.

Croce, B. *The Philosophy of Giambattista Vico.* Translated by R. G. Collingwood. London, 1913.

Donati, B. *Nuovi studi sulla filosofia civile di G. B. Vico.* Florence, 1936.

Fasso, G. *I "Quattro autori" del Vico.* Milan, 1949.

———. *Vico e Grozio.* Naples, 1971.

Fisch, Max. "Vico on Roman Law." In *Essays in Political Theory Presented to George H. Sabine.* Ithaca, N.Y., 1948. Pp. 62–88.

Flint, Robert. *Vico.* Edinburgh, 1884.

Fubini, M. *Stile e umanità di G. B. Vico.* Naples, 1965.

Garin, Eugenio. *Dal rinascimento all'illuminismo.* Pisa, 1969.

———. *La filosofia* 2:353–383 (1947).

Gemelli, A., ed. *G. B. Vico: Volume commemorato nel secondo centenario della publicazione della "Scienza nuova."* Milan, 1926.

Giambattista Vico nel terzo centenario della nascita. Naples, 1971.

Gianturco, Elio. *Joseph de Maistre and Giambattista Vico.* Washington, D.C., 1937.

Jacobelli, I. *G. B. Vico: La vita e le opere.* Bologna, 1960.

Löwith, Karl. *Vicos Grundsatz: Verum et factum convertuntur.* Heidelberg, 1968.

———. *Meaning in History.* Chicago, 1949.

Manno, A. G. *Lo storicismo di G. B. Vico.* Naples, 1965.

Manson, R. *The Theory of Knowledge in Giambattista Vico.* Hamden, Conn., 1969.

Manuel, Frank. *The Eighteenth Century Confronts the Gods.* Cambridge, Mass., 1959.

Mazlish, Bruce. *The Riddle of History.* New York, 1966. Pp. 11–58.

Meinecke, Friedrich. *Historism.* Translated by J. Anderson. New York, 1972. Pp. 37–53.

Momigliano, A. "Vico's *Scienza nuova:* Roman 'Bestinoni' and Roman 'Eroi.'" *History and Theory* 5:3–23 (1966).

Mondolfo, R. *Il verum-factum prima de Vico.* Naples, 1969.

Mooney, Michael J. *Wisdom Speaking: Language and Society in Giambattista Vico.* Princeton, N.J., 1984.

New Vico Studies 1– (1983–). Edited by G. Tagliacozzo.

Nicolini, F. *Commento storico alla seconda scienza nuova.* 2 vols. Rome, 1949.

———. *La giovanezza di Giambattista Vico (1688–1700).* Bari, 1932.

Per il secondo centenario della "Scienza nuova" di G. B. Vico (1725–1925), Rivista internazionale di filosofia del diritto 5 (1925).

Piovani, P., ed. *Omaggio a Vico.* Naples, 1968.

Pompa, Leon. *Vico: "A Study of the 'New Science.'"* Cambridge, 1975.

Quaderni contemporanei no. 2. Naples, 1968.

Ricciardelli, M., ed. "A Homage to Vico in the Tercentenary of His Birth." *Forum Italicum* 2, no. 4 (1968).

Robertson, J. G. *Studies in the Genesis of Romantic Theory in the Eighteenth Century.* Cambridge, 1923. Pp. 179–194.

Rossi, P. *Le sterminate antichità.* Pisa, 1969.

Sorentino, A. *La retorica e la poetica di Vico.* Turin, 1927.

Tagliacozzo, G., ed. *Vico and Marx.* Atlantic Highlands, N.J., 1983.

————. *Vico: Past and Present.* Atlantic Highlands, N.J., 1981.

————, M. Mooney, and D. Verene, eds. *Vico and Contemporary Thought.* Atlantic Highlands, N.J., 1980.

Tagliacozzo, G., and D. Verene, eds. *Giambattista Vico's Science of Humanity.* Baltimore, 1976.

Tagliacozzo, G., and H. White, eds. *Giambattista Vico: An International Symposium.* Baltimore, 1969.

Toulmin, S., and J. Goodfield. *The Discovery of Time.* New York, 1965. Pp. 125–129.

Vaughan, Frederick. *The Political Philosophy of Giambattista Vico.* The Hague, 1972.

Verene, D. *Vico's Science of Imagination.* Ithaca, N.Y., 1981.

BIBLIOGRAPHIES

Crease, Robert. *Vico in English: Vichian Studies* 1 (1978). Gathers and extends the material in the collective volumes edited by Tagliacozzo; published by the Institute for Vico Studies, of which Tagliacozzo is the director. A supplement has appeared (to 31 May 1979), and the work will be continued in this series and in the journal *Vico Studies,* published by the Institute.

Croce, Benedetto. *Bibliografia vichiana.* Revised and enlarged by F. Nicolini. 2 vols. Naples, 1947–1948.

Gianturco, Elio. *A Selective Bibliography of Vico Scholarship (1948–1968). Forum Italicum* supplement (1968).

Donzelli, Maria. *Contributo alla bibliografia vichiana (1948–1970).* Naples, 1973.

DONALD R. KELLEY

ALAIN-RENÉ LESAGE
(1668–1747)

A SUPERB OBSERVER of human nature, a gifted satirist, and France's greatest writer during a fleeting period of transition, Alain-René Lesage* was born in Lower Brittany. Louis XIV reigned for some forty more years before Lesage's name became known in Europe. His success as a dramatist and writer of fiction was largely due to two qualities: a sure touch as a satirist and the ability to depict entertainingly the human condition.

Lesage's work falls into three general categories. The first includes a large number of dramatic skits suitable for carnivals and fairs and the miscellaneous essays that appeared across the years. The second consists of two legitimate plays, *Crispin* and *Turcaret*, that are a high point in post-Molière comedy. The third category is comprised of his episodic novels, which as a rule conform loosely to the picaresque tradition, the chief of these being the celebrated *Gil Blas.*

On one hand, he was an outsider where the rising philosophic coterie of Voltaire and his disciples was concerned. On the other hand, he was equally a stranger among the conservative partisans of altar and throne. Nor was he honored by membership in any of France's numerous academies, least of all the prestigious Académie Française.

The fact that Lesage was Breton born may have had more to do with his traits as man and writer than is usually supposed. Brittany is a French province jutting out into the Atlantic Ocean and the English Channel from the northwest corner of the country. On the map it looks as if it were striving to break off from the mainland to become a country unto itself. Its topography and its stormy history support this impression. With its savagely picturesque coastline—its jagged rocks, towering cliffs, broad sweeping strands, minute half-concealed beaches, and spectacularly high and low tides—this terrain is unique in France. Like the numerous copper-colored vipers coiled and slumbering in the setting sun in this land of the ancient Celt, its people are tranquil enough if not too violently disturbed, but provoked, they will cling fiercely to the spirit of independence that still pervades the region.

It is from this province that renowned bards as early as the sixth century created their patriotic, historic, erotic, and spirited poetry later echoed far and wide among the troubadors. It is from the very heart of this land that, more recently, great writers and thinkers, independent and sometimes revolutionary, have unexpectedly sprung. Such was the theologian Félicité Robert de Lamennais, a priest of great personal convictions who lost his disenchanted disciples, continued his eloquent writings, incurred the wrath of the pope, and

*The name has often been published as two words: Le Sage. In those autographs known to exist, however, Lesage's surname is distinctly written as one word. This has now become the generally accepted spelling.

317

was buried as he wished in a pauper's grave. Such was François René de Chateaubriand—adventurer, statesman with grandiose visions, supreme egotist who held Lord Byron's literary genius to be but a pale mockery of his own, and whose tomb is on a cliff off Saint-Malo, where he intended the waves of the sea finally to erode rock and sepulcher and mingle his ashes with the universe. And such was Joseph Ernest Renan, often referred to by the French of his day as the most intelligent man of the nineteenth century. It is perhaps he who best caught the ambience of Brittany. For those who know it well, it remains a land of mists assuming phantom shapes, a land of legends, mysteries, and mysticism, deriving from pagan as well as Christian sources. The Breton *pardons*, those days of fetes, pilgrimages, and absolution dating from the Middle Ages, contain the region's traditions, both profane and sacred. The very character of the province, whether shaped through the forces of nature or of race, sets it apart from the rest of France, to which it acknowledges belonging only with reluctance.

Throughout his *Souvenirs de jeunesse (Recollections of My Youth)*, Renan has seized the spirit of the region but, poetically speaking, at least, no more convincingly than in the opening paragraph of the book's preface:

> One of the most popular legends in Brittany is that relating to an imaginary city called Is, which is supposed to have been swallowed up by the sea at some unknown time. There are several places along the coast that are pointed out as the site of this imaginary metropolis, and the fishermen have many strange tales to tell of it. According to them, the tips of the church spires may be seen in the hollow of the waves when the sea is turbulent, while during a calm the music of their bells, ringing out the hymn appropriate to the day, rises above the waters. I often fancy I have at the bottom of my heart a city of Is with its bells calling to prayer a recalcitrant congregation. At times I stop to listen to those gentle reverberations that seem as if they came from fathomless depths, like voices from another world. Since old age began to steal over me, I have loved, in particular during the repose that summer brings with it, to gather up these distant echoes of an Atlantis that is no more.
>
> (*Oeuvres complètes*, Paris, 1928, vol. 2, p. 713)

This myth, this fantasy, as expressed by Renan, represents a prevailing mood in the Breton character. Further along in the *Recollections* the author suggests that there was never a race of men less suited for trade and industry. A distinctive sentiment among Bretons in general has always been that material gain is unworthy of the man of spirit, that the noblest occupations are those bringing no profit to speak of: the occupations of the soldier, the sailor, the priest, the gentlemanly landowner, the magistrate, and the thinker. This turn of mind—right or wrong—is based on the theory that wealth is to be acquired only by taking advantage of others and exploiting the poor. Its corollary is that one of the more important aims in life is the freedom to act and react. This ideal was close to the heart of Lesage.

True to the indigenous and sometimes inscrutable nature of a Breton character such as his, little is known about Lesage's personal life; he left nothing that could properly be called memoirs and little by way of personal correspondence. Hardly anything but a modicum of sometimes revealing anecdotes has come down to us. Given the dearth of information, what are we to make of his early years—of his career as a whole?

The only child of Claude and Jeanne Brenugat Lesage, Alain-René was born at Sarzeau on 13 December 1668. It was the county seat of the Rhuys peninsula. His father, following the family tradition, had taken up law to become notary, counselor, and registrar in the Rhuys Royal Court of Justice. At the time, the legal profession was prestigious and awarded a relatively high standard of living.

In 1673, at the age of five, young Lesage lost his mother, and he became an orphan at fourteen when, in 1682, his father also died. The lad was left an estate of sorts, although a negligent or unscrupulous uncle or two, presumably abetted by others, stripped him of most of his inheritance. Still, he had sufficient funds to enter the Jesuit College at Vannes, where he had an excellent formative education, especially in rhetoric and the humanities. His teachers, seeing him as a student of promise, then encouraged him at eighteen to go to Paris to continue his studies in philosophy and, chiefly, law. Among other students in the Latin Quarter, where he had a room, he encountered Antoine Danchet pursuing his own studies in rhetoric and literature. The two became fast friends. One can only surmise how they spent their spare time together, probably in such famous and popular cafés as the Régence and the Procope, where students, provincials, bohemians, writers, and eminent Parisians gathered. There is reason to believe that Danchet, already fascinated by the world of letters, saw in his friend more than a spark of interest, despite Lesage's diligence in the reading of law. But Danchet, having been offered the chair of rhetoric at the College of Chartres—he was only twenty-one—accepted, leaving Lesage behind to complete legal studies and be admitted to the bar in 1692.

The letters exchanged between the two friends during these years of separation have not come down to us, but we do know that Danchet thought Lesage should begin his first years in a literary career by translating foreign works into French. In later years, Danchet, though a dramatist of modest distinction, was elected to the prestigious Académie Française. He hoped the same honor might be conferred on his friend, who, with time, had become an internationally known man of letters. But Lesage was never to show interest in seeking a chair as one of the so-called forty immortals.

How did young Lesage pass these first years of adulthood during his friend's absence from the nation's capital? He immediately set about practicing law. Because of the biting satire with which he was to treat tax farmers (those appointed to collect taxes for the king and themselves) and financiers in his writings, particularly in his early plays, it has been frequently suggested that much of his time as a fledgling lawyer was taken up with accumulating unsavory glimpses of the world of finance, first during a trial sojourn in Brittany, and then upon returning to the capital. This is supposition, however. More certain is the fact that, at the turn of the century, Lesage, more or less permanently established in Paris, was endowed with youth, subtle charm, discretion, and good looks. Moreover, it was then that he developed an attachment to a young woman of quality about whom nothing else is known. Briefly, at least, he treasured her affection and, malicious pens have added, doubtless her riches as well. Gossip has remained silent as to why or how the relationship ended.

In the fall of 1694 he married before the altars of Saint-Sulpice an extremely attractive young woman, Marie-Élisabeth Huyard, the daughter of a good, solid bourgeois of Paris. There is general agreement that this was one of those unusually successful marriages where peace, harmony, mutual respect, and affection strengthened the bond. Fifty-three years later he was to die in her arms.

To turn to writing to eke out a living on one's own was especially hard in the seventeenth and eighteenth centuries. Patronage, if proffered at all, was proffered by wealthy members of the aristocracy. For needy writers of promise it was, when forthcoming, most welcome. Advantages often worked both ways: if a privileged nobleman lent financial support to an up-and-coming man of letters, it could bring added luster to his own name. It does seem, however, that Lesage was the first important French writer to live by the pen alone—although it is doubtful that he did so at the outset.

Before long, the young couple had a son, then two more sons and a daughter. Obviously the family would have been in straitened circumstances if, by some miracle, it were not blessed with good fortune. But good fortune did come in the person of the abbé de Lionne, son of Hughes de Lionne, twice Louis XIV's ambassador to Spain as well as his most distinguished minister of state.

We do not know the circumstances under which the abbé de Lionne, a man of means, a bibliophile, and a scholar for whom Spanish language and literature had a singular attraction, made Lesage's acquaintance. According to one of Lesage's sons, though, it was the good abbé—but a rascal if we are to believe Saint-Simon's *Mémoires*—who taught his father the Spanish language and familiarized him with Spanish literature in general. Furthermore, there is explicit evidence that Lionne showered Lesage with presents and, until his death in 1721, gave the younger man a pension of six hundred livres. By then Lesage had developed a considerable reputation as a playwright and novelist and was able to live and support his family in comparative comfort. But nowhere in his writings is there reference to the abbé's name.

With the exception of Cervantes' ever popular *Don Quixote*, major Spanish sources of French literature had been pretty much neglected following Pierre Corneille's *Le Cid* (1636) and Molière's brilliantly sinister treatment of the Don Juan theme in 1665. By the end of the period of French neoclassicism, Lesage for one had abandoned all thought of drawing inspiration and example from the classics of antiquity in general, and in particular from the *Lettres galantes d'Aristenète*, the erotic gallantry of the fictional letters of the Greek Sophist Aristaenetus, which he had translated from the Latin. He turned to Spain, possibly prodded by the abbé de Lionne, in search of more fertile and doubtless more lucrative sources for translation and adaptation. His next publication, appropriately titled the *Théâtre espagnol (Spanish Theater)*, appeared in 1700. It consisted of two five-act plays, one a translation from Lope de Vega and the other from Francisco de Rojas. In the preface to the volume, Lesage explained that his purpose

was to imitate the sparkle and ingenuity of the Spanish originals while omitting poetic extravagances, pompous nonsense, and swaggering braggadocio, all of which would run counter to French taste. Despite Lesage's precautions, neither of these two plays nor another adaptation of Rojas, *Le point d'honneur* (*The Point of Honor*, 1702), had any popular appeal for the French playgoer. Still undismayed, Lesage next offered the French national theater—known as "le Théâtre Français" or the Comédie Française—a double bill, *Don César Ursin*, a five-act imitation, scene for scene, of a play by Pedro Calderón de la Barca, but touched up for French consumption, and a gay, witty, skillfully contrived one-act comedy adapted with joyful abandon from a Spanish source and titled *Crispin, rival de son maître* (*Crispin, His Master's Rival*, 1709). It was the light, farcical *Crispin* and not the more ambitious, carefully worked and reworked *Don César* that won the plaudits of the spectators.

The period of release, of liberation as a writer, had begun. In his novel *Le diable boiteux* (*The Devil upon Two Sticks*, 1707) Lesage has a poet say: "Let small talents remain within the confining bonds of imitation, without daring to break them. There is prudence in their timidity." The little one-act play *Crispin*, with its boldness, dexterity, and wit, portrays an ingeniously unscrupulous valet resembling in part a Scapin of Molière and, at the same time, foreshadowing Beaumarchais's self-made, rascally hero Figaro.

Crispin, like Figaro, is ambitious and chafes at his lowly place in society. If Figaro's most telling thrusts are at the expense of the gilded aristocracy, those of Crispin are directed toward the shabby speculations of the financiers and the ruthless conduct of that voracious breed of *nouveaux riches,* the tax farmers, who contracted with the government to collect from the poor specific sums of money for the monarchy while pocketing whatever was left over—which they and their minions made sure was considerable.

Like Figaro, on the eve of the Revolution, Crispin, also in a time of far-reaching change, soliloquizes on his lot:

> How sick I am of being a valet! Yet it's no one's fault but your own, Crispin! You've always busied yourself with trifles; it's high time for you to shine in the world of finance. . . . With my nimble brain, by Jove, I could have been responsible for more than one bankruptcy.

Crispin, slight as it may be, was one straw in the wind showing that the turn of the century was a significant period of transition morally, politically, socially. It was a time when the Sun King was slowly dying of gangrene; a libertine nobility was eager to break with the monarch's newly found piety; the state was weighed down with debts brought on by incessant warfare and the cost of building Versailles and other architectural whims of royal grandeur; and taxation of the lower classes was pushed to extreme consequences. Never had the masses in France been steeped in such widespread poverty; never had blatant opportunists in all their vulgarity been so industrious; never had the princes of church and state been so dissolute. The Regency was soon at hand with its profligate extravagance. Monarchies would come and go, but the glorious spirit of the age and the majestic reign of the Sun King would be lost forever.

The public was ready for *Turcaret,* a paradigm of this transitional period, a five-act comedy of manners according to some, a comedy of character according to others. Many critics feel it is the most consequential French play to succeed *Le bourgeois gentilhomme (The Would-Be Gentleman)* and *Tartuffe* in the grand tradition of Molière. And like *Tartuffe* half a century before, it roused the fear and bitter enmity of certain coteries as well as the warm approval of those who detested the vulgar ostentation and general boorishness of the turcarets of the day (*turcaret,* an unscrupulous financier, became part of the French language, as did *tartuffe*).

By now Lesage was becoming increasingly well known, and it is said that the financiers, many of whom had mistresses among the actresses of the Comédie Française, offered him one hundred thousand livres to keep the play off the boards. The actors of the company, having already refused to appear in Lesage's *La tontine (Annuities and Death)* and *Les étrennes (New Year's Gifts),* two shorter comedies dealing with practitioners of financial chicanery, also refused to consider *Turcaret ou le financier* (the original title), until compelled to do so by order of the dauphin.

Before its seven performances by the reluctant actors, however, the comedy was already familiar to many for, as was the custom of the day, notable or even notorious men of letters were invited to read their unpublished manuscripts before numerous gatherings, especially in the more prestigious salons of the day. Lesage was one of those marked for this distinction. One often related incident reveals a bit of his Breton pride along with what was an independent and sometimes fiery spirit. On an appointed day, the playwright was an hour late in arriving at the Paris townhouse of a duchess in whose drawing room he was to read *Turcaret* before a group of distinguished guests. The duchess, piqued at the author's tardiness, tartly reminded him that he had caused all present to lose a good hour. Lesage replied that in that case he would save the company and the duchess two hours, and so picked up the manuscript and stalked out.

In the play all vital action swirls around Turcaret, and this focus gives it the unity that a good neoclassical comedy requires. Turcaret dominates the play with his presence, his vices, and, of course, his money; he does so even when he is offstage. His character and his actions bring the plot to a head. The other characters follow his example to his detriment, and sometimes theirs, for victimization, swindling, deception of all sorts, and gullibility are the order of the day. The plot is neatly summarized by the valet, Frontin, who views the action as a continuous ricocheting of cupidity, deceit, and gullibility such as has rarely been seen.

In the world of the five-act neoclassical French comedy, Lesage had shot his bolt, as it were. He had written his vitriolic masterpiece, and he had done so with an audacity and a wit almost equal to those found in the greatest comic playwright of all, Molière, and in certain scorching satirical portraits in Jean de La Bruyère's *Les caractères* (1688). Like Molière and La Bruyère, Lesage made formidable enemies for himself. If at first *Turcaret* was only a succès d'estime, it was because the powerful financiers—who had become inordinately wealthy from the practice of usury and unscrupulous tax contracts—had, under a dying monarch and his bankrupt government, formed a well-contrived cabal against the play and its author. And yet the play made its impact in more ways than one. The famous but generally ineffective motto *Castigat ridendo mores* (It [comedy] restrains morals through laughter) of the poet Jean de Santeul (Molière's contemporary) seems to have brought results. The newly enriched money-makers, in all their fatuity, arrogance, and ruthlessness, had been held up to ridicule as the epitome of vulgarity and greeted by the average theatergoer with derisive laughter. This satire, which Lesage had launched against the *turcarets* and their hangers-on, these "sanguesues d'État, . . . sanguesues du peuple" (leeches of the state and of the masses), was so scalding that, at least from 1709 on, a perceptible change for the better was apparent in their overall behavior.

Writing in 1742, Charles Duclos underscored the difference between operators in the money market in Lesage's comedy and the financiers in his own day some two decades later. Speaking of the pre-Regency world, he tells us:

> There was a time when a man of any sort at all, plunged headlong into business firmly resolved to make a fortune without having an underpinning of cupidity and avarice; a total lack of feeling for the baseness of his first dealings; a heart free of all scruples and inaccessible to remorse after success; with these qualities a man was bound to succeed. The nouveau riche while retaining his original manners added a ferocious pride of which his wealth was the measure; he was humble or insolent according to his losses and gains, and his self-evaluation, like the money he idolized, subject to increase and decrease.
>
> Financiers of that time were uncommunicative; mistrust made all men suspect to them, and public hatred put yet another barrier between them and society.
>
> (*Les confessions du Comte****, in *Oeuvres complètes*, Paris, 1821, vol. 1, pp. 266–267)

Turcaret, son of a village blacksmith, was one of these as he rose in the world of finance and clawed his way into the Parisian pseudonobility of the day.

An ironic note emerges from all this. The actors of the Comédie Française had, from the first, been ill-disposed toward Lesage, and the feeling was mutual. But to Lesage's bitter chagrin, one of his sons, under the name of Montménil, had become one of the great actors of the day. Moreover, he was elected a member of the company in 1730, the same year in which *Turcaret* was revived. Both play and actor were greeted with acclaim. After much persuasion Lesage attended one of his son's performances as the marquis in *Turcaret*. The theater, which had long separated the father and his gifted son, finally brought them together again; Lesage was inconsolable when Montménil was killed in a fall from a horse in 1743. The play has remained in the national theater's repertory.

Lesage was the only French writer of consequence during the fifteen years or so of political, social, and literary transition at the start of the eighteenth century. At that time he completed works that are still read or performed: the plays *Crispin* and *Turcaret*, the novel *The Devil upon Two Sticks*, and the first six books of *L'Histoire de Gil Blas de Santillane* (*The Adventures of Gil Blas de Santil-*

lana). La Bruyère, France's last authentic genius during what was to become the lackluster tapering off of Louis XIV's reign, had died some twenty-five years before Lesage was recognized. As Voltaire reflected in *Le siècle de Louis XIV* (*The Reign of Louis XIV,* 1751): "It will be difficult for new geniuses to rise, unless other morals, another sort of government, give a new twist to men's minds."

A propitious moment for change did arrive. The first volumes of Lesage's *Gil Blas* had appeared in 1715, precisely the year of Louis the Great's death. The Regency came into being, offering another sort of government and another set of morals. New talent and new genius sprang up and, according to the philosopher Yvon Belaval, presaged, in one way or another, the Age of Enlightenment, which lay just ahead. Among the works of writers and painters of note that revealed aspects of the "new spirit" was Lesage's "Au siècle des lumières" ("To the Age of Enlightenment," in *Histoire des littératures,* vol. 3, Paris, 1958, pp. 571–572).

To acquire self-assurance and momentum as a man of letters, Lesage's procedure in fiction was the same as in the theater. He started out with translations or adaptations from another language or culture—almost invariably Spanish. It was considered comparatively rare for a writer to make his mark with both plays and novels. Lesage and, not long after him, Pierre Carlet de Chamblain de Marivaux were the two authors of the early Enlightenment generally accorded this distinction.

In 1704, at the age of thirty-six, Lesage published the *Nouvelle aventures de Don Quichotte de la Manche (New Adventures of Don Quixote of La Mancha).* He readily and overmodestly admitted it to be in considerable measure the work of a certain Alonzo Avellaneda, published in Spain in 1614 and now appearing in French translation for the first time. Cervantes' *Don Quixote* was then as now recognized as one of the great novels of all time, popular in France as elsewhere, repeatedly translated and retranslated; as might be

expected, it furnished the inspiration for a plethora of sequels. Avellaneda may well have been a pseudonym for some author wishing to escape Cervantes' wrath against whoever had had the temerity to invent a second part of the original *Don Quixote* before he had published his own part 2. The few remarks and critical comments of Lesage do not go far toward justifying his choice in selecting Avellaneda. But it was Lesage's first attempt in the field of narrative fiction. The results of his efforts held a number of surprises in store. In the first place, he embroidered upon both Avellaneda and Cervantes. At times he paraphrased their handling of Don Quixote and Sancho with outrageous burlesque. Then again, he mercilessly cut episodes by both Spanish authors or playfully dragged them out. He criticized or praised them by turn. He resorted to parody at appropriate moments. He even added new adventures of his own and in so doing shaped what he had taken into a novel of human experience. Almost immediately a pirated edition was published in Holland and, within fifteen years, the book ran through three more French editions, to his unfeigned satisfaction. Lesage's contemporaries were delighted with him as translator of a highly diverting Spanish novel still unknown to French readers. It was not until the 1890's that Eugène Lintilhac, the nineteenth-century specialist on Lesage, gave convincing proof that this supposed second half of Avellaneda's novel was almost entirely the innovation of Lesage himself. Lintilhac's findings have been borne out in considerable detail by Roger Laufer, the leading authority on Lesage to date.

Lintilhac and Laufer have clearly demonstrated that Lesage went far toward freeing his literary personality from servile imitation of the Spaniards. There is added evidence of this in his next novel, *Le diable boiteux.* The first edition was repeatedly translated into English as both *The Devil upon Two Sticks* and *The Devil on Two Crutches;* it was received with enthusiasm in both Great Britain and colonial America.

ALAIN-RENÉ LESAGE

As Lesage was the first to admit—in his dedicatory note to the late, once renowned Spanish author Luis Vélez Guevara—he owed the title and the concept of his novel to Guevara's *El diablo cojuelo (The Limping Devil)*, which had first appeared in Madrid in 1641, twenty-seven years before Lesage's birth. Furthermore, as he explained, it was essential that *The Devil upon Two Sticks* be adapted to the tastes, interests, and inclinations of his own country. To this he added that doubtless Guevara's forgotten novel deserved the applause it had once received in Spain, and that if his own narrative was greeted with success, it might draw Guevara's work from the oblivion into which it had sunk. Then, concluding with the assertion "I have written a new novel" (J'ai fait un nouveau livre), he plunged in medias res, immediately setting the tone, giving the mood, and launching the action with a deftness entirely his own:

> One October night with the darkness hanging heavy over Madrid, the student Cléofas, interrupted in an amorous pursuit by a handful of ruffians, fled over the housetops of the sleeping city. In his escape he entered a lighted room, empty except for the alembics, flagons, quadrants, spheres, and compasses that told him he was in the laboratory of an astrologer or magician. Suddenly out of the room's silence there came a sigh.

Out of a cluster of alembics and decanters a voice rises saying that here in a nearby flask is the victim of a necromancer. It is nothing less than an imprisoned demon pleading for his release. His deliverer's reward will be great, for the embottled imp is renowned in his own right. He is, for instance, far-famed for marriages between toothless old men and nymphets, between masters and their maidservants, between virgins poor in dowry and penniless lovers—ill-assorted matches all. Furthermore, it is he, the demon boasts, who introduced chemistry, gambling, and general debauchery to the human race. He is the devil who invented carousels, music, dancing, comedies, and the latest French fashions. In brief, he holds a place of prominence in the hierarchy of demons and is celebrated under the name of Asmodeus, or the Limping Devil. The young scholar, versed in Greek mythology, also recognizes him to be Cupidon, the god of love, honored down through the centuries by poets and artists alike. So here is the opportunity to acquire more knowledge than all the universities of Europe could offer. Moreover, it is an opportune time and means for Lesage to reveal his gifts as a prose satirist of gentle irony and caustic wit.

Since the first edition of the novel was received with much enthusiasm when it was published in 1707, that year is generally considered to mark the date of Lesage's establishing himself as a man of letters. The public was not yet accustomed to a true depiction of manners and morals drawn from everyday life, except glimpses here and there in the comedies of Molière and one or two other playwrights. It was even alluded to as *The Characters* of La Bruyère turned into a novel, and it had the same appeal about it: spicy gossip, the odor of warmed-over scandal, the indiscretions of well-known personalities, and a great variety of choice tittle-tattle. The knowing Parisian could grasp the satirical allusions with ease; others were helped out through hints supplied by current journals. The news spread like wildfire that two nobles with drawn swords had fought over the lone remaining volume of the second edition still for sale. In fact, the novel became the prototype for popular taste in books and, in consequence, was looked down upon by certain reputable men of letters. It was reported that the celebrated neoclassical critic, the undisputed arbiter in literary taste, Boileau—having little use for novels—caught his lackey surreptitiously reading *The Devil upon Two Sticks* and soundly boxed the lad's ears.

But to return to the episodic plot, Don Cléofas, enchanted with the prospect of things to come, seizes the flagon from which the voice has escaped and smashes it into a thousand pieces. Out of a dense smoke steps a grotesque hunchback, two-and-a-half feet tall, supported by crutches, wearing a turban and a white satin cape, and with eyes like glowing coals. So this is Asmodeus, the god of love and of mischief!

There is not a moment to lose if they are to elude the dreaded necromancer. Telling the student to grasp his cape, the demon whisks him out of the window and swiftly takes him to the loftiest point overlooking the city, where, by lifting the roofs from the myriad dwellings of Madrid, that is, Paris, they can see the follies and foibles of mankind and much else.

The initial appeal to the student Cléofas (as to the reader of the time) derives from the voyeuristic pleasure of peering down into the antechambers, the salons, the boudoirs, and the alcoves to overhear and witness what was happening in the strictest privacy. The more notable financiers, misers, magistrates, courtesans, ministers of state, gallants, and eccentrics spring to life on the printed page. In some instances, Lesage modified the otherwise only too easily recognized portrait of a specific notable drawn close to perfection. In others, he emphasized the physical and moral traits of hostile critics, exemplars of legal corruption, haughty ladies of quality, inept actors, against all of whom he had reason to bear animosity.

But Cléofas is not merely curious. He wishes to understand, whenever possible, the wellsprings of human emotions, desires, pretensions, ambitions, rascalities, drolleries, eccentricities; the reasons for human attachments and human failings. There is even the longing to call on the recent past that will never return, to visit the mausoleums unlidded by the magic of Asmodeus to learn what thoughts and emotions had stirred the corpses in life and what had driven them to the stillness of death. He is avid to peer down into cells of lunatic asylums to have a better idea of what anguish, solace, folly, or deception

has incapacitated the minds and bodies of those fettered creatures in the vaults below.

The series of anecdotes, stories, and even related romances comprising the nocturnal spectacle of a city temporarily devoid of its roofs ends abruptly. The powerful spell of the necromancer is again upon the little imp. Bidding his apt pupil a fond farewell, Asmodeus reluctantly returns to his attic prison amid row upon row of bottles.

The overall framework for the novel was highly satisfying for readers of the day. Acceptance of the supernatural in its various forms was strong at the time, and *The Devil upon Two Sticks*, like so many other fictional works of the day, had not only a presiding demon but also sorcerers, soothsayers, astrologers, apothecaries bent over their secret concoctions, phantoms, and even covens of witches. Lesage treated all this with sly skepticism or irony. It was also the moment when the *Thousand and One Nights* burst out in translation on startled and delighted French readers. In many quarters the arcane was taken in all seriousness. When, not long after, the Sorbonne's most distinguished medical doctors had given up in despair at the bedside of a dying king, the portals of Versailles were thrown open to welcome a burly peasant who said he had the necessary brews, powders, and art to cure the royal patient; Louis XIV died two weeks later.

To be sure, *The Devil upon Two Sticks* has its flaws and is open to justified criticism. In the impressive gallery of portraits Lesage offered the reader, some had been drawn too hastily and seemed abrupt. Other physical and moral sketches struck critics as too frivolous, lacking in substance and short on interest. Occasionally, the shafts of satire were considered sharper than necessary, although the royal censor himself, in his *Note of Approbation*, declared he found much gaiety amid the sprightly and well-deserved barbs. The intermixture of long narrative with unadorned anecdotes gave a sense of disjointedness that could have been avoided had the individual sketches, portraits, and stories been fused into a generalized panorama with a strong central character around whom the basic action of the story revolved.

Still, in *The Devil upon Two Sticks* as in his first original play, *Crispin*, Lesage demonstrated that he was able to improve on his models. He was by no means a plagiarist, as Voltaire and one or two others claimed.

Toward the end of the nineteenth century, the critic Léo Claretie made a worthy observation. According to him, *The Devil upon Two Sticks* is not only Lesage's first novel but perhaps his only novel. It is a work that he redid with other settings. In it, the characters that stand out in his fiction are already on hand. *The Devil upon Two Sticks,* Claretie concludes, is at once the beginning and the résumé of Lesage's career as a novelist.

Claretie, in mentioning Lesage's formation as a novelist, perhaps should have given more emphasis to the preparatory role provided by his many little dramatic pieces relished by the general public. Like several other witty and talented men—Alexis Piron and Michel Jean Sedaine, for instance—he was long forced to earn a living by composing a considerable number of lively, highly entertaining, though evanescent skits of one sort or another. In doing so Lesage was able to support his wife, three sons, and daughter. The Comédie Française—along with the Comédie Italienne—shared under law the exclusive privilege of staging formal plays in French. The main outlet for the talent of the Lesages of the day consisted in furnishing a large variety of dramatic material for troupes of actors, minstrels, tightrope dancers, and mountebanks who performed annually at two great Paris fairs. That of Saint-Germain ran from August through September; the Saint-Laurent fair took over from February to Easter. The companies were enormously successful, particularly because of the topical satire furnished by Lesage and others in skits, parodies, caricatures, sideshows—usually mingled with songs, dances, and acrobatic tricks. These were performed in booths or on flimsy stages in front of the booths and amid the wares on sale. All classes of French society, the nobility, the bourgeoisie, and the *peuple,* went in droves to see these popular productions that had come to be known as *le théâtre de la foire* (fairground theatricals).

The Comédie Française, seeing its receipts sorely depleted as it struggled in competition with the popular spectacles of the *foire,* succeeded in having a governmental decree enacted forbidding the performance of these warmly received satirical, farcical, and burlesque skits and playlets. The *théâtre de la foire* got around the edict through sheer ingenuity. Instead of unauthorized dialogues, it presented a cavalcade of successive monologues; the actors resorted to pantomime while a single member of the company recited the play scene by scene from the wings; an actor at an appropriate moment would unfurl a long roll of paper or hold up a placard for the audience to read. Also at well-chosen intervals, topical songs were sung to popular tunes by actors, buffoons, and acrobats; the spectators joined in. It was small wonder that Jean Baptiste Rousseau, staunch defender of the staid Comédie Française, he who was the semiofficial neoclassical poet of the day, member of the exalted Academy of Inscriptions, and pomposity personified, scornfully declared that Lesage was in his true element working with tightrope dancers (*danseurs de corde*). But for thirty-five years it afforded Lesage a comfortable living and allowed him spare moments during which he could spin out his novels and even revise them with a loving hand.

In the several plays Lesage composed before he began writing for the *foire* or saw himself chiefly as a novelist, it is quite evident that it was the Spanish theater that not only stirred his imagination but also taught him the rudiments for fashioning comedies of intrigue. Yet in *La tontine* (1708), though essentially a comedy for the established theater where so much hinged on plot construction, it was apparent that in a number of respects Lesage was following not the Spanish theater but Molière. Like Molière, he boldly attacked false piety, unmitigated pedantry, and medical quackery; thus he earned attacks from the more conservative elements of France. Like Molière's, his satire could be uncomfortably topical. And especially like Molière, he was only incidentally concerned with form, being first and foremost an observer of his fellow men. Accordingly, like Molière, after providing a suitable pretext for a sustained dialogue accompanied by appropriate gestures, he would emphasize the characteristic behaviors of different social and occupational backgrounds while plot would remain secondary.

In 1712 Lesage, impressed with the success of the *foire* and the way it flouted the reign of an aged monarch and his dramatic institution, the Comédie Française, was delighted to be received with open arms by the Comédie's arch-enemy, the *théâtre forain* (traveling shows at fairs). He feted the occasion with his first piece for the fairs, *Les petits-maîtres (The Coxcombs)*, in which a typically modish aristocratic fop of the day meets Arlequin and confesses he joyfully patronizes the fairs while he invariably yawns when attending the national "opéra" and falls asleep at the equally national "Comédie...."

By 1714 Lesage was already well on his way to becoming the foremost writer for the *théâtre forain*. It was the year when his two-act play *Arlequin colonel (Colonel Arlequin)* was performed at both the Foire Saint-Germain and the Foire Saint-Laurent. In writing for the fairs an author had to have a strong sense of immediacy, an excellent idea of the latest trends, fads, and hypocrisies. *Colonel Arlequin* touched upon the promiscuity of the *beau monde* at fashionable balls, the callousness of fathers trying to rid themselves of daughters by marrying them off to the first comer, the presumption of legal and medical quackery, and like themes, commingled with vaudevillian songs and dances.

The year 1715 witnessed the death of the Sun King, the advent of Philippe d'Orléans as the notoriously dissolute regent of France, and forebodings of economic disaster throughout the land—though John Law was yet to appear. It also brought the first six books of *Gil Blas* before the public—books Lesage had been writing since 1712 during spare moments between his dramatic outpourings for the fairs. At the age of forty-seven, Lesage had come into his own. From now on the novel vied with the stage as a vehicle for depicting his views of humanity in action.

Eugène Lintilhac, though he wrote in 1893, remains one of the few authorities on Lesage and his work. What he said nearly a century ago still holds today:

> In the satire of character or that of social conditions, in his *théâtre de la foire* and in *Gil Blas*, Lesage has no rival, if not for the bitterness of his attacks, at least for the finesse and cleverness of the criticism, for the truth of the observation, for the genuineness, the life, and the inexhaustible variety of unusual types, finally for his amusing dexterity in seizing and putting vividly on the stage, where they belonged, tittle-tattle and piquant current events. . . .
>
> (*Lesage*, p. 132)

Lintilhac saw that these effective qualities in Lesage's theater were equally evident in his novels, not only in *Gil Blas* but in his prose fiction in general.

Joseph Spence, the English essayist and chronicler, had visited Lesage in the Faubourg Saint-Jacques, where he lived for well over three decades, enjoying harmonious domesticity and turning out plays for the fairs and fiction for the booksellers with seemingly the greatest of ease. Spence describes the house in the second volume of *Observations, Anecdotes, and Characters of Books and Men:*

> An extremely pretty place to write it was. His house is in Paris in the suburbs of Saint Jacques, and so open to the country air, and the garden laid out in the prettiest manner that ever I saw for a town garden. It was as pretty as it was small, and when he was in the study part of it he

was quite retired from the noise of the street or any interruptions from his own family. The garden was only the breadth of the house, from which you stepped out into a raised square parterre planted with a variety of the prettiest flowers. From this you went down by a flight of steps on each side into a berceau which led to two rooms, or summerhouses, quite at the end of the garden. These were joined by an open portico, the roof of which was supported with columns so that he could walk from one to the other, all under cover, in the intervals of writing. The berceaux were covered with vines and honeysuckles, and the space between them was grovework. It was in the right-hand room as you go down that he wrote *Gil Blas.*

It was here, then, in the solitude of an idyllic spot that Lesage spent a large share of his waking hours depicting through his plays and novels what turned out to be a vast and, for the most part, satirical portrait of his age. While he remained sedentary, his imagination took his restless characters to the four corners of the earth. In plays and, especially, in novels he created protagonists who learned and demonstrated the ways of the world.

Having won over Paris and the rest of France as well, *The Devil upon Two Sticks* was soon translated into various European languages. Such an unexpected and amazingly quick success for a short and plotless, though appetizingly satirical, bit of disguised fact and improbable fiction had much to do with deciding the main course of Lesage's literary career. Publishers begged him to write another enticingly satirical series of animated portraits. That in itself was enough to persuade him that he had perhaps found his true bent.

It is probable that Lesage began writing the first part of *Gil Blas,* his masterwork, in 1712 or 1713. It is the autobiographical account of another youth, who is somewhat like Cléofas of *The Devil upon Two Sticks*—inquisitive by nature and possessed of a naive self-assurance and lukewarm scholarly ambitions—and who feels prepared to make his way in the world

while witnessing and experiencing human behavior at all levels of society.

Gil Blas evolved over a long period of time, in three sections contained in four volumes; each volume included several books. Each section was a novel in itself, with a beginning, middle, and end; and each new section was motivated by the success of the preceding section. During the intervals between the writing of the sections, the French political, religious, and social scene was constantly in a state of change. Moreover, both the character of Gil and Lesage himself evolved in the advancing years. Then, too, between 1715 and 1735 fiction assumed new forms, and, in due course, literary critics and the general reading public were open to new interpretations of fiction as a literary genre and, as would be expected, adopted fresh ways of looking at *Gil Blas.* As a result, the work became far more complex than it had at first seemed. Since Lesage's death, serious attempts at classifying the novel have resulted in a confusing mass of contradictions.

What was long referred to as "The Question of *Gil Blas*" had first been raised by Voltaire. The question reduced to its simplest terms was "Who really was the author of *Gil Blas?*" In the 1775 edition of his *Reign of Louis XIV,* with no love in his heart, Voltaire gave Lesage short shrift:

> Lesage, born in Vannes in Lower Brittany in 1667. His novel, *Gil Blas,* has lasted because of its fidelity to nature; it was taken entirely from *La Vida del escudero don Marcos* [*The Life of Squire Don Marcos*]. Died in 1747.

Voltaire was too intelligent to attack the novel *qua* novel in this curt notice. He erred, no doubt unintentionally, in stating that Lesage was born in Vannes and the year of his birth was 1667. Voltaire showed his maliciousness, however, by adding that the novel had been completely lifted from the half picaresque novel, half autobiography of the

Spanish poet Vicente Espinel (1550–1642). Voltaire, under various guises, had been the veiled butt of Lesage's satire on the boards of the open-air theaters of Paris. In *Gil Blas* he was especially satirized as the dramatic poet Don Gabriel Triaquero, who, during intermissions, went from one first-tier box to the next "modestly offering his head for the laurels that were his due." Voltaire finally took his revenge, but his antagonist had long since been dead.

Others followed in Voltaire's footsteps to malign Lesage's abilities as a novelist. The most notable of these was a Spanish priest, Father Isla, who declared that for the honor and glory of Spain he had translated *Gil Blas* back into the original from which Lesage had stolen it. However, "The Question of Gil Blas" has once and for all been settled. Lesage freely acknowledged both orally and in his prefaces that when he translated a work into French, he bluntly stated as much. He admitted with equal readiness that he did not hesitate to draw incidents, romances, ideas, even characters from various French, Spanish, and Italian historical and literary sources to make them his own. By the nineteenth century, the question of plagiarism had been well settled in favor of Lesage. Any partial plagiarism dug up by diligent scholars has done little to detract from the freshness and originality with which he portrayed the weaknesses and absurdities of human nature.

What sort of novel is it, then? For eighteenth- and nineteenth-century European and American readers, it was held the best-known example of picaresque fiction. Though it borrows generously from the Spanish picaresque tradition, present-day scholars are quick to point out it has not a great deal in common with such well-known Spanish picaresque novels as the anonymously written *Lazarillo de Tormes* (1554) and Mateo Alemán's equally famous *Guzmán de Alfarache* (1599–1605). Elements of the picaresque are plentiful in *Gil Blas*, but they may also be found in

Petronius' *Satyricon*, the *Metamorphoses* of Apuleius, and even the medieval *fabliaux*. But "picaresque" is an adjective deriving from the Spanish *pícaro* (rogue). In the Spanish tradition a *pícaro* is a young person of questionable morals, and often criminal intent, who outwits and is outwitted by others in the course of wandering along dusty roads from town to town. Two derivative names for the genre are the "rogue novel" and the "road novel." Such fiction usually consists of a series of loosely connected episodes following one upon the other and offering satirical sketches and interpolated stories often cynical in tone. *Gil Blas*, as we shall see, only partly fits such a description.

Gil Blas has also been called "the first important novel of manners in France," "the last of the early realistic novels," a *roman à tiroirs* or episodic novel, and even a novel of youthful education and development, such as the German Bildungsroman of the next century. The fact that so many categories present themselves is testimony to the rich development of novel types in the eighteenth century.

Between the death of Louis XIV and the Revolution, thousands of new French works of fiction were published openly or surreptitiously in France or printed in some other country and smuggled across frontiers to escape the watchful eye of governmental censors. Indeed the most daring, the most provocative, the most influential literary achievements of the age were in the domain of the novel. During the preceding era, prose fiction had been almost entirely in the hands of nonprofessionals and women, who generally kept close to the proprieties of the day.

As Georges May and others have repeatedly noted, there were in the seventeenth century few rules for the budding French novelist to follow, few challenging fictional patterns to be seized upon, whereas the respected dramatist or epic poet proceeded as if he were following the prescribed figures of a court minuet. And so what writers of fiction there were at the time—Honoré d'Urfé (1567–1625), Charles Sorel (1597–1674), Mlle. de Scudéry (1607–1701), Paul Scarron (1610–1660), Antoine Furetière (1619–1688), Mme. de La Fayette (1634–1693)—either idealized their subject matter, often extravagantly, or resorted to satire and down-to-earth realism. By the eighteenth century, however, French novelists strove to loosen their bonds. And many among them arrived at a realistic, spirited, graphically truthful presentation of life.

Doubtless Lesage would have shrugged his shoulders at the efforts of posterity to locate the proper niche for *Gil Blas.* He knew, as we do now, that it was a tale of a hundred episodes. More precisely, he knew its place and its twin purpose as a novel, and he tersely said as much. Drawing the pseudomemoirs to a close (he himself now well along in years), he had his elderly hero address the prospective reader to the effect that the contents would merely entertain some, whereas others, besides being entertained, could also learn something of the ways of the world. Richard Bjornson would seem justified in comparing the product of Lesage's pen with "an enormous comic stage where all the characters are playing roles in a kaleidoscopic sequence of scenes which reconciles the audience's sentimental expectations of poetic justice with its demand for verisimilitude."

It cannot be denied that *Gil Blas* has at the least the general underlying structure of the typical Spanish picaresque novel, where roguery plays a preponderant role, as a young person, by fair means or foul, attempts to find an appropriately agreeable place in the sun. Gil Blas, too, experiences—in one way or another—the impact of society, in his case, from its lowest dregs to the upper reaches of nobility. As the work unfolds, the protagonist develops a psychological consistency lacking in the Spanish picaresque novel. Each succeeding adventure is one more step toward his understanding of man in society and one more stage in his own evolution as a distinctive personality. Gil Blas, unlike other pícaros, looks

at himself at times as if he were someone else. And what he sees prevents him from taking himself too seriously. To read Lesage's narrative looking for elements of the French picaresque novel *à l'espagnole,* or, as some critics have done, to study it as the prototype of *The Human Comedy* (where in forty volumes Balzac attempted to give a complete picture of the society of his day), or to accept it as the chief progenitor of the nineteenth-century French *roman de moeurs* (novel of manners) is to approach it in ways that have lost much of their relevance for modern scholarship.

Nevertheless, *Gil Blas* is a universal novel, in that each reader finds evidence of his own strengths and weaknesses, hopes and chagrins, successes and failures, and recognizes himself as part of general humanity. Charles Nodier, in his "Notice sur *Gil Blas*" (1835), was persuaded that this broad appeal results from the fact that the novel represents the moral history of the average man who has experienced all conditions of life. This opinion was close to that of Nodier's eminent compeer, Charles Sainte-Beuve, who stressed the point that here was the ordinary man par excellence, no better and no worse than another.

It is customary to follow Lintilhac and, indeed, Lesage a century and a half before him, in noting that the novel falls into three distinct parts. The first part (books 1–6, 1715), the section richest in events and adventures, begins by following the general pattern of picaresque plots but ends with Gil Blas achieving moral and social equilibrium as he mends his rapscallion ways—at least for the time being—and becomes majordomo of a fine country estate. The tone of these first six books is zestful, spiced with wit and good humor and the poetry of youth.

The three books of the second part were published nine years later. The accent is on the character of the hero far more than on his countless and often diverting adventures. Both Gil Blas and Lesage alike sound older, less impulsive, more mature, and at times given over to sobering reflection. We have the impression that the author had to grow older, more mellow, in order to catch convincingly the influence of the passing years on his chief character.

In the third part (books 10–12, 1735), a little over a decade later, Lesage and his protagonist have aged perceptibly. This part, which brings the 700-page novel to a close, has a certain delicate charm about it, in the serenity with which old age feels and knows that a little time is still left, looks back with a touch of nostalgia for the past, and sees how it blends with the present. The narrative finally draws to a close in a mood of comforting self-reconciliation for author and protagonist alike.

The novel is in reality three novels, each with a beginning, a middle, and an end, each independent and yet interacting with the others. As such, it offers at times startling perspectives. Roger Laufer suggests that we are confronted with a sort of triptych. The term is apt; like altarpieces of that name, it has its three "panels," the two side panels throwing an oblique light on one another and on the center panel, which in turn gives a sense of unity by shedding light on the whole.

An elderly Gil Blas, in beginning his autobiography, reaches back through memory to when he was a lad of seventeen. The only child of respectable but humble parents, he seemed little more than a quite ordinary youth destined to become an obscure member of the lower middle class in the town of his birth. Fortunately, his mother, a lady's maid, had a brother who was both Gil's godfather and a canon in the local church. The small, pudgy clergyman had little formal learning; his main interests were eating well and receiving the regular stipend due a canon. Nevertheless, he had early taken young Gil under his wing and given him the rudiments of an education. A more learned priest was called upon to tutor him in Latin, Greek, and rhetoric. It was then that Uncle Pérez, no longer wishing to be burdened with the responsibility and continued expense of a godson, decided it was time for Gil to leave home and family to continue his studies at the University of Salamanca—a destination that would never be reached.

Gil Blas was delighted to leave his familiar surroundings and see the world. His uncle gave him a pocketful of ducats for his expenses on the way and a mule, which Gil could sell upon reaching Salamanca. Before setting out, the youth took leave of his father and mother, who enriched him with such advice as to pray for his uncle, to avoid evil ways and bad company, and, above all, to refrain from stealing what belonged to others. They then made a present of their blessing, which, Gil says ironically, was the only gift he expected from them anyway. "Behold me then on my way," he tells the reader, "master of my own conduct, of a pitiful mule, and forty good ducats, besides some extra money I had stolen from my much honored uncle." And so Gil Blas, a bit of a seventeen-year-old rogue, was en route. But he was far from the penniless abandoned figure of the traditional Spanish *pícaro* who, in his solitude, had only his wits at his disposal.

Gay, naive, carefree, self-confident, gullible, and short on scruples, young Gil Blas rode his mule in the morning sunshine, counting his ducats into his hat, when suddenly there emerged an armed ruffian to relieve him of part of his money. Arriving at an inn for the night in the next town, he was exploited unmercifully by the innkeeper, taken complete advantage of by a flatterer, and swindled by a muleteer. He had, however, received his first practical lesson in the ways of the world: in brief, the need to mistrust others. Alas, he was to be victimized numerous times before he was able to grasp the lesson fully. His travels had only just begun, and what he experienced at the inn was as nothing compared with what the future held. An extraordinary variety of episodes was to unfold throughout in quick succession. But in a short summary it would be impossible to do justice to the prodigious activity of all kinds stirred up by plain adventurers, the nobility and its lackeys, the clergy, the bourgeoisie, actors and actresses, men of letters, governors and magistrates, the police, and that great butt of Molière's gibes, the medical doctor. Scattered here and there a few honest, upright characters are to be found. Still, virtue is not a particularly fruitful topic for a writer of satire, and the decent people who do occasionally emerge in the novel are understandably less interesting to the reader than the knaves, scoundrels, reprobates, malefactors, libertines, procurers, trollops, and hypocrites.

Once well on his way, Gil Blas, falsely accused of theft and fleeing the law, falls into the clutches of a band of brigands. Forthwith, he is taken to their large subterranean habitation, for him a prison. Instead of remaining their scullion, he joins the highwaymen on their forays in plundering and slaughtering, the better to gain his liberty. He succeeds in making good his escape, taking with him a lady of quality the bandits wished to keep for their own sexual purposes.

At this juncture Lesage resorts to the time-honored tradition of Spanish and Italian romances, the interpolated story, where one person entertains others with a detailed account of unexpected turns of fate. Such misfortunes as violent and sudden death, financial ruin, the tragic loss of a loved one, betrayal, malevolent cruelty, and general heartbreak are mingled with breathtaking adventures and the capriciousness of blind chance.

This popular narrative device not only offers the reader a change of pace and a fresh set of characters every so often, it helps the novelist—sometimes short on invention—to pad his work by pilfering from an almost inexhaustible store of tales depicting the vicissitudes of fortune and retelling them in new settings. Like the great Cervantes, whose *Don Quixote* is filled with interpolated tales, Lesage resorted repeatedly to the device in *Gil Blas* and his other works of fiction. In one instance he even freely admitted that the interpolated story or novella was overly long.

In the present instance the lady, whose honor and perhaps whose life had been so gal-

lantly saved, presents Gil Blas with a sack of gold pieces and a diamond ring. He is now rich beyond his fondest dreams (but not for long). Dazzling Gil Blas with her seductive beauty and promises of things to come, a woman of the world—playing an elaborate confidence game in conjunction with her paramour—strips the lad of all his possessions.

Meeting by chance his childhood friend Fabrice, he is persuaded to give up all thought of a university education and hires himself out as a valet. An intelligent lackey, Fabrice explains, does not confine himself to menial work. He goes into a family to command rather than obey. He begins by studying his employer: he accommodates himself to his weaknesses, wins his confidence, and then leads him by the nose. If his employer has vices, the clever lackey will flatter him and turn them to his advantage. It is a procedure followed by most valets in Lesage's novels.

Fabrice's advice is doubtless excellent but can be put to little use when an aged, gout-ridden ecclesiastic, in need of "an honest valet," immediately takes Gil Blas into his service. The canon, now impotent but a great glutton, consumes each day copious quantities of the best foods and wines served up by the still attractive housekeeper and the new lackey. Gil Blas is so attentive serving food during the day and assiduous in fetching the old man's chamber pot throughout the night that the priest promises to remember his valet, along with the housekeeper, in his will.

Within three months, the elderly priest's gout takes a turn for the worse. He sends for a highly respected doctor and, at the same time, a notary to draw up his will. When the notary learns that the physician is none other than the famous Doctor Sangrado, he hastens to the bedside of the cleric knowing that under this doctor's care the patient has only a short time to live. The will is drawn up; the priest is hastened to his grave by the medical attention received; his beloved housekeeper and her supposed "niece," a girl of ten, inherit the estate, the canon's immediate family nothing, and

Gil Blas a library consisting of a few moth-eaten volumes—one of which is entitled *Le parfait cuisinier (The Complete Housewife)*. This is, with its sly innuendos (the priest has not kept his vow of celibacy), one of the better-known incidents in the first part of the novel.

Besides Gil Blas himself, probably the best-known character in this first section is the aforementioned Doctor Sangrado, who so ably hastened the canon's demise. As Katherine Carson has said, the eighteenth-century French physician enjoyed a privileged position in society that was rarely commensurate with his skill. Medical practice, little more than a continuation of procedures followed during the seventeenth century, remained a barbarous occupation. Acceptable remedies included physics, emetics, broths, poulticing, and especially bleeding. In plays and novels, it was a commonplace to depict a doctor who kills rather than cures. The name Sangrado was well chosen since *sangrador* is Spanish for bloodletter. It is probable that Lesage had in mind one of the most famous physicians of the day, Philippe Hecquet, dean of the faculty of medicine of Paris, who, in his writings, advocated incessant cuppings, a frugal table, and hot water. One of his medicinal treatises was *Les vertus médicinales de l'eau commune* (The Medicinal Virtues of Ordinary Water).

Doctor Sangrado is pleased to take on the now unemployed Gil Blas, first as a clerk, then as an apprentice physician. The doctor considers it a waste of time for the lad to engage in such studies as pharmacy, anatomy, and botany: "Know, my friend, all that is required is to bleed your patients and make them drink warm water. This is the secret of curing all the distempers incident to man." Gil Blas is soon afforded ample opportunity to practice medicine, for smallpox begins to ravage the city of Valladolid, and all the local physicians have their hands full. Doctor Sangrado and his assistant each administer their prescriptions to some dozen patients a day. None survives, which Gil Blas finds disconcerting. When the

lover of one of his patients—who has gone the way of the others—promises to dispatch the young physician with a rapier, Gil Blas gives up his new profession and moves on to Segovia, Madrid, and Toledo. Often living meagerly as a valet, he serves both masters and mistresses and keeps morally disreputable company throughout. Vanity, connivance, promiscuity, and victimization are the prevailing behavior.

Eighteenth-century French critics were inclined to reproach Lesage for depicting so many ignominious characters. Nineteenth-century critics were, on the whole, more charitable in this respect, maintaining that the author was merely portraying society more or less as it was and would always be.

Both before and after *Gil Blas*, the main theme in French fiction of the eighteenth century was love in its various forms, idealized, thwarted, or desecrated. This was especially the case in the novels of Lesage's contemporary the abbé Prévost. In *Gil Blas*, though, we are dealing with an early and at times quite stark realism. "Love" is a scenario played out in the social arena. As the first section of the novel gains momentum, the hero becomes more and more enmeshed in the toils of the *beau sexe* as he plays along with actors and actresses, men and women of the aristocracy, insolent fops as well as man- and maid-servants like himself. Lester Crocker, in *An Age of Crisis*, calls it the great game of love, a game "in which the male's role is ruthlessly to seduce and enjoy, that of the female to conquer and enslave the male—or to use the word that was to become the fashion, *fixer le mâle*."

Gil Blas is able to view such activities in Madrid from a number of vantage points. One of these is from his position as domestic in the establishment of Arsénie, a coquettish, much-sought-after actress. At first he is intoxicated by what he sees as piquant experiences among attractive soubrettes, fashionable comediennes, their wealthy pursuers, and their expectant hangers-on. Then uneasiness and disenchantment set in; Gil Blas explains to an acquaintance his sudden departure from this alluring household: "After having stayed almost a month at Arsénie's, whose style of living I found altogether unsuitable, I have just left on my own initiative in order to preserve my innocence." Considering what the protagonist has already experienced, we may conclude that the word "innocence" is used ironically. Gil Blas, however, finally attains—at least temporarily—something of a moral and spiritual equilibrium thanks to a respectable and lucrative position as steward for an aristocratic friend who has at last come into his own. And so end the six books of part 1.

Since it was almost immediately a success, Lesage slowly and deliberately set out to write a sequel. Part 2 appeared in 1724. Again episode follows episode in quick succession, and a gallery of characters is paraded before our eyes. The situation or character of a given personage is, as before, often depicted by a simple gesture or a telling remark. In a grave voice but with merriment in her eyes, a former soubrette with many lovers piously remarks, "I turned actress to preserve my morals." In part 2 there are also constant chance meetings of old friends, acquaintances, and lovers, so much so that the reader is given the impression that the universe holds ten thousand people, and they all know one another.

Still, in the 1724 sequel, Gil Blas has lost his newly found sense of honesty in behavior and purity of intentions. The novel is now in a postpicaresque stage; the emphasis has shifted from the man's adventures to the man himself. Lesage warns us through his hero's own words that there is to be a change as he again heads for Madrid: "Fate has taken me by the hand and led me there to fill more important roles than any I have performed before."

The time was propitious for such a decision. At the moment Lesage was writing, the head of state in France was the regent, Philippe d'Orléans, a gifted but odd sort of man who had taken up alchemy and drifted into a life of debauchery. He has frequently been held to be the symbol of the depravity that extended down through various layers of Parisian society during his ascendancy. Orléans's escapades were rivaled only by those of his extraordinary daughter, the duchesse de Berry, to whom he has been suspected of having more than a paternal attachment. It was a time when Lesage, the masterful satirist, could without fear—for censorship was at an ebb—proceed to give a vivid picture of various aspects of the rakish Regency, with special emphasis placed on sexual and fiscal intrigues. And it was a time when Gil Blas was convinced that a fortune could be made in the nation's capital, even by those of ordinary talents.

Before setting out for Madrid, however, Gil Blas passes through two incidents that add to his knowledge of the world and its ways. The first of these, known to every French schoolchild, is the most famous anecdote in the entire novel. Gil Blas, having been warmly recommended by a noble whose valet he had been, goes to the magnificent episcopal palace of the archbishop of Granada seeking the post of secretary to the great man. The prelate is sixty-nine years old and physically resembles Gil's uncle, the canon. Like him, the archbishop is almost as wide as he is tall, bald, and with legs bowed inward.

But our hero sees that, despite his unprepossessing physique, the archbishop, like all high dignitaries, creates an aura of grandeur about him. The moment he enters the room, his insolent officers fall into a profound and respectful silence. His Grace has been looking for a young man with a smattering of Greek and Latin and excellent penmanship, for the prelate is a "great author" whose keenest satisfaction in life is producing flawless and eloquently delivered homilies by the hundreds. For these he needs a bright young man to transcribe elegant-looking copies of sermons against avarice, gluttony, voluptuousness, female frailty, and other perils. Gil Blas fills this role admirably and soon becomes the great prelate's favorite.

ALAIN-RENÉ LESAGE

The archbishop, wise in years, tells his secretary that one day his latest homilies might show the ossification of old age. A condition of the young man's employment with him is the solemn promise that he will caution the archbishop should his eloquence ever begin to flag. He will be well rewarded for his honesty.

Before long, however, Gil Blas's ecclesiastical master suffers a stroke of apoplexy, which understandably impairs the quality of his sermons. Following the archbishop's orders, Gil tactfully warns the old man that he is slipping. His Grace becomes irate at this intimation of his decline and summarily dismisses his protégé with the charge that he is incapable of distinguishing between gold and tinsel.

The story of the prelate and his trusted secretary made a tremendous impact on Lesage's contemporaries, and the incident is very much a part of French folklore. Such vanity as his belongs to all ages. But his resemblance to certain Parisian personalities of the day was pointed out in France's leading periodical, the *Mercure de France* (June 1724). The satire here, however, was relatively mild. The archbishop was, after all, an extremely pious if somewhat vain prelate. Other men of the cloth who came under Lesage's pen, however, were on occasion drawn as exaggerated examples of stupidity, lustfulness, greed, and hypocrisy. That this should be his view is hardly surprising; the clergy of the Regency was, in his eyes, simply the reflection of the standards of the society it served.

The second and far more mundane incident near the beginning of part 2 brings Lesage's hero back to the world of actors and actresses, where, well before the archbishop of Granada incident, he had first acquired a relish for the theater and its wanton pleasures. In the nation's capital he had become a lover of the aspiring comedienne Laure and remained devoted despite her almost daily inconstancy. But, unable to reconcile himself to the flexible morals of the milieu in general and of Laure in particular, he had found himself torn with doubts as to where the joys of love lay. Awakening one morning, hearing the small voice of conscience, and without a farewell to his dear Laure, he had set out to find employment in more reputable surroundings.

Now in Granada and having been dismissed by its archbishop, he is again drawn to the theater, where the current play and its leading lady, "the divine Estelle," are the talk of the town. Seated in a packed house, he soon discovers that Estelle is none other than the Laure of former days. It is well known in Granada's taverns that her present lover is a distinguished Portuguese nobleman. But to Gil Blas's delight, when he presents himself to Laure the following morning, he is received with open arms. She passes him off as her beloved long-lost brother and presently tells him that her plans are to lend herself to three or four more wealthy aristocrats. This would provide a tidy little fortune and, since she and Gil Blas were, after all, created by heaven for one another, they could finally enjoy the bonds of marriage. Alas, she had merely built a castle of dreams. Narcisse, the one comedienne of the troupe who for years has been faithful to one man alone, her husband, is now the most promiscuous actress of the lot. Since she wants the Portuguese nobleman for one of her present conquests, she plans to expose Gil Blas for what he is, not the brother but the former lover of Laure. The hero accordingly takes measures while his skin is whole and escapes in the direction of Madrid at three o'clock the following morning. It is clear that if the depravity of the Regency had touched even the clergy, it had intensified the already notorious turpitude of those in the world of provincial theater.

Once again in the nation's teeming capital, Gil has his first significant encounter; it is with Captain Chinchilla, the protagonist for the first episode of a new series of events. This is, perhaps, as good a moment as any for a word on Lesage's use of description.

Every so often the author, or rather his hero, pauses to say that if he were to follow the

335

practice of so many other raconteurs, he would, from time to time, break off and go into a long, tedious description of a personage or of a locale merely for the sake of describing. The implication is that his own descriptions are pertinent to the narrative. He is right: they are; and they are usually arresting as well. Wishing to depict Chinchilla as an elderly, honorable, maimed officer whose services to his country have gone unrewarded, whereas the author of a few wretched sonnets might well receive a generous pension, he gives the following portrait of the old soldier. It is quite typical of the Lesage–Gil Blas preoccupation with descriptive details that prepare us for the story to follow:

> Seeing him for the first time I simply stared at him. He was a man about sixty, extremely tall and incredibly thin. He had a thick mustache that curled up to his temples on each side. Besides that, he was short of an arm and a leg, and a green silk patch took the place of a missing eye. His face had been slashed here and there. Except for that, he was pretty much like any other man. Moreover, he was not lacking in intelligence and had an air of sad dignity about him. He was morally scrupulous and prided himself on his sense of honor.
>
> (7.12)

The pride, the sense of honor, and the complete honesty of Captain Chinchilla are merely obstacles to his petition for the military pension that is his due. Through manipulations that the captain would reject as unprincipled, if he were aware of them, Gil and his friends obtain for him the pension that he so well deserves. For even the casual reader the description of the captain becomes an integral part of the incident.

Shortly after the Chinchilla affair, Gil Blas again runs into his friend Fabrice, who like himself has gravitated toward Madrid, the center of everything that is desirable, expedient, or both. Fabrice, son of the barber back in their hometown, has, through chicanery,

found himself in the minor nobility. His apartment of four rooms is, in reality, one rather large room partitioned into four sections. Gil Blas describes it with the eye of a practiced observer. Presented with the unflinching realism of a Balzac, the picture shows in minute detail a place of clutter and confusion and abominable taste. It prepares us for the figure of Don Fabrice, fashionable author and critic, who represents the new criticism and practice of the day. According to him, style must not be simple and natural, but complex and obscure. Prose and poetry should be filled with perplexities and innovations that are so many stumbling blocks for the reader. One should be a bold innovator, making changes in the language and seeking odd expressions, unfamiliar words. (The term *néologisme* did not come into general usage in France until the middle of the eighteenth century, after the publication of *Gil Blas.*) "After all," asserts Fabrice, "our design is highly commendable; and, prejudice apart, we are more valuable than those natural writers, who speak like the common run of mankind" (7.13). Lesage's description here functions on three levels: it portrays a specific individual; it gives an emblematic significance to places and things; and it satirizes intellectual and artistic pretensions.

Having passed from master to master as lackey, accountant, steward, and secretary, Gil Blas begins in earnest a new life under the tutelage of none other than the duc de Lerme, prime minister of Spain. In presenting himself to this personage, our still lighthearted young man attempts as usual to skip over as deftly as possible, without telling downright falsehoods, the more unsavory aspects of his past life. But, despite his efforts, the duke senses where the truth lies:

> "M. de Santillane," he said to me when I had finished, "it seems to me that you have been something of a picaro." "Monseigneur," I replied blushing, "Your excellency insisted that I

be sincere. I have obeyed." "I am pleased you have," he answered. "Come, my boy, you've gotten out of it cheaply. I am surprised that bad example hasn't completely ruined you. How many respectable people would become consummate scoundrels if chance put them to the same test."
(8.2)

Shortly after this interview, Gil Blas's life does indeed change. The prime minister senses that, from among his staff of secretaries, the new arrival is astute enough, adequately shrewd, and even sufficiently dependable to be taken into his confidence both in matters of court intrigue and in financial schemes. Our hero immediately shows his aptitude and soon becomes the duke's favorite. From his hero's new vantage point, Lesage reveals to us the secrets of government, administration, and the general state of affairs at this time.

Under the cover of fiction—the cadre being the reign of the Spanish king Philippe III (1598–1621)—we are, of course, in reality scrutinizing the Regency of Philippe d'Orléans. The sinister shadow of the regent's minister, the ambitious, greedy, and unscrupulous Cardinal Dubois, falls across the pages of this part of the novel. With the finances of France already in a critical state at the death of Louis XIV, and the nation on the verge of bankruptcy, the Scottish financier John Law arrived to engage Philippe in fiscal manipulations that promised prompt and easy gains for the government, for commerce, and for industry. Speculators sprang up everywhere—the regent was one of them—and fortunes were made and lost overnight. All classes in France were more money conscious than ever before in the country's history.

As this section of the novel progresses, the prime minister lets Gil Blas know that he can fatten his purse by being intermediary between petitioners and the duke in a wide variety of matters. Usually the duc de Lerme would grant these requests, and his confiden-

tial secretary, as a go-between, would be rewarded by the person seeking favors. The secretary's coffers were filled with doubloons from handling the dispensations of titles of nobility and selling letters of patent. It is understood that Gil Blas may pocket reasonable sums of money for these and other often shady practices. But he must share with the duke when large sums are involved.

Lesage's hero is already doing very well with his stock in trade, and he boasts, "I was not satisfied with making governors only; I conferred orders of knighthood, and converted some good common folk into bad gentlemen" (8.9). He is abetted in questionable practices by one of his servants, Scipión, in whom he had immediately recognized a disposition for intrigue that could admirably suit his purpose—to amass more money and to heighten his prestige. Scipión, with a history of roguery behind him, proves adept in ferreting out persons who will pay well for requests granted by the corrupt court. Consequently, Gil Blas and the indispensable Scipión both flourish.

Since it has become common knowledge that Gil is a favorite of the duc de Lerme, he is able to have a court of his own, with horses, an elegant carriage, and an antechamber full of people on hand to fawn and buy services. By his own confession he becomes more calculating, more haughty, and more vain than ever. His morals are completely corrupted in the ambience of the court. He even becomes procurer for the heir apparent of Spain.

He now considers himself a part of the aristocracy and hesitates to marry beneath him. But, persuaded by Scipión, he agrees to marry the daughter of a wealthy bourgeois because of the magnificent dowry involved—a common enough procedure. Both Gil Blas and Scipión have become steeped in rascality. The wedding plans are interrupted, however, for Gil Blas is thrown into prison by royal order for pandering to the young prince of Spain's desire for women. Scipión effects his master's release, and they set out for a little country estate given to Gil for services rendered by a grateful member of the nobility. This brings part 2 to a satisfactory conclusion.

During the next decade, Lesage brought out a new edition of *The Devil upon Two Sticks,* accompanied by a lively, short supplement, *Entretiens des cheminées de Madrid (Conversations of Madrid's Chimneys),* and a curious play, *La tontine.* More fiction—at times not far removed from the better sort of literary drudgery—was snapped up by booksellers. The first two parts of *Gil Blas* had brought Lesage international fame. We may assume that during this time he was working on part 3, which appeared in 1735.

The story picks up where it had left off ten years before. Lesage grown older seems at peace with the world, and his hero has mellowed perceptibly. On the way to his new holdings in Lirias, Gil stops off to visit his parents, long absent from his thoughts. He arrives in time for his father's death. Moved by sadness and regret, he settles an annuity on his mother and, with loyal Scipión, heads for his château and its rich farmlands. He falls in love with and marries the beautiful Antonia, daughter of his head farmer, but conjugal happiness ceases abruptly when his wife and newborn son both die.

Overcome by grief, Gil seeks a change of scene. He returns to Madrid and the royal court, where the former prince of Spain, now Philippe IV, recognizes him and recommends him to the new prime minister, the comte d'Olivares. If Lesage depicted his protagonist as a mature man in part 2, the aging author reveals him in a state of advanced maturity in part 3. This is achieved with finesse as Gil comes close to being confronted with much the same situations as those he had already experienced. In fact, the third part is, in many ways, an echo of the first and second parts of the novel. Scipión's long account of his own youthful picaresque adventures recalls to mind young Gil of part 1. When our hero returns to the Spanish capital and the court to be the confidant of the new prime minister,

that is to say, the comte, soon to become the duc d'Olivares, we are reminded of Gil Blas, confidential secretary to the duc de Lermes in the second part of a novel covering thirty years or more.

But there is a perceptible evolution in character as part 3 unfolds. Vanity, greed, perpetual intrigue, and self-aggrandizement have been replaced by compassion, generosity, and indulgence for the shortcomings of others. The Gil Blas of light amours is now capable of abiding love and marital bliss. He is able to shed tears as he develops a capacity for genuine affection. He now renders services solely from his desire to aid worthy supplicants as he continues to demonstrate a marked sense of integrity. "'You have become quite disinterested and highly moral,' said His Excellency; 'I think you were much less so under the last minister'" (11.13).

One echo from the past, however, rings less blithely. Gil Blas is persuaded to seek out a certain beautiful, charming, virtuous, youthful actress for the delectation of the king. The reader is hardly surprised that she turns out to be the daughter of Laure, whom our protagonist had twice abandoned. The affair ends disastrously in the deaths of both mother and daughter, with Gil suffering from the mixed emotions of sorrow and guilt. Nevertheless, for his hand in catering to the monarch's pleasures, a patent of nobility is—against his will—conferred on him.

If in part 2 our hero fell into disgrace, in part 3 it is the prime minister who is banished from the court and Madrid. He is followed into exile by Gil Blas, who, upon Olivares' death, receives a handsome legacy for his devotion. Time has moderated Gil's sense of pleasure and given him a strong inclination for the simple beauties of nature. And so he leaves with Scipión for the welcome seclusion of his estate at Lirias after an absence of twenty-two years. There he falls in love with an impoverished nineteen-year-old girl of the aristocracy, and despite the disparity in age, Dorothée, to his joy, gladly accepts him for her husband.

And so Gil Blas is able to bring his autobiography to a close:

> Dear reader, for three years I have led a life of unmixed bliss with people I dearly love; and to make my happiness complete, heaven has blessed me with two children, whom I piously believe to be my own, and whose education will brighten my declining years.

The novel has had a long and varied appeal. Widely popular in eighteenth-century England and Scotland, it appeared in numerous translations and editions. Among the British writers of the day, Tobias Smollett was unquestionably the most influenced by Lesage, and his *Roderick Random,* published in 1748, owes much to *Gil Blas,* a fact the English novelist was the first to acknowledge. Moreover, dissatisfied with previous translations of Lesage's fictional biography, Smollett himself translated it the following year. Among the remarks in his preface to the translation, we read:

> Of all his [Lesage's] works, that now presented to the reader is by far the most popular, and deservedly ranks very high among the productions of historical fancy. . . . Few books have been so frequently quoted, as affording happy illustrations of general manners, and of the common caprices and infirmities incident to man.

But even twenty years after *Roderick Random,* its author testifies to his continued allegiance to Lesage. In his portrait painted by Nathaniel Dance between 1766 and 1768, Smollett, seated in his library and surrounded by immense but unrecognizable tomes, holds in his hand a clearly visible copy of *Gil Blas.*

Other British writers of the period, such as Joseph Warton, John Gay, and even Henry Fielding, were to various degrees indebted to Lesage. Early in the following century Sir Walter Scott wrote an admirable biographical sketch of "this delightful author." It is a piece to which many subsequent essayists, biographers, and encyclopedists have turned for

facts and interpretation. In reference to *Gil Blas,* Scott says: "Few have ever read this charming book without remembering, as one of the most delightful occupations of their life the time which they first employed in the perusal. . . ." Then, summarizing the varied impressions the story makes in turn on the growing boy, the youth not yet turned man, and the mature, knowledgeable individual, he concludes: "The power of the enchanter over us is alike absolute. . . . If there is anything like truth in Gray's opinion, that to lie on a couch and read new novels was no bad idea of Paradise, how would that beatitude be enhanced, could human genius afford us another *Gil Blas.*"

In the French Age of Enlightenment, Voltaire, who had no fondness for Lesage, reluctantly admitted that *Gil Blas* had enduring qualities. Denis Diderot, *philosophe* par excellence, knew author and novel early and late. In 1751 he called attention to "that famous writer of *Gil Blas de Santillane,*" and, thirty years later he wrote his daughter that three times a day he was reading the novel to her mother. In book 4 of his celebrated *Confessions,* Jean Jacques Rousseau admits that, as a youth, he had read *Gil Blas* with pleasure but was then "too immature to appreciate such works." In Germany *Gil Blas* was apparently one of Goethe's favorite novels, for his diaries tell us he read it in its entirety at least three different times. Examples of enthusiasm for the work continued to multiply in various parts of the world. The consensus seems to be that in *Gil Blas* we have a novel to be read at leisure and revisited from time to time. It appears to represent the French turn of mind that found its best expression in the eighteenth century.

At the outset of his career, as we have seen, Lesage gave the impression of groping in the dark as he tried his hand at translating novels chiefly from the Spanish with only slight modifications and in a style not yet entirely his own. In the second stage, he became bolder and more self-confident; with a mastery of style, he made such a successfully loose adaptation from Spanish fiction with *The Devil upon Two Sticks* that he acquired a hitherto lacking authority, and, at the same time, though early schooled in the Spanish theater, he succeeded in acquiring virtual independence from his Hispanic predecessors with his lively one-act comedy *Crispin, His Master's Rival.* He reached his third and greatest period with two works of refreshing originality that are—each in its own way—lasting masterpieces, the play in five acts, *Turcaret,* and the novel in twelve volumes, *Gil Blas.*

Having thus proved to himself and his contemporaries his very considerable talent in drama and fiction, he turned his literary gifts to more or less secondary writings, which went far toward the family upkeep and encouraged thoughts of a serene retirement from the teeming capital.

This literary baggage consisted of potboilers—sometimes of a high order. Greatest monetary returns came from his hundred or so plays and operettas for the Paris street fairs, spanning close to a quarter of a century. Many are still worth perusing for their astonishing variety and their satirical ingenuity in reflecting the trends of the day.

Then there was a series of other full-length novels—four in number—that lie in partial obscurity under the shadow of *The Devil* and *Gil Blas.* The first of these, often neglected, is *Les aventures de M. Robert Chevalier, dit de Beauchêne, capitaine de flibustiers (The Adventures of M. Robert Chevalier, Call'd De Beauchêne, Captain of Privateers in New-France),* published in 1732. Lesage declares in the preface that he obtained the manuscript from the widow of a noted French pirate. Novels based on imaginary voyages to distant lands and on the primitive conditions of the New World were both in vogue at the time. An author's claim that a manuscript in all its detail had fallen into his hands was a subterfuge widely practiced in the eighteenth century to give a novel an air of authenticity.

It is, of course, quite possible that Lesage did come upon the manuscript, cutting here, adding there, and giving his personal touch to the absorbing account of a French-Canadian boy of seven who is carried off by Indians and takes on their traits of courage and cruelty. After reaching manhood, the lad becomes a freebooter, then a prisoner in Ireland; again resorting to piracy, he is seized by the English and abandoned in the desert to starve. Following another series of vicissitudes, he again takes to the high seas in search of more booty. Beauchêne is once more abandoned, this time by Lesage, who ends the work by saying that the continuation of the corsair's adventures is still in the hands of the widow. Lesage promises to publish the manuscript if she releases it.

If *Beauchêne* is a work by Lesage, it is a work apart. It presents settings and develops scenes that are uncharacteristic of the author of *Gil Blas;* for example, the captain of freebooters shows a capacity for remorseless brutality, at other times a compassion for his fellow man. By and large there remains an aura of mystery about this novel that, by turns, stresses piracy, exotic travels, and passion, both licit and illicit, as new protagonists are introduced. And yet there is Lesage's unmistakable touch. Perhaps *Beauchêne* was an attempt to experiment with a new type of novel. If so, it was his only effort of this kind.

There followed three novels in the tradition of *Gil Blas,* with their Spanish settings, with protagonists relating in the first person their exploits and adventures, and with numerous borrowings from sources. The first and least original of these works is *Guzman d'Alfarache* (1732), an agreeable enough translation from the Spanish, but already well known in France through the translations of Gabriel Chappuis (1600), Jean Chapelain (1619), and Gabriel de Brémond (1696). Like those of his predecessors, Lesage's translation is not literal. It is, however, more scrupulous; unlike Brémond, for instance, he adds no episodes of his own to the original and truncates passages either too salacious or too dull. According to one critic, the result is an elegant, fluent, amusing, and well-modulated endeavor.

The second, more original than *Guzmán*, is *Estevanille Gonzales, surnommé le garçon de bonne humeur* (1734), published in America as *The History of Vanillo Gonzalez, Surnamed the Merry Bachelor*. Lesage borrowed some passages from the original Spanish version, and even pillaged his own *Gil Blas*. There is clearly a sign of fatigue here; Lesage's imagination was on the wane. It is a novel close to the anecdotal, but it makes light, pleasant reading, mostly because of the sharp, well-placed barbs cast at characters who represent various human foibles. The hero sustains his humor in good times and bad, all the while greatly enjoying being alive.

Le bachelier de Salamanque (*The Bachelor of Salamanca*, 1736) is the last of his long novels and, in importance, comes directly after *Gil Blas* and *The Devil upon Two Sticks*. As became his practice, Lesage picked up situations and incidents already treated in his two best works of fiction. He even took what suited him from *Vanillo* and *Guzman*. And, as in *Gil Blas*, he offered a large, varied picture with French characters in Spanish dress representing all levels of society. Then too, as in *Gil Blas*, incident follows incident in rapid order but seemingly with little sense of procedure. And when improbability of action comes in the door, reality flies out the window. The hero, a university graduate (hence "bachelor") and sometime tutor to the children of the wealthy, is amusingly exposed to a variegated lot of parents and pupils. The hero is likable and has an appealing freshness of youth. As he grows older, however, he resorts increasingly to introspection, with skepticism and irony becoming more a part of his nature. Time and again coincidence is pushed to extremes. Yet despite the novel's weaknesses, it easily holds the attention of the indulgent reader.

In Paris, as a young man, Lesage had felt quite in his element. He and his good friend Danchet could go to the theater and even see their own plays performed now and then. He had, moreover, married a Parisian girl and took great satisfaction in her company and that of their four children. Besides his family and his writing, he had been able to absorb the ambience of the bustling city through its better-known cafés—frequented by men of letters and well-to-do patrons of the arts—its crowded thoroughfares, and its vast, sprawling market places. With time he became increasingly hard of hearing, but he found that this disability had its advantages. Though he used an ear trumpet in communicating with family or friends, he would put it aside the better to write in a world of silence. When he went to see one of his plays performed, he found, according to Diderot, that, hearing nothing, he was able to judge both the acting and the play itself better than ever before.

By the time he was sixty, Lesage had become so deaf that he could hear only when the person speaking put his mouth to the trumpet and shouted. Already before bringing the last part of *Gil Blas* to a close, he was half withdrawn from the world. Besides his final three novels, which some—including his compeer Charles Collé, the dramatist—judged to be little more than pallid duplications of his masterpiece, Lesage turned out literary odds and ends before drawing his career to a close. One, inspired by a passage in Horace, was a slim little volume titled *Une journée des parques* (1734), which appeared in Cambridge and London as *A Day's Work of the Fates*. The three old crones who, in ancient Greek and Roman mythology, controlled the lives of men, are depicted by Lesage in two séances or sittings. In one séance they spin the thread of life; in the other they sever it with scissors, all the while exchanging raucous banter on the destinies of mortals and gods. The book had considerable success and convinced readers that advancing years had not dimmed the author's mind and talents. Far less favorably received was *La valise trouvée* (1740), which, though never translated into English, could conceivably be called *A Rediscovered Satchel*.

It is nothing more than a tome stuffed with refurbished excerpts from his important works and a few touched-up epistles from his very first publication, *Lettres galantes d'Aristénète.* Three years later he offered to the public the overflow from *La valise trouvée* and gave it the verbose title of *Mélange amusant de saillies d'esprit et de traits historiques des plus frappants*—which might be translated as *An Entertaining Mixture of Witticisms and the Most Extraordinary Happenings.* Here he gave verbatim passages from other works of his and, with his memory failing, became confused in references to Greek and Roman antiquity—he who had once known his classics so well.

It was indeed time to recall to mind the aging archbishop of Granada, whose sermons had become far poorer than he himself recognized. At the age of seventy-five, Lesage, taking his famous parable of the prelate's approaching senility to heart, left for Boulogne-sur-Mer with his devoted wife and loving daughter. There, with Paris well behind them, they were taken in by their second son, a canon of the Cathedral of Boulogne. During the few remaining years Lesage worked on the *ne varietur* edition of *Gil Blas.*

In the final revision of his already famous novel, the elderly author left untouched the following passage—written at least a decade before—where Gil Blas and the former prime minister, banished from Madrid and the glamor and intrigue of the royal court, hold this conversation:

> One day being alone with him, and admiring the serenity of his countenance, I took the liberty to say, "My lord, allow me to express my joy: from the air of satisfaction in your looks, I conclude that Your Excellency begins to be accustomed to retirement." "I am already quite reconciled to it," he answered; "and . . . I am every day more and more pleased with the quiet, serene life I lead where I now am."

On 17 November 1747 Lesage peacefully died in the arms of his wife, at the age of seventy-nine.

Selected Bibliography

EDITIONS

INDIVIDUAL WORKS
Le diable boiteux (1707). Edited by Roger Laufer. Paris, 1970.

Crispin, rival de son maître (1709). Edited by T. E. Lawrenson. London, 1961.

Turcaret (1709). Edited by T. E. Lawrenson. London, 1969.

Histoire de Gil Blas de Santillane (1715–1735). Edited by René Etiemble. 2 vols. Paris, 1973.

Les aventures du Chevalier de Beauchêne, dit de Beauchêne, capitaine de flibustiers (1732). Paris, 1980.

COLLECTED WORKS
Oeuvres. Notice de J.-J. B. Audiffret. 12 vols. Paris, 1821.

Oeuvres choisies de Le Sage. 15 vols. Paris, 1783.

TRANSLATIONS

The Devil upon Two Sticks. 2 vols. London, 1708.

The Comical History of Estervanille Gonzalez, Surnamed the Merry Fellow. London, 1735.

The Bachelor of Salamanca; or Memoirs of Don Cherubin de la Ronda. Translated by Mr. Lockman. 2 vols. London, 1737–1739.

The Adventures of Robert Chevalier, Call'd De Beauchêne, Captain of Privateers in New-France. 2 vols. London, 1745.

Une journée des Parques: A Day's Work of the Fates. London, 1745.

The Devil on Two Crutches. 2 vols. London, 1750. With "Asmodeus' Crutches" and "Dialogues of Two Chimneys."

Pleasant Adventures of Gusman, of Alfarache. Translated by A. O'Connor. 2 vols. London, 1812.

The Novels of Lesage and Charles Johnstone. London, 1822.

The Lame Devil. London, 1870. An expurgated edition of *Le diable boiteux.*

The History of Vanillo Gonzalez, Surnamed the Merry Bachelor. New York, 1890.

The Thousand and One Days. Persian Tales. Edited by J. H. McCarthy. 2 vols. London, 1892.

The Adventures of Gil Blas de Santillana. Translated by Tobias Smollett. London, 1907.

BIOGRAPHICAL, CRITICAL, AND RELATED WORKS

Alter, Robert. *Rogue's Progress: Studies in the Picaresque Novel.* Cambridge, Mass., 1964.

Barbaret, V. *Lesage et le théâtre de la foire.* Geneva, 1971.

Bjornson, Richard. *The Picaresque Hero in European Literature.* Madison, Wis., 1977.

Bowe, Forrest, and Mary Daniels. *French Literature in Early American Translation.* New York, 1977. Pp. 360–363.

Brunetière, Ferdinand. *Études critiques sur l'histoire de la littérature française.* 7 vols. Paris, 1890. Lesage is discussed in vol. 3.

Carson, Katharine. *Aspects of Contemporary Society in "Gil Blas."* Studies on Voltaire and the Eighteenth Century, vol. 110. Banbury, 1973.

Chinard, Gilbert. *L'Amérique et le rêve exotique dans la littérature française.* Geneva, 1970.

————. "Les Aventures du Chevalier Beauchêne de Lesage." *Revue du dix-huitième siècle* 1:279–293 (1913).

Claretie, Léo. *Lesage romancier.* Geneva, 1970.

Cordier, Henri. *Essai bibliographique sur les oeuvres d'Alain-René Lesage.* Geneva, 1970.

Coulet, Henri. *Le roman jusqu'à la Révolution.* Paris, 1967.

Crocker, Lester G. *An Age of Crisis: Man and World in Eighteenth-Century French Thought.* Baltimore, 1963.

Dédéyan, Charles. *Lesage et "Gil Blas."* 2 vols. Paris, 1963.

Etiemble, René, ed. *Romanciers du XVIIIe siècle.* 2 vols. Paris, 1960–1965.

————. "Preface," in Le Sage, *Gil Blas de Santillane.* Paris, 1973.

Ford, Franklin L. *Robe and Sword: The Regrouping of the French Aristocracy after Louis XIV.* Cambridge, Mass., 1962.

Gaiffe, Félix. *Le drame en France au XVIIIe siècle.* Paris, 1907.

Green, F. C. *Minuet: A Critical Survey of French and English Literary Ideas in the Eighteenth Century.* New York, 1935.

————. *French Novelists, Manners and Ideas: From the Renaissance to the Revolution.* New York, 1964.

Joliat, Eugène. *Smollett et la France.* Paris, 1935.

Knapp, Lewis M. "Smollett and Lesage's *The Devil upon Crutches.*" *Modern Language Notes* 47:91–93 (1932).

Laplane, Gabriel. "Lesage et l'abbé de Lionne." *Revue d'histoire littéraire de la France* 68:589–604 (May–Aug. 1968).

Laufer, Roger. *Lesage ou le métier du romancier.* Paris, 1971.

Lintilhac, Eugène. *Lesage.* Paris, 1893.

Longhurst, Jennifer. "Lesage and the Spanish Tradition: *Gil Blas* as a Picaresque Novel." In *Studies in Eighteenth-Century French Literature,* edited by J. H. Fox, M. H. Waddicor, and D. A. Watts. Exeter, 1975. Pp. 123–137.

Malitourne, M. "Éloge de Lesage." A lecture that shared the *prix d'éloquence,* awarded by the Académie Française at its meeting of 24 August 1822. Paris, 1822.

May, Georges. *Le dilemme du roman au dix-huitième siècle.* New Haven, Conn., and Paris, 1963.

Morillot, Paul. *Le roman en France depuis 1610 jusqu'à nos jours.* Paris, 1892.

Mylne, Vivienne. *The Eighteenth-Century French Novel: Techniques of Illusion.* Manchester, 1965.

————. "Structure and Symbolism in *Gil Blas.*" *French Studies* 15:134–145 (1961).

Paulson, Ronald. "Satire in the Early Novels of Smollett." *Journal of English and Germanic Philology* 59:381–402 (1960).

Pizarro, Agueda. "Lesage, Picaresque Paradox and the French Eighteenth-Century Novel." Ph.D. diss., Columbia University, 1964.

Sainte-Beuve, Charles. *Les grands écrivains français: XVIIIe siècle, romanciers et moralistes.* Paris, 1930.

————. *Portraits of the Eighteenth Century: Historic and Literary.* Translated by Katherine P. Wormeley. 2 vols. New York, 1964. Vol. 1, pp. 71–105.

Sarrailh, Jean. *À propos de A. R. Lesage américaniste.* Paris, 1964.

Scott, Sir Walter. *The Miscellaneous Prose Works of Sir Walter Scott.* 6 vols. Boston, 1829; Paris, 1837. Vol. 3, *Biographical Memoirs of Eminent Novelists,* pp. 209–229.

Showalter, English. *The Evolution of the French Novel 1641–1782.* Princeton, N.J., 1972.

Spence, Rev. Joseph. *Observations, Anecdotes and Characters of Books and Men.* Edited by James M. Osborn. 2 vols. London, 1966.

Striker, Ardelle. "The Theatre of Alain-René Lesage." Ph.D. diss., Columbia University, 1968.

Voltaire. *Oeuvres complètes.* Edited by Louis Moland. 52 vols. Paris, 1877–1885. Vol. 14, *Siècle de Louis XIV.*

Warton, Joseph. *Ranelagh House: A Satire in Prose. In the Manner of Monsieur Lesage.* London, 1747.

OTIS FELLOWS

MONTESQUIEU
(1689–1755)

I

THE MOST ONE can say about Montesquieu's life is that it was generally uneventful. Charles-Louis de Secondat, baron of La Brède and of Montesquieu, was born in 1689 at the château of La Brède, in the Bordeaux region. He inherited the title of baron of La Brède from his mother, the property of the Secondats from his father, and the title of baron of Montesquieu from his father's elder brother. Very early in his youth he decided to follow the family tradition and study law in order to become a magistrate. In 1708 he received his law diploma and was admitted to the Bordeaux parlement as barrister. In 1716 his uncle died, leaving him, in addition to his title, his office of *président à mortier* (chief court officer). Montesquieu would fulfill his duties as *président* for several years but without genuine conviction, for, he tells us in his memoirs, he had little interest in the daily routine required by his office.

Montesquieu's real concerns were elsewhere: like many of his contemporaries, he was very much interested in scientific questions. Thus in 1716 he joined the Bordeaux Academy of Sciences, and during the period of his active membership he wrote a great number of scientific memoirs. He also spent his free time writing a fictional critique of political institutions in the form of an oriental epistolary novel. *The Persian Letters (Letters persanes)*, first published in 1721 without Montesquieu's name, was an instant success. It opened the doors for him to the best salon society. He frequented the Club de l'Entresol and the salons of Madame de Lambert, Madame de Tencin, and, later, Madame du Deffand. In 1726 Montesquieu resigned his magisterial charges and sold his office in order to consecrate himself to scientific and political work. One can infer that it was at about this time that he began to perceive the general configuration of what would later become *The Spirit of the Laws (De l'esprit des lois*, 1748).

But Montesquieu was not satisfied with his status of armchair scientist and political theorist; travel he must. In 1728 he set forth on a journey throughout Europe. During 1729 he traveled to Austria, then to Italy, Switzerland, Germany, and Holland. The Italian sojourn provided him with an opportunity to develop his aesthetic views on painting and taste in general; by contrast, he did not like Germany, which he felt lacked natural polish. In the Hague he met Lord Chesterfield, and traveled with him to London, where he would stay until 1730. There he frequented the highest aristocratic milieus and was invited to join the Royal Society. He shared in English political life and went to the sessions of both houses of the British Parliament on a regular basis, all the while slowly drafting the general terms of one of the key political concepts of *The Spirit*: separation of powers. Upon his return to La

Brède in 1731, Montesquieu consecrated all of his time—the rest of his life—to the elaboration and completion of his work on the ''spirit'' behind all law. The man whose comprehensive political vision extended so far died blind in 1755.

The question of formative influence is difficult to resolve in the case of any author. With Montesquieu it is even more complicated, because he left little documentation of his personal experiences. Except for some autobiographical remarks about the happy inclination of his character, his good health (he tells us that his ''machine is well built''), and his contentment with his personal and social situations, we know little about the sources of his genius. What can be stated with some certainty is that Montesquieu's general frame of mind owed something to his family's background (*noblesse de robe*, the nobility of office) and fairly comfortable roots (Montesquieu would never abandon his interests in viniculture); and that despite wry remarks about his travels (''In France, I make friends with everyone; in England, I make friends with nobody; in Italy, I flatter everybody; in Germany, I drink with everybody'' [quoted in Loy, *Montesquieu*, p. 32]), they played an important role in helping him develop his embryonic theories of state and of individual liberty, and his sense of government. As J. Robert Loy remarks: ''Travels form the catalyst that brings the intellectual stirrings of Montesquieu to precipitation. After them, his lifework will proceed steadily with a good sense of direction'' (p. 24). One could also add to this sketch of his person that by eighteenth-century standards Montesquieu was a good Frenchman and a true citizen of the world.

In contrast to the limited material available on Montesquieu the man, his literary production offers perhaps too much to choose from. Indeed, a glance at Montesquieu's writings will show, in addition to the well-known *Spirit of the Laws* and *The Persian Letters*, a collection of scientific memoirs on such topics

as the function of the kidneys (1718), the phenomenon of the echo (1718), the ebb and flow of the sea (1719), the physical history of the earth (1719), and gravity and transparency in bodies (1720). Other works include disquisitions on economic questions (*Considerations on the Wealth of Spain*, 1726), a philosophical tale (*A True Story*, 1731); a monograph on political history (*Considerations on the Causes of the Greatness of the Romans and Their Decline*, 1734); a treatise on aesthetics (*The Essay on Taste*, 1755); a fashionable oriental divertissement; a pastiche of classical sentimental romance; travelogues; imaginary interviews; polemical reviews; even a study on the extraction of coal in mines and a museum catalog. Can one then talk, as does Roger Caillois, the editor of Montesquieu's *Complete Works*, of a ''specific and almost natural law that presides over the development of his oeuvre'' (*Oeuvres*, Plèiade ed., 1.1)? Or rather should one recognize, as the list of selected works appearing in the bibliography testifies, that Montesquieu's writings cut across too many disciplines to provide a unified point of view? But to view Montesquieu from the perspective of disciplinary separation is precisely what ought to be avoided, for it is to go against the very logic that sustains an output ranging from one extreme (science) to the other (fiction). For even across what might seem a disparate body of writings, the substance of Montesquieu's thinking remains consistent. From one text to another, ideas are echoed, one remark complements another, paradoxes find their answers, so that we can view Montesquieu's seemingly varied works as a series of transitions in a quest for knowledge that culminates in the most monumental sociopolitical treatise of the eighteenth century, *The Spirit of the Laws*.

Under the circumstances, how can we best do justice to his work as a whole? To try to cover thoroughly all of his writings would result in the mere enumeration of his publications; to discuss only *The Spirit* would require putting aside his numerous essays and memoirs. And what of the fictional masterpiece *The Persian Letters*? Or Montesquieu's first attempt at historico-political analysis, his *Considerations on the Causes of the Greatness of the Romans and Their Decline*? The most famous texts demand their due, and yet to slight the less well-known works would also be to miss the unique diversity of a context that is crucial to an understanding of Montesquieu. What strategy can best represent the totality of a work that is, in Caillois's words, "a kind of *organic tissue*, unevenly differentiated, but where through innumerable *canals* and endlessly *branching out*, a singularly persevering body of thought *circulates*" (1.1, emphasis added)?

Caillois's use of highly exaggerated figurative language is striking. Whether consciously or not, he has grasped the most representative means of dealing with Montesquieu's work, representative in that it faithfully duplicates a procedure of metaphor making that unifies the very material about which Caillois writes. If Caillois waxes eloquent, it is no doubt because he has an antecedent style, Montesquieu's, to inspire him. And indeed, it is quite common for an author to use figurative language to communicate to his readers images of species and structures with which they may be unfamiliar. From this point of view Montesquieu is not unusual; he even asserts in the opening paragraph of *The Spirit of the Laws* that he has set himself the task of explaining the logic of institutions by analogy to physical—organic and natural—laws. Hence it seems as if the issue of Montesquieu's use of figures can be resolved once and for all as a simple expository device. And yet this is not the case, and we must insist on this point. The metaphors that Montesquieu keeps returning to—metaphors that compare man to a plant, a monarch to the sea, the body to an empire, Rome to a river, the soul to a spider in its web, the body (or even the body politic) to a machine, and so forth—are not merely devices to make a text more readable, nor empty linguistic habits drawn from the canon of the day. As we shall seek to demonstrate, the abundant figurative language that characterizes Montesquieu's writing serves the double function of expository tool and mode of comprehension. At those junctures in his thinking where Montesquieu pauses between one system and the next (natural history, geography, history, politics), he always seems to render by means of metaphor those relationships he considers the most fundamental and essential. In that sense, metaphor is neither a device for exploration nor an affirmation of coincidental similarity; rather, it spells out Montesquieu's philosophy: a profound belief and confidence in the kinship of all phenomena. Underlying differences of size or material makeup is his belief in an essential similarity that allows him to compare institutional structures to living organisms, and geopolitical principles to natural laws. It was, after all, Montesquieu who was to declare in an encyclopedia article on aesthetics ("Essay on Taste") that the soul's fundamental faculty is comparison, and in anticipation of his own dictum Montesquieu certainly practiced what he would eventually preach. The faculty of comparison is exercised not only to decide matters of taste, but in all cognitive situations. In short, it is the basic mechanism of human understanding.

In an attempt to explain the fundamental rules of his thinking, our present study will concern itself with detailing and analyzing the figures Montesquieu uses in his scientific, political, and fictional works. The consistency with which he applies the same figures and principles is enough to make us fear the charge of repetition; for whichever route one takes into his system, there is always a path that returns one to the same basic configurations: abstract principles of dependence, reciprocity, harmony, integration, or confluence, which serve as the common ground granting Montesquieu access to the same organic and phenomenal metaphors.

II

In the many volumes that comprise Montesquieu's complete works can be found numerous passages familiar to the political scientist and the historian of ideas. Montesquieu is well known as the originator of a theory of the effect of climate on politics and as the initiator of the first serious "scientific" study of governments. Yet many do not know that before he was a "political scientist" Montesquieu was a natural scientist of sorts, and that many of his contributions to the study of human behavior and human institutions can be traced to his earlier interest in what was then called "natural history." The bulk of his work in this area shows him to be largely a cautious investigator who limited himself to the corroboration of existing theories and rarely strayed into theorizing. Part of this caution resulted from his association with the Academy of Bordeaux, where, as one of its officers, he was responsible for accepting, reporting on, and verifying the findings that other scientists submitted to the academy's various competitions.

What we gather from his assessments of the work of others is that he was very much a student in the process, and that he applied criteria of informed common sense in making his judgments. What was plausible would meet with his approval; what seemed farfetched would not. Certain questions obviously fascinated Montesquieu more than others, and with respect to these, as his *Observations on Natural History* attests, it was not sufficient merely to deliberate in the abstract: direct observation was indispensable and, in fact, was undertaken with a good deal of relish.

The basic matters addressed in the *Observations* are plant propagation and plant and animal physiology. Montesquieu studied the phenomenon of vegetal parasitism and circulatory phenomena in both plants and animals. What the *Observations* reveals is a man in search of a common set of principles that

might account for as many apparently different phenomena as possible, so that, for example, reproduction and growth might be explained as continuous processes traceable to the same mechanisms. But even more important than phenomenal continuity (and an even greater challenge) was the search for a theory that would link plant and animal life, and references made in passing by Montesquieu in other contexts suggest that his ambitions might have extended even to include the so-called mineral kingdom as well in an overall theory that would explain all phenomena in their entirety.

Although the *Observations on Natural History* seems to have contributed little to the advancement of science in Montesquieu's time, it is relevant to us in our search for the source and meaning of his use of metaphors, for it plays a significant role in explaining his scientific beliefs. We will focus in particular on metaphors drawn from the realm of natural history and applied to his scientific work. It is worth stressing that those of us who are comfortable with our modern categories of knowledge, and particularly with the distinction between science and letters, will be made very uncomfortable by the links Montesquieu permits himself. We may be even more taken aback when it comes to the principles he articulates within the discipline of science itself, for his understanding of natural history in no way prefigures our modern disciplinary divisions. We look in vain for a distinct physiology or body chemistry (physics is out of the question); what we find is a scheme that explains everything it can by purely mechanical cause and effect, and the rest by fermentation, a process whose chemical aspects are largely overlooked in favor of its physical side effects. The system certainly has an appeal for a mind such as Montesquieu's, for it seeks to reduce everything to a basically physical phenomenon of displacement: of liquors in tubes, of organs relative to one another, of bodies upon one another. And because nearly every phenomenon can be reduced to a lowest common denominator, it is simple to find turning points on which to construct the revolving scheme of analogies Montesquieu erects.

Consider, for example, the life history of species within the kingdom of plants. It would be difficult to imagine a botanical theory that did not make reference to the sun, for the plant is an obviously sun-dependent organism. Yet the processes that link plants to a source of energy, as Montesquieu understood them, have nothing photosynthetic about them. The sun, through the process of fermentation, imparts motion to fluids in the soil, causing them to rise up through a series of canals inside the plant. Within this scheme, the leaf is considered not the basic workhorse but rather—like the fruit of plants—something of a by-product of processes that originate in the soil. The plant is conceived of as an entity under pressure; rising fluids push against the channels through which they travel, and may break out laterally to form branches or, at the tip, to carry buds into the open air. Montesquieu does not have a separate explanation to account for the differentiation of parts; all offshoots—stems, buds, flowers—can be traced to the same mechanical process of vital saps circulating through variously restrictive and directing channels. An adjunct phenomenon, "coagulation," is summoned to explain how the vital fluids can turn themselves into leaf or wood, for once the fluid comes into contact with the air, its forward movement is stopped short, halted by the process of coagulation, and a stem or bud will result. (Without coagulation, obviously, the plant would be an undisciplined, self-destructive entity.) Thus, the plant is born of a systematic process of alternating movement and restraint in which even the air plays its part; there are successive internal tides within the organism-mechanism, the rising and falling of which account for the full spectrum of its life processes (*Observations on Natural History*, Pléiade ed., 1.37).

Implicit in Montesquieu's description of the process is the notion that it may have something in common with at least one geographical phenomenon. First, the movement of the sea is evoked by the terminology Montesquieu uses to describe the waxing (flux) and waning (reflux) of sap; it is an ebb (reflux) and flow (flux), but the association to geographical phenomena is drawn even closer when, in a desire to help his reader visualize the process, Montesquieu suggests that "the size of branches is always proportionate to the conduits [that pass through them], which can be compared to a *little river*, in which the ligneous fibers, *like little brooks*, carry the sap" (1.31, emphasis added). These conduits are like little rivers or brooks not by virtue of shape alone; they mark the ultimate extent of a network of rivers that begins on the surface of the earth, passes through capillaries in the soil, and ends up in the branches of plant life. It is this structural continuity between what we would call the inorganic and the organic that somehow accounts for the miracle of vegetation. Although Montesquieu does not supply the most lengthy of descriptions of the process, we can reconstruct that he must have intended something like filtration, from the river outward into the floodplain, where the important elements are ultimately trapped in little canals, or geographical capillaries. At that point, there remains nothing but for the sun to provoke fermentation, and the trapped or filtered particles can begin their upward flow into another set of "little rivers." By this reasoning, of course, even the very soil is fertile (or "fecund," to use Montesquieu's term), although not with inert yet catalytic substances, as modern science believes. The substances are life-bearing and sustaining only insofar as they participate in a universal plenitude and channeling of the type we have described above. Thus, while Montesquieu specifies the animal and vegetal realms in writing that "organization, whether in plants or animals, can be nothing but the movement of liquids in tubes" (*My Thoughts*, Pléiade ed.,

1.1187), he also gives us reason to believe that this search for organizational principles of movement is all-inclusive and extends even into the third realm, the territory of the earth itself.

Although Montesquieu did not explore all the possibilities of geographical or geological organization, he did at one point announce a projected history of the earth. We assume that the project was never realized, and also, on the basis of work that has come down to us, that anatomical or physiological considerations were probably his major scientific passions. As we have suggested, there are many reasons to consider the earth and the plant or the animal as fundamentally similar, but one crucial difference must be marked and noted. While the earth and the plant may be the site of many a physical combat, they are essentially passive entities with respect to the forces that traverse them. This is obviously not the case with the animal. It thus becomes imperative to find an explanation that will bridge the gap between the passively and the actively structural, and Montesquieu does this by making the phenomenon of self-generated activity one of the mechanical principles that account for growth and change. He writes:

> When the body is at rest, the branched and oleaginous parts of the blood stop in the fatty cells, which are always open to receive them. But when the body is in motion, the nutritive parts are sent to the extremities of the fibers. The force of the blood's circulation deposits and inserts them in the fibers and in the spaces between these fibers. The fibers must accordingly become thicker, more solid, the more compact.
>
> (*Essay on Causes Affecting Minds and Characters*, Carrithers ed., p. 452)

As this description of the growth of muscle fiber does not include mention of the term "cell," it seems fair to assume that the concept of cellular growth or cellular organization is not part of Montesquieu's biological scheme. The basic unit of organization is not the cell, as one would expect, but a tube or canal. It is this particular characteristic of Montesquieu's organization of all animate matter that allows him to make comparisons between animate and inanimate processes that duplicate, on a larger scale, the structure and organization of living plants and animals. Thus, for Montesquieu, circulation and change in plants and animals, as in a river system, consist primarily of the forward motion of fluids through canal-like structures.

By far the largest portion of Montesquieu's scientific work, however, is concerned with applying physiological descriptions to the explanation of human behavior. In order to provide a detailed look at the subsystem of human anatomy that is the central nervous system, he derives a second organizational model. The second model depends on the transfer of motion not by the displacement of a fluid contained within a canal or tube, but by another process that he compares to the vibration of a spider's web or a musical instrument's strings. In this case, Montesquieu chooses the analogy of the spider's web because it is particularly apt for expressing the *pattern* of movement transmitted through the nerve network of the body: "The soul in our body is like a spider in its web" (*Essay on Causes*, pp. 428–429). Impulses can pass in both directions, from the center outward or from the edge of the network to its center, but the essential factor in determining the efficiency of the system is size. If the length of the individual strand extends too far from its center, the impulse cannot be accurately transmitted. The center will not then effectively interpret the impulse, nor will it be able to send out commands efficiently. Montesquieu comments on the quality of the stimulus thus transmitted by way of analogy to the strings of a musical instrument, where the finest strings produce the sharpest tones (*Essay on Causes*, p. 418). The musical instrument also suggests, as does the web, the dependence of the overall mechanism on its component parts:

> Just as those who play a musical instrument are careful, in order to insure that no interruption of

sound occurs, to use strings that have no knots and no places thicker or thinner, tighter or looser than others, it is also necessary, for the easy communication of movement in our machine, that all the parts of the nerves be uniform and smooth, that there be no places tighter, or drier, or less suited to receiving the activation fluid than others, that each part be joined to all the rest, that the whole constitute a unified system, and that there be no break in the network of the nerve fibers.

(p. 429)

This passage shows that Montesquieu's primary concern is that the nerve strings be uniform, continuous, and not blocked in any way; in this sense, they are exact analogues to the kind of liquid-filled conduits Montesquieu believed the nerves to be. It is not the phenomenon of vibration that led Montesquieu to choose either the spider's web or musical instrument analogy, but rather the fact that both of these structures represent closed, finite, uninterrupted systems. In that sense, both vibration-based models are consistent with his conception of the circulating system of fluids; they both account for the transmission of motion. (Obviously, Montesquieu hesitates between two different models, between genuine circulation and hydraulic displacement; but, just as obviously, he does not care to make very much of the differences, because he does not find them particularly radical as long as the same effect of transfer has occurred.) In organic entities, some things circulate and some push; some even push by circulating, and others circulate by being pushed. What is most important is that these various displacements never be at cross-purposes; that there be continuity, contiguity, and, most important of all, reciprocity, for that which is pushed must, perforce, also be able to push back. Montesquieu details the process at the most intricate level of organization, within and between the fibers themselves, calling the interaction between the blood and the muscle fiber "a kind of battle" (p. 452). Like the reciprocal action of the liquid sap and the newly coagu-

lated sap within the stem of a growing plant, the optimal organic system (the optimal system, for that matter) is one with a hearty degree of give and take such that, to use a familiar formula, for every action there should be an equal and opposite reaction: "everything is in motion, everything exerts pressure on everything else. As neighboring parts swell, those whose functions have become useless diminish, atrophy and even dry up" (*My Thoughts* 1.1189). If one organ expands, another must shrink away, or at least shrink back, until the time comes for it to regain its former place—and more—by asserting supremacy once again.

Given these principles of organization and operation, anything that upsets the pressure ratios within the body is bound to have a significant effect; and, while the notion might strike the modern reader as charmingly literal-minded, Montesquieu views sexuality as just such an organic upset. Because he imagines the animal as a finite system under pressure, he views anything that would inflate or deflate it with a good deal of misgiving, and sexuality, like any economy, has its inflationary and deflationary cycles. It is on the basis of such a notion that Montesquieu constructs his typology of the genders. In the *Essay on Causes Affecting Minds and Characters*, his concept of human physiology leads him to a lengthy discussion of the effect of circulatory and pressure changes on the characters of women and eunuchs. Modern science explains the female menstrual cycle as a hormonal reaction; according to Montesquieu, it results from the mechanics of fluid buildup in the body. Because the body is made up of organs each exerting pressure against the other, the buildup of fluids and their eventual outflow naturally alter the female character from day to day: "Since this quantity changes daily in women, their temperament and disposition must similarly change" (*Essay on Causes*, p. 425). By the same rationale, the eunuch, who for obvious reasons is not able to find any release for the buildup of extraneous fluids within his system, has a difficult and unnatural character. The normal male, however, maintains an even and consistent character because the pressure exerted internally on his organs is always constant.

Montesquieu's interest in understanding the principles of human life processes and human anatomy dated back to his academy days, when, in a speech entitled *Discourse on the Function of the Kidneys* and prepared for delivery in 1718, he admitted to being fascinated and awed by the ingenuity of the human animal:

> When we study the human body and become familiar with the immutable laws that govern *this little empire*, when we consider the innumerable parts which all work together for the common good, . . . this will which *commands as queen and obeys as slave*, these so well-regulated cycles, this *machine* which is so simple in its action and so complex in its moving parts, this continual repair of strength and life . . . what grand examples of wisdom and economy!
>
> (*Oeuvres*, Pléiade ed., 1.15, emphasis added)

In this description, Montesquieu uses two seemingly different analogies to communicate his understanding of anatomical and physiological principles. The human body is alternately an empire with immutable laws, a common good, a ruler and subjects, and a machine, complete with moving parts. The comparison of the body to a machine was common in Montesquieu's time; in fact, the term "machine" was often used synonymously with "body." Similarly, it was common to associate the political state and the body, but Montesquieu's version, where the body is described as the state and not vice versa, is an original twist. What is particular about his use of the two comparisons is that he is able to shift so easily from one to the next, without calling attention to the shift.

But having learned how Montesquieu views the body, it remains for us to ask what the empire has in common with it, and, in turn, what the organizational metaphors used in a political or historical context have in common with those scientific principles just discussed. Such a case in point, for instance, is the famous dictum that stands behind Montesquieu's preferred form of government: "These fundamental laws [those of monarchy] necessarily suppose the intermediate channels through which the power flows" (*The Spirit of the Laws*, Carrithers ed., p. 112). We have become quite used to the phrase "channels of power" and remain largely immune to the literal content of the expression; but in the light of Montesquieu's assertion that organization in both plants and animals occurs by means of "channels," his attribution of a similar mechanism to political organization takes on a new significance. It soon becomes evident to what extent his ideal form of government—monarchy—is derived from his understanding of the phenomenal world, and that it is designed to emulate the efficient, productive, natural laws as Montesquieu defines them.

This similarity extends to another level of analysis. A second of the political models developed by Montesquieu accounts for the interaction not within but between states. There, he describes a situation of give-and-take that duplicates his model of the interaction of the organs within the body. In this case, he postulates the desirability of a stalemate between the outward thrust of one state against the border of its neighbor, a force that in optimum cases is exactly countered by the second nation's own opposition. Montesquieu uses strikingly similar terms to describe his concept of political interaction—"barrier," "to force," "to repulse," "to inundate"—and his portrait of strife between opposing forces within the plant ("waxing and waning") or the animal ("a battle"), which simultaneously produces and results from the vital processes of these organisms.

In addition to the models of circulation and pressure, Montesquieu also postulates as essential to a state its ability to control its size and to preserve ties between the center of its power and its territorial jurisdiction: "within a very small orbit" (*Considerations on the Greatness of the Romans,* Lowenthal trans., p. 29), "Rome was the center of everything" (*My Thoughts* 1.1422). This principle is reminiscent of the emphasis placed on optimum size and centricity in his circular analogue of the nervous system, the spider's web, an image chosen specifically for that reason. There the soul's position relative to its nerve network directly affects its ability to assert proper control over the body, in the same way that a capital's position relative to its lines of communication irrevocably determines its ability to govern.

Those who know Montesquieu's political science know him to be a great comparer of institutions. It was by a lifetime of comparative study that he arrived at his famous system of the laws, namely that like all other things, governments are entities that have discernible parts and respond to readily identifiable forces. In all the universe there are but three types of government: those entities determined by a form that structures them (monarchy, republic, despotism) and a principle (honor, virtue, fear) that motivates them. Even in the process of formulating this artlessly simple rule we cannot help evoking the image that pervades it, the idea of a machine: "In monarchies, politics makes people do great things with as little virtue [as possible]. Thus, in the finest machines, art has contrived as few movements, springs and wheels as possible" (*The Spirit of the Laws,* p. 119); once again, the enterprise of across-the-board comparison is launched. We will direct our attention to the set of mechanistic principles that point the way to a concordance between Montesquieu's political and scientific models, before turning to his fiction and exploring how a particular mode of thinking might have generated a literary text.

III

In his *Montesquieu: La politique et l'histoire,* Louis Althusser has made a brief but penetrating study of two of the better-known metaphors found in *The Spirit of the Laws:* the image of opposing bodies used to illustrate the mechanics of power distribution in a despotic government, and the river image, which describes the same phenomenon in a monarchy. In so doing, Althusser is bent on demonstrating the political implications of this choice of metaphors, particularly with respect to the second of the two images: "the metaphor that haunts monarchy is that of a spring which flows out" (p. 74). On the surface, Montesquieu's choice of imagery reveals his preference for the monarchy, whose power distribution is both necessary, like the laws of nature, and continuous (because, mediated through channels, it can be sustained). But Althusser looks beyond the immediately apparent implications of the metaphor in order to reveal another motive for Montesquieu's choice. He begins his analysis with the first image, colliding (opposing) bodies. This, he argues, is also Montesquieu's starting point. The river image can be understood only when it stands in opposition—and as a preferable alternative —to the sudden headlong impact of two opposing forces. This is the nature of power in a despotic government, and it can only result in constant clashes between opposites; it can never be harnessed or made effective over time. To this structure of power Montesquieu proposes his alternatives: "intermediate channels, through which the power flows" (*The Spirit of the Laws,* p. 112), which transmit or distribute the monarch's power. According to Althusser's hypothesis, these channels, which control and direct the power exerted by the monarch, are necessary, like the laws of nature. The circulation image therefore allows Montesquieu to suggest a mechanism by means of which the potentially negative forces inherent in the monarch's power can be both controlled and tapped. Inherent in the image of the river are a set of structures (secondary channels, restraining barriers in the landscape) that serve his double goal: to make despotism the worst of all possible alternatives and to legitimate a tempered monarchy as the only viable solution.

According to Althusser, Montesquieu argues from the negative effect of unmediated power to its positive effects so as to allow himself to demonstrate the necessity of his own aristocratic class within a monarchical type of government. Althusser's analysis is persuasive, and a political dimension is certainly evident in Montesquieu's writings. His belief that republics have passed their prime is one example; his insistence that the people rarely act effectively in their own interest is another. But what Althusser poses as a subjective ideological problem must be attributed in fact to other factors, in particular the universal scope attempted by the methodological focus Montesquieu derived from his earlier scientific work.

For a man who viewed the world from this all-encompassing perspective, understanding the most ambitious imperialistic project on European territory must have presented quite a challenge. It is precisely the challenge of understanding how Rome worked—in all the senses of the word we have come to expect from Montesquieu—that he addresses in *Considerations on the Causes of the Greatness of the Romans and Their Decline*. His conclusion? That the empire was a noble experiment in expansionism, and that although Rome would seem to have broken all the rules and yet—for a time at least—to have survived and even prospered, ultimately the experiment collapsed because Rome contravened the rules of the body-state: "When the domination of Rome was limited to Italy, the republic could easily maintain itself" (*Greatness of the Romans*, p. 91); but as soon as Rome's ambitions carried it beyond the boundaries imposed by the rules of the body-state, its political difficulties began: "But when the legions crossed the Alps and the sea, the warriors, who had to be left in the countries they were subjugating for the duration of several campaigns, gradually lost their citizen spirit" (*Greatness of the*

Romans, p. 91). Thus it became only a matter of time before size got the best of things: "It was the greatness [bigness] of the republic that caused all the trouble" (*Greatness of the Romans*, p. 93). Soon it became impossible for Rome to remain actively at "the center of everything" (*My Thoughts* 1.1422). It had pushed well beyond the limits of viable statehood, extended its circle of dominance outward to the point where the forward drive of expansionism would necessarily dissipate, for no capital can sustain such force from a distance. As long as Rome held firm, as long as its expressions of power remained constant, the meridional peoples it had pushed back to the north could be held at bay: "While the force containing them lasted, they stayed there" (*Greatness of the Romans*, p. 153). Once Rome's power to repulse waned, what it had compressed could only recoil—a flood of people "backed against the limits of the world," as Montesquieu writes in a related context (*Greatness of the Romans*, p. 154), would inundate and reconquer Europe.

The political ideal expressed here is unmistakably analogous to the model adopted by Montesquieu as an illustration of the human nervous system—the spider in its web—which can function only if the size of the nerve filaments is proportional to the overall "mechanism"; and size in that system is quite obviously determined by distance from center to circumference. Size is an important consideration above all because it determines whether the nerve network is well centered, that is, in constant contact with the body as both recipient and agent of impulses. Consider again Montesquieu's analysis of Rome's fall: it is the result of its failure both to obey the law of the spider's web and to follow the lead of the body. Rome stretched its resources of intelligence to the limit, and the center could no longer command; at the same time, her generals lost the feeling of belonging to the whole: they could not or would not report back. This renunciation of the center could only translate itself in organic terms as a loss of vigor. Rome, so ambitious in the beginning as to aspire to a corporeal takeover, meets the ignoble fate of a noncompetitive organ. By the logic of the body, Rome should diminish, atrophy, even dry up and dwindle away, as well it does. In describing the final chapters of Roman history, there is a point beyond which Montesquieu cannot bring himself to go, in fact, beyond which he need not go, for the power of his structural vision of the ignominious ending will carry the story for him: "I do not have the courage," he writes, "to speak of the calamities which followed. I will only say that, under the last emperors, the empire—reduced to the suburbs of Constantinople—ended like the Rhine, which is no more than a brook when it loses itself in the ocean" (*Greatness of the Romans*, p. 219). The tactic is all the more poignant when we consider all the geopolitical implications contained in this tale of the river that peters out.

It should be clear by now that Montesquieu's analyses of the mechanics of statehood—which later became classical categories of political analysis—rely heavily on his scientific work. The reader will recall from our earlier discussion that, for Montesquieu, human bodies and animal bodies are governed by rules of expansion within a fairly privileged notion of space. A man presumably can grow as large as he would like until he collapses under his own weight. And while he may be threatening his own system internally, he comes up against no major external impediments to expansion. But states take their shapes across territories, and their ambitions are always bound to bring them into contact with the competing territorial imperatives of other states. The relationship among states is one of resistance, where the border is held in place by forces impinging upon it from two directions. If one state pushes against the border of its neighbor and encounters no resistance, that border will yield and the invaded state will diminish in size proportionately. Once a state encroaches in this manner upon other territories, it bears the burden of holding that border in place against the increased resistance its outward expansion has initiated. If the state cannot do so, the reaction may not only push the border back, it may even engulf the encroaching nation (*Greatness of the Romans*, p. 153). In that sense, Europe—or any recognizable geographical entity—is like a body in which the states themselves can be considered the organs, all of them pushing and jostling for a place of their own.

Not only do the neighbors make their claims, geography itself imposes limitations. In the case of Rome, for instance, the fall of the empire is all the more ironic to Montesquieu because in its expansion Rome disregarded the natural and manageable share of land allotted to her by chance. Montesquieu finds this all the more unfortunate because in order to take over all of Europe, Rome had to rise up within, expand to fill, and then overflow a natural geographical limitation that might have saved it. As long as the ambitions of the republic corresponded to the borders set by the Mediterranean Sea, surrounding the peninsula and the mountains to the north, Rome met Montesquieu's requirements for a well-centered, sensibly sized state: "In Europe natural divisions form many nations of a moderate extent, in which the government of the laws is not incompatible with the maintenance of the state" (*The Spirit of the Laws*, p. 278). Once beyond the mountains, however, Rome had taken more than the "natural share" allotted to it by geography, so that its size became the single most important cause of its downfall.

Given Montesquieu's criterion of optimum size and properly balanced internal-external relationships between states, it is understandable why, of all possible geopolitical configurations, he would favor the island-state. Islands, in general, are of suitable size, and the fixed nature of that size is self-evident. Obviously islands cannot violate the natural share allotted to them by nature, nor are they subject to external threats as are landlocked states:

> The peoples of the isles have a higher relish for liberty than those of the continent. Islands are commonly of a small extent: one part of the people cannot be so easily employed to oppress the other; the sea separates them from great empires; so that they cannot be countenanced by [are not motivated by establishing] tyranny.
>
> (*The Spirit of the Laws,* p. 283)

Among numerous other geographical limitations (rivers, mountains, deserts) discussed by Montesquieu, the sea is presented as the major physical cause that shapes and determines the formation of different types of government. The pattern of its action on the landscape over time, apart from its role as a determinant, is further used by Montesquieu metaphorically to explain how the power of a despot can be limited:

> As the ocean which seems to threaten to overflow the whole earth, is stopped by weeds and by little pebbles that lie scattered along the shore; so monarchs whose power seems unbounded, are restrained by the smallest obstacles, and suffer their natural pride to be subdued by supplication and prayer.
>
> (p. 114)

Like phenomena in the biological and natural world, governments respond to pressure principles. The power of a monarch is tempered by the industry of his people, who work constantly to oppose despotism. The reader will recall the similarity between this view of political history and the discussion of growth and change in plants and animals. In all cases, the process in question results from the give and take of opposing forces.

Ultimately, Montesquieu's notion of government is sustained by the underlying concepts of integration and pressure, where all the parts of a totality are incorporated into a system such that each individual part, in spite of itself, is directed to the good of the whole.

His ideal is, of course, a government in which individual actions are not dissipated or sublimated, but harnessed to run the state. Opposition is essential, since it is the pressure of differing opinions or actions that drives forward the whole enterprise. Montesquieu compares his ideal of government to the laws of physics, where two forces in opposition—gravity and centrifugal force—are balanced against one another and, in this give-and-take, produce a harmonious whole:

> It is with this kind of government as with the system of the universe, in which there is a power that constantly repels all bodies from the center, and a power of gravitation that attracts them to it. Honor sets all the parts of the body politic in motion; by its very action it connects them, and thus each individual advances the public good, while he only thinks of promoting his own particular interests.
>
> (p. 122)

Harmony, in Montesquieu's mind, does not mean total agreement between parties; rather it is made up of discord, and government, as he conceives of it, should be designed to thrive on such discord: "What is called union in a body politic is a very equivocal thing. The true kind is a union of harmony, whereby all the parts, however opposed they may appear, cooperate for the general good of society—as dissonances in music cooperate in producing overall concord" (*Greatness of the Romans,* pp. 93–94). At the same time, Montesquieu's ideal of government tends in the direction of simplicity. He admires the well-designed state for its efficiency of operation, a characteristic ultimately derived from the economy of its construction. He expresses that ideal in the analogy to a machine. It is certainly true that his typology of government aims at the perfect simplicity, with its reduction of political analysis to the description of the nature and principle of government—a structure through which, and a motivating principle by means of which, all governments function.

As our study of Montesquieu's botanical and anatomical models has shown, the principle of balance prevails in the properly functioning organism as well. For this reason, and because of other structural similarities that can be discerned between the state and the organism, Montesquieu's designation of the state as a *body* is far more than a casual linguistic habit. The metaphor of the body has long been associated with the structure and workings of the state. We say "body politic" without considering the etymology of the term. Yet it must be apparent by now that Montesquieu attached special importance to metaphors drawn from nature and applied to the state, and that the terms were not devoid of significance in his vocabulary. The same can be said for his use of the body metaphor. It is pertinent to note that within the context of *The Spirit of the Laws*, itself nominally a study of government, Montesquieu devotes several books to the exposition of certain features of human anatomy and physiology. On one level, this analysis is appropriate because it seeks to demonstrate the direct effect of climate upon the individual and, by extension, upon institutions. But the parallel between Montesquieu's findings there and the principles we have discussed above is striking. Like the state, the human body, for maximum efficiency, requires a well-defined border, an optimum size, and an active relationship of communication between its center and its "outlying areas."

In order to substantiate this assertion, it is essential to examine closely Montesquieu's findings in book 14 of *The Spirit of the Laws*. There he passes immediately from a discussion of the relationship between taxation and liberty to a study of climatic influences, even interrupting his own political analysis in order to present the findings of relevant scientific investigations. Montesquieu examines a sheep's tongue under a microscope; at room temperature, the tongue's surface appears to be covered with various protuberances, which he likens to small hairs, pyramids, and hillocks. Once it is frozen, many of these surface features seem to have disappeared; the microscope confirms that the surface relief is greatly reduced. Montesquieu concludes that the effect of temperature on animal flesh is drastic and, when extended to the entire body, can be expected to produce very considerable changes (*The Spirit of the Laws*, p. 245). These findings lead him to postulate two different physiological types based on climatic influence. The southern man is more vulnerable than his colder northern counterpart, whose outer covering is more resistant, less susceptible to damage. Not only are the people of the north more adequately fortified, but, because their blood tends more toward the center, their hearts are stronger and the circulation pattern within their bodies makes them more able than southern types: "People are therefore more vigorous in cold climates. Here the action of the heart and the reaction of the extremities of the fibers are better performed, body fluids are in better equilibrium, the blood moves more freely towards the heart, and reciprocally the heart has more power" (*The Spirit of the Laws*, pp. 243–244).

We recall from our discussion of the Roman Empire that an essential criterion for the efficient working of an empire was a vigorous interaction between the center and its outlying domains. For Montesquieu, the body is efficient when its fluids can be made readily available to the body's center. In the body of the southern man, however, just the opposite occurs. The influence of temperature on his muscle structure and circulation causes his fibers to slacken, to elongate. Because there is no hearty interaction between the peripheral surfaces of his body and its center, the individual loses all initiative and ethical sensibility. Not coincidentally, it is in these southern climates that despotic governments are most likely to arise, and Montesquieu's description of the territorial configuration of that type of state exactly parallels his portrait of southern physiology. They have two features in common: an unwieldy mass and a center that is one in name only. The despotic state, we learn, practices a crude kind of self-protection. To buffer itself against invasion, it devastates the surrounding land, in the middle of which it then sits, isolated and cut off from the outside world. Insofar as it occupies a center in the middle of nowhere, the despotic state becomes a dysfunctional machine. By contrast, the patchwork of European (northern) states is in fact one great mechanism governed by laws of territorial give-and-take, about which it is appropriate to conclude that, as in the body, "all space is filled. . . . Everything is in motion, everything exerts pressure on everything else" (*My Thoughts* 1.1189). The idea of mutual dependence is, of course, the key to this organic notion of statehood. It is the law that prevails within the human body, where, if one tissue or organ swells, its neighbors must shrink in compensation. The same principle governs the internal mechanics of plant growth, where each part influences the whole. Similarly, efficient government integrates opposing factions, so that "all the parts, however opposed they may appear, cooperate for the general good of society" (*Greatness of the Romans*, pp. 93–94). In each case, the parts are so intricately associated that a change in one component, however minute, alters the organism in its entirety.

Given Montesquieu's understanding of political history and social change by analogy to the principles by which the physical world operates, it should not surprise the reader to discover that the fictional world of *The Persian Letters*, in turn, follows the same logic. We say "in turn" although in fact *The Persian Letters* was written before *The Spirit of the Laws*. But since *The Persian Letters* attempts to show the consequences of the degradation of absolute power into despotic power from an experimental fictional point of view, our analysis of the structure and functioning of the seraglio will be more meaningful having first clearly established the case that *The Spirit of the Laws* makes regarding despotism—namely, that like all political systems, despot-

ism is to be understood according to the configurations of the physical body and its power structure translated according to organic metaphors.

IV

The plot of *The Persian Letters* is simple and straightforward: a wealthy and patriotic Persian, Usbeck, accompanied by his philosophical friend, Rica, leaves Persia and his seraglio to journey to Paris, where he studies the opposing life-styles of Western Europe. The reader observes how Usbeck copes with his new situation; what effects it has on his philosophical, religious, and political views of Persia; and what psychological effects it has on his relationship with his wives at home. At the same time, the reader is exposed to the changes the wives undergo in Persia as Usbeck's trip is prolonged and memory of him fades. The key to the plot is in the gradual changes Usbeck undergoes. These changes are reflected in the tone of his language, the sequence of his letters home, and of course in their content.

In line with our expectations, the figurative language that supports the seraglio structure is identical to the one we identified earlier: metaphors of the seraglio as "empire" and "machine" abound, and it would be redundant to go on listing them. Instead, we shall aim at demonstrating how these metaphors regulate, literally, the rigorous sexual (and sociopolitical) economy of the seraglio, and the implications of his approach to our understanding of Montesquieu's philosophy of political theory. Thus, rather than deal with the political reality of Asiatic regimes and their similarities to the politics of Louis XIV, we will focus on analyzing the nature of power as Montesquieu imagined it in *The Persian Letters* and the figurative and symbolic means by which he staged power relationships in the seraglio.

We recall from *The Spirit of the Laws* the

difference between the nature and principle of government: "its nature is that by which it is constructed, and its principle that by which it is made to act" (*The Spirit of the Laws*, p. 119). In book 3, chapter 1, Montesquieu adds that the principle of government is the "mainspring of the *whole* machine," thus implying that, by definition, a principle must be shared by both those who govern and those who are governed. The mechanics of power require reciprocal and reversible relationships for the system to function at all. In that sense, the seraglio, understood as a structure of power, satisfies all the requirements of a political machine. It is nonetheless a peculiar one in that it is the noncirculation of bodies, rather than their circulation, which regulates all sociopolitical relationships. The effective principle of power is thus reduced to the symbolic efficiency of the despot's body.

Before proceeding with our analysis of the mechanics of power in the seraglio, it would be useful to define its nature; our explanation will come by way of an analogy, or rather a metaphor: Montesquieu's metaphor of the seraglio-machine. To understand the seraglio as a machine, one must be able to say how and with what goals it functions: first, to situate its source of energy; second, to analyze the manner in which energy circulates; third, to determine what the machine produces and for what purposes. The reader of *The Persian Letters* will have diagnosed, at least on a thematic level, all the components that constitute the seraglio-machine. The motor ("mainspring" or "driving force") is the despot's body, whose "sex extracts a hearing from rocks and stirs even inanimate objects" (*The Persian Letters*, Loy trans., 28.83). His body feeds the machine with negative energy (negative since, as we shall see, it is produced from an illusory source; that is, an illusory body). Below the despot, the eunuchs are those who possess the technical know-how to operate (within) the machine. "I can see with pleasure that everything turns on me," says the chief eunuch (9.56). To minimize the risk of disturbances

and to make sure that the seraglio functions smoothly, it is important to provide replacement parts. Thus all the components of the machine, so as to be replaceable, must by necessity be interchangeable: the eunuchs are interchangeable by virtue of their sexual nullity, and the women by virtue of their sexual servitude. Lastly, this machine, which runs according to the personal regimen of the despot, produces nothing but the same: images of the self. Indeed, the despot cannot conceive of an otherness except to satisfy his own self-image and felicity:

> For what are all of you if not base tools that I can break at my fancy . . . you, who exist in this world only to live under my laws or to die . . . you, finally, who can hope for no other lot but submission, no other soul but my desires, no other hope save my felicity?
>
> (21.74–75)

Perhaps echoing Louis XIV's famous "L'État, c'est moi," despotic discourse always repeats the same thing: "I am the Law." By personifying the Law in the eyes of his subjects, the despot hopes to legitimize and perpetuate the cult of his personality.

Having rapidly described the structure of the seraglio-machine, it remains for us to explain the dynamics of power and the principle(s) by which its elements (citizens) are made to act and interact among each other.

The formal closure of the seraglio—a place that "no man has ever soiled with his lascivious regard" (26.80)—corresponds to a specific disposition of the body. Just as the step, cadence, and movement of the oriental body are regulated in all their forms, the order of the seraglio is organized with the purpose of instituting a state of bodily rest and "innocence, far from the reaches of all human beings" (26.80). Each wall in the seraglio enforces an interdiction of the body, since no relations between the sexes are allowed except with Usbeck's own perfect one. Considered from his perspective, the seraglio is a disciplinary machine that supervises all bodily activity in order to concentrate pleasure in a central point: the transcendent Body of the despot. Not only is this conception of the Body required for the orderly functioning of the seraglio (we shall return to this point), but all other participants of the seraglio-machine are distributed in terms of their relationship to this principle of transcendence. Each individual belongs to a class defined by a lack that is specifically related to the master's perfect Body. Eunuchs, women, children, all members of the seraglio represent negatively the one feature particular to the master; thus they provide both the visible emblem of his Body's infinite superiority and the tangible reminder of his presence, even when he is not there.

The Chief Eunuch, the White First Eunuch, and the Black First Eunuch hold positions that give them a provisional power, that in fact give them all the power except the absolute power of the Body. The authority of these master-eunuchs is paradoxical, for they are the relays and not the sources of power. Jaron, Nessir, Solim, and others become masters only because they have "by birth" renounced any claim to absolute mastery. Exercising power only in the name of Usbeck, they replace the master: they provide simulacra of authority that bring to mind their false sexuality. As Usbeck puts it: "You command as master like myself [but] remember always the void from which I drew you" (2.48). But precisely because they are impotent, cut off from all sexuality and separated forever from themselves, they seek to compensate for their central lack by blindly identifying with the master's Body. The function of the eunuch in *The Persian Letters* is systematically to emphasize the absence of the master: the eunuch features what he *lacks* by opposition to what Usbeck *has*. Discussing the White Eunuch's request to be allowed to marry Zelide, Zelis writes Usbeck about "the idea of this false marriage and the vain hope held out to Zelide by it":

What does she propose to do with that unhappy fellow? A man . . . who will always remember what he was and thus make himself remember what he is no longer. . . .

What then! Live always only in images and in phantoms! Live only to imagine!

What scorn must one have for a man of the sort, made only to guard and never to possess! *I search for love and cannot see it there.*

(53.119, emphasis added)

And yet, as the simulacrum of the master, the eunuch performs perhaps the most important function in the seraglio. Paul Valéry was the first to note with a certain perplexity the disproportionate place assumed by eunuchs in Montesquieu's novel: "Who will explain to me all these eunuchs? I have no doubt there is a secret and profound reason for the almost obligatory presence of these characters so cruelly separated from so many things, and in some way, from themselves" (preface to *The Persian Letters,* in *Variétés II,* p. 71). In response to Valéry's question, we shall demonstrate the central double function of the eunuch in *The Persian Letters.*

On one level, the eunuch is given the task of supervising the production of pleasure for the master: "I take inflamed [irritées] women to my master's bed" (9.57). But by virtue of his own sexual separation, the eunuch is "all the better a judge of women since with [him] the eyes are never troubled by movements of the heart" (96.182). Consequently, and paradoxically, the eunuch becomes the principal coordinator of sexual relations, the professional coupler who restores sexual harmony and provides for peace in the seraglio: "Disorder had arisen between the sexes because their rights were reciprocal. We have entered upon the plane of a new harmony. We have put between women and ourselves, hate; and between men and women, love" (22.75). On a more profound level, however, the eunuch performs an even more fundamental operation—fundamental in that it touches everyone in the seraglio. It is precisely because the eunuch is unable to compensate for his lack that the women have no other choice but to keep imagining the master's perfect Body. Thus, it is the eunuch's inadequate corporeality that keeps the master's Body alive in their memory. "I do not count as men those frightful eunuchs," writes Fatme, who adds that, by contrast, "my imagination furnishes me no more delightful idea than the enchanting charms of your [Usbeck's] person" (7.52). The eunuch maintains the *illusion* of Usbeck's transcendent presence in his absence: he is thus the principle of the seraglio's economy of desire. Furthermore, if it is essential for the despot to perpetuate fully the image of a transcendent presence, we can then understand the multiplication of the negative power relays provided by the eunuchs as a strategy operating to create transitory supports for the image of the despot. Each relay (eunuch) recalls by opposition Usbeck's power—now a symbolic one only, but all the stronger for being unconfirmable in reality. The eunuch is therefore the central agent in the process by which the women substitute in their imaginations a fantasy world for the reality of their life in the seraglio.

Montesquieu is undoubtedly the first writer to have staged an erotico-political fiction to demonstrate that all political systems gain in strength and stability—at least in the short run—as the imaginary realm increases at the expense of the reality principle. In the limiting case of despotism, the real must be completely annulled. It is this complete takeover by the imagination that makes the seraglio-machine so effective. It can operate at full capacity precisely because everyone, from Usbeck to the least of his subjects, fails to recognize the imaginary game in which all participate and from which none may escape once they have been taken in. Hence Montesquieu's correlative political maxim: "The reason that princes have such a false idea of their greatness is that those who raise them are daz-

zled by it themselves; they are in the first dupes, and the princes are fooled only as an after-effect" (*My Thoughts* 1.1440).

The same voluntary relation of "dupes" can be found at the beginning of *The Persian Letters* among Usbeck's subjects, and first of all among his wives. They represent interchangeable sexual objects (Zachi, Zephis, Zelis, Zelide—even their names remind us of their equivalent status in the seraglio), and in that sense it is clearly less a question for Usbeck of possessing the other sex than of possessing a multiplicity of it. Nevertheless, in the early days of his absence, the idea of Usbeck's body so pervades the wives' minds that they dress and prepare themselves as if in anticipation of his imminent return: "Although I am to be seen by no one . . . still I maintain the habit of pleasing. I never go to bed without being perfumed with the most delicious scent" (7.52). But Usbeck's absence lasts nine years! And in the meantime there is no new satisfaction, no other "presence" in sight for these women, who live "deprived of him who alone can satisfy them" (7.53). Thus they fall back on what has gone before. They take refuge in the imaginary realm and invest Usbeck's body with all the prestigious attributes their imaginations can produce. Fatme writes: "I run about throughout the whole harem as if you were still here. . . . I remember those happy times when you would come to my arms. A happy dream, seducing me, brings before me the dear object of my love. My imagination is lost in its desires" (7.52–53). Zachi wanders "from apartment to apartment, seeking you always, finding you never," but finding instead memories of past adventures that obsessively come to haunt her mind, "everywhere falling upon the cruel memory of my past felicity" (3.48).

The intensity of such image-memories erupts vividly in the correspondence. Zachi's letter in particular makes purposeful reference to the seraglio's elaborate theatrical games staged by the wives as a competitive measure to capture Usbeck's favors. But, suspending her sentence in mid-course, Zachi suddenly catches herself succumbing to the effect of her imagination: "But where have I strayed? Where does this empty recital take me?" (3.49). It is clear that, short of indulging themselves in forbidden pleasures, the wives must resort to letter writing. And although the images transcribed on paper cannot be translated into real objects, it is their way of conjuring back to the seraglio the missing body. Zachi: "Sometimes I imagine I was in that place where for the first time in my life, I took you in my arms" (3.48). Fatme: "Nights pass in dreams that belong neither to sleep nor to waking. I seek you at my side and you seem to be fleeing me" (7.53). Usbeck's body thus becomes endowed, through the force of the imagination, with an exhorbitant power: "Fire is flowing in my veins. . . . Usbeck, I should give the dominion of the whole world for a single one of your kisses" (7.53). In its new, imaginary life, the body becomes Body—all the more dazzling the longer it is absent. It must be emphasized here that the transcendent sexual force recognized by the women as an attribute exclusively held by Usbeck is the means by which his power is rendered absolute. Usbeck's Body, by becoming an object of faith (because it has been divested of any sense in reality, the wives must believe in it even more), also becomes the principle of obedience and order around which the seraglio's hierarchies are established. This illustrates Montesquieu's political belief that in despotic governments power must operate on the common basis of two complementary notions: faith and obedience, or love and fear.

But the women in the seraglio also cling to the imaginary projection of Usbeck's body as a way of protecting themselves. For any attempt, no matter how negligible, to place in question the transcendence of the master would automatically place in question the entire system of the seraglio. Zachi's early breach of faith in the system—"even in this very prison where you hold me, I am freer than you . . . your suspicions, your jealousy, and your heartaches are all so many proofs of your dependency" (62.133)—prefigures Roxane's letter, the last of the novel: "you thought I was deceived, and I was deceiving you" (161.280), which spells out her death, the collapse of the seraglio, and with it, one must assume, Usbeck's annihilation.

We have just analyzed from the point of view of seraglio life how and why Usbeck's wives reinforce—willingly or unwillingly—the process by which the image passes for the real thing. But beyond a certain point, imaginary life cannot sustain itself anymore. Usbeck's wives have undergone a bodily training that defies all the ruses of the imagination. The imaginary object of love (the Body) must take form, must produce itself as body, or else adultery and betrayal ensue. "Things have come to a pass that is no longer tolerable," writes the Chief Eunuch. "I found Zachi in bed with one of her women slaves. . . . Last evening, a young lad was found in the garden of the seraglio, and he escaped over the walls" (147.270). Solim confirms the horrible news: "A new sense of joyfulness, spread throughout the halls, is, to my mind, infallible proof of some new satisfaction" (151.272). Suddenly the imaginary mechanism collapses and the process inverts itself: instead of sustaining Usbeck's mastery, it undermines it radically. In other words, Usbeck is condemned to be only what his wives perceive him to be: a body. They no longer identify him with a symbol but make him into a sexual object. Instead of denouncing the personal and social repression Usbeck has been imposing on the seraglio, their only bone of contention is a missing body. The theme of the wives' rejected and thus devalued bodies becomes a leitmotiv in their letters. Fatme: "What do you hope will happen to a woman . . . who was used to holding you in her arms? . . . when she has not even the benefit of serving the happiness of another—useless adornment of a seraglio!" (7.52–53). But Usbeck, whose body is diminished by fatigue ("My health is not good. My body and my mind are depressed": 27.83) and alienated by too much Parisian effervescence ("I have barely walked a hundred paces before I am more bruised than if I had gone ten leagues": 240.77), understands less and less the orderly function his body serves in the life of the seraglio. He mistakes the reason behind his wives' revolt and thus attempts to restore peace by establishing with them a new type of relationship:

> I have just found out that the seraglio is in disorder and filled with quarrels and dissension. . . . I beg of you, therefore, to amend your ways. . . . For I should like to make you forget that I am your master so that I may remember only that I am your husband.
>
> (65.137)

Predictably, this language of pure husbandry fails, as the wives cannot conceive of love and authority as other than inseparable, and both are a function of Usbeck's physical presence.

Usbeck's ultimate blunder derives from his misapprehension that a letter can stand in place of a body, that authority can forever be exercised in absentia: "May this letter be like unto the thunder that falls in the midst of storms and flashes of lightning" (154.274). Far outstripping the letter's inadequacy as a medium of power is its impotence to satiate desire. Tactfully choosing a euphemism to describe that role, the Chief Eunuch writes: "But all of that, magnificent lord, is nothing without the presence of the master. . . . You temper fear with hope; you are more absolute when you caress than when you threaten. Come back then . . . and bring with you all the marks of your sway" (96.183). Only toward the end of the novel does Usbeck suddenly understand that his position of mastery is not a function of familial, social, or political links, but is directly related to the very precise sexual economy of the seraglio. In a flash, as he measures the immeasurable fascination his body still exercises on some of his wives —"I have lived through your absence, and I have preserved my love by the very force of that love. Nights, days, passing moments—all were for you" (152.277), writes Zachi in her last letter to him—Usbeck realizes his helplessness and the tragic meaning of his existence:

> I am living in a barbarous climate, in the company of everything that vexes me, far removed from everything that interests me. A somber sadness seizes me; I am falling into a frightful oppression. It seems to me that I am destroying myself and no longer find my own personality except when a dark jealousy ignites within and gives birth in my soul to fear, suspicion, hate and regret.
>
> (155.274)

But it is already too late for him, and the reader undoubtedly will have guessed the sinister result of Usbeck's final insight: the destruction of the seraglio and, ultimately, his own death.

In "Reflections," which prefaces the 1754 edition of *The Persian Letters*, Montesquieu claims that he regards the seraglio fiction as the proper framework for the presentation of his philosophical and political concerns: "The author has granted himself the prerogative of being able to mix philosophy, politics, and ethics into a novel and to bind the whole together by a secret and, so to speak, obscure chain" (p. 39). We have demonstrated that Usbeck's corporeal presence/absence is the guiding principle that joins Paris and Ispahan, history and fiction, politics and sexuality. The organic metaphor is not only confirmed but extended to a second level of analysis, one of function—the body as an operational principle—in addition to one of structure. Time and again in *The Persian Letters*, Montesquieu posits similarities of structure and function (nature and principle) between the organism and political power. The seraglio's energies, concentrated around the passions of the despot's body and the absurd economy of noncirculation that ensues, prefigure what we read in *The Spirit of the Laws* about the self-centered rather than well-centered nature of despotic government, and the lack of geopolitical and economic interaction between the capital and its devastated territories. It would not be an exaggeration to say that long before the theoretical analyses on oriental despotism found in *The Spirit of the Laws,* the seraglio fiction had formulated in a different—and more elaborate—language the organic modalities of political power.

Selected Bibliography

FIRST EDITIONS OF INDIVIDUAL WORKS

Except where otherwise noted, dates of publication are also dates of composition. All works were first published in Paris.

Discourse upon Reception into the Academy of Bordeaux. 1716.
Dissertation on Roman Policy as to Religion. 1716.
Memoir on the Debts of the State. 1716.
How Geniuses Are Different. 1717.
Discourse upon the Reconvening of the Academy of Bordeaux. 1717.
In Praise of Sincerity. 1717.
Discourse on the Causes of Echo. 1718.
Discourse on the Function of the Kidneys. 1718.
Project for a Physical History of the Earth. 1719.
Discourse on the Cause of Gravity in Bodies. 1720.
Discourse on the Cause of Transparency in Bodies. 1720.
Observations on Natural History. 1721. Written in 1719.
The Persian Letters. 1721.
The Temple of Gnidus. 1724.
Cephisa and Cupid. 1724.
Dialogue Between Sylla and Eucrates. 1724.
Discourse upon the Reconvening of the Bordeaux Parliament. 1725.
Treatise on Duty. 1725.
On Politics. 1725.
Discourse on the Motives That Should Encourage Us in the Sciences. 1725.
On Respect and Reputation. 1725.
Discourse on the Cause and Effects of Thunder. 1726.
Considerations on the Wealth of Spain. 1726.

Discourse upon Acceptance into the French Academy. 1728.
Travels in Austria. 1728.
Travelers in Italy, Germany, and Holland. 1728–1729.
A True Story. 1731.
Memoir on Mines. 1731–1732.
Considerations on the Causes of the Greatness of the Romans and Their Decline. 1734.
Reflections on Universal Monarchy. 1734.
An Essay on Causes Affecting Minds and Characters. 1736.
For Madame Geoffrin. 1738. A poem.
For Madame Le Franc. 1738. A poem.
Arsaces and Ismenia. 1742.
Invocation to the Muses. 1747.
The Spirit of the Laws. 1748.
The Defense of "The Spirit of the Laws." 1750.
Clarifications on "The Spirit of the Laws." 1750.
Replies and Explanations Given to the Faculty of Theology. 1752.
Memoir on the Constitution. 1752.
Essay on Taste. 1753–1755.

MODERN EDITIONS

De l'esprit des lois. Edited by Jean Brèthe de la Gressaye. Paris, 1950–1958.
Essai sur le goût. Edited by Charles Beyer. Geneva, 1967. Critical edition.
Histoire véritable. Edited by Roger Caillois. Geneva, 1948. Critical edition.
Les lettres persanes. Edited by Antoine Adam. Geneva, 1954. Critical edition.
Les lettres persanes. Edited by Paul Vernière. Paris, 1960.
Oeuvres complètes de Montesquieu. Edited by Roger Caillois. 2 vols. Paris, 1949 and 1951. Pléiade edition.
Oeuvres complètes de Montesquieu. General editor André Masson. 3 vols. Paris, 1950–1955. Vol. 1 edited by A. Masson. Vol. 2 edited by A. Masson and L. Desgraves. Vol. 3 edited by F. Gébelin and X. Védère.

TRANSLATIONS

Considerations on the Causes of the Greatness of the Romans and Their Decline. Translated by David Lowenthal. New York, 1965.

The Persian Letters. Translated by J. Robert Loy. New York, 1961. By far the best English translation of *Les lettres persanes,* with a valuable introduction by the translator.

The Spirit of the Laws: A Compendium of the First English Edition. Edited by David Wallace Carrithers. Berkeley, 1977. Based on Thomas Nugent's translation (London, 1750) of the text of *L'Esprit des lois* published in 1748 in Geneva. Montesquieu congratulated Nugent on the excellence of his translation. Carrithers' edition tries to take into account the changes made in the 1757 posthumous edition of *The Spirit.*

BIOGRAPHICAL AND CRITICAL STUDIES

Althusser, Louis. *Montesquieu: La politique et l'histoire.* Paris, 1969.

Aron, Raymond. *Les étapes de la pensée sociologique: Montesquieu, Comte, Marx, Tocqueville, Durkheim, Pareto, Weber.* Paris, 1967.

Barrière, Pierre. *Un grand provincial: Charles-Louis de Secondat, baron de la Brède et de Montesquieu.* Bordeaux, 1946.

Benrekassa, Georges. "Montesquieu et le roman comme genre littéraire." In *Roman et lumières au 18ᵉ siècle.* (Proceedings of the 18th-century colloquium under the sponsorship of the review *Europe.*) Paris, 1970. Pp. 27–37.

Caillois, Roger. "Montesquieu ou la révolution sociologique." *Cahiers de la Pléiade* 18:174–184 (1949).

Callot, Émile. *La philosophie de la vie au XVIIIᵉ siècle.* Paris, 1965.

Cassirer, Ernst. *The Philosophy of the Enlightenment.* Boston, 1964.

Courtney, C. P. *Montesquieu and Burke.* Oxford, 1963.

Dargan, E. P. *The Aesthetic Doctrine of Montesquieu: Its Application in His Writings.* Baltimore, 1907.

Dedieu, Joseph. *Montesquieu.* Paris, 1966.

Desgraves, Louis. *Catalogue de la bibiliothèque de Montesquieu.* Geneva, 1954.

Dodds, Muriel. *Les récits de voyages, sources de "L'Esprit des lois" de Montesquieu.* Paris, 1929.

Durkheim, Emile. *Montesquieu and Rousseau.* Ann Arbor, Mich., 1960.

Ehrard, Jean. *Montesquieu critique d'art.* Paris, 1965.

———. "Le despotisme dans *Les lettres persanes.*" *Archives des Lettres Modernes* 116:33–50 (1970).

Europe. 574 (February 1977). Special issue on Montesquieu.

Faguet, Émile. *La politique comparée de Montesquieu, Rousseau et de Voltaire.* Paris, 1902.

Fletcher, F.T.H. *Montesquieu and English Politics (1750–1800).* London, 1939.

Gearhart, Suzanne. "The Place and Sense of the Outsider: Structuralism in the *Lettres persanes.*" *MLN* 92:724–748 (1977).

Grimsley, Ronald. "The Idea of Nature in the *Lettres persanes.*" *French Studies* 5:293–306 (1951).

Grosnichard, Alain. *Structure du sérial.* Paris, 1979.

Gurvitch, George. "La sociologie juridique de Montesquieu." *Revue de métaphysique et de morale* 46:611–626 (1939).

Havens, George. *The Age of Ideas: From Reaction to Revolution in Eighteenth-Century France.* New York, 1955.

Hubert, René. "La notion du devenir historique dans la philosophie de Montesquieu." *Revue de métaphysique et de morale* 46:587–610 (1939).

Kempf, Roger. "*Les Lettres persanes* ou le corps absent." *Tel Quel* 22:84–92 (1965).

Laufer, Roger. "La réussite romanesque et la signification des *Lettres persanes.*" *Revue d'histoire littéraire de la France* 61:118–203 (1961).

Levin, Lawrence M. *The Political Doctrine of Montesquieu's "Esprit des Lois": Its Classical Background.* New York, 1936.

Loy, J. Robert. *Montesquieu.* New York, 1968.

Mason, Sheila. *Montesquieu's Idea of Justice.* The Hague, 1975.

McLelland, J. "Metaphor in Montesquieu's Theoretical Writings." *Studies on Voltaire and the Eighteenth Century* 199:205–224 (1981).

Mercier, Roger. "La théorie des climats des *Réflexions critiques* à l'*Esprit des lois.*" *Revue d'histoire littéraire de la France* 53:159–174 (1953).

Merquiol, André. "Montesquieu et la géographie politique." *Revue internationale d'histoire politique* 7:127–146 (1957).

Meyer, Paul H. "Politics and Morals in the Thought of Montesquieu." *Studies on Voltaire and the Eighteenth Century* 56: 845–891 (1967).

Oake, Roger B. "Montesquieu's Analysis of Roman History." *Journal of the History of Ideas* 16:44–59 (1955).

Ranum, Orest. "Personality and Politics in the *Persian Letters.*" *Political Science Quarterly* 84:606–627 (1969).

Roger, Jacques. *Les sciences de la vie dans la pensée française du XVIIIe siècle.* Paris, 1963.

Rostand, Jean. "Montesquieu et la biologie." *Revue d'histoire des sciences et de leurs applications* 7:129–136 (1955).

Shackleton, Robert. *Montesquieu: A Critical Biography.* London, 1961.

Singerman, Alan J. "Réflexions sur une métaphore: Le sérial dans *Les lettres persanes.*" *Studies on Voltaire and the Eighteenth Century* 185:181–198 (1980).

Vartanian, Aram. "Eroticism and Politics in the *Lettres persanes.*" *Romanic Review* 60:23–33 (1969).

BIBLIOGRAPHIES

Cabeen, David C. *Montesquieu: A Bibliography.* New York, 1947.

——————, ed. *A Critical Bibliography of French Literature (18th Century).* Syracuse, N.Y. 1951. *Supplement,* edited by Richard Brooks, 1968.

JOSUÉ HARARI
JANE McLELLAND